REGULATING CREATION

The Law, Ethics, and Policy of Assisted Human Reproduction

In 2004, the *Assisted Human Reproduction Act* was passed by the Parliament of Canada. Fully in force by 2007, the Act was intended to safeguard the health and safety of Canadians. However, a 2010 Supreme Court of Canada decision ruled that key parts of the Act were invalid.

Regulating Creation is a collection of essays built around the 2010 ruling. Featuring contributions by Canadian and international scholars, it offers a variety of perspectives on the role of law in dealing with the legal, ethical, and policy issues surrounding changing reproductive technologies. In addition to the in-depth analysis of the Canadian case, the volume reflects on how other countries, particularly the United States, the United Kingdom, and New Zealand, regulate these same issues.

Combining a detailed discussion of legal approaches with an in-depth exploration of societal implications, *Regulating Creation* deftly navigates the obstacles of legal policy amid the rapid current of reproductive technological innovation.

TRUDO LEMMENS is Professor and Scholl Chair in Health Law and Policy in the Faculty of Law, the Dalla Lana School of Public Health, and the Joint Centre for Bioethics at the University of Toronto.

ANDREW FLAVELLE MARTIN is a SSHRC Bombardier CGS Scholar and doctoral candidate in the Faculty of Law at the University of Toronto.

CHERYL MILNE is the Executive Director of the David Asper Centre for Constitutional Rights in the Faculty of Law at the University of Toronto.

IAN B. LEE is an associate professor in the Faculty of Law at the University of Toronto.

Regulating Creation

The Law, Ethics, and Policy of Assisted Human Reproduction

EDITED BY TRUDO LEMMENS,
ANDREW FLAVELLE MARTIN,
CHERYL MILNE, AND IAN B. LEE

UNIVERSITY OF TORONTO PRESS
Toronto Buffalo London

Toronto Buffalo London
www.utppublishing.com
Printed in the U.S.A.

ISBN 978-1-4426-4669-8 (cloth) ISBN 978-1-4426-1457-4 (paper)

♾ Printed on acid-free, 100% post-consumer recycled paper with vegetable-based inks.

Library and Archives Canada Cataloguing in Publication

Regulating creation : the law, ethics, and policy of assisted human reproduction / edited by Trudo Lemmens, Andrew Flavelle Martin, Cheryl Milne, Ian B. Lee.

Includes bibliographical references and index.
ISBN 978-1-4426-4669-8 (cloth). – ISBN 978-1-4426-1457-4 (paper)

1. Human reproductive technology – Law and legislation – Canada.
2. Human reproductive technology – Government policy – Canada.
3. Human reproductive technology – Moral and ethical aspects – Canada.
I. Lemmens, Trudo, author, editor II. Martin, Andrew Flavelle, 1983–, editor III. Milne, Cheryl, 1962–, author, editor IV. Lee, Ian B., 1970–, author, editor

KE3660.5 R44 2017 344.7104'19 C2016-904569-2
KF3830 R44 2017

This book has been published with the help of a grant from the Federation for the Humanities and Social Sciences, through the Awards to Scholarly Publications Program, using funds provided by the Social Sciences and Humanities Research Council of Canada.

University of Toronto Press acknowledges the financial assistance to its publishing program of the Canada Council for the Arts and the Ontario Arts Council, an agency of the Government of Ontario.

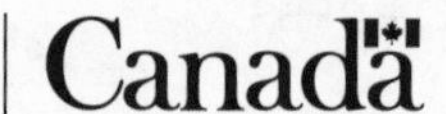

Contents

REGULATING CREATION

The Law, Ethics, and Policy of Assisted Human Reproduction

Introduction

TRUDO LEMMENS AND ANDREW FLAVELLE MARTIN

In 2004, more than a decade after a Royal Commission report urged the government to regulate the legal, ethical, and social issues associated with assisted human reproduction (AHR), the Parliament of Canada adopted the *Assisted Human Reproduction Act* (*AHRA*).[1] The Act had four main components: a set of strict prohibitions; a regulatory framework surrounding specific AHR practices; privacy rules related to AHR; and provisions related to a new Assisted Human Reproduction Agency of Canada. The final scope of the prohibitions had changed considerably throughout the various drafting processes, in line with emerging technologies that were not yet developed at the time the Royal Commission tabled its report. The Act included strict prohibitions on activities such as cloning, the creation of embryos for research, and the creation of chimeras. Other activities were surrounded by both prohibitions and regulatory restrictions. The commercial sale of human reproductive materials and surrogacy, for example, was prohibited, while compensation for reasonable expenses incurred as part of these activities was to be regulated. The Act also created a framework for the development of further regulations and the licensing of virtually all AHR services. To implement this framework, the Act established the Assisted Human Reproduction Agency of Canada and mandated the agency to review and regulate a panoply of issues associated with the rapid changes in assisted human reproduction technology.

The Act faced criticism from the moment of its enactment. Commentators raised several concerns, particularly about the use of the criminal law and the strict prohibitions on some activities. Criticism was especially strong from the research community with regard to the restrictions on research, such as the prohibition on the creation of chimeras. The original purpose of the Act had been primarily to regulate reproductive services; the debate around the use of the criminal law became primarily a debate about the alleged lack of flexibility of the criminal law in adjusting to scientific developments. Some criticized also the prohibition on the commercialization of gametes and surrogacy. The legislative scheme introduced in Canada was, however, not unique, as several countries had enacted legislation on AHR around the same time, with similarly combined prohibitions on some activities, strict regulation of others, and the establishment of a regulatory or review authority. The stark contrast between the Canadian regulatory approach and the largely unregulated market for assisted human reproduction in the United States generated additional pressure on the Canadian system. However, it was the traditional and limited question of federalism – the division of authority between the federal and provincial governments – that ultimately had the most significant impact on the future of the regulatory approach.

In 2008, the Province of Quebec challenged several provisions of the Act, in particular those related to the regulation of assisted human reproductive activities, as an inappropriate intrusion on provincial jurisdiction over the regulation of health services and facilities.[2] In 2010, the Supreme Court of Canada struck down key provisions of the Act as being outside federal jurisdiction, including those that restricted the manipulation and use of gametes and embryos to people and premises licensed by the Agency.[3] This decision hollowed out much of the regulatory apparatus in the Act and dramatically reduced the role of the Agency, which was later abolished. As a result, both the federal government and the provinces are back at the drawing board, having to reimagine how AHR could and should be regulated in Canada. The federal government's response has been limited. It has abolished the regulatory agency that was supposed to be in charge of implementing the regulatory scheme, and it has not enacted any regulations, which it is still empowered to do under the provisions that have remained in place.

This book explores a range of legal, policy, and ethical issues in the aftermath of the Supreme Court's decision. Several of the chapters were presented in earlier versions at a conference at the University of Toronto Faculty of Law in October 2011. Leading Canadian and international scholars reflect not only on the decision itself but also on diverse issues such as the potential exploitation of surrogates; the impact on women's health of AHR and of the harvesting of eggs; the commodification of human life; the societal implications of market-oriented reproduction; the dignity of women, infertile couples, and offspring; and the role of law and policy in ensuring access to AHR without discrimination. Some chapters analyse the decision itself as a development in federalism, including the scope of the federal power over criminal law and provincial jurisdiction over health care. Other chapters consider unanswered questions about the legal impact of AHR on children and families, particularly in terms of legal parentage and gamete donor anonymity. Finally, some chapters consider the implications of the decision – and particularly the judges' differing views of the proper role for the criminal law – for the commercialization of human reproductive services, the commodification of human reproductive materials, and the allocation and availability of these services and materials. All of these chapters reflect in one way or another on the daunting challenge faced by legislatures and courts in responding to the often unforeseeable and at this point perhaps still unimaginable possibilities created by new technologies; the difficulty in reassessing previously accurate ideas and assumptions about the nature of the division of powers, parenthood, and reproduction itself; and the challenge in regulating activities where often very divergent ethical norms, social values, and economic interests intersect. This challenge has been addressed wisely in some respects and poorly in others, and simply ignored in the rest.

This book provides timely reflection on many of the issues both federal and provincial legislators will face. To inform the Canadian debate, several of the international commentators reflect on how other jurisdictions – such as the United States, the United Kingdom, and New Zealand – deal with some aspects of AHR regulation. In addition, the book pays special attention to the changing international context in which AHR services occur. Since the adoption of the Act, AHR has been developing at a very fast pace at a global scale, in a complex social, medical, and industrial context. The global context has brought new issues to the fore, with concerns about reproductive tourism and its social, ethical, and legal implications. Foreign surrogacy and AHR services involving foreign donated sperm and ova, for example, raise complex questions about the applicability of national rules related to family law and immigration. People travel to obtain access to gametes or to use surrogates in countries that allow the practice. Also, people from outside Canada are using Canadian clinics for AHR procedures on themselves or on surrogates. The commercial interests of AHR clinics, sperm and ova banks, and other industries with financial stakes in the promotion of AHR – many of them operating internationally – also create special challenges and conflicts of interest.

The *AHRA*, the *Reference*, and Subsequent Developments

The *AHRA* was the fourth federal bill attempting to govern assisted human reproduction in the wake of the 1993 final report of the Royal Commission on New Reproductive Technologies.[4] The bill was introduced in February 2004 and received Royal Assent in March of that year. Parts came into force in 2004, 2006, and 2007; other sections were never proclaimed.

As mentioned above, the Act prohibited many activities outright and allowed others subject to licensure and other limitations. The key prohibitions included those against creating and using embryos for research purposes, combining human and non-human cells, cloning, and sex selection; payment for surrogacy or gametes, and any surrogacy by persons under 21; using gametes or an embryo without the contributor's consent; and using the gametes of persons under eighteen for any purpose other than creating a child to be raised by those persons. The regulated activities comprised the creation or implantation of embryos, as well as the import, export, or transfer of gametes and embryos; the combination of human and non-human genetic material; and the reimbursement of expenses for gamete contributors or surrogates. Licences were required for the persons providing AHR services and the premises in which they did so. The Act also established a specialized regime of privacy and access to information for assisted reproduction records and a specialized agency to perform the licensure and information functions.

The government of Quebec's legal challenge to parts of the *AHRA* began as a reference application to the Quebec Court of Appeal. Of the prohibitions, Quebec challenged only those on the use of gametes or embryos with the contributors' consent and the use of gametes from persons under eighteen to create a child for another person. Quebec challenged all of the provisions on regulated activities and privacy and access to information, as well as related ancillary sections of the *AHRA*. Quebec's argument was that these sections "regulate[d] the entire field of medicine relating to assisted procreation,"[5] which was a function for the provinces, given that they had jurisdiction over health care. Canada argued, unsuccessfully, that all of these provisions were valid exercises of the federal power over criminal law. The Court of

Appeal, in a unanimous decision by a panel of three judges, held that all of the sections challenged by the government of Quebec were *ultra vires* the Parliament of Canada; the court agreed that, aside from the outright prohibitions, "the Act constitutes a complete code governing all clinical and research activities relating to assisted reproduction."[6]

The federal government appealed the judgment to the Supreme Court of Canada. Two provinces and various other groups intervened on the appeal. The nine judges who heard the appeal issued three sets of reasons: one by McLachlin CJ for a total of four judges, one by LeBel and Dechamps JJ for a total of four judges, and one by Cromwell J for himself alone. Chief Justice McLachlin held that the challenged provisions were aimed at preventing moral harm as well as public health ills and security issues and were thus properly criminal law within the jurisdiction of Parliament:

> Assisted reproduction raises weighty moral concerns. The creation of human life and the processes by which it is altered and extinguished, as well as the impact this may have on affected parties, lie at the heart of morality. Parliament has a strong interest in ensuring that basic moral standards govern the creation and destruction of life, as well as their impact on persons like donors and mothers. Taken as a whole, the Act seeks to avert serious damage to the fabric of our society by prohibiting practices that tend to devalue human life and degrade participants. This is a valid criminal law purpose, grounded in issues that our society considers to be of fundamental importance.[7]

In contrast, LeBel and Deschamps JJ held that the provisions constituted regulation of health services, a provincial responsibility: "the purpose and the effects of the provisions in question relate to the regulation of a specific type of health services provided in health-care institutions by health-care professionals to individuals who for pathological or physiological reasons need help to reproduce."[8] They held that "[n]othing in the record suggests that the controlled activities should be regarded as conduct that is reprehensible or represents a serious risk to morality, safety or public health."[9] Justice Cromwell broke the tie, agreeing largely but not entirely with Lebel and Deschamps JJ. His holding, and thus the result, was that some sections – most importantly, those on the licensure of professionals and premises for the delivery of AHR services and the privacy and information regime – were *ultra vires*, whereas others – particularly the prohibitions on using gametes or embryos without consent, the restriction on the use of minors' gametes, and the provisions allowing reimbursement of expenses but not payment – were not.

In 2012, Parliament passed a series of amendments to the *AHRA*.[10] These repealed several sections, primarily those held to be *ultra vires*, and abolished the Agency and the licensure apparatus. Also, a new section was added that established safety standards for sperm and ova.[11]

Since the Supreme Court judgment, some other important legal developments have taken place in the context of AHR, which relate to a lively topic of discussion at the conference, and which are further developed in this book. Between 2008 and 2012, around the same time as the *AHRA Reference* and subsequent amendments, the case of *Pratten v British Columbia (Attorney General)* was winding its way through the courts.[12] Olivia Pratten argued that persons born through AHR had a constitutional right to information about their progenitors under the *Canadian Charter of Rights and Freedoms*.[13] She argued that such a right was created both through section 7 (which recognizes the right to not be deprived of life, liberty, or security of the person except in accordance with the principles of fundamental justice) and section 15 (which protects against discrimination). More specifically, she claimed that the lack of information violated her liberty and security by endangering her health and undermining her very identity, and that it was discriminatory to provide similar information to adopted persons but not to persons born through gamete donation. Pratten was successful in 2011 at first instance on the section 15 claim, but the Court of Appeal overturned the trial judge in 2012, and the Supreme Court of Canada in 2013 refused leave to appeal. At the time of the conference, the Court of Appeal's *Pratten* decision had not yet come out. One of the most intense moments of the conference occurred in the context of this debate, when we showed Canadian filmmaker Barry Stevens's documentary film *Bio-Dad*, and followed it with a conversation between the filmmaker and the audience.[14] The movie documents Stevens's search for the identity of his biological father. Stevens was one of the first persons to be created through AHR, at a time when the technology was entirely unregulated and concerns about the desire to know one's "biological identity" and the privacy implications of gamete donation were not on anyone's radar. The debate in the wake of the *Pratten* decision highlights in an interesting way how new concerns may arise in relation to AHR that were not imagined at the time the technology was introduced. A detailed discussion of the *Pratten* decision seemed key to this book.

Another important regulatory development relates to the funding of AHR. In late 2014, the Government of Quebec introduced a bill that, among other things, would eliminate IVF funding in the health care system and prohibit women younger than eighteen and older than forty-two from undergoing IVF.[15] Some of our chapters refer to these developments and discuss the implications of funding decisions related to AHR in terms of the right to access the technology.

Law's Struggle with the Possibilities Created by New Technology

The heart of the *Reference* and a unifying theme among the various chapters in this collection is how the law – both legislatures and courts – strives to understand and respond to the legal, ethical, and social ramifications of technological advancements. Assisted reproductive technologies, from artificial insemination to *in vitro* fertilization (IVF), surrogacy, and cloning, create situations that challenge basic assumptions about human relationships and that call into question the role of government regulation and the purpose of the health professions. When powers were first divided between the federal and provincial governments in 1867 – and for many years thereafter – there could be no meaningful consideration given to who should regulate technologies that were fantasy if not unimaginable. Similarly, it was once necessarily true that a newborn baby was the child of the woman who delivered it and a man who was sexually active with her nine months or somewhat less before, with adoption being the only situation where parent–child relations could be created outside the context of sexual relations. New reproductive technologies based on IVF created new opportunities for couples who could not naturally conceive, but it also created new challenges related to identity within a framework of parentage and privacy laws that remain founded on the assumption of natural reproduction. Most fundamentally, while all technology creates new possibilities, assisted reproductive technologies enable the creation of human life. In so doing, these technologies often harness the biology of existing humans, whether as sources of sperm and ova or as gestational carriers. This poses questions about participation in, access to, and the funding of AHR services. Particularly because of the costs of the technology and the considerable financial interests that have developed around a booming commercial AHR industry – interests that include commercial sperm and ova banks, commercial surrogacy, consultancy firms, legal practitioners, and *in vitro* laboratories – AHR also raises questions about the commodification and commercialization of human life, in a way that few medical advancements have done before.

The specific dispute that gave rise to the reference is, at one level, about federalism and the respective powers of the provincial and federal governments. At a more fundamental level, however, this constitutional question and the other legal issues turn on what exactly AHR is. Is it a fundamentally new activity, one that can give rise to problematic practices that ought to be criminalized, or is it merely one more service that modern medicine can offer? If it is just part of the many other medical services that exist, can some of its challenges be regulated like any other medical activity? Does the fact that it touches on questions of personhood and identity, related to the importance and nature of biological origin and the importance of kinship relation, make it something unique in the context of medical practice? Are the concerns about potential exploitation and commodification special because AHR involves reproduction and future human beings? If so, is this a reason to develop firmer regulatory control? If regulatory control is required, is a unique, stricter regulatory system the way to go? If it is just a medical service, should it be considered a luxury or a basic medical need? Are regulation and criminal law appropriate tools for imposing restraints on a technology that may offer boundless new applications?

Like many stories of law reform, the history of AHR in Canada, and of the *AHRA* and the *Reference* in particular, is largely a story of delay and inaction. As with any issue, one option open to governments is to do nothing. This points to a peculiar limitation of federalism cases – the courts' determination that one level of government has exceeded its jurisdiction and that only another level of government can legislate in an area is no guarantee that those governments will actually do so. Such a determination does not *compel* them. The responsibility for this delay and inaction can be attributed, albeit unequally, to all branches of government at all levels. Interestingly, the constitutional challenge to the *AHRA* may even have provided the federal government at the time with an excuse not to move forward and implement the most basic regulatory structure, though it was legally able to do so. By not enacting the regulations required to make the system work, the federal government may very well have given perfect ammunition to the critics of a strict regulatory approach and may have contributed to the demise of a legislative model it continued to publicly defend.

Background to the *Reference re: Assisted Human Reproduction Act* and Constitutional Law and Federalism Perspectives

The first part of this book introduces the context surrounding the Canadian Supreme Court reference and the *Assisted Human Reproduction Act*, as well as the key constitutional and federalism issues raised by the case. Bernard M. Dickens provides a historical introduction to the Supreme Court's decision and the *AHRA* itself. He details the referral of the legal issues raised by AHR to the Ontario Law Reform Commission in 1982; traces the work of the Commission alongside contemporary examinations in Australia and Britain; and notes the relative silence that greeted the release of the Commission's report in 1985. Dickens then turns to the Royal Commission on New Reproductive Technologies, from its establishment by the Government of Canada in 1989 to the publication of its final report in 1993. By situating political and legal responses in the context of the developments as they happened, Dickens illuminates the trepidation and controversy that these new realities invoked among the general public and the human context in which legislatures and courts operated. His account of these visceral public reactions and concerns over the implications of AHR provide a hint of the moral dimensions that dominated the reasons of McLachlin CJ in the *AHRA Reference*.

The next three chapters explore the impact of the *Reference* on constitutional law at three different levels: the scope of the criminal law power, the implications of that scope for constitutional norms, and the boundaries of the federal government's jurisdiction over health. In particular, they explore how AHR fits into and changes the historical division of powers between the federal and provincial governments. Ian B. Lee argues that the reasons in the *AHRA Reference* obscure the fundamental disagreement between the Chief Justice and Justices Lebel and Deschamps about what regulatory tools Parliament can validly employ to regulate various components of an activity that may only loosely be connected to an area of federal jurisdiction. He suggests that the decision is better understood as being not about the purpose of the impugned provisions, as the reasons nominally state, but instead about the means used to achieve that purpose. Interpreting the *Reference* in the context of previous decisions about the criminal law power, he argues that these provisions fell outside of that power because they included a licensure regime for a wide variety of activities related to AHR. He suggests that the repeal of the licensing elements by the 2012 amendments to the *AHRA* should therefore make these provisions a proper exercise of the criminal law power.

Hoi L. Kong analyses the disagreements between the Chief Justice and Justices Lebel and Deschamps as they relate to the role of provincial autonomy. His focus is on how these two main sets of reasons understand the breadth of the criminal law power and the scope of, and role for, the double aspect doctrine and the paramountcy doctrine. He identifies what he terms the norm of non-suppression – that is, that there are several recognized federalism-related values, and that none of these values should be suppressed by courts. In contrast to the reasons of Justices Lebel and Deschamps, those of the Chief Justice violate this norm by suppressing the value of provincial autonomy in applying a criminal law power that is so broad as to remove any certainty over when the federal government will intervene in matters of provincial jurisdiction.

Glenn Rivard evaluates the impact of the *Reference* on the federal and provincial governments' jurisdiction around health. As context for his analysis, he identifies the primary sources of federal powers related to health and the major legislation that draws on those sources. He emphasizes the federal government's accepted role in product safety health risks via the criminal law power – risks such as those related to food, drugs, cosmetics, medical devices, human cell tissues and organs, and semen – and contrasts this with the accepted provincial role in regulating health professionals, services, and facilities. In this context, Rivard analyses the three sets of reasons in the *AHRA Reference*. He explains that Justices Lebel and Deschamps appear to narrow the established scope of the criminal law power in holding that public health risks are only an acceptable criminal law purpose where the thing being regulated – in this case, AHR – is an "evil" to be "suppressed." He argues that although this narrowing could conceivably challenge long-standing and widely accepted federal control over product safety health risks, such an outcome is unlikely because those statutes have a more limited impact on provincial jurisdiction over health; indeed, the 2012 amendments to the *AHRA* make that Act more like those other statutes.

Together, these four chapters comprise a reflection not only on the scope of the federal criminal law power, but also on the legitimate dimensions of government regulation against moral harms and the role of public outcry as a motivator for lawmaking. They also demonstrate the challenge of situating AHR, a development with truly transformative impacts, in the context of previous and largely more mundane jurisdictional disputes between the federal and provincial levels of government.

Family Law and Children's Rights Perspectives

The next part of the book focuses on the family law implications of assisted human reproduction and children's rights. The first part grappled with how AHR impacts long-standing legal concepts around the federal and provincial division of powers; this next part addresses AHR's challenge to the basic social and legal concepts of parent and child. Fundamentally, these are questions about the relationships and responsibilities among children born through AHR, the persons providing gametes or surrogacy, and the persons who intend to raise the children. Which of these persons are parents, with all the implications that that legal status brings, and which – if any – have informational obligations to the child? Can adoption law provide a template to address these issues, or is AHR ultimately too different? Among the unproclaimed provisions struck down in the *AHRA Reference* and subsequently repealed were those on the collection, disclosure, and use of health information in the context of AHR. It now falls to the provincial legislatures, or potentially the courts, to fill this legal gap, whether by replicating the policy choices made by Parliament or by rejecting them. A particularly serious question is whether, and under what circumstances and conditions, donor-conceived offspring will have access to knowledge of and information about their origins. A related challenge at the provincial level is to address the role of gamete donors and surrogates in parentage law. This second part of the book approaches these issues from a variety of perspectives.

Carol Rogerson considers an urgent legislative challenge facing provincial governments: the need to modernize parentage laws to explicitly address parenthood where children are born using gamete donation or surrogacy. She argues that while tools such as social parenthood (recognizing persons standing in the place of a parent, i.e., *in loco parentis*), birth registration, and adoption may give some level of recognition to intended parents, these are not substitutes for the certainty and stability of established legal status as parents from birth. Moreover, she illustrates how the statutory emphasis on biological and genetic parenthood may indeed give gamete donors or surrogates unplanned and/or unwanted parental status. Rogerson concludes by assessing the Uniform Law Conference of Canada's *Uniform Child Status Act, 2010* and related legislation in British Columbia as precedents for future provincial action in this area.

Michelle Giroux and Cheryl Milne illustrate another need for provincial legislation with a critique of *Pratten v British Columbia (Attorney General)*, in which the BC Court of Appeal rejected arguments for donor-conceived offspring's right to know their genetic origins under sections 7 and 15 of the *Charter*. Giroux and Milne illustrate the negative implications of the court's holding that the section 15(1) violation – that donor-conceived offspring are discriminated against as compared to adopted children, who can access information about their biological parents – was saved by the ameliorative-purpose exception in section 15(2). They also argue that the court was overly dismissive of the section 7 claim, given the physical and mental health implications for the liberty and security of the person of donor offspring, as recognized by the trial judge's findings of fact. In particular, they argue that the court erred in rejecting the persuasiveness of related decisions applying the European Convention on Human Rights and in suggesting that the UN *Convention on the Rights of the Child* does not impact provincial governments because they are not directly parties to it. Given the holdings in *Pratten*, Giroux and Milne conclude that these issues will require legislation by the provinces.

Vanessa Gruben explores in more detail the potential for donor-conceived offspring to successfully claim a right to knowledge of their genetic origins under section 7 of the *Charter*, despite the rejection of such a claim in *Pratten*. She acknowledges that a right to know one's origin would be a positive right and that no positive rights have yet been recognized under section 7. She explains several potential interpretations of a right to know, including access to a donor's identity and personal health information, and how such a right would raise complex privacy issues for donors, donor-conceived offspring, and others. While she argues that donor anonymity should be abolished and that donor-conceived offspring should have access to donor information, like Giroux and Milne she concludes that those changes are more likely to be made by legislatures than by courts.

If legislatures are the appropriate vehicle for determining the scope of access to information for children born through AHR, the next question must be what form that legislation should take. The remaining three chapters in this part examine this question from various perspectives. Juliet R. Guichon explores the suitability of provincial and territorial adoption legislation as a model. She begins by assessing the health impacts of secrecy and donor anonymity for donor-conceived offspring, drawing on recent new research to establish the pronounced psychological and psychosocial effects. In this context, she considers the various adoption regimes used across Canada, evaluating the strengths and weaknesses of their access-to-information provisions and how those provisions could be applied to the context of donor conception. She identifies a mutual consent registry – in which identifying information is released to offspring only if the donor consents – as the minimum appropriate response.

Jeanne Snelling argues that New Zealand law provides a desirable model for Canadian provinces to legislate access to donor identity and other information by donor-conceived offspring. She notes that while the *AHRA* and the corresponding New Zealand legislation share similar principles and histories, the former facilitated anonymity while the latter provides donor-conceived offspring (or their guardians) with both non-identifying and identifying information about their donors. However, she also acknowledges several weaknesses in New Zealand law – in particular, because there are no provisions to annotate birth certificates to indicate donor conception, some offspring may not know they are donor-conceived at all.

Jennifer M. Speirs considers the impact of donor anonymity and corresponding legislation in the broader context of AHR regulation in the United Kingdom. Her focus is on the attitudes of past anonymous semen donors, including how they felt their attitudes had changed in the intervening years. She considers the role of payments for sperm donation and the ways in which that money potentially changes the relationships among donors, clinicians, and offspring. She also explores the mix of apprehension, curiosity, and ambivalence that donors feel about meeting their offspring. Using these issues as a base, Speirs then canvasses the key features of present-day legislative schemes in the UK that govern AHR – specifically, donor anonymity and payment for gametes. She concludes by reflecting on how approaches towards donor-conceived offspring's access to information about their genetic parents have been and may continue to be informed by UK adoption legislation.

Together, the chapters of this part illustrate the need for provincial legislative action to update and adapt existing family law concepts and regimes in light of the new realities created by AHR. In so doing, they also illustrate the functionality and limitations of the courts as a substitute vehicle to address these issues. By exploring analogous legislation not only from Canadian jurisdictions but also from New Zealand, Australia, and the UK, these chapters provide a rich exploration of many approaches from which the provinces might choose. At the same time, they also provide a compelling reminder of the human impact of continued inaction.

Commodification and Commercialization of AHR, Access and Funding of AHR, and the Role of Law

The final part of this book is devoted to issues around the provision of AHR services. These services challenge fundamental assumptions about the nature of disease and medical services, the proper distribution of public and private resources, and the appropriate role for domestic and global government regulation in combatting perceived harms. These chapters explore the dimensions of this challenge as it applies to commercialization and commodification, reproductive tourism, the role for the private sector in service delivery, access and discrimination, and public funding.

Lisa C. Ikemoto contrasts the Canadian and American experiences around the commercialization of assisted reproduction and the resulting implications for reproductive tourism. She traces the *AHRA*'s ban on payments for gametes and surrogacy to the Royal Commission's concerns about not only coercion and exploitation of vulnerable groups, but also the more general commodification of human life. She explains how these concerns have gained little traction among the American public and lawmakers in most states, and attributes this inattention to an emphasis on individual choice and free-market principles, combined with commercial providers' portrayal of themselves as compassionately facilitating the growth of happy and complete families. In this context, she illustrates how some American states have become magnets for those reproductive tourists who are willing and able to pay, particularly those from jurisdictions – such as Canada – where there are strong restrictions or prohibitions on the industry.

Susan G. Drummond argues that provincial law should be amended to recognize the enforceability of gestational surrogacy contracts. She illustrates the continuing dominance of the traditional approach to maternal parentage, under which the mother is the woman who gives birth to the child, and details the variation among the provinces as to the likely legal impact of a surrogacy contract. She demonstrates how the absolute rule in the Uniform Law Conference of Canada's

Uniform Child Status Act, 2010 – that surrogacy contracts are explicitly unenforceable – can paradoxically create a range of uncertainties and potentially undesirable outcomes for both the carrier and the intended parents. In contrast, she claims that enforceable surrogacy contracts would provide a more desirable distribution of risk. Finally, she argues that the existing empirical evidence, including as it relates to commodification, psychological impacts on children, and exploitation of vulnerable carriers, does not support the policy concerns about enforceability. Her critique of the criminal prohibition on commercialization contrasts in an interesting way with Ikemoto's sketch of the moral hazards associated with the untrammelled commercialization that currently dominates AHR in the United States. One question to ask when reading these two chapters is whether we are really talking here about two opposing models. As pointed out earlier, the Canadian regulatory scheme has never really been reasonably implemented, and we may therefore not have a good picture of how a well-designed regulatory system could address some of the concerns of both Ikemoto and Drummond. Nevertheless, here an American scholar faced with untrammelled marketing in the American context is calling for what looks like a more Canadian regulatory restriction on commercialization to tackle exploitation, whereas a Canadian scholar rejects the concerns about commercialization and commodification and is calling for a lifting of the Canadian restrictions, in part out of concerns for women's rights.

Stu Marvel and colleagues survey the special challenges facing LGBTQ people seeking access to assisted reproduction. They begin by noting that although the *AHRA* includes a principle of non-discrimination that specifically contemplates sexual orientation, the *AHRA Reference* itself refers to LGBTQ people only once. This inattention is particularly problematic because the current legal environment imposes barriers that disproportionately affect LGBTQ people. The supply of gametes is limited, due in part to the *AHRA*'s prohibition on gamete purchase. The use of known semen donors is more expensive and time-intensive than it may be for heterosexual couples, as there can be no exemption from the processing requirements if the donor is not the recipient's spouse or sexual partner; moreover, special authorization is required if the known donor is gay, and will be denied if he is HIV positive. The prohibition on paid surrogacy presents an analogous barrier, particularly for gay men. These legal barriers exist alongside institutional attitudes in fertility clinics that focus on the needs of infertile heterosexual families.

Colleen M. Flood and Bryan Thomas critique the regulation of IVF facilities and services after the *AHRA Reference*. They argue that current legal regimes insufficiently address quality and safety issues as well as the potential for financial exploitation of IVF patients. These risks are exacerbated because IVF is largely offered by private for-profit facilities and is typically not covered by public or private health insurance. Flood and Thomas review the existing literature comparing health outcomes in for-profit and not-for-profit facilities and argue that the potential weakness of for-profit care warrants careful consideration in the IVF context. They also explain how the commercial approach may create conflicts of interest that could result in financial exploitation. They compare the regulatory environment in Ontario, where IVF is regulated by the same general statutes and regulations that apply to health professions and other medical services, to the one in Quebec, which has adopted several additional legal tools specific to IVF. They argue that both regimes have significant deficiencies. Finally, they explore how the *AHRA*'s remaining prohibitions on payments for gametes and surrogacy, as well as the regulatory restrictions on embryo implantation in Quebec, tend to impede reproductive freedom.

Sarah Hudson assesses how a rights-based approach might support the funding of assisted reproduction under public health insurance. She explores the relationships among the concept of medical necessity under the *Canada Health Act*, the role of costs in determining health care priorities, and a narrow, illness-based concept of infertility that prioritizes the claims of heterosexual couples over those of singles and LGBTQ couples. In this context, she evaluates past and potential *Charter* claims for funding. She demonstrates that while claims to positive rights to reproductive autonomy or health care under section 7 would likely fail, discrimination claims under section 15 would have more promise, where some reproductive funding was already covered; however, much turns on the definition of infertility and the purpose of health care services. She concludes that anti-discrimination rights, as opposed to a free-standing right to reproductive assistance, have a major role to play in policy-making in this area.

Trudo Lemmens explores the arguments invoked in the debate over the commodification of human reproductive material. Building on Margaret Radin's market inalienability approach and referring also to the work of others who have emphasized the special issues raised in the context of reproduction and the special nature of reproductive goods, Lemmens argues that criminal sanctions restricting the commercialization of gametes are legitimate and aim at confirming a richer concept of individual autonomy and at protecting human dignity. He suggests that regardless of changes in how we value AHR itself, reproductive goods should continue to be awarded special status and special protection outside the commercial market. Among the reasons for special treatment, Lemmens focuses in particular on the inherent relational nature of reproductive goods, the profound link to identity and personhood, and equity. The impact of commercialization on societal values associated with reproductive goods justifies, in his view, an approach that rejects untrammelled commercialization but allows for some level of state-organized compensation. Lemmens connects this discussion to a brief rebuttal of those who have argued that a prohibition on the sale of gametes violates *Charter* rights such as the right to life, liberty, and security of the person and the right to equality.

Together, the chapters in this part examine how value judgments embodied in law, specifically as they relate to the distribution and regulation of health resources, should be rethought in light of the challenges posed by AHR. These new technological possibilities place stress on the Canadian social consensus – to the extent that such consensus does indeed exist – on the nature of health services and the degree to which those services should be commercialized. As with the previous parts of the book, the focus here is on how AHR has pressured legislatures and courts to reconsider long-standing legal concepts, in this case about the inherent and commercial value of human life and its component prerequisites.

Appendix: Expert Reports

As addenda, this book offers three expert opinion reports that were prepared in the context of the *AHRA Reference* decisions. The Quebec government commissioned an expert report to support its position on the *AHRA* at the Quebec Court of Appeal; the Canadian government did the same. These reports, which have not been published elsewhere, are valuable companions to the body of this book, as they reflect well the divergent opinions that exist in Canada with respect to the desirability of federal legislation in this area.

The report for the Government of Quebec by Bartha Maria Knoppers and Élodie Petit is reproduced in full in English translation in Appendix 1. Knoppers and Petit emphasize Quebec's long-standing and continuously evolving approach to regulating this area. They explain how and why this approach involves dynamic collaboration among the provincial government and government agencies, professional organizations, research ethics committees, and the provincial agency that funds health research. They then detail how this approach has addressed some of the major issues raised by AHR technologies, including consent, commercialization, and research oversight, and argue that this approach has made Quebec a leader both nationally and internationally. The foreword to the report, although brief, may be of particular interest. There, Knoppers draws on her experience as a member of the Royal Commission on New Reproductive Technologies to identify the limitations facing the Commission. She also emphasizes the irreconcilable conflicts among the Commission's members and the corresponding need for compromise in its work. These notes are illuminating, given the prominent role of the Commission's report for commentary about AHR and about portions of the reasons in the *AHRA Reference* itself.

In Appendix 2, Françoise Baylis provides her report for the federal government. In contrast to Knoppers and Petit, Baylis focuses on the differential impacts and effectiveness of federal versus provincial action around AHR. Her overarching message is that the need for national uniformity makes essential the federal regulation of AHR in the interests of public health and safety and public morality. Variation among the provinces would not only promote reproductive and research tourism to jurisdictions with laxer standards but also allow potential harm to Canadian social values through coercion, exploitation, and commodification. Moreover, she argues that regulation via a single specialized federal agency – Assisted Human Reproduction Canada – would minimize the shortcomings arising from regulatory collaboration by several existing bodies within each province. Finally, she emphasizes the appropriateness of the ethical principles underlying the *AHRA*, tracing them back to the parallel principles identified by the Commission on New Reproductive Technologies in its national consultations. Knoppers wrote a short reply report to Baylis' report, which is reproduced as Appendix 3. By this time Baylis had been appointed a member of the Board of Assisted Human Reproduction Canada and was not in a position to respond further.

Conclusion

In the wake of the *AHRA Reference*, the Parliament of Canada and the provincial legislatures face myriad challenging decisions. With the federalism aspect settled by the Supreme Court, both levels of government have one less excuse for further inaction. The delay to date, both before and after the Supreme Court's decision, has created substantial uncertainty for people seeking to use or participate in AHR services and for those health professionals and entrepreneurs who are willing to provide them. As the chapters in this book demonstrate, the complexities involved span a huge range and pose a real danger of unintended consequences. What ties these challenges together is the dramatic extent to which they require re-examination and adaptation of existing legal norms and structures to address previously impossible circumstances. Governmental action in these areas must be prompt, but it must also be informed and deliberate. The largest issues – the regulation of AHR services, the legal identity and rights of people conceived using these services, the rise of reproductive tourism, and the commercialization of reproduction itself – are the same ones facing politicians, policy-makers, and academics in many countries. While there may be room for a variety of reasonable responses to these issues, progress in any jurisdiction will continue to be undermined by inaction elsewhere. This book offers a rich reflection on these questions and will help create space for further discussion and deliberation among those involved in or being affected by the governance and practice of assisted human reproduction.

NOTES

1 *Assisted Human Reproduction Act*, SC 2004, c 2.
2 For a good discussion of the *AHRA* and the constitutional challenge, see Vanessa Gruben and Angela Cameron, "Quebec's Constitutional Challenge to the Assisted Human Reproduction Act: Overlooking Women's Reproductive Autonomy?," in *Fertile Ground: Exploring Reproduction in Canada*, ed. Stephanie Patterson, Francesca Scala, and Marlene K. Sokolon (Montreal and Kingston: McGill–Queen's University Press, 2011), 125, esp. 130–40.
3 *Reference re Assisted Human Reproduction Act*, 2010 SCC 61, [2010] 3 SCR 457 [*AHRA Reference*].
4 For a brief history of legislative attempts in this area, see *In the matter of a Reference by the Government of Quebec pursuant to the Court of Appeal Reference Act, R.S.Q., c. R-23, concerning the constitutional validity of sections 8 to 19, 40 to 53, 60, 61 and 68 of the Assisted Human Reproduction Act, S.C. 2004, c. 2,* 2008 QCCA 1167, [2008] RJQ 1551 at paras 4–17 [*Quebec AHRA Reference*].

5 *Quebec AHRA Reference*, *ibid* at para 26 [translation]. The official text reads as follows: « le caractère véritable des dispositions attaquées consiste à réglementer tout le secteur de la pratique médicale liée à la procréation assistée ».
6 *Quebec AHRA Reference*, *ibid* at para 121 [translation]. The official text reads as follows: « la *Loi* constitue un code complet qui régit l'ensemble des activités cliniques ou de recherche en relation avec la procréation assistée ».
7 *AHRA Reference*, *supra* note 3 at para 61. McLachlin CJ discusses public health at para 62 and security at para 63.
8 *Ibid* at para 227.
9 *Ibid* at para 251.
10 *Jobs, Growth and Long-term Prosperity Act*, SC 2012, c 19, ss 713–739.
11 *Ibid*, s 716 [not yet in force], adding a new section 10.
12 *Pratten v British Columbia (Attorney General)*, 2011 BCSC 656, 99 RFL (6th) 290, rev'd 2012 BCCA 480, 25 RFL (7th) 58, leave to appeal to SCC refused, 35191 (30 May 2013), [2013] SCCA No 36.
13 *Canadian Charter of Rights and Freedoms*, Part I of the *Constitution Act*, 1982, being Schedule B to the *Canada Act 1982* (UK), 1982, c 11 [*Charter*].
14 Barry Stevens, *Bio-Dad* (2009). See also Barry Stevens's reflections on his search for his biological identity in "Who I Came From" in Juliet R. Guichon, Ian Mitchell, and Michelle Giroux, *The Right to Know One's Origin: Assisted Human Reproduction and the Best Interests of Children* (Brussels: Academic and Scientific Publishers, 2012), 31–5.
15 Bill 20, *An Act to enact the Act to promote access to family medicine and specialized medicine services and to amend various legislative provisions relating to assisted procreation*, 1st Sess, 41st Leg, Quebec, 2014, cl 3 (introduced by Hon Gaétan Barrette, Minister of Health and Social Services, 28 November 2014), adding s 10.1 to *An Act respecting clinical and research activities relating to assisted procreation*, RSQ c A-5.01: "No *in vitro* fertilization activities may be carried out on women under 18 or over 42 years of age." See Kelly Grant, "Quebec to cut in vitro fertilization insurance coverage," *Globe and Mail*, 28 November 2014, 2014 WLNR 33673554; and Kelly Grant, "Quebec moves to ban IVF for women over 42," *Globe and Mail*, 5 December 2014, 2014 WLNR 34345749.

PART ONE

Background to the *Reference re: Assisted Human Reproduction Act* and Constitutional Law and Federalism Perspectives

1 A Historical Introduction to the Supreme Court's Decision on the *Assisted Human Reproduction Act*

BERNARD M. DICKENS

A freedom of presenting a selective social or legal history is that it has no obvious time of commencement. There are several credible points of departure for what was enacted in Canada on 29 March 2004 as *An Act respecting assisted human reproduction and related research*, with the short title of the *Assisted Human Reproduction Act* (*AHRA*). The birth that indirectly resulted in the *AHRA* occurred on 25 July 1978 when the world's first proven "test tube" baby was delivered in the northern English town of Oldham. This achievement of successful *in vitro* fertilization (IVF) by Drs Robert Edwards and Patrick Steptoe received international recognition, both acclaim and consternation at what it might portend.

Recognition that an ovum fertilized by sperm in a Petri dish (i.e., *in vitro* or in a "test tube") could remain viable when transferred to and implanted in the uterus of the source of the ovum originated with veterinary investigators and animal breeders.[1] The technique was subsequently applied in a human by Steptoe and Edwards to achieve pregnancy and, in 1978, the birth of a healthy child.[2] It was soon further recognized that transfer and implantation could also be achieved in the suitably prepared uterus of another woman, allowing ovum and embryo donation. A woman could thereby gestate a child to which she was not genetically related. If the gestating mother intended at the outset to surrender the child at birth to be reared by another person as that person's own child, the result was full surrogate motherhood.[3]

At its origin, IVF was not funded by public (government) health plans, and in Canada it remains unfunded by provincial health insurance plans. It developed – particularly in the United States – in the private sector, open to commercial entrepreneurship largely outside legislative control. Noel Keane, a lawyer in Dearborn, Michigan, became involved with infertility clinics and in 1976 began to draft private contracts for surrogate motherhood. These were initially for partial surrogacy, but with development of IVF after 1978 they were extended to full surrogacy. He was the lawyer, for instance, who brought together the parties in the much discussed, controversial custody case concerning Baby M.[4] In the late 1970s or at the beginning of the 1980s, a couple from the Toronto suburb of Scarborough received Keane's assistance in arranging for a woman from Florida to be a surrogate mother for them. It was a second marriage for the husband of the couple, who was a truck driver in his forties. The couple had failed to conceive a child naturally. They had previously applied to the local Catholic Children's Aid Society to be adoptive parents but had been rejected on grounds of the husband's advanced age and a physical disability. To facilitate surrender of the child, it was agreed that the gestating mother would undertake delivery locally at the Scarborough General Hospital.

On admission to the hospital, she provided details of her identity and religion, which was Catholic. On recovery from delivery of the child, she left and returned home without it. When the couple went to take the baby from the hospital, they were refused access, the hospital understandably declining to surrender an abandoned newborn to individuals of whom the hospital authorities knew nothing. The hospital placed the child in the custody of the authority indicated by the birth mother's recorded religion – the local Catholic Children's Aid Society. On legal advice and with medical evidence, however, the husband of the couple obtained proof of his paternity. Armed with this and legal support, he compelled the Society to respect his parental rights and surrender the child to him.

Managers and staff of the Society who remembered the father were outraged at having to give the child to a person they had assessed as unfit for adoptive parenthood, and at him evading their gatekeeping role in the placement of children for whose welfare they had become responsible. They complained to the provincial Minister of Community and Social Services, Frank Drea, who was the member of Ontario's Legislative Assembly for Scarborough and was active in the Catholic community. Drea urged legal proceedings against the couple. The legal advice from ministry senior counsel Douglas Rutherford, however, was that no law had been broken. Because of public concern expressed in the media, provincial attorney general Roy McMurtry referred the matter to the Ontario Law Reform Commission (OLRC) on 5 November 1982.

The Letter of Reference required the OLRC to "consider the legal issues relating to the practice of human artificial insemination, including 'surrogate mothering' and transplantation of fertilized ova to a third party" and to "report on the range of alternatives for resolution of any legal issues that may be identified."[5] Included within the scope of the report were to be the legal status and rights of children and safeguards for protecting their best interests, the legal rights and duties of biological parents and of any spouses of such parents, the nature and enforceability of agreements relating to artificial insemination and related practices, and child custody. Further, the report was to propose legal procedures for establishing and recognizing the parentage of children born as a result of artificial insemination and related processes of medically assisted reproduction, and the potential application of existing laws on child custody and adoption. The report was also to consider the legal rights and liabilities of medical and other personnel involved in these practices.

The OLRC's introductory observation that "there is no consensus in the community in relation to many of the issues canvassed in this Report, but, instead, often sharply conflicting positions" was reflected among the Commissioners.[6] The OLRC had previously been engaged in studies, reports, and recommendations concerning family law, but primarily the Commissioners were from a practice background in commercial and property law and were somewhat doubtful that there would be much in this Reference of interest to mainstream legal practitioners. They became more interested, however, when asked whether they would regard a cryopreserved (i.e., frozen) embryo as a "life in being" for purposes of the rule against perpetuities (the common law provision that requires a testamentary bequest to vest not later than twenty-one years after the end of a life existing at the time the will is made). They considered this to be a legitimate legal issue, since in principle an embryo could be preserved in perpetuity, but one better resolved by the courts. Some doubted that the government had any intention of legislating in this area of potential political controversy; they surmised that it was using the Reference to the OLRC only to deflect the political heat of the time. In this they may have been proven correct.

On receipt of the Reference, the Commission appointed a project consultant (myself) and a multidisciplinary Advisory Board that included Dr John F. Jarrell, then director of the Infertility Clinic at McMaster University Medical Centre, Ruth S. Parry, a professor of social work and director of Toronto's Family Court Clinic, Abbyann Lynch, a prominent bioethicist in the philosophy department at the University of Toronto's St Michael's College, and Lloyd W. Perry, Q.C., the Official Guardian of Ontario. The Advisory Board members informed the Commission staff and members of past practices, such as a history of informal artificial insemination (by turkey baster) for surrogate motherhood among Aboriginal and immigrant communities in which a couple's infertility was stigmatizing, and new developments, such as the then-novel awareness that the human immunodeficiency virus (HIV) could be spread by artificial insemination by donated sperm. Dr Paul Steinhauer, director of training in the Division of Child Psychiatry, University of Toronto Department of Psychiatry, provided insight into how children might deal with knowledge of their gestation by surrogate mothers.

With this support, the OLRC project prepared research papers into legal aspects of human assisted reproduction and developed proposals for legal approaches to accommodate new reproductive practices informed by the corresponding familial, social, and ethical contexts. Since this was a provincial project, proposals for criminal law reform were not addressed. Within their purview, however, was the potential creation of provincial offences to reinforce constitutionally valid proposals – for instance, to regulate medical and related practitioners.

The project staff were informed about comparable studies undertaken, for instance, in Australia, and they kept abreast of the various papers and reports issued by committees in Victoria, Queensland, and South Australia.[7] There was also interest in the terms of reference of the UK (Warnock) Committee of Inquiry into Human Fertilisation and Embryology, set up in July 1982, and their possible influence on the OLRC project's own terms of reference, presented in November of that year. The UK and Ontario projects were contemporaneous and of different scope, so there was no interaction between them. But because of the more public profile of the UK Inquiry, including the international attention it was garnering in the English-language media and beyond, and the relatively low profile of the Ontario project, interested observers acquired their information of the possible familial and social effects of the new technologies from the UK experience. The Ontario project was completed and its proposals approved by the Commissioners in the late summer of 1984, but the text itself was not released until the beginning of 1985. That text had to be translated into French, and presented to the provincial attorney general and tabled in the legislature, before it could be released. Because of the legislative timetable, this could not be done before this time. Many of the proposals coincided with those of the Warnock Inquiry in the UK, except, for instance, for those relating to prior judicial review of surrogate motherhood agreements, including all financial terms, analogous to Family Court adoption procedures.[8] But because the report of that inquiry had been released in July 1984,[9] and was referred to in the OLRC Report,[10] some incorrectly supposed that the Ontario project had followed the lead of the UK inquiry.

The OLRC Report, filed in the provincial legislature, was never debated there.

Similarly, the provincial government responded with silence. For a brief time, more in the United States than in Canada, the Report attracted some media attention and academic commentary. But its main effect was to feed a rising storm of resentment among an emerging community of feminist commentators, scholars, and activists, who contended that decisions about women's bodies and choices were being directed by male-dominated institutions to serve men's goals, and furthermore, that women's vulnerability was being exploited and aggravated by commercial interests – particularly those of the pharmaceutical companies whose products were expensively applied in medically assisted reproduction.[11]

The OLRC Report accepted that the genie of the new reproductive technologies (NRTs) was now out of the bottle, for good and/or ill. The Scarborough case of surrogate motherhood that resulted in the Reference to the Commission also underscored how Ontarians, and other Canadians, could access reproductive services in and through the United States that did not exist, and that might be unlawful, north of the US border. The thrust of the OLRC Report, therefore, was less promotion of the NRTs than damage control: to mitigate their most dysfunctional effects and to keep faith with the first and central principle of its mandate, "protecting the best interests of the child."[12] Priority of this principle required compromise with, and even subordination of, other principles, such as certainty of paternity and even maternity in birth registration. This first principle also presupposed that there would be a child. The Commission recognized the paradox of proposing to "protec[t] ... the child" by preventing its conception and existence.[13]

In contrast, many feminists opposed to the NRTs were calling for prohibition, in pursuit of what they saw as women's best interests. In favouring a prohibitive approach, these feminists allied themselves – largely inadvertently – with the religious opposition, particularly the hierarchy of the Roman Catholic Church. These feminists and the Roman Catholic hierarchy did not appear to be natural allies, but both seemed to fear that if Ontario legislated the OLRC's proposals, the rest of the country would follow. The feminists' strategy in particular evolved to favour Canadian nationwide legal control of NRTs and a national commission to design the means of that control.

The federal government initially failed to respond to, and then resisted, this proposal, but eventually yielded to pressure to have NRTs brought under some form of uniform management. Much of this pressure may have arisen from media coverage of the Baby M case in New Jersey, which came to public attention in 1986 in Family Court child custody proceedings. The story had in abundance the conflict, sensation, and scandal upon which media thrive, becoming an almost worldwide event due to the international dominance of US media.

Mary Beth Whitehead, a New Jersey mother of two young boys, responded to a New York recruiting agency advertisement to serve as a surrogate mother. Her own ovum was fertilized by sperm from William Stern via artificial insemination, on condition that after gestation she would surrender the child to him and his wife Elizabeth. The child was duly born and surrendered. However, the gestational mother subsequently had misgivings about giving up her new daughter, captured the child, and proposed to rear her herself. She named her Sara. The Sterns took legal proceedings to regain custody of the child, whom they had named Melissa (hence Baby M). On appeal, the New Jersey Supreme Court, confirming that surrogate motherhood custody agreements are subject to judicial rulings on the children's best interests, ordered a scheme for joint custody between the bitterly contesting and mutually antagonistic Mrs Whitehead and the Sterns. An authority on US children's law described the judgment as "indisputably the logical, reasoned, and straightforward result of existing legal concepts of parenthood, adoption, baby-selling and the like," but also as "surely the worst result possible."[14]

Realizing that the legal concerns regarding NRTs were mounting, the federal government established by Order in Council the Royal Commission on New Reproductive Technologies (RCNRT) on 25 October 1989. The Commission was chaired by Dr Patricia Baird, a distinguished professor of pediatrics and genetics at the University of British Columbia. Its mandate was "to inquire into and report upon current and potential medical and scientific developments related to new reproductive technologies, considering in particular their social, ethical, health, research, legal and economic implications and the public interest, recommending what policies and safeguards should be applied."[15] The Commission transcended some turmoil among its initial membership, including the departure of some members (who subsequently brought legal proceedings against the government) and the addition of new members. The RCNRT published its Final Report in mid-November 1993 with a membership of five, each the mother of at least two children. This was consistent with a long tradition of respected, influential Canadian Royal Commissions all of whose members were of the same sex.

In addition to its Final Report, the Commission published a number of research studies, received written submissions and opinions, participated in numerous symposia and colloquia, conducted public hearings, and commissioned public opinion surveys. All of these activities were reflected in its report and in its 293 recommendations. After several false starts, some related to the Parliamentary timetable, these recommendations resulted in the enactment of the *AHRA* on 29 March 2004. The recommendations of the UK's Warnock Inquiry, of July 1984, were enacted more than six years later in the *Human Fertilisation and Embryology Act* (1990). By this measure, the ten years between the RCNRT Final Report and the *AHRA* may not appear excessive.[16]

There were several important developments between the submission of the RCNRT Report in 1993 and the enactment of the *AHRA* in 2004, one being the passage of time itself. The RCNRT was influenced by public opinion recorded at the beginning of the 1990s in reaction to the often sensationalized media coverage of NRTs – coverage that was typically quite unfavourable if not positively hostile. The Commission pointed out that in some regards, popular perceptions were factually incorrect, such as the one that sex preference in Canada favoured male children.[17] Greater familiarity with new medical developments, including by personal exposure, often increases comfort and acceptance. Such progress was recorded by two gynecologists in 1966 regarding artificial insemination for the conception of children, when they observed:

> Any change in custom or practice in this emotionally charged area has always elicited a response from established custom and law of horrified negation at first; then negation without horror; then slow and gradual curiosity, study, evaluation, and finally a very slow but steady acceptance."[18]

In a similar vein, greater familiarity and comfort with surrogate motherhood in the UK has resulted in judicial approval of transactions involving payments for "expenses" of up to £15,000 (C$23,500) – which, under government-funded health care, do not include medical and childbirth costs.[19] Similarly, the popular opinions gathered in the early

1990s that influenced the RCNRT may have evolved by 2004 from their initial "horrified negation" stage.

Another development, in the wake of the creation of Dolly the Sheep in 1996, was recognition that human cloning was possible. This led to the introduction of legal prohibitions in Canada as elsewhere. The first of the *AHRA*'s criminal prohibitions, in section 5, is against any attempt to "create a human clone by using any technique, or transplant a human clone into a human being or into any non-human life form or artificial device." This provision is aimed at the condemned possibility of reproductive cloning.[20] However, it may also cover therapeutic cloning,[21] in which an embryo that is pluripotent (i.e., that is capable of developing all organs and tissues of a human body) is created to develop into only a particular organ or cluster of cells with a view to transplantation – for instance, into the donor of the cloned cell.[22] This could produce an organ or tissues sufficiently closely genetically matched to the cell donor to evade rejection (due to the natural immune reaction) and assume normal functions in the recipient's body. With scientific development – now barred in Canada but allowed, for instance, in the UK – this might provide a replacement organ such as a kidney or heart from the cells of a person suffering from terminal organ failure, or tissues to overcome some affliction, for instance diabetes, cancer, or spinal cord injury. As research into human therapeutic cloning advances to achieve regenerative therapies, Canada may have to revisit the scope of the ban on cloning in section 5 of the *AHRA*. Until then, Canadians may have to seek such therapies in other countries.

A further related development concerns human stem cell research, including embryonic stem cell research, based on the pioneering discovery of stem cells by the late Dr Ernest McCulloch and Dr James Till in the 1960s, at the University of Toronto. Section 5(1)(b) of the *AHRA* prohibits the creation of human embryos for any purpose other than human reproduction or reproductive research, so other human embryo–dependent research – for instance, into regenerative medicine and tissue engineering – can be conducted only on embryos created but becoming surplus within programs of IVF treatment. However, those who seek IVF may not possess the genetic characteristics that would be valuable to study for the development of particular stem cell therapies, such as for genetic disorders originating at the embryonic stage of human development that result in spontaneous abortion of embryos or fetuses, or in deaths in childhood or early adolescence. Those affected by these conditions do not survive to enter IVF programs. The development of stem cell therapies for these conditions may require study of purpose-made embryos with specified genetic attributes. That the *AHRA* has effectively precluded embryonic stem cell research into fetal, pediatric, and adolescent genetic disorders in Canada may have been incidental rather than deliberate. It presents the question, however, of whether the provisions of the Act that prevent stem cell research into disorders such as infertility due to chronic spontaneous abortion, and into fatal genetic childhood and adolescent diseases – research that the UK has changed its law to accommodate – are open to challenge under the *Canadian Charter of Rights and Freedoms*, for instance, for discrimination on grounds of age or disability, or for denial of security of the (disabled) person.

In its reference to the Quebec Court of Appeal challenging the *AHRA*, the government of Quebec did not contest the criminal prohibitions contained in sections 5, 6, or 7. Section 6, for instance, prohibits payment, brokerage, and advertising concerning surrogate motherhood arrangements, although in deference to provincial authority the section "does not affect the validity under provincial law of any agreement under which a person [who must be 21 years of age or above; see s. 6(4)] agrees to be a surrogate mother" (s. 6(5)). Quebec's largely successful challenge to the *AHRA*'s provisions affecting health service professionals and facilities was that constitutionally these are under provincial rather than federal control. The following chapters discuss how the Quebec Court of Appeal ruled[23] and how the Supreme Court of Canada upheld but limited the ruling.[24]

Pursuant to the decision of the Supreme Court, provinces are authorized – but not compelled – to legislate not only on non-criminal human reproductive procedures but also on how resulting children are registered at birth and legally integrated into the families in which they will be reared. In the absence of specific legislation on NRTs, registration and integration will continue to be managed under existing legislation and common law doctrines. After Quebec filed its Reference to the provincial Court of Appeal, it introduced amendments to the *Civil Code* to address the NRTs. Other provinces may consider what if any initiatives they might take. More than a quarter-century ago, the Ontario Law Reform Commission reported on its recommendations, but there was no response from the executive branch of the provincial government.[25] Staff in the provincial health ministry, however, are now addressing how the province may respond to the Supreme Court's decision. This may indicate a sense of engagement, though perhaps not necessarily of urgency, in considering the familial, social, and legal concerns raised by these new and now routine reproductive technologies.

NOTES

1 In contrast to parthenogenesis, in which an ovum is induced to divide and develop by itself into a parthenote (i.e., an unfertilized or single-parent embryo). See A. Paffoni, T.A.L. Brevini, E. Somigliana, L. Restelli, F. Grandolfi, and G. Ragin, "In vitro development of human oocytes after parthenogenetic activation or intracytoplasmic sperm injection" (2007) 87:1 Fertility & Sterility 77.

2 "Natural human reproduction is a process which involves the production of male and female gametes and their union at fertilization. Pregnancy is that part of the process that commences with the implantation of the conceptus in a woman." International Federation of Gynecology and Obstetrics (FIGO), "Definition of Pregnancy," in *Ethical Issues in Obstetrics and Gynecology* (London: FIGO, 2015), 113, http://www.figo.org.

3 Partial or traditional surrogate motherhood, in which a woman is impregnated by sperm to bear her own genetic child for surrender to another couple, has a history dating to biblical times (Genesis 16). This is distinguished from full or gestational surrogacy, in which the ovum is from a woman other than the woman who gestates the embryo/fetus *in utero*. See Rachel Cook, Shelley D. Sclater, and Felicity Kaganas, eds., *Surrogate Motherhood: International Perspectives* (Oxford: Hart Publishing, 2003), 1 and 101.

4 *In the Matter of Baby M*, 537 A 2d 1227 (NJ Supreme Ct, 1988), reversing in part 525 A 2d 1128 (NJ Superior Ct, 1987).

5 Ontario Law Reform Commission, *Report on Human Artificial Reproduction and Related Matters* (Toronto: Ministry of the Attorney General, 1985), 1.

6 *Ibid*, at 6.

7 For instance, the *Interim Report of the State of Victoria (Waller) Committee to consider the Social, Ethical and Legal Issues arising from In Vitro Fertilization* (Melbourne: Government of Victoria, 1982).

8 The South African law on surrogacy, for instance, has adopted the approach of prior judicial review.

9 UK Department of Health and Social Security, *Report of the Committee of Inquiry into Human Fertilisation and Embryology*, Cmnd 9314 (London: HMSO, 1984).

10 Ontario, *supra* note 5 at 3.
11 See, for example, Gena Corea, *The Mother Machine: Reproductive Technologies from Artificial Insemination to Artificial Wombs* (New York: HarperCollins, 1986); Christine Overall, *Ethics and Human Reproduction: A Feminist Analysis* (Boston: Allen and Unwin, 1987); and Catherine MacKinnon, *Feminism Unmodified: Discourses on Life and Law* (Cambridge, MA: Harvard University Press, 1987).
12 Ontario, *supra* note 5.
13 See now I. Glenn Cohen, "Regulating Reproduction: The Problem with Best Interests" (2011) 96 Minnesota L Rev 101.
14 Randall P. Bezanson, "Solomon Would Weep: A Comment on *In the Matter of Baby M* and the Limits of Judicial Authority" (1988) 16:1–2 Law, Medicine & Health Care 126; and Larry Gostin, ed., *Surrogate Motherhood: Politics and Privacy* (Bloomington: Indiana University Press, 1990), 243–50.
15 Royal Commission on New Reproductive Technologies, *Proceed with Care: Final Report* (Ottawa: Ministry of Government Services Canada, 1993), v.
16 For the history of the bill's progress to enactment, including the preliminary voluntary moratorium on certain practices, see Glenn Rivard and Judy Hunter, *The Law of Assisted Human Reproduction* (Markham: LexisNexis Canada, 2005), 18–22.
17 Royal, *supra* note 15 at 889–90.
18 Sophia J. Kleegman and Sherwin A. Kaufman, *Infertility in Women* (Philadelphia: F.A. Davis, 1966), 178.
19 See *Re An Adoption Application, [Surrogacy]*, [1987] All ER 826 (Latey J, Family Division), discussed in Eric Blyth and Claire Potter, "Paying for It? Surrogacy, Market Forces and Assisted Conception." in Rachel Cook *et al.*, *supra* note 3 at 227–42.
20 Kerry L. Macintosh, *Illegal Beings: Human Clones and the Law* (New York: Cambridge University Press, 2005).
21 Martha Nussbaum and Cass R. Sunstein, eds., *Clones and Clones: Facts and Fantasies about Human Cloning* (New York: W.W. Norton, 1998).
22 Rivard, *supra* note 16 at 7 and 91–2.
23 *Renvoi relatif à la Loi Sur la procréation assistée (Canada) (Re)*, 2008 QCCA 1167, [2008] RJQ 1551, 298 DLR (4th) 712 (Que CA).
24 *Reference re Assisted Human Reproduction Act*, 2010 SCC 61, [2010] 3 SCR 457, 327 DLR (4th) 257.
25 Ontario, *supra* note 5.

2 Licensing and the *AHRA Reference*

IAN B. LEE

Introduction

In this chapter,[1] I argue that the majority justices in the Reference[2] were justified in concluding that several of the controlled activities provisions in the *Assisted Human Reproduction Act* (*AHRA*)[3] were *ultra vires* Parliament, albeit not precisely for the reasons offered by Justices Lebel and Deschamps. In my view, the infirmity in the controlled activities provisions did not lie in their purpose, as the majority justices contended, but in one of the means they employed, specifically licensing. These features of the Act were not, moreover, sufficiently minor that they could be considered a merely ancillary feature of the scheme.

My argument proceeds in the following steps. First, I provide a brief description of the features of the *AHRA* that are material to my analysis. Second, I explain why the ostensible disagreement between the two main judgments as to the purpose of the challenged legislation is less significant than it first appears. Third, I suggest that the case in fact turns on two disagreements about what means are permissible in the pursuit by Parliament of an admittedly valid criminal law purpose. I shall defend the view that established doctrine concerning the scope of the federal criminal law power favours the Chief Justice's position on one of these disagreements, but not the other. Fourth, I explain why the problematic features of the Act could not be saved by the "ancillary powers" doctrine. In the conclusion, I briefly discuss the implications of my analysis for the scope of federal power to regulate assisted human reproduction (AHR) under the criminal law power. Specifically, I suggest that in amending the Act in 2012 so as to, among other things, repeal the licensing provisions, Parliament has brought the legislation within its powers.[4]

The *AHRA* and the Reference

The Act on which the Supreme Court opined in the Reference contained two types of prohibition. Some activities, such as human cloning, are prohibited outright ("prohibited activities").[5] Other activities, called "controlled activities," are prohibited conditionally. Specifically, the controlled activities are prohibited "except when carried out in accordance with the regulations and a licence."[6] An example of this class of activity is the manipulation of human reproductive material for the purpose of creating an embryo.[7]

In the Reference, the validity of three of the outright prohibitions was conceded. The challenge was instead directed at the other two outright prohibitions,[8] all of the controlled activities provisions, and several of the other supporting provisions of the Act, especially those concerning the issuance of controlled activities licences and the obligations of licensees.[9]

The Chief Justice, writing on behalf of four members of the Court, would have upheld all of the challenged provisions. Justices Lebel and Deschamps, also writing for four justices, were of the opposite view, holding none of them to be valid. The tie-breaking vote was cast by Justice Cromwell, who upheld the challenged outright provisions, one of the controlled activities provisions, and certain of the supporting provisions. The immediate consequence of this divided judgment can be summarized in three propositions. First, all of the outright prohibitions are valid criminal law, as is the prohibition against the reimbursement of expenses incurred by (among others) surrogate mothers and donors of reproductive material otherwise than in accordance with the regulations and a licence. Second, the provisions purporting to control other activities concerning AHR, via a requirement that they be carried out only in accordance with the regulations and a licence, are not valid criminal law. Third, the supporting provisions of the Act, such as those concerning the issuance of licences and the obligations of licensees, are valid only insofar as they relate to the outright prohibitions or the conditional prohibition against reimbursement.

What Is the Disagreement between the Two Main Judgments About?

On the surface of the three judgments, it appears that the disagreement between the Chief Justice, on the one hand, and Justices Lebel and

Deschamps and Justice Cromwell, on the other, concerns the purpose of the provisions. Since the *Margarine Reference*, the recognized requirements for valid criminal legislation have been that the law be prohibitory, that it impose a penalty, and that it have a valid criminal law purpose.[10] Neither the Chief Justice nor Justices Lebel and Deschamps doubted that the impugned provisions satisfied the first two requirements, but they disagreed about whether the provisions had a valid purpose.[11] Justice Cromwell did not comment at all on the first two requirements; like Justices Lebel and Deschamps, he treated the purpose requirement as pivotal.

What was problematic about the purpose of the provisions that were not upheld? There are two ways of describing the problem. First, in Justices Lebel and Deschamps's opinion, the provisions appeared to have as their purpose "to establish mandatory national standards for assisted human reproduction"[12] rather than, as the Chief Justice maintained, to "prohibit inappropriate practices."[13] The implication of this disagreement is, of course, that the establishment of national standards for an activity is not a permissible criminal law purpose.

Second, because it is normally the purpose of a criminal law to prevent a social harm, there appears to have been a dispute about the harmfulness, or lack thereof, of the activities targeted by the legislation. For instance, analysing each of the impugned provisions, the Chief Justice emphasized that their purpose was to prevent certain moral and other social harms.[14] Justices Lebel and Deschamps countered that, at least insofar as the controlled activities are concerned, "nothing in the record suggests that [they] should be regarded as conduct that is reprehensible or represents a serious risk to morality, safety or public health."[15]

Taking the two main judgments at face value, there appears, therefore, to be a disagreement as to what the purpose of the impugned provisions is and as to whether the criminalized activities cause sufficient harm or present sufficient risk. In my view, however, there are good reasons for doubting that these ostensible disagreements are what the case actually turns on. Consider the first disagreement – the disagreement about whether the purpose of the legislation is to prohibit inappropriate conduct or to establish standards for assisted reproduction. This is a disagreement about semantics, akin to arguing about whether the purpose of a curfew is to prevent late nights out or to establish the time for coming home. It is a dispute about two different ways of saying the same thing; it is not the kind of disagreement that can be resolved by reasoned argument.

As for the second disagreement, as to whether the criminalized conduct is risky or harmful enough, it is important to notice that the justices are not referring to the same conduct. The Chief Justice is referring to the subset of the controlled activities that are determined by the Governor in Council to be harmful.[16] By contrast, Justices Lebel and Deschamps are referring to the controlled activities in general when they assert that they do not pose serious risks to health, morality, or safety – that they are not, in short, dangerous.[17]

These observations lead me to conclude that, insofar as the controlled activities are concerned, the true ground of disagreement between the Chief Justice and Justices Lebel and Deschamps is not whether the prevention of social harm is the purpose of the legislation, or whether the harm in question is legally sufficient. Rather, it is the following: Which activities must be harmful or dangerous – the controlled activities in general or only the prohibited subset? I now turn to an analysis of this question.

The Ends and Means of the Criminal Law

The *Margarine* criteria define the permissible ends and means of federal criminal legislation. The criminal law pursues a particular end – namely, the prevention of harm to a public interest – which is why the activities against which the law is directed must be harmful or dangerous. It pursues this end by distinctive means, specifically the prohibition and penalization of the harmful or dangerous conduct.

If the justices did not dwell upon the means employed by the *AHRA*, it is likely because it is, in a sense, obvious that the impugned prohibitory provisions, including those concerned with the controlled activities, employ permissible means. They are, after all, prohibitory, and the Act imposes penalties for their violation. I nevertheless contend, with respect to the controlled activities in particular, that the divergence between the Chief Justice and Justices Lebel and Deschamps's respective analyses of the provisions' purpose is most usefully thought of as a disagreement about means.

Recall that the controlled activities are prohibited "except when carried out in accordance with the regulations and a licence." The crucial questions, therefore, are these. First, when a given activity (X) is not harmful or dangerous in general, but is harmful or dangerous when carried out in a particular manner or under particular circumstances (X′), is it permissible for Parliament to authorize the Governor in

Council to define and prohibit X′? Second, can Parliament authorize a licensing authority to define X′? These are questions about the means to which Parliament may validly resort, under its criminal law authority, in order to achieve the undoubtedly valid objective of preventing harm to a public interest.

There is an easy answer to the first question: yes, the harmful, prohibited sphere of activity can be defined by the Governor in Council. This was the principle of decision in *R v Hydro Quebec*, in which the Supreme Court upheld an environmental protection scheme containing precisely this structure.[18] Justices Lebel and Deschamps's choice to direct their analysis at the controlled activities as a whole, rather than only the prohibited subset of them, stands in some tension with the principle established in *Hydro-Quebec*. It is telling that Lebel and Deschamps JJ cite *Hydro-Quebec* only once (and for a different principle), whereas the Chief Justice cites it seven times. Depending on one's attitude towards that decision, Lebel and Deschamps's approach can be viewed either as doctrinally questionable or as a laudable attempt to limit the authority of a narrowly decided and normatively problematic precedent.[19]

The second question – whether Parliament can authorize a licensing authority to determine the harmful, prohibited sphere of activity – is where, in my view, the *AHRA* encounters serious difficulty. In *Reciprocal Insurance*, the Judicial Committee of the Privy Council held to be invalid a federal act that made it an offence to "mak[e] or carr[y] out … an insurance contract in the absence of a licence from the Minister of Finance issued pursuant to the … Insurance Act of Canada."[20] Justice Duff, sitting on the Judicial Committee, wrote: "It is one thing … to declare corruption in municipal elections, or negligence of a given order in the management of railway trains, to be a criminal offence and punishable under the Criminal Code; it is another thing to make use of the machinery of the criminal law for the purpose of assuming control of municipal corporations or of Provincial railways."[21] In other words, while it is permissible for Parliament to draw lines between lawful and unlawful conduct, it cannot "assume control" over an otherwise lawful activity by submitting it to federal licensing.

To be sure, *Hydro-Quebec* relaxes the *Reciprocal Insurance* principle to an extent, insofar as Parliament may delegate to the federal cabinet the delineation, by Order in Council, of the proscribed area of conduct. However, there is a world of difference between regulations, which establish rules of general application and are published in the Canada Gazette, and the conditions attached by a licensing authority to individual licences. *Hydro-Quebec* recognizes that ministerial regulations are analogous to statutes; it does not follow that, as far as delegated prohibition is concerned, anything goes.

Since *Reciprocal Insurance*, it has also come to be recognized that licensing is permissible, within the criminal law power, if the licensed activity is harmful or dangerous. Thus, in the *Firearms Reference*, the Supreme Court upheld a federal firearms licensing regime; however, the decision rests critically on the Court's determination that firearms are intrinsically dangerous.[22] It can be inferred from that decision that, where an activity is harmful or dangerous, Parliament may indeed "assume control" over it. But, as Justices Lebel and Deschamps observe, there is no suggestion that the controlled activities, which the *AHRA* purports to subject to federal licensing, are intrinsically harmful or dangerous. Certainly, neither Parliament nor the federal government took this position.[23]

I have suggested that, despite the justices' emphasis on the purpose of the impugned legislation, their superficial disagreement on this subject masks a more substantial divergence between them as to the means that must be employed by federal legislation in order to support its characterization as criminal law. Specifically, the key question was whether, in the pursuit of a valid criminal law purpose (the prevention of social and moral harm), it is permissible for Parliament to delegate the power to define the harmful, prohibited forms of an otherwise non-dangerous activity to (a) the Governor in Council and (b) a licensing authority. I have argued that the case law supports an affirmative answer to part (a) and a negative answer to part (b).

A Permissible Encroachment on Provincial Powers?

I have suggested that, in principle, the criminal law power does not authorize Parliament to delegate to a licensing authority the power to define the harmful, prohibited forms of an otherwise non-dangerous activity. The licensing features of the *AHRA*, of course, run afoul of this principle. However, it is the main features of an Act that determine its constitutionality, even if there is some incidental encroachment on the powers of the other level of government.[24] It follows that the licensing provisions are valid if they are incidental, or ancillary, to the prohibitory features of the Act (the "ancillary powers doctrine"). Specifically, they need to be sufficiently minor and sufficiently related to the functioning of the prohibitory features. This is, indeed, what the Chief Justice says about what she describes as the "administrative provisions" of the Act, which concern, among other things, the issuance of licences and the legal obligations of licensees. According to the Chief Justice, these provisions effect no more than a "minor incursion on provincial jurisdiction,"[25] and this incursion helps ensure the effectiveness of the prohibitions.[26]

In determining that the incursion is minor, the Chief Justice explained, in particular, that the property and civil rights power is a "very broad" power[27] and that the provisions do not "purport to create a substantive right";[28] the latter would represent a more significant invasion of the property and civil rights power. The Chief Justice's analysis proceeds, obviously, on the assumption that the significance of the encroaching provisions is to be assessed in comparison to the magnitude of the provincial power in question.

However, it is not sufficient, in my view, that the licensing provisions be minor relative to the vastness of the property and civil rights power. In order for the licensing provisions of the Act to be minor features that do not affect the overall prohibitory character of the Act, the licensing provisions also need to be minor in comparison to the rest of the Act. In making the latter assessment, certain inquiries are relevant, such as: How large is the licensed, non-prohibited sphere of activity relative to the prohibited sphere? (The prohibited sphere includes the sphere prohibited by the regulations.) And how extensive are the legal obligations imposed upon licensees? The Chief Justice's opinion does not consider these questions.[29]

Conclusion

I have argued that it is permissible, under the criminal law power, for Parliament to delegate to the Governor in Council the definition of the harmful or dangerous and therefore prohibited sphere of a generally non-dangerous activity. However, the criminal law power should not be understood as permitting Parliament to subject a non-dangerous activity to a requirement of federal licensing, at least where the licensing requirement and the obligations of licensees are not a minor part of the legislation.

In June 2012, a bill containing, among other things, amendments to the *AHRA* received Royal Assent. Under my analysis, these amendments suffice to repair the constitutional defect in the original legislation. Specifically, the 2012 amendments remove the (problematic) licensing requirement for the controlled activities,[30] leaving in place the (unproblematic) prohibition against carrying out certain of the controlled activities "except in accordance with the regulations."[31]

NOTES

1 The argument set forth in this chapter is along the lines of my argument in Ian B. Lee, "The *Assisted Human Reproduction Act Reference* and the Federal Criminal Law Power," Case Comment (2012) 90:2 Can Bar Rev 469.
2 *Reference re Assisted Human Reproduction Act*, 2010 SCC 61, [2010] 3 SCR 457 [*AHRA Reference*].
3 *Assisted Human Reproduction Act*, SC 2004, c 2, ss 10–13.
4 *Jobs, Growth and Long-term Prosperity Act*, SC 2012, c 19.
5 *AHRA*, ss 5–9.
6 *AHRA*, ss 10–12. In addition, s 13 prohibits licensees from undertaking controlled activities in unlicensed premises.
7 Subsection 10(1). This would include, for instance, artificial insemination.
8 The challenged outright prohibitions were those set forth in ss 8 and 9 (a prohibition against the use of reproductive material without the donor's consent, and a prohibition against the use of reproductive material from a donor under eighteen years of age).
9 The challenged provisions were ss 14–19 (information collection and privacy), 40–53 (licensing and inspection), 60 and 61 (offences), and 68.
10 *Reference re Validity of Section 5(a) of the Dairy Industry Act*, [1949] SCR 1, [1949] 1 DLR 433.
11 Justice Cromwell's analysis is also formulated in terms of the purpose of the legislation. He states that most of the challenged provisions "cannot be characterized as serving any criminal law purpose recognized by the Court's jurisprudence": *AHRA Reference* at para 287.
12 *AHRA Reference* at para 226 ("the purpose of the impugned provisions was to establish mandatory national standards for assisted human reproduction").
13 For example, para 24 ("The text of the Act suggests that its dominant purpose is to prohibit inappropriate practices, rather than to promote beneficial ones").
14 *AHRA Reference* at paras 89–121.
15 *AHRA Reference* at para 251.
16 Recall that the Act prohibits the controlled activities "except when carried out in accordance with the regulations and a licence." The Chief Justice's

reasoning is, in essence, that regulations promulgated by the Governor in Council will define under what circumstances and in what forms the controlled activities are morally or socially harmful, and what the Act does is prohibit this subset of the controlled activities. See *supra* note 4.

17 See *supra* note 13.

18 *R v Hydro-Québec*, [1997] 3 SCR 213, 151 DLR (4th) 32.

19 It would have been possible to distinguish the *AHRA* from the legislation upheld in *Hydro-Quebec*. In the latter case, the majority emphasized that delegation of the authority to determine and proscribe the harmful sphere of conduct was necessary in light of "the particular nature and requirements of effective environmental protection legislation" (*R v Hydro-Québec*, [1997] 3 SCR 213, at para 147). This observation, of course, invites the question whether the effective prevention of harms relating to assisted human reproduction shares, or does not share, these "particular … requirements." Moreover, the environmental protection scheme in *Hydro-Quebec* contained a definition of "toxic" such that it is reasonable to believe that the Governor in Council's determination whether to add a substance to the list of toxic substances, and in what quantity and concentration the emission of the substance should be permitted, is to be based on whether the emission would "constitute a danger to the environment … or … to human life or health" (*Canadian Environmental Protection Act*, RSC 1985, c 16 (4th Supp), s 11; now SC 1999, c 33, s 11). The absence of a similar cue in the *AHRA* requires us, to a greater extent, to accept on faith that the prohibitions will ultimately be directed at harmful or dangerous practices. These avenues were not pursued by Lebel and Deschamps JJ.

20 *The Attorney General of Ontario v The Reciprocal Insurers*, [1924] AC 328.

21 *Ibid* at pages 9–10.

22 *Reference re Firearms Act (Can)*, 2000 SCC 31, [2000] 1 SCR 783. See, for example, para 33 ("Parliament views firearms as dangerous and regulates their possession and use on that ground"); para 42 ("Guns are restricted because they are dangerous"); and para 43 ("Parliament views guns as particularly dangerous and has sought to combat that danger by extending its licensing and registration scheme to all classes of firearms").

23 For instance, s 2 of the *AHRA*, which sets forth the principles underlying the Act, contains no suggestion that Parliament considers assisted human reproduction to be dangerous, let alone harmful. Nor, in its factum, did the federal government contend that the controlled activities, outside the zone of prohibition established by the Governor in Council, are harmful or dangerous. The federal government did argue that "the practices addressed by the Act … pose unique risks to morality or health, or

both, because the practices involve the artificial creation of human life" (Appellant's Factum, para 32; see also paras 6, 134), but this falls short of a claim that the activities are harmful or dangerous. The operation of motor vehicles poses risks, too; yet a federal driver's licensing scheme would not be valid criminal legislation. See *Firearms,* at para 43. Similarly, the Chief Justice does not suggest that the controlled activities are, in general, harmful or dangerous; rather, she regards the scheme of the controlled activities provisions as one in which the Governor in Council is authorized to determine the harmful or dangerous subset of them, while leaving the others "untouched" (Chief Justice, para 101).

24 *General Motors v City National Leasing,* [1989] 1 SCR 641 at paras 46–7; Peter W. Hogg, *Constitutional Law of Canada,* s 15.9(c).

25 *AHRA Reference* at para 137.

26 *Ibid* at para 145 (for instance, the information collection obligations imposed upon licensees "help to ensure that the Act's prohibitions are respected").

27 *Ibid* at para 134.

28 *Ibid* at para 135.

29 *AHRA Reference.* In describing the "pith and substance" of the Act, the Chief Justice does assert that its "dominant effect" is to prohibit certain things (at para 32). Unfortunately, the analysis in support of this assertion is rather thin (paras 31–3); it appears to consist of an acknowledgment that the Act "has an impact on the regulation of medical research and practice and hospital administration" followed by an assertion that "dominant effect" of the Act is prohibitory despite its "impact on provincial matters."

30 *Jobs, Growth and Long-term Prosperity Act,* SC 2012, c 19, ss 717–20, 724.

31 Section 11 of the Act was repealed altogether. In ss 10 and 12, the licensing requirement was deleted, but not the requirement of compliance with the regulations.

3 The Federalism Implications of the *Assisted Human Reproduction Act Reference*

HOI L. KONG

The *Reference re Assisted Human Reproduction Act* [*AHRA Reference*][1] evidenced deep disagreements in the Supreme Court of Canada about the scope and significance of provincial autonomy. In this chapter, I set the disagreements within the Court in a theoretical context, tease out some implications of those disagreements, and offer a framework for resolving them. I focus on the criminal law power and the double aspect and paramountcy doctrines, and not on other doctrines addressed in the reasons (including the ancillary doctrine), because they clearly illustrate the debate over provincial autonomy that I intend to analyse. Elsewhere, I have argued that the concept of Canadian federalism encompasses many different values, including provincial autonomy.[2] I have argued that the judiciary, within the limits of its institutional capacity and its appropriate role in the constitutional order, should seek to ensure that no federalism value is suppressed. I label this imperative to protect against the suppression of federalism values the norm of non-suppression. In this chapter, I identify conditions in which the value of provincial autonomy is suppressed and argue that when these conditions arise, there is a violation of the norm. I begin by setting out what I mean by autonomy and its suppression.

One is autonomous, in the sense I intend here, when one is free from the influence of another's arbitrary will. This conception of autonomy has been perhaps most prominently articulated by Philip Pettit in his republican theory of freedom as non-domination.[3] One is dominated, Pettit argues, when one is subject to the arbitrary will of another, and a relationship can be characterized as dominating even when the dominated party's interests are not arbitrarily interfered with. The classic example of a relationship characterized by such domination is the master–slave relationship. Pettit notes that a slave in such a relationship is subject to domination even if the master is benevolent and does not in fact exercise his capacity to interfere arbitrarily with the interests of the slave.[4] The capacity to so interfere is sufficient for such a master–slave relationship to be characterized as one of domination.

Pettit argues that in the political sphere, government can stand in a similarly dominating position relative to citizens. According to Pettit, government is in this sort of dominating position when it fails to track interests that members of a polity perceive they share by virtue of their common membership. Pettit includes in the list of these "common, perceived interests" uncontroversial public goods such as "a stable framework for commercial and civic relations,"[5] and in my view, the norms of a constitutional order form an essential part of that stable framework. Pettit suggests two means by which we can identify when a failure to track such perceived common interests occurs. He claims that citizens in such a relationship of domination suffer from certain effects, one of which in particular is pertinent to the present analysis: a citizen so dominated will suffer from persistent uncertainty about when her interests will be interfered with.[6] Such is the case of a citizen whose interests are beholden to the arbitrary whims of a government administrator. Pettit also argues that it will be *common knowledge* in a polity when government action fails to track the common perceived interests of citizens. For example, in a society that prizes the rule of law, it will be common knowledge that an administrator who is unconstrained by law and who has the capacity to inflict indiscriminate harm on citizens who are subject to his authority has been granted a power that does not track the common perceived interest of those citizens in being free from this kind of despotism. According to Pettit, it will be common knowledge that those citizens are unfree.

How would such a conception of freedom apply to the relationship between the federal and provincial governments, and how might one identify a situation where provincial legislative autonomy is systematically suppressed? We might begin by identifying the *effects* of a federal–provincial relationship characterized by domination. If a provincial government were subject to persistent uncertainty regarding when the federal government would interfere with its constitutionally defined interests, we would say that the province's autonomy was compromised in much the same way as our hypothetical citizens would lack freedom when subject to the arbitrary will of an administrator. In the context of federalism, the uncertainty would arise because the federal government would have the power to interfere extensively in constitutionally defined areas of provincial jurisdiction, without meaningful constitutional constraint. The absence of such constraint would be significant because the constitution in a federal state like Canada is the source of legitimating reasons for federal and provincial government action, and it articulates the common perceived interests of those levels of government. The constitution, through the division of powers, provides the polity's framework of reasons for determining whether the federal government, in its interactions with the provinces, tracks their common interest in benefiting from a meaningful defined measure of autonomy. If a federal government were permitted to act unconstrained by such constitutional reasons, it would be part of the *common knowledge* of the members of the polity that the provinces' autonomy was being severely compromised. I contend that when provincial autonomy is compromised to this degree and in this way, it is systematically suppressed.[7] Note, moreover, that according to the general theory of domination that supports this conception of autonomy, the mere fact that the federal government under such conditions might *permit* provinces to regulate within the scope of their constitutional authority would not be sufficient to demonstrate that provincial autonomy had not been compromised. A province standing in relation to a federal government that granted such permission would enjoy this capacity to regulate only at the constitutionally unconstrained pleasure of the federal government.[8]

It is important to note that a given set of circumstances in a polity can generate disagreement about whether provincial government autonomy is being suppressed. There can, nonetheless, be agreement in that polity over the general principle that provincial autonomy is suppressed when provinces are persistently uncertain about whether the federal government will interfere with their common perceived interests, and when the federal government is free to act, unconstrained by constitutional reasons.[9] In what follows, I will be arguing that a particular constellation and specification of constitutional doctrines results in the systematic suppression of provincial autonomy. I accept that there may be disagreement about whether that constellation in fact yields this result, but I assume that all reasonable observers would accept my statement of the general principle of what constitutes suppression. I assume that the general principle forms part of the common knowledge of the Canadian polity and, furthermore, that those who accept my characterization of the relevant circumstances will also accept my conclusion that the doctrines in question suppress the autonomy of the provinces.

This chapter has two broad aims. First, to clarify the positions of the two main sets of reasons in the *AHRA Reference* and to specify the nature of the disagreements between them. Second, to demonstrate that the Chief Justice's reasons violated the norm of non-suppression. In particular, I will be arguing that the breadth of her interpretation of the criminal law power, and the extent of the deference she gives to Parliament, combined with the current state of the double aspect and paramountcy doctrines (which together govern cases in which provincial law enters into conflict with federal law), systematically threaten the autonomy of provincial legislatures. I begin with a brief summary of the reasons in the *AHRA Reference.*

Part I. *Reference re Assisted Human Reproduction Act*: Conceiving the Criminal Law Power

In the *AHRA Reference,*[10] the Court addressed the question of whether some sections of the *Assisted Human Reproduction Act* (*AHRA*)[11] exceeded the legislative authority of Parliament under section 91(27) of the *Constitution Act, 1867* to enact criminal law. One group of four Justices – LeBel, Deschamps, Abella, and Rothstein JJ – reasoned that all of the challenged provisions were *ultra vires* the criminal law power, except to the extent that two of the challenged provisions contained offences related to provisions not in dispute.[12] Another group of four Justices – McLachlin CJ and Binnie, Fish, and Charron JJ – concluded that some of the challenged provisions were *intra vires* the criminal law power and that although the rest were not in pith and substance criminal law, they were nonetheless valid under the ancillary powers doctrine.[13] Cromwell J, in a tersely written set of reasons, provided the swing vote. As a result of his reasons, a majority of the Court (Cromwell, LeBel, Deschamps, Abella, and Rothstein JJ) held that some of the *Act*'s challenged provisions in pith and substance regulated matters of exclusive provincial jurisdiction, including the establishment, maintenance, and management of hospitals, property, and civil rights in the province and matters of a purely local or private nature in the province.[14] A second majority of members of the Court (McLachlin CJ and Cromwell, Binnie, Fish, and Charron JJ) held that the remaining challenged provisions were valid. In this chapter, I focus on the reasons of Lebel and Deschamps JJ, on the one hand, and those of the Chief Justice, on the other, as they evince the most clearly defined theoretical positions.

The sharpest disagreements in the case were over the definition of the criminal law power. These disagreements raised issues related to the contents of the power and the institutional role of the judiciary in resolving federalism disputes. The two main sets of reasons diverge in their analysis of the breadth of the criminal law power. The Chief Justice wrote: "A crabbed, categorical approach to valid criminal law purposes is … inappropriate. On the other hand, a limitless definition, combined with the doctrine of paramountcy, has the potential to upset the constitutional balance of federal-provincial powers. Both extremes must be rejected."[15] With this statement of the range of the debate in view, let us turn now to examine the points over which the Chief Justice and her colleagues disagreed.

1. The Chief Justice's Approach: An Open-Ended Definition of the Power and a Deferential Stance towards Parliament

The Chief Justice's reasons invoked precedent and a broadly defined constitutional principle to delineate the criminal law power, and set out a deferential standard of review. The Chief Justice identified the substance of the power in a set of public purposes drawn from precedent, and she referred to the balance of federal–provincial powers as the guiding principle for interpreting the criminal law power. According to the standard formulation, cited by the Chief Justice, legislation enacted pursuant to the criminal law power must have a valid public purpose and must contain a prohibition backed by a penalty. Of particular relevance to the Chief Justice's assessment of the *AHRA* were the public purposes of morality and health. She relied on *R v Malmo-Levine*[16] to reason that "Parliament need only have a reasonable basis to expect that its legislation will address a moral concern of fundamental importance."[17] The role of the judiciary, reasoned the Chief Justice, is twofold: to verify that legislation in pith and substance relates to what "Parliament views as contrary to our central moral precepts, and that there is a consensus in society that the regulated activity engages a moral concern of fundamental importance."[18] In articulating the content of the public purpose of health, the Chief Justice drew from precedents three indicia for identifying when a legislative objective falls within the scope of this purpose: when that objective "is grounded in (1) human conduct that (2) has an injurious or undesirable effect (3) on the health of members of the public."[19] According to her interpretation of the precedents, a court assessing legislation under this purpose need only satisfy itself that Parliament had a "reasonable apprehension of harm"; and, reasoned the Chief Justice, there is no constitutional threshold of harm.[20]

2. The Reasons of Justices LeBel and Deschamps: A Narrower Definition of the Power and a Less Deferential Stance

As did the Chief Justice, LeBel and Deschamps JJ referred to precedent and principle as they interpreted the scope of the criminal law power. While the Chief Justice took as her guiding principle the broadly defined federal–provincial balance of powers, LeBel and Deschamps JJ drew from the precedents a more specific set of principles. First, the Justices invoked the principle that governments in a federation are coordinate, not subordinate,[21] drawing this principle from the *Reference re Secession of Quebec*.[22] Second, they referred to that reference, as well as to the reasons of L'Heureux-Dubé J in *114957 Canada Ltée (Spraytech, Société d'arrosage) v Hudson (Town)*,[23] to support the proposition that subsidiarity is a principle of our federal system that is tied to the democracy-facilitating features of that system.[24] Finally, the Justices drew from double aspect and ancillary powers cases the principle that the division of powers involves "a measure of flexibility that enables governments at different levels to co-operate in pursuing their legislative mandates."[25]

At first glance, LeBel and Deschamps JJ's invocation of these principles and their use of precedent do not significantly distinguish their reasons from those of the Chief Justice, who relies on similar sources of constitutional authority. Perhaps the most striking point of divergence between the principle invoked by the Chief Justice and the principles referenced by LeBel and Deschamps JJ has to do with their relative levels of generality. The principles of LeBel and Deschamps JJ are more specific and thus leave to a court applying them less interpretive room than does the open-ended principle of federal balance invoked by the Chief Justice. Compare, for example, the effects of LeBel and Deschamps JJ's non-subordination principle with the effects of the Chief Justice's balance of powers principle on a division of powers analysis.

If the baseline for determining whether the balance of power between the federal and provincial orders of government is upset is a status quo that permits substantial provincial subordination, one can have subordination without necessarily upsetting – in the sense of altering – the federal–provincial balance.[26] In addition, one can imagine circumstances in which the potential for subordination created by a confluence of constitutional doctrines is offset by on-the-ground federalism practices that allow for cooperation-as-equals between the orders of government.[27] In this instance, there may be subordination but no upsetting of the federal balance of powers, if the doctrine and practices governing federal–provincial relations are considered as a whole. In both these examples, if courts were to adopt the balance of powers principle then the question of whether the doctrinal rules should be altered would be left open, whereas if they were to adopt the anti-subordination principle, that question would be settled. The anti-subordination principle would require doctrinal change in order to lessen the extent of provincial subordination in the federal system.

Consider next the reasons' respective interpretations of the contents of the criminal law power. The interpretations diverge most sharply in their treatment of the valid public purpose requirement. LeBel and Deschamps JJ reasoned that for legislation to fall within the criminal law power, its purpose must be to "suppress an evil."[28] They added that this purpose requirement can only be satisfied if the federal government has "a concrete basis and a reasoned apprehension of harm"[29] and if the conduct targeted is "inherently harmful."[30] The Justices fleshed out what they meant by inherently harmful conduct as they worked through the precedents and identified the specific conduct in each of the cases considered that gave rise to risks of harm that could be reasonably apprehended.[31]

LeBel and Deschamps JJ's reasons have implications for how broadly they read the criminal law power and the level of deference accorded to Parliament. For LeBel and Deschamps JJ, the requirement of suppressing evil applies to all the specific examples of valid public purposes that are invoked in the case law, including morality.[32] By contrast, for the Chief Justice the valid public purpose requirement can be satisfied if legislation aims simply to address "a moral concern of fundamental importance."[33] LeBel and Deschamps JJ's version of the public purpose requirement is narrower and therefore more restrictive of Parliament's power to legislate under the criminal law power than is the Chief Justice's version. As a consequence, their reasoning is also less deferential to Parliament, as it requires more by way of justification for legislation that would purport to be enacted pursuant to the criminal law power.

Part II. Two Views of Double Aspect and Paramountcy Doctrine

In addition to the disagreements over the scope of the criminal law power, there were in the *AHRA Reference* conflicts over the scope of the double aspect doctrine's application and, by implication, the reach of the paramountcy doctrine. In this section, I place the disagreement in the context of recent developments in federalism doctrine and identify precisely the central point of disagreement. The reasons of the Chief Justice are consistent with recent developments in double aspect and paramountcy doctrine, and it is worth briefly considering those developments. As Wade Wright has argued, the Court has adopted an interpretive approach that permits significant jurisdictional overlap and intergovernmental cooperation.[34] This degree of overlap results from a particular approach to double aspect doctrine. According to that doctrine, both orders of government are permitted to regulate in areas of political, social, and economic life that can be validly characterized as falling within the legislative jurisdiction of both orders. The classic example is highway regulation, which the provinces can regulate pursuant to their jurisdiction over purely local matters or over property and civil rights, and which the federal government can regulate pursuant to its criminal law power.[35] The Court has interpreted the federal heads of powers broadly and, in addition, has permitted the orders of government to regulate in ways that have substantial "incidental effects" on each other's jurisdiction in areas of common concern.[36]

The result of these interpretive choices has been to extend the reach of the double aspect doctrine by expanding the number and scope of areas that are open to both federal and provincial regulation. As a further consequence, the Court limits exercises of legislative power under the division of powers not primarily through determinations of invalidity, but rather mainly by applying the paramountcy doctrine. In general, paramountcy doctrine specifies the conditions under which federal and provincial law conflict and mandates that when these conditions obtain, the federal law prevails over the provincial and renders the provincial law inoperative. Although the Court has adopted a broad "frustration of federal legislative purposes" test in addition to its "impossibility of dual compliance" test for determining whether there has been a conflict sufficient to trigger federal paramountcy, it has counselled courts to exercise caution in applying the broader test.[37] If applied with restraint, the Court has reasoned, the paramountcy rules, combined with a generously applied double aspect doctrine, permit considerable room for overlapping exercises of legislative power and significant opportunities for intergovernmental cooperation.

1. The Chief Justice's Interpretation of the Double Aspect Doctrine

The Chief Justice's reasons in the *AHRA Reference* reflect these doctrinal developments. According to the Chief Justice:

> "Double occupancy" of a field of endeavour, such as health, is a permanent feature of the Canadian constitutional order. It leads to a standard, "double aspect" analysis under which both aspects subsist side by side, except in a case of conflict, when the federal power prevails ... Canadian constitutional jurisprudence has consistently granted wide latitude to the federal criminal law power, despite the fact that much of the criminal law has a provincial regulatory counterpart.[38]

In this excerpt we can see key features of the emerging constitutional consensus identified by Wright. The Chief Justice, in setting out the double aspect doctrine, articulated a broad interpretation of the federal power and conceded that this results in significant overlap with areas of provincial jurisdiction. Moreover, in her rejection of her colleagues' attempt to circumscribe the scope of the criminal law power and in her affirmation of paramountcy doctrine, she exemplified the Court's general tendency to favour recourse to paramountcy rules over findings of legislative invalidity as a means of resolving federalism disputes.

In a related passage, the Chief Justice affirmed a final element of the emerging constitutional consensus, namely, the priority the Court gives to intergovernmental cooperation as a mode of regulating the division of powers. According to the Chief Justice, section 68 of the *AHRA* – which empowers the Governor in Council to declare sections of the *Act* inapplicable in a province in cases where there is an agreement that laws in force in the province are equivalent to those sections – is a mechanism for provincial–federal cooperation in an area of overlapping jurisdiction.[39] This interpretation of that section is reinforced by the Chief Justice's conception of the principle of subsidiarity. The Chief Justice in the *AHRA Reference* limited the application of that principle to circumstances in which provincial (or municipal) regulation complements federal legislation and enables federal purposes to be adapted to local circumstances.[40] The Chief Justice reasoned that the principle of subsidiarity could not, however, restrict a legitimate exercise of legislative power by Parliament. The Chief Justice summarized her disagreement with her colleagues in this way: "I cannot subscribe to the picture of Canadian federalism painted by my colleagues, where the federal criminal law power would be circumscribed by provincial competencies."[41]

2. Justices LeBel and Deschamps on Double Aspect Doctrine

It is perhaps helpful to introduce the LeBel and Deschamps JJ reasoning on the double aspect doctrine with the Chief Justice's characterization of their understanding of subsidiarity. She summarized their position in this way: "Since the provincial governments are closest to health care, the argument goes, they should exercise power in this area, free from the interference of the criminal law. Subsidiarity therefore favours provincial jurisdiction."[42] Yet LeBel and Deschamps JJ did not refer to the subsidiarity principle in order to define the scope of the heads of power. Rather, they reasoned that the principle may assist courts in determining whether legislation fits within one head of power or the other. They invoked the principle at the end of a long analysis that found that the impugned provisions of the *AHRA* were *ultra vires* because, in pith and substance, they were legislation in relation to the provinces' jurisdiction over hospitals, property, and civil rights and matters of a local or private nature.[43] Justices LeBel and Deschamps introduced the subsidiarity principle by stating that "[i]f any doubt remained, that is where the principle of subsidiarity could apply."[44] This formulation suggests that the subsidiarity principle will be relevant in cases where the extrinsic and intrinsic evidence, as well as an examination of the legal effects, all tend towards a finding of provincial jurisdiction but do not conclusively establish the finding. Since LeBel and Deschamps JJ only suggested that if the principle were to be applied, it would have led to a finding that the provisions at issue were *ultra vires*, they did not specify how the principle would be applied in a particular case. Nonetheless, it is clear that the Chief Justice's description of their position bears little resemblance to their analysis. Justices LeBel and Deschamps suggested that the principle might be incorporated into a pith and substance analysis, under specific circumstances. They did not suggest that the principle was relevant to a determination of the *definition* of the criminal law power.

This distinction is important because it helps clarify the nature of the disagreement between the two sets of reasons over the double aspect doctrine. Contrary to what the Chief Justice suggested, LeBel and Deschamps JJ did not deny the possibility of jurisdictional overlap in the area of health.[45] Indeed, with respect to the activities that were the object of the *AHRA* provisions not challenged in the *AHRA Reference*, LeBel and Deschamps JJ expressly noted the existence of such an overlap.[46] However, with respect to a range of other activities that were the object of various impugned provisions,[47] the Justices reasoned that "in light of the legislative facts adduced in evidence," regulation of them could not be characterized as falling within criminal jurisdiction, but could only be characterized as being within provincial jurisdiction.[48]

We are now in a position to characterize the nature of the disagreement between the Chief Justice and LeBel and Deschamps JJ over the double aspect doctrine. Because LeBel and Deschamps JJ defined the criminal law power more narrowly than did the Chief Justice, they will necessarily find (as they did in the *AHRA Reference*) some laws that the Chief Justice would consider *intra vires* to be beyond the jurisdiction of Parliament's criminal law power. It does not follow, as the Chief Justice's reasons would have it, that LeBel and Deschamps JJ held "that the double aspect doctrine does not apply to this field of double occupancy (health)."[49] As we have seen, the Chief Justice's colleagues expressly stated that some aspects of the field of health do give rise to the possibility of double occupancy. However, for those activities that are beyond the reach of Parliament's criminal law power (as well as any of its other powers), there is no possibility of double occupancy and therefore no room for paramountcy to operate. This conclusion is not "a new approach of provincial exclusivity."[50] It simply follows from an interpretation of the division of powers in which there are some limits on federal jurisdiction and from the principle of exhaustiveness. According to that principle, no activity can fall outside the jurisdiction of both orders of government.[51] For those areas of social, economic, and political life that are beyond the reach of federal jurisdiction, the principle of exhaustiveness requires that the provinces have jurisdiction, and that jurisdiction is by definition exclusive. Indeed, this conclusion should also follow from the Chief Justice's reasons, if we are to accept her claim that her definition of the criminal law power is not "limitless."[52] It must follow from the recognition of such limits that at least some activities are beyond the reach of the criminal law power. If Parliament does not have jurisdiction to legislate over such activities under some other head of power, the Chief Justice will necessarily conclude that the provinces enjoy exclusive jurisdiction.

3. The Norm of Non-Suppression and the Significance of Paramountcy Doctrine

To this point in this chapter, I have sought to clarify the nature of the disagreements among the Justices in the *AHRA Reference*, and I have tried to trace out some implications of their reasoning. I conclude this part by (1) claiming that the Chief Justice's reasons violate the norm of non-suppression and (2) suggesting a way of approaching the criminal law power that avoids this outcome. Recall that the norm of non-suppression states that no value that can reasonably be understood to be part of the cluster of values that define Canadian federalism should be systematically suppressed. Included among these is the value of provincial autonomy. I turn now to consider how that value is treated by the various reasons in the *AHRA Reference*.

If we leave to one side Cromwell J's reasons, we are left with a contest in the *AHRA Reference* between one interpretation of the criminal law power that is highly deferential to Parliament and another that requires Parliament to offer greater specificity in its justifications for action under that power. We have seen that the Chief Justice's broadly defined power is highly deferential to Parliament and that it affords the federal government significant leeway to legislate in areas of provincial jurisdiction. The Chief Justice only requires that Parliament have a reasonable basis for believing that it is legislating to protect an open-ended societal concern of fundamental importance. Because of the Court's history of highly deferential review when applying this kind of reasonable basis standard in its emergency powers jurisprudence respecting the peace, order, and good government power,[53] one might understand LeBel and Deschamps JJ's scepticism that this standard would function as a meaningful restraint on federal assertions of jurisdictional authority.

Moreover, as we have seen, one consequence of the Chief Justice's reasoning is that the division of powers is regulated by courts not primarily through determinations of validity but rather through application of the paramountcy doctrine. As others have noted, this tendency in the Court's division of powers jurisprudence can represent a threat to the effectiveness and scope of the provinces' legislative powers.[54] In my view, an approach to the division of powers that emphasizes open-ended and broadly overlapping jurisdictions and that grants Parliament largely unchecked deference places the ultimate power for regulating the division of powers in Parliament. To understand why this is so, consider the frustration of the legislative purposes version of the paramountcy test. According to this test, a conflict between provincial and federal legislation occurs when the former frustrates a valid federal legislative purpose.[55]

Now imagine if courts were to apply the Chief Justice's reasonable basis review standard to any claim by the federal government that it had enacted legislation pursuant to a broadly defined criminal law purpose. The Court's application of this highly deferential standard in the emergency powers cases suggests that Parliament would be permitted to legislate unconstrained by meaningful constitutional standards.[56] Imagine further that a law that Parliament claimed to have enacted pursuant to the criminal law power were to conflict with a provincial law. In these circumstances, the frustration of the legislative purposes version of paramountcy doctrine, and the Chief Justice's highly deferential stance, would combine to enable Parliament to render provincial legislation inoperative by a mere expression of federal legislative will because it would not be meaningfully limited by a requirement to provide reasons relating to the constitution. There are two consequences of limiting effective judicial review in this way: Parliament would be the ultimate arbiter of division of powers disputes in this area, and provincial autonomy would be compromised.

By contrast, LeBel and Deschamps JJ's narrower definition of the criminal law power is protective of provincial autonomy. A narrow definition of the criminal law power would limit the number of instances in which Parliament could validly legislate and be in a position to render provincial legislation inoperative. Such a definition would therefore increase the sphere of provincial legislative autonomy. Moreover, one concern with a highly deferential and open-ended criminal law standard is that it might permit Parliament to act for reasons that do not consider the relevant constitutional interests. By contrast, a more exigent standard would compel Parliament to formulate purposes that are relevant to the applicable constitutional norm.[57]

The degree of provincial vulnerability to the will of Parliament that is implied by the Chief Justice's reasons arises from the *broad range* of areas in which the federal government can potentially render provincial regulation inoperative and from the *degree of deference* granted to Parliament's actions. As we saw in the introduction to this chapter, provincial autonomy is suppressed when provinces suffer from persistent uncertainty about when the federal government will interfere in their areas of jurisdiction and when the federal government can act unconstrained by constitutional reasons. By contrast, if federal jurisdiction is conceived more narrowly (as is the case with LeBel and Deschamps JJ's reasons), the number of cases in which provincial legislation can be threatened by the operation of paramountcy doctrine is reduced. In addition, if the reasons for which a conflict could be triggered are limited and if the degree of deference granted to the federal government's characterization of its actions as falling within the criminal law power were lessened, the federal government would be placed under a greater obligation to provide constitutional reasons for legislation rendering provincial regulation inoperative. Such an obligation would avoid a federal–provincial relationship in which provincial autonomy is under persistent threat by mere exercises of federal political will, and would lead us towards a relationship regulated by constitutional reasons.

This burden of providing constitutional reasons for state action can also be considered by comparing the risks to which the Chief Justice's definition of the criminal law power in the *AHRA Reference* give rise with those to which LeBel and Deschamps JJ's definition give rise. The primary risk of the Chief Justice's reasons is that they may be applied *under*inclusively – that is, they risk permitting Parliament to act for reasons unrelated to its criminal law power, and therefore to engage in inadequate deliberation about the relevant constitutional interests.[58] By contrast, the primary risk associated with LeBel and Deschamps JJ's reasons is that they may be applied *over*inclusively – that is, they risk forbidding Parliament from acting for reasons related to its criminal law power. However, the more exigent strategy requires Parliament to act for more specific reasons and therefore imposes on Parliament a higher deliberative burden. This requirement that Parliament consider the relevant constitutional interests functions as a safeguard for the federalism-related value of provincial autonomy. Thus, LeBel and Deschamps JJ's reasons offer robust protections against the risk that that value will be suppressed; the Chief Justice's reasons do not.

Conclusion

The various contributions to this collection remind us that the implications of the *AHRA Reference* are wide-ranging, touching on diverse areas of law and social policy. This chapter has focused on the federalism implications of the judgments in the *AHRA Reference* and has sought to clarify both the reasoning in the various opinions and the nature of the debates among them. I have also sought to evaluate those reasons in light of what I have called the norm of non-suppression. As I conclude this chapter, it is perhaps helpful to consider the underlying purpose of that norm. In the introduction to this chapter, I noted that Canadian federalism entails a range of values. In my view, there can be reasonable disagreement about the relative weighting of those values, but it would be unreasonable for any participant in debates about Canadian federalism to claim that any of those values are insignificant. This emphasis on reasonable debate places a premium on deliberations that are characterized, in their substance and process, by a respect for opposing positions. The norm of non-suppression, in its application to the value of provincial autonomy, represents a *substantive* commitment to respect for the opinions of others, because it does not permit the erasure of a reasonable position from constitutional debate. My analysis of the reasons in the *AHRA Reference* suggests the contours of a *procedural commitment* to respect for opposing positions. Courts evince this procedural norm of respect when they impose upon the political branches an obligation to justify their actions in constitutional terms and when they do not permit those branches to act for reasons of political will alone. There are, of course, important questions about the relative institutional competences of courts and the political branches to facilitate reasoned deliberation and to provide constitutional justifications, but my interpretation of the *AHRA Reference* suggests that at least in some cases, courts can prevent legislatures from acting in ways that are unsupported by such justifications.

NOTES

Author's note 1: This chapter revises my previously published article, "Beyond Functionalism, Formalism, and Minimalism: Deliberative Democracy and Decision Rules in the Federalism Cases of the 2010–2011 Term" (2011) 55 Sup Ct L Rev (2d) 355.

Author's note 2: I gratefully acknowledge the financial support of the Secrétariat aux affaires intergouvernementales canadiennes for this article, the research assistance of Marie-Andrée Plante, and Andra Syvanen's assistance with the final note formatting. I also thank Ian Lee and the anonymous reviewers for their excellent comments. This text was prepared for the Assisted Reproduction Act Conference, held at the Asper Centre of the University of Toronto, 4–5 November 2011.

1 2010 SCC 61, [2010] 3 SCR 457.
2 See, for example, Hoi Kong, "Beyond Functionalism, Formalism, and Minimalism: Deliberative Democracy and Decision Rules in the Federalism Cases of the 2010–2011 Term" (2011) 55 Sup Ct L Rev (2d) 355; and Hoi L. Kong, "Republicanism and the Division of Powers in Canada" (2014) 64:3 UTLJ 359.
3 Philip Pettit, *Republicanism: A Theory of Freedom and Government* (Oxford: Clarendon Press; New York: Oxford University Press, 1997), 52 [Pettit, *Republicanism*].
4 *Ibid* at 32.
5 Philip Pettit, "Republican Freedom and Contestatory Democratization," in *Democracy's Value*, ed. Ian Shapiro and Casiano Hacker-Cordón (Cambridge and New York: Cambridge University Press, 1999), 163 at 172 [Pettit, "Contestatory Democratization"]. For a broader conception of these shared interests, see James Bohman, "Cosmopolitan Republicanism and the Rule of Law," in *Legal Republicanism: National and International Perspectives*, ed. Samantha Besson and José Luis Martí (Oxford and New York: Oxford University Press, 2009), 60 at 61.
6 Pettit, *Republicanism*, *supra* note 3 at 87.
7 By systematic suppression, I mean that the value of provincial autonomy is rendered null by this degree of vulnerability to unconstrained exercises of federal will.
8 If, for instance, the federal government were to prohibit an activity yet permit the provinces to prohibit more than that activity (see the Chief Justice's reasons in the *AHRA Reference*, *supra* note 1 at paras 27–38), the simple fact of this permission would not be sufficient to demonstrate that the provinces were autonomous. If that permission were to result from the constitutionally unconstrained choice of the federal government, the provinces' autonomy would still be severely compromised, because as we have seen above, autonomy is defined as not being subject to such choices.
9 This kind of consensus would represent what Cass Sunstein has described as a case of incompletely theorized agreement about a political principle, but divergence about the principle's concrete expression: Cass R. Sunstein, *One Case at a Time: Judicial Minimalism on the Supreme Court* (Cambridge, MA: Harvard University Press, 1999), 11.
10 *AHRA Reference*, *supra* note 1.
11 SC 2004, c 2.
12 *AHRA Reference*, *supra* note 1 at para 158.
13 *Ibid* at para 10.
14 *Ibid* at paras 285–94.

15 *Ibid* at para 43.
16 2003 SCC 74, [2003] 3 SCR 571.
17 *AHRA Reference*, *supra* note 1 at para 50.
18 *Ibid* at para 51.
19 *Ibid* at para 54.
20 *Ibid* at paras 55–6.
21 *Ibid* at para 182.
22 [1998] 2 SCR 217, 161 DLR (4th) 385.
23 2001 SCC 40, [2001] 2 SCR 241.
24 *AHRA Reference*, *supra* note 1 at para 183.
25 *Ibid* at para 184.
26 This is how one might interpret the Court's concern about drastic shifts in the balance of powers between the federal and provincial orders. For a statement of this concern, see *Canadian Western Bank v Alberta*, 2007 SCC 22, [2007] 2 SCR 3 [*Canadian Western Bank*].
27 See, for example, the discussion of the interpretive doctrines and the potential for intergovernmental cooperation in *British Columbia (Attorney General) v Lafarge Canada*, 2007 SCC 23, [2007] 2 SCR 86 [*Lafarge*].
28 *AHRA Reference*, *supra* note 1 at paras 232–3.
29 *Ibid* at para 238.
30 *Ibid* at para 251.
31 *Ibid* at para 237.
32 *Ibid* at para 238.
33 *Ibid* at para 50.
34 Wade K. Wright, "Facilitating Intergovernmental Dialogue: Judicial Review of the Division of Powers in the Supreme Court of Canada" (2010) 51 Sup Ct L Rev (2d) 625 [Wright, "Facilitating Intergovernmental Dialogue"]. For the Court's claim about the importance of intergovernmental cooperation, see *Lafarge*, *supra* note 27, and for its claims about overlap, see *Canadian Western Bank*, *supra* note 26.
35 *O'Grady v Sparling*, [1960] SCR 804, 25 DLR (2d) 145.
36 Wright, "Facilitating Intergovernmental Dialogue," *supra* note 34 at 656–7. For examples of cases in which the Court generously interpreted a federal head of power in a way that permitted significant impacts on areas of provincial regulation, see *Reference re Same-Sex Marriage*, 2004 SCC 79, [2004] 3 SCR 698 [*Same-Sex Marriage Reference*] and *Reference re Employment Insurance Act (Can.)*, ss. 22 and 23, 2005 SCC 56, [2005] 2 SCR 669. For an example of the Court finding a provincial statute valid despite significant impacts on federal jurisdiction, see *Krieger v Law Society of Alberta*, 2002 SCC 65, [2002] 3 SCR 372.

37 Wright, "Facilitating Intergovernmental Dialogue," *supra* note 34 at 674. See *Canadian Western Bank*, *supra* note 26 at paras 72–4.
38 *AHRA Reference*, *supra* note 1 at para 67.
39 *Ibid* at para 152.
40 *Ibid* at para 70.
41 *Ibid* at para 77.
42 *Ibid* at para 69.
43 *Ibid* at para 273.
44 *Ibid*.
45 *Ibid* at para 67.
46 *Ibid* at para 270.
47 LeBel and Deschamps JJ listed one set of activities that "are already found in medical practice and research" – "the use of human reproductive material (s. 10 of the *AHR Act*), transgenic research (s. 11) and the regulation of the use of premises for health care and research (s. 13)" – and referred to a second set of activities "governed by the provisions on consent and the use of genetic material obtained from minors (ss. 8 and 9), and on the reimbursement of expenditures incurred by a surrogate mother (s. 12)." *Ibid* at para 269.
48 *Ibid* at para 270.
49 *Ibid* at para 67.
50 *Ibid*.
51 *Same-Sex Marriage Reference*, *supra* note 36 at para 34.
52 *AHRA Reference*, *supra* note 1 at para 43.
53 *Re: Anti-Inflation Act*, [1976] 2 SCR 373, 68 DLR (3d) 452.
54 See, for example, Bruce Ryder, "The End of Umpire? Federalism and Judicial Restraint" (2006) 34 Sup Ct L Rev (2d) 345 [Ryder, "Umpire"]; Eugénie Brouillet, "La dilution du principe fédératif et la jurisprudence de la Cour suprême du Canada" (2004) 45 C de D 7.
55 See *Bank of Montreal v Hall*, [1990] 1 SCR 121. For insightful commentary on this test, see Robin Elliot, "Safeguarding Provincial Autonomy from the Supreme Court's New Federal Paramountcy Doctrine: A Constructive Role for the Intention to Cover the Field Test?" (2007) 38 Sup Ct L Rev (2d) 629 at 634–5, 658. See also Ryder, "Umpire," *supra* note 54.
56 See the discussion of *Re: Anti-Inflation Act*, *supra* note 53 in the accompanying text.
57 In this respect, I aim to avoid the costs of what Joseph Arvay called the "positivist aspect" of the criminal law power: Joseph J. Arvay, "The Criminal Law Power in the Constitution: And then Came *McNeil* and *Dupond*" (1979) 11 Ottawa L Rev 1 at 5.

58 Commentators have expressed similar concerns about the breadth of the federal trade and commerce power, and the degree of deference granted to Parliament when it purports to regulate under that power: Noura Karazivan and Jean-François Gaudreault-DesBiens, "On Polyphony and Paradoxes in the Regulation of Securities within the Canadian Federation" (2010) 49 Can Bus LJ 1 at 1. A discussion of the relevant constitutional doctrine is beyond the scope of this paper, but it is worth noting that recent Supreme Court of Canada authority suggests that the trade and commerce power is constitutionally constrained and subject to meaningful review. See *Reference Re Securities Act*, 2011 SCC 66, [2011] 3 SCR 837.

4 Federal and Provincial Jurisdictions with Respect to Health: Struggles amid Symbiosis

GLENN RIVARD

In the past few years, litigation has pitted federal jurisdiction pertaining to health-related matters against provincial jurisdiction pertaining to this same field. In *Reference re the Assisted Human Reproduction Act* [*AHRA Reference*],[1] a federal attempt to address the health risks associated with assisted reproduction was in large part rebuffed by a majority of the Supreme Court of Canada in favour of provincial authority over the practice of medicine. In *Canada (Attorney General) v PHS Community Services Society* [*Insite Injection*],[2] a subsequent decision of the same Court, the constitutionality of the possession and trafficking provisions of the *Controlled Drugs and Substances Act*[3] was upheld despite provincial arguments that the Act impaired the provision of health services to drug addicts. With shared jurisdiction over the complex field of health, it is perhaps inevitable that these struggles will occur from time to time, yet overall the two levels of government enjoy what can more properly be called a symbiotic relationship in the governance of the health field, with federal and provincial responsibilities mutually supportive and equally necessary to the protection of the health of Canadians. Shared responsibility functions better, however, when roles are clearly defined, and it is the unfortunate result of the *AHRA Reference* that the principles for distinguishing the federal role from the provincial are less sure than before, while *Insite Injection* does little to renew clarity in division of powers matters.

In general, the federal government seeks to reduce health risks arising from a variety of products, and its legislation has historically been seen as operating outside the scope of the patient–doctor relationship.

Conversely, the provinces focus on the governance and delivery of health care, including with respect to hospital services and the medical professions. These generalities, however, fail to adequately describe the full nature of the health-related activities of either level of government. Furthermore, the seemingly bright line between the regulation of products, on the one hand, and oversight of the provision of health care, on the other – to the extent it has ever existed – breaks down in the face of the increasing use, for therapeutic purposes, of human biological material such as cells (including sperm and ova), tissues, organs, and *in vitro* embryos. These products come from patients, are manipulated by health professionals, and in one form or another are placed again into the body of the same or another patient.

It is submitted that this close and symbiotic relationship between federal oversight of "products," including biologics, and provincial oversight of the delivery of health care will continue in the future, and, while *AHRA Reference* constitutes a setback in the context of reproductive technologies, it will have limited impact with respect to overall federal health jurisdiction.

Federal Responsibilities in the Field of Health

There is, of course, no constitutional head of power over health. Both levels of government enact legislation pertaining to this subject matter on the basis of several of their respective heads of power. The federal government's exclusive jurisdiction over criminal law serves as the primary head of power relied upon as the constitutional basis for federal health legislation.[4] The Constitution also grants the federal government authority over quarantine,[5] and pursuant to the spending power, the federal government provides the provinces with significant funds for their health care insurance plans and undertakes and supports public health programming and health-related research.

Federal health legislation prohibits conduct harmful to the health and safety of Canadians, and includes the authority to regulate so as to minimize risks to health and safety associated with a wide variety of products. Federal legislation of this nature includes the *Food and Drugs Act*, *Canada Consumer Product Safety Act*, *Hazardous Products Act*, *Pest Control Products Act*, *Tobacco Act*, *Radioactive Emitting Devices Act*, *Controlled Drugs and Substances Act*, and *Human Pathogens and Toxins Act*.[6] The Minister of Health also plays a significant role under the *Canadian Environmental Protection Act, 1999* in assessing the health risks to humans of substances released into the environment.[7] The *Quarantine Act* addresses public health risks arising from the presence of infested conveyances and infectious diseases in persons arriving in or departing from Canada.[8] The federal spending power is relied upon as the basis for several statutes pertaining to public health (*Public Health Agency of Canada Act*), health research (*Canadian Institutes of Health Research Act*), and health care (*Canada Health Act*).[9] Aspects of some federal legislation may also be based upon the trade and commerce power[10] and the peace, order, and good government power.[11]

To understand how Parliament has interpreted its criminal law power in the health field, it is instructive to examine to some degree the scope and content of a few of these statutes.

The *Food and Drugs Act* may be the best known of federal health statutes. Precursor federal statutes can be traced back to the *Inland Revenue Act* of 1875.[12] Today's *Food and Drugs Act* prohibits the sale of products – including food, drugs, cosmetics, and medical devices – that pose health risks arising from adulteration, preparation in unsanitary conditions, or other causes.[13] The same Act prohibits the advertising of products claiming to treat, prevent, or cure scheduled diseases and disorders, such as cancer, heart disease, and obesity.[14] Also prohibited are the misleading advertising of drugs and the labelling of drugs contrary to the regulations.[15] Similar authorities are created with respect to food, cosmetics, and medical devices. The prohibitions are supported by a statutory regime allowing for inspection of premises containing any regulated product and seizure of any article by means of which any provision of the Act or regulations has been contravened.[16] Extensive authorities for the creation of regulations are found in the Act, the general purpose of which is to establish the requirements that must be met before regulated products can be sold or distributed.[17] The Minister may make interim orders to address any significant risk to health, safety, or the environment.[18] The prohibitions and regulatory provisions are supported by offences for their breach, punishable by fine and imprisonment.[19]

Pursuant to the Act, regulations have been adopted with respect to food, drugs, cosmetics, semen used in assisted conception, medical devices, medical marijuana, natural health products, and cells, tissues, and organs (CTOs) used for transplantation.[20] In general, these regulations establish requirements for the production of this material and require ministerial approval for sale or distribution of the material within Canada. For example, the *Safety of Human Cells, Tissues and*

Organs for Transplantation Regulations prohibit the transplantation of CTOs unless processed in a registered establishment and determined safe for use.[21] Establishments are required to obtain the medical history of the donor, determine that the donor is not unsuitable based upon contraindications and exclusion criteria established in the regulations, perform a physical examination of the donor, and undertake the appropriate tests for diseases specified in the regulations.[22] Requirements are established for the retrieval, testing, packaging, and labelling of CTOs.[23] Quarantine periods are established for cells and tissues, along with storage requirements for cells, tissues, and organs.[24] The regulations also create reporting requirements for errors, accidents, and adverse reactions.[25] General rules are provided for records, personnel, facilities, equipment, and supplies.[26] The objective of these regulations is to help ensure the safety of CTOs that are used for transplantation by minimizing the risk of disease transmission or harm to the material through mishandling.

Federal efforts to minimize risks to the public extend beyond therapeutics, food, and cosmetics to consumer goods in general. In 2010 the *Canada Consumer Product Safety Act* was adopted and replaced Part I of the *Hazardous Products Act*. The *CCPSA* addresses the need to protect Canadians from goods that present a safety risk to consumers through poor design and manufacture. The Act relies on three primary legislative mechanisms to achieve this end. Some consumer products are completely prohibited from entering the Canadian market, including those as diverse as mobile baby walkers and urea formaldehyde insulation.[27] Other consumer products may be the subject of regulations governing their manufacture, import, advertisement, and sale.[28] Sections 7 and 8 create general safety standards applicable to all consumer products, which prohibit products that are a danger to human health or safety, have been subject to a recall notice issued under the Act, or are in non-compliance with a measure ordered under the Act.

The safety of products used in Canada to control pests is addressed in the *Pest Control Products Act*. A "pest" is an animal, plant, or other organism that is injurious, noxious, or troublesome.[29] The Act seeks to prevent unacceptable risks to people and the environment from products used to control pests.[30] Health or environmental risks are considered acceptable if there is reasonable certainty that no harm to human health, future generations, or the environment will result from exposure to or use of the product if used in accordance with the approved conditions for its use.[31] Pest control products are prohibited from use unless registered with the Ministry, which assesses the product for health and environmental risks and authorizes its use subject to conditions designed to address any identified risks.[32]

While the primary basis for federal regulatory legislation is the criminal law power, section 91(11) of the *Constitution Act, 1867* provides a specific federal authority with respect to quarantine. Pursuant to this authority, the federal *Quarantine Act* seeks to protect public health through measures intended to minimize the likelihood of the introduction and spread of communicable diseases. Under the Act, screening or quarantine officers authorized by the Minister of Health may determine whether any traveller entering or leaving Canada has a communicable disease or the symptoms of one.[33] Travellers must comply with any reasonable measure ordered by a screening or quarantine officer designed to prevent the introduction or spread of a communicable disease.[34] A traveller can be ordered to undergo a health assessment.[35] Travellers, baggage, and places can be ordered disinfested.[36] Quarantine officers may detain travellers and apply for an arrest warrant if necessary to enforce the Act or an order issued under the Act.[37]

The federal role with respect to public health matters was enhanced in 2006 with the adoption of the *Public Health Agency of Canada Act*. This Act created the Agency, headed by the Chief Public Health Officer, to aid the Minister in exercising her public health functions. Largely through research and program initiatives, the Agency addresses a variety of issues, including infectious and chronic diseases, immunization, emergency preparedness and response, and laboratory biosafety and security. The Agency is also responsible for administering the *Human Pathogens and Toxins Act*. The Act creates an obligation to take all reasonable precautions to protect the health and safety of the public when laboratories or other establishments knowingly deal with human pathogens or toxins.[38] Persons must notify the Minister if they have human pathogens or toxins in their possession.[39] Pathogens and toxins may be added to schedules under the Act, and persons who possess a scheduled pathogen or toxin must dispose of it, transfer it to a licensed facility, or obtain a licence for possession of the pathogen or toxin.[40]

Finally, any review of the federal legislation in the field of health would not be complete without mention of the *Canada Health Act*. This statute is founded upon the federal spending power and is the federal act that most closely addresses the practice of medicine in Canada. Essentially, it provides authority for the federal government to contribute funding to a province that operates a health care insurance plan that conforms to the criteria established in the Act. The insurance plan must be publicly administered, comprehensive in the sense that it insures all insured health services provided by hospitals and medical practitioners, universal by providing coverage for 100 per cent of insured persons on uniform terms and conditions, portable from province to province, and accessible in the sense of reasonably accessible to all insured persons and providing reasonable compensation to medical practitioners and hospitals.[41] Beyond these broad requirements for the operation of provincial health care plans, however, the Act does not provide for specific governance of either health care services or the medical profession.

Provincial Responsibilities in the Field of Health

Provincial responsibilities in the field of health are extensive and are founded on several heads of power, including the establishment, maintenance, and management of hospitals; local works and undertakings; property and civil rights; and generally all matters of a merely local or private nature in the province.[42]

To a significant extent, the provincial responsibilities in the field of health are more visible to the average Canadian. The provinces govern, directly or indirectly, hospitals, the health professions, and the provision of health care services in general. Provincial statutes establish and provide oversight of the self-regulating authorities for health professionals[43] and legislate with respect to medical consent[44] and the protection of health information.[45] Hospitals and independent health facilities are regulated pursuant to provincial law.[46] While the federal *Canada Health Act* may underwrite some of the cost of health care services, it is the provinces that operate the health care insurance plans that Canadians rely upon for access to health care services without charge.[47] The provinces are also active in public health with legislation pertaining to matters as diverse as drinking water and immunization.[48] They also legislate with respect to occupational health and safety.[49]

Shared Jurisdiction, Complementary Roles

The greater provincial visibility in the provision of health care arguably detracts from public and professional understanding of the mutually supportive nature of the federal and provincial roles. The courts, however, have long recognized health as a shared jurisdiction, with each level of government legislating pursuant to its respective constitutional powers. Through a series of challenges to federal legislation, some successful and others not, the contours of the use of the federal criminal law power in the health field have been established to a significant degree. The starting point for the modern understanding of the scope of the federal authority can be found in the *Margarine Reference*,[50] which marked a clear evolution from a mere formalistic definition of the criminal law power to a purposive one. While a valid criminal law statute must contain prohibitions accompanied by penalties, in the words of Justice Rand of the Supreme Court it must also serve a public purpose pertaining to "[p]ublic peace, order, security, health, morality."[51] These objectives are described as the ordinary purposes of criminal law, but were not in the eyes of the Court an exhaustive list. The purpose of the margarine legislation was to protect the dairy industry and not, as conceded by the federal government, to protect against any health risk. On that basis, the Court concluded that the legislation was not valid criminal law. Similarly, in *Labatt Breweries v Attorney-General of Canada*,[52] the Supreme Court concluded that the development of standards for "light" beer, pursuant to the *Food and Drugs Act*, was unconstitutional as the compositional standard for beer was unrelated to health.

Where, however, the courts have found the purpose of federal legislation as being to protect against a risk to health, the legislation has been upheld as valid criminal law. Jurisprudence has confirmed the application of the criminal law power to address health concerns with respect to adulterated food and drug products (*R v Wetmore*), tobacco consumption (*RJR-MacDonald v Canada*), and illicit drugs (*R v Malmo-Levine*), as well as the related issue of protection from environmental hazards (*R v Hydro-Quebec*).[53]

In large part, the shared federal and provincial jurisdiction functions well, providing layers of protection from health risks to Canadians. For example, pharmaceuticals can only be sold in Canada that have been approved for sale by the Minister of Health under the *Food and Drugs Act*. Upon receipt of an application, Health Canada reviews the submission and relevant scientific research to assess the safety, efficacy, and quality of the drug. Once approved, a pharmaceutical is given a Drug Identification Number (DIN) and will be sold with labelling and dosage information requirements. Health care professionals such as doctors and pharmacists make use of this information in prescribing and dispensing pharmaceuticals. What is true for pharmaceuticals is also true for other therapeutic products such as medical devices. To some extent, therefore, the federal requirements regarding the use of these therapeutic products affect the treatment relationship between physicians and their patients. The federal and provincial oversight, respectively, of health products and of health professions operates in symbiotic fashion to protect the Canadian health consumer. The impact of federal regulatory oversight of therapeutic products on medical practice may be limited to achieving the objective of reducing health risks arising from the product, but it is there nonetheless.

What is true for manufactured products is even more so for the therapeutic use of biologics, including the use of cells, tissues, and organs for therapeutic purposes. CTOs are removed from patients by medical practitioners and then (re)introduced into the same or another patient by, again, medical practitioners. The use of CTOs for therapeutic purposes presents significant health risks of disease transmission or failure of the CTO through improper storage or processing. The *Food and Drugs Act* addresses these risks through the *Cells, Tissues and Organs Regulations* and the *Semen Processing Regulations*. Inevitably, these regulations provide directions that are implemented by doctors and other health professionals with regard to the isolation of this material from patients, its storage and processing, and eventual use by a patient. The regulation of these health products inevitably affects the conduct of health practitioners towards their patients and with respect to these therapeutic products. This limited impact on the practice of medicine is accepted provided the federal regulatory regime remains focused on the safety of the product and strays no further afield into governance of the doctor–patient relationship. Federal regulatory oversight of CTOs reflects the reality that biologics present health risks every bit as serious as those of manufactured health products, and that their regulation requires directions to health practitioners that impact on their treatment of patients, at least to the extent necessary to address the health risks raised by these biologics.

Reference re the Assisted Human Reproduction Act

Given the long-standing federal role in regulating the safety of therapeutic products, including cells (including semen), tissues, and organs, why was the proposed regulation of semen, ova, and *in vitro* embryos to be used in assisted reproduction procedures a "bridge too far" for the majority of the Supreme Court Justices? While the components of the decision can be analysed for an answer, underlying the opinion of Justices LeBel and Deschamps is a sense that the *AHRA* would have upset the balance of federalism in the field of health care. The federal government was not insensitive to this concern, arguing that the creation of life is a unique issue and does not serve as a precedent for the oversight of medical practice in general. Put more pithily, the artificial creation of human beings is not like knee surgery. While the Chief Justice found merit in this argument, clearly this was a distinction that Justices LeBel and Deschamps found unconvincing.

Without a doubt, however, the deliberate manipulation of sperm, ova, and *in vitro* embryos to artificially create human life presents unique challenges. The use of reproductive technologies has always been seen as high in ethical content, from the days of the first "test tube baby," through the report of the Royal Commission on New Reproductive Technologies,[54] to current issues associated with cross-border reproductive care.[55] Much of the *AHRA* prohibits procedures considered to be ethically unacceptable, including cloning, sex selection, creation of an *in vitro* embryo for any purpose other than reproduction, and research involving chimeras and hybrids. The field is rapidly evolving, with new techniques regularly being developed (such as ova cryopreservation) that often raise new ethical and health issues.[56] In a fashion very similar to the therapeutic use of CTOs, the use of semen, ova, and *in vitro* embryos for assisted reproduction directly involves patients and medical practitioners in the isolation and processing of the therapeutic biological product. The health risks extend to donors and to the women undergoing assisted reproduction procedures, but also to any eventual offspring and even subsequent generations. Regulation of this field requires a high degree of sophistication and funding, yet in many Canadian provinces the use of these technologies is so limited that it may prove difficult to argue that heightened governance should be a priority, given scarce government resources.

It is against this backdrop that Quebec launched its constitutional reference with respect to many of the provisions of the *AHRA*. The core of Quebec's concerns related to section 10 of the Act, which created authorities to regulate the use of semen, ova, and *in vitro* embryos for assisted reproduction purposes. Section 10 contained several conditional prohibitions. These prohibited the use of this material for assisted reproduction unless done in accordance with regulations under the Act and a licence to be issued by the Assisted Human Reproduction Agency of Canada, an agency created by the Act. As the use of reproductive technologies inevitably involves one or more patients and medical practitioners, Quebec challenged the provisions as a colourable, or specious, incursion into the governance of medical practice and the provision of health care. In addition, Quebec challenged two other controlled activities – section 11, which established a scheme to prohibit unethical transgenic research, and section 12, which allows for the reimbursement of expenditures incurred by donors and surrogate mothers as an exception to the prohibitions of sections 6 and 7 against the commercialization of many aspects of assisted reproduction. Quebec threw the net wider, however, by also challenging several of the prohibitions under the Act, including section 8, which seeks to ensure that gametes and *in vitro* embryos are not used contrary to the wishes of their donors, and section 9, which seeks to protect minors from being used as gamete donors. The inclusion of the latter seems particularly puzzling as it is a classic criminal law provision that could just as easily have been placed in the *Criminal Code* and that fits four-square within an accepted purpose for the use of the federal criminal law power: the protection of vulnerable populations from exploitation.

The Reference: The Positions of the Parties

In defending the provisions in question, the federal government relied upon the standard formulation of the criminal law power. It argued that the impugned provisions addressed a mixture of both public morality concerns and risks to public health and safety, particularly the risk of disease transmission or the transmission of adverse genetic conditions. Thus the impugned provisions would fall within an accepted criminal law purpose instead of being a colourable attempt to regulate within the provincial sphere.

Clearly, sections 8 and 9 primarily addressed public morality concerns – respectively, to ensure that individuals and couples retained control over the eventual use and disposition of their gametes and *in vitro* embryos, and to protect young persons from exploitation. Section 11 was tailor-made to address the ethical issues of transgenic research. Such research generally poses few ethical risks beyond that of most research, but by means of a listing in the regulations, human and animal genetic combinations that could potentially raise ethical issues of interspeciation would have been prohibited. Section 12, as noted, simply acted as an exception to the non-commodification provisions of sections 6 and 7, provisions that were themselves not placed in question by Quebec.

Section 10 of the Act, however, was another matter. It would have allowed the federal government to regulate assisted reproduction procedures, with a view to addressing the associated health risks of the transmission of disease or adverse genetic conditions and any other risk arising from the procedures themselves. Quebec's view was that this amounted to regulation of the practice of medicine and was a colourable use of the federal criminal law power. Without a doubt, regulation under this section would have had to place requirements on doctors and other health professionals regarding the isolation and storage of sperm and ova, the use of these gametes to create an *in vitro* embryo, its proper handling for transfer into the womb of a woman, and other assisted reproduction procedures. Some of these processes directly implicate a patient – the female donor of ova, the female recipient of the *in vitro* embryo, and so on. Even semen donation requires oversight of the process of donation and the subsequent storage and use of the semen in order to ensure the safety of the product. Some of the processes do not directly involve patients at all – the creation of the *in vitro* embryo, for example – but do involve health professionals, including doctors, embryologists, and laboratory technicians.

The Reference: The Court's Analysis

In deciding whether the impugned provisions were valid criminal law, Chief Justice McLachlin and Justices LeBel and Deschamps begin their respective analyses from different starting points. For Chief Justice McLachlin, the point of departure is an examination of the Act in its entirety. After discussing the ordinary rule – that the impugned provisions are examined first before examining the entire legislative scheme – the Chief Justice argues for an exception given that so many of the Act's provisions were being challenged: "Under these circumstances, it is impossible to meaningfully consider the provisions at issue without first considering the nature of the whole scheme."[57] Justices LeBel and Deschamps, however, commence their analysis with the impugned provisions themselves. Citing *General Motors of Canada Ltd. v City National Leasing*,[58] they state that "the first step is to identify the pith and substance (purpose and effects) of the impugned provisions. If the pith and substance falls within the jurisdiction of the other level of government, the extent of the overflow must be assessed."[59] Arguably, much of the subsequent analyses of both decisions flows from these diverse starting points, for if one examines the Act as a whole, its criminal law character is more evident, whereas if one initially examines section 10 and the other impugned sections, particularly the controlled activities sections, their regulatory nature and impact on the health professions arguably come to the fore.

While the constitutional interpretive principle of initially examining the impugned sections appears to make practical sense, it does leave the substance of constitutional analysis peculiarly open to procedural and strategic choices of the initiating party. *AHRA Reference* illustrates this point well, for if Quebec had chosen to challenge all of the *AHRA*, the starting point for the division of power analysis would have been the same for the Chief Justice and Justices LeBel and Deschamps. This admittedly well-established approach ignores the true nature of legislation, in which, typically, each section contributes to the overall objective of the statute. Rare is it that a section operates in isolation from its statutory companions.

Returning to the *AHRA Reference* opinions, Chief Justice McLachlin and Justices LeBel and Deschamps proceed to examine the pith and substance of the federal Act or the impugned provisions, respectively, but reach quite different conclusions. The Chief Justice concludes that "the dominant thrust of the Act is prohibitory, and the aspects that concern the provision of health services do not rise to the level of pith and substance."[60]

Justices LeBel and Deschamps begin their analysis of the pith and substance of the impugned provisions with an examination of the Report of the Royal Commission on New Reproductive Technologies[61] and summarize its conclusions as follows: "Regarding the controlled activities, the Baird Commission considered that national standards were required. It took the view that Parliament could rely on the peace, order and good government power."[62]

The reliance on the Royal Commission report to help establish the purpose of the impugned sections raises several interesting questions. Typically, the purpose of legislation is determined by examining the statute itself, and if this is insufficient, recourse can be made to the Hansard record of the Parliamentary debates. Justices LeBel and Deschamps expand this contextual analysis to include an examination of the Report of the Royal Commission on New Reproductive Technologies, which preceded the adoption of the legislation by a decade. Royal Commissions, of course, are free to make whatever recommendations they wish, but what matters is how Parliament eventually addresses the issues raised in a Commission's report. Most significant in the present instance is the conceptual break between the Commission's Report and the *AHRA*. It is true that the Commission recommended the establishment of national standards and an Agency to oversee their implementation, founded on the Commission's understanding of the peace, order, and good government power. Parliament, however, adopted legislation based on the criminal law power with its established objectives of addressing matters of public morality and public health and safety. In doing so, it broke the link between the Commission's holistic approach to the field and the legislation's more targeted objectives.

After further analysis of the *AHRA*, Justices LeBel and Deschamps reach this conclusion regarding the purpose of the impugned provisions: "We concluded above that the purpose of the impugned provisions was to establish mandatory national standards for assisted human reproduction. A review of the practical consequences of these provisions shows that they have a significant impact on the practice of medicine."[63]

The divergence between the two opinions continues through their respective analysis of the purpose of the criminal law power and whether the Act fits within the confines of the power. Chief Justice McLachlin reiterates the accepted jurisprudential test – that valid criminal law must address a public concern relating to peace, order, security, morality, health, or some similar public purpose. Proposals for additional purposes must not have the potential to undermine the constitutional division of powers. In line with this, she reaffirms that "I do not intend to broaden the scope of the criminal law power, but rather apply this Court's jurisprudence."[64]

Justices LeBel and Deschamps, however, take the view that not all public health risks are amenable to being addressed through the criminal law. Instead, for an activity to fall under the criminal law, "it must be found that there is an evil to be suppressed or prevented" and that the pith and substance of the impugned provisions of the statute must be the suppression of the evil or elimination of the "reasoned risk of harm."[65]

The Justices then change the focus of their analysis to the affected field of endeavour itself: "Assisted human reproduction was not then, nor is it now, an evil needing to be suppressed. In fact, it is a burgeoning field of medical practice and research that, as Parliament mentions in s. 2 of the *AHR Act*, brings benefits to many Canadians."[66]

In their judgment, then, Justices LeBel and Deschamps create an onus on the federal government (a) to establish through evidence the risks to be addressed by the Act and (b) to establish that AHR itself is an evil that needs to be suppressed. This, of course, is something quite different from establishing that the statute is properly targeted at genuine moral concerns or health risks. It is quite possible for fields of human endeavour that are universally considered to be good and beneficial to also present moral and health risks. One only has to think of food, pharmaceuticals, or medical devices, all of which represent a public good, but all of which also present real and serious risks to the health of individuals if not managed properly. Without a doubt, as Justices LeBel and Deschamps conclude, assisted reproduction procedures represent a public good, but like so many fields of beneficial human endeavour, one that also presents risks of both an ethical and a health nature. In determining a division of powers question, the appropriate issue to consider should be whether the legislation seeks to address a harm, not whether the general field in question can be characterized as either good or reprehensible.

An essential difference between these two opinions relates to the extent to which the Court will show deference to Parliament's judgment, provided the Act or provisions in question can be shown to fit within an accepted purpose of the criminal law power. For Chief Justice McLachlin, the Court is properly preoccupied with determining whether the Act pursues a valid criminal law purpose, but if this is established, she is prepared to leave to Parliament's judgment the means of achieving the objectives of protecting public morality and health and safety. She makes this point clear in comments directed at the analysis of Justices LeBel and Deschamps:

> Their reasoning, with respect, substitutes a judicial view of what is good and what is bad for the wisdom of Parliament. Similar arguments have been rejected in other contexts. In *Malmo-Levine*, for example, it was argued that use of marijuana benefits many Canadians and not just those in medical need. My colleagues break new ground in enlarging the judiciary's role in assessing valid criminal law objectives. It is ground on which I respectfully decline to tread.[67]

On this issue, Justices LeBel and Deschamps take a fundamentally different tack. It is not enough to establish the objective of the Act; the onus is also on the federal government to present an evidentiary basis establishing the risks in question:

> Thus, when Parliament criminalizes an act, its decision remains subject to review by the courts, which will take society's attitude into account. And it must be borne in mind in this area that a broad range of philosophical and religious ideas coexist in a society as diverse as contemporary Canadian society. Although the rules in the *Criminal Code* have long been understood in light of the principles of Judeo-Christian morality, societal changes have freed them from those fetters. The coming into force of the *Charter*, for example, resulted in fundamental changes that affected offences related to sex, pornography and prostitution and demonstrated the importance of the explosion of the former conceptual framework ... The judgments on the application of the *Charter* have not of course purported to define the limits of the federal criminal law power, but they do clearly illustrate what is considered to be an evil, which is a question the Chief Justice does not deal with in her analysis relating to morality.[68]

The reference to the *Canadian Charter of Rights and Freedoms* as a touchstone for determining the limits of the criminal law power raises some interesting issues. Arguably, Justices LeBel and Deschamps are making two perhaps incompatible statements here. The first is that an evidentiary onus is being placed on the federal government to establish the risks it seeks to address. Reliance on the *Charter*, however, seems to amount to a sort of judicial shortcut to determining societal values without the need for a supportive evidentiary base. The significance of this reference is difficult to assess, for *Charter* rights were never pleaded and the *Charter* value placed at risk by the *AHRA* is never made clear.

A doctrine of reliance on the *Charter* to assess societal values, as an aspect of determining constitutional jurisdiction, carries with it the risk of creating a jurisdictional lacuna with respect to the subject matter in question. If the federal government does not have jurisdiction to legislate because to do so would offend a *Charter* value, then neither (it seems) do the provinces, which are equally subject to the *Charter*. This conclusion runs contrary to the principle of parliamentary sovereignty, which holds that all matters must fall within the jurisdiction of at least one level of government or the other.[69] It is interesting to note that in *Insite Injection*, the fear of a potential jurisdictional lacuna was one reason cited by the Chief Justice for not relying on the proposed doctrine of provincial interjurisdictional immunity to resolve the division of powers issue.[70]

The *Charter*, of course, seeks to uphold fundamental human rights and to protect citizens from incursions on their rights by overbearing governments. In this context, it is absolutely necessary for the courts to take a rigorous approach to assessing the merits of the underlying policy of the legislation in question. The resolution of division of powers issues, however, has not historically addressed the policy merits of the impugned legislation, but has sought instead to determine whether the legislating level of government has the authority to adopt the statute in question – a point made by the Chief Justice. This distinction appears to have implicitly reasserted itself in *Insite Injection*, in which the division of powers issues were addressed independently of the *Charter* issues. Arguably, in that more recent case the provincial invitation to restrain the federal criminal law power on the basis that it conflicted with the public policy goals of the provinces could have opened up the Court's analysis to conflating the division of powers issue with concerns raised in the *Charter* arguments. The Court, however, chose not make this connection.

Most of our current criminal law was developed before the *Charter* was adopted, and it would be difficult to argue that even today the creation of criminal offences begins with the identification of a *Charter* right that needs defending through the use of the criminal law. The intersection of the *Charter* and criminal law typically pertains to the rights of alleged and convicted offenders. Criminal offences, in contrast, have been developed in response to a need to address pressing societal issues – a need that, if an echo can be found in *Charter* values, is found only coincidentally. Of particular note would be the many *Criminal Code* provisions that address the protection of property, for which there is no apparent *Charter* homologue.

Justices LeBel and Deschamps's brief reference to reliance on the *Charter* to determine societal values can be contrasted with the processes of the government and of Parliament to discern these very same values. Parliament, of course, has historically been the arena for determining the social values that govern the issues of the day. With respect to reproductive technologies, this process began in 1989 with the appointment of the Royal Commission on New Reproductive Technologies. After several years of study and broad consultations, the Royal Commission in 1993 released its report, *Proceed with Care*,[71] which made over 290 recommendations. This was followed by several years of further consultation by the government itself, in which at least two other approaches to the subject matter were tried and found wanting. In 1995, the Minister of Health called for a voluntary moratorium on certain practices, which in the end produced no certain results. In 1996 a bill was introduced that addressed only absolute prohibitions, with a promise from the government to introduce a second bill to address the health risks of practices that otherwise should be allowed.[72] This approach was opposed by most stakeholders, who pressed the government for legislation that would address both types of conduct: the ethically unacceptable, and conduct that should be prohibited unless carried out in a manner so as to avoid health risks. In 2001 a draft bill with this scope was introduced and examined by the House of Commons Standing Committee on Health, which heard from more than seventy public stakeholders. The Committee recommended several changes to the bill but encouraged the government to proceed.[73] Shortly afterwards, in 2002, the government introduced the bill that was to become the *AHRA*. Again, the legislation went through review by the Health Committee of the House, which again heard from numerous stakeholders. Lively debates were had on issues such as commercialization and donor identity, and Members made decisions on the resolution of these difficult social issues. In due course, the bill travelled through the House of Commons itself, where it underwent further scrutiny. From there, the Senate Standing Committee on Social Affairs, Science, and Technology conducted its own hearings and heard from numerous stakeholders. In due course, the bill was passed by the Senate. In the decision of Justices LeBel and Deschamps one might read the implication that Parliament did not consider societal values and that, hence, the Court must do so by reliance on the *Charter*. If so, this seems an unfair criticism in light of the extensive review of this legislation. In contrast, recognition of both the responsibility and the ability of Parliament to examine difficult social issues appears to underlie the Chief Justice's greater degree of deference.

Finally, note must be made of Justice Cromwell's opinion in this matter. The concise nature of the opinion renders any analysis of its underlying rationale somewhat tentative. It appears, however, that Justice Cromwell was of the view that many of the impugned sections were overly broad in their scope. However, he distinguishes sections 8 and 9, arguing that these sections address matters of public morality. Section 8 seeks to ensure that control over the disposition of sperm, ova, and *in vitro* embryos remains in the hands of the donors and commissioning couples, while section 9 seeks to protect young persons from exploitation. Equally, Justice Cromwell sees the link between section 12, which permits reimbursement of expenditures, and the sections 6 and 7 prohibitions on payments for gametes and *in vitro* embryos. He concludes in all three cases that these provisions constitute valid criminal law in pursuit of public morality objectives.

Ten months after the release of the *AHRA Reference*, the Supreme Court released its decision in *Insite Injection*.[74] Unlike in *AHRA Reference*, the constitutionality of the statute in question, the *Controlled Drugs and Substances Act*, was not at issue. However, the Act's application to provincial spheres of responsibility was challenged, and in this fashion division of powers issues were placed before the Court for its consideration. As the Court's division of powers analysis is somewhat cursory, however, it serves to provide only limited guidance on the future resolution of such issues after the *AHRA Reference*. Writing on behalf of the entire Court, Chief Justice McLachlin concludes that the *Controlled Drugs and Substances Act* is valid criminal law that seeks to balance concerns for public safety with concerns for public health. In arriving at this conclusion, the Court rejects the argument that provincially regulated services are beyond the reach of the criminal law power: "The fact that the law at issue in this case has the incidental effect of regulating provincial health institutions does not mean that it is constitutionally invalid. A valid federal law may have incidental impacts on provincial matters ... It is therefore untenable to argue, as I understand Quebec to do, that a valid federal law becomes invalid if it affects a provincial subject, in this case health."[75]

In discussing provincial arguments in support of provincial interjurisdictional immunity, the Court reaffirms the validity of the federal *and* provincial roles in health: "The federal role in the domain of health makes it impossible to precisely define what falls in or out of the proposed provincial 'core.' Overlapping federal jurisdiction and the sheer size and diversity of provincial health power render daunting the task of drawing a bright line around a protected provincial core of health where federal legislation may not tread."[76]

As limited as the division of powers analysis is in *Insite Injection*, we do see assertion of some constitutional fundamentals, including shared jurisdiction with respect to the field of health, the acceptability of a valid federal law's incidental effects on provincial laws and institutions, and reliance on the doctrine of federal legislative paramountcy to resolve any conflicts between federal and provincial legislation. At least on these points the Court remains unanimous.

Amendments to the *AHRA*

Following the *AHRA Reference*, the *Assisted Human Reproduction Act* was amended in 2012 by Division 56 of the *Jobs, Growth and Long-term*

Prosperity Act.[77] The general purpose of the Act was to implement the Government's budget introduced earlier in the spring. The *AHRA* amendments give effect to three objectives. The first is to repeal those provisions determined to be unconstitutional in *AHRA Reference*. The second is to dissolve the AHR Agency created by the 2004 Act, reflecting the diminished federal role in this field. The third encompasses a series of amendments designed to ensure a coherent and functional federal legislative scheme that conforms to the limits of federal jurisdiction as established by *AHRA Reference*.

With regard to this third objective, the amending Act creates two new prohibitions, in a new section 10, pertaining to sperm and ova donated for third party use (other than by a spouse, common law partner, or sexual partner of the donor) unless the material is treated in accordance with regulatory requirements. This new section, however, is not yet in effect. Donated semen for assisted reproduction, therefore, currently remains regulated under the *Food and Drugs Act* as a "drug" as defined in that Act, while the use of ova for assisted reproduction currently remains unregulated. The *AHRA* amendments also include a number of changes to the administration and enforcement provisions of the Act to clarify their application within the legislative scheme.

Should the government ever decide to bring the new section 10 into force, it will prohibit any person from distributing, making use of, or importing sperm or ova to be used by a third party (other than by a spouse, common law partner, or sexual partner of the donor) for the purpose of AHR. This prohibition will apply unless the material has been tested and processed and the donor screened, tested, and assessed in accordance with regulations to be adopted. A second, similar prohibition will apply to those engaged in processing these biological products. Subsection (1) states that the purpose of the section is "to reduce the risks to human health and safety ... including the risk of the transmission of disease" arising from the use of this material for the purpose of AHR.[78]

Section 10 is focused exclusively on the biological products in question and does not extend, as did the former authority, to the medical procedures of assisted reproduction. While the former section 10 would have allowed for broad federal regulation of the procedures of assisted reproduction, including obtaining of gametes, artificial insemination, *in vitro* fertilization, and transfer of the *in vitro* embryo, the scope of the new section 10 is limited to ensuring the safety of the biological product itself. The medical procedures of assisted reproduction are no longer addressed in federal law.

As to what *is* addressed, the new section 10 is limited in scope to clear risks to human health, primarily the transmission of infectious disease, such as HIV-AIDS and hepatitis, through the use of sperm or ova donated by one individual for the use of another. As such, it reflects the Chief Justice's understanding that the criminal law power can be used to address risks to human health and safety, while also reflecting that of Justices LeBel and Deschamps that the legislation must address an identifiable evil or harm.

Sperm or ova to be used by a spouse, common law partner, or sexual partner are excluded from the scope of the section because the use of gametes donated within a relationship would not normally increase the risk of disease transmission in light of the likelihood of sexual relations.

The amendments to the *AHRA* place the statute in line with other federal legislation designed to ensure the safety of products to be used for medical purposes, including drugs, medical devices, cells, tissues, and organs. The risk to health is well established and serious, and the scope of the regulatory authorities is logically tied to those measures that can be scientifically established as necessary and effective in reducing these risks.

With the passage of time, therefore, it can be said that *AHRA Reference*, while itself reflective of judicial dissonance, has contributed to a more consistent federal approach to the oversight of products that present serious risks to human health. This approach can be described as product oriented, focused on significant risks to human health and safety, and including those measures that can be demonstrated to effectively reduce these risks. Any impact on medical practice is limited and incidental to ensuring the safety of the product itself.

Conclusion

Returning to the jurisprudence, the impact of *AHRA Reference* on future division of powers litigation, particularly within the field of health, is difficult to assess. This is due in part to the particular nature of the subject matter of the legislation in question and in part to the divided nature of the decision and the novelty of aspects of the opinion of Justices LeBel and Deschamps. Clearly, pursuit of a valid criminal law purpose such as public morality, health, or safety remains relevant to establishing the *vires* of any legislation founded on the criminal law power. It may be that the stricter test of establishing the existence of an evil or harm necessitating the use of the criminal law power is more likely to be relied upon where in the eyes of the court the federal legislation is seen to overlap substantially with provincial constitutional authorities. However, the existence of any such overlap by existing federal health legislation is limited, including with respect to the practice of medicine. Most federal legislation is long established and presents little tension with matters falling within provincial health jurisdiction. While there may be some limited incidental impact on matters governed by the provinces, the risks to human health arising from the regulated products – infection, failure of a life-saving medical device, injury, or exposure to excessive radiation, to name a few – are manifestly serious, self-evident, and sufficient to justify federal oversight of the products even in the shadow of *AHRA Reference*.

What of Justices LeBel and Deschamps's argument that the field of reproductive technology is a public good and therefore beyond the reach of the criminal law power? It is to be hoped that this aspect of the judgment does not enjoy jurisprudential longevity, for it is evident that many beneficial fields of endeavour, including the provision of food, pharmaceuticals, and medical devices, are public goods that nonetheless carry with them considerable risks to the health and safety of Canadians. Provided that federal legislation remains properly focused on preventing these risks, it should continue to be seen as consistent with valid criminal law objectives, whether conceived as protecting public health and safety or as addressing a harm or evil.

Doubtless, from time to time, new struggles will arise as both levels of government seek to carry out their respective constitutional mandates in the field of health. The symbiotic nature of their respective roles, however, can be expected to endure to the overall benefit of Canadians. Health remains a field that will continue to see much use of the constitutional value of cooperative federalism in the years ahead.

NOTES

Author's note: The opinions expressed herein are those of the author and not necessarily those of the Government of Canada. The author was co-counsel for the federal government in *AHRA Reference*.

1 2010 SCC 61, [2010] 3 SCR 457.
2 2011 SCC 44, [2011] 3 SCR 134.
3 SC 1996, c 19.

4 *Constitution Act, 1867* (UK), 30 & 31 Vict, c 3, reprinted in RSC 1985, Appendix II, No 5, section 91(27) – The Criminal Law, except the Constitution of Courts of Criminal Jurisdiction, but including the Procedure in Criminal Matters.
5 *Constitution Act, 1867*, section 91(11) – Quarantine and the Establishment and Maintenance of Marine Hospitals.
6 *Food and Drugs Act*, RSC 1985, c F-27; *Canada Consumer Product Safety Act*, SC 2010, c 21; *Hazardous Products Act*, RSC 1985, c H-3; *Pest Control Products Act*, SC 2002, c 28; *Tobacco Act*, SC 1997, c 13; *Radioactive Emitting Devices Act*, RSC 1985, c R-1; *Controlled Drugs and Substances Act*, SC 1996, c 19; *Human Pathogens and Toxins Act*, SC 2009, c 24.
7 SC 1999, c 33.
8 SC 2005, c 20.
9 *Public Health Agency of Canada Act*, SC 2006, c 5; *Canadian Institutes of Health Research Act*, SC 2000, c 6; *Canada Health Act*, RSC 1985, c C-6.
10 *Constitution Act, 1867*, s 91(2).
11 *Constitution Act, 1867*, s 91.
12 37 Vict, c 8.
13 *Supra* note 7, *Food and Drugs Act*, ss 4, 8, 16, and 19.
14 *Ibid*, s 3 and Schedule A.
15 *Ibid*, s 9.
16 *Ibid*, ss 22–9.
17 *Ibid*, s 30.
18 *Ibid*, s 30.1.
19 *Ibid*, ss 31 and 31.1.
20 *Food and Drug Regulations*, CRC, c 870; *Cosmetic Regulations*, CRC, c 869; *Processing and Distribution of Semen for Assisted Conception Regulations*, SOR/1996–254 [*Semen Processing Regulations*]; *Medical Devices Regulations*, SOR/98–282; *Marihuana Medical Access Regulations*, SOR/2001–227; *Marihuana Exemption (Food and Drugs Act) Regulations*, SOR/2003–261; *Natural Health Products Regulations*, SOR/2003–196; *Natural Health Products (Unprocessed Product Licence Applications) Regulations*, SOR/2010–171; *Safety of Human Cells, Tissues and Organs for Transplantation Regulations*, SOR/2007–118 [*Cells, Tissues and Organs Regulations*]. For a discussion of the ways in which the *Semen Processing Regulations* impact LGBTQ persons, see the chapter by Stu Marvel and colleagues in this volume.
21 *Ibid*, *Cells, Tissues and Organs Regulations*, s 4.
22 *Ibid*, ss 18–23.
23 *Ibid*, ss 24–33.
24 *Ibid*, ss 34–39.

25 *Ibid*, ss 43–49.
26 *Ibid*, ss 55–69.
27 *Supra* note 7, *Canada Consumer Product Safety Act*, s 5 and Schedule 2.
28 *Ibid*, s 6.
29 *Supra* note 7, *Pest Control Product Act*, subs 2(1).
30 *Ibid*, s 4.
31 *Ibid*, subs 2(2).
32 *Ibid*, ss 7 and 8.
33 *Supra* note 9, *Quarantine Act*, s 47.
34 *Ibid*, s 15.
35 *Ibid*, s 19.
36 *Ibid*, s 21.
37 *Ibid*, ss 27 and 28.
38 *Supra* note 7, *Human Pathogens and Toxins Act*, s 6.
39 *Ibid*, s 12.
40 *Ibid*, ss 9–11.
41 *Supra* note 10, *Canada Health Act*, ss 7–12.
42 *Constitution Act*, 1867: section 92(7) – The Establishment, Maintenance, and Management of Hospitals, Asylums, Charities, and Eleemosynary Institutions in and for the Province, other than Marine Hospitals; section 92(10) – Local Works and Undertakings other than such as are of the following Classes: …; section 92(13) – Property and Civil Rights in the Province; and section 92(16) Generally all Matters of a merely local or private Nature in the Province.
43 See, for example, *Regulated Health Professions Act, 1991*, SO 1991, c 18.
44 See, for example, *Health Care Consent Act, 1996*, SO 1996, c 2.
45 See, for example, *Personal Health Information Protection Act, 2004*, SO 2004, c 3.
46 See, for example, *Public Hospitals Act*, RSO 1990, c P.40; *Independent Health Facilities Act*, RSO 1990, c I.3.
47 See, for example, *Health Insurance Act*, RSO 1990, c H.6.
48 See, for example, *Safe Drinking Water Act, 2002*, SO 2002, c 32; *Clean Water Act, 2006*, SO 2006, c 22; *Immunization of School Pupils Act*, RSO 1990, c. I.1.
49 See, for example, *Occupational Health and Safety Act*, RSO 1990, c O.1.
50 *Canadian Federation of Agriculture v Attorney-General of Quebec*, [1949] SCR 1, [1951] AC 179.
51 *Ibid*, [1949] SCR 1 at 50.
52 [1980] 1 SCR 914, 110 DLR (3d) 594.
53 *R v Wetmore*, [1983] 2 SCR 284, 2 DLR (4th) 577; *RJR-MacDonald v Canada*, [1995] 3 SCR 199, 127 DLR (4th) 1; *R v Malmo-Levine*, 2003 SCC 74, [2003] 3 SCR 571; and *R v Hydro-Quebec*, [1997] 3 SCR 213, 151 DLR (4th) 32.

54 *Proceed with Care: Final Report of the Royal Commission on New Reproductive Technologies* (Ottawa: Minister of Government Services Canada, 1993).
55 See, for example, G. Pennings, G. de Wert, F. Shenfield, J. Cohen, B. Tarlatzis, and P. Devroey, "ESHRE Task Force on Ethics and Law 15: Cross-Border Reproductive Care" (2008) 23:10 Human Reproduction 2182; N. Hudson, L. Culley, E. Blyth, W. Norton, F. Rapport, and A. Pacey, "Cross-Border Reproductive Care: A Review of the Literature" (2011) 22:7 Reproductive BioMedicine Online 673.
56 Ova cryopreservation refers to "freezing" ova that have been removed from a woman and their preservation for later use by the same woman or another. Recent medical advances have increased the success rate of this process without attendant damage to the ova. Ova cryopreservation is increasingly an option for women undergoing cancer therapies, which has raised questions regarding the adequacy of current informed consent protocols. See, for example, Katherine E. Dillon and Autumn M. Fiester, "Sperm and Oocyte Cryopreservation: Comprehensive Consent and the Protection of Patient Autonomy" (2012) 27:10 Human Reproduction 1.
57 *Supra* note 2, para 17.
58 [1989] 1 SCR 641, 58 DLR (4th) 255.
59 *Supra* note 2, para 189.
60 *Ibid*, para 24.
61 *Supra* note 54.
62 *Supra* note 2, para 204.
63 *Ibid*, para 226.
64 *Ibid*, para 48.
65 *Ibid*, para 243.
66 *Ibid*, para 251.
67 *Ibid*, para 76.
68 *Ibid*, para 239.
69 For a further discussion of this, see Mark Carter, "Federalism Analysis and the Charter" (2011) 74 Sask L Rev 5.
70 *Supra* note 3, para 64: "Third, the doctrine of interjurisdictional immunity may overshoot the federal or provincial power in which it is grounded and create legislative 'no go' zones where neither level of government regulates."
71 *Supra* note 54.
72 *New Reproductive and Genetic Technologies: Setting Boundaries, Enhancing Health* (Ottawa: Minister of Public Works and Government Services Canada, 1996).

73 *Assisted Human Reproduction: Building Families* (Ottawa: Public Works and Government Services Canada, December 2001).
74 *Supra* note 3. In the end, the outcome hinged on the Court's *Charter* analysis, which is not examined in the current paper.
75 *Ibid*, para 51.
76 *Ibid*, para 68.
77 SC 2012, c 19. The Act received Royal Assent on June 29, 2012. Amendments to the *AHRA* that repeal unconstitutional provisions came into effect on that day. Provisions dissolving the AHR Agency came into effect on 30 September 2012 (PC 2012–1136).
78 Sections 4.1 and 4.2 of the amended *AHRA* provide that the *Human Pathogens and Toxins Act* and the *Food and Drugs Act* will not apply to the use of the biological products governed by the *AHRA*, thereby creating a single federal authority to ensure the safety of these products when used for purposes of assisted reproduction. These provisions will come into force at the same time as the new section 10. Until then, the *Semen Processing Regulations* under the *Food and Drugs Act* remain in effect.

PART TWO

Family Law and Children's Rights Perspectives

5 Determining Parentage in Cases Involving Assisted Reproduction: An Urgent Need for Provincial Legislative Action

CAROL ROGERSON

Introduction

Assisted reproduction raises important issues about the determination of parenthood. Parental status is an important starting point for assigning responsibility for the care and support of children as well as an important component of a child's identity, one that determines issues such as citizenship and broader kinship relationships. Assisted reproduction, which can include gamete and embryo donation and surrogacy (both traditional and gestational), forces a re-examination of the basis for assigning legal parenthood and an assessment of the respective significance to be attached to genetic contribution, gestational contribution, intention to parent, and being in a relationship with the child's parent. Much has been written on these topics, and it is not the purpose of this chapter to assess the merits of different proposals beyond noting a generally emerging consensus that assisted reproduction requires that greater significance be attached to intention to parent than under traditional models of parenthood, which place primary emphasis on bio-genetic connection.[1]

The main argument of this chapter is that in Canada, where we have a record of being at the forefront of legal reform in reshaping traditional definitions of the family, we have been shockingly slow to take up this challenge of comprehensively reassessing and revising our laws of parentage (or "child status" laws, as they are often called) to take account of assisted reproduction. There is a pressing need for legislative action at the provincial level to eliminate the legal hurdles and uncertainties that now face families in which children are born as a result of assisted reproduction and to provide clear rules that will establish parentage from the moment of birth, without resort to adoption or complex and costly litigation. This chapter provides a broad overview of the existing legal framework for establishing parentage in Canada, highlighting both the legislative gaps with respect to children born as a result of assisted conception and one possible model for legislative reform that has recently been developed by the Uniform Law Conference of Canada.

Provincial Jurisdiction and the *AHRA Reference*

Although jurisdictional uncertainty has surrounded many aspects of legislation dealing with assisted human reproduction in Canada, there has never been any uncertainty surrounding issues of parental status: this clearly falls within provincial jurisdiction over family law. The federal government made no attempt to legislate on these matters in the *Assisted Human Reproduction Act* (*AHRA*).[2] The only provisions in the *AHRA* that even came close to touching on issues of parenthood were those prohibiting the disclosure of donor identity without the donor's consent, thus effectively putting in place a system of anonymous donation in which legal parenthood could not attach to donors.[3] Yet the majority of provinces have not reformed their laws of parentage to deal with assisted reproduction: to date only four provinces have engaged in any significant reform of their parentage laws, and of these only two (Alberta and BC) have enacted comprehensive legislation that covers surrogacy as well as donated reproductive material.[4] As will be shown below, much of the governing legislation in the other provinces is anachronistic, rooted in bio-genetic concepts of parenthood, and contains no acknowledgment of either assisted reproduction or same-sex spousal relationships. Indeed, some provinces do not even have parentage (or child status) legislation.

This failure to legislate is something of a mystery, considering that Canada has been at the forefront of so many legal developments giving expansive recognition to family relationships beyond the traditional nuclear family consisting of a married man and woman and their biological children. We have legalized same-sex marriage (and same-sex adoption) and have embraced a broad and functional approach to defining the family that has resulted in extensive legal recognition of common law couples (both opposite-sex and same-sex) and of *de facto* or social parents.[5] However, legal parentage law itself has not been a focus of reform, and the provinces have been slow to respond to the growing use of assisted reproduction and to adopt laws that give greater weight to the intention to parent when assigning legal parentage at birth. Some possible explanations can be suggested. The general atmosphere of jurisdictional uncertainty and legal inertia that has surrounded assisted reproduction since the enactment of the *AHRA* in 2004 may have acted as a general deterrent to provincial legislative action in the area, despite the fact that provincial jurisdiction over parenthood was never in doubt. As well, the broad application of the doctrine of *in loco parentis*, which has provided a measure of legal protection to those adults who take on the role of *de facto* or social parents to children born as a result of assisted reproduction, may ironically have reduced the pressure to change laws related to legal parenthood. Finally, family law reform agendas in recent years have been dominated by pressing issues of institutional reform and access to justice; parentage laws have not been a political priority. In both Alberta and BC, the two provinces that have most comprehensively revised their parentage laws, those changes were part of a much more comprehensive and ambitious reform of the entire family law system. There are few political gains from opening up the contentious issues around assisted reproduction, particularly as they challenge conventional family norms, and it is thus no surprise that provincial legislatures have for the most part avoided comprehensive reform of parentage laws, preferring to leave unresolved issues to the courts or to enact low-profile "quick fixes" on a piecemeal basis. The relatively uncontentious nature of the reforms to parentage law in BC – which was somewhat surprising – will hopefully encourage other provinces to follow suit.

The Supreme Court of Canada's decision in the 2010 reference, which concluded that significant portions of the *AHRA* were *ultra vires* the federal government, has only increased the need for provincial legislative action. The federal provisions respecting donor anonymity are now invalid, and there is political pressure on provinces to legislate with respect to disclosure of donor information.[6] The possibility of more identified donors will lead to more disputes about parental status and parental rights and obligations. It is to be hoped that the provinces will seize the moment and comprehensively reform their parenthood legislation to take account of assisted reproduction.

Meanwhile, much work has taken place on developing models for legislative reform. The Uniform Law Conference of Canada has been working for many years to develop a model for new parentage legislation. Its *Uniform Child Status Act, 2010*, released shortly before the decision in the *AHRA Reference*, now provides a template for reform of parentage laws in those provinces that have not yet undertaken this task.[7] Besides providing a comprehensive framework that deals with both donated reproductive material and surrogacy, the model act breaks new ground by recognizing the possibility of a child having more than two legal parents. British Columbia, in the course of its recent family law reforms, has become the first province to model its new parentage legislation on that template.[8] After reviewing the current legal landscape with respect to the parentage laws currently in place in the rest of the country, this chapter will conclude with an examination of the *Uniform Child Status Act, 2010* and the new BC legislation modelled on it.

The Distinction between Legal Parentage and Social (*de facto*) Parentage

Canadian law with respect to parentage is complicated because as well as recognizing legal parentage, in some contexts it also recognizes *de facto* or social parentage. Legal parentage is a formal status – part of a child's identity – that is assigned at birth and subject to reassignment only through the formal legal procedure of adoption. Legal parentage is a lifelong status that determines the existence of a parent–child relationship across a wide range of legal contexts, including for example citizenship and inheritance. In most cases legal parentage is also the starting point for the allocation of parenting responsibilities (often referred to as custody and access) while the child is a minor, although it is not determinative, and for the imposition of the obligations of child support.

However, the concept of *in loco parentis* or "standing in the place of a parent" has taken strong root in Canadian family law, one manifestation of our strong functional approach to defining the family.[9] As a result, Canadian law, at both the federal and provincial levels, recognizes that persons who are not legal parents may have taken on parenting roles and responsibilities and will treat them as parents in particular contexts. Although the focus of this overview is on legal definitions of parenthood in Canadian law, it is important to be aware of this recognition of social or *de facto* parenthood. The limitations of this form of legal recognition in cases involving assisted reproduction underscore the need for reform of laws that assign legal parental status; at the same time, this recognition of social parenthood provides anchorage in our legal system for incorporating ideas of intentional parenthood in our laws of legal parenthood.

The doctrine of *in loco parentis* finds its most explicit anchorage in child support law, which imposes a support obligation on step-parents and others who have taken on the parental role. However, the legal recognition of social or "psychological" parents also extends to other contexts, such as applications for custody and access or rights of participation in child protection or adoption proceedings.[10] Thus in many contexts, those who act as the child's parents are treated as parents and legal parentage alone does not determine how Canadian law allocates responsibility for the care and support of children. The broad use of the concept of *in loco parentis* has allowed Canadian law to recognize and protect significant relationships in children's lives and to ameliorate the problems created by the rigidly bio-genetic definitions of legal parenthood that still largely prevail.[11]

In many cases the doctrine of *in loco parentis* will provide some legal recognition of "intentional" parents of children conceived through assisted reproduction who are not recognized as legal parents. However, the relationship of standing in the place of a parent is neither a permanent nor full legal status and rests upon uncertain discretionary judicial determinations. It is also a relationship that develops over time and that is not attained at the moment of birth. For these reasons, "intentional" parents of children born as a result of assisted conception most often desire recognition as legal parents.[12] At the same time, the widespread recognition of this form of parental status based on the assumption of the social role of parent provides some existing legal anchorage for incorporating the idea of intentional parenthood into legislation establishing legal parentage at birth.

One other implication of the use of the doctrine of *in loco parentis* to recognize social parents is that it allows for the recognition that a child may have more than two parents. The recognition of a social parent does not terminate the parental status of legal parents; it simply adds other adults to the list of those who may have rights and obligations with respect to the child.[13] In some cases involving assisted reproduction this multiplicity of parents is contrary to the wishes of the intended parents – which underscores the need for parentage legislation to reflect, for example, that gamete donors do not have parental status. Thus lesbian couples who use a known sperm donor face the risk, under older parentage laws, of the court finding the sperm donor to be a legal father, contrary to the initial intentions of the parties.[14]

At the same time, the two-parent model may be unduly restrictive and not reflective of the social diversity of parent–child relationships. Broad reliance on the concept of *in loco parentis* has accustomed us to the idea that children can have more than two parents and has helped pave the way for ground-breaking models for the reform of the law of legal parentage in Canada that would allow a child to have more than two legal parents where that arrangement reflects the intentions of all the parties.

Birth Registration Legislation and Legal Parenthood

Apart from adoption legislation, there are typically two different kinds of provincial laws that deal with the assignment of legal parentage. The focus of this chapter is on what is often referred to as "child status" legislation that sets out the basis for determining legal parentage. However, one must also keep in mind the birth registration provisions found in provincial vital statistics laws that include registration of parents as part of the documentation of the birth.[15] Birth registries are administrative tools and are not determinative of legal parentage. However, registration as a parent often acts as a presumptive determination of parenthood. As will be discussed in more detail below, several recent legal challenges to the way in which provincial law assigns parentage have been directed at the provisions governing who may register as a parent, and some provinces have chosen to quietly modify their birth registration laws and regulations rather than engage in more comprehensive reform of their laws assigning legal parentage. Because birth registries do not provide for definitive determinations of parenthood, provincial reform efforts directed at vital statistics legislation are generally an inadequate substitute for reform of legal parentage laws.[16]

Legal Parentage: The First Wave of Family Law Reform

Much of the provincial legislation governing parentage dates from the period of active family law reform in the 1970s and 1980s.[17] The template for these reforms can be found in the Uniform Law Conference's 1982 *Uniform Child Status Law*.[18] This reform of parentage laws was aimed at abolishing illegitimacy and replacing marital status with biology as the basis for assigning legal parentage. Thus section 1(1) of the Ontario *Children's Law Reform Act* establishes as the basic rule of parentage that "a person is the child of his or her *natural* parents and his or her status as their child is independent of whether the child is born within or outside marriage."[19] Reflecting the then prevailing concepts of biological parenthood, most provincial schemes from this period rest on the assumption that a child will have two parents of the opposite sex – one mother (easily identified by the act of birth), and one father (whose identification may be more difficult) – and then go on to provide certain presumptions (rebuttable by blood tests or other evidence) for determining paternity. Although there are variations among the provinces, these presumptions are generally based on a man being the mother's partner (through marriage or cohabitation) at the time of conception or birth or, alternatively, upon acknowledgment of paternity under provincial vital statistics legislation.[20] Nova Scotia stands out as an exception among the provinces, having failed to participate in even this first wave of reform of parentage laws. To date, Nova Scotia has failed to enact any form of child status legislation setting out the basic rules for assigning parentage.[21]

Parentage and Assisted Reproduction: The Current Legal Patchwork

In recent years the advent of assisted reproduction (including gamete and embryo donation and surrogacy – in both its traditional *and* gestational forms) and the legal recognition of same-sex relationships have complicated the issue of parentage. The possibility of separating the genetic and gestational contributions to the birth of a child means that the assignment of maternity is no longer straightforward; more importantly, the idea that biological connection rather than intention to parent should be the basis for assigning legal parentage at birth has come under question. Broad legal recognition of same-sex relationships, including adoption by same-sex couples, has led to the social and legal reality that children can have two mothers or two fathers. Same-sex couples, as well as opposite-sex couples using assisted reproduction, have begun to question why their relationships with the children they intend to parent cannot be legally formalized at birth rather than through adoption. The failure to provide children born as a result of assisted reproduction with the same legal certainty of parentage from birth as enjoyed by children born without resort to assisted reproduction can be considered discrimination against children on the basis of their birth circumstances or family status.[22] In the absence of clear rules governing parentage in cases of assisted reproduction, existing laws privileging bio-genetic definitions of parentage may assign legal parentage in ways contrary to the intentions of the parties, and the ensuing uncertainty and conflict may be contrary to the best interests of children.[23] In addition, parenting arrangements in some same-sex families where known donors or surrogates have continued to be involved in the child's life have raised the question of whether it might be possible for the law to formally recognize that a child has more than two parents.

However, as noted in the introduction to this chapter, Canadian law, which has been at the forefront of family law reform on many issues, and in particular on same-sex issues, has for the most part failed to deal comprehensively with the assignment of parentage in the context of assisted reproduction. The appendix at the end of this chapter provides an overview, in chart form, of the parentage laws now in place in the Canadian provinces and territories, illustrating the current patchwork of laws across the country that address the parentage issues arising in cases of assisted reproduction.[24] Particular focus is placed on how three issues related to parentage are addressed: use of donated gametes, surrogacy, and whether there is provision for more than two legal parents.

Until the Uniform Law Conference of Canada's release of its new *Uniform Child Status Law* in 2010, there were few templates for provinces wishing to amend their laws to deal with assisted reproduction. The ULCC made a limited foray into this territory in 1992 by adding some modest amendments to its *Uniform Child Status Act* to deal with parentage in cases where opposite sex couples had used artificial insemination.[25] The rules chosen reflected the intention of the birth mother and her male partner to be parents. Same-sex couples and surrogacy were not addressed, however, and as will be shown below, there was little legislative response even to this modest proposal for reform. In the 1990s Newfoundland made modest reforms to its parentage laws of the sort contemplated by the 1992 *Uniform Child Status Act*, adding some provisions to its child status legislation to deal with "artificial insemination," but only where it is used by opposite sex couples. Under these provisions, the birth mother's married or unmarried male partner is to be deemed the legal father if he consented to the insemination.[26] Similar provisions were included in relevant Yukon legislation.[27]

Prior to BC's enactment of the new parentage laws based on the *Uniform Child Status Act, 2010*, only three provinces had enacted legislation dealing in a somewhat more extensive manner with parentage in cases involving assisted reproduction. Quebec led with pioneering legislation in 2002 that allows married spouses or partners in a civil union (same-sex or opposite-sex couples), who by consent enter into a mutual "parental project" involving assisted procreation, to both be regarded as the child's parents at birth.[28] However, the Quebec legislation is not completely comprehensive. The types of parental projects involving assisted reproduction that are contemplated are those involving donation of reproductive material. There are no provisions specifically dealing with parentage in cases of surrogacy, other than a provision that surrogacy agreements are null.[29] Quebec's legislative reforms were followed by new Alberta parentage legislation in 2003 that dealt with both surrogacy and donation of reproductive material.[30] However, it was not until amendments in 2010 that same-sex couples were fully included in the Alberta legislation, following a series of *Charter* challenges.[31] Prince Edward Island's reforms to its parentage laws in 2008 included same-sex couples but, like the Quebec reforms, only dealt with situations involving gamete donation.[32] Thus of the three more extensive attempts at reform of parentage legislation prior to 2010, only the Alberta legislation dealt with surrogacy. All three schemes restricted the number of legal parents to two.[33]

The other six provinces – Manitoba,[34] Saskatchewan,[35] Ontario,[36] New Brunswick,[37] Nova Scotia,[38] and Newfoundland and Labrador[39] – have quietly modified their birth registration legislation, regulations, or administrative practices in a piecemeal fashion to deal with situations where children have been born as a result of assisted conception, without engaging in any comprehensive revision of parentage legislation. Often these changes have been made in response to successful *Charter* challenges based on arguments that current regimes discriminate on the basis of sexual orientation by failing to provide to same-sex couples and their children the same secure legal recognition of their parent–child relationships at the moment of the child's birth as that enjoyed by opposite-sex families. In Saskatchewan, Nova Scotia, and Newfoundland and Labrador, these birth registry changes are somewhat more extensive in that they apply to births as a result of surrogacy arrangements and are not restricted to those involving donated reproductive material. However, as has been noted above, registration as a parent on a birth registry is not equivalent to a legal declaration of parentage, and such piecemeal changes do not eliminate the uncertainty surrounding declarations of parentage under older laws that continue, in their literal wording, to give priority to bio-genetic definitions of parenthood.[40] Resort to litigation to clarify parentage may still be required.[41]

The result of the failure to legislate clear and comprehensive laws assigning parentage in cases of assisted reproduction has been uncertainty and the need to resort to litigation for declarations of parenthood in individual cases under anachronistic parentage legislation that courts have been more or less willing to update through creative judicial interpretation.[42] The most noteworthy decision to arise out of this context of uncertainty and individual litigation is the ground-breaking decision of the Ontario Court of Appeal in *A(A) v B(B)*,[43] in which the court, relying on the *parens patriae* power,[44] found that on the facts of the particular case it was in the child's best interests to recognize a third legal parent – his mother's lesbian partner – in addition to the two parents recognized under the existing legislation: his birth mother and his genetic father (a known sperm donor who continued to play a parental role in the child's life). This three-parent arrangement was consistent with the intentions and understandings of all the parties. The resort to the *parens patriae* power to protect the child's best interests was justified because a legislative gap was found to exist: the drafters of the *Children's Law Reform Act* parentage provisions in 1977 had simply not anticipated the social changes entailed by assisted reproduction and same-sex parenting. The decision of the Ontario Court of Appeal has been criticized for its failure to address the discriminatory nature of the legislation itself and for requiring individual court applications under the *parens patriae* power for declarations of parentage that cannot be accommodated within the anachronistic language of the *Children's Law Reform Act*.[45] However, the decision's recognition that a child can have more than two legal parents clearly broke new legal ground in Canada and demonstrated the capacity of the Canadian legal system to respond to diverse and changing family forms. As will be shown below, British Columbia has now legislatively endorsed this development.

Recent Developments: The *Uniform Child Status Act, 2010* and the BC *Family Law Act* (2011)

In 2010 the Uniform Law Conference of Canada adopted the *Uniform Child Status Act, 2010*, the culmination of many years of work devoted to developing a new model for parentage laws that would take into account the significant social and technological changes that had taken place over the past two decades with respect to human reproduction.[46] In the course of comprehensively reforming its family law system, British Columbia adopted, in 2011, a new parentage law that came into force on 13 March 2013. Found in Part 3 of the new *Family Law Act*,[47] the new parentage law reflects, with some modifications, the template provided by the new *UCSA*.[48] The modifications introduced in the BC legislation were intended primarily to reduce the need to seek court declarations of parentage.

In greatly simplified form, the main planks of legal framework for parentage in cases of assisted reproduction found in both the *UCSA* and the parentage provisions of the new BC *FLA* are as follows:

- The birth mother is always the child's parent, whether or not she is the child's genetic mother, subject to change through adoption or surrogacy.[49]
- In cases where assisted conception is used (with the exception of surrogacy) the birth mother's partner (whether married or unmarried, opposite-sex or same-sex) is presumed to be the other legal parent unless there is proof that that person did not consent to be a parent of a child of assisted conception.[50]
- Egg, sperm, or embryo donors are not parents merely by virtue of their donation of genetic reproductive material.[51]

The *UCSA* and the *FLA* deal with surrogacy somewhat differently. Both are consistent in providing that:

- surrogacy agreements are not enforceable;
- the birth mother may refuse to relinquish the child at birth and will then be recognized as the child's parent; and
- if the birth mother does agree after the child's birth to relinquish her parental status and to place the child in the care of the intended parents, they should be recognized as the child's legal parents.

However, while the *UCSA* requires a court declaration, made after the child's birth, to transfer parentage to the intended parents, under the *FLA* there is no need for an application to court and emphasis is placed, instead, on a prior written agreement between the parties that the intended parents will be the parents. If there is such an agreement, the intended parents will become parents upon the birth of the child if, after the birth, the surrogate consents in writing to surrender the child and the intended parents take the child into their care. As well, the *UCSA* surrogacy provisions only apply if at least one of the intended parents is genetically related to the child, whereas there is no such requirement in the *FLA* that gives greater independent weight to intention to parent.

One of the most novel aspects of the *Uniform Child Status Act*, incorporated into the *FLA*, is the possibility created for a child to have more than two legal parents. Generally, under both schemes, a child will have a maximum of two parents. However, following the precedent set by the Ontario Court of Appeal in *A(A) v B(B)*,[52] the ULCC concluded that it would be appropriate to recognize an additional parent or parents in circumstances where, prior to the assisted conception, there is an agreement between the parties that they will all be parents.[53]

Conclusion

Although there is sure to be ongoing discussion and debate about fine-tuning the template for new parentage laws that has been provided in the *Uniform Child Status Act, 2010* and BC's new *Family Law Act*, one can hope that other provinces will follow BC's lead and undertake a comprehensive reform of their parentage laws in light of the new templates that have been developed, thus bringing their parentage laws into the twenty-first century.[54]

Appendix: Overview of Parentage Legislation by Province/Territory with a Focus on Assisted Reproduction

Province/ Territory	Legislation	Gamete/embryo donation	Surrogacy	More than two parents?
Alberta	*Family Law Act*, SA 2003, c. F-4.5 [as amended by *Family Law Statutes Amendment Act*, 2010, c. 16], Part 1, "Establishing Parentage" • parentage legislation revised to explicitly deal with assisted reproduction through series of reforms beginning in 2003 that initially did not deal with same-sex parents but now do • except for cases of assisted reproduction or adoption, parents are birth mother and biological father, *FLA* s. 7(2)(a) • presumptions of paternity, outside of cases of assisted reproduction, s. 8(1)	– expressly dealt with in s. 8.1(5) of *FLA* – in non-surrogacy cases, parents are birth mother and birth mother's married spouse or conjugal partner – person who donates reproductive material without intention of using material for his or her own reproductive use is not, by reason of donation only, a parent, *FLA* s.7(4)	– expressly dealt with in ss. 8.1 and 8.2 of *FLA* • surrogacy agreements not enforceable • possible to get declaration after child's birth that surrogate is not a parent if surrogate consents; • if surrogate consents, where one or both intended parents have contributed their own reproductive material they are the parents; if only one intended parent contributed reproductive material, their married spouse or conjugal partner at time of conception if they consented is also a parent • if declaration is made, intended parents are deemed to be parents from birth, s. 8.2(7) • if surrogate does not consent, surrogate/birth mother is only parent • surrogate's spouse or conjugal partner is not a parent, s. 7(5) • surrogacy provisions do not apply to situations where neither intended parent contributed their own reproductive material	– no declaration to be made that would result in child having more than two parents, *FLA* s. 8.2(12)

(Continued)

Province/ Territory	Legislation	Gamete/embryo donation	Surrogacy	More than two parents?
B.C.	*Family Law Act*, SBC 2011, c. 25 • new legislation assented to on 24 November 2011 came into force on 13 March 2013 • Part 3 dealing with parentage, implements (with some modifications) Uniform Law Conference of Canada's *Uniform Child Status Act, 2010* • explicit provisions dealing with parentage in cases of assisted reproduction and surrogacy • in cases not involving assisted reproduction, child's parents are birth mother and biological father, s. 26(1)	– expressly dealt with in s. 27 of new *FLA*: • child's birth mother is parent, s. 27(2) • in addition to the child's birth mother, a person who was married to, or in a marriage-like relationship with, the child's birth mother when the child was conceived is also the child's parent unless there is proof that, before the child was conceived, the person did not consent to be the child's parent or withdrew their consent, s. 26(3) – s. 24 provides that donor of reproductive material is not parent merely by reason of the donation	– expressly dealt with in s. 29 of new *FLA*: • surrogate is birth mother but on birth intended parents will become child's parents if, after child's birth, surrogate gives consent to surrender child and intended parents take the child into their care pursuant to a prior agreement to this effect • not necessary that the intended parents have contributed any of their own reproductive material • no court declaration required	– expressly dealt with in s. 30 of new *FLA*: • in cases of assisted reproduction, may be more than two parents if parties agree to such arrangement in written agreement prior to child's birth and agreement is not withdrawn prior to child's birth • in surrogacy cases allows birth mother and intended parents to all be declared parents • in cases of gamete donation, allows birth mother, birth mother's partner, and donor who also intends to be a parent all to be declared parents

Manitoba	*Family Maintenance Act*, CCSM c. F20, Part II, "Child Status" • provides for declarations of parentage • presumptions of paternity, s. 23 • no amendment to explicitly deal with assisted reproduction or same-sex parents *Vital Statistics Act*, CCSM c. V60 • s. 3(6) deals with registration of births in cases of artificial insemination Reg 308/88, *Vital Statistics Forms, Fees and Registrations Regulation Amendment,* as amended by Reg 74/2011 • new form 4, "Registration of Birth," refers to father/other parent • new form 7, "Consent of Parents," refers to mother's spouse or common law partner	– no explicit reference to assisted conception in child status provisions in *FMA* – but birth registration provisions in *Vital Statistics Act* provide that where child is born to woman as a result of artificial insemination, birth registration shall be completed with particulars of the woman and her spouse or common law partner as the father or other parent if both woman and her spouse/partner consent	– no explicit reference in parentage or birth registration legislation	– no explicit reference to more than two parents in parentage or birth registration legislation

(Continued)

Province/ Territory	Legislation	Gamete/embryo donation	Surrogacy	More than two parents?
New Brunswick	*Family Services Act*, SNB 1980, c. F-2.2, Part IV, "Parentage of Children" • a person is the child of his or her natural parents, s. 96(1), subject to adoption • provides for declarations of parentage • presumptions of paternity, s. 103(1) • no reform to deal with assisted reproduction or same-sex parents *Vital Statistics Act*, SNB 1979, c. V-3 • no explicit amendments making reference to assisted reproduction or same-sex parents	– no explicit reference in parentage or vital statistics legislation – but birth registration governed by decision in *AA v New Brunswick (Human Rights Commission)*, [2004] NBHRBID No 4, 2004 CarswellNB 395 (NBE STD): Dept. of Health and Wellness was ordered to cease discriminating against lesbian couples by refusing to register the birth mother's same-sex partner on the birth registration; therefore same-sex partners of birth mothers allowed to have their particulars on birth registry	– no explicit reference in parentage or birth registration legislation – but see judicial decision declaring intended parents to be parents in case involving gestational surrogacy and embryo derived from intended parents' reproductive material: *JAW v JEW*, 2010 NBQB 414, 373 NBR (2d) 211	– no explicit reference to more than two parents' parentage or birth registration legislation
Newfoundland and Labrador	*Children's Law Act*, RSNL 1990, c. C-13, Part I, "Status of Children," & Part II, "Establishment of Parentage" • s. 3(1), a person is the child of his or her natural parents	– s. 12 of *CLA* explicitly deals with artificial insemination in *opposite-sex couples* only: • if couple married, mother's husband at time of insemination is father if he consented in advance to the insemination	– no explicit reference to surrogacy in *CLA* – but *VSA* deals with birth registration in cases of surrogacy	– no explicit reference to more than two parents in either *CLA* or *VSA*

	• provisions for declarations of motherhood (s. 6) and fatherhood (s. 7) • presumptions of paternity, s. 10 • only explicit reference to assisted reproduction is s. 12 dealing with "artificial insemination" in *opposite-sex* couples *Vital Statistics Act*, 2009, SNL 2009, c. V-6.01 • includes provisions dealing with artificial insemination (s. 5(5)) and surrogacy(s. 5(6))	• if couple cohabiting, male cohabiting with mother at time of insemination is the father if he consented in advance, unless it is proved that he refused to consent to responsibilities of parenthood • man whose semen is used to artificially inseminate woman to whom he is not married or with whom he is not cohabiting is not the father of the resulting child – but birth registration provisions in *VSA* dealing with artificial insemination are broader, allowing birth mother's spouse or cohabiting partner to have their particulars listed as father or "other parent" if both birth mother and her spouse/partner consent, s. 5(5)	– s. 5(6) *VSA* provides that intended parents shall be registered as parents where adoption order has been made or where a declaratory order respecting the parentage of the child has been issued under s. 6 or 7 of the *CLA* (thus implying that declarations of parentage under the *CLA* need not reflect biological parentage)	
Nova Scotia	– no distinct child status or parentage legislation, but some parentage provisions found in other statutes or regulations	– no explicit reference in legislation	– no explicit reference in legislation	– no explicit reference to more than two parents in legislation or regulations

(Continued)

Province/ Territory	Legislation	Gamete/embryo donation	Surrogacy	More than two parents?
	– some provisions dealing with establishment of paternity in *Maintenance and Custody Act*, RSNS 1989, c. 160, *Vital Statistics Act*, RSNS 1989, c. 494 • no explicit reference to assisted reproduction or same-sex parents re birth registration; but see regulations, below • provision for declarations of paternity *Birth Registration Regulations* under the *Vital Statistics Act*, NS Reg 390/2007 • provides that woman who gives birth must be registered as mother, s. 4 • deals with birth registration in cases of assisted conception, s. 3 • deals with declarations of parenthood in cases of surrogacy, s. 5	– however, the *Birth Registration Regulations* under the *Vital Statistics Act* deal with assisted conception in s. 3: • s. 3(1) provides that if the mother of a child who was conceived as a result of assisted conception is married, the birth must be registered showing the mother's spouse as the other parent • s. 3(2) provides that if the mother of the child who was conceived as a result of assisted conception was unmarried, and the person acknowledged by the mother as the other parent and that person files a statutory declaration acknowledging that they intend to assume the role of parent, the birth must be registered showing that person as the child's other parent	– however, the *Birth Registration Regulations* under the *Vital Statistics Act* deal with both parentage and birth registration in surrogacy cases in s. 5: • s. 5(2) allows courts to make declaratory order with respect to parentage on application by intended parents; limited to cases where one of intended parents has a genetic link to child and woman who is to carry and give birth to child does not intend to be the child's parent (note: no requirement of post-birth consent by surrogate) • once declaratory order made, court may make order that names of intended parents be registered on birth registry and name of surrogate be removed, s. 5(3)	

Ontario	*Children's Law Reform Act* RSO 1990, c. C.12, Part I, "Equal Status of Children," and Part II, "Establishment of Parentage" • a person is the child of his or her natural parents, s. (1) • provision for declarations of parentage, s. 4 • presumptions of paternity, s. 8 • no amendment to explicitly deal with assisted reproduction or same-sex parents *Vital Statistics Act*, RSO 1990, c. V.4 • no explicit reference to assisted reproduction or same-sex parents; however, see regulations below	– birth registration context explicitly dealt with in Reg 1094, RRO 1990 under the *Vital Statistics Act* as amended by O Reg 410/06: • allows an "other parent" to register the child. • s. 2(1) defines "other parent" as "a person whom a child's mother acknowledges as the other parent, who wishes to be acknowledged as the other parent and who agrees to certify the statement with respect to the child *where the father is unknown* and conception occurred through assisted conception"	– no explicit reference in parentage or birth registration legislation – but see judicial decisions re birth registration and declaration of parentage in cases of gestational surrogacy: • *JR v LH*, [2002] OJ No 3998 (SC) (QL) and *MD v LL*, 90 OR (3d) 127, 52 RFL (6th) 122 (SC) (gestational surrogacy, declarations that intended parents who were also genetic parents were child's mother and father, births to be registered consistent with declarations) • *KGD v CAP*, [2004] OJ No 3508 (SC) (QL) (gestational surrogacy, intended father single gay male who uses own sperm, anonymous egg donation, declaration of parentage under *CLRA* in favour of intended father/sperm donor and order that he be only parent on birth registration)	– no explicit reference in parentage or birth registration legislation – but see judicial decision using *parens patriae* power to respond to legislative gap and make declaration of parentage resulting in three legal parents (birth mother, birth mother's partner, and identified sperm donor): *A(A) v B(B)* (2007), 83 OR (3d) 561, 278 DLR (4th) 519, 35 RFL (6th) 1 (CA).

(Continued)

Province/ Territory	Legislation	Gamete/embryo donation	Surrogacy	More than two parents?
	Reg 1094, RRO 1990, under the *Vital Statistics Act* as amended by O Reg 410/06 • explicitly deals with birth registration in cases involving assisted conception	• this amendment followed *Rutherford v Ontario (Deputy Registrar General)* (2006), 81 OR (3d) 81, 270 DLR (4th) 90, 30 RFL (6th) 25 (SC), which found that the birth registration provisions of Ontario's *Vital Statistics Act*, which did not allow the lesbian partner of a birth mother to be registered as a co-parent in situations where the male partner of a woman who conceived using donate sperm, violated s. 15 of the Charter; birth registration provisions found not to reflect only biological parentage – no explicit reference to assisted conception in parentage provisions of *CLRA*, but judicial decisions have looked beyond biological parenthood and have declared husbands of women inseminated with donor sperm to be fathers: • L(TD) v L(LR) [Low v Low] (1994), 114 DLR (4th) 709, 4 RFL (4th) 103 (Ont Gen Div) • *Zegota v Zegota-Rzegocinski* (1994), 114 DLR (4th) 709, 4 RFL (4th) 103 (Ont Gen Div)	• *MD v LL* (2008), 90 OR (3d) 127, 52 RFL (6th) 122 (SC) (gestational surrogacy, declaration of parentage in favour of *opposite-sex* couple who were both intended parents and genetic parents; surrogate and her husband declared not to be parents) • *AWM v TNS*, 2014 ONSC 5420, [2014] OJ No 5793 (QL) (gestational surrogacy, declaration of parentage in favour of male same-sex couple; declaration that gestational carrier not the legal mother)	

P.E.I.	*Child Status Act*, RSPEI 1988, c. C-6, Part I, "Equal Status of Children," and Part II, "Establishment of Parentage" • birth mother deemed to be mother even if not genetic mother, s. 9(7) • presumptions of paternity, s. 9(4) • explicit amendments in 2008 to deal with assisted conception	– but ONCA has ruled that *CLRA* cannot be interpreted to allow two women to be declared mothers: *A(A) v B(B)* (2007), 83 OR (3d) 561, 278 DLR (4th) 519, 35 RFL (6th) 1 (CA), need to rely on *parens patriae* power-explicit provisions in *CSA* dealing with assisted conception: • birth mother deemed to be mother, s. 9(7) • person cohabiting with or in conjugal relationship with mother at time of insemination presumed to be parent unless no advance consent and no demonstration of settled intention to treat child as his or her child, s. 9(5) • person who donates semen or ovum not parent by that reason alone, s. 9(6)	– no explicit reference to surrogacy in *CSA*- birth mother (i.e., surrogate mother) will be deemed to be mother even if not genetic mother, s. 9(7)	– no explicit reference in *CSA* to more than two parents – presumptions of parenthood in *CSA* not to be applied if would result in more than one person being considered to be a parent in addition to the mother, s. 9(8)
Quebec	*Civil Code of Quebec*, LRQ, c. C-1991, ch. 1, "Filiation by Blood," and ch. 1.1, "Filiation of Children Born of Assisted Reproduction" (arts 538–42) • ch. 1.1 added in 2002	– filiation in cases of assisted procreation explicitly dealt with in ch. 1.1 of *Civil Code*:	– *Civil Code* contains no provisions allowing parental status to be granted to intended parents in cases of surrogacy	– no provision in *Civil Code* for more than two parents:

(Continued)

Province/ Territory	Legislation	Gamete/embryo donation	Surrogacy	More than two parents?
		• contribution of genetic material for purposes of third-party parental project does not create any bond of filiation between contributor and child (art. 538.2) • however, contribution of genetic material provided by sexual intercourse may give rise to bond of filiation if established within one year of birth (art 538.2) • relationship of filiation established between woman who gives birth and child (art. 538.1) • if child is born as a result of a parental project involving assisted procreation between married or civil union spouses the spouse of the woman who gave birth is presumed to be the child's other parent (art. 538.3) • birth mother's spouse may contest the filiation by showing no mutual parental project (art. 539)	– only reference to surrogacy is art. 541, which renders surrogacy agreements null – see also judicial decision refusing adoption by intended mother because of prohibition on surrogacy agreements: *Adoption-091*, 2009 QCCQ 628, [2009] RJQ 445	• code provisions assume one mother and one father • in cases of assisted procreation, if both parents women, legal rights and obligations of the father are assigned to the mother who did not give birth (art. 539.1)

Saskatch- ewan	*Children's Law Act*, 1997, SS 1997, c. C-8.2, Part VI, "Child Status and Parentage" • person is child of his or her natural parents, s. 40(1) • provision for declarations of parentage • resumptions of paternity, s. 45(1) • no amendment to deal with assisted reproduction *Vital Statistics Act, 2009,* SS 2009, c. V-7.21 • provisions for registration by "other parent" in addition to birth mother and biological father	– no explicit reference in *CLA* – but re birth registration under *Vital Statistics Act*, intended parent also allowed to sign birth registry: • "mother" defined as woman who gives birth, s. 2(1) • "father" defined as person who acknowledges himself to be biological father • "other parent" who is also allowed to sign birth registry defined as "person other than the mother or father who is cohabiting with the mother or father at the time of the child's birth and who intends to participate as a parent in the upbringing of the child"	– no explicit reference in *CLA* – but re birth registration under *Vital Statistics Act*, intended parent also allowed to sign birth registry: • "mother" defined as woman who gives birth, s. 2(1) • "father" defined as person who acknowledges himself to be biological father • "other parent" who is also allowed to sign birth registry defined as "person other than the mother or father who is cohabiting with the mother or father at the time of the child's birth and who intends to participate as a parent in the upbringing of the child" – thus the surrogate, the sperm donor/intended father, and his partner/intended parent could all sign the birth registration as parents – see also judicial decision declaring under *CLRA* that gestational surrogate not the legal mother and ordering that her name be removed from the birth registry, leaving the intended parents as parents, one of whom had contributed the sperm: *WJQM v AMA*, 2011 SKQB 317, 339 DLR (4th) 759	– no explicit reference in *CLA* to more than two parents, but birth registration provisions of *Vital Statistics Act* allow other parents to register in addition to birth mother and biological father

(Continued)

Province/ Territory	Legislation	Gamete/embryo donation	Surrogacy	More than two parents?
Northwest Territories and Nunavut	*Children's Law Act*, SNWT 1997, c. 14, Part I, "Status of Children," and Part II, "Establishment of Parentage" • person is child of his or her natural parents, s. 2(1) • provisions for declarations of parentage • presumptions of paternity, s. 8(1) • no amendments to explicitly deal with assisted reproduction or same-sex parents	– no explicit reference in legislation	– no explicit reference in legislation	– no explicit reference in legislation to more than two parents
Yukon	*Children's Act*, RSY 2002, c. 31 • presumptions of paternity, s. 12(1) • provisions dealing with artificial insemination in *opposite-sex* couples, s. 13	– s. 13 of *Children's Act* explicitly deals with parentage in cases of artificial insemination in *opposite-sex* couples (same provisions as in Newfoundland and Labrador *CLA*, see above)	– no explicit reference in legislation	– no explicit provision for more than two parents in legislation

NOTES

1 For a review of some of this literature, see Susan Boyd, "Gendering Legal Parenthood: Bio-genetic Ties, Intentionality, and Responsibility" (2007) 25 Windsor YB Access Just 63.
2 SC 2004, c 2.
3 *AHRA*, s 10, which allowed for the disclosure of health information, but not of donor identity.
4 As will be discussed *infra*, Quebec and Prince Edward Island have dealt with conception involving donated reproductive material but not with surrogacy, and some provinces have amended their birth registration legislation but not their parentage legislation. Since the writing of this chapter, the Manitoba Law Reform Commission has studied the issue: "Assisted Reproduction: Legal Parentage and Birth Registration," Issue Paper, April 2014, http://www.manitobalawreform.ca. While the Commission made some recommendations, which have not yet been acted upon, it was unable to reach conclusions on parentage in surrogacy cases or on the issue of a child having more than two legal parents without further research, consultation, and consideration. Legislation implementing the recommendations of the Commission was introduced in June 2015 but was never passed (Bill 33, *The Family Law Reform Act (Putting Children First)*). In September 2014 the Law Commission of Ontario announced that it would be undertaking a new project on redefining parentage; see http://www.lco-cdo.org/en/new-projects-announcement. This has been pre-empted by legislative developments in the form of a private member's bill, Bill 137, *Cy and Ruby's Act (Parental Recognition), 2015*, introduced in November 2015.
5 See Nicholas Bala and Rebecca Jaremko, "Context and Inclusivity in Canada's Evolving Definition of the Family" (2002) 16 Int J L Pol'y & Fam 145; and Carol Rogerson, "Canada: A Bold and Progressive Past but an Unclear Future," in *The Future of Child and Family Law: International Predictions*, ed. Elaine Sutherland (Cambridge: Cambridge University Press, 2012), 77.
6 See *Pratten v British Columbia (Attorney General)*, 2011 BCSC 656, 99 RFL (6th) 290, in which the court declared that British Columbia's failure to provide donor offspring with the same access to information about their biological origins as adopted children constitutes an unjustifiable violation of equality rights under s 15 of the *Canadian Charter of Rights and Freedoms*, Part I of the *Constitution Act, 1982*, being Schedule B to the *Canada Act 1982* (UK), 1982, c 11. The decision was reversed on appeal, on the ground that the violation of s 15(1) was saved by s 15(2): 2012 BCCA 480, 25 RFL (7th) 58, leave to appeal to SCC refused, [2013] SCCA No. 36. The earlier decision

seems in line with articles 7 and 8 of the UN *Convention on the Rights of the Child*, 20 November 1989, 1577 UNTS 3, which have been interpreted as supporting the child's right to knowledge of genetic origins. Reviews of Canada's compliance with the convention have noted the failure of Canadian laws governing both adoption and assisted reproduction to ensure that children have access to the identity of their biological parents: see concluding observations on Canada's second periodic report, 27 October 2003, CRC/C/15/add.215, paras 30 and 31. On this issue and on the *Pratten* case, see the chapters by Giroux and Milne, Guichon, Gruben, and Snelling in this volume.

7 An annotated version of the Act is available at http://www.ulcc.ca/en/uniform-acts-new-order/current-uniform-acts/86-josetta-1-en-gb/uniform-actsa/child-status-act/1371-child-status-act-2010. The Uniform Law Conference of Canada is a volunteer organization, many of whose members are government policy lawyers and analysts. Its civil law section directs its efforts to the development of uniform statutes to facilitate the harmonization of provincial and territorial laws.

8 *Family Law Act*, SBC 2011, c 25 (assented to 24 November 2011; came into force 13 March 2013). Part 3 of the new act deals with parentage.

9 This is true of the common law provinces, but not of Quebec, where the civil law is more resistant to recognition of *de facto* relationships, whether spousal or parent–child.

10 At the federal level, see the *Divorce Act*, RSC 1985, c 3 (2nd Supp), s 2(2), which defines "child of the marriage" as including any child for whom a spouse "stands in the place of a parent." This definition applies to the child support and to the custody and access provisions of the *Divorce Act*. Similar provisions exist in most of the common law provinces. In Ontario, see the *Family Law Act*, RSO 1990, c F.3, s 1(1), which uses the language of "a settled intention to treat a child as child of [one's] family." For overviews of this area of law, see Alison Harvison Young, "This Child Does Have 2 (or More) Fathers … Step-parents and Support Obligations" (2000) 45 McGill LJ 107; Carol Rogerson, "The Child Support Obligation of Step-Parents" (2001) 18 Can J Fam L 9; and Nicholas Bala and Meaghan Thomas, "Who Is a 'Parent'? 'Standing in the Place of a Parent' and Canada's *Child Support Guidelines* s. 5," *Queen's Faculty of Law, Legal Studies Research Paper Series*, No. 07–11 (12 July 2007), online: Social Science Research Network Electronic Paper Collection http://papers.ssrn.com/sol3/papers.cfm?abstract_id=10238955.

11 See *BHW v DJR*, 2007 ABCA 57, 280 DLR (4th) 90. (Same-sex partner of biological father of child born as a result of a surrogacy found to stand *in loco parentis* because he had participated in raising the child for three years

and thus presumptively was entitled to access. The biological father and the surrogate mother, who had also remained involved in the child's life, had tried to prevent the father's same-sex partner from having access.) For the sequel to the case with respect to the access order, see *BHW v DJR*, 2009 ABQB 438, 70 RFL (6th) 341. For a further sequel yet, see *DWH v DJR*, 2011 ABQB 608, 7 RFL (7th) 84 in which, after finding that the provisions of the Alberta parentage legislation in place at that time violated s 15 of the *Charter* because they did not extend the concept of parentage established by intention to same-sex couples, only opposite-sex couples, the court by way of remedy granted the same-sex partner of the biological father a declaration of legal parentage. This decision was upheld on appeal: *DWH v DJR*, 2013 ABCA 240, 34 RFL (7th) 27.

12 See *A(A) v B (B)*, 2007 ONCA 2, 83 OR (3d) 561, 278 DLR (4th) 519, 35 RFL (6th) 1, leave to appeal to SCC refused, 2007 SCC 40, [2007] 3 SCR 124, for a recognition of the significant legal consequences that flow from the assignment of legal parentage. In this case, which will be discussed in more detail below, the court used its *parens patriae* power to issue a declaration of parentage to a lesbian co-mother without requiring the termination of the known sperm donor's parental status.

13 See *Young*, *supra* note 10.

14 See Boyd, *supra* note 1; and Fiona Kelly, "(Re)forming Parenthood: The Assignment of Legal Parentage within Planned Lesbian Families" (2008–9) 40 Ottawa L Rev 185.

15 This applies to the common law provinces. In Quebec, both sorts of provisions are found in the *Civil Code of Quebec*, LRQ, c C-1991.

16 For a fuller discussion of the distinction between birth registration and parentage laws, see the report of the Uniform Law Conference of Canada, which provides the background to its *Uniform Child Status Act, 2010*: Uniform Law Conference of Canada, Civil Law Section, "Assisted Human Reproduction: Report of the Joint ULCC-CCSO Working Group" (Ottawa, Ontario: 9–13 August 2009), http://www.ulcc.ca/en/uniform-acts-new-order/current-uniform-acts/637-child-status/1497-assisted-human-reproduction-working-group-report-2009?showall=1&limitstart=, paras 14–31.

17 Most provinces enacted some form of child status legislation during the first wave of modern family law reform; in some cases it was a separate statute, in others it was included as a distinct section in another piece of family law legislation. However, some provinces did not enact any child status legislation; see, for example, Nova Scotia, as discussed below, note 21.

18 The 1982 *Uniform Child Status Act* was modelled on legislation adopted in Ontario in 1977. Ontario was the first province to remove distinctions

based upon the marital status of the child's parents. See discussion in Law Reform Commission of Nova Scotia, *The Legal Status of the Child Born Outside of Marriage: Final Report* (March 1995), http://www.lawreform.ns.ca/Downloads/Status_FIN.pdf.

19 RSO 1990, c C.12 [emphasis added].

20 Alberta, however, has rejected the presumptions based merely upon cohabitation at the time of birth or conception, and a twelve-month period of cohabitation is required to give rise to a presumption of paternity; see *Family Law Act*, SA 2003, c F-4.5, s 8(1). As has often been noted, although these presumptions are presented as presumptive evidence of biological fatherhood, in practice they also reflect *de facto* arrangements of social parenting that will be legally recognized if the presumptions are not challenged. To that extent these presumptions are legal fictions.

21 Introduction of child status legislation was recommended by the Law Reform Commission of Nova Scotia in 1995, but its recommendations were not implemented; see Law Reform Commission of Nova Scotia, *supra* note 18. Some parentage provisions are "hidden" in other legislation. Under the province's *Vital Statistics Act*, RSNS 1989, c 494, authority is granted to make declarations of paternity and the *Birth Registration Regulations*, NS Reg 390/2007 provide for declarations of parentage in cases of surrogacy. As well, some presumptions related to the establishment of paternity are set out in the province's *Maintenance and Custody Act*, RSNS 1989, c 160. There was also no comprehensive child status legislation in BC before enactment of the section of the new *Family Law Act* dealing with parentage, *supra* note 8; provisions setting out the basic rules of parentage were found in the *Law and Equity Act*, RSBC 1996, c 253.

22 This discrimination could be in violation of s 15 of the *Charter* and also in violation of Canada's obligations under the UN *Convention on the Rights of the Child*, article 2 of which obligates states to protect children against discrimination, article 3 of which requires states to recognize that the child's best interests are a primary consideration in matters concerning the child, and article 7 of which requires states to ensure that the parent–child status is protected from birth.

23 For example, as discussed in Boyd and Kelly, both *supra* note 14, in cases where lesbian couples have used a known sperm donor, there is always the risk that the sperm donor will be found to be the legal father. For one example, see *MAC v MK*, 2009 ONCJ 18 (known sperm donor listed as father on birth registration subsequently refusing to follow terms of agreement and consent to adoption by lesbian birth mother's partner; court refusing to dispense with his consent).

24 In compiling this overview I have drawn upon Boyd, *supra* note 14; Kelly, *supra* note 14; Kelly Jordan, "ART Class: Assisted Reproductive Technology Class – Six Questions Answered" (2009) 28 CFLQ 71; Karen Busby, "Revisiting *The Handmaid's Tale*: Feminist Theory Meets Empirical Research on Surrogate Mothers" (2010) 26 Can J Fam L 13; Joanna Radbord, "GLBT Families and Assisted Reproductive Technologies" (paper presented at the CBA Canadian Legal Conference and Expo, Niagara, 15–17 August 2010) [unpublished]; and Ministry of the Attorney General (BC), Justice Services Branch, Civil and Family Law Policy Office, "Family Relations Act Review, Chapter 10, Defining Legal Parenthood: Discussion Paper" (August 2007), http://www.courthouselibrary.ca/docs/default-source/asked-answered/ministry-of-attorney-general-justice-services-branch-civil-and-family-law-policy-office-2007-discussion-papers/chapter10-defininglegalparenthood_apr9-2014.pdf?sfvrsn=2. More recent reviews have been undertaken since the initial writing of this chapter: see Fiona Kelly, "One of These Families Is Not Like the Others: The Legal Response to Non-Normative Queer Parenting in Canada" (2013) 51 Alta L Rev 1; and Wanda Weigers, "Assisted Conception and Equality of Familial Status in Parentage Law" (2012–13) 28 Can J Fam L 147.

25 http://www.ulcc.ca/en/uniform-acts-new-order/withdrawn-uniform-acts/707-child-status-act-1992/70-child-status-act-1992.

26 See *Children's Law Act*, RSNL 1990, c.C-13, s. 12(1). As will be discussed further below, amendments to the province's birth registration laws also allow the same-sex spouse or cohabiting partner of the birth mother to register as an "other parent" even though the *CLA* parentage provisions dealing with artificial insemination only expressly apply to opposite-sex couples.

27 See *Children's Act*, RSY 2002, c 31, s 13(1).

28 Quebec's pioneering reforms in 2002 added a new chapter 1.1 "Filiation of children born of assisted procreation" (arts 538–542) into the *Civil Code of Quebec*, LRQ, c C-1991. The Quebec reforms are discussed in Robert Leckey, "'Where the Parents Are of the Same Sex': Quebec's Reforms to Filiation" (2009) 23 Int'l JL Pol'y & Fam 62.

29 Article 541.

30 *Family Law Act*, SA 2003, c F-4.5

31 See *Family Law Statutes Amendment Act*, SA 2010, c 16.

32 *Child Status Act*, RSPEI 1988, c C-6, s 9(1).

33 In Alberta, s 8.2(12) of the *FLA* provides that no declaration is to be made that would result in a child having more than two parents. In PEI, s 9(8) of the *CSA* provides that the presumptions of parenthood contained in

the Act are not to be applied if they would result in more than one person being considered to be a parent in addition to the mother. The Civil Code provisions in Quebec dealing with filiation assume two parents: one mother and one father. In cases of assisted conception, article 539.1 provides that if both parents are women, the legal rights and obligations of the father are assigned to the mother who did not give birth.

34 See *Vital Statistics Act*, CCSM c V60, s 3(6), which covers cases of artificial insemination, providing that, with the consent of both parties, the particulars of the mother's spouse or common law partner shall be shown as those of the father or other parent.

35 Saskatchewan enacted new vital statistics legislation in 2009 without changing its laws of child status and parentage found in the *Children's Law Act*, SS 1997, c C-8.2. The *Vital Statistics Act, 2009*, c V-7.21, allows the mother, father, and "other parent" to have their particulars set out on the birth registration. Under s 2(1), the Act defines "mother" as the woman who gives birth, "father" as the "person who acknowledges himself to be the biological father of a child, and "other parent" as "a person other than the mother or father who is cohabiting with the mother or father of the child in a spousal relationship at the time of the child's birth and who intends to participate as a parent in the upbringing of the child."

36 In Ontario, *Rutherford v Ontario (Deputy Registrar General)* (2006), 81 OR (3rd) 81, 270 DLR (4th) 90, 30 RFL (6th) 25 (SC) involved a successful s 15 *Charter* challenge to the birth registration provisions of Ontario's *Vital Statistics Act*, RSO 1990, c V.4, which did not allow the lesbian partner of a birth mother to be registered as a co-parent in situations where the male partner of a woman who conceived using donated sperm would be. Following the decision in *Rutherford*, Reg 1094, RRO 1990 under the Act was amended by O Reg 410/06 to allow an "other parent" to register the child. Section 2(1) defines "other parent" as "a person whom a child's mother acknowledges as the other parent, who wishes to be acknowledged as the other parent and who agrees to certify the statement with respect to the child where the father is unknown and conception occurred through assisted conception." Note that this possibility of two lesbian mothers being registered as parents is limited to cases where the father is unknown.

37 In New Brunswick, only the administrative practices under the *Vital Statistics Act*, SNB 1979, c V-3, have been changed without any formal amendment of the legislation or regulations. As a result of the decision in *AA v New Brunswick (Human Rights Commission)*, [2004] NBHRBID No. 4, 2004 CarswellNB 395 (NBESTD), the Department of Health and Wellness

was ordered to cease discriminating against lesbian couples by refusing to register the birth mother's same-sex partner on the birth registration.

38 In 2007, regulations were enacted under Nova Scotia's *Vital Statistics Act*, RSNS 1989, c 494, that deal with birth registration in cases of assisted conception and also make provision for declarations of parentage in favour of the intended parents in surrogacy cases, which can then be used to alter the birth registration; see *Birth Registration Regulations*, NS Reg 390/2007.

39 In Newfoundland and Labrador the *Vital Statistics Act, 2009*, SNL 2009, c V-6.01, contains provisions dealing with birth registration in cases involving both artificial insemination and surrogacy. With respect to artificial insemination, while the *Children's Law Act* only deals with parentage in cases where opposite-sex couples use artificial insemination, the provisions in the 2009 *Vital Statistics Act* dealing with artificial insemination also include same-sex couples, with s 5(5) allowing the mother's spouse or cohabiting partner to complete the birth registration. The *Vital Statistics Act, 2009* also deals with birth registration in the case of surrogacy, even though there is no mention of this in the province's child status legislation. Section 5(6)(e) requires the registrar to register the intended parents as the parents of the child where there has been an adoption order or where there has been a declaratory order respecting parentage under ss 6 or 7 of the *Children's Law Act*.

40 The exception is the changes to the Nova Scotia birth registration regulations, which included provisions allowing for declarations of parentage in surrogacy cases; see *supra* note 38. This "burying" of parentage laws in birth registration legislation is in part the result of Nova Scotia having no child status legislation; see *supra* notes 17 and 21.

41 Thus in Saskatchewan, see *WJQM v AMA*, 2011 SKQB 317, 339 DLR (4th) 759 (in case of gestational surrogacy where surrogate and both intended parents had signed the birth registry under the post-2007 amendments, judicial declaration under *Children's Law Act*, SS 1997, c C-8.2 required to establish that surrogate not the legal mother).

42 In two Ontario cases, for example, courts granted declarations of parentage under the *Children's Law Reform Act* to husbands of women who had been inseminated with donor semen, taking the view that parentage under the Act could go beyond biological parentage to include social or intentional parentage: see *L(TD) v L (LR)* [*Low v Low*], 4 RFL (4th) 103, 114 DLR (4th) 709, 1994 CarswellOnt 398 (Gen Div); and *Zegota v Zegota-Rzegocinski* (1994), 114 DLR (4th) 709, 4 RFL (4th) 103 (Ont Gen Div). However, in *A(A) v B(B)*, below note 43, the Ontario Court of Appeal ruled that the legislation could not be interpreted to allow for a declaration that would

result in a child having two mothers; such a declaration could only be made under the *parens patriae* power.

43 *Supra* note 12.

44 The *parens patriae* power refers to an inherent power in superior courts to intervene to protect the vulnerable. It is most often used to protect the best interests of children in circumstances where there has been a legislative "gap," that is, a legislative failure to fully provide for or anticipate the needs of children.

45 See Radbord, *supra* note 24.

46 *Supra* note 7. For background and an explanation of the choices made by the ULCC,see the report of the working group, *supra* note 16.

47 *Supra* note 8.

48 As part of the reform process, a background discussion paper on defining legal parentage was produced; see *supra* note 24. The recommendations for reform were then laid out in the *White Paper on Family Relations Act Reform: Proposals for a new Family Law Act* (Victoria: Ministry of Attorney General, 2010), http://www2.gov.bc.ca/assets/gov/law-crime-and-justice/about-bc-justice-system/legislation-policy/fla/family-law-white-paper.pdf. The specific background discussion paper on parentage is available at http://www.courthouselibrary.ca/docs/default-source/asked-answered/ministry-of-attorney-general-justice-services-branch-civil-and-family-law-policy-office-2007-discussion-papers/chapter10-defininglegalparenthood_apr9-2014.pdf?sfvrsn=2 . An information package on the new parentage legislation is available at http://www2.gov.bc.ca/assets/gov/law-crime-and-justice/about-bc-justice-system/legislation-policy/fla/part3.pdf . The BC White Paper differs from the ULCC's model legislation in that it requires court declarations of parentage in fewer situations. The BC surrogacy provisions also apply in cases where neither of the intended parents is genetically related to the child.

49 *UCSA*, s.3(2), *FLA*, s 27(2). This is justified by the need to provide the child with certainty and security of parenthood at the moment of birth.

50 *UCSA*, s 5, *FLA* s 27(3).

51 *UCSA*, s 6(6), *FLA* s 24.

52 The ULCC also drew upon the recommendations of the New Zealand Law Commission, which recommended a process for recognizing a known donor as an additional parent; see New Zealand Law Commission, *New Issues in Legal Parenthood, Report 88* (Wellington: Law Commission, 2005), http://www.nzlii.org/nz/other/nzlc/report/R88/R88.pdf.

53 *UCSA*, s 9 and *FLA*, s 30. The UCSA contemplates that a child may have up to six parents, whereas the *FLA* only allows for recognition of three legal

parents (either the surrogate/birth mother and the two intended parents or the birth mother, her partner, and a donor). See Uniform Law Conference of Canada, Civil Law Section, "Uniform Child Status Act: A Joint Project of the Uniform Law Conference of Canada and the Federal/Provincial/Territorial Coordinating Committee of Senior Officials on Family Justice" (Halifax: 22–26 August 2010), http://www.ulcc.ca/en/uniform-acts-new-order/current-uniform-acts/637-child-status/1495-uniform-child-status-act at 19: "In theory, under this provision, a child could have a maximum of six parents – the birth mother, her spouse or common-law partner, the two donors who agreed prior to conception to be parents of the child (where the resulting embryo is carried by the birth mother), and the spouses or common-law partners of the donors. However, in most instances, it will result in a maximum of three parents – the birth mother, her spouse or common-law partner, and the donor who all agreed prior to conception to be the child's parents."

54 See the recent moves in this direction by Manitoba and Ontario, *supra* note 4.

6 The Right to Know One's Origins, the *AHRA Reference*, and *Pratten v AGBC*: A Call for Provincial Legislative Action

MICHELLE GIROUX AND CHERYL MILNE

Introduction

On 27 November 2012 the British Columbia Court of Appeal dismissed the claim by Olivia Pratten under the *Canadian Charter of Rights and Freedoms*[1] that persons conceived through assisted human reproduction (AHR) had a right to disclosure of identifying information about their genetic origins.[2] This chapter raises concerns about the Court of Appeal's decision and argues that the Court gives short shrift to the constitutional arguments made on behalf of donor offspring and to the psychological security and privacy interests demonstrated through the evidence. While acknowledging that donors and legal parents have competing interests, this chapter argues that the aftermath of the case, which was refused leave to appeal to the Supreme Court of Canada,[3] has been a legislative vacuum that will require the intervention of provincial governments to balance the conflicts and interests among parents, donors, and offspring.

Background to the Decision

Olivia Pratten was conceived in 1981 through assisted human reproduction (AHR) with the sperm of an anonymous donor. Ms Pratten's mother and father agreed to the anonymity of her donor; however, there was no other way to access the procedure at that time. She sought information about him from the doctor who had performed the insemination but was given very little information: that he was a Caucasian medical student with a stocky build, brown hair, blue eyes, and type "A" blood. She was informed that the records had been destroyed in a manner consistent with the rules of the College of Physicians and Surgeons of British Columbia. The doctor had kept them for the minimum six years following the last entry in the record before destroying them.[4]

In 2008, Ms Pratten commenced an application in the Supreme Court of British Columbia against the Attorney General for British Columbia and the College of Physicians and Surgeons of British Columbia challenging the Province's adoption disclosure legislation, which facilitates the disclosure of identifying information to adoptees. She claimed that the Province was required to enact similar identity information legislation for persons conceived through gamete donation and to compel physicians in British Columbia to maintain records of donors to facilitate disclosure.

The application was initially challenged by the Attorney General on the basis that Ms Pratten lacked standing as a litigant, having neither a private interest nor a public interest in the proceedings. It was also challenged for mootness, in that no records existed for Ms Pratten. The case proceeded on the basis that those whose records remained in the control of medical professionals could have a possible claim based on the arguments put forward by Ms Pratten as a public interest litigant.[5] Evidence, by way of affidavits, was also put before the court of the individual experiences of people who were born through assisted reproduction. Their stories evidenced harms attributed to the anonymity of the donors, including depression, anxiety, anger, and frustration; lack of medical history that impacted treatment for serious illness, including misdiagnosis and, in one instance, the lack of a transplant donor match; and lack of information about siblings that were known to exist, leading to concern about the potential for inadvertent incest.[6]

On the pre-trial motion respecting the medical files, the judge granted an injunction against the destruction of records province-wide, which was confirmed by the British Columbia Supreme Court.[7] That Court ultimately found in favour of Ms Pratten in a 124-page judgment.[8] On 27 November 2012 the Court of Appeal overturned this decision.[9] The Supreme Court of Canada dismissed the application for leave to appeal on 30 May 2013.[10]

The Parties' Arguments

Due to the anonymity rule, half of Ms Pratten's genetic make-up remains unknown. She argued that on that basis, part of her identity is missing. She also expressed concerns about her health and the health of her future children, in addition to the risk of unknowingly forming a romantic relationship with a half-sibling. Ms Pratten claimed, on her own behalf and on behalf of all donor offspring,[11] that her rights to liberty and security of donor offspring protected under section 7 of the *Charter* had been violated. She argued for a free-standing constitutional right to know one's origins and genetic heritage[12] within section 7 of the *Charter*. The alleged constitutional violation was based on government inaction: the failure of the Province to legislate in order to ensure protection of fundamental aspects of persons conceived through AHR. She phrased the argument as follows: "Here, health services are provided in BC in a way that alienates donor offspring from one biological parent and extinguishes records about their origins. The government has known since at least 1993 this is harmful to children. Thus the state has a role in events which breach people's liberty and security of person interests to know their origins, and state action to counterbalance the breaches is required."[13]

Ms Pratten also argued that the failure to include donor offspring within the scheme of the adoption disclosure legislation was discriminatory with the meaning of subsection 15(1) of the *Charter* on the analogous ground of "manner of conception." The argument, accepted by the application judge, was that the *Adoption Act* ("the Act")[14] was directed at the harm caused by the dissociation from a biological parent. Ms Pratten argued that excluding donor offspring from the benefits of the Act[15] amounted to substantive discrimination as donor offspring were sufficiently similar to adoptees in respect of this dissociation. The application judge agreed with this submission and also agreed with Ms Pratten that the exclusion of this particular group undercut the overall purpose of the program and was likely discriminatory. The next stage of the analysis looked at whether the government could raise subsection 15(2) to defend the distinction. Ms Pratten argued that, although the Act is a genuinely ameliorative program (i.e., designed to improve the circumstances of adopted persons and children in need of adoption, a disadvantaged group in society), the Province had failed to show that including the claimant group would "undermine," "undercut," "compromise," "hamper," and "potentially hollow out" the ameliorative object of the Act, nor had it shown that "it was rational to conclude that *excluding donor offspring* would contribute, serve or advance its ameliorative purpose."[16]

The Attorney General of British Columbia argued on appeal that the trial judge had erred in finding that the benefits sought were prescribed by law; it claimed that the essence of Ms Pratten's claim was the lack of legislation. Counsel also argued that the judge further erred in not accepting, under subsection 15(2) of the *Charter*, that the adoption legislation was targeted, ameliorative legislation.[17] The Attorney General argued that the legislation was targeted towards those whose legal status and legal identity had been changed by virtue of court-ordered adoption, an argument that was rejected by the trial court. With respect to Ms Pratten's section 7 arguments, the Attorney General suggested that section 7 only protected a fundamental right to privacy (a right held by the anonymous donor) and not a free-standing right to security of the person, and thus did not provide for a right to know one's origins and genetic heritage. He argued also that the trial court had been correct in not giving credence to Ms Pratten's argument that her liberty interests were engaged as well, noting that "there is no legal requirement that parents share medical, social or cultural information with children."[18] According to the Attorney General, there were no international instruments that support the proposition that there is a fundamental right to know one's genetic heritage.[19] The Attorney General also noted the changes over time in the practice of donor insemination: "The result is that, today (as compared with the 1980s), a woman in B.C. seeking donor insemination can be provided with detailed social and medical information on the sperm donor and his family, even when the donor is anonymous."[20]

Court Decisions

On the issue of discrimination under section 15 of the *Charter*, the BC Supreme Court held that the omission of donor offspring from the benefits and protections provided to adoptees under the *Adoption Act* and *Adoption Regulation*[21] created a distinction between adoptees and donor offspring. Moreover, the Supreme Court held that the legislation was perpetuating stereotypes about donor offspring. Therefore, the omission of donor offspring from the provisions of the legislation was discriminatory.[22] The BC Court of Appeal overturned the BC Supreme Court decision in its entirety, finding that the adoption provisions were saved under subsection 15(2) of the Canadian *Charter* and, therefore, that no subsection 15(1) analysis was necessary. Both the Supreme Court and the Court of Appeal found that there was no free-standing positive right applicable in respect of liberty or security of the person under section 7 of the Canadian *Charter*.

I. *Issues of Concern in the Court of Appeal's Decision*

There are a series of issues of concern in the Court of Appeal's decision. In particular, the use of subsection 15(2) in this case leaves questions as to the court's willingness to examine the effects of an ameliorative program on those disadvantaged groups left out, especially as in this case it is arguable that leaving disadvantaged groups out of the scheme may in fact further or enhance the stereotyping and stigma attached to being a member of that group. It implies that identity concerns of donor offspring are less worthy of attention than those of adoptees. The case also gives short shrift to the analysis under section 7 in respect of both positive rights and the nature of the impact on the security of persons who are deprived of identifying information that could pertain to the promotion of both physical health and mental well-being. In this regard, the decision conflates the right to know with the need to know, and by jumping to the conclusion that there is no right to know, it ignores the compelling evidence of the need to know for many donor-conceived children. Finally, the court is dismissive of the international law treatment of this issue, going so far as to suggest that the UN *Convention on the Rights of the Child*[23] is not relevant in British Columbia.

A. USE OF SUBSECTION 15(2) AS A SHIELD TO CLAIMS OF DISCRIMINATION

As noted above, the government conceded that "manner of conception" was an analogous ground under subsection 15(1), and the Court proceeded on the basis that the distinction was drawn on this ground. Following the reasoning in *R v Kapp*,[24] the Court of Appeal held that once subsection 15(2) is relied upon by the state, the analysis begins with determining whether the distinction has been shown to be on an enumerated or analogous ground, then is followed by the consideration of the applicability of subsection 15(2). In this case, the Court held that the impugned adoption legislation qualified as an ameliorative program aimed at remedying the disadvantages created by the "state sanctioned dissociation of adoptees from their biological parents."[25] The Court focused on only one aspect of the adoption regime – that adoptees' legal status is changed – rather than the effect of alienation more generally, which on the evidence clearly affected donor offspring as well.

Many concerns were expressed when the Supreme Court articulated its approach to subsection 15(2) in *R v Kapp*, such as Sophia Moreau's suggestion that the test articulated by the Supreme Court was incomplete in a serious way due to the exclusive focus on the government's purpose rather than actual effects. She notes, "[t]he test seems to give disadvantaged groups no recourse in cases where a program has an ameliorative purpose but is under-inclusive."[26] Denise Réaume commented, following the release of *Alberta v Cunningham*[27] (a more recent articulation of the approach to subsection 15(2)), that it would "invite governments to claim that benefit programs aimed at a legitimate equality seeking group could exclude other similarly *disadvantaged* groups with impunity. This has been labeled the problem of under-inclusive ameliorative programs."[28] The deferential approach taken by the Supreme Court in *Kapp* and then again in *Cunningham* had simply been applied to this case as well.[29] No analysis of the effect of excluding another similarly disadvantaged group from the benefits of the ameliorative program was deemed necessary by the Court.

The result of *Pratten* is the conclusion that governments will be given significant deference on the strength of their say-so that a program is ameliorative and must be targeted only at the group they identify and define. Clearly, the Court of Appeal adopted the reasoning in *Cunningham*, which gives considerable leeway to governments to set priorities or, as is arguable in this case, pick favourites – an approach that amounts to very strong deference without the burden on the government that would normally apply to justify discrimination under section 1 of the *Charter*.

B. SECTION 7 ANALYSIS: THE RIGHTS TO LIBERTY AND SECURITY DESERVE MORE SCRUTINY

The section 7 analysis focused on the positive right to know one's origins; there was little discussion of how government actions and inaction have impacted "security of the person," including psychological security as well as the medical implications found as an unchallenged fact by the trial court. The analysis is very dismissive of identity issues. As predicted by Vanessa Gruben elsewhere in this book, the Court was unwilling to recognize positive rights to identity, or to know one's origins.[30] While the legal arguments on both sides extensively reviewed the jurisprudence, including *Gosselin*[31] and *Chaoulli*,[32] the Court of Appeal simply focused on its conclusion that this right to know was not grounded in a fundamental *Charter* right or freedom. Missing in the analysis is a more nuanced treatment of the case law, which suggests there is a heavier onus on government where security interests relate to family relationships, or where government action and inaction establishes the framework within which the harms claimed are manifest.

The Supreme Court specifically acknowledged that the integrity of the family and psychological security associated with the parent–child relationship was a protected right under section 7 in *New Brunswick Child and Family Services v G(J)*.[33] In that case, the Court imposed on the government an obligation to ensure that parents had legal representation in child protection hearings. It is important to note that the section 7 infringement in *G(J)* was not the state's threat to remove a child from the claimant parent, but the failure to provide legal counsel, arguably a positive obligation on the government.[34] Indeed, the failure by governments to address harms they were cognizant of under section 7 was characterized by the Supreme Court as arbitrary in that case, as well as in *Chaoulli* and *PHS*.[35]

A serious question must be posed as to whether this was the best positive rights case to go forward, as the Supreme Court of Canada has at most hinted that socio-economic rights, framed as positive rights, might be made out where the evidence is clear.[36] Most advocates for positive rights do so in the context of basic needs such as food, shelter, water, and basic social assistance and health care, which are often framed as social minimums.[37] It is not clear, especially given the unsuccessful litigation in the lower courts in Ontario,[38] that the right to know one's origins would succeed where the arguments for basic socio-economic rights remain undeveloped. Furthermore, the Court held the view that "the potential implications of a free-standing constitutional right to know one's biological origins are uncertain and may be enormous."[39] Also, one could say that the case was decided in the context of a favourable conclusion under section 15, and thus with a diminished need to rule on section 7. As noted by Adair J, "[i]n my view, [the section 7 rights claimed] go far beyond anything that might be required to address Ms. Pratten's complaints in this case, particularly given my conclusion that her rights under s. 15 have been breached."[40]

Ms Pratten's assertion that the infringement amounted to state action was based upon the claim that the Province allowed the destruction of the files, depriving her of basic personal information necessary for her physical and psychological health. The Province had enacted the *Adoption Act* and the *Adoption Regulation* whereby information about the biological origins and family history of adoptees was gathered and preserved in order for adoptees to eventually obtain that information. It was also argued that the medical records that included similar information about donor offspring were collected under a regulatory regime that existed under the *Regulations* pertaining to the professional standards applicable to the College of Physicians and Surgeons. Indeed, the rules respecting retention of medical records have recently been revised to be compatible with extended limitation periods set out in provincial legislation.[41] So, why were donor offspring records viewed differently?

By arguing that no analysis of the limitations on rights internal to section 7 of the *Charter* was necessary because a positive "stand-alone" obligation existed to protect her liberty and security of the person, Ms Pratten precluded arguments that might have been more consistent with the Supreme Court's approach in *G(J)*.[42] Furthermore, the Court's conclusion failed to analyse with any depth the nature of the privacy interests at stake. As noted by Hamish Stewart, it is "generally accepted that individual interests in privacy can engage section 7, either via the interest in security of the person [...] or via the liberty interest."[43] While the Ontario case of *Marchand*[44] held that the liberty interest did not include the right of an adoptee to obtain information respecting a birth parent, more recently *Cheskes*[45] has acknowledged the privacy interests of both birth parents and adoptive children in respect of the information in question, requiring an "opt-out" option for those who had participated in an adoption at a time when secrecy was the norm.

In *Marchand*,[46] the claimant sought information about her birth father through a challenge to the *Vital Statistics Act*[47] and the *Child and Family Services Act*.[48] She argued that the denial of information deprived her of the ability to make basic choices going to the core of what it means to enjoy individual dignity and independence. The court held that there was no liberty right to obtain identifying information about a person who has expressly refused to consent to its disclosure. It also held that she had failed to show that she had suffered serious state-imposed psychological stress. In *Cheskes*[49] the applicants challenged the constitutional validity of the Ontario law that retroactively opened confidential adoption records on the basis that they violated section 7. The court allowed the application on the basis that the disclosure of birth and adoption records in circumstances where a reasonable expectation of privacy had been created constituted a breach of the privacy rights inherent in the right to liberty under section 7, as it was an invasion of the dignity and self-worth of the individual applicants.

The Court's analysis of the very personal nature of the information – that is, one's own identity – as being protected under the liberty interest of section 7, could arguably ground a claim that this information should be made available to the very person to whom it is most relevant – the child. However, the Court in *Pratten*,[50] and arguably in *Cheskes*,[51] failed to fully engage with the nature of the privacy interests (i.e., whose information is it?) and the balancing of rights that would have to be explored if both parents and children were equally acknowledged as rights holders. It appears that, contrary to the approach in other jurisdictions, the right to maintain secrets trumps the right to know even basic biological information about oneself.

II. The Fundamental Problem in Pratten*: The Need to Know versus the Right to Know*

A. A RECOGNITION OF THE NEED TO KNOW ONE'S ORIGINS

Despite the decision to dismiss Ms Pratten's application, the factual findings of the Supreme Court of British Columbia were not challenged at the Court of Appeal. Unchallenged were significant findings respecting the psychological and medical needs of donor offspring, which were held to be substantially the same as those of adoptees; the strong commitment of donor offspring to search for information about the other half of their genetic make-up; and the stress, anxiety, and frustration caused by not knowing.[52] Also acknowledged were the legitimate fear of inadvertent consanguinity and the devastating effects of secrecy.[53] In particular, the trial judge held, "donor offspring and adoptees experience similar struggles, and *a similar sense of loss and incompleteness*. However, donor offspring do not have the benefit of the kind of positive institutions and legislative support provided to and for adoptees in B.C. [emphasis added]."[54]

Published research results back up these factual findings, which have recognized that the same questioning occurs in respect of the need to know for adoptees and children conceived through AHR and that the approach taken with adoptees should exemplify the approach to be taken towards the need to know for children conceived through AHR.[55] Some institutions, such as the Senate of Canada and the Government of Quebec, have made recommendations consistent with this approach.[56]

One thing is clear: more children conceived through AHR are now adults, and some of them say they need the information in order to construct their identity. While this desire may not be universal (consistent with adoption),[57] for children who need the truth, mechanisms should be available to provide them with it.

B. A LACK OF CONSIDERATION OF THE FUNDAMENTAL RIGHT TO KNOW ONE'S ORIGINS

Acknowledgment of offsprings' need to know their origins does not entail the recognition of a fundamental right to know one's origins through section 7 or 15 of the *Charter*. The BC Court was not ready to accept that argument:

> Assuming that s. 7 of the *Charter* is capable of guaranteeing positive rights, and accepting that there has been movement in Canada and elsewhere toward more openness with respect to the type of information Ms. Pratten seeks, I am not persuaded that the right "to know one's past" is of such fundamental importance that it is entitled to free-standing constitutional recognition.[58]

Similarly, the Court was extremely dismissive of the right to identity and of Ms Pratten's arguments with respect to international law:

> In attempting to establish a fundamental right to know one's biological origins, Ms. Pratten relies on *a case from England, an international treaty to which Canada is not a party, and a United Nations convention to which Canada is a party.*[59]

The English case of *Rose*,[60] the relevance of which is summarily dismissed by the Court of Appeal,[61] concerned two persons who were conceived by AHR with a sperm donor and who wanted to have information about their progenitor. After the Secretary of State refused to give them the non-identifying information they sought, they brought the case to court. They argued that different treatment was afforded to persons born of AHR before the adoption of the *Human Fertilisation and Embryology Act* of 1990 than to those who were born after the adoption of the *Act*[62] in respect of access to information. They based their argument on the non-discrimination principle recognized in Article 14 of the *European Convention on Human Rights* ("*ECHR*") in conjunction with Article 8 (the privacy right), stating that they were not given the same treatment as adopted persons.

In its judgment, the British Columbia Court of Appeal minimized the impact *Rose* had by saying that "the [ECHR] judge did not decide whether the Secretary of State's inaction constituted a violation of Art. 8 [of the ECHR]." The Court of Appeal appeared to be unaware that the case of *Rose* has led to a consultation on access to one's origins in the United Kingdom and that the court stayed its decision to wait for the result of this consultation. Furthermore, in staying the decision, the judge reaffirmed that the right to privacy in Article 8 of the *ECHR*, as was decided in *Odièvre v France*,[63] protects the right to access to all information (nominative or non-nominative) about the progenitor. The judge in *Rose* also held that the State has some positive obligations in respect of the individual's right to access information. Finally, since the UK legislation was subsequently reformed to allow every child conceived by AHR to access information about their progenitor,[64] the court never had to decide whether there was a violation of those rights. At the very least, the British Columbia Court of Appeal judgment understated the impact of this English case.

Further in the judgment, Justice Frankel added: "What is noteworthy about the decision in *Rose* is that it does not rest on Art. 5(1) of the *E.C.H.R.* which partially mirrors s. 7 of the *Charter*."[65] There is, however, an explanation for this. The issue of identity, including the right to know one's origins, has always been addressed under Article 8 of the *ECHR*. Article 8 explicitly recognizes the right to privacy, which is indirectly protected within section 7 of the Canadian *Charter*.[66]

Furthermore, while it is true that the *European Convention on Human Rights*[67] is clearly not a convention to which Canada is a party, the case law that has been developed under Article 8 of that instrument is very relevant to the growing recognition of both the right to know one's biological origins and consideration of the perspective of the child, not just that of the adults.[68] The universal nature of these rights and their similarity to the rights recognized in the *Charter* suggest that close attention should be paid to the developing international jurisprudence. In September 2012, in *Godelli v Italy*, the European Court of Human Rights repeated the protection for the right to know one's origins in the context of a birth that was kept secret:

> The Court notes that the expression "everyone" in Article 8 of the Convention applies to both the child and the mother. On the one hand, the child has a right to know its origins, that right being derived from the notion of private life (see paragraph 47 above). The child's vital interest in its personal development is also widely recognised in the general scheme of the Convention (see, among many other authorities, *Johansen v. Norway*, 7 August 1996, § 78, *Reports of Judgments and Decisions* 1996-III; *Mikulić*, cited above, § 64; or *Kutzner v. Germany*, no. 46544/99, § 66, ECHR 2002-I). On the other hand, a woman's interest in remaining anonymous in order

> to protect her health by giving birth in appropriate medical conditions cannot be denied.[69]

It also repeated the positive obligation derived from the Article 8 of the ECHR:

> The Court reiterates that although the object of Article 8 is essentially that of protecting the individual against arbitrary interference by the public authorities, it does not merely compel the State to abstain from such interference: in addition to this primarily negative undertaking, there may be positive obligations inherent in an effective respect for private life. These obligations may involve the adoption of measures designed to secure respect for private life even in the sphere of the relations of individuals between themselves (see *X and Y v. the Netherlands*, 26 March 1985, § 23, Series A no. 91).[70]

It furthermore stated that

> [t]he Court considers that the right to an identity, which includes the right to know one's parentage, is an integral part of the notion of private life. In such cases, particularly rigorous scrutiny is called for when weighing up the competing interests.[71]

In that case, the majority (6 votes to 1) decided that Italy was in contravention of Article 8 of the ECHR because it had failed to strike a balance between the competing interests at stake. The complainant was awarded damages for the moral prejudice she suffered (viz. anguish from the impossibility of accessing information about her origins).[72]

On this point the British Columbia Court of Appeal decision also understated the impact of the ECHR in the context of the recognition of a right to know one's origins. It would have been more appropriate to recognize the difficulty of the task and to refer it to the legislature, where competing interests can be better addressed. Until today, the interests of the donors and the parents, not to mention the medical AHR clinics, have been given priority over those of offspring. A better balance is necessary.[73]

On the issue of the *Convention on the Rights of the Child*, Justice Frankel starts with an aside: "I note that British Columbia, which constitutionally has legislative jurisdiction over adoption, is not a party to the *C.R.C.*"[74] This is not relevant – section 132 of the *Constitution Act,*

1867 makes clear that the federal government has the power to ratify treaties. Besides, as the Ministry of Child and Youth Development of British Columbia emphasizes, "[t]he Convention on the Rights of the Child (CRC) was adopted by the UN General Assembly in 1989, and has since been ratified by Canada and endorsed by the Government of British Columbia."[75] Of the provinces, only Alberta had refused for a time to endorse the CRC.[76]

The Court presented an incomplete portrait of the history of Article 8 of the CRC.[77] If one looks at the "object and purpose" of the CRC, the fact that Article 8 was inspired by the history of children's abduction in Argentina makes it clear that the intent of the legislators was to recognize an unqualified right to identity.[78] Furthermore, the CRC should be interpreted in a dynamic way, as suggested by Article 31 of the Vienna Convention.[79] For Jaap Doek, "the Convention is a living instrument and its interpretation should reflect new developments that may arise in the area of children's rights."[80] Therefore, a dynamic interpretation of Articles 7 and 8, supported by the history of the CRC, confirms the existence of a right to identity. Similarly, Jaime Sergio Cerda, while defending Article 8, stated the following: "In the future, Article 8 should perhaps be interpreted independently of the author's intentions or motivations. The nature of the new right created by this article will, in fact depend on the development of the legal systems of the countries concerned rather than on the specific phenomenon that initially prompted the sponsoring countries to introduce this new idea."[81]

With respect to its impact, the Court of Appeal further stated "[t]hat neither Art. 8 nor any other provisions of the *C.R.C.* is viewed internationally as supporting the right 'to know one's past' is further evinced by the observations of the UN Committee on the Rights of the Child."[82] The court omits to develop a complete case law analysis of the European Court of Human Rights, which in its evolution is quite favourable to the recognition of a right to know one's biological origins.[83] The Court hence presented a debatable interpretation of the text of the CRC and an unconvincing analysis of the comments of the UN Committee on the Rights of the Child.[84]

Another crucial issue is that the question of one's origins is often conflated with the concept of parentage; these are two different notions. This generates constant confusion in the public discourse and judicial analysis of the issues. Access to information about the donor's identity (*who is the progenitor or gamete donor?*) and the legal mechanism for proclaiming filiation (*who is the legal parent?*) are often taken to be one and the same, when in fact they are two different questions with potentially different answers. A gamete donor is not or should not be the legal parent. In some provinces, this question remains unclear and contributes to confusion. Legal reforms of parentage frameworks would be required in these provinces and territories to delineate clearly this distinction.[85] As Julie Wallbank observed, "[u]sually, sperm donors have no desire to act as fathers. There is no reason to believe that this would change if they were identifiable."[86] Martin Richards added that the circumstance of "[k]nowing the manner of your conception and the identity, and perhaps some other information, about the gamete provider is not, of course, the same thing as having a social relationship with that person."

In the same vein, Wallbank suggests that "[f]ulfilling the child's right to know should not automatically lead to the child having a relationship with her donor or any other third party," because "[t]o contribute one's genes to the creation of a child is not congruent with the social role of parenthood."[87]

The multiple faces of families today force the law to find new ways to take into consideration these new social realities.[88] Legislative policy should balance the different roles played by different people in the family. The step-parent and the gamete donor or progenitor are not the legal parents, but the reality of their existence ought to be recognized.

Conclusion

The BC Court of Appeal decision expresses a very superficial analysis of the rights at stake in this case and a glaringly incorrect interpretation of the CRC. By summarily dismissing the section 7 claims, and permitting the government to wield subsection 15(2) as a complete defence to discrimination without having to justify the impact on the excluded group, the Court of Appeal may have unwittingly made it more difficult for legitimate positive rights claims and claims of discrimination to come forward. While no reasons are given for refusing leave to appeal to the Supreme Court of Canada, one could argue that, by refusing to intervene in *Pratten*, the Supreme Court may have reinforced its decision in the *Reference* by leaving the action to the provincial and territorial legislatures.

The situation certainly calls for provincial action. Different registries are now being used by the children to find out the truth, even if the law is keeping the information confidential. This might be another good reason to stop the practice of secrecy. Given the existence of other ways to find out the truth, the promise of anonymity to a donor cannot be respected anymore.

After all, a court decision in favour of the right to know one's origins would have called for a legislative intervention in order to balance the conflicts of rights and interests between parents, donors, and offspring. Only balanced legislation could fairly mediate between the competing interests of the parents, the gamete donor, and the child.

NOTES

Authors' note: We wish to thank Aoife Quinn for editing the endnotes.

1 *Canadian Charter of Rights and Freedoms*, Part I of the *Constitution Act*, 1982, being Schedule B to the *Canada Act 1982* (UK), 1982, c 11 [*Charter*].
2 *Pratten v British Columbia (Attorney General)*, 2012 BCCA 480, 25 RFL (7th) 58 [*Pratten* BCCA]. While this chapter contains a detailed discussion of *Pratten*, the case is also the focus of the chapters by Gruben, Guichon, and Snelling in this volume.
3 *Pratten v British Columbia (Attorney General)*, 35191 (30 May 2013), [2013] SCCA No 36 [*Pratten* SCC].
4 *Pratten v British Columbia (Attorney General)*, 2010 BCSC 1444, 325 DLR (4th) 79. The interim ruling held that the evidence was equivocal about whether the records were destroyed, and if so, when and how.
5 *Ibid*.
6 *Ibid*, at paras 36–73.
7 *Pratten v British Columbia (Attorney General)*, 2011 BCSC 656, 99 RFL (6th) 290 [*Pratten* BCSC] at para 335(c).
8 *Ibid*.
9 *Pratten* BCCA, *supra* note 2. Note that this injunction was also overturned by the Court of Appeal.
10 *Pratten* SCC, *supra* note 3.
11 *Pratten*, BCSC, *supra* note 7 at para 7.
12 *Pratten*, BCSC, *supra* note 7 at para 7.
13 Factum of Respondent at para 85.
14 *Adoption Act*, RSBC 1996, c 5.
15 *Ibid* at para 22.
16 Respondent's Factum, paras 35 and 37, referring to *Alberta (Aboriginal Affairs and Northern Development) v Cunningham*, 2011 SCC 37, [2011] 2 SCR 670, paras 73, 77–8.

17 Appeal Factum of the Attorney General for British Columbia, paras 53–6.
18 Factum on Cross Appeal of the Attorney General of British Columbia, at para 27.
19 *Ibid*, at para 40.
20 *Pratten* BCSC, *supra* note 7 at para 11.
21 *Adoption Regulation*, BC Reg 291/96.
22 Except for ss 4(1)(e) and 4(1)(h) of the Regulation which set out the type of information to be collected from birth parents of adopted children.
23 *United Nations Convention on the Rights of the Child*, 20 November 1989, 1577 UNTS 3, (entered into force 2 September 1990) [CRC].
24 2008 SCC 41, [2008] 2 SCR 483 [*Kapp*].
25 *Pratten* BCCA, *supra* note 2 at para 36.
26 Sophia Moreau, "*R. v. Kapp*: New Directions for Section 15" (2008–2009) 40 Ottawa L Rev 283 at 295.
27 Respondent's Factum, at para 85.
28 Denise Réaume, "Equality Kapped: Alberta v Cunningham" The Women's Court of Canada (22 July 2011), [unpublished, on file with author].
29 Joseph Marcus, "Sometimes Help Hurts: Imagining a New Approach to Section 15(2)," (2013) 18 Appeal 121–38 at 136.
30 See the chapter by Vanessa Gruben in this volume for a more detailed analysis of the potential for a successful claim under section 7.
31 *Gosselin v Québec (Attorney General)*, 2002 SCC 84, [2002] 4 SCR 429 [*Gosselin*].
32 *Chaoulli v Quebec (Attorney General)*, 2005 SCC 35, [2005] 1 SCR 791.
33 *New Brunswick (Minister of Health and Community Services) v G. (J.)*, [1999] 3 SCR 46 at para 91–93, 177 DLR (4th) 124 [*New Brunswick v G(J)*].
34 *New Brunswick v G(J)*, *ibid*, at para 91.
35 *Canada (Attorney General) v PHS Community Services Society*, 2011 SCC 44, [2011] 3 SCR 134.
36 *Gosselin*, *supra* note 32 at para 327, referring to *Dunmore v Ontario (Attorney General)*, 2001 SCC 94, [2001] 3 SCR 1016 [*Dunmore*] at para 22; *Gosselin*, Arbour J (dissenting), paras 364–5; discussing that these issues should be evaluated under s 7 and not s 15. See also criterion for validity of underinclusion complaints in *Dunmore* at paras 24–6.
37 Jeff King, *Judging Social Rights* (New York: Cambridge University Press, 2012) at 17; Hamish Stewart, *Fundamental Justice: Section 7 of the Canadian Charter of Rights and Freedoms* (Toronto: Irwin Law, 2012) at 56; Vanessa A. MacDonnell, "The Protective Function and Section 7 of the Canadian Charter of Rights and Freedoms" (2012) 17:1 Rev Const Stud 53 at 66;

Louise Arbour, "'Freedom from Want' – from Charity to Entitlement" (LaFontaine–Baldwin Lecture, delivered at Quebec City, 3 March 2005), in *Dialogue on Democracy: The LaFontaine–Baldwin Lectures: 2000–2005*, ed. Rudyard Griffiths (Toronto: Penguin Canada, 2006), 153 at 164–5, 169–70, 172, also available at Office of the High Commissioner for Human Rights, http://www.ohchr.org/EN/NewsEvents/Pages/DisplayNews.aspx?NewsID=3004&LangID=E.

38 *Marchand v Ontario* (2006), 81 OR (3d) 172 (SC), aff'd 2007 ONCA 787, 88 OR (3d) 600, leave to appeal to SCC refused, [2008] SCCA No. 37 [*Marchand*]; *Cheskes v Ontario (Attorney General)*, 87 OR (3d) 581, 288 DLR (4th) 449 (SC) [*Cheskes*].

39 *Pratten* BCSC, *supra* note 7 at para 290. Note that this was the view of the Court, but there was very little evidence to support a "sky is falling" fear of including donor offspring within the established adoption disclosure regime.

40 *Pratten* BCSC, *ibid*, at para 290.

41 *Limitation Act*, SBC 2012, c 13.

42 *New Brunswick v G(J)*, *supra* note 33 at para 59: "It is clear that the right to security of the person does not protect the individual from the ordinary stresses and anxieties that a person of reasonable sensibility would suffer as a result of government action. If the right were interpreted with such broad sweep, countless government initiatives could be challenged on the ground that they infringe the right to security of the person, massively expanding the scope of judicial review, and, in the process, trivializing what it means for a right to be constitutionally protected."

43 Stewart, *supra* note 37 at 78–9.

44 *Marchand*, *supra* note 38. Pratten's argument that this case was wrongly decided is quite compelling: "The trial court decision in *Marchand* that an individual has a constitutionally protected right to cause the state to withhold information when his paternity is in dispute and the applicant for such information may be his own progeny is offensive and cannot be correct. It leads to the absurd result that applications for a declaration of paternity are unconstitutional. A person who conceives a child bears the responsibility that their lives are intertwined at a biological level. The offspring is entitled to know the identity of the person from whom half their genetic make-up is derived." Respondents Factum, 29 November 2011.

45 *Cheskes*, *supra* note 38.

46 *Ibid*.

47 RSO 1990, c V.4.

48 RSO 1990, c C.11.
49 *Ibid.*
50 *Supra* note 2.
51 *Supra* note 38.
52 *Pratten* BCSC, *supra* note 7 at para 17.
53 *Ibid.*
54 *Ibid.*
55 See, namely, Julie Feast, "Using and Not Losing the Messages from the Adoption Experience for Donor-Assisted Conception" (2003) 6 Human Fertility 41; M. Crawshaw, "Lessons from a Recent Adoption Study to Identify Some of the Services Needs of, and Issues for, Donor Offspring Wanting to Know about Their Donors" (2005) 5 Human Fertility 6. See also Michael Freeman, "The Rights of the Artificially Procreated Child," in *The Moral Status of Children: Essays on the Rights of the Child*, ed. Michael Freeman (Boston: Martinus Nijhoff, 1997), 185 at 191; E. Haimes, "Secrecy': What Can Artificial Reproduction Learn from Adoption" (1988) 2 International Journal of Law and the Family 46.
56 Commission de l'éthique en science et en technologie (CEST), *Ethique et procréation assistée: des orientations pour le don de gamètes et d'embryons, la gestation pour autrui et le diagnostic préimplantatoire* (Québec: Gouvernement du Québec, 2009), recommendation 2, http://www.ethique.gouv.qc.ca/fr/assets/documents/PA/PA-avis-et-errata-FR.pdf [French], http://www.ethique.gouv.qc.ca/fr/assets/documents/PA/PA-avis-et-errata-EN.pdf [English]. Others have made a distinction between the importance of banning secrecy, but not anonymity: see Comité consultatif national d'éthique (CCNE) (France), *Avis n° 90 Accès aux origines, anonymat et secret de la filiation* (24 novembre 2005), http://www.ccne-ethique.fr/fr/publications.
57 Susan Golombok *et al.* (2013), "Children Born Through Reproductive Donation: A Longitudinal Study of Child Adjustment" (2013) 54 Journal of Child Psychology and Psychiatry 653, doi:10.1111/jcpp.12015. See also Juliet Guichon, Ian Mitchell, and Michelle Giroux, eds., *The Right to Know One's Origins: Assisted Human Reproduction and the Best Interests of Children* (Brussels: Academic and Scientific Publishers, 2012).
58 *Pratten* BCCA, *supra* note 2 at para 62.
59 *Pratten* BCCA, *supra* note 2 at para 51 [emphasis added].
60 *U.K. R (On the application of Rose and another) v Sec. of State for Health and another*, [2002] EWHC (ADMIN) 2522, (2002) 3 FCR 731 [*Rose*].
61 *Ibid* at paras 53–4.
62 *Human Fertilisation and Embryology Act 1990* (UK) 1990, c 37.

63 *Odièvre v France* [2003] 1 FCR 621 ECtHR.

64 See the following opinions: "[This] case heard by the High Court in the United Kingdom in 2002 was partially responsible for consequent legislation banning anonymous gamete donation": Vardit Ravitsky, "Conceived and Deceived: The Medical Interests of Donor-Conceived Individuals" (2012) 42:1 Hastings Center Report 17–11 at 18. See also Mariana De Lorenzi and Verónica B. Piñero, "Assisted Human Reproduction Offspring and the Fundamental Right to Identity: The Recognition of the Right to Know One's Origins under the European Convention of Human Rights" (2009) 6:1 Personalized Medicine 79 at 89. "The [British] Court acknowledged that the claimants were "trying to obtain is [*sic*] information about their biological fathers, something that goes to the very heart of their identity, and to their make-up as people" and that Article 8 of the ECHR was engaged. Nevertheless, the Court found that "[t]hat question, which may fall to be decided on a further occasion, involved consideration of other matters and may depend on any future action taken by the Secretary of State."

65 *Pratten* BCCA, *supra* note 2 at para 54.

66 *R v O'Connor*, [1995] 4 SCR 411, 130 DLR (4th) 235; *Marchand*, *Cheskes*, *supra* note 38.

67 *European Convention for the Protection of Human Rights and Fundamental Freedoms, as amended by Protocols Nos. 11 and 14*, 4 November 1950, ETS 5, (Entered into force 3 September 1953) [*EHRC*].

68 See namely Michelle Giroux, "Le droit fondamental de connaître ses origines biologiques," in Tara Collins *et al.*, *Droits de l'enfant: actes de la Conférence internaionale, Ottawa 2007 = Rights of the Child: Proceedings of the International Conference, Ottawa 2007* (Montreal: Wilson & Lafleur, 1998), 353. It is noteworthy that it is a fact not contested in the BC Court of Appeal decision that the interest of the adults and donor always trumped the one of children, at para 17(h).

69 *Godelli v Italy* ECHR 347 (2012) at para 50 (original decision in French written by Justice Françoise Tulkens).

70 *Ibid*, at para 47.

71 *Ibid*, at para 52.

72 *Ibid*, at para 74–76. See also Sylvia-Lise Bada, "Droit à la connaissance de ses origines (Art. 8 et 14 CEDH): Le principe de l'anonymat des donneurs de gamètes passe le cap du Conseil d'État," in *Lettre "Actualités Droits-Libertés"* du CREDOF (4 July 2013), La Revue des Droits de l'Homme, http://revdh.org/2013/07/04/principe-de-lanonymat-des-donneurs-de-gametes-passe-le-cap-du-conseil-detat.

73 Julie Cousineau suggests to use the ethics of care to resolve this conflict: see *L'anonymat des dons de gamètes et d'embryons au Québec et au Canada. Essai théorique sur l'internormativité entre le droit positif et l'éthique de la sollicitude dans la résolution du conflit* (DCL Thesis, McGill University, 2011).
74 *Pratten* BCCA, *supra* note 2 at para 57.
75 See, namely, Ministry of Children and Family Development of British Columbia, "Strong, Safe and Supported, A Commitment to B.C.'s Children and Youth" (2008) at 9, [on file with author]. The Senate of Canada has stated that "Canada must begin to take its international human rights treaty obligations more seriously[...]" and recognized the existence of one's right to know one's origins: Senate, Standing Committee on Human Rights, *Children: The Silenced Citizens: Effective Implementation of Canada's International Obligations with Respect the the Rights of Children* (April 2007) (Chair: Hon. Raynell Andreychuk) at ix [Chair's Forward] and 113, respectively, Parliament of Canada, http://www.parl.gc.ca/Content/SEN/Committee/391/huma/rep/rep10apr07-e.pdf.
76 Catherine Ford, *Against the Grain: An Irreverent View of Alberta* (Toronto: Random House, 2009), 230.
77 *Pratten* BCCA, *supra* note 2 at para 58. See a more detailed analysis in Michelle Giroux and Mariana De Lorenzi, "Putting the Child First: A Necessary Step in the Recognition of the Right to Identity in Canadian Law" (2011) 27:1 Can J Fam L 53 at 74–78; see also Carmen Lavallée and Michelle Giroux, "Le droit de l'enfant québécois à la connaissance de ses origines évalué à l'aune de la Convention internationale relative aux droits de l'enfant" (2013) 72 R du B 147.
78 Sarah Wilson, "Identity, Genealogy and the Social Family: The Case of Donor Insemination" (1997) 11 Int'l JL Pol'y & Fam 270 at 278ss. Cerda states that during the drafting process of the CRC, everyone agreed that this right existed: Jaime Sergio Cerda, "The Draft Convention on the Rights of the Child: New Rights" (1990) 12 Hum Rts Q 115.
79 Vienna Convention on the Law of Treaties, 23 May 1969, 1155 UNTS 331 art 31 (entered into force 27 January 1980).
80 Jaap Doek, *A Commentary on the United Nations Convention on the Rights of the Child, Articles 8–9: The Right to Preservation of Identity and the Right Not to Be Separated from His or Her Parents* (Leiden: Martinus Nijhoof, 2006)12; Cerda, *supra* note 78 at 117, is of the opinion that Article 8 can serve a larger interest than what was considered when it was drafted.
81 Cerda, *ibid* at 116–17.
82 *Pratten* BCCA, *supra* note 2 at para 59.

83 See, namely, Laurence Brunet, "Le principe de l'anonymat du donneur de gamètes à l'épreuve de son contexte. Analyse des conceptions juridiques de l'identité" (2010) 20:1 Androl 92.

84 *Pratten* BCCA, *supra* note 2 at paras 59–61.

85 We repeat on that point what has been said in Giroux and DeLorenzi, *supra* note 77. See also the chapter by Carol Rogerson in this volume.

86 Julie Wallbank, "The Role of Rights and Utility in Instituting a Child's Right to Know Her Genetic History" (2004) 13:2 Social & Legal Stud 245 at 260.

87 Martin Richards, "Assisted Reproduction and Parental Relationships," in *Children and their Families: Contact, Rights and Welfare*, ed.Andrew Bainham *et al.* (Oxford: Hart Publishing, 2003) 301 at 309.

88 See the chapter by Susan Drummond in this volume.

7 A Number but No Name: Is There a Constitutional Right to Know One's Sperm Donor in Canadian Law?

VANESSA GRUBEN

Introduction

To date, many donor offspring have embarked on a quest for information about their sperm donor.[1] What does he look like? What are his interests? Is he healthy? Does he have other children? What is his name? These questions are based on a sincere need to know about one's genetic origins. Donor offspring have sought to answer these questions by enrolling in registries like the Donor Sibling Registry[2] or by undertaking their own independent investigations using DNA samples, donor numbers, and archived records.[3] Some have been successful. Others have not. The dearth of information available to donor offspring and the absence of any legal mechanism requiring the collection and disclosure of donor information to offspring have prompted some, like British Columbia's Olivia Pratten, to turn to the courts.[4] There are many good reasons to move towards greater openness in gamete donation in Canada. Many donor offspring express a *need* to receive information about their sperm donor, but does the Constitution confer upon them a *right* to know their donor?[5]

This article considers whether section 7 of the *Canadian Charter of Rights and Freedoms* (the *Charter*) protects the right to know one's genetic origins as claimed by donor offspring.[6] The right to life, liberty, and security of the person protected by section 7 is considered to be a right with significant potential.[7] The Supreme Court of Canada has noted that this right is associated with fundamental human interests such as assisted suicide and abortion.[8] Furthermore, Canadian courts have recognized various novel applications of section 7 of the *Charter* in the context of health care and homelessness.[9] And although the Supreme Court has not yet recognized a positive rights claim under section 7, it has left the door open to such a possibility. Nevertheless, a right to know one's genetic origins faces several obstacles that I believe make the recognition of the right to know under section 7 of the *Charter* unlikely at this time.

In the first part, I offer a brief introduction to the history of donor anonymity and donor registries. I then turn to explore the challenges facing a constitutionally protected right to know one's genetic origins. In Part II, I discuss the struggle for the recognition of positive rights claims under section 7 of the *Charter*. In Part III, the definitional problems associated with the right to know are considered. Is this right simply a right to know the identity of one's donor or offspring? Does it include the right to receive certain information about the donor? Is this right prospective or retroactive? These definitional issues raise questions about privacy and retroactivity that are considered in Parts IV and V respectively. Finally, in Part VI, I explore the implications of recognizing a right to know one's genetic origins – implications that are likely to be wide-ranging and potentially troubling. I believe that greater openness in gamete donation in Canada is needed. As with adoption, donor offspring should be entitled to information about their biological progenitors. However, in my view, section 7 of the *Charter* is not the most promising route to end donor anonymity in Canada. This task is best left to the legislature.

I. A Brief Overview of Donor Anonymity and Donor Registries in Canada and Beyond

Donor anonymity exists in Canada today by default; that is, there is no legislation requiring that the identity of a gamete donor be disclosed, nor is there any legislation that protects the anonymity of donors.[10] However, this legislative gap has not always existed. Until recently, Canadian law protected the anonymity of gamete donors. It did so by virtue of the *Assisted Human Reproduction Act* (*AHRA*), which prohibited the disclosure of identifying information about the donor without his or her consent.[11]

The *AHRA* created an elaborate framework for the collection, use, and disclosure of identifying and non-identifying "health reporting information" of gamete donors and donor offspring.[12] The *AHRA* charged the Assisted Human Reproduction Agency of Canada (the Agency) with creating a registry of this information.[13] The Agency was authorized to use and disclose the registry information for a number of purposes, including disclosing certain non-identifying information about the donor to the offspring,[14] and advising two individuals having reason to believe that one or both were conceived by means of an assisted reproductive technology (ART) using donated human reproductive material whether they were genetically related.[15] The *AHRA* only authorized the Agency to disclose the identity of a donor without his consent if, in the Agency's opinion, the disclosure was necessary to address a risk to the health or safety of the offspring.[16] In December 2010, however, the Supreme Court of Canada in *Reference re Assisted Human Reproduction Act* declared these provisions, together with several others, to be outside the legislative authority of Parliament.[17] Although the Court concluded that the regulation of donor anonymity and the creation of a donor registry fell to the provincial legislatures, no province has taken steps to enact such legislation.

Whether sperm donors should remain anonymous and what information should be collected from donors and disclosed to offspring are contentious questions that require the interests of donors, intended parents, and offspring to be balanced.[18] Stakeholders hold sharply different views on these questions. On one side are those who favour disclosure and openness on the basis that it is in the best interest of the offspring. On the other side are individuals concerned about the privacy of donors, the impact of known donors on the integrity of the family unit, and the consequences of a prohibition on anonymity on the supply of sperm available for the creation of Canadian families.[19] The decision to allow anonymous gamete donation has been the subject of significant public debate and disagreement spanning many years. Indeed, the Royal Commission on New Reproductive Technologies[20] and the Standing Committee on Health[21] presented starkly different recommendations to Parliament on this issue: the former recommended that donor anonymity continue, and the latter concluded that it should be prohibited. Donor anonymity was also "passionately" debated by stakeholders in testimony before the Standing Committee on Social Affairs, Science, and Technology prior to the introduction of the *AHRA*.[22]

Notably, the federal and provincial approach to gamete donation stands in stark contrast to that of adoption: many provincial legislatures have created adoption registries and opportunities for adoptees and birth parents to obtain identifying and non-identifying information about each other.[23] Indeed, a province's failure to legislate directly in respect of gamete donation was the subject of the recent *Pratten* litigation.[24] Olivia Pratten was a donor offspring searching for information about her sperm donor. She argued that British Columbia's *Adoption Act*, which establishes a mechanism through which adoptees can access certain information about their birth parents depending on whether they were adopted before or after 1996, violates section 15 of the *Charter* because it is underinclusive.[25] Furthermore, Ms Pratten argued that she had a free-standing constitutional right to know her biological origins protected by section 7 of the *Charter*. Alternatively, she argued that the failure to know her donor breached her right to security in that she had suffered physical and psychological harm as a result, as well as breaches her right to liberty in that this knowledge fell within the sphere of fundamental decisions, with implications for her individual dignity and independence.[26] The British Columbia Supreme Court rejected Ms Pratten's section 7 claim but found that her section 15 rights had been violated and that the violations were not saved by section 1; however, the Court of Appeal held that the violation of subsection 15(1) was saved by subsection 15(2).[27]

Canada's approach to gamete donation also stands in stark contrast to that of a number of other countries that have abolished donor anonymity and established donor information registries.[28] These countries include the United Kingdom,[29] Sweden,[30] the Netherlands,[31] and several states in Australia.[32] Notably, in each of these countries, information disclosure to offspring resulted from legislative reform and not litigation. To date, no court has concluded that there is a free-standing right to know one's genetic origins.

The prohibition on donor anonymity and the disclosure of certain donor information is consistent with much of the recent empirical research on the effects of secrecy and anonymity on donor offspring. Studies suggest that offspring who learn that they were conceived using donated sperm, gradually and at a young age, generally suffer no psychological harm and in most cases appear to be quite well-adjusted.[33] Unfortunately, there are significantly fewer studies regarding the impact, be it positive or negative, of knowing the donor's identity (which may include knowing the name of the sperm donor or may extend to contact with the donor) on the donor offspring.[34]

There are, however, some very troubling court decisions where known sperm donors have been awarded access to their offspring against the wishes of the legal parents, in the context of both lesbian-led and single-mother families. These concerns are particularly acute in Canada, where many provinces have not yet addressed the parental status of gamete donors.[35] These cases raise fundamental questions about the importance of preserving donor anonymity to protect the integrity of women-led families, which I have addressed elsewhere.[36]

There is no question that a legislative gap exists in Canada that must be filled. Donor offspring should be provided with certain information about their donor. The question this chapter explores is whether the courts will lead the much-needed law reform in this area by recognizing that section 7 protects a right to know one's genetic origins. As will be seen, the recognition of such a right faces several obstacles.

II. The Struggle for Recognizing Positive Rights under Section 7 of the *Charter*

The first challenge to recognizing a free-standing constitutional right to know one's genetic origins is that, no matter how defined, it is a positive right. That is, the state must undertake positive action in order to give effect to the right. While there are strong arguments in favour of expanding section 7 of the *Charter* to protect positive rights, in my view, it is unlikely that the court will do so in this context. First, the right to know arises outside the administration of justice; the courts have been slow to recognize claims arising outside of the administration of justice as falling within the ambit of section 7. Second, a court may be reluctant to overstep its institutional role and wade into the contentious debate on donor anonymity that has been ongoing in Canada for decades. Third, a court will likely be hesitant to recognize a positive right to know out of concern that this will almost certainly open the door to other positive rights claims.

To date, Canadian courts have refused to extend section 7 to recognize positive rights claims against the state.[37] Instead, section 7 has been limited to protecting individuals from state action causing a deprivation of their right to life, liberty, or security of the person. The Supreme Court has not, however, shut the door on the possibility that section 7 could impose a "positive obligation on the state to ensure that each person enjoys life, liberty or security of the person."[38] Furthermore, a number of courts have demonstrated a willingness to take an expansive approach to section 7, albeit within the context of negative rights claims. For example, in *Chaoulli*, three members of the Supreme Court concluded that a state prohibition on purchasing private health insurance contracts violated section 7 and explicitly acknowledged that they were "moving away from a narrow approach to section 7."[39] In addition, many scholars have raised compelling arguments that an interpretation of the *Charter* that creates a false dichotomy between positive and negative rights should be rejected.[40] Nevertheless, Canadian courts have consistently shied away from finding that section 7 protects positive rights.

Canadian courts have invoked a number of reasons for refusing to find that section 7 confers positive rights upon individuals. First, the wording of section 7 itself poses some difficulty to an interpretation that protects a free-standing positive right. Section 7 states that "[e]veryone has the right to life, liberty and security of the person and the right not to be deprived thereof except in accordance with the principles of fundamental justice."[41] To date, section 7 has been interpreted as protecting *one* right and not two rights – requiring the claimant to prove *both* that the state has deprived him or her of the right to life, liberty, or security of the person *and* that the deprivation is not in accordance with the principles of fundamental justice.[42] As such, the jurisprudence is restricted to breaches of section 7 where the state has *deprived* a claimant of life, liberty, or security of the person.

Furthermore, Canadian courts have struggled to reach a consensus on whether section 7 violations can be found to exist outside of the administration of justice.[43] Although this issue arises with respect to both negative and positive rights, most of the cases where claimants have sought to expand the application of section 7 to confer a positive duty on the state arise in the context of socio-economic rights, such as the right to an adequate standard of living in *Gosselin* or the right to adequate housing in *Grant*.[44] These rights typically arise outside the adjudicative context and in the context of the legislative process. As Wilkie and Gary explain, positive rights "can be violated by mere inaction on the part of government, which implicates public policy decisions, rather than the justice system."[45]

The courts have also expressed a reluctance to interpret section 7 as conferring positive rights on claimants out of deference to the legislature. The adjudication of positive rights by courts raises both institutional and budgetary concerns. There are usually significant financial costs associated with the protection of positive rights, which are often socio-economic rights. The courts have recognized that positive government action and the expenditures of funds are often required to comply with the *Charter*.[46] However, they have been increasingly reluctant to impose costly obligations on the government.[47] Furthermore, the courts have consistently held that requiring the government to undertake "responsive action to a finding that a law violates s. 7" that involves the expenditure of funds is distinct from the adjudication of positive rights.[48]

In addition, the courts may be hesitant to recognize positive rights out of concern for maintaining proper institutional boundaries between the judiciary and the legislature. The courts have historically had regard for the "preservation of a constitutional separation of powers" – that is, the distinct institutional roles of the judiciary and the legislature.[49] Justice MacTavish, in *Canadian Doctors for Refugee Care*, recently stated that "it has long been recognized that decisions as to the setting of priorities and the allocation of scarce resources are matters not for the Courts, but for governments."[50]

The right to know one's genetic origins implicates some of these concerns but not others. This is in part because, although the right to know is a positive right, it is not a socio-economic right. I address each of these challenges in turn. First, it may very well be possible to overcome the textual difficulties associated with section 7. More than ten years ago, Arbour J in *Gosselin* offered a compelling alternative interpretation of section 7 that supports a free-standing positive right: she proposed reading the two clauses of section 7 separately to create two distinct rights.[51] Thus, section 7 would protect the right to life, liberty, and security of the person (a free-standing positive right) *and* also protect the right not to be deprived of one's life, liberty, or security of the person except in accordance with the principles of fundamental justice (the negative right). The positive right would be limited only by section 1 of the *Charter*. In other words, under this approach section 7 would require the state to ensure that the rights to life, liberty, and security of the person are protected, *even if* the principles of fundamental justice are not engaged.

Second, the right to know does not arise in the adjudicative context and has no connection to the administration of justice – a connection without which the courts have been slow to find a breach of section 7. The right to know is not at all related to the judicial system or its administration, but falls squarely within the realm of public policy. Although the jurisprudence in this area remains somewhat unsettled, the Supreme Court has indicated that it is possible for a breach of section 7 to exist outside of the administration of justice.[52] For example, in *Chaoulli*, a minority of three judges found that a statutory prohibition on private insurance breached section 7 – thereby implicitly recognizing that such a breach could arise outside the administration of justice. The dissenting judges confirmed this possibility although they noted that it will be "a rare case where s. 7 will apply in circumstances entirely unrelated to adjudicative or administrative proceedings."[53] Thus, the fact that the right to know does not arise in an adjudicative context may give the courts pause but will not necessarily be fatal to the recognition of this novel right.

Third, and perhaps most challenging, judicial recognition of a right to know may be seen by a court as overstepping its proper role. Although there is minimal cost associated with a right to know, the question of whether donor offspring are entitled to information about their sperm donor engages a number of difficult legal questions, including the definition of "donor" in family law legislation, the consequences of a prohibition on anonymity on the supply of sperm available for the creation of Canadian families, and the proper scope of a donor information registry. As is discussed in greater depth below, the multifaceted nature of this issue may lead a court to conclude that donor anonymity and associated legal issues should be dealt with comprehensively by the legislature rather than in a piecemeal fashion by the courts.

Finally, the recognition of a positive right to know one's genetic origins will almost certainly open the door to other positive rights claims under section 7. Although a number of courts have indicated a willingness to find that section 7 protects positive rights, no court has yet done so. In my view, there are many good reasons for interpreting section 7 to protect positive rights and rejecting an interpretation that creates a false dichotomy between positive and negative rights.[54] However, many scholars have questioned whether the courts will take such a progressive approach to section 7 in light of their historical reluctance to do so and their deferential stance vis-à-vis the legislature in other contexts.[55] The court will be acutely aware that, although there may be minimal costs associated with the right to know, acknowledging that right will set an important precedent that will open the door to many novel positive rights claims that may have significant financial implications.

III. The Trouble with Defining "the Right to Know One's Genetic Origins"

The second challenge the court will face is defining the scope of the "right to know one's genetic origins." Is the right to know simply a right to know the identity of one's donor or offspring? Does this right include access to certain information about one's biological progenitor, such as health and social information? Does the right include the right to know the manner of one's conception – that is, that one is donor-conceived? Who enjoys the right to know – the offspring only, or also the donor? Does the right to know apply both prospectively and retroactively? As the following discussion illustrates, the right to know could be narrowly defined as simply the right to know the donor's identity, or it could be broadly defined to include an entitlement to a range of information from one's donor. These definitional difficulties stem, in part, from the nature of the harms alleged to arise from donor anonymity. For the right to know to have meaning, it must address the harms suffered by donor offspring. As will be seen, these potential harms are wide-ranging and thus the definition of the right to know is potentially quite broad.[56] In my view, the struggle to define the right to know one's genetic origins poses an important challenge to the recognition of this right. The court may be hesitant to weigh the complex social science evidence regarding the harms suffered by donor offspring and opine on the potentially extensive and intrusive legislative measures that must be adopted to address these harms. Ultimately, the courts may conclude that the legislature is better placed to do so.

First, is the right to know one's genetic origins simply a right to the name of one's sperm donor? As discussed throughout, donor anonymity precludes the offspring from knowing *who* their sperm donor is and thus prevents the offspring from identifying the donor and, if so desired, from forming a relationship with him. Some donor offspring, although certainly not all, have expressed a strong need to know the identity of their donor. The failure to know the identity of one's donor – including the offspring's failure to know enough *about* the donor, to know *who* the donor is, and perhaps to form a *relationship* with the donor – has been found to lead to various physical and psychological harms, described below.

Some have argued that, like adopted children, certain donor offspring may suffer from "genealogical bewilderment" because of their lack of knowledge about their genetic heritage.[57] The lack of knowledge results in feelings of abandonment.[58] Others report that some offspring express a strong need to know their genetic origins and a powerful desire to search for their donor. This need to know is more than mere curiosity. One adult offspring explains: "I needed to know whose face I was looking at in the mirror – I needed to know who I was and how I came to be – it was a very primal and unrelenting force which propelled the search and it was inescapable and undeniable."[59]

This "need to know" has been expressed by both child and adult offspring.[60] Some offspring have reported a sense of loss or a feeling of incompleteness at not knowing their genetic history.[61] For some, this feeling of incompleteness has affected their sense of identity, which they describe as being "'tied up' with family and genetic history."[62] Indeed, Justice Adair concluded in *Pratten* that knowledge about one's donor, including his identity, is important to "completing" the offspring's personal identity.[63]

Second, does the right to know one's genetic origins include the right to receive certain social and health information about one's donor? The right to know the donor's identity does not necessarily extend to receiving certain information from him. Many argue, and Justice Adair agreed, that a lack of information about the donor may threaten the physical health of donor offspring.[64] Although a snapshot of the donor's health information is often provided to the intended parents, this was not routinely done until recently, and there is still no legal obligation on the donor to provide a family medical history. As a result, some donor offspring may not have any health information about one of their biological progenitors.

Yet many consider an individual's genetic and family medical history to be essential to the protection and promotion of his or her health and well-being. One's family history is increasingly important in the treatment and prevention of disease. This is certainly true for diseases that are linked to or associated with specific genes such as Huntington's disease or breast cancer.[65] A family history of disease may prompt one to test for the presence of a certain gene. Furthermore, if there is a family history of a certain condition, this may influence the offspring's behaviour. For example, a family history of colon cancer may prompt one to undergo a colonoscopy at an earlier age.[66] The exponential growth of biobanks, which store biological samples for future genetic testing and longitudinal studies and which allow for research into the relationship between genetics and disease, points to the importance of one's genetic history.[67] One way to address the potential health risks faced by donor offspring is to create a personal health registry, like the one previously found in the *AHRA*, that would contain the donor's health information and require non-identifying health information to be disclosed to the offspring. This would address, at least in part, the absence of the medical and genetic history of one biological progenitor. However, these registries generally only include a snapshot of information taken at the time the donation was made.

In light of the importance of one's family and medical history, some have asked whether the right to know should include a right to receive relevant health information from the donor on an ongoing basis. Typically donors are young and healthy at the time they donate sperm. However, the donor may develop a relevant health condition, such as colon cancer, long after his donation. If the offspring is made aware of this, she may decide to alter her lifestyle to minimize the risk or may undergo screening at an earlier age. In the absence of this information, she is unaware of the potential risk to her health. Thus, to fully satisfy the offspring's needs, ongoing disclosure of the donor's health information would likely be required. This may, however, pose a number of practical and legal problems, including those relating to the privacy interests or rights of the donor, which are discussed below.[68]

Third, does the right to know one's genetic origins extend to a right to know the manner of one's conception? Donor anonymity and secrecy are closely linked, but they result in distinct harms. Donor anonymity precludes the offspring from knowing *who* their sperm donor is. However, donor anonymity also enables secrecy surrounding the manner of the offspring's conception. Donor anonymity facilitates this secrecy because the donor does not know who the offspring is and so cannot disclose the manner of conception to that person.

The harms arising from secrecy are well-established.[69] The potential harm to the offspring where the manner of their conception is kept secret arises not just from having insufficient information about the donor but also from the fact that they do not know about the manner of their conception – in other words, that they are donor-conceived.

Empirical studies demonstrate that secrecy regarding the use of donor sperm can have a negative impact on offspring, many of whom report having a sense that there is something the family is keeping from them.[70] Furthermore, accidental disclosure or learning at an older age that one is donor-conceived can cause the offspring significant emotional distress[71] – in Justice Adair's words, "devastating effects."[72] Keeping the manner of conception and the use of donated sperm secret from the offspring is a long-standing practice that continues to be followed in some heterosexual families.[73]

Secrecy regarding the manner of conception may also threaten the offspring's physical health. Where the use of donated gametes remains a secret, the offspring will erroneously believe that he has access to his complete family medical history and that his legal parent(s)' medical history is relevant to his medical care. The offspring will be completely oblivious to the fact that she is missing relevant information that could affect her health. Access to a personal health registry will be meaningless for someone who does not know he or she was conceived using donated sperm. To protect the health and well-being of donor offspring, it is arguably necessary to end the secrecy surrounding the use of reproductive technologies. Abolishing donor anonymity may *discourage* secrecy. But it may not be enough to address the harms arising from secrecy.

If the right to know includes the manner of one's conception, what measures are required to ensure this right is not breached? The legislature does play a role – albeit quite an attenuated one – in preserving the secrecy of the use of donor sperm. It does so by failing to impose a duty on parents who have used such sperm to create their families to disclose the manner of conception to the offspring. To give effect to a right to know the manner of one's conception – which is undoubtedly a positive right, with the attendant difficulties described above – the legislature could either impose a legal duty on parents to disclose or (perhaps more feasibly) require an annotation to the offspring's birth certificate stating that the child was conceived using donor sperm.[74] Notably, I could find no country that has yet imposed such an intrusive duty on parents or the state.[75] It is questionable, therefore, whether the Canadian courts will be the first to do so.

Fourth, who enjoys the right to know? Generally, the right to know has been claimed by offspring in respect of the donor. However, it is possible that an offspring could claim that the right to know includes the right to know the identity of half-siblings. It is also possible that the right to know could be claimed by donors who are searching for information about their offspring. As discussed elsewhere in the text, there may be good reason to limit the right to offspring, as has been done in New Zealand, in order to prevent the unwanted intrusion of the donor on the family unit.[76]

Fifth, is the right to know one's genetic origins a prospective or retroactive right? In other words, do donor offspring who were conceived under the anonymous regime have a right to know their genetic origins? Does the right to know include the right to access the confidential records of a gamete donor where the donation was made with an expectation that he would remain anonymous? Or does the right to know apply prospectively to future sperm donors and offspring only? Other jurisdictions have struggled with these questions. For example, in the Australian state of Victoria, legislation now permits donor-conceived offspring to apply to have their previously anonymous donor's identifying information released, with the donor's consent.[77] In Canada, these difficult questions relate to our laws governing privacy and retroactivity, to which I now turn.

IV. The Protection of Privacy in Canadian Law

The protection of privacy in Canadian law is long-standing.[78] In the context of gamete donation, the issue is the extent to which the historical protection of privacy will influence whether a court will recognize a right to know. In my view, the strong legal protection afforded to individual privacy in Canadian law generally, and in the context of adoption in particular, presents another significant obstacle to the recognition of a constitutional right to know one's genetic origins. Privacy concerns arise with both a prospective right to know – for example, by imposing an ongoing disclosure requirement on sperm donors – and a retroactive right to know, because of the reasonable expectation of privacy for those who donated or were conceived under the anonymous regime. Given the importance of privacy rights in Canadian law, the courts may be reluctant to recognize a right that may erode the long-standing legal protection of individual privacy. Furthermore, the court may very well conclude that balancing the privacy interests of the donor with the offspring's interest in information is a task better left to the legislatures.

A brief review of Canadian law reveals that individual privacy is robustly protected in many contexts.[79] Although there is no free-standing right to privacy, this right underlies a number of *Charter* rights. The purpose of section 8 of the *Charter*, which protects against unreasonable search and seizure, is the protection of individual privacy, including informational privacy, which is at stake in this context.[80] The right to informational privacy is "the right of the individual to determine for himself when, how and to what extent he will release personal information about himself."[81] The Court has explained that the protection of informational privacy is founded on the "dignity and integrity of the individual" and is "essential for the well-being of the individual."[82] The protection of privacy is also entrenched in section 7 of the *Charter*. In *R. v O'Connor*, the Court explained that "respect for individual privacy is an essential component of what it means to be free" and as such engages an individual's right to liberty.[83] The liberty interest also protects the "right to an irreducible sphere of personal autonomy wherein individuals may make inherently private choices free from state interference."[84] In addition to constitutional protection, a number of federal and provincial privacy statutes, such as the *Personal Information Protection and Electronic Documents Act* (*PIPEDA*) and the *Privacy Act*, protect individual privacy.[85] Indeed, the Ontario Court of Appeal recently recognized a common law tort for the invasion of personal privacy based, in part, on the long-standing protection of privacy in Canadian law.[86] Notably, the constitutional, statutory, and common law protections of privacy are not absolute. Such protection varies with the context.

In the context of gamete donation, the legal protection of privacy may very well influence the recognition of a prospective right to know one's genetic origins. A court may be reluctant to recognize a right that erodes an individual's right or interest in privacy generally. In other contexts, the right to privacy has been held to be paramount to the competing interest in the disclosure of information.[87] Here, the right to know one's genetic origins may be in direct conflict with the privacy interests of the donor. For example, a right to know one's genetic origins that requires the ongoing disclosure of health information by the donor would likely conflict with the donor's right to privacy of his health information.[88] The right to know may also conflict with the privacy interests of the intended parents, who may argue that a state prohibition on donor anonymity interferes with their ability to create their desired family form. That is, they may wish to avoid the unwanted intrusion of the sperm donor, or perhaps there is not enough sperm available to create their family.[89]

The right to privacy is also engaged with respect to a retroactive right to know one's genetic origins. A brief discussion of the right to privacy in the adoption context, where parties have unsuccessfully argued for a right to know their genetic origins, reveals the legal challenges for offspring. Many argue that this is an apt comparison because these are "processes which create families in which the child is not genetically related to one or both parents."[90] Indeed, Justice Adair in *Pratten* found as much by concluding that adoptees and donor offspring are comparable groups for the purposes of section 15 of the *Charter*. However, others argue that this comparison is inapt because the donor offspring, unlike the adoptee, is often the biological child of one of his parents (except where conceived using a donor embryo); similarly, the donor offspring, unlike the adoptee, integrates with the gestational mother during the pregnancy.[91] Furthermore, some argue that there is a fundamental difference between a donor offspring who is *created* by his or her intended parents and the adoptee who is relinquished at birth by his or her biological parents.[92] While it is difficult to say whether the courts will follow the adoption jurisprudence, it is a useful point of departure for examining the nature and scope of the privacy interests that may arise in gamete donation.

Canadian courts have repeatedly confirmed the importance of safeguarding privacy interests in adoption. First, the courts have found that the privacy interests of *all* members of the adoption triad must be considered.[93] It is not only the birth parent whose privacy interests are at stake. In many instances, the privacy of the adoptee is engaged because he or she does not wish to be identified. Second, the courts have described birth and adoption information as "intensely private" and as "some of the most sensitive information in our society,"[94] acknowledging that its release could be "traumatic" to the individual resisting disclosure.[95] Third, the courts have concluded that an individual's decision about whether to disclose identifying adoption information is a "fundamentally personal decision with enormous implications" that is protected by the liberty interest in section 7.[96] Individuals have a reasonable expectation of privacy in this information. A law that requires the disclosure of this information *without* consent, therefore, violates section 7. Fourth, the courts have identified a principle of fundamental justice that is contravened where confidential birth and adoption records are disclosed to their parties without consent: "where an individual has a reasonable expectation of privacy in personal and confidential information, that information may not be disclosed to third parties without his or her consent."[97] Fifth, in the context of section 15 of the *Charter*, the courts have concluded that the "assurances and expectations of privacy and confidentiality" relied on by birth parents are relevant in determining whether a law that restricts information disclosure in adoption is reasonable and justifiable pursuant to section 1 of the *Charter*.[98]

Notably, the courts in the adoption context have not weighed the right to privacy against the right to know one's genetic origins. This is because, to date, no court has recognized that an adoptee has a right to know his or her genetic origins.[99] The Ontario Superior Court of Justice in *Marchand v Ontario* concluded that the adoptee had not established an evidentiary foundation for her liberty claim, and that in any event, her right to liberty was constrained by the privacy interest of her potential birth father, who chose not to reveal his identity.[100] Furthermore, she had failed to establish that her desire to know her birth father's identity rose to the requisite level of psychological stress, and she had not established that the impugned provisions had a serious and profound effect on her psychological well-being.[101] Later, the Ontario Court of Appeal concluded that no principle of fundamental justice was engaged: "the unconditional disclosure of identifying personal information of third parties, even if they are birth parents of the claimant, without regard to the privacy and confidentiality interests of the persons identified and without regard to any serious harm that might result from disclosure, fails to meet the above criteria."[102] In addition, the Superior Court of Justice in *Cheskes* concluded that "the right of searching adoptees or birth parents to gain access to confidential adoption information, although important and heart-felt, is not a *Charter*-protected right."[103]

What might these adoption cases mean in the context of gamete donation? I offer a few preliminary thoughts. First and foremost, the privacy interests that are engaged are not simply those of the donor. Some offspring may not want their identity or other personal information disclosed to the donor or half-siblings. Second, genetic information about one's donor, offspring, half-siblings, and other familial relationships is highly sensitive. Third, many of the same concerns regarding the disclosure of information and the desire for informational privacy in adoption will likely give rise to a reasonable expectation of privacy in this information for third-party reproduction. Some donors and offspring may have a strong sense of privacy and believe that the disclosure of their identity and other personal information is theirs alone to make. For a donor who has donated under the condition of anonymity, it may be that he has not advised his family that he has donated; thus, the disclosure of this information could have a significant and harmful impact on them. By contrast, an offspring may not want to disclose her identity to her donor or half-siblings as it may have a destabilizing or traumatic impact on her family, including her legal parents, siblings, or children. All told, the long-standing protection of privacy in law generally, together with the lower courts' recognition of privacy in adoption, will likely make the court reluctant to recognize a constitutional right to know one's genetic origins in the context of gamete donation.

V. Retroactivity: Concerns about Notice and Fairness

For those who donated or were conceived under the anonymous regime, the right to know raises questions not only about the reasonable expectation of privacy of donors and offspring, but also about retroactivity. As discussed above, the right to know one's genetic origins is difficult to define and could create a legal obligation to disclose on donors who donated, and offspring who were conceived, under the anonymous regime. This raises concerns about retroactivity because it deems the law to be different than what it was in the past. Although retroactive or retrospective legislation outside the criminal context is not unconstitutional *per se*, the courts may be dissuaded from recognizing a constitutional right that requires the legislature to enact a law that has a retroactive or retrospective impact on certain individuals or that offends the principles that underlie these doctrines.

A law that is retroactive or retrospective is one that "attaches new legal effects to situations that had occurred entirely or partly in the past."[104] There has been significant confusion in the use and application of these terms by the courts.[105] The Supreme Court of Canada in *Benner v Canada*, in an effort to clear up this confusion, adopted the following definitions developed by Driedger:

> A retroactive statute is one that operates as of a time prior to its enactment. A retrospective statute is one that operates for the future only. It is prospective, but it imposes new results in respect of a past event. A retroactive statute *operates backwards*. A retrospective statute *operates forwards*, but it looks backwards in that it attaches new consequences *for the future* to an event that took place before the statute was enacted. A retroactive statute changes the law from what it was; a retrospective statute changes the law from what it otherwise would be with respect to a prior event [emphasis in original]."[106]

Nevertheless, confusion has persisted.[107]

Regardless of the confusion, the concerns underlying the terms retroactivity and retrospectivity are well-established. These concerns relate to the rule of law, a bedrock principle underlying the Canadian legal system. Laws that apply retroactively are considered to be problematic because they are a "direct assault" on the principle that individuals must have adequate notice of the law.[108] To comply with the law, an individual must know what the law says. A retroactive law violates this principle because it deems the law to have said something different in the past, thereby precluding an individual from acting with knowledge of the law. Laws that apply retroactively also raise fairness concerns. As Sullivan explains, "[i]t is unfair to establish rules, invite people to rely on them, then change them in mid-stream, especially if the change results in negative consequences."[109] The importance of a principled approach in this context cannot be overemphasized given the difficulties with terminology and application of these rules.

Questions of retroactivity or retrospectivity are legally relevant for several purposes. When interpreting a statute, the court will presume that the legislature does not intend for that legislation to applied retroactively.[110] Closely related, although less established, is the presumption that the legislature does not intend that legislation be applied retrospectively unless it confers a benefit or protects the public.[111] However, these statutory presumptions have not, with one exception, risen to the level of a constitutional principle. To date, the Court has not recognized a guarantee against retroactivity under section 7 of the *Charter*.[112] Nor does the unwritten constitutional principle of the rule of law include a right to prospective legislation.[113] A guarantee against retroactivity is only constitutionally protected in the criminal context by virtue of sections 11(g) and (i) of the *Charter*.[114] Thus, generally speaking, Parliament and the legislatures are permitted to pass retroactive laws. Nevertheless, courts have real concerns about retroactive and retrospective laws that will need to be addressed in this context and may discourage the courts' intervention in this area.

Whether or not the legislation that gives effect to the right to know is characterized as retroactive or retrospective, it will engage the principles of adequate notice and fairness.[115] This is because the donor provided sperm when the law guaranteed his anonymity and did not require the disclosure of his identifying information without consent. To now require the donor's identity to be disclosed, together with other identifying information, deems the law to be different than what it was at the time of donation. In other words, the donor did not have notice of the law at the time he made his decision to donate sperm. This change in the law undermines the donor's agency and may be considered unfair because the assurance of anonymity that the donor relied on and that may have been an important condition to donation has been removed (i.e., the donor no longer has an opportunity to reconsider whether to donate). Similarly, the recipient of the donor sperm has relied on the assurance of anonymity when creating his or her family and may consider this change, which could have a significant impact on the family unit, to be unfair.

Questions of retroactivity and retrospectivity may influence the development of a right to know one's genetic origins in several ways. First, whether such a disclosure obligation is categorized as retroactive or retrospective, the court may be hesitant to recognize a constitutional right that would require the legislature to enact a law that would interfere with the settled legal expectations of donors and recipients. Thus, the court may conclude that if a right to know exists, it does so only prospectively. Second, should the court recognize a right to know that has retroactive effect, it may encourage the legislature to address the competing concerns of the donors through other mechanisms. For example, an equivalent of the disclosure veto that exists in some adoption laws would provide the donors with an opportunity to block the disclosure of information and to ensure that their legal expectations are thereby respected.

VI. The Potential Consequences of a Right to Know One's Genetic Origins

The final challenge to the recognition of a right to know one's genetic origins is that the implications, no matter how narrow or broad, are likely to be wide-ranging and potentially troubling. Whether the right to know simply includes the right to know the identity of one's biological progenitor or is a broader right to receive certain health information from that progenitor, the recognition of such a right will almost certainly have consequences far beyond the context of gamete donation. The court will certainly be mindful of the potential legal and social consequences of recognizing a positive right to know one's genetic origins, as it has been in past cases, and on this basis may be wary of recognizing such a right.[116] A few examples illustrate how the right to know could represent a sea change in several areas of law.

Should the court recognize a right to know the identity of one's biological progenitor in the context of gamete donation, this will provide a strong basis for recognizing a similar right in other contexts. There are a number of people who, like donor offspring, do not have an *opportunity* to know who their biological progenitor is. The most frequent comparison is with adoptees. Some provinces have recognized this disadvantage and have sought to remedy it through open adoption legislation, which requires the disclosure of identity and other information – such as health information – about the birth parent in certain circumstances.[117] However, as noted above, the courts have consistently refused to recognize that an adoptee has a right to know his or her birth parent(s).[118] If, however, such a right was recognized in the context of third-party reproduction, this could create a new right for adoptees in those provinces where open adoption regimes do not currently exist.

Similarly situated individuals include those who were conceived naturally; however, the mother has chosen not to disclose the father's identity. Should these offspring have a right to know his identity? Currently, there is no blanket legal obligation to declare the identity of the biological father on a child's birth certificate.[119] Although a comprehensive review is beyond the scope of this chapter, vital statistics legislation permits a woman to exclude the name of the biological father from the birth certificate in some circumstances, including when it is not in the best interests of the child. Perhaps most compelling are cases of incest, rape, and abuse. A woman who has been abused by her partner or who has conceived as a result of a rape or incest may quite rightly decide not to reveal his identity to the child.[120] Furthermore, forcing a woman to disclose the identity of the biological father represents an important incursion into her autonomy and privacy, one that has been harshly criticized by feminist scholars.[121] Recognizing a right to know one's genetic origins could very well erode the circumstances in which a woman can choose to keep private the identity of her offspring's biological progenitor.

Individuals who are mistaken as to the identity of their biological father are in a similar position to donor offspring, albeit unknowingly. It is trite that some individuals believe that their father is also their biological progenitor when in fact he is not. If the court recognizes a right to know for donor offspring, this could provide a legal basis for arguing that the same right should exist for these individuals on the ground that they are subject to the same risk of harm as donor offspring. The law currently makes no provision for these offspring, despite a mistaken paternity rate in Canada that is estimated at around 4 per cent.[122] There is no free-standing legal obligation imposed on an individual to advise a child of his or her biological parentage. For example, where families undergo genetic testing in cases of certain diseases and discover that the father is not biologically related, geneticists have no obligation to advise the family.[123] Nor does the law compel an individual to undergo DNA testing in order to determine paternity.[124] The creation of such an obligation would represent an important shift in the law, for it would result in new legal disclosure obligations for a potentially wide range of individuals – including mothers – as well as mandatory DNA testing in certain situations.

Besides creating these new legal obligations, the consequences of a free-standing right to know one's genetic progenitor could spill over into family law. One example is child support. Currently, child support is owed by a biological parent *or* by an individual who stands in the place of a parent.[125] This obligation arises even in cases of mistaken paternity.[126] In other words, a non-biological father who mistakenly believes he is a child's biological father owes child support because he is a *de facto* parent of the child. Some have argued that this constitutes "paternity fraud" and that, as such, these men should be exempt from paying child support.[127] This would, in effect, erase child support obligations for a non-biological parent. The emphasis on biological connections that underlies the right to know could lend support to this approach, one that is arguably at odds with the best interests of the child, which is a foundational principle of family law.

Separate and apart from identity, if the right to know includes a right to receive certain information about one's sperm or egg donor, this could lay the groundwork for a broad right for any individual, regardless of the manner of his or her conception, to receive health information about his or her genetic progenitors. The donor offspring's argument that he or she should receive relevant health information about his or her donor is compelling. As discussed above, a complete family medical history, especially of one's genetic progenitors, is important to one's health. Arguably, this type of health information is equally important to individuals who are not donor-conceived. Yet there is no general legal entitlement to receive any health information from one's biological progenitors.[128] Indeed, quite the opposite is true. And although many parents will choose to disclose relevant health information to their offspring, this is not always the case. With few exceptions, privacy laws preclude the disclosure of individual health information without consent to most people under any circumstances, including to one's family.[129] It is difficult to say whether the *opportunity* to ask one's biological progenitor for this information is a sufficient basis on which to distinguish the disclosure of health information to a donor offspring and thus whether this argument would find success in the courts.

Conclusion

I believe there are many laudable reasons in support of greater openness in gamete donation in Canada. The informational needs of donor offspring are pressing and must be addressed. Donor offspring have legitimate physical and psychological concerns that can only be answered by donor information. The question is, how will these changes be effected? Will it be through the court's recognition of a constitutional right to know one's genetic origins or through legislative reform? As has been discussed, there are a number of obstacles to recognizing a constitutional right to know: the fact that it is a positive right that the courts have been reluctant to recognize; that its scope is difficult to define and potentially quite broad; that it may raise privacy and retroactivity concerns, two well-entrenched principles in Canadian law; and that the consequences of recognizing a right to know could be wide-ranging and quite troubling. As a result, it is unlikely that the courts will recognize such a right. However, this in no way negates the pressing need for law reform in this area. In some respects, the legislature is well placed to address the informational requirements of donor offspring. Indeed, it is better able than the courts to ensure the needs of all parties are met and to address the difficult questions of parentage, privacy, retroactivity, and others that may arise in this context.

NOTES

Author's note: I would like to thank Andrew Lanouette and Emily Villeneuve for their excellent research assistance and Professors Natasha Bakht and Adam Dodek for their comments on earlier versions of this chapter.

1 This paper focuses on anonymous sperm donation, which has been better studied than ova donation for several reasons. Sperm donation is much more common than ova donation: S. Purewal and O.B.A. van den Akker, "Systematic Review of Oocyte Donation: Investigating Attitudes, Motivations and Experiences" (2009) 15 Human Reprod Update 499. Further, these donation processes are distinct. Unlike sperm donation, donating ova is physically intrusive and carries with it serious risks such as ovarian hyperstimulation. As a result, ova shortages are far greater than for sperm: Ilke Turkmendag, Robert Dingwall, and Therese Murphy, "The Removal of Donor Anonymity in the UK: The Silencing of

Claims by Would-Be Parents" (2008) 22 Int'l JL Pol'y & Fam 283 at 297.

2 The Donor Sibling Registry, https://www.donorsiblingregistry.com.

3 See, for example, Barry Stevens's search for his donor in his documentary film *Bio-Dad* (2009).

4 *Pratten v British Columbia (Attorney General)*, 2011 BCSC 656, 99 RFL (6th) 290 [*Pratten*], rev'd 2012 BCCA 480, 25 RFL (7th) 58, leave to appeal to SCC refused, [2013] SCCA No 36. For a more detailed discussion of *Pratten*, including the background to the case and the arguments of the parties, see the chapter by Giroux and Milne in this volume. *Pratten* is also the focus of the chapters by Guichon and Snelling.

5 A number of scholars have written in favour of non-anonymous gamete donation. See, for example, Mhairi Cowden, "'No Harm, No Foul': A Child's Right to Know Their Genetic Parents" (2012) 26 Int'l JL Pol'y & Fam 102; Michelle Dennison, "Revealing Your Sources: The Case for Non-Anonymous Gamete Donation" (2007) 21 JL & Health 1; Josephine Johnson, "Mum's the Word: Donor Anonymity in Assisted Reproduction" (2003) 11 Health L Rev 51; Pino D'Orazio, "Half of the Family Tree: A Call for Access to a Full Genetic History for Children Born by Artificial Insemination" (2006) 2 J Health & Biomedical L 249 at 252; Glenn McGee, Sarah-Vaughan Brakman, and Andrea Gurmankin, "Gamete Donor Anonymity: Disclosure to Children Conceived with Donor Gametes Should Not Be Optional" (2001) 16:10 Hum Reprod 2033 [McGee *et al.*].

6 *Canadian Charter of Rights and Freedoms*, Part I of the *Constitution Act, 1982*, being Schedule B to the *Canada Act 1982* (UK), 1982, c 11 [*Charter*].

7 See, for example, Margot Young, "Section 7 and the Politics of Social Justice" (2005) 38 UBC L Rev 539.

8 *Rodriguez v British Columbia (Attorney General)*, [1993] 3 SCR 519, 107 DLR (4th) 342, *R v Morgentaler*, [1988] 1 SCR 30, 44 DLR (4th) 385, and *Carter v Canada*, 2015 SCC 5.

9 See, for example, *Chaoulli v Quebec (Attorney General)*, 2005 SCC 35, [2005] 1 SCR 791 [*Chaoulli*], where three members of the Supreme Court concluded that a state prohibition on purchasing private health insurance contracts violated section 7, and *Victoria (City) v Adams*, 2009 BCCA 563, 313 DLR (4th) 29 [*Adams*], where the British Columbia Court of Appeal concluded that a municipal by-law that prohibited persons from erecting any form of temporary shelter at night violated section 7.

10 Identity release donors are sperm or egg donors who have agreed to the disclosure of their identity at a specified time, often upon the offspring reaching the age of majority: Mary Patricia Byrn and Rebecca Ireland,

"Anonymously Provided Sperm and the Constitution" (2012) 23 Colum J Gender & L 1. In Canada, unlike in many other countries where donor anonymity is prohibited, the disclosure of the donor's identity is governed by contract.

11 *Assisted Human Reproduction Act*, SC 2004, c 2, ss 14–18 [*AHRA*].

12 These provisions were not yet in force and many of the details had been left to the regulations: *ibid* at s 78.

13 *AHRA*, *supra* note 11 at s 17.

14 *Ibid* at s 18(3).

15 *Ibid* at s 18(4).

16 *Ibid* at s 18(7).

17 *Reference re Assisted Human Reproduction Act*, 2010 SCC 61, [2010] 3 SCR 457. Parliament repealed these provisions: *Jobs, Growth and Long-term Prosperity Act*, SC 2012, c.19, ss 713–45.

18 Different countries have balanced these rights through different legal mechanisms and registries: see Eric Blyth and Lucy Frith, "Donor Conceived People's Access to Genetic and Biographical History: An Analysis of Provisions in Different Jurisdictions Permitting Disclosure of Donor Identity" (2009) 23 Int'l JL & Pol'y 174.

19 Regarding the impact of known donors on the integrity of the family unit, see Angela Cameron, Vanessa Gruben, and Fiona Kelly, "De-anonymising Sperm Donors in Canada: Some Doubts and Directions" (2010) 26 Can J Fam L 95. Regarding concerns about decreased supply as a result of prohibitions on donor anonymity, see Turkmendag *et al.*, *supra* note 1.

20 Canada, *Proceed with Care: Final Report of the Royal Commission on New Reproductive Technologies*, vols 1–2 (Ottawa: Minister of Government Services Canada, 1993), 476.

21 House of Commons, Standing Committee on Health, *Assisted Human Reproduction: Building Families* (December 2001) (Chair: Bonnie Brown), Parliament of Canada http://www.parl.gc.ca/content/hoc/Committee/371/HEAL/Reports/RP1032041/healrp02/healrp02-e.pdf at 24.

22 *Debates of the Senate*, 37th Parl., 3rd Sess., No. 141 (9 March 2004) at 1420, Standing Committee on Social Affairs, Science and Technology (Hon. Michael Kirby).

23 Five provinces have open adoption legislation, although each has different features: *Adoption Act*, RSBC 1996, c 5; *Access to Adoption Records Act*, SO 2008, c 5; *Adoption Act*, SNL 1999, c A-2.1; *Adoption Act*, RSA 2000, c C-12; *Adoption Information Disclosure Regulations*, YOIC 1985/149, made under the *Children's Act*, RSY 2002, c 31.

24 *Pratten, supra* note 4.

25 British Columbia's *Adoption Act, supra* note 23, requires the collection of information about the medical and social history of the adoptee's biological family, provides for the making of openness agreements for the purpose of facilitating communication between the adoptee and the biological progenitors, and provides adoptees (adopted after 1996) with the opportunity to learn the identity of their biological progenitors by applying for copies of their original birth registrations and adoption orders. For those adopted prior to 1996, identifying information may only be disclosed with the consent of the birth parent.

26 *Pratten, supra* note 4 at para 295.

27 *Ibid.*

28 See, generally, Blyth and Frith, *supra* note 18. See also Pim M.W. Janssens, Annemiek W. Nap, and Laszlo F.J.J.M. Bancsi, "Reconsidering the Number of Offspring per Gamete Donor in the Dutch Open-Identity System" (2011) 14 Hum Fertil 106 at 108.

29 *Human Fertilisation and Embryology Act 1990*, c 37.

30 *Swedish Law on Artificial Insemination* (1985), No. 114O/1984. See also Ken Daniels, "The Swedish Insemination Act and Its Impact" (1994) 34 Aust NZ J Obstet Gynaecol 437.

31 P.M.W. Janssens *et al.*, "A New Dutch Law Regulating Provision of Identifying Information of Donors to Offspring: Background, Content and Impact" (2006) 21:4 Hum Reprod 852.

32 Western Australia, Victoria and New South Wales prohibit anonymous gamete donation: Cowden, *supra* note 5 at 105.

33 K. Vanfraussen *et al.*, "Why Do Children Want to Know More about the Donor? The Experience of Youngsters Raised in Lesbian Families" (2003) 24 J Psychosom Obstet Gynaecol 31 at 36; J.E. Scheib *et al.*, "Adolescents with Open-Identity Sperm Donors: Reports from 12–17 Year Olds" (2005) 20:1 Hum Reprod 239 at 248; Tabitha Freeman and Susan Golombok, "Donor Insemination: A Follow-Up Study of Disclosure Decisions, Family Relationships and Child Adjustment at Adolescence" (2012) 25 Reprod Biomed Online 193 at 194; Vasanti Jadva *et al.*, "The Experiences of Adolescents and Adults Conceived by Sperm Donation: Comparisons by Age of Disclosure and Family Type" (2009) 24:8 Hum Reprod 1909 at 1910; E. Lycett *et al.*, "School-Aged Children of Donor Insemination: A Study of Parents' Disclosure Patterns" (2005) 20:3 Hum Reprod 810.

34 Kate Godman *et al.*, "Potential Sperm Donors', Recipients' and their Partners' Opinions Towards the Release of Identifying Information in Western Australia" (2006) 21:11 Hum Reprod 3022 at 3025, noting that

"by providing personal information about the donor, a perceived emotional link between the child and donor could be created. This may cause a significant problem if the majority of sperm donors do not wish to have contact with recipients or any involvement with biological offspring born as a result of their donation."

35 Angela Cameron, "A Chip Off the Old (Ice) Block?: Women-Led Families, Sperm Donors and Family Law," in *Women and the Law*, ed. Jennifer Kilty (Toronto: Canadian Scholars' Press, 2014), 246.

36 Cameron, Gruben, and Kelly, *supra* note 19.

37 Most notable is *Gosselin v Quebec (Attorney General)*, 2002 SCC 84, [2002] 4 SCR 429 [*Gosselin*], where a majority of the Supreme Court of Canada rejected a claim by a welfare recipient that her welfare benefits were so inadequate as to give rise to a breach of section 7 of the *Charter*. See also *Flora v Ontario (Health Insurance Plan, General Manager)*, 2008 ONCA 538, 91 OR (3d) 412, where the Ontario Court of Appeal dismissed the applicant's claim that the province's failure to pay for a liver transplant outside of Canada violated section 7 of the *Charter*. See also *Grant v Canada (Attorney General)* (2009), 77 OR (3d) 481, 258 DLR (4th) 725 (SC) [*Grant*], where Cullity J of the Superior Court of Justice struck a section 7 claim to adequate housing on the basis that on the facts pled, no principles of fundamental justice applied. And most recently, see *Canadian Doctors for Refugee Care v Canada (Attorney General)*, 2014 FC 651 at para 571, 28 Imm LR (4th) 1 [*Canadian Doctors for Refugee Care*].

38 *Gosselin*, *ibid* at paras 82–3. See also Young, *supra* note 7 at 543.

39 *Chaoulli*, *supra* note 9 at para 197. Similarly, in *Adams*, *supra* note 9, the British Columbia Court of Appeal found that a municipal by-law prohibiting persons from erecting any form of temporary shelter at night violated section 7.

40 Cara Wilkie and Meryl Gary, "Positive and Negative Rights under the Charter: Closing the Divide to Advance Equality" (2011) 30 Windsor Rev Legal Soc Issues 37 at 38; Jamie Cameron, "Positive Obligations under Sections 15 and 7 of the Charter: A Comment on Gosselin v Quebec" (2003) 20 SCLR (2d) 65 at 71; Mel Cousins, "Health Care and Human Rights after Auton and Chaoulli" (2009) 54 McGill LJ 717 at 725. See also Lawrence David, "A Principled Approach to the Positive/Negative Rights Debate in Canadian Constitutional Adjudication" (2014) 23 Constit Forum 41.

41 *Charter*, *supra* note 6.

42 *Gosselin*, *supra* note 37.

43 Peter W. Hogg, *Constitutional Law of Canada*, looseleaf, 5th ed. supplemented (Toronto: Carswell, 2007) vol. 2, ch. 47 at ss 47.7(b), 47.8.

44 *Gosselin*, *supra* note 37 and *Grant*, *supra* note 37.
45 Wilkie and Gary, *supra* note 40 at 43.
46 See, for example, *New Brunswick (Minister of Health and Community Services) v G(J)*, [1999] 3 SCR 46, 177 DLR (4th) 124, where the Supreme Court found a limited right to state-funded counsel to ensure a fair hearing.
47 See, for example, *Newfoundland (Treasury Board) v NAPE*, 2004 SCC 66, [2004] 3 SCR 381, where the Supreme Court of Canada found that legislation that deferred the commencement of wage adjustment payments violated section 15 of the *Charter* but concluded that this violation was justified under section 1 because of the fiscal crisis facing the province at the time; *Cameron v Nova Scotia (Attorney General)* (1999), 204 NSR (2d) 1, 177 DLR (4th) 611 (CA), leave to appeal to SCC refused, [1999] SCCA No. 53, where a majority of the Court of Appeal found that the failure to fund *in vitro* fertilization violated section 15 of the *Charter* but concluded that this violation was justified under section 1 because of the province's limited financial resources; and *British Columbia (Attorney General) v Christie*, 2007 SCC 21 at para 14, [2007] 1 SCR 873 [*Christie*], where a majority of the Supreme Court of Canada weighed the potential costs associated with recognizing a right to be represented by a lawyer in a court or tribunal.
48 *Adams*, *supra* note 9 at para 96.
49 Young, *supra* note 7 at 556. See generally Lorne Sossin, *Boundaries of Judicial Review: The Law of Justiciability in Canada* (Toronto: Carswell, 1999).
50 *Canadian Doctors for Refugee Care*, *supra* note 37 at para 535.
51 *Gosselin*, *supra* note 37 at paras 386–7.
52 *Gosselin*, *ibid* at paras 78–80. See generally James Hendry, "Alternatives for Advancing Social Justice" (2009–2010) 27 NJCL 93.
53 *Chaoulli*, *supra* note 9 at para 196.
54 Wilkie and Gary, *supra* note 40; Young, *supra* note 7.
55 See, for example, Wilkie and Gary, *supra* note 40; Hendry, *supra* note 52; and Young, *supra* note 7.
56 Several studies are cited below, *infra* notes 57, 58, 64, 69. While these studies indicate that that secrecy and anonymity may result in real harm, it is important to acknowledge their limitations. First, the sample sizes in each of the studies are quite small. Second, many of the studies examined both secrecy and the need to know one's donor, prompting some to ask whether the "negative feelings … were centered round the shock of disclosure, feelings of deceit and mistrust" rather than "to the donor origin in itself": Vanfraussen *et al.*, *supra* note 33 at 36. Third, many of the scholars acknowledged that the subjects of these studies cannot be considered representative of all donor-conceived offspring because many scholars

recruited from offspring-support networks, which might have biased the results in favour of individuals who need to resolve identity issues: T. Freeman *et al.*, "Gamete Donation: Parents' Experiences of Searching for Their Child's Donor Siblings and Donor" (2009) 24:3 Hum Reprod 505 at 506; Jadva *et al.*, *supra* note 33 at 1911. This selection bias is difficult to overcome in light of the secrecy surrounding the use of ARTs, making it impossible to study the impact of secrecy on offspring in certain families.

57 Dennison, *supra* note 5 at 16.

58 A.J. Turner and A. Coyle, "What Does It Mean to Be a Donor Offspring? The Identity Experiences of Adults Conceived by Donor Insemination and the Implications for Counseling and Therapy" (2000) 15:9 Hum Reprod 2041 at 2047; Amber Cushing, "I Just Want More Information about Who I Am: The Search Experience of Sperm Donor Offspring, Searching for Information about Their Donor and Genetic Heritage (2010) 15:2 Information Research at 1.

59 Turner and Coyle, *ibid* at 2046.

60 Vanfraussen *et al.*, *supra* note 33 at 36; Turner and Coyle, *ibid* at 2046. It has also been expressed by parents who are searching for their child's donor: Freeman *et al.*, *supra* note 56 at 514.

61 Turner and Coyle, *ibid* at 2046. See also Dennison, *supra* note 5 at 16; Johnson, *supra* note 5 at 53; and Lisa Shields, "Consistency and Privacy: Do These Legal Principles Mandate Gamete Donor Anonymity?" (2003) 12 Health L Rev 39 at 42.

62 Turner and Coyle, *ibid* at 2047.

63 *Pratten*, *supra* note 4 at para 111.

64 *Pratten*, *supra* note 4 at para 303. See also Vardit Ravitsky, "Conceived and Deceived: The Medical Interests of Donor-Conceived Individuals" (2012) 42 Hastings Center Report 17 at 17; Dennison, *supra* note 5 at 14; Johnson, *supra* note 5 at 53; D'Orazio, *supra* note 5 at 252.

65 A mutation in the BRCA1 and BRCA2 gene is the most commonly detectable cause of hereditary breast cancer: Mark Robson and Kenneth Offit, "Management of an Inherited Predisposition to Breast Cancer" (2007) 357 N Engl J Med 154.

66 See, for example, Shilpa Grover *et al.*, "Physician Assessment of Family Cancer History and Referral for Genetic Evaluation in Colorectal Cancer Patients" (2004) 2 Clinical Gastroenterology and Hepatology 813.

67 Trudo Lemmens and Lisa Austin, "The End of Individual Control over Health Information: Governing Biobanks and Promoting Fair Information Practices," in *Principles and Practice in Biobanks Governance*, ed. Jane Kaye & Mark Stranger (Farnham: Ashgate, 2009), 243.

68 For example, ongoing collection, use, and disclosure may threaten the privacy of donors, those undergoing assisted human reproduction procedures, and donor-conceived offspring: Vanessa Gruben, "Assisted Reproduction without Assisting Over-Collection: Fair Information Practices and the Assisted Human Reproduction Agency of Canada" (2009) 17 Health LJ 229.

69 A.J. Turner and A. Coyle, *supra* note 58; A. Brewaeys *et al.*, "Donor Insemination: Child Development and Family Functioning in Lesbian Mother Families" (1997) 12:6 Hum Reprod 1349; Jadva *et al.*, *supra* note 33; Daniels, *supra* note 30; A. Lalos *et al.*, "Recruitment and Motivation of Semen Providers in Sweden" (2003) 18:1 Hum Reprod 212; K. Vanfraussen, I. Ponajert-Kirstoffersen, and A. Brewaeys, "Why Do Children Want to Know More about the Donor? The Experience of Youngsters Raised in Lesbian Families" (2003) 24 Journal of Psychosom Obstet and Gynecol 31; F. Shenfield and S.J. Steele, "What Are the Effects of Anonymity and Secrecy on the Welfare of the Child in Gamete Donation?" (1997) 12:2 Hum Reprod 392.

70 Turner and Coyle, *ibid* at 2045.

71 *Ibid* at 2044–5.

72 *Pratten*, *supra* note 4 at para 111.

73 A. Lalos *et al.*, "Legislated Right for Donor-Insemination Children to Know Their Genetic Origin: A Study of Parental Thinking" (2007) 22:6 Hum Reprod 1759 at 1766. Secrecy is not an issue in lesbian-led families because of the absence of a male partner. Numerous studies indicate that many heterosexual couples intend to keep the use of donated sperm secret, although more and more couples plan to disclose the use of donated sperm to their offspring: Brewaeys, *supra* note 69 at 1357. In this study all lesbian mothers except one had already told their children that a sperm donor was used by the time the child was between four and eight years old. Of the heterosexual parents, only 8 out of 38 had the intention of telling, and only one had. Later studies indicate a greater tendency towards openness: Jadva *et al.*, *supra* note 33. See also D.R. Beeson *et al.*, "Offspring Searching for Sperm Donors: How Family Type Shapes the Process" (2011) 26:9 Hum Reprod 2415; Rikke Rosholm *et al.*, "Disclosure Patterns of Mode of Conception among Mothers and Fathers: 5 Year Follow-Up of the Copenhagen Multi-centre Psychsocial Infertility (COMPI) Cohort" (2010) 25:8 Hum Reprod 2006.

74 Pasquale Patrizio, Anna C. Mastroianni, and Luigi Mastroianni, "Disclosure to Children Conceived with Donor Gametes Should Be Optional" (2001) 16:10 Hum Reprod 2036 at 2037 [Patrizio *et al.*]. See also McGee *et al.*, *supra* note 5.

75 Although there has been some discussion of this possibility: Cowden, *supra* note 5.
76 See the chapter by Jeanne Snelling in this volume.
77 *Assisted Reproductive Treatment Further Amendment Act 2014*. The Victoria government is currently considering additional reform that would remove the consent provision and replace it with a contact veto: http://docs2.health.vic.gov.au/docs/doc/A-Right-to-Know.
78 The right to privacy is also protected in international law by virtue of article 12 of the *Universal Declaration of Human Rights*, GA Res 271 (III), UNGAOR, 3d Sess., Supp. No. 13, UN Doc A/810 (1948) 71 and article 17 of the *International Covenant on Civil and Political Rights*, 19 December 1966, 999 UNTS 171.
79 An exhaustive examination of the extensive jurisprudence on privacy is beyond the scope of this article.
80 *Hunter v Southam*, [1984] 2 SCR 145, 11 DLR (4th) 641. The Court has recognized three zones of privacy: rights involving territorial or spatial aspects, rights related to the person, and rights that arise in the information context. This paper is concerned with the latter: *R v Dyment*, [1988] 2 SCR 417 at 428–9, 55 DLR (4th) 503 [*Dyment*]; *R v Tessling*, 2004 SCC 67, [2004] 3 SCR 432 at paras 19–23 [*Tessling*]. The Court in *Tessling* at para 23, citing Alan F Westin, *Privacy and Freedom* (New York: Atheneum, 1970) at 7, stated: "Informational privacy has been defined as 'the claim of individuals, groups or institutions to determine for themselves when, how, and to what extent information about them is communicated to others.' Its protection is predicated on the assumption that all information about a person is in a fundamental way his own, for him to communicate or retain … as he sees fit."
81 *R v Duarte*, [1990] 1 SCR 30 at 46, 65 DLR (4th) 240.
82 *Dyment*, *supra* note 80 at 427.
83 *R v O'Connor*, [1995] 4 SCR 411 at para 114, 130 DLR (4th) 235.
84 *R v Malmo-Levine*, 2003 SCC 74, [2003] 3 SCR 571 at para 85.
85 *Personal Information Protection and Electronic Documents Act*, SC 2000, c 5 [*PIPEDA*], *Privacy Act*, RSC 1985, c P-21. In Ontario see *Personal Health Information Protection Act, 2004*, SO 2004, c 3 [*PHIPA*], *Freedom of Information and Protection of Privacy Act*, RSO 1990, c F.31; *Municipal Freedom of Information and Protection of Privacy Act*, RSO 1990, c M.56; *Consumer Reporting Act*, RSO 1990, c C.33.
86 *Jones v Tsige*, 2012 ONCA 32, 108 OR (3d) 241. In addition, British Columbia, Manitoba, Newfoundland, and Saskatchewan have created a statutory tort of invasion of privacy: *Privacy Act*, RSBC 1996, c 373; *Privacy*

Act, RSM 1987, c P125; *Privacy Act*, RSS 1978, c P-24; and *Privacy Act*, RSN 1990, c P-22. Furthermore, the right to privacy is explicitly protected by section 5 of the *Charter of Human Rights and Freedoms*, RSQ c C-12.

87 *HJ Heinz Co of Canada Ltd v Canada (Attorney General)*, [2006] 1 SCR 441, 2006 SCC 13 at para 26.

88 In Ontario, see, for example, *PHIPA*, *supra* note 85.

89 Regarding the unwanted intrusion of the sperm donor, see Cameron, Gruben, and Kelly, *supra* note 19; and regarding the supply concern, see Turkmendag *et al.*, *supra* note 1.

90 *Pratten*, *supra* note 4 at para 204, citing the Adoption Council.

91 Patrizio *et al.*, *supra* note 74.

92 *Ibid*.

93 *Cheskes v Ontario (Attorney General)* (2007), 87 OR (3d) 581, 288 DLR (4th) 449 (SC) [*Cheskes*]; *Pringle v Alberta (Human Rights, Multiculturalism and Citizenship Commission)*, 2004 ABQB 821, 372 AR 154 [*Pringle*].

94 *Cheskes*, *ibid* at para 61.

95 *Ibid*.

96 *Ibid* at para 95. See also *R v WDD* (1997), 114 CCC (3d) 506, 90 BCAC 191 [*WDD*].

97 *Cheskes*, *ibid* at para 132.

98 *Pringle*, *supra* note 93 at para 58.

99 See, for example, *Cheskes*, *supra* note 93, *Pringle*, *supra* note 93, and *Marchand v Ontario*, 2007 ONCA 787, 88 OR (3d) 600, leave to appeal to SCC refused, [2008] SCCA No 37, aff'g *Marchand v Ontario* (2006), 81 OR (3d) 172 (SC), 142 CRR (2d) 25 [*Marchand*]. See also the decisions of various privacy commissioners: *Re British Columbia (Ministry of Children and Family Development)* (11 November 2004) 04–35, Office of the Information and Privacy Commissioner for British Columbia, https://www.oipc.bc.ca/orders/889 ; *Re British Columbia* (*Ministry of Children and Family Development*) (5 July 2005) F05–20, Office of the Information and Privacy Commissioner for British Columbia, https://www.oipc.bc.ca/orders/866.

100 *Marchand* (SC), *ibid* at para 111.

101 *Ibid* at paras 117–21.

102 *Marchand* (CA), *supra* note 99 at para 12. Note that the Ontario Court of Appeal did not comment on the nature and scope of the liberty or security interests: para 12.

103 *Cheskes*, *supra* note 93 at para 28.

104 Ruth Sullivan, *Sullivan on the Construction of Statutes* (Markham: Lexis Nexis, 2008) at 670.

105 *Gustavson Drilling (1964) Ltd v MNR*, [1977] 1 SCR 271, 66 DLR (3d) 449; [*Gustavson Drilling*]. See also E.A. Driedger, "Statutes: Retroactive Retrospective Reflections" (1978) 56 Can Bar Rev 264.
106 *Benner v Canada*, [1997] 1 SCR 358 at paras 39–40, 143 DLR (4th) 577.
107 See, for example, *Kalin v Ontario College of Teachers* (2005), 75 OR (3d) 523, 254 DLR (4th) 503 (Div Ct).
108 Sullivan, *supra* note 103 at 667.
109 Sullivan, *ibid* at 668.
110 *Gustavson Drilling*, *supra* note 104.
111 Sullivan, *supra* note 104 at 689.
112 *British Columbia v Imperial Tobacco Ltd*, 2005 SCC 49, [2005] 2 SCR 473 at para 69.
113 *Ibid*.
114 *Charter*, *supra* note 6. These sections provide:

11. Any person charged with an offence has the right
    (g) not to be found guilty on account of any act or omission unless, at the time of the act or omission, it constituted an offence under Canadian or international law or was criminal according to the general principles of law recognized by the community of nations;
    ...
    (i) if found guilty of the offence and if the punishment for the offence has been varied between the time of commission and the time of sentencing, to the benefit of the lesser punishment.

115 If the court recognizes a constitutional right to know one's genetic origins, it will need to address whether retroactive or retrospective legislation will be required to give effect to this right. It is difficult to say whether such a law would be considered retrospective or retroactive. If the sperm donation is considered to be a past situation whose legal consequences are fixed at the time of donation, a law that requires that his identity be disclosed changes the past legal effect, anonymity, of a past situation, donation. In other words, the law is deemed to be different than what it actually was when the facts occurred (retroactive). If, on the other hand, the act of donating sperm is seen as an ongoing situation because the genetic relationship between donor and offspring continues after the time of donation, a law that now requires the disclosure of identifying information about the donor could be seen as a law that changes the future effect, knowing the identity of one's biological progenitor, of a past situation, donation (retrospective).
116 See, for example, *Christie*, *supra* note 47 at paras 13–14, where the court refused to recognize that the rule of law includes a right to legal assistance in all proceedings.

117 See *supra* note 23.
118 See *supra* note 99.
119 British Columbia's *Vital Statistics Act*, RSBC 1996, c 479, s 3(1)(b) authorizes a biological mother to submit a statement of live birth on her own and to choose whether to acknowledge the father.
120 Lauren Taub, "Major Privacy Concerns When Minor Sues for Paternity" (2008) 26 Wash UJL & Pol'y 459 at 476–78. Indeed, in *WDD*, *supra* note 95, the British Columbia Court of Appeal refused to order a paternity test where the accused was defending himself against criminal charges of rape and incest for the reason that it was not in the best interests of the child to be informed of the potential circumstances of her conception or the identity of her biological father.
121 A number of feminists have harshly criticized the Supreme Court of Canada's decision in *Trociuk v British Columbia (AG)*, 2003 SCC 34, [2003] 1 SCR 835, including Emily F Carasco, "What's in a Name? Whose Name Is It Anyway? A Comment on Trociuk v. B.C." (2004) 37 UBC L Rev 259. See also Taub, *ibid*, who emphasizes the importance of a mother's privacy where her offspring is seeking the identity of his or her biological father.
122 Wanda Wiegers, "Fatherhood and Misattributed Genetic Paternity in Family Law" (2011) 36 Queen's LJ 623 at 625.
123 Carolyn Abraham, "Mommy's Little Secret," *Globe and Mail*, 14 December 2004, F1, Canadian Children's Rights Council, http://canadiancrc.com/Newspaper_Articles/Globe_and_Mail_Moms_Little_secret_14DEC02.aspx.
124 In Ontario, the Court may make an order for blood or DNA testing to determine paternity but a party is not required to undergo the test: *Children's Law Reform Act*, RSO 1990, c C-12, s 10. See, for example, *Silber v Fenske* (1995), 11 RFL (4th) 145, [1995] OJ No 418 (QL) (Gen Div), where the Court found that sections 7 and 8 of the *Charter* were not violated because the *CLRA* did not force an individual to give a blood sample; rather it only allowed the court to draw an adverse inference about the party who refuses to participate in the testing. See also *TW v JC*, [2000] OJ No 5646 (QL).
125 Section 2(2) of the *Divorce Act*, RSC 1985, c 3. See also s 1(1) of Ontario's *Family Law Act*, RSO 1990, c F-3.
126 *P(GN) v G (LA)*, 2001 NSSC 165, 198 NSR (2d) 175 (SC).
127 Abraham, *supra* note 123.
128 See, generally, Gillian Nycum, Bartha Marie Knoppers, and Denise Avard, "Intra-Familial Obligations to Communicate Genetic Risk Information: What Foundations? What Forms?" (2009) 3 McGill JL & Health 21.
129 In Ontario see *PHIPA*, *supra* note 85.

8 The Priority of the Health and Well-Being of Offspring: The Challenge of Canadian Provincial and Territorial Adoption Disclosure Law to Anonymity in Gamete and Embryo Provision ("Donor" Conception)

JULIET R. GUICHON

1. Introduction

The Supreme Court of Canada rendered its opinion[1] in December 2010 that much of the *Assisted Human Reproduction Act* (*AHRA*)[2] is *ultra vires* the Government of Canada. This opinion makes clear that an important and contentious legislative issue is within the jurisdiction of the provincial and territorial governments. That issue is whether statutes should grant people born through the application of assisted human reproductive technologies the right and opportunity to know (1) the fact that they have been conceived with the gametes of people who are not their rearing parents, and (2) the identity and medical, social and cultural history of their progenitors.

An important section of the *AHRA* remains in force and states what is to be the highest value:[3]

> 2. The Parliament of Canada recognizes and declares that
> (*a*) the health and well-being of children born through the application of assisted human reproductive technologies must be given priority in all decisions respecting their use[.]

This chapter aims specifically to address the health and well-being interests of people conceived by provider gametes ("Offspring").[4] It addresses the concepts of secrecy and anonymity in the context of gamete provision, discusses some of the health and well-being effects these practices have on the resulting people, and considers how the need for people to know the identity and social, cultural, and medical history of their progenitor is protected for a relevantly similar group, adoptees. The chapter compares disclosure rights offered to adoptees with those of Offspring, calls for an end to secrecy and anonymity in the practice of gamete provision, and proposes that legislation be created in provinces and territories, even to address cases where Canadians purchase gametes and embryos from other nations.

2. The Twin Problems of Secrecy and Anonymity

The practice of gamete provision has been characterized by two accompanying practices. The first has been secrecy. For the purposes of this chapter, "secrecy" is the decision made by a number of actors, including the people who rear the resulting child, not to tell the child about the fact of third-party gamete use in the child's conception. "Anonymity" is the decision either not to create records about the identity (including social, cultural, and medical history) of the third-party gamete provider, or not to release such records to the gamete provider's Offspring. The problems of secrecy and anonymity can be conflated. The right of information access is contingent upon the protection of the right to know about the unusual conception.[5]

The significance of secrecy and anonymity to Offspring can perhaps be best understood by reference to anecdotes. Stories of how individuals felt upon learning the truth about their conception and about wishing to know the identity of their progenitor communicate the significance of these practices for the individual and the emotions to which they can give rise. It is not known whether any particular person's experience is representative. The anecdotes used in this chapter, from a variety of sources, are chosen to illustrate the reactions that secrecy and anonymity can elicit.

In cases where the gamete recipient is single or in a homosexual relationship, secrecy about the conception is not typically the norm. Yet research suggests that, among heterosexual couples, most parents do not tell their children the truth about how they used provider gametes in their conception.[6] In other words, secrecy regarding the use of provider gametes is often practised.

Some Offspring have reported that the effects of secrecy are significant. For example, when the secrecy ended for a thirteen-year-old Canadian girl, she was angry and heartbroken. She writes:

> I nodded and walked far enough ahead that you wouldn't think I was with them. I'M ARTIFICIALLY INSEMINATED??? ONE PART OF ME IS WORTH 20 BUCKS? THAT'S ALL?? THIS "DAD" OF MINE IS NOT ACTUALLY HIM. WELL WHO IS HE? SOME RANDOM GUY THAT JUST MOVED IN THE FAMILY! WHO IS HE? GET OUT OF MY LIFE! GO AWAY! YOU'RE PROBABLY JUST SOME STALKER IN MY LIFE. WHERE'S MY REAL DAD? WHERE IS HE? I CAN'T MEET HIM ... I can't meet him ... I can't know him ... [...] We got back to the hotel and I hid under my covers, tears streaming down my cheeks.[7]

Offspring who learn in adulthood that they were conceived with provider gametes have described their identity fragmenting, being the victim of a lie, and having been deprived of an honest relationship with the social father. Alison Davenport, an Offspring in the United Kingdom, wrote:

> I found the news of my conception shocking ... [I]n a single moment, I felt that I had lost 50% of my understanding of myself and where I came from. My sense of self was disintegrated as a result.[8]

British barrister David Gollancz states that secrecy is the perpetration of falsehood, which has profound harmful personal effects:

> [F]or the donor-conceived, their story is a lie. When my father told me the truth back in 1965, I felt as though someone was standing in front of me, tearing up my autobiography page by page ... [T]he sentimentalists say, "But of course you are entitled to your name, of course the culture and background of your paternal family belongs to you" – and of course they are not entirely wrong; those things can be claimed [...] but it is not the same. Being entitled to choose to claim a family heritage is not the same as simply owning it.[9]

Some Offspring have expressed strong feelings that the anonymity of their gamete provider is not in their health and well-being interests. For example, a twelve-year-old girl writes:

> The amount of information that I know about my sperm donor is very limited. I've always been looking for answers that aren't available to me. The curiosity is always there, as to who my sperm donor is. As I walk down the street, I could be walking past him. I could have a dozen half-siblings that I don't even know about. And, I will probably never know, because a sperm donor's identity is kept confidential.[10]

An Australian adult, Damien Adams, argues that the problem of anonymity grows over time and takes new shape when one becomes a parent:

> As I became an adult, more questions came up all the time [...] These inquiries cumulated with the epiphany I had when my own children were born [...] I was missing the ground that nearly everyone else has: a heritage, a connection with the past, a connection with kinfolk and my lineage. It was about family and what makes the family unit so special and unique to human kind. It is not something that is just missing from my own life; it is something that is now missing from my children's as well. The disconnection that I have experienced continues into the next generation. My children too will miss out on kinship, heritage, culture, biological identity based on genetic background, and a family medical history.[11]

In anecdotal comments, Offspring often do not hold parents as accountable for secrecy and anonymity as they do physicians and the state. As the practice becomes increasingly commercialized, it is unclear whom future Offspring will hold responsible. Offspring, especially adult Offspring, can articulate an understanding of their parents' motivations, particularly when a physician instructed the parent to practise secrecy and imposed anonymity. As David Gollancz writes:

> There are a number of reasons why parents lie to their children about the circumstances of their births: people want to believe that their infertility problem has been cured – that they are the family they would have been without infertility. Acknowledging the donor as a real person makes that more difficult. Infertile parents, particularly men, often feel profound shame and grief about their inability to beget their own children; again, denying that the donor exists may make it easier to avoid those painful feelings. My own father, and others I have known, have been afraid that

if the truth were revealed, their children would not love them. And our understanding of the real importance of genetics in both physical health and personal development is extremely recent and still growing. Until relatively recently, sperm was seen as just fertiliser, rather than what it really is: the carrier of DNA, the book in which half the recipe for a new human being is written.[12]

Likewise, architect Bill Cordray writes sympathetically about his parents, who

were instructed [by the physician] not only to hide the truth from me but also never to seek to learn the identity of my genetic father. The gynaecologist even required them to sign a document to this effect, causing them to believe that they were contractually bound. Although my parents complied with the doctor's stipulations, it would be wrong to say that they freely consented; their emotions and social isolation put them in a very weak bargaining position.[13]

But, even as some Offspring forgive their parents, they can believe that actors other than parents must change their behaviour to eliminate secrecy and anonymity. The thirteen-year-old girl writes:

I would appreciate if the government gave me permission to meet my birth father and not be against it. As I said, my father was the one to tell me I was artificially inseminated so he has no problem with the fact that he is not my birth father, sometimes he says he even forgets that we aren't blood related, but to him it doesn't matter. If I could wave a magic wand, and change the law any way I wanted, I would allow permission to meet my birth father [...] I wish I could meet my birth daddy.[14]

More forcefully, David Gollancz argues that, while the parents' actions might be understandable, the state's actions are inexcusable:

[T]he state should not be party to such deceptions: the birth certificate of the donor-conceived person is a state fraud and that is wrong. [...] I think everyone has the right not to be deliberately deceived, or deprived of significant information, about their essential personal history. In other words, our stories are ours, among our most precious goods, and while we cannot prevent individuals from lying to us, the state must not connive.[15]

3. Health Science Research

The themes identified in anecdotal comments by Offspring are corroborated by health scientists as being significant or potentially significant to Offspring health and well-being. Such research, published elsewhere, was commissioned to provide an analysis of research then extant in the disciplines of health and social sciences; and to summarize the clinical knowledge of two practitioners in the domains of psychology and genetics.[16] The question each addressed was, "Is secrecy regarding the fact of donor conception and gamete provider anonymity in the health and well-being interests of Offspring?" The varying answers to this question are discussed here.

3.1 Research Regarding Psychosocial Outcomes

There is disagreement among researchers over whether the available data are sufficient to know outcomes. Health scientists Ben Gibbard and Stacey Page each argue that the psychosocial outcome data are preliminary. Ben Gibbard, a paediatrician specializing in the development of children, reviewed the medical literature to assess whether it is in the best interests of Offspring to know about their conception in terms of psychosocial outcomes.[17] Gibbard found that the current psychosocial outcome research focuses only on those who know they were conceived by provider gametes, and the research explores only their emotional reactions. Gibbard argues that, to know the effect of disclosure status on how Offspring develop, one must understand whether Offspring differ according to whether they are the subjects of secrecy or not, and whether they benefit from disclosure depending upon the age at which the secrecy ended. Moreover, Gibbard states that research should analyse all variables that affect psychosocial development when assessing the outcomes for Offspring. He proposes that future qualitative and quantitative research should review the details of risk and adaptation regarding individual, family, community, and cultural variables because these together create positive and negative psychosocial outcomes for Offspring. He recommends that future research explore family therapy and adoption literature concerning whether disclosure is indeed best from the perspectives of both the outcome for the child and family dynamics.[18]

Page conducted a review of studies on psychosocial outcomes for Offspring and concluded that the influence of being conceived with provider sperm cannot be fully understood in contexts where secrecy is prevalent.[19] The existing research has been conducted on families in which the children tend not to know about their conception with provider gametes. She reports that it is difficult to generalize the information generated by the studies because they have small sample sizes, they repeatedly observe the same groups, and the research has depended on what is probably only a subset of rearing parents: those who are willing to participate and who endorse the practice of donor conception. Many of these rearing parents maintain secrecy. This fact raises research ethics challenges. The children are not told that the purpose of the study is to learn whether they have been affected by donor conception, yet current research ethics norms require that research be of benefit[20] to the child and that a child of sufficient maturity be asked to assent to the research.[21, 22] Assent requires full information. Moreover, the research has tended to focus on discerning the views of the social parents in preference to those of the Offspring. Page concludes that researchers will be able to gain a more complete understanding of the consequences of being conceived with provider gametes only once Offspring are informed of their origins and able to provide their own opinions.

In contrast to Gibbard and Page, Jean Benward claims that we have sufficient information to conclude that secrecy and anonymity are harmful to Offspring. Benward, a licensed clinical social worker who counsels Offspring and their families, argues that it is now possible to reach a conclusion.[23] She states that secrecy and anonymity are both harmful because they impede the important task of identity development. Identity formation is a universal and vital task of human development by which each person finds answers to essential questions such as "Who am I?" and "How am I like or different from others in appearance, traits, personality, and talents?" Benward holds that secrecy regarding one's conception is not beneficial to Offspring identity development; she claims that, in fact, early disclosure is almost certainly best because it supports identity development as the child grows. Moreover, early disclosure avoids the pain and disruption of deconstructing and reconstructing one's identity as an adult. Anonymity is not beneficial to Offspring because, according to Benward, individuals can form their identities better when they can see genetic resemblance in relatives, hear family members engage in resemblance talk (e.g., "You look just like your great aunt!"), and understand where they fit with respect to the generations that preceded and will succeed them. Benward laments the historical and institutional forces that have fostered secrecy; lack of creation, preservation, and transmission of information about providers; and lack of access to gamete providers by their Offspring. Benward argues that gamete provision is now understood to have ongoing psychological meaning in the lives of Offspring, with long-term effects. Benward states that all parties associated with gamete provision ought to understand the importance of family and kinship connections, and those families who use provider gametes must respect the complexity of their children's relationships.[24]

3.2 Research Regarding Outcomes in Genetic Counselling

Medical geneticist Julie Lauzon concludes that neither secrecy nor anonymity is in the health and well-being interests of Offspring from the perspective of clinical genetics.

Lauzon argues that secrecy about the truth of one's genetic parents can cause individuals falsely to believe that the genetic history of a non-biological parent is their own genetic history.[25] False family history can lead to misdiagnosis of a genetic condition and perhaps to screening for a condition for which the individual is not at risk.

Lauzon argues also that anonymity denies patients access to one half of their family medical history and thus prevents them from fully benefiting from early detection of disease, improved treatment, and optimal health promotion with targeted prevention and screening strategies. For example, if the gamete provider has a serious condition of which the Offspring is unaware, then the Offspring will not be in a position to tell a family doctor about his or her progenitor's condition and thereby to benefit from screening and treatment at a young age.[26] Moreover, anonymity can lead to unwitting incest and its negative effects for resulting children. Anonymity can harm gamete providers as well, because a child who develops symptoms of a genetically transmitted condition can reveal that one of the biological parents also has the genetic condition. Such vital information can be communicated only if the provider and Offspring can be linked through records and knowledge of each other. Lauzon cites the case of a twenty-three-year-old man who was found to have a serious genetic heart condition called "hypertrophic cardiomyopathy" (HCM) after one of his donor Offspring was diagnosed with HCM.[27] According to Lauzon, "[w]hile donors and others who participate in conceiving a child have a general right to privacy, [these] adults [...] ought to be informed of the importance to the child of their family history and understand that the child has a moral right to it. Ultimately, the first duty of adults who bring a child into being is to the health of the child."

4. Findings of Fact in the British Columbia Supreme Court Case

The issues addressed by the health science and medical researchers described above have been judicially considered in a case of first impression in British Columbia, *Olivia Pratten v Attorney General of British Columbia and College of Physicians and Surgeons of British Columbia*.[28, 29] Olivia Pratten, who was conceived from provider sperm, argued that Offspring have constitutional rights to the creation, preservation, and disclosure of records of their genetic parents and that these rights were being denied by the Government of British Columbia and its delegate, the College of Physicians and Surgeons of British Columbia.

The Court ruled that the British Columbia *Adoption Act*[30] and *Adoption Regulation*[31] were discriminatory, contrary to s. 15 of the *Canadian Charter of Rights and Freedoms*[32] (the *Charter*).[33, 34] The Court's important findings included these, paraphrased as follows:

1. Like adoptees, Offspring need social, psychological and medical information about biological parents. Even if well intentioned, serious harm can be caused by cutting off a child from his or her biological roots.[35]
2. The circumstances of donor Offspring affecting their physical and psychological health are too important to leave unregulated. This would not be tolerated in the area of adoption, where there is a strong commitment to identifying and then, through legislation, facilitating measures considered to be in the best interests of children.[36]
3. The private sector, which now collects more information from gamete providers than it did in the past, cannot be an adequate substitute for government protection and regulation. Private sector practices cannot be a full answer to the circumstances of donor Offspring. It is unreasonable to say that donor Offspring should be content to rely on those practices in matters fundamental to their health and well-being. The suggestion reflects stereotypical thinking about donor Offspring.[37]

4. Based on the whole of the evidence, assisted reproduction using an anonymous gamete donor is harmful to the child, and it is not in the best interests of donor Offspring.[38]
5. As with adoption legislation, the primary legislative response needs to come from provincial legislatures, not Parliament.[39]

The British Columbia Court of Appeal overturned the lower court decision and ruled that the *Adoption Act* does not violate s. 15. Stating that the *Adoption Act* qualifies as an ameliorative program within the meaning of s. 15(2), the court held that "it is open to the Legislature to provide adoptees with the means of accessing information about their biological origins without being obligated to provide comparable benefits to other persons seeking such information."[40] The court held further that there was no right to know one's origins protected by s. 7 of the Charter.[41] The Court of Appeal permitted the Attorney General's appeal and dismissed Ms Pratten's cross-appeal.[42] Olivia Pratten was denied leave to appeal by the Supreme Court of Canada.[43]

5. Canadian Legislative Response Regarding Release of Identifying Information in Adoption Records

The Canadian legislative response regarding adoption records is important to consider because, this chapter argues, Offspring and adoptees are similarly situated. This was the finding of the first instance *Pratten* decision, a finding not overturned on appeal. Madame Justice Adair held that "donor offspring, alienated from the donor, suffer harm similar and comparable to that suffered by adoptees."[44] She stated that "[b]oth groups express a strong need to know their birth origins, for reasons that include completing their sense of identity, obtaining valuable and necessary information relevant to their health and to help them avoid intimate relationships with close genetic relatives. The Adoption Counsel [sic] of Canada has acknowledged similarities between adoptees and donor offspring, in areas relevant to Ms. Pratten's claims, as did the Royal Commission."[45]

To the extent that there are differences between the practice of adoption and of gamete provision, these differences are relevant to the preferences of adults and not to the needs of resulting children. Adoption is a practice that addresses the need to find a home for a child who is either born or about to be born. Gamete provision assists in the creation of a child for the benefit of an adult or adults. Because the justifications for the two practices are different, some might argue that the practices are different in important ways. From the resulting child's perspective, however, there is no material difference regarding the need and desire to know one's origins; in fact, there are many similarities.

These similarities include the following: separation from the biological family; potentially a strong feeling of loss associated with the separation and disconnection; the dissociation from progenitors' family, including half-siblings, grandparents, aunts, uncles, and cousins; and a common inability to trace one's lineage.[46] Consequently, some offspring, like adoptees, suffer from genealogical bewilderment, difficulty in constructing identity, and lack of a complete medical history. Like adoptees, many Offspring have not traditionally been encouraged to accept and address the feelings of grief associated with these losses, and as a consequence, they suffer disenfranchised grief.[47]

The *Pratten* decision accepted the relevant similarities of gamete provision and adoption. Given the first instance decision's suggestion that provincial and territorial adoption disclosure might be a template for the creation, preservation, and disclosure of gamete provider information to Offspring, this section describes that legislation and its focus on the interests of the child. These legislative attributes could also characterize legislation on gamete provision.

Each provincial and territorial adoption regime announces that the paramount consideration of its adoption legislation is the "best interests of the child."[48] There is a marked legislative trend towards ensuring that records are open to parties in future adoptions. Nevertheless, no province provides adult adoptees an unfettered right to know the identity of their birth parents.[49] In this chapter, the range of provincial and territorial adoption disclosure legislation is discussed in order of most government and individual restrictions on disclosure to least restrictions on disclosure. The information disclosed is that typically recorded by birth mothers on a Vital Statistics long form birth registration and that collected and recorded typically by social workers in discussion with birth mothers and the adoptees' other family members.

5.1 Release of Non-Identifying Information

Non-identifying information is typically social, cultural, and medical information provided by one or more genetic parents before the adoption and placed in the adoption file. The practice in Canada is to require[50] or to request[51] that parents give such information about themselves before placing a child for adoption. For example, in Prince Edward Island, the *Adoption Act* states that "[a]ny person placing a child shall provide in writing to the person receiving the child a summary of non-identifying information concerning the background and circumstances of the child including cultural heritage, medical history, family history as it might affect the child's rearing, reasons for the placement, and such other information as may be prescribed in the regulations."[52]

British Columbia specifies in great detail the kind of information that is to be obtained and requires that the person placing the child for adoption provide as much information as is practicable.[53] The value of non-identifying information is perhaps most clear when the information is medical and the consequences of withholding medical and social background information from adoptive parents proves serious.[54]

Such information held by government in the adoption file can be very important to the adoptee, but it can become dated. In some provinces, the government representative can ask parties who refuse permission to disclose identifying information or to permit contact if they will nevertheless provide current medical, social, and cultural information about themselves.[55] The government official is obligated to give any information thus provided to the adoptee.[56]

This non-identifying medical, social, or cultural information is available in all provinces and territories to adoptees at the age of majority or shortly thereafter[57] (or earlier with permission of their adoptive parents[58]) and at the age of fourteen in Quebec.[59]

In cases of medical severity or to address the health, safety, or welfare of the child, Saskatchewan,[60] Ontario,[61] Quebec,[62] New Brunswick,[63] Prince Edward Island,[64] Newfoundland and Labrador,[65] the Northwest Territories,[66] and Nunavut[67] have specific statutory provisions to permit access to adoption records. In British Columbia, the Director may actually contact the adoptee, the birth parent(s), or a relative of a birth parent for such information.[68] Other jurisdictions would probably entertain court applications for access in the interests of the child.

5.2 Release of Identifying Information

Even though non-identifying information is relatively easy for adoptees to obtain, it is often not enough to satisfy them. According to the Ontario Superior Court of Justice, most adoptees want to know their birth parents' names and even to make contact with them.[69] Adoptees seek identifying information often because of the "extraordinary level of grief, anxiety, and stress" caused by their "lack [of] personal and family information."[70] Studies of search motives among adoptees state the following reasons most frequently: [T]hey were curious about their genealogical background; they wanted medical history; they wanted to answer the question, 'who do I look like?' [;] they wanted more detailed information about their 'roots'; and they felt 'out of place' in their adoptive family."[71]

For medical practitioners' purposes, non-identifying information can be insufficient.[72]

Canadian jurisdictions have adopted a range of models for the release of identifying information from registries. These can involve explicit consent and/or vetoes and often take a different approach to past and future adoptions.

In response to what an Ontario court has termed a "compelling and heartfelt"[73] desire of adopted adults and biological parents for more openness in adoption, each Canadian provincial and territorial legislature has created a registry that releases identifying information with the mutual consent of the parties.[74] The opportunity afforded by mutual consent registries appears popular. For example, in Ontario by 2009, approximately 75,000 people had registered with Ontario's voluntary Adoption Disclosure Register, which was established in 1979.[75]

The most common and least intrusive legislative response is to create a mutual consent registry in which the government plays only a passive role. Yet passive registries, by definition, fail to give administrators the authority actively to assist a registrant; a person might wish to be found by a relative who is searching but might not know about the registry. Governments that are passive can impede the effective functioning of their mutual consent registry.[76]

Many Canadian provinces improve the effectiveness of their mutual consent registries by giving administrators authority to examine the adoption file to learn the name of the person sought; the administrator may then conduct a search and discreetly advise the person that a biologically related person is attempting to find him or her. The provinces and territories that grant an active role to administrators are British Columbia, Saskatchewan, Manitoba, Quebec, New Brunswick, Prince Edward Island, Newfoundland and Labrador, Yukon, the Northwest Territories, and Nunavut.[77] These jurisdictions have varying waiting times for searches to begin. In Nova Scotia, for example, searches are conducted generally on a first-come, first-served basis, although priority is given to medical emergencies and to cases where the birth parents are over sixty-five years of age.[78]

Even when administrators have the power to search, registries can be ineffective because adoptees might not know where they were born and, therefore, where they should register. A federal registry would circumvent this problem, but such a registry does not exist.

Moreover, mutual consent registries can be ineffective for searchers because the person searching may go away empty-handed. The relative might not have registered or might be unwilling to register if contacted by a government agent. What many adoptees want is to be treated similarly to non-adoptees. Non-adopted people may request and receive their birth certificates without the consent of their birth parents. Thus, whether government plays an active or passive role, mutual consent registries do not always meet the need for self-affirmation that many adoptees claim attaches to their freedom to receive an original birth certificate.[79]

Four provinces continue to maintain only a mutual consent registry: Quebec,[80] Nova Scotia, New Brunswick, and Prince Edward Island.[81]

Other jurisdictions have moved beyond a mutual consent system to consider how best to enable adoptees to receive their original birth certificate while still protecting the privacy expectations of birth parents.

Four provinces and one territory have, since 1990, amended their adoption information disclosure rules to make it easier for adoptees to receive identifying information. In BC,[82] Alberta,[83] Ontario,[84] Newfoundland and Labrador,[85] and Yukon,[86] adoptees may access as adults identifying information even on a retroactive basis, but subject to some constraints. Regarding an adoption finalized before the new legislation came into force, adoptees and birth parents may file "a written veto prohibiting the disclosure of a birth registration or other record."[87] They may also file a no-contact veto. This is notice by one party to the government adoption registrar "that he or she wishes not to be contacted" by the other party to the adoption.[88] A disclosure veto prohibits the Registrar of Adoptions (or equivalent official) from revealing identifying information.[89] A "no-contact veto" prohibits people from attempting to make contact with the person who files the veto on pain of a fine; in Ontario, the fine is up to $50,000 for an individual or $250,000 for a corporation.[90] Alberta has an unusual provision that allows *adoptive* parents to prevent the adult adoptee from accessing information about his or her biological parents.[91] In effect, this controversial legislation is government assistance to adoptive parents to maintain secrecy regarding the very fact that the person is adopted.

In each of these four provinces and in Yukon, no veto is permitted regarding adoptions that have occurred since the legislation came into effect.[92] These jurisdictions hold that the right to information should be superseded only where the State has created and encouraged a privacy expectation that is asserted by the relevant party. For adoptions that have taken place since the law came into effect, there cannot be an expectation of privacy: under an openness regime, parents know that their identities will be disclosed.

This system of open records allows adoptees to receive their original birth certificate provided that the parent has not actively opposed the transfer of information by filing a disclosure veto. This system is better than a registry alone because the adoptee will receive the information unless the birth parent actively prevents the release.

In Saskatchewan, the mutual consent registry was maintained for those adoptions that took place before the new adoption act.[93] In other words, disclosure of identifying information requires mutual consent if the adoption was finalized before 1 April 1997. If the adoption took place after 31 March 1997, then identifying information is available to an adoptee at the age of eighteen years six months,[94] so long as the birth parents have not filed a disclosure veto.[95]

The least restrictive means by which governments engage in disclosure is to release identifying information retroactively. The Ontario legislature attempted to pass such legislation but was ultimately unsuccessful.

In November 2005 the Ontario Legislative Assembly enacted the *Adoption Information Disclosure Act*.[96] This statute amended the *Vital Statistics Act* to permit birth parents and adopted children to apply for the release of adoption information that had previously been confidential. By this amendment, Ontario would have moved from a closed records system to a system that was almost completely open. Neither birth parents nor the adoptee could veto the disclosure of information. However, the government's Child and Family Services Review Board could receive applications for a "non-disclosure order"; it would grant such applications only if the Board was satisfied that "because of exceptional circumstances, the order is appropriate to prevent sexual harm or significant physical or emotional harm to [the adopted person or birth parent]."[97] This legislation came into effect on 17 September 2007.[98]

Two days later,[99] however, the Ontario Superior Court of Justice struck down the *Adoption Information Disclosure Act* and its amendments to the *Vital Statistics Act* relating to disclosure of information in adoption registries. In *Cheskes v Ontario (Attorney General)*,[100] Belobaba J stated that birth parents and adoptees can have a "privacy expectation" that is "a reasonable expectation that their adoption or birth registration information, absent health or safety reasons, would remain private and would not be disclosed without their permission."[101] The ruling seems to entail that the expectation may exist in the birth parent(s), the adopted parent(s), and even the adoptee (who would not usually have known of any government promises of privacy).[102] Justice Belobaba held that the legislation violated s. 7 of the *Charter*[103] in a manner inconsistent with the principles of fundamental justice and was not saved by s. 1.

Ontario did not appeal the decision[104] and instead passed regulations[105] that permitted birth parents and adopted children to receive birth and adoption records only once the time for filing a disclosure veto has elapsed. On 1 September 2008 the province enabled adopted adults and birth parents to file disclosure and contact vetoes if their adoption order was made before that date. After an eighteen-month period elapsed, adoptees and birth parents could begin to seek identifying information about each other as of 1 June 2009, provided that a veto had not been filed.[106]

Only about 1 per cent of eligible persons filed disclosure and no-contact vetoes: as of 1 May 2009, of a total of about 250,000 Ontario adoptions that had occurred since 1921, fewer than 2,500 people had filed vetoes.[107]

Even though Ontario's attempt to open records to adoptees and birth parents was struck down, two territories effectively have a system of retroactive release of identifying adoption information. Where an adoption was completed in the Northwest Territories or Nunavut prior to 1 November 1998,[108] transmission of identifying information generally requires consent, which the Registrar will attempt to obtain.[109] Yet territorial legislation waives the requirement of consent "if the person cannot be found after the search has continued for at least one year."[110] For adoptions completed after 31 October 1998, parties may receive original birth certificates as of right.

5.3 Conclusion

This section has demonstrated that adoptees across Canada have rights concerning the creation, updating, preservation, and disclosure of identifying and social, cultural, and medical information of their progenitors.

6. Law Regarding Disclosure of Information Regarding Genetic Parents in Gamete Provision in Canada

For people conceived by provider gametes, however, there is no effective government-regulated system in Canada – whether federal or provincial/territorial – that is similar to what is provided to adoptees.

The federal *AHRA*[111] contained provisions regarding information and created an agency, Assisted Human Reproduction Canada, to manage this information.[112] Gamete provider consent was necessary for the collection,[113] preservation,[114] and disclosure[115] of information concerning a gamete provider's identity, personal characteristics, genetic information, and medical history. A majority of the Supreme Court of Canada struck down, *inter alia*, these provisions.[116] The federal government announced the closure of Assisted Human Reproduction Canada by 31 March 2013.[117]

A second federal statute addresses the collection of identifying information about gamete providers. It concerns the providers of human semen only. Sections 12 and 13 of the regulations regarding semen[118] enacted under the *Food and Drugs Act*[119] require processors and distributors of human semen to create and operate a system that would enable a semen provider to be identified in order to track infectious disease. But there are no provisions to permit or to require semen processors and distributors to disclose that identifying information to the people conceived.

At the provincial and territorial level, no statutes or regulations stipulate what information, if any, a person conceived by gamete provision may receive about his or her genetic parent(s) who provided the reproductive material.

7. Comparison of Disclosure of Information Regarding Genetic Parents in Adoption and Gamete Provision in Canada

The preceding discussion of law in Canada related to records of adopted children and Offspring has revealed nine key points of comparison.

First, effective state regulation varies greatly between adopted children and Offspring. There is a marked difference in how governments regulate the collection and disclosure of information related to adoption and gamete provision. Adoption information is rigorously regulated by provinces and territories with the stated aim of focusing on the best interests of the child. By contrast, information about gamete provision has no effective regulation in Canada and is addressed – if at all – by physicians and commercial providers and distributors. These parties tend to be concerned about the best interests of the adult patient – and perhaps also with the interests of the fertility clinics and commercial operators themselves.

Second, the state has responded to changes in social mores regarding adoption but not to similar changes concerning gamete provision. Adoption originated in an atmosphere of stigma, shame, and secrecy, which has tended to dissipate.[120] So, too, has gamete provision.[121] But whereas in adoption, provincial and territorial governments have responded to adoptees who desire or need to know their genetic families, federal law created in 2004 to govern, *inter alia*, gamete provision does not appear to have accepted lessons learned in adoption about the need to know one's origins.

Third, the state takes a strong role in the collection and documentation of information to create accurate certificates of parentage for adopted children, but not for Offspring. The state creates and preserves information about the birth and the original parentage of an adopted child. These documents rely for their accuracy on the birth mother's willingness to reply truthfully and comprehensively, including in identifying the father. Social workers work to ensure the accuracy of the documents. For Offspring, however, no Canadian jurisdiction creates and preserves information regarding the identity of their biological parents.

Fourth, there is also significant contrast in the collection and creation of accurate social and cultural records. The biological parents of children to be adopted are typically requested or required to provide identifying and non-identifying information and social and cultural information to the agency that will be placing the child for adoption. No Canadian government currently requests or requires the transmission of such information about gamete providers, recipients, and Offspring to a government registry for preservation and disclosure to the Offspring.

Fifth, this contrast also applies to state collection and storage of medical information. In adoption, officials and agency workers seek comprehensive identifying and non-identifying medical information about birth parents. For Offspring, however, medical information of the gamete provider tends to be collected by commercial collectors and distributers, and while perhaps this information is given to the recipient, it may or may not be communicated to the Offspring.

Because governments permit anonymous gamete provision, the medical information that is initially provided can be very difficult to keep current. Moreover, no Canadian government verifies the accuracy of such information. This is an important consideration because gamete sellers have an incentive to falsify their medical history when telling the truth might cause them to be ineligible.

The sixth point relates to the disclosure of medical information in cases of medical severity. Provinces and territories permit adoptees in cases of medical severity to receive medical information about their birth parents upon request or court application. By contrast, there is no government collection of such information for Offspring.

The seventh point of contrast relates to mutual consent registries. Every provincial and territorial government funds and maintains a registry to help adoptees and birth parents exchange identifying information if they mutually consent. No Canadian government has created a mutual consent registry for gamete providers, recipients, and Offspring.

Eighth, there is marked contrast in the establishment of state search facilities. Some Canadian governments help adoptees or birth parents contact the other party by actively making discreet inquiries and telling that party about the registration so that the party can register to unite with the searching party. For Offspring, no government search service is available, let alone government officials who actively facilitate reunions.

Finally, Offspring have yet to achieve the prospective right to know, a right that has been provided to some adoptees. The trend in adoption legislation is to grant adoptees rights to all information that the state holds about them. Although Manitoba, Quebec, New Brunswick, and Prince Edward Island will disclose identifying information only with consent, the majority of provinces and territories (generally speaking[122]) will reveal information provided that the other party does not take an active step to oppose. By contrast, in gamete provision, there is no state recognition of Offsprings' right to know their origins.

It is clear that Offspring are disadvantaged, even though they are similar in relevant respects to adoptees. In the practice of gamete provision in Canada, there is no effective state regulation of the field; no state data collection to create non-identifying medical, social, and cultural information; no state creation of accurate records of parentage; no state method of contact in cases of medical necessity; no state mutual consent registry; no state search facility; no ability to know whether a proposed sexual partner is genetically related; and no opportunity in future gamete provisions for disclosure as of right.

8. Conclusion

Canada appears to have no effective legal mechanism by which Offspring may obtain the type of identifying and even non-identifying records of their progenitors that adoptees may receive. Commercial gamete provider agencies might collect and store such information, but these agencies tend to be in the United States, where there is no central registry and where compliance with professional guidelines regarding record keeping is voluntary.[123]

Whether the disparity in legal treatment of these similarly situated groups can be justified under s. 15 of the *Charter* is now a question for legislatures.[124] Such legislatures must ask, "Is it appropriate for reproductive physicians and commercial agencies to create in gamete providers an expectation of privacy that the state must protect – even if this protection harms the health and well-being of their genetic children?" Even if gamete providers are granted privacy protection by another country, what steps can our governments take to permit those who wish to be known to each other to reunite?

It is within the constitutional power of provincial and territorial legislatures to address the issues of secrecy and anonymity in gamete provision. Although these issues affect only a small percentage of the population, their effects on Offspring health and well-being are significant. Provincial and territorial governments can make it a requirement for fertility clinics to create, make current, preserve, and disclose accurate records of gamete provision and facilitate mutual consent registries and reunions, just as occurs in adoption. Canada has demonstrated in its semen regulations that it has the capacity to require records of foreign gamete providers to be created and preserved. Provincial and territorial legislators could collaborate with the federal government to ensure that such records form the basis of at least a mutual consent registry.[125]

Parliament's declaration that the health and well-being of Offspring be given priority; the provincial and territorial family statutes that give priority to the best interests of the child; and the findings of some research that the health and well-being of Offspring is negatively affected by secrecy and anonymity, ought to compel provincial and territorial legislators to consider why a growing number of Canadian children are not granted even the limited rights of adoptees to know their origins. As Offspring Barry Stevens claims, "I deserve the dignity of knowing the identity of the man whose body gave me life."[126]

NOTES

1 *Reference re Assisted Human Reproduction Act*, 2010 SCC 61, [2010] 3 SCR 457 [*AHRA Reference*].
2 *Assisted Human Reproduction Act*, SC 2004, c 2.
3 *Ibid*, s 2(a).
4 Every person is an offspring of his or her genetic parents. This paper uses a capital letter in "Offspring" to indicate that the individual, to whom the word refers, was conceived by gamete provision.
5 Lucy Frith, "Telling Is More Important Than Ever: Rights and Donor Conception," Comment, *BioNews* 542, 19 January 2010, http://www.bionews.org.uk/page_53094.asp.
6 Ken Daniels, "Donor Gametes: Anonymous or Identified?" (2007) 21:1 Clinical Obstetrics & Gynaecology 113–28.
7 J.S., "How I Learned the Truth and What Else I'd Like to Know," in *The Right to Know One's Origins: Assisted Human Reproduction and the Best Interests of Children*, ed. Juliet R. Guichon, Ian Mitchell, and Michelle Giroux (Brussels: Academic and Scientific Publishers, 2012), 38 at 39 ["Guichon, Mitchell, and Giroux," "J.S."].
8 Joseph J. Arvay, Alison M. Latimer, and Sean Hern, "Factum of the Applicant, Olivia Pratten" [Rule 9–7 Hearing: 25 October–5 November 2010, in *Olivia Pratten v Attorney General of British Columbia and College of Physicians and Surgeons of British Columbia*, in the Supreme Court of British Columbia [*Arvay Factum*].
9 David Gollancz, "Time to Stop Lying," *The Guardian*, 2 August 2007, http://www.theguardian.com/society/2007/aug/02/childrensservices.humanrights.
10 Naomi Williams (pseudonym for a twelve-year-old girl), "Everyone Is Here for a Reason," in Guichon, Mitchell, and Giroux, *supra* note 7, 36 at 36.
11 *Arvay Factum*, *supra* note 8 at para 40.
12 Gollancz, *supra* note 9.
13 Bill Cordray, "Does the Right to Know Matter?" in Guichon, Mitchell, and Giroux, *supra* note 7, 40 at 41.
14 JS, *supra* note 7 at 39.

15 Gollancz, *supra* note 9.
16 The research by Gibbard, Page, Benward, and Lauzon was commissioned by this author, funded by the Alberta Law Foundation, and published in Guichon, Mitchell, and Giroux, *supra* note 7. For a consideration of research on the psychological effect of gestational carriage agreements, see the chapter by Susan Drummond in this volume.
17 W. Ben Gibbard, "The Effect of Disclosure or Non-Disclosure on the Psychosocial Development of Donor-Conceived People: A Review and Synthesis of the Literature," in Guichon, Mitchell, and Giroux, *supra* note 7 at 151.
18 *Ibid*.
19 Stacey A. Page, "A Review of Studies That Have Considered Family Functioning and Psychosocial Outcomes for Donor-Conceived Offspring," in Guichon, Mitchell, and Giroux, *supra* note 7 at 124.
20 Canadian Institutes of Health Research, Natural Sciences and Engineering Research Council of Canada, and Social Sciences and Humanities Research Council of Canada, *Tri-Council Policy Statement: Ethical Conduct for Research Involving Humans* (2014), article 4.6, Panel on Research Ethics, http://www.pre.ethics.gc.ca/eng/policy-politique/initiatives/tcps2-eptc2/Default.
21 *Ibid*, article 3.10.
22 A significant contributor to research on outcomes for Offspring, Susan Golombok, acknowledged at a September 2011 Canadian Fertility and Andrology Society meeting in Toronto the importance of this ethical concern. She said it would be improper to continue to study the psychosocial outcomes for Offspring who do not know that their social parents are not also their biological parents. Professor Golombok stated that she would drop from her current study those members of the cohort whose parents engage in secrecy when they are next observed at age thirteen.
23 Jean Benward, "Identity Development in the Donor-Conceived," in Guichon, Mitchell, and Giroux, *supra* note 7 at 166.
24 *Ibid*.
25 Julie Lauzon, "The Health Benefits to Children of Having Their Genetic Information: The Importance of Constructing Family Trees," in Guichon, Mitchell, and Giroux, *supra* note 7 at 192. See also Glenn McGee, Sarah-Vaughan Brakman, and Andrea D. Gurmankin, "Gamete Donation and Anonymity: Disclosure to Children Conceived with Donor Gametes Should Not Be Optional" (2001) 16:10 Human Reproduction 2033.
26 See, for example, the GeneTests website, http://www.genetests.org.
27 Barry J. Maron *et al*., "Implications of Hypertrophic Cardiomyopathy Transmitted by Sperm Donation" (2009) 302:15 JAMA 1681–972.

28 Secrecy of the fact of the conception using provider gametes was not the focus of the judgment.
29 *Pratten v British Columbia (Attorney General)*, 2011 BCSC 656, 99 RFL (6th) 290 [*Pratten*], rev'd 2012 BCCA 480, 25 RFL (7th) 58, leave to appeal to SCC refused, [2013] SCCA No. 36. For a detailed discussion, including the background to the case and the arguments of the parties, see the chapter by Giroux and Milne in this volume. The *Pratten* case is also the focus of the chapters by Gruben and Snelling.
30 RSBC 1996, c 5, ss 6(1)(a), (c), (d); ss 8(1), (2)(a), (b), (c); s 9(b); s 32; ss 48(1), (2)(a), (b), (3); s 56; ss 58–71 [*BC Act*].
31 BC Reg. 291/96, ss 4(1), (2), (3); ss 19–24 [*BC Reg*].
32 Part I of the *Constitution Act, 1982*, being Schedule B to the *Canada Act 1982* (UK), 1982, c 11.
33 *Pratten, supra* note 29 at para 335(c).
34 Ms Pratten had also argued that the failure of the Province of British Columbia and the College of Physicians and Surgeons to create, preserve, and disclose records of genetic parentage to Offspring in circumstances of medical necessity or otherwise deprives her and other donor Offspring of their right to liberty and security of the person, contrary to s 7 of the *Charter*. On that ground, she was unsuccessful. *Ibid* at para 316.
35 *Ibid* at para 207.
36 *Ibid* at para 210.
37 *Ibid* at para 210.
38 *Ibid* at para 215.
39 *Ibid* at para 211.
40 *Pratten v British Columbia (Attorney General)*, 2012 BCCA 480, 25 RFL (7th) 58 at para 37.
41 *Ibid* at para 62.
42 *Ibid* at para 63.
43 [2013] SCCA No 36; see also, "Reversed sperm-donor disclosure ruling a 'setback,' plaintiff argues," *CTVNews.ca*, 28 November 2012, http://www.ctvnews.ca/health/reversed-sperm-donor-disclosure-ruling-a-setback-plaintiff-argues-1.1056920#ixzz2FvYuDHDL.
44 *Pratten, supra* note 29 at para 230.
45 *Ibid* at para 232.
46 Damian H. Adams, "Is a Donor Conceived Person "Half Adopted?," *Australian Journal of Adoption* 7, no. 2: 1 at 2.
47 Kenneth J. Doka, ed., *Disenfranchised Grief: Recognizing Hidden Sorrow* (Lexington: Lexington Books, 1989).

48 *BC Act*, *supra* note 30, s 2; *Child, Youth and Family Enhancement Act*, RSA 2000, c.C-12, s 58.1 [*Alta Act*]; *Adoption Act*, SM 1997, c 47, CCSM c A2, s 2 [*Man Act*]; *Child and Family Services Act*, RSO 1990, c C.11, s 1(1); *Civil Code of Quebec*, article 543 CCQ; *Family Services Act*, SNB 1980, c F-2.2, s 71(1) [*NB Act*]; *Children and Family Services Act*, SNS 1990, c 5, s 2(1) [*NS Act*]; *Adoption Act*, RSPEI 1988, c A-4.1, s 2(a) [*PEI Act*]; *Adoption Act*, SNL 1999, c A-2.1, s 3 [*Nfld Act*]; *Child and Family Services Act*, SY 2008, c 1, s 2(a) [*Yukon Act*]; *Adoption Act*, SNWT 1998, c 9, s 2(a) [*NWT Act*]; *Adoption Act*, SNWT (Nu) 1998, c 9, s 2(a) [*Nu Act*]. Saskatchewan does not explicitly state that the child's best interests are the paramount factor and appears to assume that this is the case by explicating how a child's best interests are to be determined: *Adoption Act*, SS 1998, c A-5.2, s 3.

49 The Northwest Territories and Nunavut will open records without consent one year after a search began. See *infra* at note 110.

50 *BC Reg*, *supra* note 31, s 4; *Adoption Regulation*, Alta Reg 187/2004, s 13(3); *Adoption Regulations, 2003*, RRS c A-5.2, Reg 1, s 18 [*Sask Reg*]; *Adoption Regulation*, Man Reg 19/99, s 10(1); *General*, RRO 1990, Reg 70, s 54(1); *Youth Protection Act*, RSQ, c P-34.1, s 71; *PEI Act*, *supra* note 48, c A-4.1, s 7(1).

51 In New Brunswick, birth parents are requested to complete a twenty-page form prior to placement for adoption titled New Brunswick, "Birth Family Medical and Social History" (as received from Tracey Burkhardt, Director, Communications New Brunswick [Social Development Unit], 22 September 2010). In Nova Scotia, parents are not obligated to provide medical, social, or cultural information, but it is the routine practice of social workers to seek it: telephone conversation with Ms Janet Nearing, Department of Department of Community Services, PO Box 696, Halifax NS B3J 2T7, tel: (902) 424–2755. In Newfoundland and Labrador, and in Yukon, the Director of Adoptions has a duty to obtain as much information as possible about the medical and social history of the child's birth family and preserve the information for the child; see *Nfld Act*, *supra* note 48, s 7(1)(b); *Yukon Act*, *supra* note 48, s 97. In the Northwest Territories and in Nunavut, the director has a duty to record and preserve whatever medical, social, and cultural information has been obtained by the social worker: *Adoption Regulations*, NWT Reg. 141–98, s 41; *Adoption Regulations*, NWT Reg. (Nu) 141–98, s 41.

52 *PEI Act*, *supra* note 48, s 7(1).

53 *BC Reg*, *supra* note 31, s 4.

54 See, for example, *Foster v Bass*, 575 So 2d 967 (Sup Crt Miss 1990) at 971; Deborah Franklin, "What a Child Is Given," *New York Times Magazine*, 8 September 1989.

55 *BC Act*, *supra* note 30, s 65(3); *Man Act*, *supra* note 48, ss 112(4), 113(3); *Vital Statistics Act*, RSO 1990, c V.4, s 48.5(7), s 1(1) [*Vital Statistics*]; *Adoption Information Act*, SNS 1996, c 3, s 19(5) [*NS Information Act*]; *PEI Act*, *supra* note 48, s 2; *Nfld Act*, *supra* note 48, s 3; *Yukon Act*, *supra* note 48, s 143(3); *NWT Act*, *supra* note 48, s 62; *Nu Act*, *supra* note 48, s 62.

56 But in Nova Scotia, the director may withhold non-identifying information that he or she has decided may pose a risk to the health, safety, or well-being of any person to whom the information relates: *NS Information Act*, *supra* note 55, s 11(2).

57 *BC Act*, *supra* note 30, ss 65(4), 66(7); *Alta Act*, *supra* note 48, s 74.2(2) – adoptive parents may apply to block transmission of non-identifying information if the adult adoptee does not know of the adoption and the minister finds that conveying information would be extremely detrimental to the adopted person, s 74.2(9); *Sask Reg*, *supra* note 50, ss 26(1) (c), (e); *Man Act*, *supra* note 48, ss 112(4), 113(4); *Adoption Information Disclosure*, O Reg 464/07, s 11(2) [*Ont Reg*]; *NB Act*, *supra* note 48, s 92(1); *NS Information Act*, *supra* note 55, ss 10–11; *PEI Act*, *supra* note 48, s 48(1); *Nfld Act*, *supra* note 48, s 48; *Yukon Act*, *supra* note 48, s 143(4); *NWT Act*, *supra* note 48, ss 63–4; *Nu Act*, *supra* note 48, ss 63–4.

58 *Man Act*, *supra* note 48, s. 111(b).

59 Art 583 CCQ; Origins Canada, "Quebec Adoption Records," http://www.originscanada.org/adoption-records/by-province/quebec-adoption-records/.

60 *Sask Reg*, *supra* note 50, s 33.

61 *O Reg*, *supra* note 57, ss 16–21.

62 Art 584 CCQ.

63 *NB Act*, *supra* note 48, s 92(2)(h).

64 *PEI Act*, *supra* note 48, s 48(2).

65 *Nfld Act*, *supra* note 48, s 45.

66 *NWT Act*, *supra* note 48, s 67(1).

67 *Nu Act*, *supra* note 48, s 67(1).

68 *BC Act*, *supra* note 30, s 68.

69 *Cheskes v Ontario (Attorney General)* (2007), 87 OR (3d) 581, 288 DLR (4th) 449 (SC) at para 68, Balobaba J [*Cheskes*].

70 *Ibid*.

71 *Ibid* at para 64.

72 Lauzon, *supra* note 25.

73 *Cheskes*, *supra* note 69 at para 64.

74 *BC Act*, *supra* note 30, s. 69; *Alta Act*, *supra* note 48, s 75; *Sask Reg*, *supra* note 50, ss 27–32; *Man Act*, *supra* note 48, s 108; *O Reg*, *supra* note 57, ss 9–10;

article 583 CCQ; *NB Act, supra* note 48, s 92(5); *NS Information Act, supra* note 55, s 9(1); *PEI Act, supra* note 48, ss 49–50; *Nfld Act, supra* note 48, s 44; *Yukon Act, supra* note 48, s 146; *NWT Act, supra* note 48, s 66; *Nu Act, supra* note 48, s 66.

75 "Adoptees Have Option to Learn Identity of Birth Parents Come Monday," *Canadian Press*, 31 May 2009.

76 See, for example, Joan Heifetz Hollinger, ed., *Adoption Law and Practice* (New York: Lexis, 2000) vol. 2 at para 13–5 ("Aftermath of Adoption: Legal and Social Consequences").

77 *BC Act, supra* note 30, s 71(1); *Sask Reg*, s 31(1); *Post-Adoption Registry Regulation*, Man Reg 22/99, s 5; Adoption Council of Canada, "About Adoption, Search and Reunion: Quebec," http://adoption.ca/searching-and-reuniting; *NB Act, supra* note 48, s 92(3); *NS Information Act, supra* note 55, s 19(1); *PEI Act, supra* note 48, s 50(3); *Nfld Act, supra* note 48, s 56; *Yukon Act, supra* note 48, s 147(1); *NWT Act, supra* note 48, s 66(4); *Nu Act, supra* note 48, s 66(2).

78 Province of Nova Scotia, "Information on Adoption Disclosure," http://www.novascotia.ca/coms/families/adoption/AdoptionDisclosure.html.

79 See, generally, John Triseliotis, *In Search of Origins: The Experiences of Adopted People* (London: Routledge and Kegan Paul, 1973); Elizabeth J. Samuels, "The Idea of Adoption: An Inquiry into the History of Adult Adoptee Access to Birth Records" (2001) 53 Rutgers L Rev 367.

80 Quebec reconsidered the rights of persons adopted in Quebec to seek identifying information about their progenitors. The proposed law would have distinguished between adoptions that took place before and after the law came into force. For adoptions that preceded the new law, the adoptees could, among other things, have received information if the person has been deceased for two years and had not filed a disclosure veto. For adoptions after the law came into force, the accessibility of identifying information would be the norm unless one of the parties had taken steps to prevent transmission of that information by filing vetoes. See *Avant-projet de loi, Loi modifiant le Code civil et d'autres dispositions législatives en matière d'adoption et d'autorité parentale*, 1re sess, 39e lég, Québec, 2009 (déposé par Mme Kathleen Weil, Ministre de la Justice, le 30 octobre 2009); Québec, *Pour une Adoption Québécoise a la Mesure de Chaque Enfant: Rapport du groupe de travail sur le régime québécois de l'adoption* (Quebec: Ministère de la Justice et Ministère de la Santé et des Services Sociaux, 2007) (président: Carmen Lavallée), Justice Québec, http://www.justice.gouv.qc.ca/francais/publications/rapports/pdf/adoption-rap.pdf.

81 Arts 582–3 CCQ; *NB Act*, *supra* note 48, ss 91–2; *NS Information Act*, *supra* note 55, s 19; *PEI Act*, *supra* note 48, s 7.
82 *BC Act*, *supra* note 30, s 63.
83 *Alberta Act*, *supra* note 48, s 74(3).
84 *Ont Reg*, *supra* note 57, s 9.
85 *Nfld Act*, *supra* note 48, s 50.
86 *Yukon Act*, *supra* note 48, s 140.
87 *BC Act*, *supra* note 30, s 65(1).
88 *Vital Statistics*, *supra* note 55, s 56.1.
89 See, for example, *Vital Statistics*, *ibid*, s 48.1(9).
90 *Vital Statistics*, *ibid*, ss 48.4(1), 56(5).
91 *Alta Act*, *supra* note 48, ss 74.2(4), 74.2(9).
92 *BC Act*, *supra* note 30, s 65(1); *Alta Act*, *supra* note 48, s 74.2; *Vital Statistics*, *supra* note 55, s 48.5(1); *Nfld Act*, *supra* note 48, s 50(1); *Yukon Act*, *supra* note 48, s 143.
93 *Sask Reg*, *supra* note 50, s 28.
94 *Ibid*, s 29(3).
95 *Ibid*, s 30(2).
96 SO 2005, c 25.
97 *Vital Statistics*, *supra* note 55, ss 48.5(7), 48.7(3), as amended by SO 2005, c 25, s 9.
98 Proclamation, 1 September 2007, (2007) 140–35 O Gaz 3167; Ontario Minister of Community and Social Services Madeleine Meilleur, News Release, "Ontario Fulfills Its Commitment to Deliver New Adoption Information Laws," 4 September 2007, Canada Newswire, http://www.newswire.ca/en/releases/archive/September2007/04/c4819.html .
99 Kerry Gillespie, "Adoptee Urges Flexibility in Ontario Legislation," *Toronto Star*, 2 November 2007, A17.
100 *Cheskes*, *supra* note 69.
101 *Cheskes*, *supra* note 69 at para 69.
102 *Cheskes*, *supra* note 69 at para 132.
103 *Supra* note 34.
104 Katie Rook, "No Appeal of Adoption Record Ruling," *National Post*, 14 November 2007, A6.
105 *Ont Reg*, *supra* note 57; *Disclosure of Adoption Information*, O Reg 272/08.
106 Minister Meilleur News Release, *supra* note 100.
107 Canadian Press, *supra* note 77.
108 *NWT Act*, *supra* note 48, s 66(1); *Nu Act*, *supra* note 48, s 66(1).
109 *NWT Act*, *supra* note 48, s 66(4); *Nu Act*, *supra* note 48, s 66(2).
110 *Ibid*.

111 *AHRA, supra* note 2.
112 *Ibid*, s 21.
113 *Ibid*, s 14(1).
114 *Ibid*, s 16(2).
115 *Ibid*, s 18(2).
116 Sections 14 to 19 established a system for the management and disclosure of information relating to assisted reproductive activities. In the *AHRA Reference, supra* note 1, five justices found Sections 14 to 19 to be *ultra vires* the Government of Canada: LeBel, Deschamps, Abella, Rothstein, and Cromwell JJ. The minority on this issue (McLachlin CJ, and Binnie, Fish, and Charron JJ) held that the information management provisions in ss 14 to 19 represented a minor incursion on provincial powers.
117 Gloria Galloway, "Human Reproduction Agency Has Little to Show for $30-Million," *Globe and Mail*, 31 May 2012. See also amendments to the *AHRA* made by *Jobs, Growth and Long-term Prosperity Act*, SC 2012, c 19, Division 56.
118 *Processing and Distribution of Semen for Assisted Conception Regulations*, SOR/96–254 [*Semen Regulations*].
119 RSC 1985, c F-27.
120 See generally Triseliotis and Samuels, *supra* note 79.
121 Cordray, *supra* note 13.
122 In Alberta, adoptive parents may apply to the minister for a disclosure veto on the grounds that the adoptee does not know that he or she has been adopted and that the release of personal information "would be extremely detrimental" to the adopted person. If the minister is satisfied, based on the information provided by the adoptive parents, then the minister may deem that a disclosure veto has been registered by the adoptee. *Alta Act, supra* note 48, ss 72(1) and 74.2(2)(b)(9). In the Northwest Territories and Nunavut, adoptees may reçeive state-held information about their progenitors provided that the biological parents have not registered an objection and if the registrar fails to find their birth parents within one year of searching. *Adoption Act NWT* and *Adoption Act Nu, supra* note 48.
123 Vardit Ravitsky and Joanna E Scheib, "Donor-Conceived Individuals' Right to Know," *Hastings Center Bioethics Forum*, 20 July 2010 (blog), http://www.thehastingscenter.org/Bioethicsforum/Post.aspx?id=4811&blogid=140.
124 *Pratten, supra* note 29.
125 *Semen Regulations, supra* note 118, s 13.
126 Stevens, "Who I Come From," in Guichon, Mitchell, and Giroux, *supra* note 7, 31 at 34–5.

9 A Time for Change? The Divergent Approaches of Canada and New Zealand to Donor Conception and Donor Identification

JEANNE SNELLING

Introduction

Despite striking similarities between Canada's federal *Assisted Human Reproduction Act* (*AHRA*) and New Zealand's *Human Assisted Reproductive Technology Act 2004* (*HARTA*), the approach to donor-conceived individuals' access to information adopted by these two statutes diverged markedly on the issue of donor anonymity. However, many of the *AHRA* provisions have been abrogated as a result of the Supreme Court of Canada's decision in *Reference re: Assisted Human Reproduction Act*[1] (the *Reference*) and ensuing federal legislative amendments.[2] These events in conjunction with provincial developments[3] provide a significant opportunity for Canada to revisit donor conception laws, particularly the issue of donor anonymity.

The *AHRA* adopted a compromise position. While it contained provisions governing the collection, management, and disclosure of health reporting information to donor offspring and other involved parties, it also facilitated donor anonymity. However, the health reporting information provisions were struck down by the *Reference* as outside the jurisdiction of the federal government. Although the provisions were never proclaimed in force, their abrogation is nevertheless of concern to many who advocate the establishment of standardized, mandatory information collection and disclosure regimes as well as the abolishment of donor anonymity.

Following the *Reference* and the subsequent repeal of multiple *AHRA* provisions, the collection and management of health reporting information now falls to the discretion of the provinces and territories. A failure to enact regulations governing information collection, management, and disclosure regimes clearly jeopardizes donor-conceived individuals' access to donor-related information.[4] Consequently, the decision of the Supreme Court of British Columbia in *Pratten v British Columbia (Attorney General)*[5] constituted an important development regarding the appropriate extent of legislative protection of donor offspring interests in Canada.

In *Pratten*, Adair J held that a woman conceived as a result of anonymous sperm donation was entitled to access the same information that adoptees are statutorily entitled to obtain regarding a biological parent. In BC, adoptees may access information regarding birth parents on reaching the age of majority by virtue of the *Adoption Act* and *Adoption Regulation*.[6] However, no similar regulatory mechanism exists to ensure that donor-conceived offspring may access equivalent information, including identifying information regarding the donor.

Justice Adair held that the BC government, by its differential treatment of adoptee and donor-conceived individuals' access to information regarding genetic parents, had breached s. 15(1) of the *Canadian Charter of Rights and Freedoms*, which confers the right to equal protection and equal benefit of the law without discrimination. The ruling went significantly farther in terms of facilitating access to donor-related information than did the now-defunct provisions of the *AHRA*. However, the decision was subsequently overturned on appeal.

The BC Court of Appeal found that the adoption provisions impugned by Adair J were valid. Invoking the test in *R v Kapp*, it held that the provisions constituted an attempt to institute "remedial schemes" to assist "disadvantaged groups."[7] Given that the purpose of the *Adoption Act* and *Adoption Regulation* provisions was to remedy the "disadvantages created by the state-sanctioned dissociation of adoptees from their biological parents,"[8] they qualified as an *ameliorative* program under subs. 15(2) of the *Charter*. Ultimately (and somewhat extraordinarily), the court held that although the legislature was at liberty to "provide adoptees with the means of accessing information about their biological origins," it was not obligated "to provide comparable benefits to other persons seeking such information."[9] Olivia Pratten's subsequent application to appeal was declined by the Supreme Court of Canada.

Despite the result, the decisions do not undermine the substantive arguments in *favour* of extending the same access to information to adult donor-conceived offspring. Furthermore, as Gruben and Gilbert have previously observed, legislative reform across the provinces and territories to establish a harmonized framework tailored to the unique circumstances of donor conception is ultimately preferable to invoking equality arguments based on s. 15 of the *Charter*.[10] What is of concern, however, is that the policy blueprint provided by the federal *AHRA* provisions may now be replicated by the provinces, instead of full information collection and disclosure regimes being established.

This chapter compares New Zealand's statutory framework with the one originally prescribed by the *AHRA*. New Zealand is one jurisdiction among a growing minority that have legislated to ensure a standardized information collection regime and the removal of donor anonymity. It is also one of the few jurisdictions where the move away from donor anonymity *preceded* the introduction of a statutory framework. It constitutes a particularly relevant comparator given that the *AHRA* and New Zealand's equivalent law were enacted almost contemporaneously; also, despite the different approaches to regulating donor conception, the two countries are strikingly similar with respect to the principles underpinning their legislative schemes. While this chapter is essentially comparative, it also highlights residual issues that are not directly addressed by either the New Zealand legislative scheme or the former Canadian one. First, the arguments made in regard to donor conception and the issue of donor anonymity are briefly flagged.

Contextualizing the Controversy

Proponents of donor anonymity generally make two types of arguments. First, there are rights-based arguments that claim a donor's right to privacy as well as parental rights to privacy.[11] Related to this is a particular view of the importance of social parenthood, which, it has been claimed, may be undermined when the significance of biological ties is overemphasized.[12] Second, there are arguments based on clinical expediency, such that removing donor anonymity would lead to a shortage of donor gametes.[13] Conversely, arguments based on a right to know one's genetic origins are generally premised on the adverse effects of donor anonymity for donor offspring and fall into several categories. The first category involves the argument from identity.

Social science research has established that, just as with adoption, biological or blood relations can assume significant importance.[14] For some individuals, knowledge of one's genetic origins is integral to developing a healthy self-identity,[15] and this is problematic for those who were conceived through anonymous donor conception.[16] A particular issue concerns what is often a dearth of information regarding the health and medical history of the donor, which may have implications for the donor-conceived individual's future health.[17] A further issue is the risk of inadvertently forming an intimate relationship with a biological half-sibling. However, while there is general agreement that non-identifying health information regarding a donor should be available for donor-conceived offspring, the issue of removing donor anonymity remains controversial.[18]

Nevertheless, some governments have assumed responsibility for ensuring access to identifying donor information to ameliorate the adverse experiences of donor-conceived individuals. Jurisdictions such as New Zealand, the Australian state of Victoria, and the United Kingdom have introduced regulations facilitating such access to information, which includes establishing mandatory donor registries.[19] Of course, access to such information is meaningful only for those individuals who are aware that they are donor-conceived.

The Pre-Legislative Context in New Zealand

The interest of donor offspring in knowing their genetic origins was acknowledged, and respected, in New Zealand long before the *HARTA* was introduced in 2004. The *Act* merely formalized and operationalized an existing practice. Many factors contributed to New Zealand fertility service providers' early adoption of identifiable-donor policy in the early 1990s.

First, New Zealand established a statutory open adoption policy in the mid-1980s.[20] Although this did not immediately translate into a similar legislative response in relation to donor insemination, it contributed to the move away from donor anonymity.[21] In addition, legislation was introduced in 1987 that severed the legal rights and liabilities of donors of sperm, ova, or embryos (created wholly or partly from donated gametes), deeming the woman who gave birth following donation and her husband/*de facto* partner (if any and subject to the partner's consent) to be the legal parents of the child.[22]

Māori cultural concepts also played a significant role. The earliest official statement of Māori values in the context of assisted reproduction was made in the late 1980s. A working party from the Ministry of Māori Affairs/Manatu Māori specifically considered the implications of assisted reproductive technology for Māori as part of an interdepartmental committee set up to monitor developments in assisted reproduction. It subsequently formulated the *Guidelines for the Use of Assisted Reproductive Technology*.[23]

The *Guidelines* were premised on the partnership established by the Treaty of Waitangi between Māori and the Crown and on the Crown's subsequent responsibility for ensuring that reproductive policy protected Māori cultural values.[24] The *Guidelines'* precepts recognized Māori as *tangata whenua* (people of the land)[25] and were subsequently described as providing the "foundation for Māori opinion in this area."[26] As the *Guidelines* explained, the concept of *whakapapa* (genealogy) is at the heart of Māori cultural identity. According to traditional Māori values, a child is the offspring not only of its biological parents but also of the *whanau* (extended family), *hapu* (subtribe), and *iwi* (tribe).[27] *Whakapapa* enables *whanau* (family) members to establish links to an eponymous ancestor. This concept determines individual status; it also formalizes relationships with others similarly linked to a common forebear and contributes to establishing a cultural identity and heritage. The *Guidelines* stated that the need to protect *whakapapa* required that "all children born as a result of ART have unconstrained access to information that readily identifies the child's biological parents."[28] The working party also noted that while the *Status of Children Amendment Act 1987* might have been a pragmatic measure to absolve the rights and obligations of the donor, it did not address the social, cultural, or emotional needs of the individual born because it obfuscated the donor's genetic contribution and the donor-conceived individual's genetic lineage. This created a cultural tension militating towards donor openness. Additional support for revoking donor anonymity was provided in a 1991 report commissioned by the New Zealand Medical Council.[29]

Later, in 1994, the government appointed a two-person Ministerial Committee on Assisted Reproductive Technologies (MCART) to examine and report on general developments in the field.[30] Drawing on the recently released report of the Canadian Royal Commission of Inquiry into New Reproductive Technologies, MCART endorsed the Royal Commission's adoption of broad ethical principles to guide regulation.[31] However, MCART recommended a right not proposed in the Canadian report: to know one's genetic origins.

MCART noted that enabling access to information regarding an individual's genetic origins was "a constant theme" in submissions.[32] Indeed, the Department of Social Welfare claimed in its submission that "[t]here is now general agreement amongst the parties involved in ART (including social parents) that children born as a result of donated material have a right to know their genetic identity/whakapapa."[33] The New Zealand Infertility Society – a primarily but not solely consumer-constituted organization – articulated its preference that only donors willing to be identifiable be recruited.[34] Ken Daniels, a prominent commentator in the area of donor conception, claims that the small size of New Zealand was also a significant factor,[35] for it enabled professionals and patients to actively engage with one another in discussing assisted conception issues.[36]

All of this culminated in one fertility clinic voluntarily instituting a policy of non-anonymous donation in the early 1990s; the remaining clinics soon followed suit.[37] These developments together influenced the legislative regime that was finally enacted in 2004.[38]

Enacting the *AHRA*

Canada's *AHRA* was based largely on recommendations made by the Royal Commission of Inquiry into New Reproductive Technologies in its multi-volume tome *Proceed with Care*, released in 1993.[39] These recommendations were the polar opposite of the consensus developing in New Zealand at that time. Specifically, the Commission recommended that sperm donation occur only on the basis of donor anonymity, with the exception that identifying information would be released *if* a court deemed it a matter of medical necessity.[40] Furthermore, it recommended that altruistic egg donation be restricted to the donation of surplus ova following IVF, or to eggs retrieved prior to surgical sterilization,[41] and occur only on the basis of donor anonymity with the exception of medical necessity.[42] The framework subsequently established by the *AHRA* incorporated some but not all of the Commission's recommendations.

Although now repealed, the information collection and disclosure provisions contained in the *AHRA* are still relevant. The constitutional challenge to the *AHRA* involved federalism and required the Supreme Court to determine whether the federal Parliament had encroached on matters that were within the jurisdiction of the provincial legislatures.[43] Thus it was argued not that the impugned provisions constituted bad law, but that they were *ultra vires* the federal government. The end result is that the regulatory framework provides a possible blueprint for provincial and territorial legislatures, which are now responsible for drafting laws in this context. Consequently, the following analysis compares the original federal legislative approach with the corresponding New Zealand statute.

Legislative Similarities: The *AHRA* and the *HARTA*

Both the *AHRA* and the *HARTA* were enacted in 2004 after long and difficult legislative processes. The *AHRA* received assent in March, the *HARTA* in November.

The *AHRA* establishes two categories of activities: those that are expressly prohibited, and those that are "controlled" and may only be performed in accordance with any relevant regulations.[44] The *AHRA* also sets out specific principles that the Canadian Parliament "recognizes and declares"[45] as well as penalties for any breaches of the regulatory scheme.[46]

The *AHRA* established the Assisted Human Reproduction Agency of Canada (the Agency).[47] The Agency's objectives were "to protect and promote the health and safety, and the human dignity and human rights, of Canadians" and "to foster the application of ethical principles, in relation to assisted human reproduction."[48] The Agency was empowered to provide advice to the Minister; monitor and evaluate developments in assisted human reproduction (AHR); consult persons and organizations within Canada; provide information to the public and to the professions; and designate inspectors and analysts to enforce the Act.[49] However, the formulation of regulations to implement the Act's provisions remained, and continues to remain, the responsibility of Health Canada, a federal department.[50] Consequently the Agency, since disestablished by the Canadian Parliament,[51] had no formal policy-making role under the Act.

The *HARTA* similarly establishes specific categories of assisted reproductive procedures: those that are prohibited,[52] those that are regulated and may only be performed with prior written ethical approval,[53] and those that have been declared "established" and thus may be performed routinely without prior approval.[54]

The *HARTA* has established an Advisory Committee on Assisted Reproductive Technology that provides advice to the Minister of Health.[55] Unlike the Canadian agency, it has a formal policy-making role and is responsible for formulating guidelines for the conduct of regulated procedures.[56] An Ethics Committee on Assisted Reproductive Technology has been established as well and is responsible for considering applications to perform regulated procedures.[57] Such procedures are approved only if the application is consistent with Advisory Committee guidelines.[58]

Significantly, the *HARTA* incorporates several of the principles contained in the *AHRA*. The first purpose declared in the *HARTA* is expressed in almost identical terms to one of the core principles of the *AHRA*.[59] It aims "to secure the benefits of assisted reproductive procedures, established procedures, and human reproductive research for individuals and for society in general by taking appropriate measures for the protection and promotion of the health, safety, dignity, and rights of all individuals, but particularly those of women and children, in the use of these procedures and research."[60]

The *HARTA* establishes a set of principles that must guide "all persons exercising powers or performing functions under the Act"; the *AHRA* similarly contains a list of principles that the Canadian Parliament "recognizes and declares."[61] The first principle in both Acts addresses the importance of the welfare of the child born following assisted reproduction.

The *HARTA* provides that "the health and well-being of children born as a result of the performance of an assisted reproductive procedure should be an *important* consideration in all decisions about that procedure."[62] The welfare provision originally stated that the health and well-being of children should be a *paramount* consideration, but this was altered during the legislative process. When amending the provision, the Health Select Committee indicated that it preferred a nuanced approach: "We consider it more appropriate that the risks of assisted human reproduction procedures be balanced against the benefits to children, families, and society in general. We intend decisions to be weighted in the best interest of the child, recognizing that there will still be an element of risk."[63]

In contrast, the *AHRA* provides that "the health and well-being of children born through the application of assisted human reproductive technologies must be given *priority* in all decisions respecting their use" (emphases added).[64]

The second *HARTA* principle, which declares that "the human health, safety, and dignity of present and future generations should be preserved and promoted," does not have a direct equivalent in the Canadian Act.[65] However, the next principle is again derived from the *AHRA* core principles.[66] Section 4(c) of the *HARTA* provides that "while all persons are affected by assisted reproductive procedures and established procedures, women, more than men, are directly and significantly affected by their application, and the health and well-being of women must be protected in the *use* of these procedures."

The justification for including such a clause in the *AHRA* was that "[t]he physical and social burdens and risks of reproduction are borne primarily by women," consequently this "should be acknowledged and reflected in reproductive policy."[67]

Both statutes contain principles protecting the right to informed choice and consent.[68] Both Acts also reflect a particular social justice perspective in that each seeks to prevent the commercialization of human reproduction. Thus a purpose of the *HARTA* is "to prohibit certain commercial transactions relating to human reproduction,"[69] while the *AHRA* contains a principle that "trade in the reproductive capabilities of women and men and the exploitation of children, women and men for commercial ends raise health and ethical concerns that justify their prohibition."[70]

The *AHRA* also provides that "persons who seek to undergo assisted reproduction procedures must not be discriminated against, including on the basis of their sexual orientation or marital status."[71] Although there is no similar provision in the *HARTA*, the New Zealand *Human Rights Act 1993* achieves the same result.[72]

Two additional *HARTA* principles have no equivalents in the Canadian Act. The first provides that "the needs, values, and beliefs of Māori should be considered and treated with respect."[73] The second is that "the different ethical, spiritual, and cultural perspectives in society should be considered and treated with respect."[74]

Both Acts demonstrate a similar legislative spirit and intent; however, any similarity ends with respect to donor conception.

The *AHRA* Regulatory Framework for Donor Conception

The *AHRA* prohibits the purchase, or advertising for purchase, of sperm, ova, *in vitro* embryos, or a human cell or gene.[75] Donors may not be paid; however, s. 12 permits the reimbursement of expenditures incurred in the course of donating sperm or ova *if* they arise in accordance with any applicable regulations *and* if receipts are provided in relation to those expenditures.[76] However, as s. 12 is yet to be proclaimed in force and regulations have not been drafted,[77] reimbursement of incurred expenditures may currently occur in the absence of such regulations.[78]

Sections 14–18 of the *AHRA* dealt with the collection, management, and disclosure of health reporting information. The Act defined health reporting information as "the identity, personal characteristics, genetic information and medical history of donors of human reproductive material and *in vitro* embryos, persons who have undergone assisted reproduction procedures and persons who were conceived by means of those procedures."[79] The Agency was required to maintain a registry containing such information.[80] Sections 14–18, which were struck down and subsequently repealed, established a regulatory framework that failed to adequately address the interests of donor-conceived individuals.[81]

The Act only permitted disclosure of health reporting information relating to either a donor, the individual who had undertaken the reproductive procedure, or the donor-conceived individual, and *only* with the written consent of the donor or the other involved person.[82] While the Act permitted open donation, the donor retained ultimate control of the disclosure of any identifying information. Indeed, the Act provided that the identity of the donor could *not* be disclosed without consent, nor could any "information that can reasonably be expected to be used in the identification of the donor,"[83] except in exceptional circumstances. But even in such circumstances, donor offspring were not entitled to learn the identity of the donor if the donor wished to remain anonymous. Rather, the Agency could disclose the donor's identity to a physician *if* the Agency considered that a risk existed to the health or safety of a person who had undergone a donor-assisted reproductive procedure, or to an individual conceived by such a procedure. However, the physician was not permitted to disclose that identity.[84]

The *AHRA* made limited provisions for donor-conceived individuals to determine sibling relationships – primarily for those who were concerned about inadvertent consanguinity. The Act provided that with regard to two offspring who "have reason to believe" that one or both of them were donor-conceived, the Agency was authorized to disclose whether they were genetically related and the nature of the relationship.[85] The Act did not provide for tracing all half-genetic siblings in general.

The original *AHRA* was clearly concerned with facilitating donor anonymity. Notwithstanding the *AHRA*'s core principle that "the health and well-being of children born" following assisted reproduction "must be given *priority* in all decisions," the interests of others assumed greater importance in the context of donor conception.[86]

In contrast, the decision in *Pratten* initially achieved what the *AHRA* had not – at least in British Columbia. Justice Adair accepted evidence (unchallenged by the Attorney General in the BC Supreme Court and the Court of Appeal) that donor-conceived individuals are exposed to the risk of – or indeed experience – psychological and medical harm in the absence of access to general as well as identifying information regarding donors.[87] Nevertheless, donor-conceived individuals still do not have the right to obtain donor-identifying information as adults or to trace genetic siblings.

The *HARTA* Regulatory Framework: Promoting Donor Offspring's Interest in Knowing Their Genetic Origins

In contrast to the *AHRA*, a specific purpose of the *HARTA* is to "establish a comprehensive information-keeping regime to ensure that people born from donated embryos or donated cells can find out about their genetic origins."[88] It includes a guiding principle that "donor offspring *should be made aware* of their genetic origins and be able to access information about those origins."[89]

To these ends, Part III of the Act details providers' duties regarding information collection[90] and information keeping in respect of donors of donated embryos and cells as well as donor-conceived offspring. Fertility service providers must notify the Registrar-General (of Births, Deaths, and Marriages) of any subsequent birth and provide information regarding the identity of the offspring and the donor.[91] The Act also sets out provisions regarding access to donor information by donor offspring, as well as donor access to information about donor offspring.

Donor offspring who are eighteen years or older may access information regarding their donor from either the fertility service provider or the Registrar-General.[92] If under eighteen, the individual may only access non-identifying information,[93] although their guardian may access full donor information.[94] An agency may refuse access to information if, on reasonable grounds, it is considered that disclosure is likely to endanger any person.[95] Donor offspring who are sixteen years or older may apply to the Family Court for an order that they be treated as if they are eighteen in order to access, or consent to disclosure of, information kept under the Act.[96] The Act requires the relevant agency to notify the donor whenever a person is permitted access to donor-identifying information.[97]

Under the *HARTA* (unlike under the *AHRA*), donor-conceived offspring over eighteen may access information as to whether any other individual has been conceived using the same donor.[98] (If the offspring is under eighteen, that person's guardian may access this information.[99]) However, information identifying genetic siblings may only be released *if* that other donor-conceived person (or their guardian, if under eighteen) consents to access.[100]

Like the *AHRA*, the *HARTA* enables donor-conceived offspring to remain anonymous. While providers must tell a donor, if requested, whether any individuals have been born as a result of donation and their sex,[101] providers may only disclose identifying information if the donor-conceived individual has given consent to disclosure.[102] Donor offspring over eighteen may consent in writing to the disclosure of identifying information by the Registrar-General to the donor.[103] Consequently in the case of a donor who is unknown to the recipient(s) (as opposed to a known donor such as a friend/acquaintance/relative), the Act does not facilitate unwanted contact with a family by the donor unless the donor offspring is over eighteen and wishes to disclose his or her identity.

Importantly, the Act imposes extensive information storage requirements to eradicate any possibility of destruction or loss of records. Donor information must be retained by a provider for fifty years and forwarded to the Registrar-General if the provider ceases to be a provider and does not have a successor; or if fifty years has elapsed since the birth of a donor-individual.[104] Thereafter the Register-General must keep such information indefinitely.[105]

The Act prescribes specific information that a provider must ensure is given to a donor prior to donation and to the prospective guardian of a donor-conceived individual prior to a procedure.[106] This encompasses the information that is obtained and kept by providers and the length of time such information is kept; why information is obtained and kept; what information is forwarded to and retained indefinitely by the Registrar-General; the rights conferred on the offspring, the guardians, and others regarding access to information about donors; the rights conferred on donors and other regarding access to information about donor offspring; the importance of disclosing to offspring the nature of their conception; and the availability of counselling. Although the Act is not retrospective, a voluntary register exists for donations that occurred prior to the Act coming into force.[107]

Residual Issues

Despite these significant legislative initiatives, there are several residual issues that have attracted recommendations for legal reform.

Limits on the Number of Births from a Single Donor

An issue that has not been directly legislated by the Canadian and New Zealand statutes is the maximum number of offspring that may be born from a single donor. Indeed, it was recently reported in the Canadian media that Toronto filmmaker Barry Stevens estimates that he has between five hundred and one thousand genetic half-siblings, while a US sperm donor reportedly fathered 150 children.[108] Repromed, the fertility business that runs the only sperm bank now operating in Canada, limits offspring from a single donor to 3 births per 100,000 persons in a given geographic area.[109] But as Tom Blackwell notes, this could equate to seventy-five offspring born in a city the size of Toronto.[110] The impact of discovering multiple "complex genetic networks"[111] cannot be underestimated.[112] While the *HARTA* does not impose standardized limits on the number of offspring born from a donor, the *Fertility Services* Standard, against which fertility clinics are audited, requires that fertility service organizations "ha[ve] a policy that limits the number of children from one donor."[113] Given this, New Zealand clinics have voluntarily adopted a policy of limiting the number of children born to a single sperm donor to up to ten children in four families.[114]

Annotating Birth Certificates

The *HARTA* protects a right of access to information but does not *require* that donor-conceived individuals be informed of the nature of their conception. This is problematic for those who claim an "unequivocal right" to know.[115] While "right" to know arguments are contested, it is difficult to counter the claim that donor-conceived offspring have a right not to have the biological origins of their conception obfuscated by law. As noted above, the importance of acknowledging genetic lineage was identified as of considerable importance to Māori culture in particular in New Zealand.

The *HARTA* stops short of imposing a statutory duty on parents to disclose; it does, however, impose a duty on providers to advise prospective parents regarding the *importance* of making children aware that they were donor-conceived,[116] clearly demonstrating a preference for parental disclosure to offspring.[117] Yet this compromise is in tension with the ethical and cultural values that informed the move away from donor anonymity originally. One possible solution is to annotate birth certificates to ensure that donor-conceived individuals can become aware of the nature of their conception in the event that their parents do not tell them.[118] This particular issue is attracting attention internationally.[119]

In 2010 the Australian state of Victoria introduced amendments requiring the annotation "donor conceived" to be placed on a child's birth certificate if a birth registration statement indicates that the child was born as a result of donor conception.[120] An individual who applies for a birth certificate after the age of eighteen is notified that there is further information held on the birth register that s/he may access. Significantly, this approach does not impinge on a parental prerogative not to disclose to their child(ren) when they are minors, but it does provide a mechanism for adult donor-conceived individuals to become aware that additional information regarding their birth exists should they wish to access it.

The New Zealand Law Commission (NZLC) first considered this issue in 2004. It recommended (to no avail) that *all* birth certificates be annotated to indicate that additional information is contained in the Births, Deaths, and Marriages register. The Commission reasoned that alerting individuals to the existence of this additional (and generally benign) information could lead those "with a sense of difference" in their family to access it.[121]

As yet, no other Australian state besides Victoria has introduced a similar regime of birth certificate annotation. The UK's Nuffield Council on Bioethics recently considered, and rejected, birth certificate annotation.[122] Nevertheless, it can be argued that when the state is actively involved in regulating donor conception, for it to fail to introduce a mechanism to ensure that the resulting person is made aware that there were special circumstances associated with their birth is for it to facilitate, and be complicit in, the possible deception of that individual.

Legal Parenthood and Agreements between Parents and Known Donors

The rules regarding the legal status of children conceived as a result of AHR in New Zealand are now contained in Part II of the *Status of Children Act 1969* (*SoC Act*). The Act provides that a woman who gives birth following sperm, egg, or embryo donation and her non-donor partner are the legal parents of any offspring if the procedure is performed with the non-donor partner's consent[123] and that a non-partner ovum or semen donor "is not, for any purposes, a parent" of the child.[124] As of 2004, if the woman giving birth has a female partner, the female partner is deemed to be a parent of the child.[125] Similarly, a single woman is deemed to be the legal parent of the donor-conceived offspring[126] and the egg, embryo, or sperm donor "is not, for any purpose, a parent" of the child.[127] In the event that a single woman later enters into a partnership with the donor, the ovum or sperm donor is subsequently deemed to have the rights and liabilities of a parent.[128]

In the case of known donors, s. 41 of the *Care of Children Act 2004* (*CoC Act*) makes specific provision for formalizing agreements between parents and donors concerning contact between the donor(s) and the child and/or the role a donor has in relation to the child's upbringing.[129] Although such an agreement cannot be enforced, a party may apply to the Court for an order that, subject to the consent of all parties, embodies some if not all of the terms of the agreement.[130] If the order relates to a donor(s) contact with the child, it may be enforced as "if it were a parenting order relating to contact."[131] If any of the parties cannot agree on a matter regarding the role of the donor(s) in the upbringing of the child, the court can make any order in relation to the matter it thinks proper.[132] While the Act provides for recognition of agreements in this manner, it does not confer the status of a legal parent on a donor.[133]

Significantly, there is wide discretion for a court to vary a disputed agreement, and this has attracted criticism.[134] As the NZLC observes, such discretion enables a court to significantly alter the terms of a pre-conception agreement against the wishes of the recipient couple/single woman.[135] The NZLC (which premises its recommendations on preserving the parties' original intentions regarding parenthood – i.e., the pre-conception "intentional parenthood" approach) posits that if a known donor provides gametes on the understanding that s/he relinquishes parenthood, that decision should be "determinative from the point of conception" unless (as is currently the law) the donor assumes a relationship with the birth mother, or alternatively, all of the parties agree.[136] Thus it recommended law reform to provide that a s. 41 agreement is presumptively enforceable unless it is "demonstrably in the child's best interests to vary it."[137] However, the government's response to this recommendation echoes the sentiment earlier expressed by Heath J in *P v K*[138] to the effect that such agreements should not be treated as if they were commercial contracts; rather, contact should be determined according to the child's best interests. Accordingly, the enforcement, or variation, of s. 41 agreements falls to the discretion of a judge on a case-by-case basis.[139] In the case of known donors, whether a state adopts an "intentional parenthood" or a "best interests" approach has significant implications for the parties should disputes between a donor (or donors) and the legal parents subsequently occur.

Legal Parenthood and Known Donors Who Wish to Be Legal Parents

An altogether different problem arises if the parties all intend/agree that a known donor will be an active participant in the child's life and wish the donor to be recognized as a legal parent with the attendant rights and responsibilities. Given its intentional parenthood approach, the NZLC considered that – for what is likely to be a discrete and small group of people – the *Status of Children Act 1969* should be amended to permit a donor to "opt into" parenthood *if* the single mother or recipient couple agree, effectively reversing the deeming provisions.[140] In this situation a child would potentially have multiple legal parents if the recipient couple and the known donor agree that s/he will raise the child jointly with the couple. The New Zealand government has conceded that the concerns that inform the NZLC recommendations are valid. Although an important issue given the significant rights and obligations that legal parenthood confers,[141] legal reform is yet to occur.[142]

Conclusion

New Zealand and similar jurisdictions prioritize donor-conceived individuals' interests in knowing their genetic origins over competing interests. Significantly, New Zealand's policy evolved on the basis that the rights and liabilities of a donor are extinguished once a child is born and that the mother and her consenting partner (if any) are deemed the legal parents of the donor-conceived child. The *HARTA* has established a mandatory information-keeping regime and a presumption of intra-familial openness. But this is not to suggest that facilitating and regulating donor conception does not continue to pose regulatory challenges.

Gamete donation is a significant and involved process for both donors and recipients, procedurally and emotionally.[143] Anecdotal evidence suggests that the demand for donor gametes in New Zealand exceeds the supply.[144] In particular, gay couples find it more difficult to obtain donor gametes, largely because donors may place "boundaries" on the use of their reproductive material.[145] Consequently, known donors, such as friends or family, constitute approximately half of all ova and sperm donations.[146] While legislation has been enacted to provide a mechanism for formalizing agreements between the donor and the legal parents, problematic issues may arise if a known donor wishes to play a greater role in the child's life than that originally agreed by the recipient couple/single woman. In these circumstances, the court has wide discretion to vary such an agreement, and this has attracted criticism because it enables a court to significantly alter the terms of a pre-conception agreement. Conversely, the current law precludes a known donor from being recognized as a legal parent regardless of whether the relevant parties wish the donor to be recognized as such. Consequently the legal rights, if any, that should be attributed to known donors remain the subject of debate. In addition, annotating birth certificates to indicate that an individual was donor-conceived (should their parents not inform them) is a matter that, although advocated by the NZLC, has not received support from the New Zealand government. This is ostensibly because of concerns that it could be confusing for third parties relying on the certificate.[147]

Given recent developments, Canada is clearly at a crossroads in terms of regulating donor conception. The (now repealed) provisions of the *AHRA* adopted a compromise position that facilitated donor anonymity. There is no standardized, mandatory information collection and management regime, and as a consequence, it is not ensured that the interests of donor-conceived individuals are protected and promoted. As Adair J observed in *Pratten*, "practices developed by private sector providers" cannot "be a full answer to the circumstances of donor offspring."[148]

It is to be hoped that, at a minimum, Canadian provinces and territories will adopt a standardized information collection, management, and disclosure system. Furthermore, and especially in view of developments globally, donor anonymity should be abrogated. Further on a pragmatic note, direct-to-consumer access to international genetic genealogy databases means that an individual may be able to discover genetic relatives in the future, despite attempts to facilitate donor anonymity.[149] Ultimately, it is not just the issue of donor identification itself that is at stake. While it remains a vital issue, there are a raft of associated issues to be addressed by legislators and policy-makers.

NOTES

1 Reference re: *Assisted Human Reproduction Act*, 2010 SCC 61, [2010] 3 SCR 457.

2 See *Jobs, Growth and Long-term Prosperity Act*, SC 2012, c 19, division 56 [*JGLPA*].

3 *Pratten v British Columbia (Attorney General)*, 2011 BCSC 656, 99 RFL (6th) 290; *Pratten v British Columbia (Attorney General)*, 2012 BCCA 480, 25 RFL (7th) 58, leave to appeal to SCC refused, [2013] SCCA No. 36. For a more detailed discussion of *Pratten*, including the background to the case and the arguments of the parties, see the chapter by Giroux and Milne in this volume. The case is also the focus of the chapters by Gruben and Guihon.

4 See Francoise Baylis, "Supreme Court of Canada Decision on the *Assisted Human Reproduction Act* Creates Urgent Need for Action" (2011) 33 J Obstet Gynaecol Can 317 at 319.

5 *Pratten*, *supra* note 3.

6 Section 63 of the *Adoption Act*, SBC 1995, c 48, provided adoptees over the age of nineteen the right/opportunity to obtain the identity of their biological parent by applying for a copy of their original birth registration and adoption order. Section 65 of the Act permitted a disclosure veto to be obtained by either a birth parent or an adopted person in respect of individuals adopted prior to the Act coming into force in 1996 so that no identifying information would be available. Section 66 permitted a birth parent or an adopted person to file a written no-contact declaration so although the identity of the birth parent or adopted individual may be available it is accompanied by a no-contact declaration. The Adoption Regulation detailed the information to be collected when a child was placed for adoption, and included physical, cultural, health, and social information. See now RSBC 1996, c 5; BC Reg 291/96.

7 *Pratten v British Columbia (Attorney General)*, 2012 BCCA 480 at para 34.

8 *Ibid*, at para 37.

9 *Ibid*, at para 42.

10 Vanessa Gruben and Daphne Gilbert, "Donor Unknown: Assessing the Section 15 Rights of Donor-Conceived Offspring" (2011) 27 Can J Fam L 247.

11 Ken R. Daniels and Karyn Taylor, "Secrecy and Openness in Donor Insemination" (1993) 12 Politics and the Life Sciences 155; Lawrie McFarlane, "Donor Case Strikes at Basic Family Foundations" *Times Colonist* (Victoria), 15 July 2011.

12 Kimberley Leighton, "Addressing the Harms of Not Knowing One's Heredity: Lessons from Geneological Bewilderment" (2012) 3 Adoption and Culture 63 at 84.

13 Vanessa L. Pi, "Regulating Sperm Donation: Why Requiring Exposed Donation Is Not the Answer" (2009) 16 Duke J Gender Law & Pol'y 379. In the United Kingdom, one of the more recent countries to remove donor anonymity, a significant drop in donor registrations was witnessed around the time that amendments removing anonymity were introduced.

However, anecdotal evidence suggests that recruitment of sperm donors has since increased. See Eric Blyth and Lucy Frith, "Implementing an Altruistic Sperm Donation Program in Canada" (2011) 33 J Obstet Gynaecol Can 484. See also U. Shukla *et al.*, "Sperm Donor Recruitment, Attitudes and Provider Practices – 5 Years after the Removal of Donor Anonymity" (2013) 28 Hum Reprod 676.

14 Jacqueline A. Laing, "Artificial Reproduction, Blood Relatedness and Human Identity" (2006) 89 Monist 548 at 549.

15 Mary Lyndon Shanley, "Collaboration and Commodification in Assisted Procreation: Reflections on an Open Market and Anonymous Donation in Human Sperm and Eggs" (2002) 36 Law & Soc'y Rev 257; Jospehine Johnston, "Mum's the Word: Donor Anonymity in Assisted Reproduction" (2002) 11:1 Health L Rev 51.

16 See Sonia Allan, "Donor Conception, Secrecy and the Search for Information" (2012) 19 JLM 631 at 636; A. Ravelingien, P. Provost, and G. Pennings, "Donor-Conceived Children Looking for their Sperm Donor: What Do They Want to Know?" (2013) 5 Facts, Views & Vision in ObGyn 257; Geraldine Hewitt, "Missing Links: Identity Issues of Donor-Conceived People" (2002) 9 Journal of Fertility Counselling 14; Tim Watkin, "The X and Y Files" *Listener* (New Zealand), 31 January 1998, 18.

17 In *Pratten* the Court heard evidence from a woman who only discovered that she was donor-conceived when she was diagnosed with a rare form of lymphoma and needed a bone marrow transplant. Because the donor was anonymous, she was limited in finding a close enough tissue match for bone marrow donation. In Australia a donor-conceived woman with heritable bowel cancer was unable to contact eight other individuals conceived by the same anonymous donor to warn them of the familial risk. Sonia Allan, "All Donor-conceived People in Victoria now have the Right to Donor Information" Bionews (UK), 29 February 2016, http://www.bionews.org.uk/.

18 See Katherine van Heugten and Judy Hunter, "Assisted Human Reproduction," in *A Brave New World: Where Biotechnology and Human Rights Intersect* (Ottawa: Government of Canada, 2005), 2–17, http://publications.gc.ca/collections/Collection/Iu199-6-2005E_Biotech_CH2.pdf.

19 This includes Sweden, Austria, Switzerland, the Netherlands, Norway, the United Kingdom, New Zealand, Finland, and the Australian States of Victoria, Western Australia, New South Wales, and (most recently) South Australia. See Eric Blyth and Lucy Frith, "Donor-Conceived People's Access to Genetic and Biographical History: An Analysis of Provisions in Different Jurisdictions Permitting Disclosure of Donor Identity" (2009)

23 International Journal of Law, Policy and the Family 174. A recent report of the Standing Committee of the Australian Senate recommended that the remaining Australian states and territories that have not yet introduced laws prohibiting donor anonymity do so. See Senate, Legal and Constitutional Affairs References Committee, *Donor Conception Practices in Australia* (2011), http://www.aph.gov.au.

20 *Adult Adoption Information Act 1985*, 1985/127. While the adopted individual can register a veto on contact by his/her birth parent (s 7), a birth parent that gives a child up for adoption after 1 March 1986 cannot exercise a veto.

21 See Barbara Nicholas, "Community and Justice: The Challenges of Bicultural Partnership to Policy on Assisted Reproductive Technology" (1996) 10 Bioethics 212 at 217.

22 *Status of Children Amendment Act 1987*, 1987/185. If a woman was single, or undertook the procedure without the consent of her husband/*de facto* partner, the donor remained the child's legal parent but any rights or liabilities were extinguished. (See ss 5, 7, 9, 11, 13, 15.) The *Status of Children Act 1969*, 1969/18, was again amended in 2004 (*Status of Children Amendment Act 2004*, 2004/91).

23 Manatu Māori Working Party for ART, *Guidelines for the Use of Assisted Reproductive Technology* (Wellington: 1991).

24 The Treaty of Waitangi was signed in 1840 by representatives of the British Crown and Māori. Although it is not part of domestic law, the Treaty forms part of New Zealand's constitution alongside the *New Zealand Bill of Rights Act 1990* and the *Constitution Act 1986*.

25 Manatu Māori, *supra* note 23 at 1.

26 Report of the Ministerial Committee on Assisted Reproductive Technologies, *Assisted Human Reproduction: Navigating Our Future* (Wellington: Department of Justice, 1994) at 2 ["MCART Report"].

27 For an explanation of Māori family concepts, see W.R. Atkin, "New Zealand: Children versus Families – Is There Any Conflict?" (1988–1989) 27 J Fam Law 231.

28 Manatu Māori, *supra* note 23 at 6.

29 Bioethics Research Centre, *Biotechnology Revisited: Ethical and Legal Issues in the Application of Biotechnology to Medical Practice* (Bioethics Centre Otago, Report Prepared for the Medical Council of New Zealand, 1991), 2.

30 MCART Report, *supra* note 26.

31 See Royal Commission on New Reproductive Technologies, *Proceed with Care: Final Report of the Royal Commission on New Reproductive Technologies* (Ottawa: Minister of Government Services Canada, 1993), 52–3

["Royal Commission"]. The principles identified were individual autonomy, equality, respect for human life and dignity, protection of the vulnerable, non-commercialization of reproduction, appropriate uses of resources, accountability, and balancing individual and collective interests.

32 MCART Report, *supra* note 26 at 76.

33 *Ibid* at 77.

34 *Ibid*.

35 Ken Daniels, "New Zealand: From Secrecy and Shame to Openness and Acceptance," in *Third Party Assisted Conception Across Cultures*, ed.Eric Blyth and Ruth Landau (London: Jessica Kingsley, 2004), 148 at 150.

36 Ken Daniels and Alison Douglass, "Access to Genetic Information by Donor Offspring and Donors: Medicine, Policy and Law in New Zealand" (2008) 27 Med & Law 131.

37 See Katrina Hargreaves and Ken Daniels, "Parents Dilemmas in Sharing Donor Insemination Conception Stories with Their Children" (2007) 21 Children & Society 420 at 423.

38 The first attempt to enact specific legislation occurred in the form of a private member's bill introduced in Parliament in 1996 (Human Assisted Reproductive Technology Bill 1996 195–1]).

39 Royal Commission, *supra* note 31.

40 *Ibid* at 482, R 94(i)(k)(l).

41 *Ibid* at 592, R 166; and at 593, R 167.

42 *Ibid* at 590, R 163.

43 The Act was passed as an exercise of the federal criminal power pursuant to s 91(27) of the *Constitution Act 1987*. It was accepted that some provisions were legitimate matters of criminal law; however, the Quebec Attorney General argued that others attempted to regulate all assisted reproductive medical practice and research, which were provincial matters. Consequently the impugned provisions' "real character – their pith and substance – was the regulation of medical practice and research in relation to assisted reproduction" and thus arguably not within the proper exercises of federal jurisdiction. *Reference*, *supra* note 1 at para 7.

44 *AHRA*, ss 10, 12.

45 *AHRA*, s 2.

46 *AHRA*, s 60.

47 *AHRA*, s 21.

48 *AHRA*, s 22, repealed by *JGLPA*, s 722.

49 *AHRA*, s 24, repealed by *JGLPA*, s 722.

50 *AHRA*, s 65.

51 See Françoise Baylis, "The Demise of Assisted Human Reproduction Canada" (2012) 34 J Obstet Gynaecol 511; *JGLPA*, *supra* note 2.
52 See *HARTA*, Part 2, subpart 1 and schedule 1 of the Act.
53 *HARTA*, s 16.
54 For example, artificial insemination and the collection of eggs or sperm for the purposes of donation are established procedures. HART Order 2005, Part 1 of the Schedule.
55 *HARTA*, ss 32, 35(b).
56 *HARTA*, s 35.
57 *HARTA*, s 28.
58 *HARTA*, s 19(2). Donor conception procedures that are regulated subject to ACART guidelines include "Guidelines on Donations of Eggs or Sperm between Certain Family Members"; "Embryo Donation for Reproductive Purposes"; and "Guidelines on the Creation and Use, for Reproductive Purposes, of an Embryo Created from Donated Eggs in Conjunction with Donated Sperm," Advisory Committee on Assisted Reproductive Technology, http://acart.health.govt.nz/.
59 *AHRA*, s 2(b).
60 *HARTA*, s. 3(a).
61 *HARTA*, s 3; *AHRA*, s 2.
62 *HARTA*, s 4(a).
63 See Report of the Health Committee, Human Assisted Reproductive Technology Bill, 6 August 2004, 195–2 at 5.
64 *AHRA*, s 2(a).
65 *HARTA*, s 4(b).
66 *AHRA*, s 2(c).
67 See Health Canada, *New Reproductive and Genetic Technologies: Setting Boundaries, Enhancing Health* (Ottawa: Minister of Supply and Services Canada, 1996), 16.
68 *HARTA*, s 4(d); *AHRA*, s 2(d).
69 *HARTA*, s 3(c). Commercial surrogacy is prohibited (s 15), as is the commercial supply of human embryos or gametes (s 13).
70 *AHRA*, s 2(f).
71 *AHRA*, s 2(e).
72 *Human Rights Act 1993*, 1993/82, s 44(1) and s 21.
73 *HARTA*, s 4(f).
74 *HARTA*, s 4(g).
75 *AHRA*, s 7. Section 7 came into force in 22 April 2004.
76 *AHRA*, ss 12(1),(2).

77 However, a public consultation was undertaken by Health Canada in 2007. See Health Canada, *Reimbursement of Expenditures Under the Assisted Human Reproduction Act: Public Consultation Document*, http://www.hc-sc.gc.ca.
78 See *AHRA*, s 71, which is a transitional provision that permits controlled activities to be undertaken if they were performed within the year prior to sections 10–13 being proclaimed in force. See also Dave Snow, Françoise Baylis, and Jocelyn Downie, "Why the Government of Canada Won't Regulate Assisted Human Reproduction: A Modern Mystery" (2015) 9 McGill JL & Health 1.
79 *AHRA*, s 3.
80 *AHRA*, s 17, repealed by *JGLPA*, s 720.
81 Reference re *Assisted Human Reproduction Act*, 2010 SCC 61; *JGLPA*, s 720.
82 *AHRA*, s 18(2), repealed by *JGLPA*, s 720.
83 *AHRA*, s 18(3), repealed by *JGLPA*, s 720.
84 *AHRA*, s 18(7), repealed by *JGLPA*, s 720.
85 *AHRA*, s 18(3), repealed by *JGLPA*, s 720.
86 *AHRA*, s 2(a).
87 2011 BCSC 656 at para 111.
88 *HARTA*, s 3(f).
89 *HARTA*, s 4(e).
90 Section 47 of the Act lists specific donor information that providers must obtain, including identifying, ethnic, and health information. If Māori, information regarding the *whanau*, *hapu*, and *iwi* of the donor must be obtained if the donor "is aware of those affiliations." Further information, if considered significant by the provider, may be obtained regarding not only the donor's medical history but also that of the donor's parents, grandparents, children, or siblings. The provider must also document the donor's reasons for donation. The provider must accept any updating information provided by the donor regarding the above.
91 *HARTA*, s 53. The provider must provide the Registrar-General with the date of birth, sex, and name of the child born and the names and addresses of the guardians, the donor(s') name, address, and date of birth/country of birth. Births, Deaths and Marriages (housed within the Department of Internal Affairs) is responsible for maintaining the Human Assisted Reproductive Technology Register.
92 *HARTA*, s 50(1). A guardian of a donor-conceived individual may also request information if the donor-conceived individual is under 18 (s 50(2)).
93 *HARTA*, s 50(3).
94 *HARTA*, s 50(2).

95 *HARTA*, s 50(4).
96 *HARTA*, s 65.
97 *HARTA*, s 50(6).
98 *HARTA*, s 58(1).
99 *HARTA*, s 58(1).
100 *HARTA*, s 58(2).
101 *HARTA*, s 60(1),(2).
102 *HARTA*, s 60(2).
103 *HARTA*, s 59.
104 *HARTA*, s 48(2).
105 *HARTA*, s 3.
106 *HARTA*, s 46.
107 *HARTA*, s 43, s 63.
108 Tom Blackwell, "Limit Pregnancies by Same Sperm Donor: Fertility Clinics," *National Post* (Canada), 8 September 2011.
109 *Ibid.*
110 *Ibid.*
111 Eric Blyth *et al.*, "The Implications of Adoption for Donor Offspring Following Donor-assisted Conception" (2001) 6 Child Fam. Soc. Work 295 at 304.
112 Neroli Sawyer, "Sperm Donor Limits That Control for the 'Relative' Risk Associated with the Use of Open-identity Donors" (2010) 25 Human Reproduction 1089 at 1093.
113 Standards New Zealand, *Fertility Services* (NZS 8181:2007) at 45. (Fertility services must be certified under the *Health and Disability Services (Safety) Act 2001*, 2001/93, and comply with the relevant service standards. See *HARTA*, s 80.)
114 See Blyth and Frith, *supra* note 19 at 178.
115 See Blyth and Frith, *supra* note 19 at 185.
116 *HARTA*, s 46(3)(g).
117 Studies indicate that although the rates of parental disclosure are not high in New Zealand, it has comparatively higher disclosure rates than elsewhere. See Anna Rumball and Vivienne Adair, "Telling the Story: Parents' Scripts for Donor Offspring" (1999) 14 Human Reproduction 1392. (Of 181 parents surveyed, 30 per cent had told their children. Of those that hadn't, 77 per cent intended to tell them in the future when their child was able to understand.)
118 Eric Blyth *et al.*, "The Role of Birth Certificates in Relation to Access to Biographical and Genetic History in Donor Conception" (2009) 17 International Journal of Children's Rights 207 at 215.

119 Law Commission, *New Issues in Legal Parenthood* (NZLC R88, 2005) at para 10.40; Senate, Legal and Constitutional Affairs References Committee, *supra* note 19 at para 7.63.

120 Assisted Reproductive Treatment Act 2008 (Vic), s 153(1), inserted new sections 17A and 17B into the Births, Deaths and Marriages Registration Act 1996.

121 Law Commission, *supra* note 119 at para 10.62.

122 See Nuffield Council on Bioethics, *Donor Conception: Ethical Aspects of Information Sharing* (London: 2013).

123 *SoC Act 1969*, 17(2), s 18(2). Consent is presumed in the absence of evidence to the contrary (s 27).

124 *SoC Act 1969*, s 19(2), 21(2).

125 *Status of Children Amendment Act 2004*, 2004/91, s 14.

126 *SoC Act 1969*, s 17(2), 22.

127 *SoC Act 1969*, s 20(2), 22(2).

128 *SoC Act 1969*, s 23, 24.

129 This followed protracted litigation between a lesbian couple and a known sperm donor. See *P v K*, [2003] 2 NZLR 787, [2003] NZFLR 489 (HC); [2004] NZFLR 752 (FC); [2004] 2 NZLR 421 (HC); *P v K*, [2006] NZFLR 22 (FC).

130 *CoC Act 2004*, s 41(3).

131 *CoC Act 2004*, s 41(4).

132 *CoC Act 2004*, s 41(6).

133 However, a donor can apply to be appointed as an additional guardian under section 27 of the *Care of Children Act* (2004).

134 Law Commission, *supra* note 119 at para 6.76. See also Angela Cameron, Vanessa Gruben, and Fiona Kelly, "De-Anonymising Sperm Donors in Canada: Some Doubts and Directions" (2010) 26 Can J Fam L 95 at 128.

135 The Commission utilizes *P v K* (*supra* note 116) as an example of this. Although the case predates the enactment of section 41, the same outcome could occur under the Act. In *P v K* a preconception agreement permitting a donor at least fourteen days access a year was varied against the wishes of the legal parents, permitting the donor/biological father graduated access for up to seven days a month and appointing him an additional guardian. Contact was subsequently increased by the family court when it made parenting orders under s. 48 of the Care of Children Act 1969 providing for contact every second and fourth weekend of every month, as well as half the school term holidays.

136 Law Commission, *supra* note 119 at para 6.53.

137 *Ibid* at para 6.84.

138 *P v K*, [2003] 2 NZLR 787 at para 207.
139 Ministry of Justice, *Government Response to Law Commission Report on New Issues in Legal Parenthood* (Wellington: 2006) at para 25, http://www.justice.govt.nz.
140 Law Commission, *supra* note 119 at para 6.52, Recommendation 9, Recommendation 10.
141 For a discussion, see *AA v BB*, 2007 ONCA 2 at para 14, 83 OR (3d) 561, 35 RFL (6th) 1.
142 Ministry of Justice, *supra* note 139 at para 11. It observed that "a genetic father who intends and wishes to take on all the rights and responsibilities of parenthood should not lose that legal relationship with his child purely because of the method of conception." Law Commission, *supra* note 119 at para 6.51.
143 Donors are required to meet with an approved counsellor and undertake screening for infections and genetic conditions. See Standards New Zealand, *supra* note 113 at 27–8.
144 Michelle Cooke, "Redhead Sperm Donors Welcome, Says Doctor," *Stuff* (New Zealand), 21 September 2011, http://www.stuff.co.nz. Sunday, "One Couple a Week Heading Overseas for a Baby" *One News* (New Zealand), 22 May 2011.
145 Isaac Davison, "Payments Urged for IVF Donations" *NZ Herald* (New Zealand), 30 August 2010, http://www.nzherald.co.nz. See also Standards New Zealand, *supra* note 113, clause 1.11.1(j).
146 Isaac Davison, *ibid*.
147 Rather, it preferred such a reference, if any, to be placed on birth certificate application forms. See Ministry of Justice, *supra* note 139 at para 41.
148 *Pratten*, *supra* note 3 at para 177.
149 Joyce Harper, Debbie Kennett, and Dan Reisel, "The End of Donor Anonymity: How Genetic Testing Is Likely to Drive Anonymous Gamete Donation out of Business" (2016) Human Reproduction 1.

10 What Adoption Law Suggests about Donor Anonymity Policies: A UK Perspective

JENNIFER M. SPEIRS

In this chapter I describe briefly the current laws in the United Kingdom governing child adoption, as well as regulation in the field of assisted human reproduction (AHR), as a contribution to the debates about AHR regulation in Canada. I note some fundamental differences of principle in these laws on adoption and on AHR and how they compare with the views of past semen donors regarding the long-term implications of donor anonymity. Ultimately I will suggest that the complex and sometimes overlooked and misunderstood entanglement of reserved and devolved legislation in the UK with respect to donor-assisted conception points to ambivalence about donor anonymity and has led to the marginalization of the long-term needs of people with a personal involvement.

Past Semen Donors' Reflections on Their Anonymous Donating

There has been little research into the long-term impact on semen donors of having donated anonymously and no information as to why there has been little research. Certainly in the UK there is the challenge of locating research participants, given the destruction of records – where these existed – before the legal requirement to keep them. There has also been the assumption that in contrast to human egg donors, semen donors simply had no long-term consequences to contend with. However, important research has been carried out into the views of past semen donors about sharing information with offspring, and one study revealed that since they had donated, donors had changed their thinking about the need for anonymity.[1]

I carried out ethnographic doctoral research between 2001 and 2007[2] focusing on what it meant to semen donors that they had donated anonymously when they were young medical students. After considerable time and effort lasting up to a year, I found fifteen men who agreed to meet with me after being contacted by an intermediary or who offered to meet after learning of my research. All had donated anonymously between twenty and forty-five years previously, before treatment with donated gametes became subject to regulation. Eleven of the men had donated during or not long after completing their medical studies, four others as students in other faculties. One donor had been informed that his semen had not been used. The other donors did not know whether their donations had created successful pregnancies, but assumed they had. Research methods included participant observation, one-to-one interviews, and a small survey of UK infertility clinics' policy-making regarding the use of known donors. Information was also obtained through sessional work as a lay inspector for the Human Fertilisation and Embryology Authority, through serving on the committee of the British Fertility Society's executive committee, and from many discussions with non-donor doctors and infertility clinic workers – doctors, scientists, embryologists, nurses, and counsellors. Social anthropological theories particularly about kinship, gifts, and risk were used for analysis of the findings.[3]

The aim of the research was to get behind the arguments and disagreements about donor-assisted conception, particularly on the matter of whether donor anonymity should be retained – a debate that was growing louder in the UK in the early 2000s. I had noticed claims by apparently self-appointed advocates who were stating what semen donors were feeling and thinking, as if they were reporting donors' views. The voices of the donors themselves were seldom heard. The claims on behalf of donors struck me as being too clear-cut, and I wondered whether the ambivalences, hopes, and anxieties of donors were being ignored. One example, from the time when there was increasing speculation in the media about the possibility of a change in the legislative requirement for donor anonymity, came from the then president of the National Union of Students Scotland. He was quoted in the *Daily Record* newspaper: "A lot of students do this because they are so desperate for cash. They have the choice of doing something like this or dropping out because of debt. Students will do anything for money. But they certainly don't expect to be traced later by a child with whom they had no intention of having any contact at all."[4] Such claims suggested that donors were in a vulnerable position[5] but took no account of the possibility that donors' views might change during their life course, especially if their youthful donations had been due to financial need.

The main objective of my research was to explore what it meant to semen donors in the UK that they had donated anonymously when they were young. I concentrated on doctors who had been donors partly because at the time they were donating, they were learning about genetics. It occurred to me that it might now seem paradoxical for them that their donations had been anonymized or even – when sperm mixing was carried out – totally anonymous.

All of the fifteen donors had been anonymous to potential recipients and any donor offspring, but their donating was not a secret: all of the donors had told someone else about it. In one case it was just the donor's student flatmates, but for others the information had been shared with girlfriends, wives, mothers, grown-up children, colleagues, and friends. A few had forgotten exactly who they had told. It was, as one wife described it to me, "leaky information" and what the sociologist Erving Goffman might have described as a free secret rather than an inside secret.[6]

Regrets and Ambivalence

Some donors, including former medical students, had regrets about donating, especially those who specifically mentioned that they were embarrassed now about having been paid money for their donations.[7] In discussing reasons for donating, one donor specifically suggested that there was something wrong about having done so for money. He said that it was the fact that earning money for providing semen might be seen as shameful by his children that had so far prevented him from telling them he had donated semen as a student. For him, the donating had been "a financial transaction." By contrast, another donor felt reassured because he had been rewarded financially: "I'm happy that I donated for money. Makes it clear that you could draw a line under it." Being paid meant that there was no need for further thought about the donating and its long-term implications. It had been a short-term commercial transaction.

One donor was explicit in condemning what he described as the exploitation of financially needy immature young men and was adamant that he and his young friends in no way had given informed consent in the sense in which it is understood nowadays. This donor reported that his wife was equally unhappy about him having donated anonymously.[8] Several donors described their lack of respect at the time for the recruiting doctors working in private practices, who were making a profit from the neediness of infertile couples. "He was not a proper doctor, I remembered thinking as I looked at him," one donor told me. For some, this lack of respect has remained, especially towards today's very wealthy clinicians in some for-profit infertility clinics. One donor who is a general practitioner commented scathingly that the fees paid nowadays to these clinicians by patients with fertility problems would pay for "another wheel on the Ferrari." Another donor described how it was clear to him when he was donating that the doctor in charge of the clinic was running a "lucrative business." According to the donor, he had shown no care at all towards the young donors.

It was clear from my research that some of the donors were aware of the mismatch between the stereotypical wild young student of the past who had donated for financial rewards and the respectable professionals they had become. They managed this in two ways. Firstly, there was frequent joking, a device that serves to marginalize inappropriate or transgressive actions. Infertility clinic workers in the UK are familiar with this, and especially with the use of the *double entendre*. I encountered many examples of this during my fieldwork, including this recollection from a man who had donated as a medical student: "There was another friend of mine who got involved really because he wanted some money … and he was quite amusing, he said that we were all members of the Semen's Union … and we actually held out for a pay rise, I remember that, um, we felt it was about time we got a pay rise. I remember we actually … threaten[ed] to withdraw our services."

Secondly, donors acknowledged the extent to which maturity changes perspectives. At the time of donating, most had felt some sympathy for the childless couples whom they had been told they were helping, even if their donations were for money. That was a factor in motivating them to donate, but they did not give any thought to the future needs of donor-conceived people. Today, they would, and all of the donors expressed the hope that things had turned out well for the donor offspring. For example, one donor told me, "I hope that they are at peace, strong, fulfilled, if they exist." He complained about not knowing whether they existed, and as a doctor he was astonished to learn that proper records had not been kept.

Was the fact of having donated a current concern? For a few, it was not something they had thought about until I was put in contact with them, or if they had thought about it, it was in the context of conversations with close friends. For other donors there were concerns that included the anger and embarrassment already referred to; there was also a realization that when their teenage children started dating, unwitting incest might occur. Generally the donors played down the risk of this on the grounds that it was statistically unlikely, but donors with teenage daughters admitted to feeling less certain. In addition, the public debates about changing the regulations on donor anonymity[9] had raised worries for a few donors about "a knock on the door" from donor offspring, mainly because the media seldom highlighted the fact that the change would not be retrospective, but also because of legal uncertainty regarding whether their donor offspring could make a claim on their estates.

Possible Contact with Donor Offspring

One donor stated that he had no regrets about having donated and that his concern about the absence of anonymity nowadays was that actually meeting with donor offspring would arouse feelings of responsibility towards the person that could interfere with his prior loyalties to the children of his marriage. In his opinion it would not breach the contract made with him if a donor offspring made contact with him. In addition, he would not find it a problem to meet with that person provided that it did not "take away from" his children by his marriage. By this he meant that he would not want donor offspring to divert the involvement he has with his family.

Some of the donors said that they would be happy to meet with donor offspring or simply to provide information about themselves and their genealogy. Several expressed curiosity as to what their donor offspring might look like, and one wanted to have a party for them all. However, the possibility of resemblance also worked to support ambivalence about contact. This was put most eloquently by a donor who feared that if he met with a donor offspring in the near future, he would be unable to resist trying to draw him or her into his family, and the timing would not be right: "The minute you look at someone and they look like you, you know that that link is there … It's incredible." He went on to describe meetings with adult cousins for the first time: "People who look like you, like my brothers and sisters, people who look like me and at the same time, same characteristics, same stubbornness, same bad temper, whatever, same build it is just incredible, genetic, seeing my mother and father even though they have passed away. I am seeing them in my daughter, I can see my father's smile."

His worry about connection was that if he were to open the door to a donor offspring who looked like any of his family, he would be unable to prevent himself from inviting the person into the house, and that would be "very embarrassing." However, he believed that his views about connection were "a constantly evolving thing" and that in the future, when his own child was an adult, face-to-face contact with donor offspring might be all right. At the moment, however, it would be "OK to be contacted, provided no knock at the door." And he added: "I think that at this moment I'd be quite happy to do everything that I could to give them everything that I could of, details of myself, that would not mean in any way that the child could find me and come and meet me and et cetera, et cetera, et cetera, and so that's where I think the line should be drawn." For this donor, the worry about a face-to-face meeting was that it might happen before he felt ready to manage it, and that would create an awkward situation for everyone.

The discussions with other donors revealed that they too did not intend to take active steps to search for donor offspring. Only one donor I interviewed had registered with UK DonorLink, the voluntary contact register for pre-1990 donors and donor offspring in the UK, which operated from 2004 to 2013. The concept for such a register was derived from the work of Birthlink, which set up and runs the adoption contact register for Scotland[10] and was promoted by the British Association of Social Workers (BASW) as a needs-led service for helping donors and donor offspring to exchange identifying information in a safe and confidential way.[11] A core characteristic of UK Donorlink was that, like Birthlink, it was underpinned by professional social work values and practice in recognition of the sensitivity and complexity of the issues faced by donors and donor conceived-people and their families.[12] These issues include concerns about unwitting incest, feelings of distrust and loss, and lack of information about genetic inheritance.[13]

However, for other semen donors I interviewed, registering with UK DonorLink would have been too uncertain a step to make. They were not sure how they would manage the situation if contact were made. Nearly all of the donors had little or no information about contemporary adoption laws and practices in the UK, nor did they have any knowledge about why many adopted people and their birth relatives want to exchange identifying information and perhaps meet in person. Thus they have no script to adapt for use in the context of contact with strangers who are genetic relatives. I believe that it is significant that it was the two donors who had some knowledge of how post-adoption reunions work in the UK who showed the most understanding of the implications for donor offspring of donor anonymity and, to some extent, of the lifelong implications for themselves and their families. For them, having donated semen in the past was not a closed-off chapter in their biography.

Legislative Context of Regulated Infertility Treatment

Strictly speaking, the UK does not have a constitution as the word is understood in more recently formed states. The United Kingdom of Great Britain and Northern Ireland comprises the four nations of England, Northern Ireland, Scotland, and Wales, and for historical reasons each has its distinct laws as well as those shared with the UK as a whole or, in the case of Wales, with England. Scotland retained its separate jurisdiction when its Parliament and that of England and Wales joined together in 1707. However, all jurisdictions in the UK share the impact of European laws. Following referendums in Scotland and Wales in 1997, and in Northern Ireland in 1998, the UK Parliament transferred a range of its powers to the new national Parliament in Scotland or to the assemblies in Wales and Northern Ireland. After the passing of the *Scotland Act 1998* and the *Government of Wales Act 1998* and the re-establishment of the Northern Ireland Assembly in 1998, many laws were devolved, but with different arrangements reflecting the varied histories and administrative structures of the nations. At the time of writing, responsibility for defence, foreign relations, customs and excise, welfare benefits and national insurance, and income tax and VAT (value-added tax) remains reserved to the UK.

The regulation of infertility treatment was introduced in the UK as a means of providing public confidence in IVF, tempering experimentation, and defining the legal relationships between donors, donor-conceived children, and the latters' nurturing parents. Despite the devolution of many laws and powers from the UK Parliament, the regulatory legislation, including its enforcement administration, has remained as a reserved matter. The *Human Fertilisation and Embryology Act 1990* (*HF&E Act*) is UK legislation, and there has been no significant pressure to devolve its provisions, even though health services in general are devolved. However, the *HF&E Act* and the subsequent *Human Fertilisation and Embryology Act 2008* both contain separate provisions for England and Wales, Scotland, and Northern Ireland in matters such as legal capacity, courts of appeal, and parental responsibilities. The *HF&E Act* mandated the establishment of the Human Fertilisation and Embryology Authority (HFEA), which is responsible for licensing and inspecting clinics providing infertility treatments (including *in vitro* fertilization). The HFEA also licenses the recruitment of gamete donors, and the storage and use of donated gametes. The Act allowed donors of semen, eggs, and embryos to remain unidentifiable to people conceived from the use of their gametes. After considerable lobbying by the BASW and in recognition of the human rights argument, non-retrospective regulations were introduced in 2005 that provided for donors to be identifiable to donor offspring born after 2006.[14]

The Conservative–Liberal Democrat coalition government 2010–2015 announced after it was elected in May 2010 that in the interests of efficiency and cost-savings there would be a reduction in the number of arm's length central government bodies,[15] in what became known as the "bonfire of the quangos."[16] These quasi-autonomous non-governmental organizations were subjected to legislative scrutiny in 2011–12, and this led to the *Public Bodies (Reform) Bill*, which has now been enacted.[17] Only a few weeks before the list was officially made public, the HFEA was added to the list of organizations to be abolished.[18] The reduction in the number of quangos was supposedly for the sake of improving accountability and cutting costs,[19] but it was not made clear how this was relevant to the HFEA. Most importantly, there was no indication that this ideologically driven action had at its heart the best interests and long-term welfare of infertility patients and of people with a personal involvement in donor-assisted conception – parents, donors, donor-conceived people, and their families. It was of great concern that no consideration appeared to have been given to what would happen to the registers of donor information held by the HFEA and its Donor Sibling Link service, should the HFEA be abolished.[20, 21]

The government issued a consultation in June 2012[22] on its proposals to transfer the HFEA's functions to the Care Quality Commission (CQC) and other existing bodies, offering three options:

1. Transfer all of the HFEA's functions to the CQC except those relating to research, which would be transferred to the Health Research Authority (the government's preferred option).
2. Transfer the functions of the HFEA to a range of bodies.
3. Allow the HFEA to retain its existing functions, but more efficiently.

The CQC was set up in 2009 to regulate health and social care in England[23] following a problematic merging of three predecessor organizations that regulated hospitals, social care, and mental health establishments. It would have had to be given UK-wide powers in order to deal with the functions of reserved legislation such as the *HF&E Act*, and the devolved administrations were consulted on how that might be achieved. However, in July 2013 the government announced that the HFEA would remain the independent regulator of assisted reproduction and embryo research in the UK after all, but that an independent review of its operations would be carried out.[24]

At the time of writing, the future of the HFEA may again be reviewed, following the announcement by prime minister David Cameron on 19 September 2014 of a commission to take forward the devolution commitments on further powers for the Scottish Parliament. The commission's report recommends that there be discussion about the devolution of legislation on abortion, embryology, surrogacy, and genetics.[25] The suggestion has generated views from fertility specialists both for and against. One advantage of devolution would be that it would provide the opportunity to close current gaps in the provision of services for donor-conceived people, donors, and their families.[26]

Payments to Donors

The HFEA permits payments in the form of "compensation" to donors who provide gametes.[27] An awkwardly designed public consultation[28] was carried out seeking views about anonymity, payments to donors, and interfamilial donation, among other things, but it seems that the majority of views were disregarded. The HFEA considered how much and what sort of compensation and benefits in kind sperm and egg donors should be permitted to receive, and decided that donors should be paid fixed sums: £35 per clinic visit for sperm donors and £750 per cycle of donation for egg donors.

Interestingly, a number of medical practitioners declared in their responses to the consultation that they were in favour of payment as well as the reinstatement of donor anonymity.[29] Since there is no evidence that such practices are necessary for recruiting donors in the UK, it may be that they are a response to concerns about the need to keep donors at a distance from donor offspring and their parents. Many infertility treatment providers are uneasy about or opposed to donor-conceived people searching for information about their donors, and to donors meeting with potential recipients and donor offspring, because of perceived risks. Furthermore, when donors are paid, the relationship between clinic and donor becomes a commercial one rather than one in which the donor has the status of a volunteer who acts from altruism. Payment avoids the need for reciprocity in the form of gratitude from clinic staff, and it cuts off relationships. In some clinics, payment also allows clinics to treat semen donors without sufficient respect and courtesy, and without ensuring that they are fully aware of the lifelong implications of donation by providing them with adequate counselling services. As volunteers, donors should be treated well; as gamete sellers, they can be exploited.[30]

Adoption Laws in the UK

The nations of the UK have separate adoption laws. Scotland is the only one where its original adoption legislation, the *Adoption of Children (Scotland) Act 1930*, did not remove adopted people's right to access their original birth certificate.[31] In England, Wales, and Northern Ireland, the right of access came only after 1975 (informed by research findings in Scotland on adopted people),[32] and, unusually for UK legislation, it was retrospective.[33] To give some protection to birth mothers from the possible impact of this, adopted people in those nations had to meet with an adoption counsellor before receiving a copy of their original birth certificate. However, the new access to the birth certificate did not mean that adopted people had the right to view the record of the court process of their adoption – an existing right in Scotland.[34] This record has been especially useful for older people whose adoptions were not arranged by an adoption agency but through a third party such as a doctor. It contains information about the birth parents that the adopted person can use to search for them as well as to build up the story of their adoption and their origins.[35] Thus adoption law in Scotland was not structured upon a policy of an irrevocable break between an adopted person and their birth relatives. Indeed, adopted people in Scotland were allowed to receive legacies from their birth parents until the law changed in the 1960s allowing them thereafter to inherit from their adoptive parents.[36]

The difference in adoption law has been reflected in how the status of children born through surrogacy arrangements has been legalized. Surrogacy regulations were first drafted in 2001 under s. 30 of the *HF&E Act*. Under the regulations for England, Wales, and Northern

Ireland, the birth certificate of a person born of a surrogate mother, issued after the Parental Order has been made in court, would look to an untutored individual exactly like the original. In other words, the fact of the birth having involved surrogacy has in effect been disguised. If the conception of the child involved donated gametes, then the amount of genealogical information being hidden would be even greater.[37] However, in Scotland the styles of the certificates followed those of adoption law in Scotland: an original birth certificate for which the subject could apply at the age of sixteen, a shortened version of that (e.g., for employment purposes), and a new second certificate with the names of the adopting parents. The staff of the Registrar General's office in Edinburgh advised me at the time that they would not be following the example of the other UK nations and were adamant that the *Parental Order Regulations* for Scotland would resemble the adoption regulations for Scotland as closely as possible. They were aware that there were political pressures in England for parental orders to be very different. The strong impression that I gained then and at all other times in my contacts with them over the years is that connection between people and their genealogical relatives is something that civil servants in Scotland support.

In 2009 the UK's Department of Health held a public consultation on its review of the Parental Order regulations intended to bring them into line with the adoption legislation that had been passed since the *HF&E Act* was implemented. However, although the regulations were part of the reserved legislation governing human fertilization and embryology, they impinged on family law, which is devolved; also, there was a problem with insufficiently robust "devolution-proofing"[38] of the draft regulations.[39] A small but significant change was made that removed the duty on local authorities in Scotland to make counselling available to surrogacy-born people applying after the age of sixteen for their original birth certificate. Now, instead, the new regulations place the responsibility on the Registrar General to inform anyone born of a surrogacy arrangement, and who is applying for their original birth certificate, "about the availability of any counselling services providing counselling in relation to the implications of compliance with the request." Also, applicants must be given a suitable opportunity to receive counselling before being given their original birth certificate.[40] Yet providing information to people about sources of counselling and information was what the Registrar General for Scotland staff were doing already. The explanation for the change, as stated in the summary report of the public consultation,[41] is that the previous system is not possible because there are no intermediary agencies for parental orders as there are for adoption. This is perplexing, since adoption agencies and local authorities in Scotland are not intermediary agencies anyway. It might appear as if the change was to save costs for local authorities in Scotland, but the report does not state whether they were consulted. Unfortunately, what could have been an opportunity to make it a UK-wide *duty* to provide counselling to people born from surrogacy arrangements and others with a personal involvement – their parents, the surrogate mothers, and the donors – was lost, and instead an existing provision for Scotland was removed.

Discussion

The differing adoption legislation in the UK, and the differing approaches taken to the surrogacy regulations that I have briefly described, reflect differing cultural beliefs about the roles of social and genetic parenthood, as well as differing attitudes towards risk-taking in creating and maintaining social relationships. In donor-assisted conception, as with adoption policy in the past in some of the UK nations with regard to keeping adopted people and their birth relatives unknown to each other, there is still some concern that without anonymity, donors might interfere with the upbringing of donor-conceived people. Anonymity is conceived as a device for keeping people apart, as the doctors who pioneered donor insemination (DI) clinics in the UK well understood. One perceived risk of DI, then, was the use of a personal donor (i.e., a donor known personally to the recipients), on the grounds that this had adulterous connotations and would disrupt existing social relationships. A clinician at the meeting of a study group held at the Royal College of Obstetricians and Gynaecologists in London is recorded as insisting on anonymity between donor and recipient:

> There is a certain logic in using the father or brother of the husband, and couples will occasionally request this. However, the possibility of subsequent emotional problems of a sexual nature, or in relation to ownership of the child, far outweigh any potential advantages. I would not agree to such an arrangement, although apparently successful cases of family donors have been recorded ... The use of friends entails even greater emotional dangers and lacks the genetic comparability advantage of relatives.[42]

Two specific disadvantages are perceived to arise from this kind of donation: the possibility of sexual feelings on the part of those involved, and the risk that being the genetic father of the child would entitle a donor to claim the right to be treated also as the legal father of the child. The perceived increased risk inherent in using the help of a friend is that a friend would not be constrained by being in a pre-existing family relationship to the child, such as grandfather or uncle. However, the use of personal donors has become more acceptable in the UK in recent years, encouraged by the expectations of same-sex prospective parents and the clarity in UK law that gamete donors who donate at a licensed clinic will not be treated as the father of any resulting children.

Yet the emphasis in UK legislation concerning AHR on the medical and scientific aspects of helping childless people to become parents has in a number of ways been at the expense of recognizing and ameliorating, or even avoiding, the negative long-term impacts of donor anonymity. These have been well expressed in the UK with respect to donor-conceived people but not for semen donors. Semen donation, just like adoption in many jurisdictions tended to be in the past, has been viewed as an event rather than a process. However, the brief data extracts from my study of what anonymous donation meant to a small sample of semen donors of the past indicate that for most of them there have been and will continue to be implications throughout their life course that were denied or not foreseen by infertility clinics and the young men themselves at the time of donating. Concerns about unwitting incest, the welfare of donor offspring, the reactions of their own children, and how to manage the conflict between the wish for and the fear of making a connection have been largely ignored by AHR legislation.

This suggests that policy-makers for AHR need to be informed by the lessons that have been learned in adoption practice in countries such as the UK and particularly in Scotland. Firstly, professional support and mediation services for people separated from genetic relatives have value. Secondly, the "legal control of secrecy" may be unnecessary and unhelpful.[43] Supporters of donor anonymity have argued that no similarities can be drawn between adoption and donor-assisted conception.[44] They tend to make a comparison between adopted people and donor-conceived people,[45] and they claim to have found insufficient similarities to allow donor offspring access to identifying information about donors. However, these claims are not based on research evidence; they also neglect the comparison of semen donors with birth fathers, who also may have concerns and regrets over their life course.[46]

Thus the continuing challenge for the UK, as for Canada, is how to promote safe, effective and accountable donor-assisted conception services while keeping the long-term needs of those with a personal involvement as the primary consideration of legislation.[47]

NOTES

1 K. Daniels *et al.*, "Previous Semen Donors and Their Views Regarding the Sharing of Information with Offspring" (2005) 20:6 Human Reproduction 1670.

2 Jennifer M. Speirs, "Secretly Connected? Anonymous Semen Donation, Genetics and Meanings of Kinship" (PhD diss., University of Edinburgh, 2007), Edinburgh Research Archive, https://www.era.lib.ed.ac.uk/handle/1842/2649. The research was funded by an ESRC 2001–2 Advanced Course Quota studentship: grant number 2001010541 and an ESRC 2003–6 Studentship: grant number PTA-042–2003–00001. I am grateful to the ESRC also for funding a Postdoctoral Fellowship that enabled me to travel to Toronto.

3 See, for example, James Carrier, *Gifts and Commodities: Exchange and Western Capitalism since 1700* (London and New York: Routledge, 1995); David Cheal, *The Gift Economy* (London: Routledge, 1988); Mary Douglas, "No Free Gifts [Preface]," in Marcel Mauss, *The Gift: the Form and Reason for Exchange in Archaic Societies* (1925), trans. W.D. Halls (London: Routledge, 1990); James Laidlaw, "A Free Gift Makes No Friends" (2000) J Royal Anthropological Institute (NS) 617; Jonathan Parry, "The Gift, the Indian Gift and the 'Indian Gift'" (1986) 21 Man (NS) 453; Ann Oakley and John Ashton, eds., Richard Titmuss *The Gift Relationship: From Human Blood to Social Policy*, updated and expanded ed. (London: London School of Economics, 1997); Ulrich Beck, "From Industrial Society to the Risk Society: Questions of Survival, Social Structure and Ecological Enlightenment" (1992) 9:1 Theory, Culture & Society 97; Mary Douglas, *Risk and Blame: Essays in Cultural Theory* (London: Routledge, 1992); Anthony Giddens, BBC Reith Lectures, "Risk" – Lecture 2, 1999, BBC http://news.bbc.co.uk/hi/english/static/events/reith_99/week2/week2.htm; and Caitlin Zaloom, "The Productive Life of Risk" (2004) 19:3 Cultural Anthropology 365.

4 "Test Tube Baby Plan Will Deepen Crisis in Donors," *Daily Record*, 26 July 1999.

5 Ken Daniels, "Protecting the Vulnerable in Collaborative Reproduction," in *Towards Reproductive Certainty: Fertility and Genetics Beyond 1999: The Plenary Proceedings of the 11th World Congress on In Vitro Fertilisation and Human Reproductive Genetics*, ed. Robert Jansen and David Mortimer (New York: Parthenon, 1999).

6 Erving Goffman, *The Presentation of Self in Everyday Life* (Middlesex: Pelican, 1971). An inside secret identifies a person as a member of a particular group, whereas a free secret can be revealed without affecting the status of the person involved. It would be one that any member of the doctor's social network could reveal without imperilling trust.

7 Some donors recalled being paid in kind, such as with new shirts for their sports team.

8 The findings of recent research on the views of the donors' wives are currently under analysis.

9 Lucy Frith, "Gamete Donation and Anonymity: The Ethical and Legal Debate" (2001) 16:5 Human Reproduction 818–24.

10 See http://www.birthlink.org.uk.

11 Letter to Anne Milton, Parliamentary Under Secretary of State (Public Health), Department of Health from Project Group on Assisted Reproduction, British Association of Social Workers, Birmingham, 9 November 2011.

12 Marilyn Crawshaw and Lyndsey Marshall, "Practice Experiences of Running UK DonorLink, a Voluntary Information Exchange and Contact Register for Adults Related through Donor Conception" (2008) 11:4 Human Fertility 231.

13 See Jennifer M. Speirs, "Eddies of Distrust: 'False' Birth Certificates and the Destabilisation of Relationships," in Margit Ystanes and Vigdis Broch-Due, eds., *Trusting and Its Tribulations: Interdisciplinary Engagements with Intimacy, Sociality, and Trust* (New York: Berghahn Books, 2016), 148. Concerns about unwitting incest tend to be downplayed by infertility clinics because of a perceived low probability of it happening, but to be noted by advocates of donor identification. See, for example, Mark Hamilton *et al.*, "Working Party on Sperm Donation Services in the UK" (2008) 11:3 Human Fertility 147. For a view from Israel, see http://shorashim.link/israeli-offspring-facts-and-figures/.

14 Department of Health, *Human Fertilisation and Embryology Authority (Disclosure of Donor Information) Regulations 2004*, SI 2004/1511 (London: HMSO, 2004).

15 Denis Campbell, "Quango Cull of Health Bodies Is Coalition's Third Assault on NHS," *The Guardian* (UK), 14 October 2010.

16 The expression "bonfire of the quangos" is in common use and certainly was an election pledge used by former UK Prime Minister Margaret Thatcher in 1979. See Tom Gash with Sir Ian Magee, Jill Rutter, and Nicole Smith, *Read before Burning: Arm's Length Government for a New Administration* (London: Institute for Government, 2010), 10, http://www.instituteforgovernment.org.uk/sites/default/files/publications/Read%20before%20burning.pdf .

17 Sandy Starr, "New Law Empowers UK Government to Transfer HFEA's Functions," *BioNews* 638, 19 December 2011, http://www.bionews.org.uk/page_115729.asp.

18 "Quango List Shows 192 to Be Axed," *BBC News*, 14 October 2010, http://www.bbc.co.uk/news/uk-politics-11538534.

19 *Ibid*.

20 Eric Blyth, Marilyn Crawshaw, Lucy Frith, Caroline Jones, and Jennifer Speirs, "Wither the HFEA and the Fate of Donor Registers?," *BioNews* 572, 23 August 2010, http://www.bionews.org.uk/page_69470.asp.

21 Cait McDonagh, "Quangoing, Going, Gone: What Should Happen to the HFEA?," *BioNews* 674, 24 September 2012, http://www.bionews.org.uk/page_182787.asp.

22 Department of Health, *Consultation on Proposals to Transfer Functions from the Human Fertilisation and Embryology Authority and the Human Tissue Authority*, National Archives, http://webarchive.nationalarchives.gov.uk/20130107105354/http://www.dh.gov.uk/health/2012/06/consultation-regulators.

23 *Health and Social Care Act 2008*, c 14.

24 HFEA, Press Release, "HFEA to Remain as Independent Regulator of Assisted Reproduction," 17 July 2013, HFEA, http://www.hfea.gov.uk/7934.html.

25 UK, *Report of the Smith Commission for Further Devolution of Powers to the Scottish Parliament* (Lord Smith of Kelvin, Commissioner) (Edinburgh: The Commission, 2014), paras 61 and 62, http://www.smith-commission.scot/wp-content/uploads/2014/11/The_Smith_Commission_Report-1.pdf.

26 Ruth Wilde, Alison McTavish, and Marilyn Crawshaw, "Family Building Using Donated Gametes and Embryos in the UK: Recommendations for Policy and Practice on Behalf of the British Infertility Counselling Association and the British Fertility Society in Collaboration with the Association of Clinical Embryologists and the Royal College of Nurses Fertility Nurses Forum" (2014) 17:1 Human Fertility 1.

27 Walter Merricks, "Perhaps the Government Is Right to plan to Abolish the HFEA," *BioNews* 630, 24 October 2011, http://www.bionews.org.uk/page_110436.asp.
28 HFEA, "Donating Sperm and Eggs: Have Your Say" (a consultation review of the HFEA's sperm and egg donation policies) (2011), http://www.hfea.gov.uk/5605.html.
29 Alison McTavish, "Human Fertilisation and Embryology Authority Review of Donation Policies" (Spring 2011), British Fertility Society Newsletter 5, http://www.fertility.org.uk/news/newsletters/newsletters/11-05-Spring.pdf [subscription required, on file with author]: 54 per cent of respondents wanted donors to be anonymous.
30 Regulation and professional standards do not always ensure respect for donors. See Dr Laura Machin for the National Gamete Donation Trust, "Egg, Sperm and Potential Donors Satisfaction Survey – Interim Report March 2012," NGDT, http://www.ngdt.co.uk/donor-satisfaction-survey.
31 For a good description, see Eric Blyth, "Parental Orders and Identity Registration: One Country Three Systems" (2010) 32:4 J Soc Welfare & Fam L 345.
32 John Triseliotis, *In Search of Origins: The Experience of Adopted People* (London: Routledge and Kegan Paul, 1973).
33 *Adoption Act 1976*, c 36, s 51(1), allows adopted people at age eighteen to access their birth records.
34 *Act of Sederunt (Sheriff Court Rules Amendment) (Adoption and Children (Scotland) Act 2007) 2009*, Scot SI 2009/284, Schedule, http://www.legislation.gov.uk/ssi/2009/284/made.
35 See, for example, Birthlink, www.birthlink.org.uk.
36 *Succession (Scotland) Act 1964*, c 41.
37 The discovery was made by Deborah Cullen, the then legal consultant to the British Agencies for Adoption and Fostering, and reported to me and other members of the British Association of Social Workers' Project Group on Assisted Reproduction (PROGAR). It was never discovered whether this was by accident or design. However, see Eric Blyth, *supra* note 31, for a good description of the subtle differences and the effect of policy changes made by individuals.
38 "Devolution-proofing" is a widely used expression to describe the processes that require policy-makers in the UK government to ensure that the needs and interests of the devolved nations will be met when UK legislation is being considered.

39 The response to the consultation by PROGAR stated: "We are unsure from our reading of the Draft Regulations whether they will result in the removal of counselling being available at the age of 16 from the local authority (in Scotland) and instead placing the responsibility on the Registrar General to provide information about possible sources of counselling alone. If so, we believe this to be a retrograde step."

40 Provisions of the *Adoption and Children (Scotland) Act 2007*, 2007 ASP 4, s. 55(5), as modified by the *Human Fertilisation and Embryology (Parental Orders) Regulations 2010*, SI 2010/985.

41 Department of Health, Consultation Report on the Human Fertilisation and Embryology (Parental Orders) Regulations 2010, National Archive, http://webarchive.nationalarchives.gov.uk/+/www.dh.gov.uk/en/Consultations/Responsestoconsultations/DH_111659.

42 M. Brudenell *et al.* (eds.), *Artificial Insemination: Proceedings of the Fourth Study Group of the Royal College of Obstetricians and Gynaecologists* (London: Royal College of Obstetricians and Gynaecologists, 1976) at 62.

43 Geraldine Van Beuran, "Children's Access to Adoption Records – State Discretion or an Enforceable International Right?" (1995) 58:1 Mod L Rev 37.

44 Eric Blyth *et al.*, "The Implications of Adoption for Donor Offspring Following Donor Assisted Conception" (2001) 6:4 Child & Family Social Work 295.

45 Ruth Deech, "Family Law and Genetics" (1998) 61:5 Mod L Rev 697.

46 Gary Clapton, *Birth Fathers and their Adoption Experiences* (London and Philadelphia: Jessica Kingsley, 2003).

47 For analysis of donor anonymity and the impact of adoption legislation on access to donor information in Canada, see the chapters by Giroux and Milne, Gruben, and Guichon in this volume. For a comparative analysis of Canadian legislation and New Zealand legislation, see the chapter by Snelling in this volume.

PART THREE

Commodification and Commercialization of Assisted Human Reproduction, Access and Funding of AHR, and the Role of Law

11 Assisted Reproductive Technology Use among Neighbours: Commercialization Concerns in Canada and the United States, in the Global Context

LISA C. IKEMOTO

Introduction

In 2004 the *Assisted Human Reproduction Act* (*AHRA*) clearly situated Canada on one side of an emerging divide. The divide is forming among countries in which assisted reproductive technologies (ARTs) are available. On one side of the divide, countries like Canada ban payment to a woman for surrogacy services and prohibit purchase of human gametes and embryos. Countries on the other side permit payment for surrogacy services and/or third party gamete and embryo procurement.

The Canadian commercialization bans were issued as an expression of the country's stated social values, including concerns about commodifying human reproduction and human gametes and embryos.[1] The US approach to ART use contrasts starkly with Canada's. Commodification concerns have rarely surfaced in legal or public discussion of ART use. Thus far, a market-based approach flourishes.[2] The US federal government and the states have enacted very few laws that specifically regulate the commercial aspects of ART. This has enabled the development of a purely commercial sector comprised of intermediaries who arrange surrogacy agreements or the acquisition of gametes for others' use. In comparison, the *AHRA* prohibits payment to intermediaries. While some commercial intermediary activity may persist in Canada, it persists despite the *AHRA*. In the United States, the market-based approach has enabled ART use to become the basis of a multi-billion-dollar industry.[3]

The *AHRA*'s commercialization bans provide a starting point for considering the dearth of public discourse about commodification concerns and about regulation of ART use in the United States. There have been few, if any, moments when concerns about commodifying human reproduction and human gametes could have become dominant. Instead, prevailing views have either overlooked or dismissed such concerns. The practices that have accompanied the formation of the fertility industry seemingly illustrate the substance of the commodification concerns expressed in the *AHRA*. Yet a peculiar mix of family formation narratives, neoliberalism, and liberal politics has both obscured and naturalized commercialization's effects in the United States.

Not surprisingly, the *AHRA*'s restrictive approach and the US embrace of commercialization have situated the two countries differently in the global market for ARTs. The *AHRA*'s insistence on a uniform federal regulatory approach to ART use arose, in part, from a desire to deter reproductive tourism within Canada.[4] Yet Canada's refusal to treat female surrogates, gametes, and *in vitro* embryos as the subject of payment may spur more to travel from Canada to other countries for contract pregnancy and use of others' reproductive materials. The United States has become a major destination for reproductive tourism. Proximity to Canada and the availability of surrogacy services and gametes have made the United States attractive to Canadians seeking access to ARTs.

This paper maps the public discourse about commercialization's effects in both Canada and the United States. The analysis situates both countries in the broader context of the global fertility market and international reproductive tourism. It then describes the "Wild West" of ART use in the United States and assesses the peculiar political culture that explains the US market-based approach. Finally, the chapter speculates about future implications of the gap between the two countries' approaches to commercialization. Canada's anti-commodification approach is part of a growing global trend to prioritize women's status, health, and ethics over economics. This raises the possibility that the United States, like Canada, may eventually prioritize ethics and equality over market forces.

Commercialization Concerns

Canada

The sources of the *AHRA*'s commercialization bans are well-documented. A precedent document of the *AHRA*, *Proceed with Care:*

Final Report of the Royal Commission on New Reproductive Technologies, determined that "certain activities conflict so sharply with the values espoused by Canadians and by this Commission, and are so potentially harmful to the interests of individuals and society, that they must be prohibited by the federal government under threat of criminal sanction."[5] The activities recommended for criminal sanction included "the sale of human eggs, sperm, zygotes, fetuses, and fetal tissue, and advertising for or acting as an intermediary to bring about a preconception arrangement, receiving payment or any financial or commercial benefit for acting as an intermediary, and making payment for a preconception arrangement."[6] Over the ten years during which the Commission's recommendations were shaped into the *AHRA*, the guiding principles stayed remarkably constant. The Commission's report identified eight principles, including "non-commercialization of reproduction."[7] The *AHRA* set out seven principles that included a more detailed iteration of non-commercialization: "trade in the reproductive capabilities of women and men and the exploitation of children, women and men for commercial ends raise health and ethical concerns that justify their prohibition."[8]

The Commission defined commercialization in a straightforward way – "activities involving the exchange of money or goods and intended to generate a profit or benefit for those engaging in this exchange."[9] The ethical concerns arise from both direct and indirect effects of commercialization. Commercialization's problematic effects include the risks of coercion, exploitation, and commodification. Coercion and exploitation can be understood as direct effects of commercialization. The offer of more money than necessary to cover expenses incurred by surrogates or gamete providers may prove coercive to some. Put more plainly, the risk is that paying for gametes and surrogacy will undermine consent to undergo pregnancy or provide gametes for others' use. The use of money allocates risk to those with fewer opportunities to acquire an equivalent amount by other means. The risk of coercion falls unequally.

Exploitation means use for another's profit. In a sense, exploitation is part of the definition of commercialization. But the term *exploitation* connotes that the use itself is depleting or otherwise harmful. Exploitation also suggests that the use takes advantage of a power imbalance. The Commission's eight principles included "protection of the vulnerable."[10] "Vulnerability to exploitation may also arise from [a] person's socioeconomic status, membership in a minority group, or disability."[11] Leveraging the power imbalance for one's own benefit produces the harm, in that it undervalues the status as well as the contribution of the exploited. Commercial surrogacy and gamete procurement have consistently raised concerns about the role of class and race divisions between purchasers and sellers.

The commodification concern is less tangible than the risks of coercion and exploitation. Commodification's effects may also be more pervasive. The Commission defined commodification as the "treatment of human beings or body tissues and substances as commodities – as means to an end, not as ends in themselves."[12] The harm is to human dignity.[13] The process of commodifying human reproduction changes the way we define the participants in reproduction. Treating human beings and human tissues as commodities does not necessarily or quickly make them such. Yet paying women to undergo conception, gestation, and childbirth, and paying others to provide sperm and ova, shifts the weight given human life from the immeasurable and qualitative towards the determinable and quantitative.[14] The Commission's definition of commodification focuses on how humans are treated but also encompasses the effects that resonate from such treatment.

The United States

In the United States, the first state high court decision on surrogacy addressed payment in terms similar to those used by the Royal Commission's report and the *AHRA*. In the 1988 case *In re Baby M*, the New Jersey Supreme Court determined "the payment of money to a 'surrogate' mother illegal, perhaps criminal, and potentially degrading to women."[15] Yet that strong condemnation of commercial surrogacy has not prevailed. Several state legislatures have followed New Jersey's lead and prohibited surrogacy[16] or commercial surrogacy,[17] or have declared the contracts void.[18] The substantial majority of states, however, have not prohibited commercial surrogacy. Several states expressly permit commercial surrogacy. More simply have not addressed the enforceability and payment issues. Even while the laws or lack thereof in many jurisdictions create uncertainty for those participating in surrogacy, commercial surrogacy has become a widespread practice in the United States.

The commercialization of other aspects of ART use has received even less attention from lawmakers. Payment for sperm and eggs has remained unregulated. Few laws exist that specifically address practices used by surrogacy agencies, sperm banks, egg agencies, and embryo donation centres. While those agencies are subject to laws generally applicable to businesses and fertility clinics are governed by laws generally applicable to medical practice, the fertility industry is not regulated as such.

Perhaps not surprisingly, public discourse about ART reflects lawmakers' inattention to commodification. That discourse has only sporadically acknowledged that commercialization may create risks of coercion, exploitation, and commodification. Perhaps the strongest outcry against commercialization arose in the early days of the fertility industry. At that time, radical feminists argued that commercial surrogacy would reinforce biological essentialism and reconstitute women as wombs.[19] They pointed to the possibility of creating a reproductive caste system composed of wealthy women contracting out pregnancy to poor women.[20] The *In re Baby M* opinion echoed those concerns.

The views that emerged as dominant valorized high-tech medicine and greater reproductive choice amidst the range of ART options. They also placed confidence in the ability of individual agency to withstand commercialization's risks. While the radical feminist critique has persisted, it is liberal to neoliberal characterizations that have shaped mainstream understandings of ART. A view that highlights the importance and strength of individual agency as a bulwark against commercialization's potential harms goes hand in hand with a market approach to virtually every aspect of ART use.

The fertility industry formed at a time when neoliberalism's influence was surging in US law and politics.[21] Embrace of the market-based approach was not unique to the fertility industry. It also reshaped the broader health care system. A market competition model of health care financing and delivery ascended during the same period that the fertility industry was expanding. In both the fertility setting and primary care, the market approach brought about privatization and deregulation.

The backlash against market-based health care has expressed commodification concerns. In law, that backlash led to restrictions on the use of managed care mechanisms perceived to put cost containment over quality of care. In public discourse, liberals objected to situating health care as a product and patients as consumers. Yet this objection, which closely mirrors the rationale for the *AHRA*'s ban on the commercialization of surrogacy and gamete and embryo use, has gained little traction in the US fertility setting.

Concerns about the risks of coercion and exploitation arising from ART have surfaced in remarkably discreet ways. For example, as mentioned, commercial surrogacy has been widely accepted in the United States. The preference for gestational surrogacy and its dependence on the availability of purchased gametes has received little comment outside of the scholarly literature. Yet media coverage of surrogacy in other countries such as India has prompted some public concern over the risks of coercion and exploitation outside the United States.

A second example illustrates both the discursive and legal responses when the risks are undeniably domestic. Federal and state funding of human embryonic stem cell research has prompted consideration of whether to pay women to provide eggs for research. The health and coercion risks have been central in the resulting debate. The two major counterarguments have been that payment restrictions would reduce supply and thus impede research and that payment restrictions are paternalistic and impair women's autonomy. A national consensus has not emerged. New York permitted payment after the supply problem surfaced. On the other hand, federal policy and California state regulations permit reimbursement of reasonable expenses but prohibit additional payment. The intangible risks of commodification remain the least explored concern in US public discourse on human reproduction. Fears that ART may produce "designer babies" and trait selection more generally may be the strongest expression of concern about commercialization's effects on human dignity. Some scholars, policymakers, and journalists have made serious efforts to stimulate discussion of issues such as disability discrimination, eugenic trait selection, and the commodification of children. Broader public discussion has framed these issues in ways that limit their implications. For example, much of the media coverage of "designer babies" has described scenarios that are scientifically unfeasible and seemingly extreme. This has cast the issues as more titillating and less real. In addition, much of the "designer babies" discourse segregates the genetic selection process from pregnancy and birth, thus screening out commodification's effects on women from public discourse.

In Global Context: Reproductive Tourism

The contrasting approaches in Canada and the United States take place in a globalized fertility market. The practice of offering and seeking ART across jurisdictional or national boundaries is called "reproductive tourism," "cross-border reproductive care," or "reproductive travel."[22] It is not only the intended parents who cross borders to access ART. Physicians, clinics, and other providers solicit patients from, and establish facilities in, other jurisdictions. Surrogates and gamete donors also move across borders to fulfil contract obligations. Agencies facilitate contact between providers and patients, assist with travel arrangements, and broker agreements with women who provide surrogacy and ova for others' use. Reproductive tourism occurs intra-country and between provinces, states, or territories, as well as transnationally. Reproductive travellers will cross regional as well as national borders. Intended parents from the United Kingdom travel to India. Some travel from Japan to the United States, and so on. Some who live in destination spots travel to other destinations, so that some countries are both destination spots and points of departure.

While the narratives about ART use centre on the doctor–patient and parent–child relationships, a longer list of players constitute the global market in assisted human reproduction. The participants include entrepreneurial physicians and the clinics, hospitals, and laboratories that provide clinical services to those who undergo the medical procedures. Intended parents, many of whom become patients, are the other most highly visible participants. Surrogates who carry the pregnancy and give birth to the child, and men and women who provide sperm and eggs for others' use, are positioned as "third parties," although they participate directly in the reproductive process. There are, of course, the children born as the result of ART. And there are the many entities that provide necessary materials and services and that act as the "glue" of the fertility industry: surrogacy agencies, egg brokers, sperm banks, egg and embryo banks, the pharmaceutical industry, medical professional organizations, and agencies established to create cross-border care arrangements and/or travel services.

In the global market, some jurisdictions serve primarily as destination spots and some as points of departure for those seeking services. The factors that determine these locations vary considerably from place to place. Those factors include law, cost disparities, the availability of technology and services, and bioavailability, but there are others.[23] The types of laws that operate as drivers include both those that restrict ART use and those that provide certainty of desirable outcomes.[24] Cost disparities for ART exist between the point of departure and the destination spot.[25] If ART services cost so much less in another jurisdiction that the cost difference justifies travel, that difference acts as a driver.

The availability of technology and services acts as a driver for those who reside in countries without ART.[26] Bioavailability or the availability of bodily resources in the form of surrogates and gamete donors[27] (and this includes the availability of desirable racial, ethnic, and religious identities among gamete donors and surrogates) enables surrogacy and gamete markets to form.[28] Other factors, including long waiting times and low quality of care in the home country or a desire for privacy or secrecy, are also given as reasons for reproductive travel.[29]

The destination spots and points of departure take a wide variety of regulatory approaches to ART. Countries characterized as restrictive are those with national regulations that ban particular technology uses, restrict who may use ART, and/or prohibit the commercialization of surrogacy and gametes. The restrictive laws that provide incentives to seek ART in another jurisdiction include those that ban surrogacy,[30] commercial surrogacy,[31] and use of[32] (or payment for use of) others' gametes.[33] Laws that require disclosure of those who provide gametes for others' use effectively reduce the number of persons willing to provide gametes, even for compensation, and thus limit the use of assisted insemination, *in vitro* fertilization, and gestational surrogacy.[34]

Other countries are relatively permissive. Some of these jurisdictions have laws that authorize high-demand services, including commercial surrogacy. Some have permissive regulations or guidelines, or they have guidelines that are often disregarded. Some jurisdictions have little or no regulation. Permissive jurisdictions include the United States, Israel, and Romania.[35] Not surprisingly, many countries do not fit neatly into these categories as I have used them. The International Federation of Fertility Societies categorizes regulatory approaches differently and identifies the United States as a guideline country.[36] The US, in fact, has a few scattered laws and some guidelines, and is also, in large part, unregulated.

The *AHRA* has placed Canada among the restrictive countries, even after the Supreme Court's decision. Neither Canada nor the United States is solely a destination spot or a departure point.[37] Not surprisingly, however, the limited data collected so far suggest that more depart from Canada than travel to Canada. The data also suggest that Canadians have travelled to the United States but also to India, Mexico, and the Czech Republic.[38] Those travelling from Canada most often sought *in vitro* fertilization using their own gametes, IVF with others' ova, or surrogacy.[39]

While high costs in the United States drive many to seek ART use elsewhere, that country is one of the major destination spots in the global market.[40] In the absence of comprehensive or even coordinated regulation, the entrepreneurial spirit reigns there. Many describe the state of the law and ART in the United States as the "Wild West."[41]

California, in particular, is a destination spot for domestic travellers and for those from other countries.[42] State statutes, judicial decisions, and the handful of federal rules provide sufficient certainty for intended parents and wide scope for clinicians and agencies that operate in that state. Federal and state laws require the testing of sperm and of persons who provide eggs or *in vitro* embryos for sexually transmissible diseases, as well as HIV. California's parentage laws provide legal certainty for those using others' sperm. By judicial decision, California has extended that assurance to the use of others' eggs[43] and to gestational surrogacy.[44] In September 2012, statutory rules enabling commercial gestational surrogacy were signed into law.[45] One proponent described the law as "needed legislation in California to address our burgeoning surrogacy industry and provide safeguards to prevent future scandals that could further scar this field."[46] The referenced scandals involved commercial surrogacy agencies. Both schemes used women who agreed to be surrogates as pawns, and exploited the hopes of intended parents.[47] The new legislation enshrines large agencies' practices into law. Thus, in response to evidence that commodification concerns are real and produce tangible harms, California chose to shore up its position in the global market, and did so in a way that seems to confer advantage on the large agencies.

Commercialization in the "Wild West"

What does commercialized surrogacy and gamete procurement look like in the "Wild West"? To start with, surrogacy and gametes are expensive. They remain priced as luxury goods, despite the proliferation of clinics, sperm banks, and egg agencies.[48] Providers tend to present their services in terms that emphasize professionalism or compassion.[49] That may go a long way to explain the high cost of ART.

Agencies and intermediaries use a wide range of marketing tactics. While many deploy the family formation narrative and present themselves as professional and/or compassionate, some of the most successful, high-volume, and visible brokers offer services with an "anything goes" or "will try anything" spirit that befits the "Wild West."

For example, trait pricing for gametes is standard.[50] California Cryobank, one of the world's largest sperm banks, has a "Donor Look-A-Like" search function that permits those selecting a donor to match donor appearance to that of celebrities.[51] The home page also advertises popular donors and "scholastic all-star donors." One of the oldest and most established surrogacy and egg agencies uses glamour shots of surrogates and refers to surrogates as angels. For example, the website of The Egg Donor Program & The Surrogacy Program includes a photograph of a pregnant woman in gauzy angel wings.[52] The egg donation page offers a "superdonor" database.[53] Advertisements for egg "donors" call for high college achievement test scores and often specify race, ethnicity, and certain abilities.[54]

Commercial practices intertwine with clinical practices, and so far, few of the resulting technology uses have proven unacceptable.[55] Preimplantation genetic diagnosis for social sex selection is available. Other sex selection methods are entering the market.[56] Some surrogacy agencies package their services. A common package combines egg donation with surrogacy. Planet Hospital, a medical tourism agency based in California, has gone a step further. In a recent iteration of its website, Planet Hospital offered an "India Bundle," consisting of two surrogates who would simultaneously undergo IVF for a set price.[57] The package was intended to maximize the intended parents' chances of taking home a baby. More recently, a well-respected clinic has offered a way to reduce the costs of *in vitro* fertilization. The clinic purchases sperm and eggs and uses the gametes to create *in vitro* embryos. The clinic divides up the resulting batch of embryos to offer to several patients.[58] This process saves money for the patients but shifts control of the embryos to the clinic.

Safety concerns are often overlooked. For example, professional medical guidelines limit the number of embryos per transfer in the IVF process, but the number of multiple births to women undergoing IVF indicates that providers often exceed the guidelines.[59] The American Society for Reproductive Medicine (ASRM) has guidelines for physicians who provide fertility services.[60] These guidelines, however, are not enforceable at law. The ASRM can exclude providers who violate the guidelines from membership, but evidence suggests that breach of some guidelines occurs not infrequently and is typically overlooked.

A newer practice illustrates again how market goals may supersede safety concerns. Despite the Food and Drug Administration's classification of egg cryopreservation as experimental, clinics now advertise egg banking along with their other services. Egg freezing centres have become one of the newest entrepreneurial entities in the fertility market.[61] Until recently, egg cryopreservation was offered only to women about to undergo cancer treatment that would damage the eggs. Today, egg freezing is advertised to women as a "chance to store their eggs during their reproductive prime for use when they wish to start or expand their families."[62] The Egg Freezing Center's website previously had an interactive feature on its homepage that calculates "your chances of having a baby" once you enter your birthdate.[63] This strategy seeks to increase the market for egg freezing even while the technology remains experimental.

These practices seem to make the risks of commercialization obvious. As discussed, commercialization is widely accepted, yet its risks receive relatively little prominence in public discourse. Comparison to Canada's *AHRA* highlights a question: Why do commercialization's risks raise so little concern in the United States? The explanation is multifaceted and may not surprise those familiar with US political and cultural mores. Yet those who would challenge the market-based approach have not developed a coherent analysis. The explanation discussed here, while no doubt incomplete, sets out several of the key factors.

There are two prevailing narratives about ART that intertwine with each other and with other narratives. Despite the political tensions they incorporate, these narratives form a barrier to a coordinated regulatory approach in the United States. First, the standard narrative of ART is about family formation for those in need of fertility therapy. Thus, ART use is about "building families" and "creating families." Both phrases and variations of them are used as tag lines in fertility clinic advertising.[64] The narrative is often told in ways that tap into pre-existing socially conservative, pro-natalist accounts of family formation. ART use, framed as infertility treatment, directs attention to the doctor–patient relationship and to the hoped-for, intentional pregnancy. Fertility clinics, spurred by one of the few federal laws applicable to ART use,[65] define "success" in terms of the number of live births.

By spotlighting the doctor–patient relationship and the desired pregnancy, the family formation narrative diverts attention from the commercial aspects. Commercial practices are carefully couched so as to leave the intrinsic value ascribed to family free from the taint of purchase. Those who provide gametes are called "donors," even though nearly all receive compensation. Surrogacy centres emphasize the altruistic intentions of women paid to become pregnant and to give birth to a child that others will raise. Agencies carefully describe payment to "donors" and "surrogates" as compensation for services, and not for the gametes or the child. Some even characterize payment as "gifts" from grateful intended parents.

The family formation narrative is closely intertwined with a narrative that valorizes agency in free-market terms to justify the technologies offered and selected. Thus, ARTs offer an increasing range of choices to anyone who chooses to participate, as seller or buyer. In this narrative, the market is a level playing field. The rhetoric of choice minimizes equality concerns, including concerns about coercion and exploitation.

The abortion rights movement that preceded *Roe v Wade* fought for reproductive freedom as part of the fight for gender equality.[66] In *Roe v Wade*, the Supreme Court's opinion recognized the link between the right to decide whether to terminate a pregnancy and women's ability to participate in political and economic life. But the Court's decision to ground the right to decide in the right of privacy and its underlying value, autonomy, made privacy and autonomy the legal end-all and be-all for reproductive rights in the United States. The decision facilitated the conceptual and legal delinking of reproductive liberty and gender equality. In the resulting gap, choice in the fertility market has slipped into free market individualism, a construct that obscures the workings of subordination in the formation and effects of the market.

The resulting free market family construct has forged an uneasy, tacit alliance between traditional family proponents, some LGBTQ family advocates,[67] and many pro-choice liberals. In the unregulated market, niches serve the gay men and lesbians who hope for children, even as the mainstream market remains focused on perpetuating the marriage-based heterosexual family. Liberal concerns about commercialization's effects are counterbalanced by fear of regulation's effects. There are two fears in operation, and both are probably well-founded. There is fear that any regulation of ART use can and will be translated into further regulation of abortion. Liberals and many in the LGBTQ communities also fear that social conservatives will use legal efforts to prevent commercialization's effects and to protect health and safety as a means to push for status regulations based on marriage and sexual orientation.[68]

The legal regulation that everyone embraces is the doctrine of informed consent, and the disclosure requirement in particular. For liberals, knowledge equals power; disclosure of information strengthens autonomy and smooths concerns about coercion and exploitation. Within neoliberalism, disclosure proves the point that while the product may cost dearly, the decision to sell or buy was freely made. Furthermore, as a result of judicial decisions highly favourable to the biotechnology industry,[69] legally sufficient disclosure effectively transfers control over human cells and tissue for others' commercial benefit.[70] Informed consent, then, has become both a bulwark against additional regulation of the fertility market in the United States and an important legal mechanism for commodifying human reproductive materials.

The narratives that shape ART use also draw from broader institutionalized forces in the United States. First, the medical profession and the pharmaceutical industry are powerful stakeholders in the fertility industry and typically oppose efforts to regulate in ways that might affect their practices. Providers breach their own standards even while pointing to self-policing as the better alternative to regulation.[71] Second, the United States has few structures and practices that provide technology assessment.[72] There, unlike in Canada, the precautionary principle is an unfamiliar one.[73] Rather, technology use and innovation signal progress for many. The reliable embrace and acceptance of emerging ART uses seems to reflect that assumption. Finally, while globalization has been rigorously contested in public discourse, its proponents have prevailed in the United States, whose position as a major destination for reproductive tourism validates that view. It also enables Americans to express concerns about commercialization's effects in India, a competitor in the global market, while taking comfort in the "superiority" of US commercialization.

Thus, the narratives of intimacy between doctor and patient, and between parent and child, direct the gaze away from the commercial aspects of ART use and the risks of coercion and exploitation. The narratives of intimacy also belie, or perhaps justify, commodification. Liberal political communities paralysed by strategic concerns have become complicit in preserving the resulting free market family. At the same time, the market-based approach to ART makes the US fertility industry highly competitive in the global market. In part, it is the country's participation in the global market that allows it to minimize the domestic effects of commercialization. The claim to technocultural superiority over competitors allows the United States to assert that Western agency shields us all from coercion, exploitation, and commodification.

The Functional Border

In the global market for ART, the functional border between Canada and the United States is the gap between their divergent approaches to the commercialization of pregnancy and of gametes provided for others' use. Given the gap, Canada will remain more a departure point than a destination spot, and many Canadian travellers will depart for the United States. Some suggest that reproductive travel operates as a safety valve for the point of departure. This view posits that "patient migration reduces moral conflicts and contributes to the peaceful coexistence of different ethical and religious view."[74] If true, the possibility of reproductive tourism will alleviate political pressure on the *AHRA* and the availability of the United States as a reproductive destination will help preserve the *AHRA*'s commercialization bans. In turn, the flow of business from the north may help maintain the vigour of the US fertility industry and its framing narratives. In other words, the safety valve thesis suggests that the gap will become the status quo between the *AHRA* and the Wild West. But in a global market with so much unregulated trade, there is a lot of room for excesses and abuses. The safety valve justification does not address those risks.

There are at least two other possible outcomes. One is that the presence of the Wild West next door may reinforce opposition to the commercial bans within Canada and even encourage breach of the bans.[75] The second is that the United States may perceive that the *AHRA* is part of a desirable global trend to evaluate ART use through the lens of ethics and equality rather than that of the market. France, Greece, Korea, the Netherlands, Turkey, and the United Kingdom are also part of this trend.[76]

Within the United States, the inklings of regulatory need may be surfacing. For example, concern about the physical and mental health of children conceived by persons who provided gametes but not identity information has strengthened into organizational efforts to support identity release programs and identity disclosure requirements.[77] Identity disclosure requirements tend to reduce gamete supply.[78] Willingness to adopt identity disclosure laws would signal a softening of free market individualism and perhaps a strengthening of liberal backbone. A growing body of data showing that some ART procedures pose health risks to women undergoing them and children conceived by them suggests the need to evaluate commercial and medical protocols and to change the federal law's definition of "clinic success." These inklings may reinforce the marginalized but persistent critique of commercialization that last peaked in the 1980s. In the meantime, the presence of the *AHRA* next door may increasingly suggest that the market-based approach to ART is in need of change.

NOTES

1 *Assisted Human Reproduction Act*, SC 2004, c 2, s 2(f). See also Françoise Baylis, Expert Report, *The Regulation of Assisted Human Reproductive Technologies and Related Research: A Public Health, Safety and Morality Argument* (August 2006) at 10, as presented in an appendix of this volume.
2 See George J. Annas, "Assisted Reproduction – Canada's Supreme Court and the 'Global Baby'" (2011) 365 New Engl J Med 459 at 460.
3 Debora L. Spar, *The Baby Business: How Money, Science, and Politics Drive the Commerce of Conception* (Boston: Harvard Business School Press, 2006), 3.
4 Baylis, *supra* note 1 at 12.
5 Canada, Royal Commission on New Reproductive Technologies, *Proceed with Care: Final Report of the Royal Commission on New Reproductive Technologies*, vol. 2 (Ottawa: Minister of Government Services Canada, 1993), 1022.
6 *Ibid.*
7 *Proceed with Care, supra* note 5, vol. 1 at 53.
8 *AHRA*, s 2(f).
9 *Proceed with Care, supra* note 5 at 55.
10 *Ibid.*
11 *Ibid.*
12 *Ibid.*
13 *Proceed with Care, supra* note 5 at 56.
14 For an account of commodification showing that commodification is not an either/or phenomenon, such that commodification occurs on a sliding scale and that extrinsic and intrinsic value can coexist, see Vivianna A. Zelizer, *The Purchase of Intimacy* (Princeton: Princeton University Press, 2005).
15 109 NJ 396, 411 (1988).
16 See, for example, DC Stat §16–402 (2012).
17 See, for example, Louisiana Stat Annot Rev§ 2713 (2012).
18 See, for example, Indiana Code Ann §31–20–1-1 (2009).
19 See Gena Corea, *The Mother Machine: Reproductive Technologies from Artificial Insemination to Artificial Wombs* (New York: Harper and Row, 1985); and Janice G. Raymond, *Women as Wombs: Reproductive Technologies and the Battle over Women's Freedom* (San Francisco: Harper, 1993).

20 Margaret Radin, "Market Inalienability" (1987) 100 Harv L Rev 1849 at 1930.

21 David Harvey, *A Brief History of Neoliberalism* (Oxford: Oxford University Press, 2005), 92–3; Al Campbell, "The Birth of Neoliberalism in the United States: A Reorganisation of Capitalism," in *Neoliberalism: A Critical Reader*, ed. Alfredo Saad-Filho and Deborah Johnson (London: Pluto Press 2005), 187–98.

22 For a more detailed description of reproductive tourism, see Lisa C. Ikemoto, "Reproductive Tourism: Equality Concerns in the Global Market for Fertility Services" (2009) 27 JL & Inequality 277 at 281–301.

23 See Ikemoto, *ibid*; Eric Blyth and Abigail Farrand, "Reproductive Tourism – a Price Worth Paying for Reproductive Autonomy?" (2005) 25 Critical Social Policy 91 at 96–9.

24 Howard W. Jones *et al.*, eds., *International Federation of Fertility Societies Surveillance 2010* (Mt Royal, NJ: International Federation of Fertility Societies, 2010), 12, International Federation of Fertility Societies, http://www.iffs-reproduction.org.

25 See L. Culley *et al.*, "Crossing Borders for Fertility Treatment: Motivations, Destinations and Outcomes of UK Fertility Travelers" (2011) 26 Human Reproduction 2373 at 2375.

26 See Blyth and Farrand, *supra* note 23 at 97.

27 Andrea Whittaker and Amy Speier, "'Cycling Overseas': Care, Commodification, and Stratification in Cross-Border Reproductive Travel" (2010) 29 Medical Anthropology 363 at 375; Eric Blyth, "Fertility Patients' Experiences of Cross-Border Reproductive Care" (2010) 94 Fertility and Sterility e11 at e13.

28 Whittaker and Speier, *ibid* at 377–8.

29 Blyth 2010, *supra* at note 27; Florencia Luna, "Assisted Reproductive Technology in Latin America: Some Ethical and Sociocultural Issues," in *Current Practices and Controversies in Assisted Reproduction: Report of a Meeting on "Medical, Ethical and Social Aspects of Assisted Reproduction,"* ed. Effy Vayena, Patrick J. Rowe and P. David Griffin (Geneva: World Health Organization, 2002) 31, online: World Health Organization, http://www.who.int/reproductivehealth/publications/en.

30 IFFS 2010, *supra* note 24 at 108.

31 *Ibid*.

32 *Ibid* at 43.

33 *Ibid* at 44.

34 *Ibid* at 62.

35 *Ibid*. The United States, India, and Israel use guidelines, not enforceable statutes or other laws. In Spain, ART is governed by statute, but the

statutes permit most of the practices used in other major destination spots. Permitted practices include use of third-party gametes, surrogacy, and preimplantation genetic diagnosis.

36 The IFFS groups nations into those with legislative oversight, those with voluntary guidelines, and those with neither legislation nor guidelines. IFFS 2010, *supra* note 24 at 10 and 15.

37 Edward G. Hughes and Deirdre DeJean, "Cross-Border Fertility Services in North America: A Survey of Canadian and American Providers" (2010) 94 Fertility and Sterility e16 at e17–e19; Whittaker and Speier, *supra* note 27 at 367.

38 Blyth 2010, *supra* note 27 at e12.

39 *Ibid;* Hughes and DeJean, *supra* note 37 at e18.

40 See Karl Nygren *et al.*, "Cross-Border Fertility Care – International Committee Monitoring Assisted Reproductive Technologies Global Survey: 2006 Data and Estimates" (2010) 94 Fertility and Sterility e4 at e6.

41 See, for example, Debora L. Spar, "Wild West of Fertility," *New York Times*, 13 September 2011; Alexander N. Hecht, "The Wild Wild West: Inadequate Regulation of Assisted Reproductive Technology," Note/Comment, (2001) 1 Hous JL & Pol'y 227; Meredith Leigh Birdsall, "An Exploration of the 'Wild West of Reproductive Technology': Ethical and Feminist Perspectives on Sex-Selection Practices in the United States" (2010) 17 Wm & Mary J Women & L 223; Judith F. Daar, "Federalizing Embryo Transfers: Taming the Wild West of Reproductive Medicine" (2012) 23 Colum J Gender & Law 257; and Alkorta Idiakez, "Regulation of Reproductive Medicine in North America or the Wild West of Medicine (Part I)" (2003) [January–June] Rev Derecho Genoma Hum 23.

42 Debora Spar, "Reproductive Tourism and the Regulatory Map" (2005) 352 N Engl J Med 531 at 532.

43 *KM v EG*, 117 P3d 673 (Cal 2005).

44 *Johnson v Calvert*, 851 P2d 776 (Cal 1993).

45 California Family Code §§7960–7962 (2012), http://www.leginfo.ca.gov/cgi-bin/displaycode?section=fam&group=07001-08000&file=7960-7962.

46 Andrew Vorzimer, "Governor Jerry Brown Signs California's New Surrogacy Bill into Law" *The Spin Doctor*, 27 September 2012 (blog), http://www.eggdonor.com/blog/2012/09/27/governor-jerry-brown-signs-californias-surrogacy-bill-law.

47 The owner of Surrogenesis, a California-based surrogate and egg donation agency, was recently convicted of defrauding intended parents and surrogates of at least $2 million deposited into client accounts to cover surrogacy fees, medical fees, and associated costs: "Former Modesto

Surrogacy Agency Owner Admits Fraud" *Modesto Bee*, 19 February 2013, http://www.modbee.com/news/local/article3149582.html. In a second case, a prominent lawyer who specialized in surrogacy arrangements recruited women as surrogates, sent them to Ukraine to undergo *in vitro* fertilization, and, when the women reached the second trimester of pregnancy, offered the contracts for sale on the pretext that prior arrangements had fallen through: Alyssa Newcomb, "Baby-Selling Enterprise Busted, Three Plead Guilty," *ABC News*, 10 August 2011, http://abcnews.go.com/US/attorney-pleads-guilty-baby-selling-ring/story?id=14274193.

48 Spar, *The Baby Business*, *supra* note 3.

49 For a detailed analysis, see Jim Hawkins, "Selling ART: An Empirical Assessment of Advertising on Fertility Clinics' Websites" (2013) 88 Ind LJ 1146.

50 Jason Keehn *et al.*, "Recruiting Egg Donors Online: An Analysis of *in vitro* Fertilization Clinic and Agency Websites' Adherence to American Society for Reproductive Medicine Guidelines" (2012) 98 Fertility and Sterility 995 at 997. ("The ASRM's guidelines address the concern of commodification of human life by stating that compensation should reflect the 'time, inconvenience, and discomfort' associated with the oocyte donation process, which should be 'distinguished from payment for oocytes themselves … [and] to avoid putting a price on human gametes or selectively valuing particular human traits … However, our study found that 49% of websites violate the guidelines of ASRM's intent to 'avoid … selectively valuing particular human traits.'")

51 California Cryobank homepage, http://www.cryobank.com/index.

52 The Egg Donor Program and the Surrogacy Program, http://www.eggdonation.com.

53 *Ibid*.

54 Kimberly D. Krawiec, "Price and Pretense in the Baby Market" in Michele Bratcher Goodwin, ed., *Baby Markets: Money and the New Politics of Creating Families* (Cambridge: Cambridge University Press, 2010), 41 at 43.

55 The Abraham Center of Life offered made-to-order embryos briefly in 2006 before shutting down, following strong negative comments in public discourse. See JuJu Chang and Deborah Apton, "Designing Babies? Embryos from 'Ph.D. Sperm' and 'Attractive Eggs' for Sale," *ABC News Nightline*, 22 February 2007, http://abcnews.go.com/Business/LifeStages/story?id=2895615&page=1; Abraham Center of Life, Press Release, "Abraham Center of Life No Longer in Embryo Business," 30 May 2007, EWorldWire, http://www.eworldwire.com/pressrelease/17092.

56 For example, MicroSort International is a branch of the Virginia-based Genetics and IVF Institute and offers a sperm-sorting technique that MicroSort claims "increases the probability of having a baby of the desired gender." See http://www.microsort.com.

57 Douglas Pet, "Make Me a Baby as Fast as You Can," *Slate*, 9 January 2012, http://www.slate.com/articles/double_x/doublex/2012/01/reproductive_tourism_how_surrogacy_provider_planethospital_speeds_up_pregnancies_and_lowers_costs_.html.

58 Alan Zarembo, "An Ethics Debate over Embryos on the Cheap," *LA Times*, 19 November 2012, http://articles.latimes.com/2012/nov/19/local/la-me-embryo-20121120.

59 IFFS 2010, *supra* note 24 at 11.

60 American Society for Reproductive Medicine Practice Committee Guidelines, ASRM, http://www.asrm.org/Guidelines; see, for example, the Practice Committee of the American Society for Reproductive Medicine and the Practice Committee of the Society for Assisted Reproductive Technology, "Criteria for Number of Embryos to Transfer: A Committee Opinion" (2013) 99 Fertility and Sterility 44.

61 See, for example, Extend Fertility, http://www.extendfertility.com/; Egg Freezing Center, http://eggfreezingcenter.com/.

62 North Shore Fertility, "Egg Freezing, Fertility Preservation," http://www.northshorefertility.com/egg-freezing.html.

63 Egg Freezing Center, http://eggfreezingcenter.com. [This feature is no longer available.]

64 See, for example, California IVF, "Helping People Grow Families," http://www.californiaivf.com; Center for Surrogate Parenting, "Creating Families Since 1990," http://www.creatingfamilies.com/; Global Fertility Services, "Helping to Build Families with Ovum Donation and Surrogacy," http://www.globalfertilityservices.com/.

65 *1992 Fertility Clinic Success Rate and Certification Act* (Pub L No 102–493, 42 USC §263a-1 et seq) requires the Centers for Disease Control and Prevention to publish the ART Success Rates Report on an annual basis. See http://www.cdc.gov/art.

66 Rickie Solinger, *Pregnancy and Power: A Short History of Reproductive Politics in America* (New York: NYU Press, 2007), 182.

67 See, for example, Martha M. Ertman, "What's Wrong with a Parenthood Market? A New and Improved Theory of Commodification" (2003–2004) 82 NCL Rev 1.

68 See, for example, Martha Ertman, "The Upside of Baby Markets," in Goodwin, ed., *supra* note 54, 23 at 36–7.

69 See *Moore v The Regents of the University of California*, 1990 51 Cal 3d 120; *Greenberg v Miami Children's Hospital Research Institute*, 264 FSupp 2d 1064 (SD Fla 2003); *Washington University v Catalona*, 490 F3d 667 (8th Cir 2007), cert denied, 128 S Ct 1122 (2008).

70 See Ikemoto, *supra* note 22 at 776.

71 See, for example, American Society of Reproductive Technology, *Oversight of Assisted Reproductive Technology* (Birmingham: ASRM, 2010), 11, http://www.asrm.org/Oversight_of_ART; Keehn, *supra* note 50.

72 The history of the US Office of Technology Assessment is emblematic of the role that technology assessment plays in the United States. Congress created the Office of Technology Assessment in 1972. During its twenty-three-year lifespan, political pressures and a narrow vision for the role of technology assessment in the United States limited its function and authority. See Robert M. Margolis and David H. Guston, "The Origins, Accomplishments, and Demise of the Office of Technology Assessment," in *Science and Technology Advice for Congress*, ed. M. Granger Morgan and Jon M. Peha (Washington: RFF Press, 2003), 53 at 66. Shortly after the 1994 Republican takeover of Congress, the Office of Technology Assessment was eliminated: *ibid* at 70–1.

73 There is an emerging call for implementation of the precautionary principle in US environmental law and scholarship. See Albert C. Lin, "The Unifying Role of Harm in Environmental Law" (2006) 2006:1 Wis L Rev 897 at 911, 976; Joel A. Tickner and Sara Wright, "The Precautionary Principle and Democratizing Expertise: A U.S. Perspective" (2003) 30 Sci & Pub Pol'y 213. Discussion of the precautionary principle in biomedicine and bioethics has, thus far, been sparse, and has been largely concentrated on issues of environmental health. See, for example, Mitchell S. Turker, "Banning Bisphenol A in the United States and Canada: Epigenetic Science, the Precautionary Principle, and a Missed Opportunity to Protect the Fetus" (2012) 8 J Health & Biomed L 173.

74 Anna Pia Ferraretti *et al.*, "Cross-Border Reproductive Care: A Phenomenon Expressing the Controversial Aspects of Reproductive Technologies" (2010) 20 Reprod Biomed Online 261 at 262.

75 See Françoise Baylis, "Are Canadian Fertility Services Breaking the Law?," *Hastings Center Bioethics Forum*, 1 May 2012 (blog), www.thehastingscenter.org/Bioethicsforum/Post.aspx?id=5815&blogid=140.

76 France, Korea, and the Netherlands are among the countries that have laws restricting payment for gamete procurement: IFFS 2010, *supra* note 29 at 44. Greece and the UK prohibit payment to birth mothers for surrogacy: *ibid* at 108. Several countries prohibit the use of donor gametes and contract

pregnancy altogether, for a variety of reasons. See, for example, Zeynep B. Gürtin, "Banning Reproductive Travel: Turkey's ART Legislation and Third-Party Assisted Reproduction" (2011) 23 Reprod Biomed Online 555 at 557.

77 See, for example, Donor Sibling Registry, https://www.donorsiblingregistry.com/about-dsr/history-and-mission: "The DSR's core value is honesty, with the conviction that people have the fundamental right to information about their biological origins and identities."

78 Naomi Cahn, "Reproducing Dreams" in Goodwin, ed., *supra* note 54, 147 at 152.

12 Fruitful Diversity: Revisiting the Enforceability of Gestational Carriage Contracts

SUSAN G. DRUMMOND

Introduction

The aspirations of those who sought a set of national policies on reproductive technologies in Canada have been considerably dampened by the last five years of judicial and executive action at the federal level. In December of 2010, large portions of the federal *Assisted Human Reproduction Act* (*AHRA*) – the product of years of scholarly and policy deliberation – were ruled *ultra vires* by the Supreme Court of Canada in *Reference re Assisted Human Reproduction Act*.[1] Left with an eviscerated mandate, it was only a matter of time before the largely dysfunctional federal agency[2] tasked with implementing and enforcing the act – Assisted Reproduction Canada – was abolished in the federal budget cuts of early 2012.[3] A tattered patchwork of federal provisions remain in the *AHRA*, mostly held together by the federal criminal law power; however, their coverage is thin, given that the scaffolding of regulation requisite for their effective coverage remains absent for some critical provisions of the Act (notably s. 12 of the Act, which relates to the reimbursement of expenses relating to gestational carriage) and given the almost complete absence of enforcement of the provisions that relate to gestational carriage and gamete donation.[4]

As a result of these developments, Canada's federal government currently has a weak regulatory presence in the field of assisted reproduction, especially gestational carriage. And the will to renew a national legal project appears phlegmatic despite (and no doubt because of) assisted reproduction norms – moral and market – that have been thriving, effectively unchecked, on the ground.[5] By a considerable measure, provincial governments have remained uninvolved in the last twenty years of drama surrounding assisted reproduction while the federal government has attempted to define the proper legislative and regulatory controls to govern the field. As a result, the provinces have largely refrained from occupying fields allocated to them under the constitutional division of powers. This is acutely evident in the area of parentage law, where many provinces have failed to legislatively update their concepts of legal parentage to keep pace with the astonishing and various news ways in which families are now being created.

The clearing left over the past two decades for legislatively ungoverned norms to flourish means there is a considerable amount of empirical data as well as a swell of anecdotal tales in traditional and social media that might inform juridical norms. The governance lag – a lag that often seems perpetual in the area of assisted reproduction – has produced an auspicious moment to measure the appropriateness of explicit legislative frameworks that render gestational carriage contracts unenforceable, as well as those provincial regimes (which remain the majority) in Canada that have not passed comprehensive (or even any) legislation in this area. Under both explicit statutory regimes and those governed by default common law or outdated legislation, the woman who gives birth to a child becomes thereby the legal mother of the child, whether or not she has a genetic link to the child and whether or not she intended to occupy that position. This is the ancient common law rule of *mater est quam gestatio demonstrat* (hereinafter *mater est*) – by gestation the mother is demonstrated. This is the understanding of maternal legal parentage that for the most part prevails in common law Canada in the absence of legislated regimes;[6] or is supplemented by child status legislation that references the "natural" mother (although drafted in a period when assisted reproduction was unimaginable); or is obliquely recapitulated in vital statistics legislation that defines birth as the complete expulsion or extraction of a child from its "mother." This chapter will argue that an alternative that barely dared speak its name in Canada after the 1988 *Baby M* debacle in the United States[7] – the primacy of intentional parenting over gestational parenting in legal parentage – may finally have enough normative and empirical solidity to unseat the ancient rule.

The practical attenuation of the criminal prohibitions in the *AHRA* has left room for a considerable shift in the substratum of values associated with assisted reproduction. With the hobbling of legislation relating to assisted reproduction at the national level, the time is auspicious for private law (principally provincial) to respond to the surprising and complex family law implications of the last twenty years of conceiving children differently. This chapter will argue that the most appropriate response to developments would be to create legislative and regulatory frameworks under which gestational carriage contracts are enforceable.

Current Provincial Laws on Gestational Contracts: Gestation over Intention

The 1988 *Baby M* case in New Jersey generated a staggering amount of contradictory scholarly literature on the family law implications of assisted reproduction. The tensions in the case were writ large on the academic stage, where legal scholarship focused on the tension between contract law and the rights of gestational carriers and children as vulnerable parties. At the centre of the case was a surrogate, Mary Beth Whitehead, whose egg was combined with intended parent William Stern's sperm. Stern was thus both a genetic and an intended father. The sole contribution of his wife Elizabeth, who had neither a biological nor a genetic stake in the child's conception and delivery, was her intention to become the mother of the offspring. The intentions of each of these parties were embodied in a gestational carriage contract that stipulated that Whitehead would relinquish her parental rights in favour of Elizabeth Stern postnatally. Absent the contract, Whitehead's parental rights were implicit in the theretofore unchallenged assumption that the status of motherhood follows gestation, an assumption that Whitehead drew upon in her postnatal decision to keep the child as her own. The Sterns' legal challenge to have the child recognized as the legal daughter of Elizabeth Stern as per the contract did not succeed, as gestational carriage contracts were held to be void as contrary to public policy. However, the father – who was on equal footing as a genetic parent with Whitehead vis-à-vis parentage – was granted custody on the basis of the child's best interests. The dispute was settled, in other words, on the basis of facts that sounded in custody, not parentage, law: the best interests of a particular child.

The characterization of the contest as one between status and contract – a legal elevation of the contest between biology and intention – was taken up in the academic literature. Linking the status of motherhood with gestation reproduced a state of affairs so obvious that it went without saying, the means for establishing maternity historically almost universally going without explicit mention in legislation dedicated to establishing legal parenthood for children.[8] The linkage also intersected with more contemporary concerns about protecting the vulnerabilities of women, particularly in the face of asymmetries of class and anxieties about the commodification of children.[9] Entrenching the status of motherhood through biology provided a bulwark against the encroachment of the unbridled market embodiment of intention in contract, and in particular commercial contract.

As detailed in the *AHRA Reference*, the federally instituted Royal Commission on New Reproductive Technologies in Canada – created one year after the American Baby M spectacle – generated one set of policy responses to assisted reproduction that led eventually to legislation that could unify national policy by subsuming policy under the federal criminal law power. Shortly thereafter, in 1992, the Uniform Law Conference of Canada created the *Uniform Child Status Act*, which was accepted by the Bar Associations of Canada as a model for addressing the civil – and therefore provincial – implications of assisted reproduction.[10] The model legislation, which reflects the will of no government or political authority, entrenched gestation over intention as the core determinant of legal maternal parentage by deeming a child's mother to be the woman who gives birth to him or her, whether or not her egg was used to conceive the child. While the model act provides basic rules speaking to a range of issues relating to parentage, the 2010 updating of the act reproduces the 1992 primacy of gestation over contract when it stipulates that "[a]n agreement in which a surrogate arranges to relinquish a child conceived for that purpose is unenforceable."[11] The thrust of public policy with respect to gestational carriage contracts appears to have remained static over the last twenty years. I will argue that the model law in this regard is no longer adequate to deal with the complexities – legal, political, and emotional – of gestational carriage.

It would be incorrect to characterize the *Uniform Act, 2010* as forever precluding the possibility of intention surmounting gestation as a means of establishing parentage in the context of a gestational carriage arrangement. Indeed, the Act lays out a straightforward procedure whereby intended parents can become legal parents following the birth of a child through gestational carriage through mutual agreement between the parties conjoined with declaratory relief. This agreement, however, is not rooted in the carriage contract but rather antedates it. I will return to the mechanism proposed in the *Uniform Act*. First I want to lay out parentage law as it currently exists in provincial common law and statute.

Legal parentage is a lifelong status that determines the existence of a parent–child relationship across a wide range of legal contexts and is the usual (although not determinative) starting point for allocating parenting responsibilities while the child is a minor. I will not be covering parentage law in detail in this analysis but will rather focus principally on those aspects of parentage law that relate to determinations of motherhood.

Parentage law (or filiation in Quebec) covers not only the relationship between child and mother but also all of the ways by which fathers become legal parents to children.[12] While legal parentage for fathers can be rooted in unrebutted legal presumptions such as the name on the birth certificate or the relationship with the birth mother, legal parentage of mothers has historically been uniquely based on birth (the *mater est* rule). For the purposes of this chapter, I will focus mainly on the link between the gestational and intended parents, who may or may not have a genetic link to a child born of gestational carriage. This issue is spotlighted by the potential conflict at the heart of this chapter – namely, the rare and juridically untested case in Canada where both the gestational carrier and the intended parents claim legal parentage.[13] Working through the statistically rare case of a conflict between parties to a gestational carriage contract – in the light of public policy and the most current empirical evidence – provides an opportunity to clarify the interests at stake in gestational carriage arrangements.[14]

In the rare event that a gestational carrier were to decide postnatally that she wants to be a mother to the child, Quebec provides a clear and certain rule about the legal outcome of the inevitable conflict that would ensue with the intended parents, an outcome that requires no further legal action on the carrier's part. As the first province to extensively regulate assisted reproduction in the context of family law, Quebec passed Article 541 of the *Civil Code of Quebec* in 1991 under which "[a]ny agreement whereby a woman undertakes to procreate or carry a child for another person is absolutely null." Regardless of who provides the sperm and egg that constitute the child's genetic makeup, and regardless of what the original intentions of all parties were regarding who would be the child's parent(s) and raise him or her, the woman who gives birth to the child is the presumptive mother – a status that can only be overcome by an adoption that breaks the links with the biological mother and creates "fictional" links with new parents.[15] Quebec is the only jurisdiction in Canada that compels intended parents in the context of gestational carriage, regardless of genetic link to the child, to proceed with an adoption in order to become that child's legal parents.

The common law provinces and territories have a mix of provisions that facilitate the creation of legal parentage in intended parents; however, almost all of them have provisions rooted in common law or statute that recognize the woman who gives birth to a child as his or her mother. With the possible exception of Nova Scotia and Newfoundland and Labrador, none of them have opened the door for a grounding of legal parentage in the gestational carriage contract itself. Quebec, Alberta, and British Columbia are the only provinces in Canada that have taken the *explicit* position that such contracts are null and void, to wit, unenforceable. However, it would be incorrect to characterize the situation in the remaining common law provinces and territories as one in which such contracts are enforceable. Indeed, with the possible exception of Newfoundland and Labrador and perhaps Nova Scotia, Canadian provinces and territories tend not to recognize legal parentage on the grounds of the gestational carriage contract alone. In some cases, provincial law makes clear what legal result would ensue should the carrier choose to parent the child postnatally; in other cases, it does not.

In common law provinces that have not passed legislation explicitly dealing with legal parentage in the context of gestational carriage, outdated common law prevails and parties must rely on judicial intervention in the event of a postnatal conflict between the intended parents and the gestational carrier. In the absence of legislation, provinces draw upon the *mater est* rule, a rule generated in an epoch when it was unthinkable that motherhood might vest in parties other than the biological mother (and also in her husband or male partner under rebuttable presumptions of paternity). Where legislation supplements this common law biological understanding of motherhood, two types of provincial legislation are typically drawn on: vital statistics legislation and child status legislation. The former, an administrative tool, permits the registration of parents as part of the documentation of birth. The resulting birth certificate creates a presumption of parenthood but is not itself determinative of legal parentage. The vast majority of parents create a lifelong status for their child through this original document that determines the existence of a parent–child relationship across a wide range of legal contexts, never needing to draw upon child status legislation that allows for judicial declarations of parentage affirming or denying the presumption created by a birth certificate.

For the most part, both vital statistics and child status legislation historically entrenched the common law rule that links motherhood to gestation and birth.[16] Very slowly, provincial legislatures have begun to catch up with the realities of assisted reproduction to permit other mechanisms whereby intended parents might be registered as the child's parents or secure declarations of legal parentage.

BC has passed the most recent legislation to deal with assisted reproduction and gestational carriage. A larger revision to the provincial *Family Law Act* that came into effect in March 2013 explicitly addresses parentage through gestational carriage by laying out the criteria and a mechanism for creating legal parentage in intended parents. The legislation requires a written contract providing for legal parentage to the intended parents, but that contract alone is insufficient to overcome the *mater est* rule. The gestational carrier further needs to consent *postnatally* to the transfer of legal parentage, and the legislation permits the carrier to withdraw consent to the contract prior to birth.[17] The new legislation does not require a court order for the transfer of parentage. Registration consistent with the consent requirements of the *Family Law Act* will suffice, and a birth can be registered to intended parents on the day of birth; however, if the gestational carrier refuses to provide consent, a court order cannot vest legal parentage in accord with the original contract. The legislation is explicit that gestational carriage contracts are unenforceable and may not be used as evidence of the carrier's consent to a transfer of legal parentage; however, the contract may be used as evidence of the intended parents' intentions with respect to parentage if a dispute arises after the child's birth so that if intended parents refuse to take steps to assume parentage postnatally despite the contract and the gestational carrier's consent to relinquish, the contract can be used to impute parentage to them.[18]

A number of those common law provinces that have passed child status legislation that specifically addresses gestational carriage similarly render the contract unenforceable on its own terms. Alberta also added a provision on surrogacy to its *Family Law Act* in 2003; following Quebec's lead, it explicitly provided that "[a]ny agreement under which a surrogate agrees to give birth to a child for the purpose of relinquishing that child to a person a) is not enforceable and b) may not be used as evidence of consent of the surrogate [to a declaration of change of legal parentage to the intended parents]."[19] Unlike in Quebec, however, intended parents do not need to go through the adoption process in order to acquire legal parentage; they can seek a declaration that permits them to register themselves as the legal parents of a child. However, as in BC, this process requires the gestational carrier to give birth to the child, to understand that she is the parent of the child by virtue of having given birth (the *mater est* rule), and to consent to the application to change parentage.[20]

Nova Scotia provides analogous provisions that allow intended parents to become legal parents in the context of assisted reproduction without adoption; however, these provisions on gestational carriage are captured in the regulations to the *Vital Statistics Act* alone, and not in child status legislation.[21] While they do not specifically address the enforceability of gestational carriage contracts, these regulations enable intended parents to register the child provided that the "woman who is to carry and give birth to the child *does not intend to be the child's parent*."[22] This provision does not impose a positive obligation for the registration to be accompanied by the carrier's consent. The gestational carriage contract then might provide evidentiary weight in conjunction with the absence of the carrier's objection. However, the ability of the gestational carrier to override a gestational contract postnatally by expressing an intent to parent renders such contracts unenforceable on their own terms, even if the "arrangements" (as they are called in the regulations) provide the foundation for successful registration. Furthermore, consistent with Alberta's legislation, one of the intended parents must have a genetic link to the child.[23] Despite the inability of gestational carriage contracts to modify legal parentage on their own terms, Nova Scotia does lay out some bare minimums that such contracts would need to meet for the regulations to apply, namely, that the "arrangements" had to have been initiated by the intended parents and must have been planned prior to conception.[24] Nova Scotia, in with BC, is specifying the requisite content that gestational carriage contracts require before legal parentage can be transferred to intended parents. BC's requirements are more detailed and echo the requirement that the gestational carriage be organized in advance of conception. Neither province requires that the carrier be legally represented by independent counsel.

Newfoundland and Labrador, like Alberta, permits declaratory orders of legal parentage that override the common law *mater est* rule.[25] Even though an oblique reference to the *mater est* rule can be found in the definition of birth as "the complete expulsion or extraction from its *mother*" in the *Vital Statistics Act* and the provision in the provincial child status act that "a person is the child of his or her *natural* parents,"[26] the child can be registered subsequent to a declaration of legal parentage as the child of the intended parents. This rule issues from a 2009 amendment to the *Vital Statistics Act* that explicitly took into account gestational carriage.[27]

Unlike in Alberta, however, the legislation is silent on whether the gestational carrier has to consent to the transfer of legal parentage, although this is implied by the oblique *mater est* references. The province's vital statistics and child status legislation are almost silent on the mechanism by which this presumption might be rebutted, noting only that "[w]here the court finds on the balance of probabilities that a woman is or is not the mother of a child, the court may make a declaratory order to that effect."[28] This leaves open the possibility that the gestational carriage contract might be used as the only evidence to vest intended parents with legal parentage, such that Newfoundland and Labrador come closest to giving gestational carriage contracts such potential weight. Alberta and BC, which also allow the contract to serve as an evidentiary foundation for assigning legal parentage, positively require the written consent of the carrier to the transfer postnatally.

Prince Edward Island amended its *Child Status Act* in 2008 to deal with assisted reproduction; however, the legislation does not directly address gestational carriage, thus leaving the status of these arrangements in a similar position to what is found those provinces that lack comprehensive legislation on legal parentage in the case of gestational carriage.[29] The legislation is clear, however, that "[a] woman who gives birth to a child is deemed to be the mother of the child, whether the woman is or is not the genetic mother of the child."[30] This makes the transfer of legal parentage to intended parents contemplated in gestational carriage contracts effectively dependent on the carrier's consent.

In Ontario, Saskatchewan, New Brunswick, and Manitoba, and the three territories, the possibility is present for a declaratory order of legal parentage to be granted to the intended parents despite the lack of explicit legislation outlining the process for legal parentage in the case of gestational carriage and despite incidental embedding of the *mater est* rule in both child status and vital statistics legislation. The rule is embedded in language such as that found in Ontario's *Family Law Act*, which stipulates that "for all purposes of the law of Ontario a person is the child of his or her *natural* parents."[31] "Natural" is not defined in the legislation. In these provinces, vital statistics legislation implicitly further entrenches the *mater est* rule, for example, by defining birth as "the complete expulsion or extraction from its *mother* of a fetus that did any tim[e] after being completely expelled or extracted from the mother breathe or show any other sign of life."[32]

Intended parents who want to clarify and register their role as legal parents have needed to draw upon the scant case law in these provinces (most of which have no reported cases) in which judges have granted declaratory relief in scenarios where the gestational carrier consents to, or declines to contest, an application made by intended parents.[33] A judicial *declaration* of parentage is required if the registration is to override the common law biological presumption. Despite the lack of explicit legislation on gestational carriage, the leading Ontario case on point grounded the transfer of legal parentage in a provision of the *Children's Law Reform Act* that allows "any person having an interest to apply to court for a declaration that a male person is recognized in law to be the father of a child or that a female person is the mother of the child."[34] This judicial interpretation of child status legislation has been shored up by a second Superior Court judgment from Ontario, which found that there was a "gap" in the provincial *Vital Statistics Act* because its embedded definition of "mother" through birth no longer accorded with developments in assisted reproduction. The "gap" that was relied upon in the *AA v BB* case that allowed for the registration of three parents on a birth certificate through an invocation of the court's *parens patriae* jurisdiction[35] was used to find legal parentage in intended parents despite the archaic language of the Act.[36]

Given that the oblique reference to the *mater est* rule in these types of legislation is vulnerable to supplemental judicial lawmaking, and given the broad reading of "any person having an interest" that includes intended parents, there may be a narrow door open in these provinces for gestational carriage contracts to be the *evidentiary* source of a declaration of parentage for intended parents. However, the alternative implication of residual *mater est* rules is that a contract will not be enforced on its own terms, as the child is born the child of the gestational carrier and there is no statutory room for the contract to apply of its own force to supplant this status.

This is indeed how the Court of Queen's Bench in Manitoba interpreted the provincial *Vital Statistics Act* in the face of an application by intended parents for a pre-birth order for a declaration that the hospital documentation of the child's birth show them to be the "natural and legal parents" of the child delivered through gestational carriage. The court relied on the definition of birth as "the complete expulsion or extraction from its *mother*" and denied the application.[37] This interpretation of the oblique and dated *mater est* references in *Vital Statistics Acts* and child status laws is, however, by no means settled in law, particularly given the growing tendency of courts to use their *parens patriae* jurisdiction where they perceive a legislative "gap." That leaves the legal status of gestational carriage contracts in considerable limbo.

Despite the oblique persistence of the *mater est* rule, on the strength of the handful of cases that recognize declaratory orders as a mechanism for assigning legal parentage to intended parents, declaratory relief has become routine in those provinces that have failed to pass explicit legislation that deals with legal parentage in the context of gestational carriage, with the effectively untested proviso that the gestational carrier does not contest the application.[38]

There is only one case on record in Canada of a carrier – in this case a surrogate as per the definition in note 1 – contesting the parentage provisions outlined in a gestational contract.[39] In that BC case both the carrier and the intended father were genetically linked to the child. Postpartum, both parties sought custody, and the surrogate refused to give consent to the intended mother's adoption. The genetic father and his wife had custody, and on an interim judgment this arrangement persisted, with the carrier denied interim access. This is all that is on record of this case, which was an unusual one in the context of current practice around gestational carriage in that the surrogate was also genetically related to the child, as well as an unsatisfying one with respect to clarifying the outcome of a contest between intended parents and gestational carriers.

To summarize the status of gestational carriage contracts in the common law provinces and territories of Canada: Only Alberta states explicitly that the contracts are unenforceable and cannot be used as evidence. With the possible exception of Newfoundland and Labrador and Nova Scotia, all other common law jurisdictions either have not legislatively overridden the *mater est* rule (in which case the status of gestational carriage contracts remains somewhat obscure) or explicitly provide that a declaration or registration of legal parentage in the intended parents cannot proceed without the consent of woman who has given birth to the child or children. Nova Scotia and Newfoundland and Labrador leave open the possibility that a court might find, on a balance of probabilities, that a gestational carriage contract is sufficient to find that gestational carrier is not the mother of a child. Nova Scotia and BC are alone in laying out some minimum standards that gestational "arrangements" need to meet in order to position an intended parent to claim legal parentage. In the context of this diverse patchwork of provisions on legal parentage relating to assisted reproduction, it is fair to say that Canada has barely begun to deal with the growing reality of gestational carriage: five provinces (PEI, Ontario, Manitoba, New Brunswick, and Saskatchewan) and the territories lack any legislation dealing directly with the new reality; two provinces have only thin legislation (Newfoundland and Labrador and Nova Scotia); and only three provinces have passed anything resembling a comprehensive approach to assisted reproduction that includes treatment of gestational carriage (Quebec, Alberta, and BC).

Unifying Canadian Parentage Law: The *Uniform Child Status Act*

The *AHRA* was meant to unify national policy around assisted reproduction by subsuming large parts of the field under the federal criminal law power. In the above private law context, the *Uniform Child Status Act* of 2010 seeks to generate a unified national policy for the private law aspects of assisted reproduction, including gestational carriage. The *Uniform Act* proposes comprehensive legislation covering all aspects of child status, including the more common parentage scenario where assisted reproduction is not involved; but it also looks hard at several aspects of how assisted reproduction has changed the rules of parentage. Section 8, in particular, is devoted to declaratory orders respecting parentage where gestational carriage has been involved.

The model law remains aspirational, given that it was generated by government policy lawyers and analysts, private lawyers, and law reformers rather than legislatures. Rather than cover the entire section that deals with declarations of parentage relating to gestational carriage contracts, I want to focus on those provisions that stand to affect their status as enforceable agreements,[40] principally because I want to argue that they serve as a poor model for provincial legislation around legal parentage with respect to gestational carriage contracts, and that the rationale invoked to support the model is inadequate to a proper analysis of the field. I will argue that the inadequacy of the model legislation indicates that the framework of those American states that explicitly regulate enforceable gestational carriage contracts would be better suited to the realities of gestational carriage that have emerged over the past two decades.[41]

The *Uniform Act* starts with an explicit entrenchment of the *mater est* rule: "The following persons are the parents of a child: his or her birth mother."[42] This is followed by a set of presumptions about how other parties become legal parents that are common to all child status legislation; and the mechanism of declaration of parentage by a court that is already common to most child status legislation in Canadian provinces.[43] In this regard the *Uniform Act* differs from Quebec in not requiring intended parents to adopt a child who is born the legal parent of the birth-mother-née-gestational-carrier. They need only have an interest, which would be generated by intention to parent plus a genetic link to the child or a spousal relationship with the former party. The *Uniform Act* proposes explicit provisions that deal with both assisted reproduction and gestational carriage.

For the *Uniform Act*, gestational carriage agreements can serve as an evidentiary foundation for the legal parentage of intended parents, but only to the extent that they provide evidence of the latters' intention to parent postnatally. This provision would serve admirably to lessen the chances that a gestational carrier might find herself the legal parent of a child that she did not set out to gestate for that purpose. It does not, however, bind the intended parents to their original intention, for gestational carriage contracts are unenforceable under the *Uniform Act*.[44] The contract cannot serve as evidence of the carrier's consent to relinquish legal parentage, no matter how explicit the terms of the contract. These provisions shore up the Act's explicit *mater est* rule, which makes the gestational carrier the legal mother upon birth until a declaratory order to the contrary is made. Both she and the intended parents would have to share parental rights and responsibilities pending the order (although such a declaratory order can have retroactive effect to the time of birth). Consent for a relinquishment of legal parentage, in other words, can only issue postnatally. Evidentiary considerations aside, the *Uniform Act* is clear that gestational carriage contracts, on their own terms, are unenforceable and at most provide evidentiary weight in favour of a carrier's intention *not* to parent. These provisions are consistent with Alberta's *Family Law Act*.

In the comments that accompany these provisions of the Uniform Act, the rationale invoked is the following: "Subsection (11) clarifies that surrogacy agreements are unenforceable. It is not consistent with public policy or with the court's overarching *parens patriae* responsibilities to allow surrogacy contracts to be enforceable. Note *Jane Doe v Alberta*, (2007), 278 D.L.R. (4th) 1, which references the inability of an agreement between the parties to bind the hands of the court."

In *Jane Doe*, it was held that it is not in the best interests of children that their parentage can be contractually designated or limited in advance.[45] A couple in a romantic relationship wished to contractually limit the male partner's parental status and obligations with respect to a child, conceived through sperm donation, whom the mother wanted to parent exclusively. They wanted to contractually preclude the *de facto* acquisition of the status of social parent for the man, as his ongoing relationship with the mother might generate the kinds of relationship and reliance that ordinarily enable a court to attribute fatherhood, with its attendant rights and obligations. The rights and obligations of *de facto* parents have been affirmed by the *Chartier* case, which is briefly discussed below.[46]

The *Jane Doe* case did not turn on the best interests of the particular child, which had not been argued, but on whether the policy in the provincial legislation permitting courts to override private parental agreements violated the contracting parties' liberty as protected by s. 7 of the *Canadian Charter of Rights and Freedoms*.[47] The Alberta Court of Appeal upheld the trial judge's finding that Jane Doe's spouse would "stand in place of parent" as per the provincial *Family Law Act* regardless of his intent to not parent. The statute says that a person stands in the place of parent if he or she is the spouse of the child's parent or is "in a relationship of interdependence of some permanence" with the parent, and has demonstrated a settled intention to treat the child as his or her own. As to the determination of settled intention, the court weighed Jane's spouse's actions and the nature of the spouse's relationship, but they also found that his choice to remain in the common law relationship with the mother indicated his reality as parent to her child. His future conduct might manifest a settled intention to treat Jane's child as his own. The Court of Appeal regarded the emergence of this relationship as effectively inevitable.[48] The commentary to the *Uniform Child Status Act* finds analogy between gestational carriage contracts and the proposed contract between Jane Doe and her spouse.

An Alternative Model for Canadian Parentage Law: Intention over Gestation

This chapter will scrutinize this rationale by contrasting the policy driving the model law (unenforceable gestational carriage contracts) with the policies that drive the alternative (enforceable contracts). It will also address the empirical realities that challenge other long-standing justifications for minimizing the place of the intention of the parties to such a contract. The proposed alternative would preclude the situation that, at any time following birth, parents from two families who are otherwise strangers in law would continue to share rights and responsibilities that flow from legal parentage. Rather than create certainty by rendering gestational carriage contracts null and void (as Quebec has done), the alternative would create certainty by rendering the contract enforceable in that it provides all the requisite evidence for the consent of both carrier and intended parents for legal parentage to vest in the intended parents; and it would be a new self-standing foundation for declaratory orders of parentage: the enforceability of contract. This certainty would just as effectively clarify responsibilities and rights from the moment of birth onwards.

This certainty has been characterized as "heartless" by the preponderance of Canadian policy analysts on this topic since the Baby M case in New Jersey. Rosemarie Tong's sentiments, for example, have found an echo in Canadian policy when she notes that

> women as a *whole* will benefit from an approach that stresses their right, not their duty, to be mothers (and not simply baby machines). The adoption approach, with its change of heart clause, replaces what strikes me as the *heartless* contract approach. A deal is not always a deal – at least not when one is trading in some of the deepest emotions human beings can ever feel. Any approach that *binds* women to reproductive decisions – as does the contract approach – must be regarded with deep suspicion.[49]

The "heartlessness" of gestational carriage contracts has long been advanced as one reason – among many – for resisting their enforceability on public policy grounds. I will revisit these arguments momentarily. For now I want to lay out the alternative as it is articulated in California's new surrogacy law. That jurisdiction has been immersed in a very different policy climate around assisted reproduction over the past two decades. The differences in context are often jarring enough that Canadian policy analysts and law reformers almost reflexively turn away from the Californian model. That reflex may be impulsive.

California judicially considered the very issue of the enforceability of gestational carriage contracts two decades ago in a case where the intended parents both had a genetic link to the child that another woman carried and gave birth to. The argument that gestational carriage is appropriately analogized to adoption, which affords a period for "change of heart" postnatally, was weighed in *Johnson v Calvert*.[50] The court also considered whether the gestational carrier had at least an equal right to legal parentage upon birth due to the strong emotional connection created by carrying a child, and it considered the argument that the tie-breaker between those equal claims should be consideration of the best interests of the child.[51] Ultimately, however, in *Johnson*, none of these arguments prevailed in the majority decision. The Court endorsed the view of Professor Hill that "while all of the players in the procreative arrangement are necessary in bringing a child into the world, *the child would not have been born but for the efforts of the intended parents.* [T]he intended parents are the first cause, or the prime movers, of the procreative relationship." The court also held that the one who intended to "bring about the birth of a child that she intended to raise as her own – is the natural mother under California law" (italics added).

The primacy of intention over biology in matters of legal parentage was extended to cases where intended parents have neither genetic nor biological links to the child. Five years after *Johnson*, the court in *Re Marriage of Buzzanca*[52] clarified that the enforceability of gestational carriage contracts "was not limited to just *Johnson*-style contests between women who gave birth and women who contributed ova, but to any situation where a child would not have been born 'but for the efforts of the intended parents.'" With the results in these two cases, gestational carriage contracts enforceably determined legal parentage thereafter in Californian parentage law for similar situations. And intended parents have been able to get pre-birth orders that clarify that they have all of the rights and responsibilities of legal parentage upon birth.

California recently passed a gestational carriage law, effective since the beginning of January 2013, that entrenches and formally regulates the common law generated by *Johnson* and *Buzzanca*.[53] While the law was originally an extensive attempt to regulate a wide range of practices associated with assisted reproduction in California, it was ultimately whittled down to a codification of best legal practices associated with gestational carriage contracts.[54]

The clarification of legal requirements for enforceable gestational carrier contracts was in some measure stimulated by the outrage surrounding an international scam with roots in California in which American women were recruited to travel abroad for the implantation of embryos created by brokers in the absence of intended parents. Once past their first trimester of pregnancy, the gestational carriers and the fetuses they were carrying were marketed to prospective parents for $150,000 on the ruse that the original intended parents had backed out of the agreement. The lawyers and coordinator who perpetrated the scam were convicted of wire fraud and monetary transactions in property derived from illegal activity.

Stimulated by this debacle, California's *Surrogacy Law* now requires that intended parents and gestational carriers be represented by separate counsel and that their agreement be notarized for binding effect. The execution and notarization of the agreement has to be completed prior to the administration of medications used in assisted reproduction or any embryo transfer procedure and requires the parties to the contract to attest, under penalty of perjury, to their compliance with the provisions of the Act. The Act further codifies past practice in permitting intended parents to establish a parent-and-child relationship in law consistent with the intent expressed in the agreement prior to the child's birth by filing a parentage action under the *Uniform Parentage Act*.[55] In this manner, upon birth, legal parentage can be clarified from the moment that potential medical decisions need to be made along with the exercise of other parental rights and responsibilities; also, the parent(s) who needs to register the birth is known from the start.

California's *Surrogacy Law* need not be taken as the be-all-and-end-all of gestational carriage contract law. There are features of Canadian parentage law and clinical practice that might be drawn upon to supplement these elements. While not permitting pre-birth orders and still requiring the postnatal consent of the gestational carrier for legal parentage to be ordered consistent with the contract, the BC *Family Law Act* echoes California's requirement that a written agreement be made prior to conception for the arrangement to qualify as gestational carriage. It further stipulates content to the agreement for its validity – to wit, the agreement must provide that the carrier will not be a parent of the child, that the carrier will surrender the child to the intended parent or parents, and that the intended parent(s) will be the child's parent(s).[56] A sensible gestational carriage contract that reflects dominant clinical practice might also require that gestational carriers have completed their own families, that they not use their own gametes or those of their spouses, and that they have clarified their wishes, feelings, motivations, and intentions through a counsellor who specializes in gestational carriage.[57]

If Canadian provinces were to adopt the provisions of California's *Surrogacy Law* (perhaps amplified with Canadian law and practice as well as drawing on other jurisdictions that regulate enforceable contracts), the remnants of the *mater est* rule in vital statistics law would need to be revised in such a way that the definition of "birth" did not foreclose the possibility of a displacement of biological motherhood by a gestational carriage contract. This would not require the elimination of the *mater est* rule (although it would probably need to be more explicit than current oblique references in vital statistics and child status legislation). After all, outside the context of assisted reproduction and gestational carriage, the rule is certainly useful to the extent that most women who give birth are unequivocally the legal mothers of their children short of adoption or a finding of unfitness. Child status legislation would have to add a provision that recognizes the possibility of legal parentage arising from a gestational carriage contract either through declaratory order or birth registration. Those provinces that have created explicit rules requiring post-birth consent from the gestational carrier for a transfer of legal parentage would have to revise their regimes; *a fortiori* those provinces that explicitly rule gestational carriage contracts unenforceable. Before such legislative reforms could even be contemplated, the public policy rationales for the current regimes would need to be revised and reconsidered. And it is to this undertaking that I now turn.

Risk and Certainty

In those provinces that have created an explicit statutory trump for the gestational carrier with respect to legal parentage, the virtue of the approach is underlined by the certainty it generates in advance of the child's birth and in advance of conflict between intended parents and gestational carriers. Ostensibly, no one need go to court as the outcome of a legal parentage dispute is clear in advance. The child and his or her family can set about consolidating the family around this certainty from the outset of birth. However, in those provinces that declare gestational carriage contracts null and void, the consequences of such certainty are borne by all parties, but in different measures. Of the risks (some of which are theoretical in that there is no empirical evidence that they have recently, commonly, or ever arisen), the trump of gestation over intention exposes the implicated individuals and their kin differently. And there are many configurations of misery that can flow from this apparently certain rule.

In light of the absence of comprehensive statutory clarity regarding the treatment of gestational carriage contracts – both in provinces that explicitly declare them unenforceable and of limited evidentiary value and in those that are silent on both issues – there is residual uncertainty about the outcome should intended parents refuse, on birth, to adopt the child, or to seek a declaration of legal parentage in their favour, or register their names on the birth certificate. While Quebec, for example, has amended its civil code to account for "parental projects" involving assisted reproduction, the language of the provisions is directed to those situations where "a person alone decides or spouses by mutual consent decide, in order to have a child, to resort to the genetic material of a person *who is not party to the parental project*."[58] A genetically related intended parent *is* a party to a parental project – just not the one in consideration in the amended code; and genetically unrelated intended parents are completely outside of consideration. Quebec is thus silent on what would happen if intended parents declined to apply for an adoption as per the terms of a contract that the civil code regards as null and void.

A recent Canadian situation illustrates an instance where such a scenario might arise. The gestational carrier in a story cited in the *National Post* originally refused to abort a fetus with Down syndrome, despite the instructions of the intended (and genetic) parents and a contract that stipulated that the surrogate would become the legal mother if she did not respect the intended parent's instructions on termination.[59] Canadian law does not allow anyone but the woman carrying a child to control her body (e.g., her diet, her medical treatment, and her weight), and this includes the decision to terminate a pregnancy. That constitutional limitation, however, does not control all of the private law implications of her decision – namely, whether a woman can be obliged to become a legal parent to a child she carries for intended parents. BC's new *Family Law Act* would not transfer legal parentage to intended parents if the gestational carrier refuses to consent to the transfer; however, if the intended parents refuse to apply for legal parentage, the contract can be used as evidence regarding parentage intentions. But in this case, the terms of the contract provide ambiguous evidentiary assistance. It is not clear that they intended to bring this particular child into the world; there is evidence that that was explicitly *not* their intention – just as there is evidence that it was.[60]

As it stands in BC, a genetic link to the intended parents coupled with their (qualified) intention to parent creates the likely prospect of an imputation of legal parentage, presuming that the gestational carrier (now birth mother) makes an application as a "person with an interest" to attribute parentage. As gestational carriage contracts have not had the occasion to be judicially reviewed in Canada, it is not clear whether family law, which delineates obligations on genetic intended parents, would prevail over the contract or whether the latter could override family law obligations; nor is it clear what would happen if neither intended parent had a genetic link to the child.

This scenario speaks to a serious peril in regimes in which contracts[61] are unenforceable: the child may have legal parents from two different families. Given that child status laws define parentage for a whole range of parental rights and obligations defined in other areas of family law including child support, custody, and access, the perils are both financial and psychosocial on a life-changing scale. There are various permutations of risk involved, from carriers becoming parents against their wishes to intended parents sharing parental rights and responsibilities with carriers against their original intentions, to carriers sharing parental rights and responsibilities with intended parents against their wishes, to intended parents losing all rights and responsibilities for children they intended (and yearned) to bring into the world. These permutations of peril differ from province to province. In those provinces that have not passed child status legislation dealing with gestational carriage, the situation is very uncertain, although there remain risks in provinces like Alberta, Quebec, and BC that *have* done so and also risks under the model proposed by the *Uniform Act*.

For those provinces lacking statutory guidance, there are a mere handful of cases that lay out the course that courts and parties might follow in the event of a breakdown in the "arrangement." The *JR v LH* case in Ontario provides a type of roadmap but struggles to articulate ratios beyond the confines of the facts in that case – a "good news case" that involved two genetically related intended parents, a gestational carrier, and her husband, all four of whom were in agreement with the intended parents' application for legal parentage.[62] As Judge Kitely noted, "[t]here is no issue as to the enforceability of the gestational carriage agreement."[63] The case cannot stand for a judicial ruling on how gestational carriage contracts should be read in the event of a dispute regarding parentage.

As noted above, s. 4(1) of Ontario's *Children's Law Reform Act* allows "any person having an interest" to apply for a declaration of parentage.[64] This language is common to many child status laws in Canada.

For genetically related intended parents, this section could be invoked by the carrier (or her male spouse) for parentage to vest in the intended parents. This kind of provision is the usual route whereby mothers apply for declarations of legal parentage for genetic (or "natural," in the language of many statutes) fathers who might otherwise deny paternity. Legal parentage can be attributed to both men and women who have made a genetic contribution to a child on this basis; however, provincial legislation generally precludes the attribution of legal parentage to gamete donors who did not intend to parent.[65] But genetically related intended parents clearly do intend to parent, or did intend at some time to do so, so are both liable to a declaration of parentage against their wishes and able to apply for a declaration of parentage as "interested parties."

This may be a matter of concern if only one of the intended parents made a genetic contribution but both intend(ed) to parent the child; but it might also be a matter for concern where intended parents used donated sperm and egg. Indeed, the uncertainty generated by this kind of situation spills over into Nova Scotia's and Alberta's legislation (and the *Uniform Act*), given the statutory requirement in both provinces for a genetic link to at least one of the intended parents in order for a parentage order to properly vest in intended parents. This leaves the result more uncertain when such a link is absent in both intended parents.[66]

For those common law provinces with no explicit statutory language dealing with gestational carriage (or thin language), the roadmap in *JR v LH* is sketchy at best. Judge Kitely cites the genetic relation of the intended parents as the reason for the ready application of s. 4(1) *CLRA*, leaving it less clear what would happen in the absence of this connection.[67] And it was this genetic link with the intended parents that further allowed a rebuttal of the presumption in child status legislation that the birth mother's spouse was the father.[68] While the judge recognized that child status legislation does not permit a court to make *negative* declarations as to parentage (such as declaring a gestational carrier to be a non-parent), a resolution for the collective aspirations of the two families was found in the *Courts of Justice Act* that provides for a superior court to make a binding declaration of right; this is the mechanism by which the gestational carrier was declared to be *not* the mother of the twins, despite the oblique *mater est* rule in the *Vital Statistics Act* that definitionally links "birth" to "mother." But Judge Kitely is also clear that the court's ability to invoke the *Courts of Justice Act* in this way depends on the lack of opposition to the transfer of legal parentage.

While the reference to lack of opposition in *JR v LH* was to the gestational carrier's opposition, the opposition of the intended parents might also pose a problem: "If the application had been opposed, the omission from the application [of a request for declaratory relief] may have been problematic." That the failure of the intended parents to seek declarative relief might also pose a problem is highlighted by the judge's reference to the *Johnson v Calvert* case from California, discussed above, in which the gestational carriage contract was contested. Judge Kitely notes in *obiter* that "[i]f such a conflict existed, I would have to consider whether s. 4(1) enables a declaration that there is more than one mother."[69] In light of the lack of clarity in a situation where intended parents refuse to pursue their undertakings in the gestational carriage, the risks are considerable not only to the gestational carrier and her family, but also to any child born in these circumstances.

In the absence of the contract's enforceability on its own terms, the mechanism by which a judge would assign parentage in this scenario is somewhat obscure, particularly if there is no genetic link to a party, and particularly in those provinces that do not legislatively state the evidentiary weight that might be attributed to the contract. The best interests of the child standard from custody law (proposed by the dissent in *Johnson v Calvert*) will have little purchase in these circumstances. The standard for functional parenthood (based not on genetic or biological connections to children but on having stood in place of parent)[70] or the *status quo ante* will not have any play in the early weeks of the child's life.

Chartier v Chartier is the leading case in Canada that creates parentage rights and responsibilities in "functional" parents, or those who stand in place of a parent. The Court held that a step-parent who is found to be *in loco parentis* cannot unilaterally withdraw from the family relationship. The determination of whether an adult stands in the role of parent is made by taking account of a number of factors, including whether the child participates in the extended family in the same way as would a biological child; whether the person provides financially for the child (depending on ability to pay); whether the person disciplines the child as a parent; and whether the person represents to the child, the family, the world, either explicitly or implicitly, that he or she is responsible as a parent to the child; as well as the nature or existence of the child's relationship with the absent biological parent. But in the case of contested parentage relating to gestational carriage, no one has yet occupied the functional role of parent, and no pattern of parenting has been established so as to create a status quo that should be maintained in the child's best interest – one of the other criteria for determining custody under the best interests rule.

In addition to the risks to carriers and their families of the unenforceability of contracts, and the risks to the children of genetically linked intentional parents, there are the risks to the intentional parents, which are more manifest in the event of a dispute about parentage between the carrier and intended parents. If intended parents are also genetic parents, in light of current laws that link custody and support to genetic connections[71] they risk being responsible for children who are torn between families from the outset. As noted with respect to Ontario, which has child status laws similar in this respect to those of many other common law provinces of Canada, "any person having an interest" can seek a declaration of parentage and can clearly do so with respect to intended parents with a genetic link to a child. A carrier who decides to withhold consent to a transfer of legal parentage retains the ability to have a genetically related intended parent of either gender declared a legal co-parent for purposes such as child support. The language used by Judge Kitely in *JR v LH* to attribute exclusive parentage to genetically related intended parents could be imported virtually without change, with "obligatorily" substituted for "entitled to" in such a context, reflecting the reality that parenthood involves responsibilities as well as rights: "The blood tests indicate that the probability that [genetic contributors] are [legal parents] is greater than 99.99%. I find that on a balance of probabilities they are the genetic parents. Pursuant to s. 4(1), [such an intended parent] is [obligatorily] 'recognized in law' as the [parent] of a child."[72]

The intended parent would be responsible for a child they are precluded from exclusively parenting as per their best-laid plans. Indeed it is possible they would be responsible for supporting a child financially that they are parenting not at all or very little. While legal parentage can be assigned to them on the foundation of their genetic link and intention to parent, determinations about custody and access are made in the best interests of particular children. These are fact-driven determinations, and there is no legal necessity linking joint legal parentage with a joint physical custody order. The case law compelling legal parents to persist in joint physical custody of children despite ongoing conflict is thin. Alternatively, child support obligations are routinely assigned to legal parents who do not share a residence with a child.

In light of uncertainties about the evidentiary weight of contracts for those intended parents without a genetic link outlined above, all intended parents are at risk of being assigned parenting responsibilities for children they are not raising, or not raising exclusively in accordance with the contract. As noted, Alberta and BC are quite explicit about the ability to use contracts as evidence of the parties' intentions with respect to parentage if a dispute arises after the child's birth. There may be some mitigation of the risk under Alberta legislation as it is explicit that an application attributing legal parentage cannot result in the child having more than two parents.[73] The *Uniform Act* also has this limitation in its general parentage provisions, which limit the number of parents a child can have by declaratory order.[74]

This limitation goes against the grain of an emerging common law mechanism that allows more than two parents to be registered on birth certificates under vital statistics laws – for example, two lesbian mothers and the known gay man who donated the sperm, each of whom intend to jointly parent the child.[75] But more to the point, such a provision does not prevent the two legal parents from being the birth mother-neé-gestational-carrier and a genetically related intended parent. This can happen if the carrier has no spouse. The genetically related intended parent would be the other legal parent. But it is also possible for two families to be raising a child born of gestational carriage even if both parties have spouses. The spouses of both the carrier and genetically intended parent (if such parties are present) may well be found to be social parents,[76] as the presumption of paternity in the carrier's male spouse could be rebutted by genetic fatherhood in another party, particularly given that the carrier's spouse had no original intention to parent the child. Following *Jane Doe*, canvassed above, the carrier's husband could not unequivocally preclude the status of social parent being assigned to him or her. It is difficult to see why the reasoning in that case – here modified to the facts of gestational carriage contracts gone wrong – would not prevail here as well:

> The "settled intention" to remain in a close relationship [with the birth-mother-neé-carrier] thrust[s] [the carrier's spouse] from a practical and realistic point of view, into the role of parent to this child. Can it seriously be contended that he will ignore the child when it cries? When it needs to be fed? When it stumbles? When the soother needs to be replaced? When the diaper needs to be changed?[77]

The same reasoning would apply to the genetically related parent's spouse. As both the *Jane Doe* case and *Chartier* lay out, the rights and obligations of those standing in place of parent do not obliterate rights and obligations of legal parents but are able to operate alongside them. Both a "natural" father, for example, and a stepfather can owe child support.

In the case of BC, the evidence generated by the gestational carriage contract does not bear solely upon those intended parents who made a genetic contribution to the child, as that statute does not require a genetic link in at least one of the intended parents. The incomes of both intended parents (if there are more than one) may be implicated under child support legislation.

That intended parents do not necessarily disappear as legal parents (although they might wish to) in the face of a decision by the carrier to retain legal parentage points to a further set of possibilities that could jettison each of the parties (including the child or children and any other family members) in an uncertain and fraught set of multiple family relations. This scenario would be precluded in Quebec, where an adoption is required to create legal parentage in the intended parents – an adoption that can be blocked by the birth-mother-née-gestational-carrier. But in the common law provinces, intended parents are poised to become legal parents.

Through the same mechanism in child status laws that allows an imputation of legal parentage to unwilling intended parents, "any person having an interest" can allow intended parents, particularly if genetically related to the child, to insert themselves as co-parents into the families of carriers that retain legal parentage. As the evidentiary weight of the contracts has not been judicially tested, the ability of intended parents with no genetic link might also fall into this category. It ought not to be assumed that intended parents who have invested financially, emotionally, and likely genetically in the birth of a child will want to disappear from that child's life once the gestational carrier opts to pursue legal parentage. This scenario of multiple legal parents between more than one family, each of whom is a legal stranger to the others outside of the gestational arrangement, is strongly intimated in Judge Kitely's obiter that in the case of conflict "I would have to consider whether s. 4(1) enables a declaration that there is more than one mother." This would introduce a newborn child into the centre of a vortex in which multiple parents would be poised to claim custody and access – a context that would likely be fraught, given the decay of agreement from the outset of the child's life.[78] While divorce has risks for all children, in these cases children would be *born into* a divorce-like scenario at the centre of the centrifugal forces of two families that had no original desire to be entwined with each other.

If the various scenarios in which legal parentage can be attributed to both intended parents and a gestational carrier who opts to retain legal parentage seem far-fetched, the British case of *CW v NT & Anor* gives some pause.[79] In that case the intended father, who was genetically related to the child, owed child support payments to the surrogate (who was also the genetic mother) as an aspect of the same default rules around child support that exist in Canada – namely, that genetic parents owe child support. This was despite the fact that the surrogate retained full custody of the child – contrary to the original intentions of the parties – and the intended parents voluntarily relinquished access to the child so that the child would not be split between two homes that had never intended to be connected.

Where the carrier opts to retain legal parentage, the scenario of intended parents being ascribed legal parentage against their wishes or choosing to pursue co-legal parentage with the gestational carrier/birth mother and her spouse presents considerable risks for intended parents, for gestational/birth parents, and for the children caught up in such possible scenarios. But intended parents might also opt to abandon all claims to parentage of their intended child when the gestational carrier claims legal parentage. Here the risk is high for intended parents in another sense – or rather a risk present from the beginning of the project materializes. With the lack of enforceability of gestational carriage contracts, intended parents always bear the risk of the loss of whatever financial contribution they have made to the child's creation and gestation as well as their intense emotional and psychological investment in plans to become parents with the carrier's assistance. They are perpetually vulnerable to this shattering of aspirations when gestational carriage contracts are unenforceable on their own terms. Leaving these vulnerabilities unprotected might be construed as heartless as readily as the contracts themselves have been described as heartless. In both cases, one is "trading in some of the deepest emotions human beings can ever feel."[80]

The rule that gestational carriage contracts are void is intended to protect general interests such as the best interests of children and the vulnerabilities of women as well as particular carriers and individual children. The policy of protecting these general interests can leave other vulnerable groups at risk. It might not just be individual intended parents who are more exposed under the *mater est* rule in gestational carriage situations, but also a significant percentage of those who use assisted reproduction and are members of marginalized groups within society. The case of a Michigan gestational carrier who decided to retain parentage and custody of twins because of the intended mother's "mental illness" hints at how problematic might be the birth mother's discretion to keep the child following the *mater est* rule.[81] In that case the intended mother and her husband were the genetic parents of the children. Under Michigan law, as in Quebec, the gestational carrier is the presumptive mother of children born through surrogacy and legal parentage is only transferred to intended parents through the process of a formal adoption, which requires the birth mother's consent and is subject to a "change of heart" provision. The twins had already been yielded to the intended parents for a month when the gestational carrier "discovered" at the preliminary hearing for an adoption determination that the intended mother had a minor criminal record and a "mental illness" and decided not to consent to the legal transfer of parentage. As a result, the carrier and her husband retained custody.

The surrogate's personal assessment that the intended mother was unfit to parent, despite expert testimony to the contrary, underscores how morally messy the non-enforcement of gestational contracts can be. Supporting the argument that gestational carrier contracts should not be enforced is an awareness that there are currently no public policy limits on such contracts that would align them with general interests such as the best interests of children and women. But there is a counterpart to anxieties about insufficient attention to public policy on the side of those who argue that the contracts should be enforced – namely, that blanket unenforceability has no public policy limits that engage central social values such as non-discrimination. The change of heart can be provoked by a whim as easily as it might be provoked by retrograde social values such as racism or homophobia. Without enforceability, the arrangement is shielded from legal scrutiny. Given the high rate of non-traditional families formed out of assisted reproduction (including single and LGBTQ parents, for example),[82] it is not difficult to imagine how marginalized groups may confront a precarious situation as a consequence of the *mater est* rule.

In summary, the rule that gestational carriage contracts are unenforceable on their own terms provides some prospective certainty regarding a dispute as to legal parentage in gestational carriage contracts. But it is also attendant with risks and further uncertainties that are redistributed elsewhere – and not only, as we have seen, to the intended parents, but also to carriers, their families, and the children born of the arrangements. A rule that the contracts *are* enforceable redistributes risk differently but does not eliminate it altogether.

A law favouring a presumption of parenthood as laid out in the gestational carriage contract would also create certainty. Intended parents and carriers would know in advance which party would prevail in a legal contest over parentage: the intentions embodied in the contract would in principle prevail, barring the faults that otherwise nullify contracts generally and barring the context-specific contractual safeguards that might be added in keeping with legislation such as California's *Surrogacy Law*. Here, too, risks would be potentially borne by all parties, but in different measures.

In addition, more general risk-bearers would also emerge from such a legal rule: surrogates as a class, women as a group, and children. The gestational carrier risks the removal of a child to whom she has grown attached throughout the pregnancy, attendant with all of the anguish (although in a different, more embodied way) that the intended parents would experience under the alternative legal rule. In the scenario in which intended parents are identified as parents early in the process (at birth, or shortly thereafter, or even before birth), the individual child has more certainty around who his or her parents will be, and that certainty is unmuddied by the possibility of two families having co-parentage status. However, a risk to children in general emerges from the context of a child having been created by forces more aligned with the marketplace and contract than with the "natural" forces of affection or attraction of the traditional family. This risk to children in general created by the context of gestational carriage is mirrored by a risk to women and carriers in general arising out of the creation of a group or class of women whose reproductive capacities are put at the disposal of third parties, a risk magnified by the possibility that economic asymmetries might induce into surrogacy women who might not otherwise be disposed to the potential difficulties and risks of pregnancy and the corresponding risks of attachment. In light of constitutional guarantees of women's autonomy and integrity throughout pregnancy, the intended parents bear the risk of becoming parents to a child they might not themselves have carried to term and the risk of becoming parents in circumstances that may have changed unfavourably from the date of the original contract.

There is, then, the virtue of certainty that arises from a clear rule about the enforceability, or lack thereof, of gestational carriage contracts.

The related risks fall differently and in different measures on different parties depending on which rule is chosen.[83] The enforceability of gestational carriage contracts would also preclude the need to conduct a fact-driven assessment of the best interests of the child, which is the golden rule for determinations relating to children within family law. As noted above, this avoidance of fact-based assessments makes sense in the context of gestational carriage in that most of the standard criteria used for interpreting a particular child's best interests – such as stability, status quo, and determination of the primary caregiver– do not have a temporal foundation on which they can be built at the very moment when parentage might be contested (i.e., at or around birth).

In light of how gestational carriage does not square easily with custody law, a rule regarding the enforceability of the contracts might be better established on the basis of policy determinations about the best interests of *children* in general, as opposed to a specific *child*. And this general standard is in fact one of the justifications provided in the commentary by the *Uniform Child Status Act, 2010* for its proposal that provinces pass legislation rendering gestational carriage agreements unenforceable. A legal policy of enforcing gestational carriage contracts (as in California) carries risks, as does a policy of refusing to enforce them. As I have tried to lay out, both policies have some potentially heartless consequences. Turning to a more scrupulous consideration of the public policy concerns and to the evidence of the empirical studies around gestational carriage might generate better ways of allocating the risks. A closer scrutiny of the rationales underlying the *Uniform Child Status Act, 2010* is a profitable starting point for this rethinking.

Contracts and Family Law: The Aptness of *Doe* in the Gestational Carriage Context

As noted above, the comments to s. 8(11) of the 2010 *Uniform Act* draw upon the Alberta Court of Appeal's 2007 decision in *Jane Doe* as the legal rationale for voiding contracts that delineate legal parentage in advance. The *Jane Doe* case itself was not uncontroversial with respect to social parentage and the ability of parties to contractually create the type of family that suits their individual interests. Brenda Cossman, notably, was critical of the imposition of a narrow nuclear conception of family and parenthood on the potential creativity arising from how individuals contractually construct their conception of family.[84] In Cossman's view the ongoing relationship between spouses should not *necessarily* impinge on an exclusive parental relationship between one of the spouses and a child.[85] In particular, she felt that women's ability to choose distinct romantic and parenting relationships was impeded by the ability of a court to impose a parental relationship regardless of contractual parental intention. Cossman's emphasis on intentional parenting fits into an emerging alternative to the traditional nuclear family that emphasizes a new paradigm of families by choice – or created families.[86] The paradigm of intentional parenthood extends to the scenario of the *Jane Doe* case, but it also speaks well to the scenarios of same-sex partners/spouses and of families created by reproductive technologies – which are not infrequently overlapping family forms.[87]

Beyond the critique Cossman offers regarding the suppression of contract in the context of parties who will continue to be in some kind of relationship with a child, it is not evident that the analogy promoted by the *Uniform Act* is effective in the context of gestational carriage contracts. The type of contract envisaged in *Jane Doe* is fully contemplated within the family law model of domestic contract. Family law legislation across the country contemplates limitations on the kinds of contracts that already constituted "families" can enter as a means of avoiding default legislative regimes. Hence it is, across Canada, acceptable to contract out of the default property regimes imposed by family law statutes that more or less divide assets equally between spouses upon dissolution. It is now possible to enter domestic contracts that deal with division of spousal assets before, during, and at the termination of the relationship. Courts are generally reluctant to set aside a domestic contract on matters of assets unless there is a clear violation of basic rules of contract law (such as unconscionability, fraud, error, or duress).[88] In contrast, parties are generally precluded from agreeing how they wish, between themselves, to deal with possession of the matrimonial home or custody of children until the point of separation. As for custody, courts are able to review contracts not only for standard contractual adequacy, but also for the best interests of children. As an indication of how far the supervisory reach of the court goes on matters of children, it is possible for a court to bar a divorce if a judge determines that child support arrangements are inadequate.[89]

But this anxiety about contracts relating to children, custody, and support is directed to families that are more or less already constituted around a traditional conception of the family; they are "domestic" to the extent that there is a recognizable family domain, which the contract aspires to regulate, even in its dissolution. They are not contracts between strangers. In the case of a gestational carriage contract, however, there is *no* already constituted family. In fact what is at stake is the constitution *de novo* (with the child) of a family. To presume that gestational carriage contracts fall under the rubric of domestic contracts generates the question about which family the child, as between two possible groups of effective strangers to each other, will enter into a domestic arrangement with. Before the contract is enforced (or not), there is no ongoing domestic relationship. Furthermore, the intention of the parties to a contract is generally to preclude the emergence of a domestic relationship arising among the carrier, intended parents, and child.

Furthermore, if a gestational carriage contract is honoured and kinship links are contractually severed between the gestational carrier and the child, there will be no place for any but the intended parents to be social parents. Unlike in the Jane and John Doe scenario, where the contract between the parties contemplated ongoing opportunities for functionally parental (or "parent-like") relationships to develop, there will be no place for carriers to develop a settled intention to treat the child as their own if the contract is honoured; no emotional or financial reliance will develop between the child and the gestational carrier.[90] The idea that family law should govern gestational carriage arrangements because the agreements made in contemplation of the birth of a child through this means are "domestic contracts" skews both the nature of family law and the nature of these arrangements.[91] Family law issues such as custody and the special limits on domestic contracts only come into play once the issue of parentage is already determined, particularly when the gestational carrier has no genetic link to the child, as is overwhelmingly the case in current clinical practice.[92] Custody arose as an issue in the Baby M case only by virtue of Mr Stern's competing genetic link with the child. If he had no genetic connection, family law as it then was would have had no purchase. If Mary Beth Whitehead had had no genetic link, then the question of the set of parents to which family law should apply would have arisen in a very different manner. Calling the arrangement a custody issue rather than a contract issue construes Whitehead's and Stern's status as respectively maternal and paternal from the outset. And the policy issue of why gestational carriage contracts should not be honoured remains unanswered. Whether it is a family matter is precisely what is in question, for the matter of which set of adults will become the child's family is yet unanswered.

In light of the ways in which a gestational carriage contract is distinct from a domestic contract, and in light of the absence of the risks contemplated in *Jane Doe* of children relying on the settled intentions and conduct of adults who interact with them for prolonged periods "as if" they were parents, it seems more appropriate to regard the gestational carriage contract as a contract between strangers, or perhaps as a *sui generis* contract in family law that has a distinct policy content that limits contractual freedom – content, that is, such as the best interests of children (in the plural) and the social and economic interests of women (in the plural). Whether those policy concerns are best dealt with by the proposal that all gestational carriage contracts be viewed as null and void is a question to which I will return. But first I want to turn to the ways in which assisted reproduction expands the place of contract and intention in the creation of new family forms in a manner consistent with trends away from status-based conceptions of the family – whether that status arises through marriage or biology.[93] When conjoined with same-sex family models and the rise of single parenthood, intention-based parenthood contributes to more diverse and individually tailored conceptions of the structure of the family.

Issues regarding the structure of the family and its place in contemporary society were exploding in venues other than assisted reproduction at the same moment that technology was opening up other means of locating the place of children (in fact and in law). Several commentators noted the shift from status to contract in family law that characterized the last forty years of the twentieth century.[94] Whereas family law historically fixed family relationships and obligations in a sphere in which the scope for individual choice and personal proclivity was officially constrained – parties were born into gendered bodies with overdetermined scripts and then ushered into preconfigured institutions like marriage – the late twentieth century opened up to the prospect of greater individual tailoring of how marriage (and non-marital cohabitation) could meet the needs of its respective parties.

The centrality of status was eroded in the 1970s with the elimination of the concept of legitimacy for children of marriage; this was swiftly followed by a place for pre-marital legal agreements – "meretricious" agreements – in which parties to a marriage contemplated its dissolution and dealt prospectively with their assets.[95] Judicial respect for domestic contracts – for the bargains of the parties themselves in derogation of state-generated default models – has only grown since their validity was recognized.[96]

The idea that contract is uniquely associated with commerce and therefore inappropriate to the protected domain of emotion and intimacy of the family long ago gave ground to the idea that contract law can be affiliated with, and tailored to, a range of different contexts that suggest particularized limitations. Juliet Guichon has recently promoted the idea that contract law has no place in family law, noting that "contract law is an essential tool of commerce and regards a deal as a deal. It assumes that people are autonomous, rational, self-interested and equal. However, family law accepts that people are interdependent, capable of irrationality, self-giving and vulnerable."[97] In fact, contract law is much broader than commercial contract law and has had a place in regulating the dissolution of adult interdependent relationships since a range of domestic contracts and their limitations were structured into family law legislation and case law in Canada over the last part of the twentieth century. If, as Guichon notes, family law "supervises the unraveling of solemnly made marriage vows in divorce,"[98] it does so very often by regulating the perfectly legal domestic contracts that the parties to the dissolution themselves create. The allure of the imagery of a stark divide between the private and public realms can generate a romantic fog about the family. The idea that "family law focuses on the body, emotions and changing intentions" is oblivious to the fact that a considerable bulk of family law is about property, custody, and support at the *dissolution* of emotional entanglements. The narrow (and incorrect) view that contract law is the equivalent of the narrower field of commercial contract, when extrapolated into the reproductive domain, facilitates imagery that associates reproductive arrangements with "products" and "widgets" and "commodification" and with the assumption, as Françoise Baylis gratuitously puts it, that "the child is seen by the commissioning parents as a product."[99]

While family law establishes some context-specific limitations on domestic contracts through legislation and case law, taking into account the particular ways in which bargaining may not be equal between spouses, the practical reality is that courts largely and increasingly tend to honour such contracts.[100] Many of these domestic contracts deal with both child custody and child support, but this does not mean that family law has "commodified" children or failed to take account of their best interests, or that it views them as a "product" or "property" of the parents.

Contracts and Family Diversity

Marriage is no longer important for establishing the legitimacy of children. Beyond that, the concept of marriage has been broadened to the point that it bears a tenuous relation to previous patriarchal conceptions. The *locus classicus* of this transformation is same-sex marriage. The same movement that began to privilege individual choice and diversity over a pre-scripted status, as seen in these latter developments in family law, manifested itself in the fading importance of the institution of marriage itself to socially acceptable conceptions of the family. With the explosion in diverse socially and legally recognized ways of creating family came a commensurate loosening of the structures of family law, attended by struggles to find adequate alternative models to ground categories such as custody and spousal support.[101] Overall, respect has been increasingly granted for the arrangements made between parties. Enlargement of the scope for contracts within family law corresponded to increasing social recognition and respect for the diversity and flexibility of family possibilities outside of a narrowly construed use of status. Enlarging the place of contract in family law consolidated that individually constructed diversity.

That family law has increasingly recognized the place of contract suggests not only that status-derogating bargains are tolerated in concert with the shifting substratum of social values over the past half century, but also that increasing latitude is opening up for individuals to alter previously fundamental parts of the social structure. Gestational carriage contracts fit squarely into that social transformation as the status of parenthood – in particular motherhood – opens up to alterations driven by individual tailoring. Just as regulation of domestic contracts, rather than their prohibition, is now readily used to overcome potential problems stemming from the familial context, it is worth asking whether the policy concerns – the conceivable individual and social risks of gestational carriage contracts – can be modulated by context-specific limitations on contract.[102] Just as the substratum of values has shifted with the movement from status to contract in family law and with the attendant diversity and flexibility of individual tailoring, the realities that subtend the practices surrounding assisted reproduction have provided a substratum of empirical evidence against which to measure policy concerns. If the evidence confirms that the risks, both social and individual, are considerable and unmitigable, then the regulation proposed by the *Uniform Act* is well-advised. However, if those risks have been greatly overplayed, then the structure of contract can be marshalled to create policy limitations in the *sui generis* area of gestational carriage contracts, just as domestic contracts are shored up by sensitivities to the particularities of the family context.

Empirical Evidence

An overall picture of the empirical realities of gestational carriage arrangements as they have developed in both regulated and unregulated settings suggests ways that contract law might be tailored to the specific context of reproductive technology. Limitations on freedom of contract can incorporate the vulnerabilities of women and children as demonstrated by observed, rather than anticipated, phenomena.

The evidence shows that the risk of intended parents failing to honour their part of the bargain and assume parental responsibility for the child carried by the surrogate is extremely minimal, to the point of being effectively non-existent in practice.[103] The evidence also reveals that the incidence of carriers failing to honour the intentions entrenched in gestational contracts has been extremely low in Canada, the United States, and the United Kingdom since the Baby M case in 1988.[104] It might seem sensible, then, to keep the status quo unchanged instead of legislatively making gestational carriage contracts enforceable. Why tinker with something that is not broken and for which informal norms appear to govern effectively the needs and intentions of all contracting parties?

Furthermore, there is evidence that those rare cases where the contract does not go well stem from a breakdown of the relationship between the carrier and the intended parents.[105] It seems that the current rule – that contracts cannot be enforced – compels intended parents, through the risk of losing the child they have fostered in their hearts and imaginations, to "husband" the pregnancy in an honourable, caring, and respectful manner. Residual uncertainty in provinces that have not explicitly declared gestational contracts unenforceable seems to have the added and unstated bonus of policing disreputable conduct in intended parents.

The exceptional cases, however, underline the extreme conflict and emotional turmoil that can result when the intentions embedded in the contract are not honoured. Furthermore, the subjective measure of honourable treatment leaves a considerable and weighty discretion in the private hands of the carrier – discretion that can depart radically from laudable social objectives, such as the minimization of discrimination on the grounds of marital status, sexual orientation, or disability. And dishonourable conduct might also include the exploitation by gestational carriers of the vulnerable and dependent position in which intended parents remain until they are declared legal parents – a vulnerability that the lack of enforceability entrenches. The profile of carriers as an emerging professional class also suggests that an overemphasis on the governance of the relationship by analogy to respectful and supportive spouses may no longer align with the way that carriers and commissioning parents have been constructing and construing the arrangement over the past twenty-five years.

These considerations aside, respecting the *mater est* rule in gestational carriage contracts may nevertheless be justified if there are more compelling social interests that override these problems. As noted above, the principal social interests cited to justify the non-enforceability of gestational carriage contracts are those of women and children. However, the empirical evidence suggests that those concerns, while once legitimate prospectively, are in fact overblown.

With respect to children, the anxiety underlying the unenforceability of gestational carriage contracts is that the individual child, born to a carrier and raised by intended parents, would feel abandoned by the woman who, it is assumed, would feel to them most like their mother. With respect to children in general, the concern was that financial remuneration for gestational carriage services would tend to normalize the commodification of children.[106] There is no empirical evidence that supports these worries. With children of gestational carriage contracts becoming a normal phenomenon over the last quarter-century, there is no evidence that such children lament the loss of the woman who birthed them. Edelman summarizes the empirical literature by noting that there are "few, if any, psychological differences between children conceived by [assisted reproductive technologies] and those conceived naturally with regard to emotions, behaviour, the presence of psychological disorders or their perceptions of the quality of family relationships."[107] Indeed, some studies suggest that there are higher levels of warmth and interaction within assisted reproduction families than in other families. One 2006 study concluded that "it appears that the absence of a genetic and/or gestational link between parents and their child does not have a negative impact on parent–child relationships or the psychological well-being of mother, father or children at age 3."[108]

Adoption is a respected practice even though the biological and genetic mother yields parentage and custody to intended/social parents. As well, there is some evidence that some adopted children yearn for their biological and genetic progenitors,[109] yet the practice of adoption has not been eliminated on this ground.

There is also evidence that some children who have a genetic link through gamete donation can yearn to connect with their genetic predecessors.[110] However, the evidence that the yearning to connect with a gestational carrier is present with children born of gestational carriage is highly limited – most particularly where the carrier is not genetically related to the child (which is the case in 95 per cent of contemporary carriage arrangements).[111]

Cumulative research indicates that gestational carriage is regarded by the gestational carriers themselves as a compensable service contract rather than a contract for sale of goods. As noted above, the contractual relationship is falsely squared with commercial contract; domestic contracts, to provide a relevant example, are not commercial contracts. As with domestic contracts, the fact that the arrangement is consolidated via contractual instruments does not transform the children contemplated within them into commodities or property.[112]

Furthermore, a woman who is a genetic *and* biological parent can decide to terminate the pregnancy of a disabled fetus without her decision implying that she views children, including her current or future children, as "commodities." A critical disability analysis is available to assess parental choice to terminate the pregnancy in both gestational carriage and conception through coitus; that analysis finds that neither group of parents has more or less of a tendency to see a child "as a product, and a ... substandard product because of a genetic condition," as Françoise Baylis puts it.[113] The misconstrual of the place of contract in family law facilitates facile analogies that are not tethered to the empirical realities of how parents (intended, social, genetic, or biological) conceive their offspring and make choices regarding them and with respect to the lives of each of them.

The fear that gestational carriage, even paid carriage, brings children closer to being conceived as commodities has not played out among the parties associated with the contracts. The case of the American surrogacy brokerage that impregnated carriers with embryos in the absence of intended parents and then sought to sell the children under the ruse that the intended parents were declining their part of the bargain has met with considerable opprobrium and Canada's first investigation under the *AHRA*. It stands out as a criminal anomaly against the backdrop of the payment-for-service model of standard carriage contracts – a model that creates children who join families as robustly loving as those who conceive through coitus.

The evidence regarding the vulnerabilities of carriers also calls into question the assumption that the non-enforceability of contracts protects those whose social and economic vulnerability would be compromised by such bargains. Two concerns have been associated with the presumed vulnerability of carriers: that they cannot give meaningful consent to relinquish a child without knowing how the experience of pregnancy might alter their feelings towards the child; and that the socio-economic asymmetries between intended parents and carriers makes them ripe for exploitation.[114] Neither of these concerns have played out in the empirical evidence.

Busby's survey of the empirical literature on gestational carriage, to her own surprise, turns many of the feminist concerns that drove Canada's national policy on carriage on their head.[115] The feminist voices that predominantly shaped the Royal Commission on Reproductive Technology in the early 1990s construed gestational carriage as a form of prostitution or slavery and regarded the carrier's undertaking not to bond with the child she was carrying as delusional and dehumanizing. Yet the voices of the women who work as gestational carriers go strongly against the grain of that analysis. The growing body of empirical research does not support concerns about prenatal bonding or emotional instability during pregnancy. Gestational carriers consistently report that they are able to detach early from connecting emotionally with the child and to maintain that detachment throughout pregnancy and post-delivery. This detachment is facilitated by the overwhelming trend for gestational carriage arrangements to be gestational and not traditional – that is, the carrier does not use her own ova.[116] Gestational carriage has thus moved 180 degrees away from the practice at the time of the Baby M case, when most surrogacies were traditional. Carriers consistently report thinking of the fetus as being for the commissioning parents (as their child), a position facilitated by their sense that the carriage is a job or a service with professional overtones and requirements. They reject the analogy to commercial contracts and the sale of goods; they overwhelmingly view their work as providing a meaningful and altruistic service, no different from services such as teaching, firefighting, or medicine. The construal of their undertaking as a service – and their associated ability to detach emotionally from the fetus – is facilitated by the clear contractual (and enforceable) nature of the undertaking and by payment for the service.

Concerns about the exploitation of carriers arising from socio-economic asymmetries between them and intended parents also appear to be largely attenuated by the evidence of practices that have emerged on the ground. It has been found that carriers are more likely than the general population to be self-sufficient, independent thinkers, as opposed to the socio-economically fragile women contemplated in the prostitution/slavery analogies, Karen Busby summarizes the research:

> The profile of surrogate mothers emerging from the empirical research in the United States and Britain does not support the stereotype of poor, single, young, ethnic minority women whose family, financial difficulties, or other circumstances pressure her into a surrogacy arrangement. Nor does it support the view that surrogate mothers are naively taking on a task unaware of the emotional and physical risks it might entail. Rather, the empirical research establishes that surrogate mothers are mature, experienced, stable, self-aware, and extroverted non-conformists who make the initial decision that surrogacy is something that they want to do.[117]

Almost all carriers are familiar with the experience of family, having already had children and completed their own families; indeed, clinical practice reflects a trend towards working only with women in these circumstances. This ensures that carriers have a sense of what it will be like to surrender a child upon birth as well as a sense of the realities of pregnancy.[118]

The empirical research also reveals that the fears that a racialized underclass of carriers will develop in North America have not panned out. Carriers tend to be Christian and Caucasian, but even when there are racialized differences between carriers and intended parents, carriers have interpreted this as something that facilitates their detachment from the fetus and their understanding that the child belongs to the commissioning parents. Carriers have varying degrees of education, but their incomes tend strongly *not* to be within the range of financial distress. Their family incomes are most often modest (as opposed to low), and there is no convincing evidence that women on social assistance are significantly represented in the class of carriers. No empirical study in the materials reviewed by Busby indicates that carriers became involved with surrogacy because of financial distress. Rather than support the anxiety about vulnerable exploitable women, the research appears to consistently confirm that carriers feel empowered by their ability to use their bodies in a manner that generates a meaningful service.[119]

Conclusion

All of this growing body of empirical research cited by Busby in her overview of the literature indicates that the overarching policy concerns that informed decisions to render gestational carriage contracts unenforceable – and, incidentally, to criminalize payment for services – are misplaced. The vulnerabilities of women and children are not non-existent; however, the empirical research indicates that those vulnerabilities may not be sufficiently acute, where they exist at all, to override the policy concerns (including the best interests of children) that might be furthered by enforcing regulated carriage contracts.

Furthermore, the certainty created by treating gestational carriage contracts analogously to domestic contracts – that is, they will be enforced unless they fail to meet context-specific limitations on the validity of contract, such as unconscionability, fraud, error, or duress, that take into account the unique settings of physical intimacy in which they are conceived – has the prospect of consolidating the emerging professional model of gestational carriage. Carriers are on notice from the outset of their undertaking that the children they give birth to will not be their legal children. This is the understanding of the service most carriers embrace as members of a professional community. Potential emotional losses are easier to contemplate and prepare for psychologically under a certain rule that the contract will be enforced. Those women who are uncertain whether they can manage the arrangement without ambivalence would be confronted with a clear rule that post-natal ambivalence will not be supported and with a more certain outline of what the contract is asking of them. The current situation, where it is uncertain whether a carriage contract will be enforced, reinforces ambivalence throughout a pregnancy and up until the very moment that the child's legal parentage is lined up with intention. Also, the certainty that gestational carriage contracts are null and void in jurisdictions like Quebec prolongs ambivalence until the moment of adoption. The ambivalence persists even though, unlike adoption, the pregnancy in assisted reproduction is never entered into haphazardly or without awareness of the consequences of fertilizing ova and allowing the resulting embryo to develop in a nurturing womb.

If the contracts were enforceable in law, a woman who enters a gestational carriage contract would be doing so knowing that the law speaks clearly on the implications of her decision – a result that would eliminate the harsh consequences for intended parents, who are currently beholden to the carrier's potential ambivalence and exposed to considerable risks of emotional and financial loss and, in the current legal context, ongoing parental responsibilities if they are genetically related to the child (and quite possibly if they are not). The intended parents in gestational carriage contracts are after all not complete strangers to the child: they are the parties but for whom the pregnancy would not have been initiated,[120] and they *intend* from the outset to be actively involved in the child's care, whereas the gestational carrier does not.

All of these empirical and policy arguments comport with the emergence of a scholarly literature that favours intention over gestation in carriage contracts.[121] Emerging in tandem with increasing use and normalization of gestational carriage is an awareness that the practice generates little tangible harm and that those residual harms would best be addressed by explicit regulation. The general hiatus in modifying child status legislation to deal explicitly with gestational carriage (with the exceptions of Quebec, Alberta, and BC) has afforded a pause to more thoughtfully balance the risks to all parties without the alarm and hostility that followed on the Baby M case. It would be regrettable at this juncture and given what we now know about gestational carriage to follow a model, such as the one proposed in the *Uniform Child Status Act*, that hinges on an outdated understanding of the realities on the ground.

NOTES

Author's note: Throughout this chapter I have favoured the term "gestational carrier" over "surrogate" where possible as more reflective of the way in which the woman who carries the child and his or her intended parents view the relationship. I reserve the term "surrogacy" (often called "traditional surrogacy" in the literature) for the small fraction of the situations associated with this means of bringing children to term in which the woman who carries the child is also genetically related to him or her. (See statistics cited in Busby, *infra*, note 114.) The terminology of "gestational carriage" also has the virtue of not begging the legal question at issue in this chapter, which is focused on the determination of legal parentage. To call a woman the surrogate "mother," even if borrowing colloquial usage, is to prejudge the legal outcome. I recognize that the term "intended *parent*" also begs the legal question; however, this terminology has more universal currency in the literature, along with "commissioning parent" – and usage in this case also comports with the argument I will be making in this chapter.

1 2010 SCC 61, [2010] 3 SCR 457 [*AHRA Reference*]; *Assisted Human Reproduction Act*, SC 2004, c 2.
2 See Parliament, Standing Committee on Health, *Evidence*, 40th Parl., 3d Sess., No. 37, 16 November 2010, at 1–25 (Françoise Baylis *et al.*), http://www.parl.gc.ca/content/hoc/Committee/403/HESA/Evidence/EV4782428/HESAEV37-E.PDF; see also Françoise Baylis, "The Demise of Assisted Human Reproduction Canada" (2012) 34:6 J Obstet Gynaecol Can 511–13.
3 See Anne Kingston, "Assisted Human Reproduction Canada: The Budget Cut Everyone Missed," *Maclean's*, 2 April 2012; see also Sara Cohen, "Bill Impacts Assisted Human Reproduction in Canada," *AdvocateDaily.com*, 25 September 2012, http://www.advocatedaily.com/2012/11/bill-impacts-assisted-human-reproduction-in-canada-ready/.
4 See Alison Motluk, "The Human Egg Trade; How Canada's Fertility Laws Are Failing Donors, Doctors, and Parents," *The Walrus*, April 2010, http://thewalrus.ca/the-human-egg-trade.
5 See *ibid*.
6 For a review of the common law rules and statutory regimes that apply in provincial regimes across the country, see Angela Campbell, "Conceiving Parents Through Law" (2007) 21 Int'l JL Pol'y & Fam 242; Roxanne Mykitiuk, "Beyond Conception: Legal Determinations of Filiation in the Context of Assisted Reproductive Technologies" (2001) 39:4 Osgoode Hall LJ 771–815; and Susan Boyd, "Gendering Legal Parenthood: Bio-Genetic Ties, Intentionality and Responsibility" (2007) 25 Windsor YB Access Just 63. These scholarly articles are somewhat dated, and this chapter will update provincial statutory and common law accordingly.
7 *In re Baby M*, 537 A2d 1227, 109 NJ 396 (NJ 02/03/1988); the *Baby M* case involved traditional surrogacy in the sense outlined in note 1. I will discuss this case in more detail.
8 See Mykitiuk and Campbell, *supra* note 6.
9 This was the conclusion of the Royal Commission on New Reproductive Technologies, *Proceed with Care: Final Report of the Royal Commission on New Reproductive Technologies*, vol. 2 (Ottawa: Minister of Government Services Canada, 1993) [RCNRT], for example at xxxii, 15, 22, 52, 107, 199, and Recommendations 199–205. The conclusions of the Royal Commission were supported by a large number of Canadian feminists. For a summary of these views and references to much of this literature, see Karen Busby, "Revisiting the Handmaid's Tale: Feminist Theory Meets Empirical

Research on Surrogate mothers" (2010) 26 Can J Fam L 13 ["Revisiting Handmaid's"]; for extensive references to the leading dominant feminist position supported by the Royal Commission, see note 6 in particular.

10 *Uniform Child Status Act*, 1992, Uniform Law Conference of Canada, http://ulcc.ca/en/uniform-acts-new-order/withdrawn-uniform-acts/707-child-status-act-1992/70-child-status-act-1992; *Uniform Child Status Act*, 2010, Uniform Law Conference of Canada, http://ulcc.ca/en/uniform-acts-new-order/current-uniform-acts/86-josetta-1-en-gb/uniform-actsa/child-status-act/1371-child-status-act-2010.

11 Section 8(11), *Uniform Child Status Act*, 2010. For a discussion of the uniform act's parentage provisions, see the chapter by Carol Rogerson in this volume.

12 See Mykitiuk, Campbell, and Boyd, *supra* note 6; see also Fiona Kelly, "(Re)forming Parenthood: The Assignment of Legal Parentage within Planned Lesbian Families" (2009) 40 Ottawa L Rev 185.

13 I will address the *HLW and THW v JST and JT*, 2005 BCSC 1679, [2005] BCJ No. 2616 case below – but that case sounded in custody as well as consent to adoption, and the only reported decision from the case relates to the interim issue of custody.

14 As the overwhelming majority of contemporary cases where a woman carries a child through pregnancy for other (intended) parents do not involve a genetic linkage between her and the child, I will be restricting my analysis to that scenario – and suggesting that the enforceability of gestational carriage contracts be restricted to that form of gestational carriage – and leaving aside the possible implications of legal parentage for "traditional" surrogacy in which the woman carries a child to whom she has a genetic link.

15 Notoriously, one Quebec judge refused to permit such an adoption to proceed on the basis that surrogacy contracts are null and void in Quebec, leaving the child parentless (*Adoption – 091*, 2009 QCCQ 628); however, subsequent cases in Quebec have declined to follow the precedent set by this case and have permitted intended parents to adopt the children whose birth they facilitated through gestational carriage. *Adoption – 09184*, 2009 QCCQ 9058; *Adoption – 09367*, 2009 QCCQ 16815; *Adoption – 10330*, 2010 QCCQ 17819; and *Adoption 10329*, 2010 QCCQ 18645.

16 See, for example, *Family Services Act*, SNB 1989, c F-2.2, s 96(1); *Children's Law Act*, RSNL 1990, c C-13, s 3(1); *Children's Law Act*, SNWT 1997, c 1, s 2(1); *Children's Law Reform Act*, RSO 1990, c C.12, s 1(1); *Child Status Act*, RSPEI 1988, c C-6, s 1(1); *Children's Law Act*, SS 1997, c C-8.2, s 40(1); and *Family Law Act*, SA 2004, c F-4.5, s 2(1).

17 See *Family Law Act*, SBC 2011, c 25, ss 29(3)(a), (b)(i), which came into force in 2013.

18 *Ibid*, s 29(6).

19 Section 8.2(8) of the *Family Law Act*, SA 2003, c F-4.5. This language is the same as the language in the Uniform Child Status Act, s 8(11).

20 Sections 2(2)(b)(c) and (f) of Alta Reg 148/2005 under the Alberta *Family Law Act*. Alberta also requires that one of the intended parents be genetically linked to the child.

21 See section 5(2) of the *Birth Registration Regulations*, NS Reg 390/2007, made under s 51 of the *Vital Statistics Act*, RSNS 1989, c 494.

22 *Ibid*, section 5(2)(c) [emphasis added].

23 *Ibid*, section 5(2).

24 The fact that other provinces tend to regard gestational carriage contracts as unenforceable means that little attention has been given to what ought to go into these contracts to safeguard the interests of the parties and larger public policy interests that are only intimated in Nova Scotia's regulations and British Columbia's child status legislation. There is no statutory prohibition in the other provinces on a gestational carriage contract being entered into one day before birth, leaving the distinction between gestational carriage and adoption somewhat blurry. I will address this concern when I review California's new surrogacy law.

25 Sections 3 and 6 of the *Children's Law Act*, RSNL 1990, c C-13.

26 [Emphasis added]; "natural" is not defined.

27 Section 5(6) of the *Vital Statistics Act, 2009*, SNL 2009, c V-6.01.

28 Section 6(2), *Children's Law Act*, RSNL 1990, c C-13. This is standard language in many child status laws across the country.

29 See section 9(1) of the *Child Status Act*, RSPEI 1988, c C-6, as amended by the *Domestic Relations Act*, SPEI 2008, c 8, s 2(4).

30 See section 9(7), *Child Status Act*, RSPEI 1988, c C-6.

31 Section 1(1), *Children's Law Reform Act*, RSO 1990, c C.12 [emphasis added].

32 Section 1, *Vital Statistics Act*, RSO 1990, c V.4 [emphasis added]. Other provinces have similar definitions of birth: see *Vital Statistics Act*, RSPEI 1988, c V-4.1, s 1; *Vital Statistics Act*, SS 2009, c V-7.21, s 2(1); *Vital Statistics Act*, CCSM c V60, s 1; *Vital Statistics Act*, SNB 1979, c V-3, s 1.

33 See *JR v LH*, [2002] OJ No 3998 (SC); *MD v LL* (2008), 90 OR (3d) 127 (SC); *JAW v JEW*, 2010 NBQB 414, 373 NBR (2d) 211; and *WJQM v AMA*, 2011 SKQB 317, 339 DLR (4th) 759.

34 *JR v LH*, *ibid*, citing s 4(1) of the *Children's Law Reform Act*.

35 *AA v BB*, 2007 ONCA 2, 83 OR (3d) 561, 35 RFL (6th) 1 [*AA v BB*]; the *parens patriae* jurisdiction is defined in that case at para 27 as follows: "The court's

inherent *parens patriae* jurisdiction may be applied to rescue a child in danger or to bridge a legislative gap."

36 *MD v LL* (2008), 52 RFL (6th) 122 (Ont SC).

37 *JC v Manitoba*, 2000 MBQB 173, 12 RFL (5th) 274 [emphasis added].

38 Karen Busby cites the following statistics: "One Ontario lawyer has handled more than 1500 surrogacy arrangements while an Alberta lawyer's website states that she has 'helped hundreds' with surrogacy contracts. A British Columbia lawyer testified that he made applications in more than seventy-five surrogacy cases between 2003–11, and a Vancouver ART clinic states that it 'performs gestational carrier surrogacy for 15–20 couples each year.'" Cited in "Of Surrogate Mother Born." Paper in author's possession.

39 *HLW and THW v JST and JT*, 2005 BCSC 1679, [2005] BCJ No. 2616.

40 The general provision on "Declaratory orders respecting parentage – surrogacy" can be found at s 8 of the model act; and those provisions that relate to the enforceability and evidentiary value of gestational carriage contracts can be found at s 8(11).

41 See Elizabeth S. Scott, "Surrogacy and the Politics of Commodification" (2009) 72.3 Law & Contemp Probs 109. For more comparative work, see also Judith F. Daar, *Reproductive Technologies and the Law* (Newark: LexisNexus Matthew Bender, 2006).

42 *Supra* note 10, s 3(2)(a) *Uniform Act*, 2010.

43 *Ibid* at s 3(2)(b)(iii).

44 *Ibid* at s 8(11).

45 *Doe v Alberta*, 2007 ABCA 50, 404 AR 153 [*Jane Doe*].

46 See *infra* note 71.

47 *Canadian Charter of Rights and Freedoms*, Part I of the *Constitution Act, 1982*, being Schedule B to the *Canada Act 1982* (UK), 1982, c 11.

48 "The Appellants ask how can it be said that a person has demonstrated a 'settled intention' to take on a parental obligation when there is a personal statement of intent from the outset which is contrary to that? In my opinion, the answer is to be found in the context of the relationship between Jane and John Doe. The 'settled intention' to remain in a close, albeit unmarried, relationship thrust John Doe, from a practical and realistic point of view, into the role of parent to this child. Can it seriously be contended that he will ignore the child when it cries? When it needs to be fed? When it stumbles? When the soother needs to be replaced? When the diaper needs to be changed?" *Jane Doe* at paras 21–2.

49 Rosemarie Tong, "Feminist Perspectives and Gestational Motherhood: The Search for a Unified Legal Focus," in *Reproduction, Ethics, and the*

Law: Feminist Perspectives, ed. Joan C. Callaghan (Bloomington: Indiana University Press, 1995), 55 at 75.

50 851 P2d 776 (1993) [*Johnson*].

51 These were the arguments that were favoured by the dissent in the case.

52 *In re Marriage of Buzzanca*, 61 CalApp4th 1410, 72 CalRptr2d 280 (Ct App 1998) [*Buzzanca*].

53 See sections 7960 and 7962 of the *California Family Code* [*California Surrogacy Law*]. California is not the only American state to recognize the enforceability. See Scott, *supra* note 41; and for more comparative work, see also Daar, *supra* note 41.

54 Judy Daar, "California Surrogacy Bill Reacts to Lawyer Bad Acts," Harvard Petrie-Flom Centre (blog), 17 September 2012, http://blogs.harvard.edu/billofhealth/2012/09/17/california-surrogacy-bill-reacts-to-lawyer-bad-acts/.

55 *Uniform Parentage Act*, Cal Fam Code Div 12, Part 3.

56 Sections 29(2)(a) and (b) of the *Family Law Act*

57 These requirements would comport with current clinical practice. Empirical studies indicate that almost all gestational carriers have had children and completed their family; see summary of research in Busby, "Revisiting Handmaid's," *supra* note 9 at 48. Busby's article also covers the empirical studies that indicate that clinics and agencies only agree to work with women who have given birth; also at 48.

58 Article 538, *Civil Code of Quebec*, LRQ c C-1991 [emphasis added].

59 See Tom Blackwell, "Couple Urged Surrogate Mother to Abort Fetus Because of Defect," *National Post*, 6 October 2010.

60 The resolution of the tension in this case did not ultimately result from an interpretation of the contract or any other legal intervention: the gestational carrier eventually chose to have the abortion, partly because of her own family obligations. If anything, this scenario makes clear that greater regulatory attention to the gestational carriage contracts is required – an attention that has been lacking partly because they are effectively unenforceable in Canada under the *mater est* rule or explicit statutory language.

61 Hereafter, "gestational carriage contract" will be used interchangeably with "contract"; and "gestational carrier" with "carrier."

62 *JR v LH*, *supra* note 33.

63 *Ibid* at para 8.

64 This language is standard in many pieces of child status legislation across the country.

65 See, for example, s 24(1) of *Family Law Act*, SBC 2007, c 25; s 12(6) *Children's Law Act*, RSNL 1990, c C-13; s 4(6) *Child Status Act*, RSPEI 1988, c C-6; Article 538.2 *Civil Code of Quebec*, LRQ c C-1991.

66 Section 8.2(1), *Family Law Act*, SA 2003, c F-4.5: "An application may be made to the court for a declaration that … (b) a person whose human reproductive material or embryo was provided for use in the assisted reproduction is a parent of that child." Also see section 5(2) of the *Birth Registration Regulations*, NS Reg 390/2007 made under s 51 of the *Vital Statistics Act*, RSNS 1989, c 494.
67 "The blood tests indicate that the probability that JR and JK are the mother and father respectively is greater than 99.99%. I find that on a balance of probabilities they are the genetic parents of the twins. Pursuant to s 4(1), JK is entitled to be 'recognized in law' as the father of the children and JR is entitled to be 'recognized in law' to be the mother of the children." *JR v LH*, para 11.
68 "[T]he gestational carrier's husband did not contribute genetic material. He is not the biological father. He is involved because he is the husband of the woman who is the gestational carrier and, pursuant to section 8(1) of the Children's Law Reform Act, he is presumed to be the father of the children. The presumption has been rebutted." *JR v LH, supra* note 33 at para 12.
69 *Ibid* at para 18.
70 See *Chartier v Chartier*, [1999] 1 SCR 242 [*Chartier*].
71 With the exception of anonymous donor insemination, which breaks the kinship link (and attendant obligations) between genetic progenitors and children.
72 Substituted language from *JR v LH, supra* note 33 at para 11.
73 See section 9(7)(b) of *Family Law Act*, SA 2004, c F-4.5.
74 Section 6(8)(b), *Uniform Act*.
75 *AA v BB, supra* note 35; see also Kelly, *supra* note 12.
76 Following *Chartier, supra* note 70.
77 See *Jane Doe, supra* note 45 and associated text.
78 That the Whiteheads called Baby M "Sara" while the Sterns called her "Melissa" is the tip of the iceberg of possible ways in which a child might be torn in several directions from the outset of their lives.
79 *CW v NT & Anor* [2011] EWHC 33 (Fam) (21 January 2011).
80 See Tong, *supra* note 49.
81 See Stephanie Saul, "Building Baby, with Few Ground Rules," *New York Times*, 12 December 2009.
82 Stu Marvel notes that "in 2008 it was estimated that as much as 15–25% of client traffic at Toronto-area fertility clinics is comprised of people from LGBTQ communities." Cited in Stu Marvel, "Tony Danza Is My Sperm Donor?: Queer Kinship and the Impact of Canadian Regulations Around Sperm Donation" (2013) 25:2 CJWL 221.

83 The lability in the field of assisted reproduction and in the social norms associated with the technology suggests that a synopsis of foreseeable risks may well be incomplete and only as partial as the section of the field of possibilities to which we have already been exposed.

84 See Brenda Cossman, "Parenting beyond the Nuclear Family: Doe v. Alberta" (2007) 45 Alta L Rev 501–13.

85 This argument could be extrapolated to the case of a carrier's spouse where the former decides to retain legal parentage postnatally in Alberta and under the *Uniform Act*, both of which limit the number of parents a child can have to two. I argued above that the spouses of the carrier and genetically related intended parent could be ascribed status as social parents with the latter being the two legal parents. Cossman's argument is not really available for this purpose, however, given that the overall thrust of the Alberta law and the *Uniform Act* is to undermine intention in the creation of families, something that Cossman's argument is structured to shore up.

86 See, for example, Martha Albertson Fineman, "Our Sacred Institution: The Ideal of the Family in American Law and Society" (1993) 1993:2 Utah L Rev 387, 389 n.8; Elvia R Arriola, "Law and the Family of Choice and Need" (1997) 35 U Louisville J Fam L 691, 694; R. Alta Charo, "And Baby Makes Three – or Four, or Five, or Six: Redefining the Family after the Reprotech Revolution" (2000) 15 Wis Women's LJ 231, 242; Richard Storrow, "Parenthood by Pure Intention: Assisted Reproduction and the Functional Approach to Parentage" (2001–2002) 53 Hastings LJ 597; Brenda Cossman and Bruce Ryder, "What Is 'Marriage-Like' Like? The Irrelevance of Conjugality" (2001) 18 Can J Fam L 269.

87 *Jane Doe, supra* note 45.

88 See the leading cases of *Miglin v Miglin*, [2003] 1 SCR 303 and *Hartshorne v Hartshorne*, [2004] 1 SCR 550.

89 See s 11(1)(b) of the *Divorce Act*, RSC 1985, c 3 (2nd Supp).

90 I will address later the presumed emotional ties between gestational carrier and child that are claimed to arise from the intimate bodily experience of carrying him or her.

91 For the contrary argument, namely, that determinations of parentage, even in cases of assisted reproduction, should be made according to the principles of family law, not contract law, see Juliet Guichon, "The Body, Emotions and Intentions: Challenges of Preconception Arrangements for Health Care Providers" (2007) 176 CMAJ 479.

92 Cf. Karen Busby: "While most surrogate mothers until the late-1980s would have been impregnated by assisted insemination and therefore

are the genetic mothers of the children, by 1994, about 50 percent of surrogacies involved the implantation of an embryo created using the genetic materials of others. This figure climbed to 95 percent by 2003." Karen Busby citing Heléna Ragoné, "Of Likeness and Difference: How Race Is Being Transformed by Gestational Surrogacy," in *Ideologies and Technologies of Motherhood – Race, Class, Sexuality, Nationalism*, ed. Helena Ragoné and France Winddance Twine (New York: Routledge, 2000), 56 [Ragoné, "Of Likeness and Difference"] and David P. Hamilton, "She's Having Our Baby: Surrogacy Is on the Rise as In Vitro Improves," *Wall Street Journal*, 4 February 2003, in Busby, "Revisiting Handmaid's," *supra* note 9.

93 I will return to, and elaborate on, this distinction between contractual and status-based understandings of the family.

94 See, for example, Janet Dolgin, *Defining the Family: Law, Technology, and Reproduction in an Uneasy Age* (New York: NYU Press, 1997); and, earlier, Mary Ann Glendon, *The New Family and the New Property* (Toronto: Butterworths, 1981).

95 Child status legislation was modified in the 1970s province by province to eliminate the distinction between legitimate children (those issuing from a marriage) and illegitimate children (those born out of wedlock). For an early-twentieth-century decision that found domestic contracts unenforceable on the grounds that such agreements in anticipation of divorce were outside the realm of contract altogether, see *Balfour v Balfour* [1919] 2 KB 571 (Eng CA). Provincial family law reform following the 1968 Divorce Act provided for the enforceability of domestic contracts; the role of contract expanded beyond that juncture to include non-married spouses, same-sex spouses, and the enforceability of contracts entered into post-marriage.

96 See the leading cases of *Miglin* and *Hartshorne*, *supra* note 88.

97 Guichon, "The Body, Emotions and Intentions: Challenges of Preconception Arrangements for Health Care Providers," *supra* note 91.

98 *Ibid*.

99 Both Guichon and Baylis construe reproductive arrangements as means of transforming children into "products," "widgets," and "commodities." See Blackwell, *supra* note 59.

100 *Miglin* and *Hartshorne*, *supra* note 88.

101 See Law Commission of Canada, *Beyond Conjugality: Recognizing and Supporting Close Personal Adult Relationships* (Ottawa: 2001); Cossman and Ryder, *supra* note 86.

102 As noted above, the California Surrogacy Law may be the beginning of how to imagine the requisite safeguards.

103 Beyond reviewing the studies that researched the frequency of intended parents declining to pursue legal parentage – and finding the rate at the vanishing point – Busby notes that "there is no evidence of commissioning parents rejecting children who do not meet their expectations": "Revisiting Handmaid's," *supra* note 9 at 78. That the diversity of examples on the ground are emerging more quickly than the law and research can keep up with is perfectly illustrated by recent cases where precisely this scenario has unfolded. See, for example, http://www.smh.com.au/national/explosive-allegations-in-baby-gammy-saga-20140917-10ievn.html. The clarification that a gestational carriage contract consolidates the intended parents' responsibility for all children that result would tend to expedite resolutions in this kind of scenario; however, the exposure of children to discrimination and abandonment on the basis of disability remains acute, as it does for children conceived through coitus.

104 Busby reviews the handful of cases where the intentions of the parties to a gestational carriage contract were not honoured in "Revisiting Handmaid's," *ibid*, at 24 et seq.

105 See review of empirical literature on this topic at 59 et seq. of "Revisiting Handmaid's," *ibid*.

106 See reference, *supra* note 7.

107 R.J. Edelmann, "Surrogacy: The Psychological Issues" (2004) 22:12 Journal of Reproductive and Infant Psychology 123. For a different perspective on the psychological impact on offspring, see the chapter by Juliet Guichon in this volume.

108 Sandra Golombok, Clare Murray, Vasanti Jadva, Emma Lycett, Fiona MacCallum, & J. Rust, "Non-Genetic and Non-Gestational Parenthood: Consequences for Parent–Child Relationships and the Psychological Well-Being of Mothers, Fathers and Children at the Age of 3" (2006) 21 Human Reproduction 1918.

109 The *Pratten* case in the Supreme Court of British Columbia recapitulates the legislative history that accompanied the understanding that closed adoption was not in the best interests of adopted children. See *Pratten v British Columbia (Attorney General)*, 2011 BCSC 656, 99 RFL (6th) 290 ([*Pratten*] at para 178 et seq., rev'd on other grounds (violation of s 15(1) saved by s 15(2)), 2012 BCCA 480, 25 RFL (7th) 58, leave to appeal to SCC refused, [2013] SCCA No. 36.

110 These concerns are well represented in *Pratten*, *ibid*.

111 Ragoné, *supra* note 92.
112 See the studies summarized in Busby, "Revisiting Handmaid's," *supra* note 9 at 67, as well as the general empirical literature canvassed regarding the motivations and perspectives of gestational carriers.
113 *Supra* note 99 (Baylis).
114 *Supra* note 9.
115 See Busby, "Revisiting Handmaid's," *supra* note 9. It is important to underline that Busby's research does not focus on developing countries; and as such it does not address the more significant possibilities for, and evidence of, exploitation emerging from significant asymmetries of wealth and knowledge across global divides.
116 Ragoné, *supra* note 92.
117 "Revisiting Handmaid's," *supra* note 9 at 51–2.
118 See the studies summarized in Busby, "Revisiting Handmaid's," *ibid*, at 41 et seq., under sub-heading "Social, Racial, and Psychological Characteristics of Surrogate Mothers."
119 Busby summarized a long list of empirical studies on these demographic characteristics of gestational carriers in "Revisiting Handmaid's," *ibid* at 42–4 (with references to the studies cited in notes 69 and following).
120 As per *Johnson*, *supra* note 50, and *Buzzanca*, *supra* note 52.
121 See, for example, Kirsty Horsey, "Challenging Presumptions: Legal Parenthood and Surrogacy Arrangements" (2010) 22:4 Child & Fam LQ 449; see also Scott, *supra* note 41; and for earlier articles, Marjorie Maguire Shultz, "Reproductive Technology and Intent-based Parenthood: An Opportunity for Gender Neutrality" (1990) 2 Wis L Rev 297; John Lawrence Hill, "What Does It Mean To Be a 'Parent'? The Claims of Biology as the Basis for Parental Rights" (1991) 66 NYU L Rev 353; Storrow, *supra* note 86.

13 Listening to LGBTQ People on Assisted Human Reproduction: Access to Reproductive Material, Services, and Facilities

STU MARVEL, LESLEY A. TARASOFF,
RACHEL EPSTEIN, DATEJIE GREEN,
LEAH S. STEELE, AND LORI E. ROSS

Introduction

In the wake of the December 2010 Supreme Court decision on the constitutional legitimacy of the *Assisted Human Reproduction Act* (*AHRA*),[1] Canada finds itself facing continued regulatory uncertainty in the area of reproductive technology. While next steps have yet to be defined by both provincial and federal authorities, this lacuna is of particular importance to lesbian, gay, bisexual, trans, two-spirit, and queer (LGBTQ) people in Canada.[2] LGBTQ people are uniquely dependent on assisted human reproduction (AHR) services to create biologically related children, with estimates suggesting that LGBTQ people represent 15 to 25 per cent of clientele at some urban fertility clinics.[3] Yet in a lengthy 167-page decision, the Supreme Court justices make only a single mention of LGBTQ users of AHR services. The reasons written by Chief Justice McLachlin failed to discuss LGBTQ people at all, while the judgment written by LeBel and Deschamps JJ paused briefly to note that AHR "represents the only option for homosexuals who wish to reproduce."[4]

In this chapter we argue that the present legal regime has been crafted with scarce consideration of the reproductive needs of "homosexuals," let alone others in the LGBTQ spectrum. Yet LGBTQ people in Canada who wish to become parents remain heavily dependent on both adoption and AHR services.[5] These are bureaucratically onerous and/or expensive options, leaving LGBTQ communities vulnerable to legislative gaps and judicial decisions that do not account for their particular needs.[6] The *AHRA Reference* once again emphasizes this gap,[7] leaving increased legal uncertainty alongside the virtual erasure of LGBTQ people in Canada from the discussion of how and why AHR technologies are to be used in the future.

As was clear in the *AHRA Reference*, the infertile heterosexual couple is contemplated as the exemplary user of AHR services. Other dependent populations, including non-partnered men or women, are either ignored (as in the McLachlin CJ decision) or marked only in passing (as in LeBel and Deschamps JJ). Such a judgment is based on the assumption that cisgender,[8] heterosexual couples constitute the norm, with all other demands for reproductive technology to be understood within this guiding frame. Thus, LGBTQ people's concerns may warrant no more than a passing acknowledgment, as the standard of the heterosexually reproductive family can presumably expand to accommodate all forms of kinship.[9]

This chapter aims to challenge such a perspective and to demonstrate the specific issues faced by LGBTQ people seeking AHR services. We argue that the needs of LGBTQ people do not always overlap with those of heterosexuals, while LGBTQ reproductive projects are too often misread under the common rubric of "infertility" that currently drives the law and science of AHR.[10] We write this as members of a qualitative, community-based study that has aimed to shed light on the experiences of LGBTQ people in Ontario who have used or have considered using AHR services to have biologically related children. In line with community-based research principles, this study was guided by an advisory committee of AHR service providers and service users. In total, sixty-six LGBTQ people from across Ontario were interviewed about their experiences with AHR services. Representing to our knowledge the largest project of its kind, this pilot study was conducted collaboratively by researchers at the Centre for Addiction and Mental Health, the Sherbourne Health Centre, and Osgoode Hall Law School.[11]

Based on this research, we point out the gaps and limitations in the current regulatory framework and offer suggestions to ensure a more equitable access and utilization of AHR services by LGBTQ people in Canada. The chapter draws upon data from the "Creating Our Families" study to demonstrate how reproductive policy affects LGBTQ people in distinctive ways.[12] Although there are other areas of law that impact how LGBTQ people access and use AHR services, this chapter will take up the pressing consideration of access to reproductive materials, services, and facilities.[13] Our research shows that questions of access pose unique challenges for LGBTQ people accessing AHR, few of which have been addressed within Canadian case law or legislation. These challenges are the consequences of restrictive law crafted without LGBTQ people's needs in mind, and of unclear or vague jurisprudence that presents a particular hurdle for LGBTQ couples and individuals. Part I deals with the restricted access to legal means of gamete acquisition in Canada and the disproportionate impact of this on LGBTQ people. Part II looks at how known semen donors are managed under current regulations and the difficulties faced by families seeking to use a known donor. Part III explores the issue of semen donation by gay and HIV-positive men, while Part IV provides an overview of the impact, faced by gay men in particular, of the criminalization of commercial surrogacy in Canada. Finally, Part V surveys the ways in which legislative uncertainty has affected access to services at fertility clinics and the impact this has had on LGBTQ families in particular. The chapter concludes by suggesting possible areas of policy development and judicial analysis. In highlighting these areas of inequality and differential access to reproductive assistance and materials, we hope to encourage future developments in AHR legislation to take into account the specific concerns of LGBTQ parents and parents-to-be.

There have already been positive steps in this direction. The Canadian Bar Association (CBA) has explicitly recognized the special requirements of LGBTQ people in relation to AHR. In a submission to Health Canada, the CBA noted that while the availability of fertility services affects all segments of the population, "limits to that availability are likely to systemically discriminate against single people, and the lesbian, gay, bisexual and transgendered communities, who more often rely on assisted reproductive technologies to have children."[14]

This concern is echoed by the statement of principles laid out in the *AHRA* itself, which also explicitly aims to prevent discrimination against persons who seek to undergo AHR procedures, "including on the basis of sexual orientation and marital status."[15] This provision flows directly from the concern of the Royal Commission on New Reproductive Technologies (the Baird Commission) on prevailing discrimination against lesbians and single women in Canadian society. In its 1993 report, the Baird Commission expressed the strong view that "it is wrong to forbid some people access to medical services on the basis of social factors while others are permitted to use them; using criteria such as a woman's marital status or sexual orientation to determine access to donor insemination, based on historical prejudices and stereotypes, amounts to discrimination as defined under human rights law and contravenes the Commission's guiding principle of equality."[16]

Given this long-standing recognition of the reproductive barriers faced by non-heterosexual families, it was particularly distressing to witness the virtual elision of LGBTQ people from the *AHRA Reference* decision. It is our hope that a concern for all manner of families will remain at the fore as federal and provincial jurisdictions alike move to draft new legislation concerning AHR. This is a position also reflected by the *Canadian Human Rights Act,* which was amended in 1996 to include sexual orientation, following the declaration by Parliament that gay and lesbian Canadians are entitled to "an opportunity equal with other individuals to make for themselves the lives they are able and wish to have."[17] Present-day rules about access to AHR and the disproportionate impact experienced by LGBTQ families stand to threaten this guarantee of equality.

LGBTQ Access to Reproductive Material, Services, and Facilities

This area of law may be generally characterized in terms of *access to reproductive material, services, and facilities*. It encompasses access to human gametes such as sperm and ova, as well as access by commissioning or intended parents to reproductive surrogates, be they traditional or gestational.[18] It also includes access to fertility clinics and gamete banks, which draw upon reserves both domestic and imported, besides helping individuals freeze and store their own gametes (eggs, sperm, and embryos).

Access to third-party reproductive material is a crucial issue for LGBTQ people who wish to have biological children. Lesbians require sperm donation, gay men require ova donation (as well as a reproductive surrogate), bisexuals may require sperm or ova, and trans people may require sperm, ova, and/or a surrogate, depending on the particulars of their situation.[19] While some lesbians, bisexuals, and trans people may avoid the clinical system entirely and pursue home-based solutions with known donors, this is not an option for many cisgender gay men.[20] When creating children with third-party gametes, LGBTQ parents-to-be must first determine whether they will select known or unknown gamete donors; each choice leads to very different legal pathways.

In this section we outline five mechanisms of existing legal doctrine that infringe upon or negatively impact LGBTQ people's access to reproductive material, services, and facilities. While some of these issues may also be faced by heterosexual couples seeking reproductive assistance (e.g., gamete acquisition or a gestational surrogate), our contention is that such matters squarely and often disproportionately affect the LGBTQ community. Again, while AHR services typically assume that clients are heterosexual, cisgender, partnered, or married with access to a double income, and that they are dealing with fertility issues, some or none of these things may be the case for LGBTQ clients.[21] The following five sections outline key areas in which the care that LGBTQ people require may differ from what is typically offered.

I. Restricted Access to Legal Means of Gamete Acquisition

The acquisition of ova and gametes is strictly regulated in Canada, and under the *AHRA* it remains a criminal act to privately purchase human reproductive materials.[22] Section 7 was unchallenged in the reference case and continues to prohibit the purchase of sperm or ova from Canadian donors. This legislation works in concert with Health Canada regulations regarding the transport, freezing, handling, purchase, and cross-border traffic of human gametes, most notably the *Processing and Distribution of Semen for Assisted Conception Regulations (Semen Regulations).*[23] Together, the *Semen Regulations* and s. 7 of the *AHRA* constitute the legal terrain for all Canadians seeking to gain access to third-party semen and ova.[24]

Canada's legislation concerning gamete donation is currently among the strictest in the world.[25] This has limited the available supply of Canadian-donated sperm, both anonymous *and* known.[26] The supply of anonymous semen has been throttled by an onerous threshold for donation that prevents gay and bisexual men from donating; meanwhile, as will be seen below, all known donors who are not also sexual partners must navigate the secondary directives of the *Semen Regulations.*

Canada's restrictive donor legislation has had an accentuated impact on LGBTQ people. It was estimated in 2011 that there are only around thirty-five active sperm donors in the entire country; the numbers are even more uncertain regarding ova donors.[27] To meet demand sperm is being imported from abroad, with some commentators estimating that 95 per cent of Canadian needs for donor sperm are being met by sperm banks located outside the country.[28] Evidence suggests that

LGBTQ people are drawing upon a relatively small pool of available anonymous donors, making it possible for related "donor sibs"[29] to be concentrated within urban LGBTQ communities.[30] Our research suggests that LGBTQ people are far more likely to be using the same donor and learning of the shared biology of their children through queer community ties. One lesbian couple from our study attended a queer prenatal yoga class in Toronto, where they met another set of lesbian parents who had conceived with the same anonymous sperm donor. The women subsequently connected with fifteen more donor sib parents through online media and Facebook, most of whom were other lesbian couples.

These tight networks pose particular issues for people of colour, who face even fewer options in terms of semen donors.[31] Carol,[32] a bisexual woman, conceived a child with her lesbian partner using anonymous donor insemination. In their case, they had to go to the United States to find a donor who matched their racial background. As she recounted: "the sperm supply is quite limited in Canada. There's not tons of it … [especially] for people from other, um, like ethnic minorities … If you're not looking for a white donor you have to look a little bit harder."

Gay and bisexual men are also restricted by the ban on commercial transactions of donor ova. If pursuing gestational surrogacy, they must first locate an altruistic donor willing to undergo the invasive process of egg extraction.[33] While there are options for purchasing donor ova from the United States and elsewhere, these are prohibitively expensive avenues that raise questions about the legality of cross-border gamete purchase.[34] Most of the gay men we interviewed felt that payments to egg donors and surrogates should be legal, although regulated, with additional legislation required to protect both ova donors and commissioning parents.

II. Known Semen Donors Who Are Not Sexual Partners Are Viewed as Anonymous Third-Party Donors

For reasons such as cost, convenience, shared parenting arrangements, and intentional kinship creation, some people prefer to carry out assisted conception with a known donor instead of purchasing anonymous sperm from a sperm bank.[35] For the purposes of the *Semen Regulations*, "assisted conception" refers to "a reproductive technique performed on a woman for the purpose of conception, using semen from a donor who *is not her spouse or sexual partner*."[36] This definition places *all* donor semen in the same category, meaning that an anonymous vial ordered online will be treated with the same dispassionate rigour as a donation from a brother-in-law, a childhood friend, or an intended father in a multi-parent arrangement.

In practice, this means that the semen of a known donor is subject to the same testing and quarantine requirements as an anonymous donation. Even if a known donor has a clean bill of health and all parties agree to use a fresh specimen that has been tested and washed in the laboratory prior to insemination, the *Semen Regulations* prohibit the use of fresh sperm *unless there has been a sexual relationship* between the donor and the person being inseminated. Instead, the sperm sample must be frozen for a minimum of 180 days for infectious disease screening, with the donor's blood extracted and tested at the time of sample provision and again six months later when the semen is thawed and finally used. This same routine must be followed for any subsequent specimens the donor may produce.[37] This is a costly and time-consuming process that treats a known donor, who is often a close friend or member of a partner's family, with the same epidemiological suspicion as an anonymous stranger.[38]

We interviewed a female couple, Tonya and Jacqueline, who decided to avoid the clinic altogether after being faced with these protocols.[39] The women planned for Tonya to be inseminated with Jacqueline's brother's sperm, in order to foster genetic alignment in their family and create a child that would resemble both its mothers. The couple sought out the assistance of a local fertility clinic to help with the process and carry out standard testing for both Tonya and Jacqueline's brother. However, once they encountered the six-month quarantine period and associated costs mandated by the *Semen Regulations*, they decided to undertake the process at home instead. As they described, while their initial preference was for the clinic to manage the collection of Jacqueline's brother's semen, the known donor fees and procedural hurdles proved a frustrating barrier:

> Jacqueline: I'm serious, like I'm still angry to this day about, about that clinic experience. 'cause I think that a lot of people that are going in with known donors or friends, they virtually put a barrier up and it makes so that if you want an anonymous donor it's already out of the price range but if you have a known donor or you want to co-parent or anything like this, it just makes the cost even more. And for the average family it's already expensive, so can you imagine what it does if they're going to

> store this stuff for six months and do these extra procedures ... Financially [it] can be impossible for some families.

Another female couple we interviewed had also opted to use home insemination with a known donor. They explained that "a big part" of their decision to avoid the clinical system was that the third-party donor sperm would have had to be frozen. They were both in their mid-thirties and did not feel that they could afford the additional delay in moving forward with insemination and wanted to begin trying for a child as soon as possible. Bev, one of the women, had the following to say about the *Semen Regulations* and its restrictions on third-party donors: "Trust women. Let them make decisions about their own bodies and their own safety rather than trying to impose safety standards that assume that women who are trying to get pregnant are incapable of rational decision-making."

Note that these regulations do allow women seeking insemination by a *sexual partner* to bypass quarantine requirements. Women in opposite-sex relationships may use fresh semen from a conjugal partner without delay, thereby avoiding the six-month waiting period as well as the fees associated with the storage of donated semen. Indeed, should a lesbian or bisexual woman walk into a fertility clinic and falsify a sexual relationship with her male companion, she can request immediate insemination without the requirements of freezing or quarantine.[40] Rachel Epstein, writing on behalf of the LGBTQ/AHRA Working Group, a collective of Toronto-based service providers and researchers concerned with issues of access to AHR services, put the matter of harm as follows:

> While we understand that the intent of this practice is to protect people from undetected risks, in fact there are no fewer risks in being inseminated with the sperm of someone one is having sex with, than there is being inseminated with the sperm of a known donor one has been inseminating with. The risks are the same. If one is willing to assume the risk of insemination from a sexual partner, one should also be able to assume the risks of insemination from a known donor. The situation outlined above has put people who are using known sperm donors in the position of lying when they approach fertility clinics. If they present their donors as sexual partners, they can access the services they require. If they tell the truth, they are denied. As well this means that in the case of a lesbian couple, the non-birth parent is left out of the process, which results in undue hardship

> to her. She is left out of the very personal and significant process of her child's conception.[41]

In other words, a woman may assume the "risk" of being inseminated by her sexual partner but not the "risk" of being inseminated by a loved one with whom she is not having intercourse. The *Semen Regulations* presume an anonymity and fear of contamination that is simply not the case with a known sperm donor. This presumption, which has been crafted with cisgender, heterosexual couples firmly in mind, is unable to account for the important role played by known sperm donors within potential LGBTQ families.[42]

III. Gay Men and HIV-Positive Men Require Special Permission to Be Known Donors and Are Barred from Anonymous Donation

The *Semen Regulations* also incorporate a document titled the *Technical Requirements for Therapeutic Donor Insemination* (Directive),[43] which excludes a comprehensive range of prospective donors determined to be in the "high risk" category or genetically unfit. These exclusions include men over forty years of age and "men who have had sex with another man, even once, since 1977."[44] Thus, even when presenting with a known third-party donor and attempting in good faith to follow the dictates of the *Semen Regulations*, a lesbian will find her donor in the "high risk" category and be prevented from readily using sperm if it is from a gay or bisexual friend. Yet our interviews indicate that many lesbians, bisexuals, and trans men would like to use sperm from a cisgender male or trans woman[45] friend. In some cases this may even lay the groundwork for an intentional multi-parenting arrangement.[46]

One lesbian couple we interviewed was prevented from using a known donor, and found themselves presented with confusing and contradictory information about their friend's sexuality. At the clinic they were told that because he was gay, their chosen donor would not be eligible to donate. Justine recalled: "They [said we] would have to do a year quarantine, then that would include several samples throughout that year to be tested ... We actually had confided in one of the nurses that Rob [our known donor] was gay and they said that he wouldn't even be able [to do it] ... His donation would not be taken at all."

Frustrated by the extended quarantine period and the complex regulations regarding gay men as donors, this couple eventually decided to use an anonymous donor. Justine described their exasperation:

JUSTINE: I mean we wanted to use Rob. I mean that was our first choice and we weren't able to …

INTERVIEWER: But the nurse was discouraging.

JUSTINE: Yeah, very discouraging in that sense. She said that they probably wouldn't even test him … If they know. And it's like, well what does it matter? What, I mean what does it? You're testing for HIV anyway. Is it just a given because he's gay he's gonna have it? No. It's, I mean, it's a given that he's gonna have sex with men, yes … If you answer honestly as a gay man, yeah, you're basically excluding yourself. Do you lie? I mean, is that what we've come to now … that for Rob to be able to, you know, to donate he has to lie about who he is? I don't think that's right.

As Epstein suggests, the equating of gay men and risky sexual practice is inaccurate, not to mention "steeped in the homophobic and discriminatory view that 'gay' men are synonymous with HIV/AIDS."[47]

For a gay man who is excluded under the Directive's criteria but who wishes to donate, there is recourse. After first testing negative for infectious diseases such as HIV and hepatitis, he may apply for special authorization from his doctor under the Donor Semen Special Access Program (DSSAP). If the DSSAP is granted, he may then undergo the six-month semen testing and quarantine period.

In 2007 the Ontario Superior Court of Justice ruled on a challenge to the constitutionality of the *Semen Regulations*. The lesbian applicants in *Susan Doe v Canada*[48] had argued that considerations such as conceptions of autonomy and community values played an important part in determining their reproductive choices and that the donor exclusion list posed a discriminatory barrier not experienced by heterosexual couples or donors. In the judgment, Dambrot J maintained that the donor exclusions as listed did not discriminate against lesbian women or gay men. According to the court, these regulations were based on a protectionist health approach to reproductive matters, by which there was a necessity to prevent the public from acquiring infectious diseases. In finding that the health argument overruled other considerations, Dambrot J concluded that any differential treatment was justified by the original intention of the regulations.[49] Yet even if one accepts the court's dismissal of questions of prejudice and stereotyping, public health approaches to reproductive matters and HIV transmission have changed dramatically since these guidelines were first developed.

At the time of writing, HIV-positive men are banned from anonymous third-party sperm donation. Nor is surrogacy is an option in Canada for HIV-positive single men or HIV-positive men in a same-sex couple, despite a large body of evidence suggesting that reproductive technologies can allow HIV-affected men to safely conceive.[50] Indeed, a 2007 multi-centre study on inseminations of women with HIV-positive semen reported that when using current sperm-washing technologies, "the calculated probability of HIV contamination is equal to zero."[51] The recommendation of that research team, based on this and other correlate studies, is that "it is neither ethically nor legally justifiable to exclude individuals from infertility services on the basis of male HIV-infection."[52]

Advances in technology have minimized the risk of infectious disease transmission and call on us to revise the terms of protectionist arguments made in cases such as *Susan Doe v Canada*. In light of the onerous burden the Directive places on gay and bisexual men and HIV-positive men, as well as on the recipients of their donor sperm, we may ask what public interest is truly being served by continuing to uphold these outdated standards.[53]

IV. The Criminalization of Commercial Surrogacy

Gay men who desire to create a genetically related family without the involvement of a female co-parent will require the services of a reproductive surrogate, as may some bisexual and trans-identified couples and individuals.[54] This places gay men in a situation of complex dependency and engagement with the people willing to bear their children. Our research makes clear that Canada's criminalization of commercial surrogacy has had a powerful impact on gay men hoping to create biologically related children, while legislative hesitancy to address the bioethics of surrogacy has created uncertainty around allowable reimbursement for surrogate expenses.[55]

Surrogacy refers to the practice whereby, through prior arrangement, a woman carries and gives birth to a child that she does not intend to parent.[56] Instead, parenting responsibilities are assumed by the intended or "commissioning" adults. Surrogacy may be *traditional*, wherein a surrogate's own egg is fertilized by donor sperm, or *gestational*, in which the surrogate is implanted with an egg and sperm to which she has no genetic tie.[57]

Two sections of the *AHRA* come to bear on surrogate transactions. Section 6 prohibits the payment or advertisement of payment to surrogate mothers or intermediaries and places a minimum age restriction of twenty-one years on potential surrogates. The maximum criminal penalty for transgressing s. 6 is $500,000 and ten years' imprisonment.[58] Section 12 recognizes, however, that some reimbursement of expenditures is necessary on the part of surrogates (and gamete donors) and makes allowance for their limited compensation.[59] This was one of the few sections of the *AHRA* to withstand constitutional scrutiny by the Supreme Court and was deemed an important safeguard to public morality in the reasons of McLachlin CJ; its constitutionality was subsequently affirmed by the swing vote of Cromwell J.[60]

As Health Canada has not yet promulgated regulations for Section 12 the details of allowable compensation are uncertain. At this point, all that commissioning parents know is that receipts must be kept, and that a surrogate must not be reimbursed for the loss of work-related income incurred during her pregnancy unless "a qualified medical practitioner certifies, in writing, that continuing to work may pose a risk to her health or that of the embryo or foetus."[61] Thus, a strictly altruistic system is being enforced in Canada, as surrogates are not legally entitled to claim remuneration beyond out-of-pocket expenses and may only be compensated for missing work if their health is at risk.

But what kinds of expenses for reproductive labour may be compensated? Health Canada has taken the position that all "reasonable" expenses incurred in the course of donation or surrogacy may be reimbursed, without actually defining what reasonable entails.[62] This remains a confounding area of law, as indicated by our research participants:

> INTERVIEWER: When you say mandating of payment [to the surrogate], what do you mean?
>
> JAMES: I think it should be better worded 'cause "reimbursement for expenses" for me was never very clear and I don't think anybody really understands it. If it's sort of the middle of the road before you say "Yes you can pay" or "No you can't pay" if that's the way it's gonna have to be, it's okay I guess but I – I don't understand why they can't make it clearer (A gay man, who with his partner, now has two children via anonymous egg donor and gestational surrogate).

At present, only the intended parents may reimburse a surrogate for expenses. They are left to their own devices in determining the "reasonableness" of expenditures in accordance with contracts between the parties. In practice, this is generally done in consultation with a lawyer, who is an intermediary third party who *may* be paid for his or her services in helping negotiate the surrogacy contract, despite regulatory uncertainty around acceptable contractual boundaries.[63] Other third parties who may receive compensation currently include fertility physicians, gamete banks, and pharmaceutical companies, although none are allowed to help connect potential surrogates and parents. Sally Rhodes-Heinrich, who helms the popular website *Surrogacy in Canada*, warns about this ban on intermediaries: "I think you will see more disasters and tragedies in surrogacy if you don't have people who do some preliminary screening, people who are educating and providing support."[64]

This selective approach to compensated support and professional advice is paternalistic, and privileges an educated class of practitioners – doctors, lawyers, and pharmaceutical firms – over the actual surrogates being commissioned. One's legal counsel may be remunerated for their labour, but not the surrogate at the centre of the transaction. Concerns over the commercialization of reproductive labour have been a central thrust of the *AHRA* since the Baird Report was tabled.[65] Arguments over the moral validity of commercial surrogacy have raged for decades, only growing more complicated in recent years with the globalization of reproductive surrogate markets into locations such as India, Thailand, and Eastern Europe.[66]

While some feminist commentators have argued that practices such as commercial surrogacy serve to embody and institutionalize the patriarchal domination of women, others have sought to understand surrogacy within terms of women's agency and the difficulties of contractual decision-making.[67] These are complex issues, as surrogacy arrangements vary significantly depending on geographic, economic, and social conditions.

Drawing from a meta-analysis of research on surrogacy in Canada, the United States, and the United Kingdom, a 2010 study by Karen Busby and Delaney Vun wades into this debate to interrogate the power differentials of surrogacy and presumptions of exploitation.[68] As they report, "empirical research concerning women who become surrogate mothers in Britain and the United States does not support concerns that they are being exploited by these arrangements, that they cannot give meaningful consent to participating, or that the arrangements commodify women or children."[69] Busby and Vun call for a more nuanced legal regime to ensure that women who enter into altruistic *or* paid surrogacy contracts will receive the full protection of the law.[70]

As a practitioner in fertility law and legal counsel to surrogacy arrangements, Toronto lawyer Sara Cohen poses the following question: "If women obtain medical advice, independent legal advice, and psychological counselling and choose to engage in surrogacy or egg donation, why should the state protect them from themselves when they do not need or want protecting?"[71] A number of the gay male couples we interviewed commented on the perceived independence of their surrogates while also lamenting the lack of guidance around how to navigate this complex social experience. Paul, a gay man, and his male partner are in the process of having a child via an anonymous egg donor and a gestational surrogate. "Should we buy her something nice?" he asks. "You know what I mean? You don't know what to do – it's like unchartered territory."

Clearly, Canadian laws prohibiting commercial surrogacy are having a real and disproportionate effect on LGBTQ people and are developing without consideration of the reproductive dilemma faced by gay men in particular. The indeterminacy of guidelines for reimbursement has not halted the practice but *has* piled greater anxiety onto what is an already fraught and emotional process. James and Brad are a gay couple who have had two children via an anonymous egg donor and a gestational surrogate.

BRAD: I think the whole ambiguity of the process scares people. I think even being in the process you kind of feel like you're doing something wrong … I think if it's very clear then people will know that it is legal and you're paying someone to, you know, help you with your …

JAMES: Have your child.

BRAD: Because I still have people saying to me: "Ooh isn't that illegal?"

Recent research indicates that paid surrogacy is still occurring; it has merely been driven underground.[72] While broad empirical data are scarce, it appears that after the *AHRA* criminalized the domestic practice of commercial surrogacy, people simply turned online to locate surrogates – many of whom are located in the United States, where paid surrogacy is legal.[73] Says Brad: "People were putting up information – 'I'm ready to be a surrogate' or 'I'd like to be a surrogate' or 'Are you looking for eggs?' or whatever. So there were certain sites that I would go and visit and click on certain areas and e-mail people and have information. The majority of them were in America, though."

For the time being, the uncertainty of s. 12 may actually be of benefit, for it allows surrogates to be compensated within a broadly defined "grey area." However, this indeterminacy comes with its own stresses, and – as discussed – relies on the paternalistic hypocrisy of allowing some industries and professionals to benefit financially, while the surrogates themselves cannot. If and when s. 12 regulations are promulgated, we believe it is of paramount importance that LGBTQ people's concerns and the voices of actual Canadian surrogates be taken directly into account.[74]

V. Legislative Uncertainty Impacts Access to Service at Fertility Clinics

At present, there is no consistency of formal qualifications for health professionals performing controlled AHR activities as laid out in the *AHRA*.[75] Nor is there a consistent standard of practice to which clinics are held, either federal or provincial. No mandatory licence or accreditation is required for private fertility clinics, and in the absence of binding clinical practice guidelines for the provision of reproductive care, it is left to individual clinics or practitioners to set their own fees and standards.[76] As the Ontario Expert Panel on Infertility and Adoption concluded in 2009, "without mandatory provincial accreditation, there are no common provincial standards for clinic operations, the services they should offer nor the prices that clinics should charge for their services."[77]

However, while fertility clinics are largely self-regulated, medical practitioners such as reproductive endocrinologists, nurses, and other health professionals are members of regulated professions and are required to meet the standards of practice set out by their regulatory colleges. Fertility counsellors represent an important exception to this rule, as there is no agreement among those in the field concerning the minimum qualifications necessary to provide appropriate AHR counselling services.[78]

While attempts have been made to develop national standards for fertility practice, the *AHRA* ruling has made it virtually impossible for binding regulations to be promulgated at a national level.[79] The bulk of controlled activities regulated under the *AHRA* are now contained under the provincial power in matters of health, although provisions outlining consent to use and allowable compensation for gamete donors and surrogates are still validly enacted at the national level.[80] Clinics may choose to be accredited by Accreditation Canada,[81] but "the clinics and physicians' offices that provide assisted reproduction services are not required to be accredited and information about their practices and success rates is not easily available."[82]

In the absence of definitive standards for fertility clinics, the Canadian Fertility and Andrology Society (CFAS) has developed clinical practice guidelines for physicians as well as guidelines and standards for certification for other fertility-related service providers such as counsellors. While LGBTQ people's perspectives are beginning to find a modicum of purchase in CFAS, the society's draft clinical practice guidelines do not account for any breadth of experience or embodiment; instead, lesbian couples (the only mention of LGBTQ people), when present, are compared solely against a heterosexual norm. For example, while the CFAS guidelines on AHR counselling practice do refer specifically to lesbians and single women, the text quickly offers the reassurance that lesbians "do not differ from heterosexuals in their parenting skills."[83] While the intention is surely to comfort the (presumptively) heterosexual reader, once again this discourse revolves around a conceptual model that presumes a heterosexual couple as the exemplary AHR client. The CFAS guidelines also fail to include any discussion of gay men, bisexuals, or trans people.

Although we do not intend to stake a claim here for the exceptional character of lesbian parenting, it *is* important to note that even well-meaning reassurances serve to mask substantial differences between heterosexual and LGBTQ AHR clients. These differences begin at the clinic's front door. In contrast to cisgender, heterosexual couples, who tend not to solicit fertility services until a problem is discovered, LGBTQ prospective parents generally seek out clinical advice quite early on their journey to conceive. Yet despite the large numbers of LGBTQ people now using fertility clinics, the overwhelming presumption facing new clients is that of reproductive pathology. Clinics structured around the heterosexual model of fertility are geared towards alleviating "infertility"[84] in conjugal partners and often mandate a series of intrusive, sometimes painful and laborious diagnostic tests before service provision can even begin.[85] Miriam, a single queer woman who ultimately avoided AHR services and conceived outside of the clinic with known donor sperm, put it this way:

> I think not having access to sperm is a really different thing than trying to get pregnant with sperm and having trouble, right … The idea that queerness in and of itself, like being a lesbian in and of itself, is a fertility problem is ridiculous and the fact that people are kind of going through the same measures as folks who have tried less invasive ways to get pregnant … *I think it needs a whole rethink in order for it to really make sense to everybody who is accessing it* [AHR services] (emphasis added).

There are also a range of gatekeeping and bureaucratic elements that hamper LGBTQ people from carrying out their reproductive intentions. Epstein and colleagues note:

> [I]n very recent history some Canadian fertility clinics required psychiatric assessment of lesbians before they were granted access to donor insemination services. We also know of at least one Toronto physician who required lesbians requesting access to donor insemination to write a "letter to the doctor" in order to convince him that they should be granted access to services. Other clinics and physicians simply denied access to lesbians and single women.[86]

Sadly, trans people are now, in some instances, facing similar gatekeeping decisions with regard to their access to AHR services and are having to debunk arguments about their rights and abilities to parent.[87]

Furthermore, many of the "Creating Our Families" study participants noted that fertility clinic intake forms do not take account of their particular identities and family configurations, nor do clinic environments include representations of their identities and families. Presumptions of heterosexuality and infertility saturate these clinical spaces, littering cultural as well as substantive barriers in the path of LGBTQ people seeking AHR services.[88] As national guidelines for AHR clinicians, nurses, and counsellors are produced, it is vital that LGBTQ voices be part of the discussion. Increased cultural competency and sharpened awareness of LGBTQ people's specific needs are badly needed at this critical juncture of legislative development.

Conclusion

The *AHRA Reference* has left Canadians with more uncertainty than clarity. What has not changed, however, is the sidelining of LGBTQ people with regard to how AHR services are legislated and regulated. LGBTQ people now comprise a significant proportion of clientele at Canadian fertility clinics, and the numbers are only poised to grow. Outdated understandings of "infertility," discriminatory treatment of known sperm donors, limited sperm reserves, misinformation about the "risk" of HIV-positive sperm donors, and vaguely defined commodification concerns in relation to surrogacy must be revised to conform to contemporary realities. The present regime reflects dusty approaches based on outdated science, limited empirical data, and discriminatory assumptions.

We have explored the many "grey areas" that plague Canadian legislation concerning access to reproductive material, services, and facilities. The standards of clinical practice that exist are based on the dyadic cisgender, heterosexual family norm. As queer intentional parenting arrangements move further from the normative ideal, they find themselves in ever more precarious and uncertain territory.

Despite explicit reference in the preamble of the *AHRA* to the importance of preventing discrimination "including on the basis of sexual orientation and marital status," our research has shown that LGBTQ people seeking AHR services are not being adequately served by the present legal order. In this chapter, we have highlighted five areas of law that require immediate and comprehensive attention in order to guarantee equitable access to AHR services for LGBTQ people. While our research has begun to explore these issues and is the first study of its kind to include the voices of GBQ men and trans people, the analysis we have presented will be broadened and enriched by accounts from of a greater number of gay men and trans people, as well as from low-income and racialized people, single parents, surrogates, donors and their families, people living with disabilities, and First Nations people seeking AHR. Until these voices are heard, many residents of Canada who rely on AHR will continue to struggle through a regulatory regime inappropriately designed for the normative white, cisgender, financially resourced heterosexual couple. Despite *Charter*-backed guarantees of equality and access, judicial decisions such as the *Reference re Assisted Human Reproduction Act* have been unable to account for the cultural specificity and community values of LGBTQ people in Canada. A re-evaluation of reproductive values is required as we move forward to ensure equitable access to AHR services for all those in Canada who wish to become parents.

NOTES

1 *Reference re Assisted Human Reproduction Act*, 2010 SCC 61, [2010] 3 SCR 457 [*AHRA Reference*]. See also *In the matter of a Reference by the Government of Quebec pursuant to the Court of Appeal Reference Act, R.S.Q., c R-23, concerning the constitutional validity of sections 8 to 19, 40 to 53, 60, 61 and 68 of the Assisted Human Reproduction Act, S.C. 2004, c 2*, 2008 QCCA 1167, 298 DLR (4th) 712 [*Quebec Reference*].

2 *Lesbian* is a term for a female whose primary sexual orientation is to other women. *Gay* is a term for a male whose primarily sexual orientation is to other men. This term is sometimes used by lesbians (i.e., gay woman). *Bisexual* is a term for a person whose sexual orientation is directed towards individuals of more than one sex or gender, although not necessarily at the same time. *Trans* is an umbrella term referring to people who do not embrace traditional binary gender norms of masculine and feminine and/or whose gender identity or expression does not fit with the one they were assigned at birth; it can refer to transgender, transitioned, transsexual, and genderqueer people, as well as to some two-spirit people. *Transgender* is a term used by individuals who fall outside of traditional gender categories or norms. It literally means "across gender" and conveys the idea of transcending the boundaries of the gender binary system. It, however, is not necessarily a desire to be of the "opposite" sex. A *transsexual* is someone who feels that their gender identity does not match the sex they were assigned at birth. Many transsexual people choose to go through sex reassignment, including hormone treatment and surgeries, so that their sex and gender identity match. *Transition* refers to the process of changing from the sex one was assigned at birth to one's self-perceived gender. It may involve dressing in the manner of the self-perceived gender, changing one's name and identification, and undergoing hormone therapy and/or sex reassignment surgeries to change one's secondary sex characteristics to reflect the self-perceived gender. *Two-Spirit* is an English-language term used to reflect specific cultural words used by First Nations people who have both a masculine and a feminine spirit or to describe their sexual, gender, and/or spiritual identity. *Queer* is a term that has traditionally been used as a derogatory and offensive word for LGBTQ people. Many have reclaimed this word and use it proudly to describe their identity and/or as an umbrella term for LGBTQ people or communities. Some people use "queer" as a way of identifying their non-heterosexual orientation while avoiding the sometimes strict boundaries that surround lesbian, gay, bisexual, and trans identities. "Queer" can also signify one's rejection

of heteronormative sexual identities, normative gender constructions, or essentialist identity politics. Please note that because ideas and attitudes are constantly changing within LGBTQ communities and among society at large, these definitions may be used differently by different people and in different regions. Many of these terms have been adapted from the following sources: Angela M. Barbara, Gloria Chaim, and Farzana Doctor, *Asking the Right Questions 2: Talking about Sexual Orientation and Gender Identity in Mental Health, Counselling and Addiction Settings*, rev. ed. (Toronto: Centre for Addiction and Mental Health, 2007), 55–60 (Glossary); Greta R. Bauer *et al.*, "'I Don't Think This Is Theoretical; This Is Our Lives': How Erasure Impacts Health Care for Transgender People" (2009) 20:5 J Assoc Nurses AIDS C 348–361; Eli R. Green and Eric N. Peterson, "LGBTQI Terminology" (2003–4), LGBT Campus Research Center, UCLA, http://www.lgbt.ucla.edu/documents/LGBTTerminology.pdf.

3 Rachel Epstein for the AHRA/LGBTQ Working Group, *The Assisted Human Reproduction Act and LGBTQ Communities* (Toronto: Sherbourne Health Centre, 2008), 1.

4 *AHRA Reference*, *supra* note 1 at para 254 (decision of LeBel, Deschamps, Abella, and Rothstein JJ, written by Lebel and Deschamps): "Rather, both those who testified before the Baird Commission and those who participated in the parliamentary debates acknowledged that the development of assisted human reproduction amounts to a step forward for the constantly growing number of people dealing with infertility. *Moreover, it represents the only option for homosexuals who wish to reproduce*. The risks for the health and safety of people who resort to these technologies do not distinguish the field of assisted human reproduction from other fields of medical practice that have evolved after a period of experimentation, such as that of organ transplants or grafts" [emphasis added].

5 For more information about LGBTQ people's experiences with adoption, see Lori E. Ross *et al.*, "Policy, Practice and Personal Narratives: Experiences of LGBTQ People with Adoption in Ontario, Canada" (2009) 12:3–4 Adoption Quarterly 272–93; Lori E. Ross *et al.*, "Policy and Practice Regarding Lesbian, Gay, Bisexual, Transgender, Transsexual and Two-Spirit Adoption in Ontario" (2009) 35:4 Can Pub Pol'y 451–67; Lori E. Ross *et al.*, "Lesbian and queer mothers navigating the adoption system: the impacts on mental health" (2008) 17:3 Health Sociology Review 254–66. For a discussion of how lesbian and bisexual women are navigating the provision of AHR services, see: Lori E Ross, Leah S Steele & Rachel Epstein, "Lesbian and Bisexual Women's Recommendations for Improving the Provision of Assisted Reproductive Technology Services" (2006) 86:3

Fertility and Sterility 735–8; Lori E. Ross, Leah S. Steele, and Rachel Epstein, "Service Use and Gaps in Services for Lesbian and Bisexual Women during Donor Insemination, Pregnancy and the Postpartum Period" (2006) 28:5 Journal of Obstetrics and Gynaecology Canada 505–11.

6 As an example, trans people have only recently gained recognition of their gender identity as an enumerated grounds for discrimination in provincial and territorial human rights legislation. The Northwest Territories was the first jurisdiction to add "gender identity" to its human rights legislation in 2002 (*Human Rights Act*, SNWT 2002, c 18, s 5(1)). Manitoba added "gender identity" to its Human Rights Code in June 2012, as did Ontario, which also added "gender expression." *Human Rights Code*, SM 1987–88, c 45, CCSM c H175, s 9(2)(g), as amended by *Human Rights Code Amendment Act*, SM 2012, c 38, s 5(2); *Human Rights Code*, RSO 1990, c H.19, s 1, as amended by *Toby's Act (Right to be Free from Discrimination and Harassment Because of Gender Identity or Gender Expression), 2012*, SO 2012, c 7, s 1. Prior to these amendments, the grounds of "gender" under the Ontario Code in particular had been held to include "gender identity," but recent developments now make the legislation explicit. The term "gender identity" refers to a person's own identification of being masculine, feminine, male, female, or trans. Gender identity is unrelated to sexual orientation; not all trans people identify as lesbian, gay, bisexual, or queer. Gender expression is the public expression of gender identity: actions, dress, hairstyles, and so on, performed to demonstrate one's gender identity.

7 *Supra* note 3.

8 Cisgender refers to a person whose gender identity matches the gender they were assigned at birth; someone who is not trans.

9 In regard to LGBTQ rights, Brenda Cossman has described how a functional equivalency argument – wherein same-sex relationships are described as being "just like" heterosexual relationships – utilizes a discourse of sameness that may serve to collapse LGBTQ difference. As she writes, "[f]unctional approaches to the family are invariably measured against a set of norms about what families do or ought to do" (Brenda Cossman, "Lesbians, Gay Men, and the *Canadian Charter of Rights and Freedoms*" (2002) 40 Osgoode Hall LJ 223 at 226–7). This "set of norms" is commonly rooted in the heteronormativity of law – the assumption, in individuals or in institutions, that everyone is heterosexual and that heterosexuality is superior to homosexuality and bisexuality. "Heteronormativity refers to the privileging of heterosexual relationships and identities through the establishment of said relationships and

identities as the norm by which all others are evaluated." Mary E. Hylton, "Heteronormativity and the Experiences of Lesbian and Bisexual Women as Social Work Students" (2005) 41:1 Journal of Social Work Education 67–82 at 69. This chapter argues that the privileging of heterosexual relationships and identities is foundational to the operation of the fertility clinic, as well as the legal regime through which it is regulated.

10 While this chapter will apply a specifically queer lens to analyse the weakness of infertility as a diagnostic, we are not the first to question the utility of the term. For a discussion on the shortcomings of "infertility" as a conceptual rubric for both demographers and reproductive endocrinologists, see S. Gurunath *et al.*, "Defining Infertility – a Systematic Review of Prevalence Studies" (2011) 17:5 Human Reproduction Update 575–588.

11 This chapter was developed based on a Canadian Institutes of Health Research–funded study "Creating Our Families: A Pilot Study of the Experiences of Lesbian, Gay, Bisexual and Trans People Accessing Assisted Human Reproduction Services in Ontario" (FRN–103595). The study was developed in 2009 by Lori E. Ross (Re:searching for LGBTQ Health, Centre for Addiction and Mental Health), Leah S. Steele (St Michael's Hospital), and Rachel Epstein (LGBTQ Parenting Network, Sherbourne Health Centre). Stu Marvel joined the project in 2010 as a Co-Investigator and conducted a portion of the interviews in 2010 and 2011. Staff for the project included datejie green, Lesley A. Tarasoff, and Scott Anderson. Other staff and students from the Re:searching for LGBTQ Health team also contributed to this project (see http://www.lgbtqhealth.ca). In line with community-based research principles, this study was guided by an advisory committee of AHR service providers and service users. Cf. Barbara A. Israel *et al.*, "Review of Community-Based Research: Assessing Partnership Approaches to Improve Public Health" (1998) 19 Annual Review of Public Health 173–202. In total, sixty-six LGBTQ people from across Ontario were interviewed about their experiences with AHR services. We would like to thank the Creating Our Families (COF) research team for their comments on this piece, and the COF study participants for sharing their stories with us.

12 While the points made herein are broadly applicable for LGBTQ people in Canada, it is important to note that the majority of participants in our qualitative study were aged thirty-one to forty, married or in a common law relationship, white, and university educated and had an annual household income of greater than C$66,000 (i.e., they are not necessarily representative of the larger LGBTQ population).

13 The other three areas of law that exert a differential impact on LGBTQ people are access to reproductive funding, determinations regarding the legal parentage of donor-conceived offspring, and the rights of donor-conceived offspring to knowledge of their birth.

14 Canadian Bar Association, *Reimbursement of Expenditures under the Assisted Human Reproduction Act* (Ottawa: CBA, 2007), 2, http://www.cba.org/cba/submissions/pdf/07-47-eng.pdf. The CBA policy position paper makes a series of recommendations to Health Canada, urging greater flexibility and the avoidance of narrow definitions for the reimbursement of gamete donors or surrogates: *ibid* at 1–8.

15 *Assisted Human Reproduction Act*, SC 2004, c 2 [*AHRA*], s 2(e).

16 Royal Commission on New Reproductive Technologies, *Proceed with Care: Final Report* (Ottawa: Minister of Government Services, 1993), vol. 1 at 455–6.

17 *Canadian Human Rights Act*, RSC 1985, c H-6, s, 2, as amended by SC 1996, c 14, s 1.

18 A note on definitions: A *gestational surrogate* is a person who volunteers to have an embryo implanted in the uterus and carry the pregnancy on behalf of the intended parent or parents. A gestational surrogate is not genetically related to the resultant baby. A *traditional surrogate*, on the other hand, is someone who volunteers to conceive through insemination and carry the pregnancy on behalf of the intended parent or parents. A traditional surrogate contributes half the genetic complement of the resultant baby.

19 Of course these situations may prove more complex, with lesbian and bisexual couples or individuals also requiring an egg as well as a surrogate, and gay men also requiring a sperm donor. The scenarios listed above represent the minimum of third-party gametes required by LGBTQ parents-to-be.

20 For example, a 2011 study of thirty gay men who used AHR services concluded that "gay men increasingly seek parenthood through assisted reproduction using an oocyte donor and a gestational carrier": Dorothy A. Greenfeld and Emre Seli, "Gay Men Choosing Parenthood through Assisted Reproduction: Medical and Psychosocial Considerations" (2011) 95:1 Fertility and Sterility 225–9 at 226. A preference for gestational surrogates – not least because of uncertainty over maternal parentage – means that gay men may find themselves completely reliant upon AHR services and the legal uncertainty this entails. For example, a US study of gay fathers included a couple who were obliged, due to legal barriers to surrogacy in their state of residence, to hire "an egg donor from one state, a surrogate mother from another state, a surrogate agency in another state, the paternity clinic in a fourth state, [while they] were in a fifth state":

Dana Berkowitz and William Marsiglio, "Gay Men Negotiating Procreative Identities" (2007) 69 Journal of Marriage and Family 366–81 at 377. Another gay father in the United States, who had opted for a traditional surrogate because of the difficulty of accessing gestational services, mused that "we were lucky that there was never a question for our surrogate of her role in the children's lives, but as I look back, we were taking quite a risk. If she had changed her mind, or fought for custody, I suspect that our stable home life would've been disrupted in a homophobic system that would not have recognised my partner and I as the real parents": quoted in Arlene Istar Lev, "Gay Dads: Choosing Surrogacy" (2006) 7:1 Lesbian & Gay Psychology Review 72–6 at 73.

21 datejie green, Lesley A. Tarasoff, and Rachel Epstein, "Meeting the Assisted Human Reproduction (AHR) Needs of Lesbian, Gay, Bisexual, Trans and Queer (LGBTQ) People in Canada: A Fact Sheet for AHR Service Providers," LGBTQ Parenting Network (Toronto: Sherbourne Health Centre, 2012).

22 The *AHRA* prescribes a maximum penalty of $500,000 and ten years' imprisonment: *supra* note 17. For details of the first prosecution under the prohibited sections of the *AHRA*, see *infra* note 59.

23 The *Processing and Distribution of Semen for Assisted Conception Regulations*, SOR/96–254 [*Semen Regulations*], was enacted under the *Food and Drugs Act*, RSC c F-27. The *Semen Regulations* came into force in June 1996 and are aimed at reducing the likelihood of infectious disease transmission. They set up a range of stringent health and safety requirements for the semen used in assisted reproduction.

24 Although amendments to s 10 of the *AHRA* have been made under s 716 of the *Jobs, Growth and Long-term Prosperity Act*, SC 2012, c 19, such provisions are not yet in force.

25 Canada's sperm regulations are stricter than those enacted in many US jurisdictions, which makes it difficult for Canadians to import sperm from other countries. As reported by the Sperm Bank of California, a large semen distributor located in Berkeley, California: "Shipping semen samples to Canada is restricted because *Health Canada* has instituted strict regulations on donor testing that are not tenable for most US sperm banks to follow. However, we are able to sell sperm to recipients in Canada if they register with a US medical professional, cross the border to receive shipments and inseminate in the US" [emphasis in original] (Sperm Bank of California, promotional material).

26 While Canadians are able to import sperm from other countries, the regulations on allowable imports are strict, as indicated in the footnote

above. This combination of restrictive domestic legislation and high international standards may collude to unduly impact certain people, and in particular those seeking sperm from a specific non-White racial background. For example, our interview participants included an interracial lesbian couple who were unable to find Filipino sperm within the limited Canadian stock. They selected a Filipino donor from US sperm bank reserves but encountered significant barriers when attempting to import the specimens due to partial non-compliance with *Health Canada* regulations. Despite repeated attempts to import an available Filipino donor, the couple was ultimately prevented from bringing the desired samples into Canada and obliged to physically drive across the border into the United States for insemination.

27 Note that this number emerges largely from popular media, not scientific sources, and from a May 2011 article written by Toronto journalist Danielle Groen, who investigated the status of ReproMed as Canada's last domestic sperm bank. Groen interviewed a number of clinical practitioners, including the medical director of ReproMed, Dr Alfonso Del Valle, who offered the following statement: "Before these laws came into place, we would have 100 donors at any given time ... As it stands now, we must scramble to have 30 or 35 donors active." Groen also interviewed Samantha Yee, a social worker at Mount Sinai's Centre for Fertility and Reproductive Health, who corroborated this scarcity: "People are very surprised at how few donors there are in the Canadian catalogue." See Danielle Groen, "Down for the Count: There Are Only 35 Sperm Donors Left in All of Canada. Holy Mama, We've Got a Problem," *The Grid* [Toronto], 19 May 2011, http://www.thegridto.com/city/local-news/down-for-the-count. As of the time of writing, Groen's article is hosted on the ReproMed website, http://www.repromed.ca.

28 Tom Blackwell, "Limit Pregnancies by Same Sperm Donor: Fertility Experts," *National Post*, 8 September 2011, http://news.nationalpost.com/2011/09/08/limit-pregnancies-by-same-sperm-donor-fertility-experts.

29 *Donor sibs* is a colloquial term used to discuss the other children who are the offspring of one's sperm donor. It is not universally applied, but those that utilize it seek to describe the genetic relationship between their children and other offspring of the same donor, which may not translate into a social relationship. See Rosanna Hertz and Jane Mattes, "Donor-Shared Siblings or Genetic Strangers: New Families, Clans, and the Internet" (2011) 32:9 Journal of Family Issues 1129–55 at 1136.

30 For an in-depth analysis of this looming impact on queer people in Canada, see Stu Marvel, "Tony Danza Is My Sperm Donor?: Queer Kinship

and the Impact of Canadian Regulations around Sperm Donation" (2013) 25:2 CJWL 221–48.

31 *Ibid*. See also Ross, Steele, and Epstein, *supra* note 5.

32 All names have been changed.

33 For an investigation of how Canadians are accessing donor ova and the attendant medical risks to donors, see Alison Motluk, "The Human Egg Trade: How Canada's Fertility Laws Are Failing Donors, Doctors, and Parents," *The Walrus* (April 2010), 30–7, http://thewalrus.ca/the-human-egg-trade.

34 See the chapter by Susan Drummond in this volume.

35 While Canadians cannot *privately* transact the purchase of human sperm under criminal penalty, they may purchase donor semen from licensed sperm banks. While this article will not explore the ethical hypocrisy of allowing payment for commercially traded gametes from other legal jurisdictions, it does call into question the *AHRA*'s interdictions against payment for human reproductive material. This ban originates in the wording of the Baird Report, which stated: "To allow commercial exchanges of this type [buying and selling embryos, use of financial incentives, etc.] would undermine respect for human life and dignity and lead to the commodification of women and children": *supra* note 18, vol. 2 at 718.

36 *Supra* note 26 at s 1 [emphasis added].

37 Health Canada, Health Products and Food Branch Inspectorate, *Guidance on the Processing and Distribution of Semen for Assisted Conception Regulations* (GUIDE-0041) (Ottawa: Government of Canada, 2004), http://www.hc-sc.gc.ca/dhp-mps/compli-conform/info-prod/don/gui_41_tc-tm-eng.php.

38 For an analysis of the impact of the *Semen Regulations* on LGBTQ people in Canada, see R. Epstein, "The Relationship That Has No Name: Known Sperm Donors, the Canadian Semen Regulations, and LGBTQ People," in *Queering Motherhood: Narrative and Theoretical Perspectives*, ed. M.F. Gibson (Toronto: Demeter Press, 2014).

39 All participant names have been changed.

40 Epstein for the AHRA/LGBTQ Working Group, *supra* note 3 at 6.

41 *Ibid* at 7. There is also the related issue of custody, should a known donor choose to later claim legal parentage of the child. The documentation from a fertility clinic in which a known donor was masquerading as a sexual partner would have the known donor registered as "partner." This may make it more difficult for the mother to prove intent in case of custodial challenge.

42 For a philosophical meditation on the psychic lives of those who live outside of normative kinship, with specific reference to children born through donor insemination, see Judith Butler, "Is Kinship Always Already Heterosexual?" (2002) 13:1 Differences: A Journal of Feminist Cultural Studies 14–44.

43 Health Canada, Therapeutic Products Program, *Technical Requirements for Therapeutic Donor Insemination* (Ottawa: Government of Canada, 2000), http://www.hc-sc.gc.ca/dhp-mps/brgtherap/applic-demande/guides/semen-sperme-acces/semen-sperme_directive-eng.php.

44 *Ibid* at 4, s 2(1)(e). A challenge to the constitutionality of this policy in specific relation to blood donations by men who have since 1977 had sexual relations with other men was dismissed by an Ontario court in 2010, determining that the *Charter* did not apply as the respondent was a private rather than a governmental entity. See *Canadian Blood Services v Freeman*, 2010 ONSC 4885, 217 CRR (2d) 153. See also *infra* note 54 on the latest position of Canadian Blood Services.

45 Trans woman: a male-to-female transsexual (MTF); someone who was assigned as male at birth and identifies as female. Trans man: a female-to-male transsexual (FTM); someone who was assigned as female at birth and identifies as male. While hormone replacement therapy and surgical treatments will lead to loss of reproductive potential in male-to-female transsexuals, if they have stored spermatozoa before starting hormonal therapy these gametes may be used in the future. See also Paul De Sutter, "Gender Reassignment and Assisted Reproduction: Present and Future Reproductive Options for Transsexual People" (2001) 16:4 Human Reproduction 612–14.

46 *AA v BB*, 2007 ONCA 2, 83 OR (3d) 561 is perhaps the best-known Canadian example of a case in which a man was actively co-parenting with two lesbian women, wherein the court awarded joint parental rights to all three parties. See also *C(MA) v K(M)*, 2009 ONCJ 18, 94 OR (3d) 756 for a more contentious example, in which the parental rights of a lesbian couple were challenged by the gay man who was also the sperm donor.

47 See Epstein for the AHRA/LGBTQ Working Group, *supra* note 3 at 7. *Sexual orientation* is a term for the emotional, physical, romantic, sexual, and spiritual attraction, desire, or affection for another person (e.g., gay, straight, bisexual, lesbian), whereas *sexual identity* refers to one's identification to self (and others) of one's sexual orientation. Sexual identity is not always the same as sexual orientation and/or sexual behaviour (what people do sexually).

48 *Susan Doe v Canada (Attorney General)* (2006), 79 OR (3d) 586, 25 RFL (6th) 384 (SC), aff'd 2007 ONCA 11, 84 OR (3d) 81.

49 For an extended treatment of the case, see Sandra Dughman, *Doe v. Canada: Lesbian Women, Assisted Conception, and a Relational Approach to Rights*, LLM Thesis, University of Toronto Faculty of Law, 2009, T-Space University of Toronto Research Repository, https://tspace.library.utoronto.ca.

50 According to recently approved Canadian HIV Pregnancy Planning Guidelines, "as all fertility clinics should be operating using Canadian Standards Association procedures for universal precautions and infection control, *there are no scientific grounds on which to refuse services to people living with HIV*": Mona R. Loutfy *et al.*, "Canadian HIV Planning Pregnancy Guidelines" (2012) 34:6 Journal of Obstetrics and Gynaecology Canada 575–90 at 587 [emphasis in original].

51 This was the first multicentre study of the use of sperm washing in HIV-1-serodiscordant couples, the largest series published to date, and the first with sufficient case numbers to confirm the safety and efficacy of assisted reproduction where sperm washing was used as the primary means of avoiding HIV infection in the female partner. Louis Bujan *et al.*, "Safety and Efficacy of Sperm Washing in HIV-1-Serodiscordant Couples Where the Male Is Infected: Results from the European CREATE Network" (2007) 21:14 AIDS 1909–1914 at 1909. See also James D.M. Nicopoullos *et al.*, "A Decade of Sperm Washing: Clinical Correlates of Successful Insemination Outcome" (2010) 25:8 Human Reproduction 1869–1876; Lynn T. Matthews and Joia S. Mukherjee, "Strategies for Harm Reduction Among HIV-Affected Couples Who Want to Conceive" (2009) 13 Suppl 1 AIDS and Behavior S5–S11.

52 Bujan *et al., ibid*, at 1913.

53 Canadian Blood Services has publicly acknowledged that these criteria may be outdated in regard to blood donation, and announced in 2013 that it had "received approval from Health Canada to reduce the current men who have sex with men (MSM) deferral period from indefinite to five years from last MSM activity," and would implement this change effective 22 July 2013: Canadian Blood Services, News Release, "Changes to Blood Donor Guidelines: Deferral Policy for Men Who Have Sex with Men Reduced from Indefinite to Five Years," 22 May 2013, http://www.blood.ca/CentreApps/Internet/UW_V502_MainEngine.nsf/page/MSM.

54 See *supra* note 23 on the multiplicities of embodiment and kinship formation within LGBTQ communities.

55 Eight years after the *AHRA* received Royal Assent, key sections of the Act that survived the constitutional challenge and remain *intra vires* are still

not in force. See *infra* note 60 for Health Canada's position on allowable expenses under s 12. See also *infra* note 69 for a position that challenges the presumed exploitation and corrosive power dynamic of paid surrogacy arrangements.

56 Trans men may of course also act as surrogates; however, we know of no such cases to date.

57 See *supra* note 22 for a detailed description of different types of surrogacy.

58 In 2013, the RCMP charged Leia Dawn Picard with three counts under *AHRA* s 6(1) [pay, offer to pay, or advertise payment to a female person to be a surrogate mother] and three counts under s 6(2) [accept consideration to arrange the services of a surrogate mother, or advertise or offer to make the arranging], as well as five counts under s 7(1) [purchase, offer to purchase, or advertise for purchase of sperm or ova], and five counts under the *Criminal Code*, RSC 1985, c C-46 [forgery]; Canadian Fertility Consulting Ltd, of which Picard was the CEO, was charged with three counts under 6(1), five counts under 7(1), and four counts under s 367. See RCMP, News Release, "RCMP Charge Owner of Human Fertility Consulting Business," 15 February 2013, RCMP, http://www.rcmp-grc.gc.ca/on/news-nouvelles/2013/13-02-15-newmarket-eng.htm. These appear to be the first criminal charges under the *AHRA*: Alana Cattapan and Audrey L'Espérance, "Strict Enforcement of Assisted Human Reproduction Act is a Backward Step" (editorial opinion), *Toronto Star*, 1 March 2013,: *Toronto Star* http://www.thestar.com/opinion/editorialopinion/2013/03/01/strict_enforcement_of_assisted_human_reproduction_act_is_a_backward_step.html. Picard and CFC pled guilty and were fined $60,000; the forgery charges were dropped: Tom Blackwell, "Canadian Fertility Consultant Received $31K for Unwittingly Referring Parents to U.S. 'Baby-Selling' Ring," *National Post*, 15 December 2013, http://news.nationalpost.com/2013/12/15/canadian-fertility-consultant-received-about-30000-for-unwittingly-referring-parents-to-u-s-baby-selling-ring. This was the first prosecution under the *AHRA*: Blackwell, *ibid*. On the RCMP investigation, see Tom Blackwell, "Ontario Fertility Raid Linked to U.S. 'Baby-Selling' Scandal," *National Post*, 5 March 2012, http://news.nationalpost.com/2012/03/05/ontario-fertility-raid-linked-to-u-s-baby-selling-scandal.

59 Section 12 is not yet in force and Health Canada has not yet issued regulations. They have provided the following clarification regarding this regulatory vacuum: "Regulations regarding reimbursement are currently being developed to clarify what types of expenditures will be allowed and how the activity will be licensed. Until the licensing scheme

and regulations are in place, donors may be reimbursed up to the actual amount of their legitimate expenditures without a licence." Health Canada, "Frequently Asked Questions," http://www.hc-sc.gc.ca/hl-vs/reprod/hc-sc/faq/index-eng.php.

60 With regard to the validity of impugned provisions of the *AHRA* in upholding the criminal law power and protecting public morality, McLachlin CJ reasoned as follows: "In summary, morality constitutes a valid criminal law purpose. The role of the courts is to ensure that such a criminal law in pith and substance relates to conduct that Parliament views as contrary to our central moral precepts, and that there is a consensus in society that the regulated activity engages a moral concern of fundamental importance" (*supra* note 1 at para 51). The Chief Justice also drew specific attention to the role of s 12 in preventing Canadian morality from "crossing the line" into commercialized reproductive activities: "This [s 12] is the line that prohibits that which is considered inappropriate commodification, and permits that which is considered acceptable reimbursement. *Threat of drawing this line raises fundamental moral questions*" [emphasis added] (*supra* note 1 at para 111).

61 *AHRA, supra* note 17, ss 12(1)–(3), quoting s 12(3)(b).

62 Sherry Levitan, "Surrogacy in Canada," http://www.fertilitylaw.ca/surrogacy.shtml.

63 With regard to the promulgation of regulations under section 12, Toronto lawyer Sherry Levitan writes: "It's been eight years, and I don't expect to see them in my lifetime … All I can do is lay it out for a client, and they can tell me where their comfort level is": quoted in Michael McKiernan, "Fertility Lawyers Press Ahead Despite Legal Vacuum," *Law Times*, 9 July 2012, http://www.lawtimesnews.com/Focus-On/Fertility-lawyers-press-ahead-despite-legal-vacuum. See also the chapter by Susan Drummond in this volume.

64 Tom Blackwell, "Canada's Murky Legal World of Surrogate-Consultants and Human-Egg Buyers," *National Post*, 9 March 2012, http://news.nationalpost.com/2012/03/09/canadas-murky-legal-world-of-surrogate-consultants-and-human-egg-buyers.

65 As Maneesha Deckha argues convincingly, anxiety over a potential marketplace of human commodities is one of the two central factors that have propelled the *AHRA*. The other is what she terms "species anxiety," or "the phobia that individuals manifest at the thought of the human body intermingling with another species at the reproductive, genetic, cellular, or other body part level": Maneesha Deckha, "Holding onto Humanity: Commodification and Species Anxiety in Canada's Assisted

Human Reproduction *Act*" (2009) 5:1 Unbound: Harv J Legal Left 21–54 at 22.

66 For discussions of reproductive tourism and the bioethical and feminist issues at play within the globalization of commercial surrogacy, see Eric Blyth and Abigail Farrand, "Reproductive Tourism – a Price Worth Paying for Reproductive Autonomy?" (2005) 25:1 Crit Soc Pol'y 91–114; C.A. Jones and L.G. Keith, "Medical Tourism and Reproductive Outsourcing: The Dawning of a New Paradigm for Healthcare" (2006) 51:6 International Journal of Fertility and Women's Medicine 1–5; Richard F. Storrow, "Quest for Conception: Fertility Tourists, Globalization and Feminist Legal Theory" (2005) 57 Hastings LJ 295–330; Richard F. Storrow, "*The Handmaid's Tale* of Fertility Tourism: Passports and Third Parties in the Religious Regulation of Assisted Conception" (2005) 12 Tex Wesleyan L Rev 189–211.

67 For examples of the radical feminist view, see Gena Corea, *The Mother Machine: Reproductive Technologies from Artificial Insemination to Artificial Wombs* (New York: Harper & Row, 1985); Janice Raymond, *Women as Wombs: Reproductive Technologies and the Battle over Women's Freedom* (New York: Harper, 1993); and Jocelyn Scutt, ed., *The Baby Machine: Reproductive Technology and the Commercialisation of Motherhood* (London: Merlin, 1990). For commentators who argue for more nuanced views of women's autonomy and choice, see Rosalind Petchesky, "Reproductive Freedom: Beyond 'A Woman's Right to Choose'" (1980) 5:4 Signs 661–85; Judith Lorber, "Choice, Gift, or Patriarchal Bargain? Women's Consent to *in vitro* Fertilization in Male Infertility" (1989) 4:3 Hypatia 23–36; Marilyn Strathern, *Reproducing the Future: Anthropology, Kinship and the New Reproductive Technologies* (Manchester: Manchester University Press, 1992); and Sarah Franklin, *Embodied Progress: A Cultural Account of Assisted Conception* (London: Routledge, 1997).

68 Karen Busby and Delaney Vun, "Revisiting *The Handmaid's Tale*: Feminist Theory Meets Empirical Research on Surrogate Mothers" (2010) 26 Can J Fam L 13–93.

69 *Ibid* at 46.This is substantiated by other studies carried out in English-speaking countries, including Bree Kessler's estimation that military wives accounted for 50 per cent of gestational surrogate carriers at clinics in Texas and California in 2008: Bree Kessler, "Recruiting Wombs: Surrogates as the New Security Moms" (2009) 37:1–2 Women's Studies Quarterly 167–82.

70 Busby and Vun, *ibid*, at 55.

71 Sara Cohen, "Dear Margaret, It's Me, Sara," *Fertility Law Canada*, 5 April 2012 (blog), http://www.fertilitylawcanada.com/1/post/2012/04/dear-margaret-its-me-sara.html.

72 "Paid Surrogacy Driven Underground in Canada: CBC Report," *CBC News*, 2 May 2007, http://www.cbc.ca/news/technology/paid-surrogacy-driven-underground-in-canada-cbc-report-1.691254; Shireen Kashmeri, "Unraveling Surrogacy in Ontario, Canada: An Ethnographic Inquiry on the Influence of Canada's Assisted Human Reproduction Act (2004), Surrogacy Contracts, Parentage Laws, and Gay Fatherhood," MA thesis, Concordia University, 2008.

73 There are a large number of online resources designed to connect surrogates with intended parents, many of which specifically target Canadians. While none of the following websites explicitly detail the illegal fees one may be expected to pay when hiring a surrogate, many of the forums and classified ads do discuss the transfer of payment. To list just a few: Surrogate Mother (http://www.surrogatemother.com), Surromoms Online Classifieds (http://www.surromomsonline.com/classifieds/index.htm), Canadian Surrogacy Options (http://www.canadiansurrogacyoptions.com), Invitro Fertilization New Jersey (http://www.ivfnj.com/html/can-patients.html), Circle Surrogacy Online (http://www.circlesurrogacy.com/index.php/en?lang=gb-en), Surrogacy in Canada Online (http://surrogacy.ca). See also Motluk, *supra* note 36.

74 Cf. Epstein for the AHRA/LGBTQ Working Group, *supra* note 3.

75 See Committee on Professional Standards, CFAS ART Lab Special Interest Group, *Guidelines for Qualification and Responsibilities for Each Assisted Reproductive Technology Laboratory Professional Position in Canada* (approved 27 February 2009 by the Canadian Fertility and Andrology Society Board of Directors), www.cfas.ca. While organizations like CFAS are working to develop standardized guidelines for mandatory application across Canada, this has not yet been implemented.

76 While national accreditation for assisted reproductive technology does exist in Canada (see *infra* note 82), it is not mandatory. Suggested clinical practice guidelines for reproductive endocrinology and infertility have been advanced by the Society of Obstetricians and Gynaecologists of Canada, but as of writing these are not binding in any province or territory. See http://sogc.org/clinical-practice-guidelines.

77 Ontario, *Raising Expectations: Recommendations of the Expert Panel on Infertility and Adoption* (Toronto: 2009) (chair: David Johnston) at 100, Ontario Ministry of Children and Youth Services,http://www.children.gov.on.ca/htdocs/English/infertility/report/index.aspx.

78 Counselling Special Interest Group, Canadian Fertility and Andrology Society, *Assisted Human Reproduction Counselling Practice Guidelines*

(December 2009), http://www.cfas.ca/images/stories/pdf/csig_counselling_practiceguidelines__december_2009_.pdf.

79 Canadian constitutional law expert Peter Hogg made this remark during a conference held at the University of Toronto, "*Reference Re Assisted Human Reproduction Act*: Implications of the Supreme Court's Decision," 4–5 November 2011.

80 Under section 92(7) of the *Constitution Act, 1867* (UK), 30 & 31 Vict, c 3, reprinted in RSC 1985, App II, No. 5, the provincial level of government is granted exclusive authority over the "establishment, maintenance, and management of hospitals, asylums, charities, and eleemosynary institutions in and for the province, other than marine hospitals." In practical terms, the awards the majority of legislative power in the area of health care to the provinces. The *AHRA Reference* has maintained sections 8 and 12 *intra vires* the federal government.

81 Accreditation Canada is a national organization that helps health service organizations improve the quality of care and service they provide to their clients. They have developed 'Qmentum' standards at a system-wide level for Leadership for Assisted Reproductive Technology, and service excellence standards in the following three areas: Assisted Reproductive Technology Standards for Clinical Services; Assisted Reproductive Technology Standards for Laboratory Services; and Assisted Reproductive Technology Standards for Working with Third Party Donors. None of these standards are publicly available without fee.

82 *Supra* note 78 at 96. This is not to suggest that no standards are in place. Health Canada regularly inspects the offices and clinics of all physicians who are distributors of semen. Physicians are required to meet certain minimum requirements in terms of documentation of compliance with the technical specifications.

83 CFAS *Assisted Human Reproduction Counselling Practice Guidelines*, *supra* note 79 at 11.

84 A recently published glossary of AHR terms defines "infertility (clinical definition) [as] a disease of the reproductive system defined by the failure to achieve a clinical pregnancy after 12 months or more of regular unprotected sexual intercourse": F. Zegers-Hochschild *et al.*, "The International Committee for Monitoring Assisted Reproductive Technology (ICMART) and the World Health Organization (WHO) Revised Glossary of ART Terminology, 2009" (2009) 92:5 *Fertility and Sterility* 1520 at 1522. This standard, heterosexist definition cannot account for many forms of sexual behaviour among LGBTQ people, which may be regular and unprotected but will never result in a pregnancy. When

this model of infertility is in play, LGBTQ people fall out of the diagnostic system.

85 As there are no standard practices across fertility clinics in Canada (or even across a single province), each clinic will differ regarding what it determines to be mandatory testing.

86 Epstein, *supra* note 3 at 3.

87 See, for example, William Buckett, "Infertility Treatment for Non-Traditional Families" (Fall 2011), Infertility Awareness Association of Canada, http://www.iaac.ca/en/632-613-infertility-treatment-for-non-traditional-families-by-william-buckett-md-mrcog-fall-2011.

88 For a more detailed discussion of the barriers that LGBTQ people commonly experience when accessing AHR services, as well as recommendations to counter such barriers, see Ross, Steele, and Epstein, "Lesbian and Bisexual Women's Recommendations for Improving the Provision of Assisted Reproductive Technology Services," *supra* note 5. See also Epstein for the AHRA/LGBTQ Working Group, *supra* note 3.

14 Regulatory Failure: The Case of the Private-for-Profit IVF Sector

COLLEEN M. FLOOD AND BRYAN THOMAS

Introduction

In December 2010, the Supreme Court of Canada ruled that significant portions of the *Assisted Human Reproduction Act* (*AHRA*) were *ultra vires* federal jurisdiction. This decision essentially found that only the provinces have the authority to regulate *in vitro* fertilization, while allowing for a federal ban with criminal law penalties on the buying and selling of sperm, ova, and surrogacy services.[1] In our view it is an astonishing oversight that the SCC in its decision did not mention or reflect the market context of IVF services in Canada – that is, on the fact that the vast majority of IVF services are delivered in private, for-profit clinics and are privately financed. Quebec became the notable exception in August 2010, when it moved to provide public funding for three cycles of the procedure.[2] Recent developments indicate that the move may be short-lived: the Quebec government, faced with rising costs, brought forth draft legislation in late 2014 that will drastically curtail public funding for IVF services and impose various barriers to access.[3]

The literature on regulating IVF has focused largely on ethical concerns as they relate to the exploitation of persons through the commercialization of surrogacy and the commercial procurement of eggs and sperm.[4] There has been almost no emphasis on the need to regulate IVF to protect individuals and couples seeking IVF services in terms of quality, safety, and consumer protection. We will argue that these concerns are particularly salient in the context of IVF delivery in Canada, given that the provider market is dominated by private for-profit interests.

The problem of underregulation is not unique to IVF. Publicly financed health care attracts considerable regulation and oversight across Canada, whereas privately financed health care attracts comparatively little.[5] Interestingly, in Quebec, the move to publicly finance IVF coincided with a move to regulate the practice, further supporting our thesis that public care attracts more regulation than private care, despite the equal or greater need for regulation in the private sector.[6] Unfortunately, federal regulation in this area, which the Supreme Court has now largely overturned, and the laws promulgated in Quebec, speak primarily to restricting reproductive freedom rather than improving the safety and quality of IVF services or strengthening consumer protections. This perhaps can be attributed to the initial use of the federal criminal law power to regulate the field and the consequent need to define IVF as "harmful" or "morally wrong." We do not dispute the SCC's finding that much of the regulation needed for the IVF sector would properly fall under provincial purview (e.g., advertising, informed consent, and licensing for quality and safety). However, the jurisdictional debate has framed the regulatory challenges in criminal law terms, which arguably has coloured the regulatory choices discussed and the regulations adopted at the provincial level, as we will illustrate in the Quebec context.

In what follows we analyse the regulatory governance of IVF in Ontario and Quebec, arguing that existing regulations are insufficient to address concerns regarding quality, safety, and consumer protection. We acknowledge that private financing can make access to such services a challenge for many; thus our regulatory prescriptions seek to be as efficient as possible, so as to enhance the safety and quality of IVF services without unduly increasing the potential cost of services. We do not advocate for or against public funding for IVF; rather, we simply ask what regulations are necessary to protect patients in light of the existing context of private delivery and/or financing. Our argument is that regulatory attention needs to focus less on arbitrary restrictions of reproductive freedom and more on protecting patients.

The Context of IVF Delivery and Financing in Canada

To understand the risks inherent in the fertility industry and to better analyse the existing regulatory responses to those risks, we need to understand the context of IVF funding and delivery in Canada. We explore this context here.

First, with respect to delivery, there are currently just under thirty IVF clinics in Canada, most of which are for-profit.[7] For example, in

Ontario, there are eleven private IVF clinics that perform the procedure outside of a public hospital. In contrast, five public hospitals (i.e., run on a not-for-profit basis) are classified as IVF hospitals, and of these, only three currently run IVF clinics (which are not necessarily run on a not-for-profit basis).[8] Quebec seems to be an outlier in this regard. There are five IVF clinics in the province, three of which are run on a not-for-profit basis through public hospitals. The private clinics, however, have multiple branches, so the private sector still has a strong presence in IVF delivery.[9] The Quebec government had anticipated an even larger role for not-for-profits when it introduced public funding;[10] it is too early to say how its subsequent decision to retrench public funding (explored below) will affect this.

Second, with respect to financing, throughout Canada (apart from Quebec) most IVF is privately financed. Some provinces, like Manitoba, offer couples an income tax refund for a portion of the costs of infertility treatment, but the couples must still finance the treatment out of their own private funds.[11] Usually, private financing means that a couple will have to cover the cost of treatment out of their own pockets since private health insurance companies in Canada generally do not cover IVF.[12] Some private insurance plans will cover the cost of fertility drugs, but a single cycle of IVF may still cost over $10,000,[13] and individuals/couples may have to endure multiple cycles of IVF before a successful conception and many may never conceive.

There are two exceptions to private financing. In Ontario, IVF is publicly insured through the Ontario Health Insurance Plan (OHIP) when the indicator of infertility is a bilateral tube blockage (i.e., both fallopian tubes in the female are blocked), but only if this condition has not been caused by a voluntary sterility procedure.[14] This is a narrow exception, constituting approximately 20 per cent of all IVF procedures in Ontario in 2004.[15] Every other indicator of infertility is uninsured and must be covered privately; that includes all forms of male infertility. Interestingly, IVF was fully covered in Ontario from 1983 to 1993; however, at that time, the procedure could only be performed in public hospitals (which are subject to much greater regulation).

For what may turn out to have been but a brief window, the second (major) exception to private financing is/was the province of Quebec. As of August 2010, residents enlisted under the provincial health insurance plan, RAMQ, could be funded for up to three stimulated cycles of IVF or up to six natural or modified natural cycles of IVF, provided that only one embryo was transferred at a time (to a maximum of two or three embryos, depending on the patient's age).[16] The scheme – public funding, combined with limits on multiple transfers – was meant to avert the heightened medical expenses associated with multiple births. Accordingly, private financing of IVF services was forbidden unless the patient had unsuccessfully undergone the insured IVF services (with associated limitations on multiple implantation) or the patient did not qualify for RAMQ coverage because of age or residency status.[17]

The fact that Quebec at present publicly finances IVF, has higher levels of public delivery of IVF, and has specific legislation regulating the practice of IVF has made the province exceptional three times over. Although the scheme has succeeded in lowering multiple births, unanticipated demand for IVF services has meant that its overall costs are now deemed unsustainable, and at time of writing Quebec has proposed shifting to a tax credit scheme. Under the proposed "sliding scale" tax credits, families earning less that $50,000 a year would receive a tax credit covering 80 per cent of the procedure, while families earning over $120,000 would be covered for only 20 per cent.[18] But as in Manitoba, couples would have to finance the care at first out of pocket – if able – and seek the tax credits at a later date.

Regulatory Challenges Associated with IVF and Privatized Health Care

Invasive medical procedures generally entail certain risks, and IVF is no exception. The IVF process itself carries risks for both the mother and the potential future child. For example, if more than one embryo is transferred at a time, there is a risk that multiple pregnancies will occur, a condition that can cause anaemia, toxaemia, and kidney trouble for the mother, in addition to a more difficult delivery and a longer recovery time.[19] There is a higher risk of premature birth and consequently low birth weight in children born in multiples (i.e., twins or higher).[20] There is also a risk of infection associated with the extraction of ova as part of the IVF process, which in turn can cause or exacerbate existing fertility problems. Studies have found that this occurs in 0.6 to 1.3 per cent of cases.[21] Moreover, the fertility drugs used as part of IVF treatment carry the risk of ovarian hyperstimulation syndrome for the mother, and especially for younger women. In very rare cases, this can be life-threatening.[22]

These are risks associated with IVF regardless of where the procedure is performed and how it is financed; however, private clinics may engage in activities that exacerbate health risks in order to improve profits. As far as we are aware, there are no studies analysing the differential risk of the delivery of IVF services in public or not-for-profit settings as opposed to private for-profit hospitals and clinics. Nonetheless, evidence from other areas of delivery should inform the appropriate regulatory approach (at least until more specific research is conducted). Important evidence in this regard is provided by Devereaux and colleagues, who conducted a meta-analysis of fifteen smaller studies (reviewing a total of 26,000 hospitals and 38 million patients). This study compared the adjusted mortality rates of not-for-profit and for-profit hospitals between 1982 and 1995.[23] Adjusting for factors such as the facility's teaching status and the severity of illnesses treated, the analysis found that private for-profit hospitals are associated with an increased risk of death (relative risk [RR] 1.020).[24] The authors note that not-for-profit facilities serve populations with greater disease severity, which suggests that the disparity in mortality rates may even be an underestimate.[25] When explaining this disparity, the authors note that investors in for-profit facilities expect a return of 10 to 15 per cent – a profit that has to be earned while competing with non-profits that enjoy tax exemptions and offer smaller reimbursement packages to senior administrators. For-profit administrators are rewarded for achieving or exceeding this profit margin, thus creating a significant motivation to cut costs.[26] The study avoided, where possible, adjusting for variables under the control of hospital administrators that may be influenced by profit considerations and that may affect mortality, including staffing levels (e.g., nurses per bed, pharmacists per bed).[27] Other evidence suggests that understaffing may be a cause of the heightened mortality in for-profits: two studies that did adjust for staffing levels (in particular, for registered nurses as a proportion of all nurses and for the proportion of board-certified specialists among all physicians) found that well-staffed for-profit facilities had reduced mortality rates.[28]

A second systematic review and meta-analysis conducted by Devereaux and colleagues, this time comparing the mortality rates of private for-profit and private not-for-profit dialysis facilities in the United States, similarly associated a higher mortality rate with for-profit clinics (RR 1.08).[29] The study combined the results of eight observational studies with a median of 1,342 facilities per study, amounting to 500,000 patient-years of data. Of these studies, six showed significant increased mortality in for-profit dialysis facilities and one showed non-significant increased mortality.[30] This study is significant because it was conducted entirely within the realm of *publicly funded* medicine, as the US government since 1973 has funded dialysis under Medicare (the public insurance plans for Americans over sixty-five).[31] It thus suggests that merely including for-profit facilities *within* a public insurance scheme will not in and of itself reduce concerns regarding quality and safety. Moreover, the implications of this study's findings are deeply troubling. Between 20 and 25 per cent of in-centre hemodialysis patients in the United States die each year. Based on the 8 per cent relative risk of death and the fact that 75 per cent of patients attend for-profit facilities for this treatment, the authors estimate that there are 2,500 excessive premature deaths annually in the United States in for-profit dialysis centres.[32] As in the previous study, Devereaux and colleagues note that the issue is at least partly one of cost-cutting through inadequate staffing. Studies show that for-profit dialysis centres employ fewer personnel per dialysis run and less highly skilled personnel in general.[33] The study also found that for-profit facilities use shorter durations of dialysis treatments, which are associated with higher mortality.[34]

A 2005 systematic review by Michael Hillmer on nursing home ownership and profit status and quality of care since 1990 likewise found that for-profit ownership is more strongly associated than not-for-profit ownership with poor quality of care.[35] The review, which encompassed thirty-eight studies, screened for adequate risk adjustment and looked at indicators such as structural quality (e.g., staffing levels), process quality (e.g., the use of restraints), and outcomes (e.g., pressure ulcers, falls, and mortality). Of eighty-one results drawn from these studies, thirty-three results found that for-profit status resulted in lower quality of care whereas only six results found that not-for-profit status resulted in lower quality of care.[36] For instance, not-for-profit nursing homes were found to have a higher staff skill mixture and lower nursing turnover rate, both of which have been linked to better patient outcomes. One study suggested that for-profit institutions substitute medication for staffing levels.[37] The review also found that for-profit centres had a higher rate of pressure ulcers. This could be a further result of lower staffing levels, or perhaps the result of admitting more patients with pressure sores. The authors commented that this would be unlikely given that these patients would be more expensive to care for and thus a counterintuitive choice for a profit-maximizing enterprise.[38]

Despite the aforementioned studies, there remains significant disagreement among scholars as to the connection between profit status and quality of care. McClellan and Staiger, for example, while noting that on average not-for-profit status appears to be associated with lower mortality rates, emphasize that there is substantial variation in quality of care *within* these ownership types and suggest that the location and size of a hospital may have a greater impact on mortality than profit status *per se*.[39] In general, there tends to be a strong negative relationship between patient volume and mortality.[40] In a study of specific heart disease outcomes (mortality and complications) among elderly US Medicare patients from the mid-1980s to the early 1990s, McClellan and Staiger found that when not-for-profit, for-profit, government-owned, and teaching hospitals were compared, higher mortality in for-profit and government-owned hospitals could be explained by the fact that these hospitals are generally smaller than not-for-profit and teaching hospitals.[41]

The essay concluded that there was huge variation within profit status groups, even if not-for-profit hospitals seem better in the national average.[42] In other words, to merely point to the national differences between for-profit and not-for-profit may be to mask the underlying factors affecting quality that are unrelated to profit status *per se*. The study also pointed to some potentially beneficial effects from having a mix of for-profit and not-for-profit facilities within a health system: for-profit hospitals arguably provide an impetus for others to improve; they also tend to locate in areas of poor quality and to leave areas in which quality is rising (for business reasons).[43]

In our view, on balance, there is compelling evidence that for-profit clinics give rise to special cause for concern regarding quality and safety, although the exact reasons for this have yet to be teased out (e.g., perhaps such clinics are more likely to be small and thus to have lower quality, or perhaps the profit motive is incentivizing cuts in quality, or perhaps both these factors are in play). Because of the debate in the literature, we are cautious about overattributing quality concerns to for-profit clinics. Nonetheless, the scale of the studies conducted by Devereaux and others at the very least gives us reason to pause and consider the dangers that a profit motive could pose in the delivery of health care services. We argue that policy-makers must keep in mind the factors identified by Devereaux and others when considering the most appropriate regulatory framework for IVF services, given that for-profit delivery is characteristic of much of this sector.

Apart from concerns regarding measureable differences in quality and safety outcomes, the commercial context of privately financed treatments delivered by for-profit institutions raises other concerns from the perspective of patients. It is widely accepted that there is an information asymmetry between the physician and the patient, irrespective of where treatment is procured. In other words, patients often rely on physicians to disclose medical information about risks, quality, safety, and so on. When combined with the profit motive of many private clinics, this problem of information asymmetry has the potential to become a conflict of interest that could lead physicians to prescribe unnecessary treatments, to present the risks associated with IVF in a certain light, to neglect to inform a patient about non-medical or less invasive alternatives, or to otherwise present information to a patient in a self-interested way. These are regulatory concerns in their own right, and moreover, they carry the risk of compounding safety and quality concerns.

In IVF treatment there is an incentive to transfer multiple embryos at one time so as to increase the likelihood that one will implant and result in pregnancy. This would increase a clinic's pregnancy rate; it would also be an attractive option for couples without the financial resources to undergo multiple cycles of expensive IVF treatment. Unfortunately, this practice increases the risk of multiple pregnancy, which, as we noted earlier, poses health risks to both mother and child as well as significant costs for the public health care system.[44] If private clinics want the additional business these couples could bring, this may affect how these risks are presented to patients.

Another concern regarding for-profit IVF clinics is how they advertise their services. A clinic may present only those statistics that reflect favourably on its practice. For example, a given clinic's fertilization, pregnancy, and live birth rates can vary widely,[45] and thus it could paint a very different picture of its success by omitting factors that affect the IVF process, such as maternal age and health and the number of embryos transferred. Since patients rely heavily on their physicians to provide all of the relevant information they will need to make a decision, this has huge implications for the quality of the patient's consent.

Self-referral by doctors is another concern. Choudhry and colleagues note that a physician who works part-time in the public *and* private sectors may, at a much higher rate than normal, refer public patients to a private clinic where he or she has an ownership or other economic interest.[46] Similarly, many IVF clinics offer their own diagnostic services and have the expertise to diagnose infertility and prescribe treatment.[47] This creates a risk that physicians may diagnose infertility and then sell IVF treatment as well as costly add-ons such as intracytoplasmic sperm injection (ICSI) in order to make a profit, even when it is not strictly necessary or in the patient's best interests.

In summary, in addition to the regulatory concerns surrounding IVF in any context, the private for-profit context introduces or heightens a number of additional concerns because of the potential for conflicts of interest. With regard to safety and quality of care, there are concerns that for-profit clinics may skimp on factors associated with higher quality, such as the volume of trained staff, in order to maximize profits. With regard to informed consent, there is a concern that clinics will not fully or properly apprise patients of the real risks of certain practices, such as multiple embryo transfer. From a consumer protection perspective, there is a concern that clinics will advertise only average success rates (as opposed to their own particular success rate) in order to gain business. Likewise, there is a concern that physicians engaging in self-referral or other kickback arrangements will favour the interests of their clinic over the interests of their patients. Next we turn to ask to what extent the existing regulatory framework governing IVF (direct and/or indirect) addresses these concerns.

The Inadequacy of Existing Regulations: Ontario as a Case Study

In 2004 the federal *AHRA* divided activities associated with the practice and study of AHR into those that are prohibited and those that ought to be controlled. The province of Quebec asked the SCC to decide whether certain provisions of the *AHRA* that dealt with "controlled activities," such as IVF, were *ultra vires* federal jurisdiction. The Attorney General of Quebec targeted these provisions, arguing that they constituted an attempt to regulate medical practice, an area that has historically fallen within provincial jurisdiction under ss. 92(13) and 92(16) of the *Constitution Act, 1867*.[48] The Attorney General of Canada defended these provisions as a valid use of the federal criminal law power under s. 91(27) of the *Constitution Act, 1867*.[49] In a 4–4–1 split decision released in December 2010, the Court allowed the appeal in part, striking down the provisions that empowered the federal Assisted Human Reproductive Agency to license and regulate the practice of IVF. Relying substantially on the recommendations of the Baird Commission, which had prompted the legislation, Justices LeBel and Deschamps writing the joint reasons for judgment (with Justices Abella and Rothstein concurring) found the pith and substance of these provisions to be regulatory.[50] Moreover, they argued that for a regulatory scheme to be valid criminal law, it must target either a harm or a moral evil, otherwise the criminal law power becomes too broad.[51] In the case of the impugned provisions, no moral evil or harm was identified; indeed, the Baird Commission considered the "controlled" activities beneficial.[52] Note that the Act's "prohibited" activities set out in ss. 5 to 7 were not challenged and therefore remain in force. These include human cloning, screening for sex for non-medical purposes, permanently altering the genome of an embryo so that the alterations would be passed down to descendants, creating chimeras or animal hybrids, paying surrogates or intermediaries to a surrogacy contract, using a surrogate mother under the age of twenty-one, and the sale of gamete material.[53]

As mentioned above, the court essentially ruled that the regulation of the delivery of IVF services lies primarily in the hands of the provinces. Few would contest that it does lie within the power of provinces to regulate the provision of IVF services, but until recently none have taken up this challenge let alone come to a national consensus that would see harmonization of such regulations across the country. The first child conceived through *in vitro* fertilization was born in 1978, the first Canadian child in 1983.[54] It took twenty-one years for the federal government to attempt to (unsuccessfully) regulate the practice through the *AHRA*. In 2010, Quebec became the first province to directly regulate IVF, twenty-seven years after the technology's appearance in Canada. To date, most provinces in Canada resemble Ontario in eschewing direct regulation of the IVF sector, taking instead a light and indirect approach. In what follows we discuss this "light" approach in both Ontario and Quebec and how the status quo does not sufficiently address or attend to the safety, quality, and consumer concerns arising from the delivery of IVF services in the context of private, for-profit clinics.

Safety and Quality of Care

In Ontario, concerns about the safety and quality of IVF procedures in private for-profit clinics are governed by the regulatory regime that applies to health care and health care professionals in general. The *Regulated Health Professions Act* (*RHPA*) empowers the Ontario College of Physicians and Surgeons (CPSO) Discipline Committee to act in cases of professional misconduct.[55] In addition, *Regulation 114/94*, made under the *Medicine Act*, has established a Quality Assurance Committee, also administered through the CPSO.[56] Quality of care and safety in private Ontario clinics are thus subject to professional self-regulation.

Self-regulation can be beneficial in that it provides oversight by experts in the field.[57] However, it has a number of drawbacks. First, it tends not to be proactive. In terms of prevention, there is no regular inspection mechanism in place to uncover breaches of the standards of care. Enforcement generally requires patient complaints to bring concerns to light, which is problematic because patients may not necessarily be able to detect failings in quality and safety. Moreover, patients may not report their complaints if they are concerned about jeopardizing the physician–patient relationship – a particular problem in specialty IVF clinics, which may be monopolies in certain areas. Second, there is a danger that self-regulation will cater to the needs of the profession rather than the needs of the public.[58] For example, under a system of self-regulation, only the most egregious breaches of care tend to attract sanctions. The emphasis is placed on retraining rather than on discipline. While continued education may be a laudable goal, it is arguably a weaker deterrent.

The facilities themselves may likewise be regulated in Ontario. The *Independent Health Facilities Act* (*IHFA*)[59] applies to private non-hospital facilities offering diagnostic or ambulatory care services. Again corroborating our thesis that regulation follows public financing, the *IHFA*'s licensing and regulatory regime applies *only* to providers that deliver publicly insured services and then bill "facility fees" to the province. Regulations currently enacted under the *IHFA* exclude facility fees for costs associated with IVF ("oocyte retrieval or embryo transfer").[60]

Private IVF clinics are, however, subject to the Out-of-Hospital Premises Inspection Program (OHPIP), designed and overseen by the Colleges, which was created in 2010 and applies to facilities that use anaesthetics in their procedures.[61] The Out-of-Hospital Premise Standards, issued in May 2010, are meant to provide detailed standards to guide the inspections,[62] and encompass such matters as infection control, equipment maintenance, emergency protocols, and record keeping. An analysis by the *Toronto Star*, published in 2014, found that 13 per cent of private clinics (of which IVF clinics are but a subset) had not met inspection standards – a failure and conditional pass rate worse than one finds under Ontario's restaurant inspection regime.[63] Moreover, OHPIP standards do not address the IVF-specific concerns about quality, safety, and consumer protection raised above. The indirect regulations and mechanisms currently in place are therefore, in our view, inadequate.

Conflicts of Interest and Informed Consent

In Ontario, the *Health Care Consent Act* (*HCCA*)[64] and the common law apply to all health care settings, including private, for-profit clinics. The *HCCA* requires a patient to be informed of the nature of the treatment, the expected benefits, the material risks, the material side effects, alternative courses of action, and the consequences of forgoing the treatment.[65] The common law on informed consent requires a patient to be informed of the material risks as well as alternative courses of treatment. The physician must also ensure that the patient understands the risks.[66] However, the fact that these laws exist does not mean they are enforced effectively. The *HCCA* is in theory enforced through the *Professional Misconduct Regulation*, made under the *Medicine Act*, which allows physicians to be sanctioned with a suspension or revocation of their licence, conditions placed on their licence, or a substantial fine.[67] Unfortunately, it is unclear precisely how this regulation is enforced, since no monitoring mechanism is specifically laid out.

The common law on informed consent can be enforced through the civil court system, but litigation is a weak deterrent. First, a patient may not be aware of his or her rights. Second, IVF is very costly, as is pursuing a lawsuit. Patients may be unable to afford expensive legal claims, especially in addition to their medical expenses. The Canadian Medical Protective Association, the primary insurer of physicians, aggressively litigates claims in Ontario and insulates physicians from damages.[68] This doubly weakens the deterrent because it discourages patients from pursuing litigation and it means that even where litigation is successful, physicians are not hit with the full costs of their negligence. Third, the burden of proof on the patient is a high hurdle to success. Even if a patient is able to establish that her physician did not properly apprise her of the risks, she must then establish causation on the basis that a reasonable person in her shoes would not have undertaken the treatment given the risks disclosed. There are also very broad defences available to physicians.[69] As a result, the success rate for informed consent litigation in the medical context in Ontario is extremely low. Similar problems arise out of the general regulations of informed consent found in Quebec's *Civil Code* and *Professional Code*.[70]

These weaknesses in the protections for informed consent exist in the public *and* private sectors. However, the concerns are amplified in the context of private, for-profit clinics, given the potential for conflicts of interest. Therefore, there is a need for stronger regulations for commercialized procedures such as IVF, to ensure that patients are making decisions based on the fullest information possible. Also necessary are mechanisms to ensure that these regulations are enforced.

Conflicts of Interest and Consumer Protection

Beyond direct physician-to-patient disclosure of medical risks, it is important to ensure accuracy in advertising and in disclosure of financial conflicts of interest. In Ontario, *Regulation 114/94*, made under the *Medicine Act*,[71] prohibits false, misleading, or exaggerated claims in advertising; however, this provision is largely unused. Other activities that may result from a conflict of interest in the delivery of health care services are regulated under the *Health Professionals Procedural Code*, which states that medical duties must always supersede any corporate or proprietary duties,[72] and *Regulation 114/94*, which states that it is a conflict of interest for a member to order a diagnostic or therapeutic service to be performed by a facility in which the member or a member of his or her family has a proprietary interest unless that conflict is disclosed to the patient.[73]

Compounding the weakness of these regulations is inadequate enforcement. In Ontario, it is up to the College of Physicians and Surgeons to enforce these regulations. As we argued above, relying on self-regulation alone is inadequate given the information asymmetry inherent in health care and the desire for patients to maintain care relationships with their physician, both of which result in underreporting of safety and quality issues. The non-IVF-specific regulations on consumer protection and conflicts of interest therefore neglect to address the real risks that patients face in the private, for-profit sector.

The Inadequacy of Existing IVF-Specific Regulations: Quebec as a Case Study

The regulation of assisted reproduction implicates strongly held and fiercely contested ideas about motherhood and parenting, the exploitation of donors and surrogates, and concerns for the dignified treatment of gametes. Thus, even when a province has undertaken to regulate IVF specifically, the resulting "targeted" legislation may insufficiently protect patients and instead focus on limiting reproductive autonomy. In August 2010, the *Act respecting clinical and research activities relating to assisted procreation*[74] and the *Regulation respecting clinical activities related to assisted procreation* came into force in Quebec.[75] To date, Quebec is the only province to enact IVF-specific regulation. Unfortunately, in our view, these regulations do not actually fill in the gaps left by pre-existing provincial laws that address IVF indirectly.

Safety and Quality of Care

In terms of quality and safety, the new Quebec regulations take several measures to mitigate the risks associated with the practice of IVF. First, like the (now overturned) federal *AHRA* before, it sets out a licensing scheme for all clinics that offer IVF services. Licences are issued by the Quebec Minister of Health and Social Services for three-year terms and are subject to renewal.[76] Moreover, licences may be conditional, suspended, revoked, or refused if it is in the public interest or if the facility's practices fall below the standards of quality, safety, or ethics, in the opinion of the Ordre professionnel des médecins du Quebec (i.e., the College of Physicians).[77] To be licensed, IVF facilities must be owned and operated by physicians in good standing (in the case of a corporation, 50 per cent of shares and operational control must rest with physicians), and they must be directed by a physician with a specialist's certificate in obstetrics/gynaecology.[78] Section 4 of the Act also requires a percentage of the members of the board of directors of a clinic to work at the clinic.[79] Furthermore, there is a requirement that the physician who operates the clinic have entered into a service agreement with a hospital so that a patient may be directed there if complications arise.[80] Conducting IVF procedures in a facility that does not have a licence or otherwise does not meet the scheme's requirements constitutes an offence that carries with it a fine of $2,000 to $30,000 for natural persons and $6,000 to $90,000 for legal persons (i.e., corporations).[81]

The licensing requirement for clinics that wish to perform IVF does provide a mechanism through which the province can set standards and monitor clinics; however, the renewal process occurs only every three years. Although the Act empowers the province to appoint inspectors, there does not seem to be a regular inspection mechanism in place to enforce this law. This suggests that there is no proactive regime to prevent harm in the first place – for any action to be triggered, a patient must complain. Moreover, the placing of conditions or suspensions on licences continues to be at the discretion of the College of Physicians.

In other words, even though a government ministry issues the licences, the issuing of sanctions is still a matter of self-regulation. Another problem with enforcement is the potential inadequacy of the penalties. While seemingly severe, the fines an individual or corporation could face for breaking any of the regulations pale in comparison to the very high prices charged for IVF services and the potential for profits. In our view, these enforcement mechanisms may accomplish very little overall in terms of deterrence.

Even assuming these provisions are properly enforced, there are problems with the provisions themselves that likely limit their effectiveness in terms of quality and safety. The requirement that a clinic be owned and operated by doctors is likely an attempt to ensure that the owners/operators are all subject to the code of ethics by which all physicians must abide. It could also be an attempt to guarantee a certain level of care so that patients can trust that qualified individuals are running the clinic without having to do independent research. But the fact that the clinic is owned by doctors does not necessarily mean that every physician working there is experienced in the often complicated procedures associated with IVF. Presumably, a collective of family physicians could own an IVF clinic and still hold a licence. In any event, the evidence that physician-owned clinics perform better in terms of quality of care is mixed at best. One study compared the services provided by physician-owned and corporate-owned clinics in the US dialysis industry and found a correlation between physician ownership and higher quality of care.[82] Other studies have found no difference in the quality of care provided by physician-owned and non-physician-owned facilities.[83] Thus, an ownership requirement may merely lull patients into a false sense of security vis-à-vis the quality of care provided.[84] On the other hand, the requirement that the director be a specialist in obstetrics/gynaecology certainly provides a level of expert oversight. The requirement that a percentage of the board of directors be physicians who work at the clinic likewise ensures that the clinic is operated by physicians in the field. This provides additional oversight similar to that provided by the director, albeit to a lesser degree, since there is no mention of what special qualifications, if any, they must hold. Unfortunately, it does not follow from the director's qualifications that every physician providing services in the clinic will have the same qualifications, or that overall staffing levels will be sufficient, which, as mentioned earlier, is a problem often associated with for-profit clinics more generally.

Quebec's scheme fails to outline or define quality and safety standards for IVF. In terms of safety, the main plank of legal protection is that the procedure is now offered with public financing. Generally, individuals seeking IVF treatment are prevented from accessing private services and must comply with restrictions, such as the restriction on multiple embryo implants, in order to receive government funds.[85] This diminishes the chances of multiple births and the attendant health and safety risks for mother and child. However, these broad-stroke measures to which public financing is tied create additional costs for some patients. We will discuss the drawbacks of these restrictions later in this chapter. Aside from the embryo transfer limits, the *Act* and *Regulation* provide no standards to ensure quality and safety. The scheme seems to depend entirely on the oversight of a director and the board.

Conflicts of Interest and Informed Consent

The new Quebec scheme shows some promise in addressing the issue of informed consent. Under the regulations, there are rules setting out what information must be provided to an IVF patient in order for consent to be truly informed or "enlightened." In particular, the patient must be told of the risk of multiple pregnancies and must be told the specific procedures used and their rates of success.[86] But even this more IVF-tailored informed consent requirement does not fully correct for the information asymmetry so as to protect patients. The success rates among particular IVF clinics vary widely.[87] The law does not specify whether the success rate reported must be the personal rate of the physician or clinic or whether a national average will suffice. Nor does it define what "success rate" actually means. It could refer to the fertilization rate, the implantation rate, the clinical pregnancy rate, the birth rate, or the live birth rate. Ideally, informed consent would mean that the patient is given all of this information. Moreover, as a number of factors may have an impact on the efficacy of IVF treatment, including patient age and health, the indicator of infertility (different forms of infertility carry very different prognoses, not all of which can be treated with IVF), and the number of embryos transferred, success rates should be broken down accordingly. This is a critically important protection when patients are paying privately for treatment, but also when IVF is publicly funded, given the stress and risks associated with IVF treatments. Patients are entitled to know the *true* rates of success of particular clinics. Furthermore, clinics that do not provide accurate information should be sanctioned, and these kind of transgressions need to be made public.

While the Act allows the Minister to create regulatory offences,[88] the regulations do not explicitly state that failing to provide sufficient information is an offence. Thus, the legislation provides no more recourse than in other areas of care for failing to provide full information. Furthermore, the penalty for a person (natural or legal) under the Act ranges from $1,000 to $10,000 – significantly less than the cost of a single course of IVF.[89] On the deterrent side of informed consent, the IVF-specific regulations again miss the mark.

Conflicts of Interest and Consumer Protection

Besides the fact that the disclosure requirement is incomplete, the new legislation on IVF does not offer any additional consumer protection provisions and does not provide any regulations to prevent practices that result from conflicts of interest in the private sphere (e.g., self-referral). It could be that because Quebec anticipated a shift in the delivery of IVF to the not-for-profit sector, the government did not regard this issue as pertinent. Unfortunately, this gap leaves current consumers of IVF services vulnerable. Furthermore, public financing of IVF does not necessarily eliminate the profit motive of private clinics. The meta-analytical study by Devereaux illustrates this point, as the study was conducted in a situation of *full* public funding (US Medicare) but delivery by way of private, for-profit hospitals/clinics.[90] Thus, public funding may be an insufficient tonic for regulatory concerns associated with for-profit delivery.

The Impact of Regulations on Reproductive Freedom

We turn now to the broader question of why we currently see these regulatory failings in both Ontario and Quebec. Here, it is helpful to understand that the focus of both scholarship and general discourse in this area has been on the "harmful" or "morally wrong" aspects of AHR. In our view, this perspective has restricted reproductive freedom, even as regulations have failed to adequately protect IVF patients from the risks inherent in the procedure and the industry. In Quebec, even after public financing for IVF was implemented so as to greatly improve access, public funding was denied to certain groups. As a result, patient autonomy with regard to treatment is at times severely limited by the restrictions tied to public financing.

At present, various regulations restrict reproductive freedom in Canada: the national ban on commercial surrogacy and the sale of gamete material (sperm and ova), the law in Quebec that states that only one embryo may be transferred into a woman in any particular cycle, and the law in Quebec that forbids an embryo from being transferred into a woman who is "no longer of childbearing age."[91] Quebec's proposed legislative amendments will limit reproductive freedom further, notably by prohibiting IVF services for all women over the age of forty-two even if paid for privately.

Several sections of the *AHRA* have remained intact since the SCC reference. Notably, the SCC upheld the provision related to the ban on commercial surrogacy that empowered the Assisted Human Reproduction Agency[92] to regulate a surrogate's compensation for expenses; however, this provision has yet to come into force.[93] Similarly, Quebec's *Civil Code* requires that all gamete donations be without payment and that any financial reward be restricted to compensation for loss and inconvenience.[94] Thus, it is currently illegal to pay for surrogacy services or for gamete material, and the compensation that a surrogate or donor may receive for her legitimate expenses remains a grey area.

As a consequence of these laws, the pool of donated material available to infertile couples has been significantly reduced. Moreover, the laws on surrogacy and gamete donation lack clarity, with a consequent impact on access to services. Clinics may be deterred from offering ovum donation services due to the lack of legal clarity regarding what constitutes "reasonable" expenses for which a donor may be compensated – leading to longer wait times overall or even to individuals or couples being unable to access treatment altogether. This is a particular concern for same-sex couples, whose infertility can only be treated with donated gametes (and often a surrogate).

For the same reasons as above, these laws reduce patient choice. Canada once had forty sperm banks nationwide. Now there is only one bank (the Toronto Institute of Reproductive Medicine), and there are currently only thirty to seventy donors.[95] Couples looking for a donor with features similar to their own will have perhaps three options. South Asian couples (for example) may have fewer still.[96] The laws have thus significantly reduced access and choice, perhaps even to the point of endangering public health as the number of half-siblings from a single donor in a given area increases. It is clear that the laws on IVF have had an impact on reproductive freedom.

At the same time, it is not clear that these laws actually achieve their intended purposes. Our proximity to the United States, where commercial surrogacy and the gamete market are legal and flourishing, makes it impossible for the law to eliminate the commercialization of reproduction by Canadian couples.[97] Some clinics have connections to US fertility agencies to help their clients procure ova from paid American donors.[98] Also, the ReproMed bank and some fertility clinics will import purchased donated material from the United States for use in Canada.[99] Besides this, there is a growing global reproduction market. Many Canadians are choosing to enter surrogacy arrangements in India, Latin America, or the United States when they cannot find an altruistic Canadian donor or surrogate.[100] Thus, the ban on commercialization of reproduction at best merely prohibits the sale of *Canadian* gamete material and *Canadian* surrogacy services, at the cost of reproductive freedom.

To be clear, we are not necessarily arguing in this chapter that the various criminal law bans on the commercialization of IVF are wrongheaded; our point, rather, is that a philosophy of restriction and control has crept into the regulation of IVF services more broadly and overwhelmed what should be the primary goal, which is to ensure the safety of all participants in the IVF sector. For example, the Quebec law states that only one embryo may be transferred at a time, to a maximum of two for women under thirty-five and three for women over thirty-five, in extraordinary circumstances, and a more recent proposal would forbid all IVF services for women over forty-two. At first glance, perhaps these provisions are justified as an attempt to improve the quality and safety of IVF procedures to and save RAMQ the costs associated with treating complications, by limiting the number of multiple pregnancies. But, this rationale does not factor in that the prognosis of infertility differs from patient to patient. The safety and advisability of multiple embryo transfer is a controversial topic in the literature, and more research must be done in this area. According to available information, age is one factor in the equation, but so is the particular indicator of infertility. Young women may have reduced egg quality or another condition, affecting the likelihood that a single embryo will implant and result in pregnancy.[101] These are not "extraordinary circumstances" that need to be carved out, but frequently occurring conditions that are simply not recognized as such by the black-and-white view adopted by the legislation – arguably the result of staring too long through the criminal law lens.

There is a risk that this ban will have a chilling effect on doctors by once again placing them in a position of conflict with their patients. A doctor, not wanting to face penalties, may hesitate to transfer more than one embryo into a patient whose eggs are of slightly lesser quality, even if doing so would be in her best interest. This concern must of course be weighed against the concern that private clinics may be inclined to recommend multiple embryo transfer despite the risks because it would likely boost their success rates. But that is arguably an issue best addressed by consumer protection legislation. Clinicians, and more importantly patients, should be afforded some degree of choice. By restricting the number of embryos entirely by the patient's age, without any meaningful discretion extended to the physician to take into account the patient's actual prognosis, the law may be denying these women the treatment that is best suited to their condition, and constitute an unjustified restriction on reproductive freedom.

The *Act respecting clinical and research activities relating to assisted procreation* presently prohibits the transfer of an embryo to a woman who is "no longer of childbearing age."[102] This provision, which again seems to be aimed at preventing "harmful" practices, denies access to fertility treatment based on age. As noted earlier, the province has also recently tabled legislation that would prohibit IVF for women over forty-two, and impose fines of up to $50,000 on physicians who violate this prohibition or who refer women to out-of-province IVF clinics.[103] In our view, there is no satisfactory medical justification for such blanket bans. Studies have shown that there is nothing about the postmenopausal uterus that is inhospitable to implantation. The age of the woman may affect the quality of the ova; however, this can be corrected using donated gametes (and Bill 20 makes no allowances for this).[104] Some studies have reported lower success rates of IVF in older women or increased complications and health risks in pregnancy and childbirth in older women. But as other studies have pointed out, these studies fail to take into account that age increases the likelihood that a woman has underlying health problems, which may interfere with pregnancy.[105] The law does not reflect this, instead relying on age as a crude proxy of a woman's health and assumed capacity to parent.

It is highly unusual for governments to categorically deny a health service to an entire class of citizens out of a fear that the procedure might be unsafe for some members of that class. This is a *prima facie* case of age-based discrimination, for which one would expect and demand a clear and compelling justification from government. Some have defended the age-based prohibition on grounds of cost, noting that the state may bear the costs of pregnancy complications.[106] It is true that advancing maternal age carries higher costs: according to the Canadian Institute for Health Information, the added costs associated with in-hospital births for mothers over thirty-five was approximately $61.1 million for the three-year period from 2006 to 2009.[107] However, this sum is spread across almost 195,000 births to mothers in the thirty-five-and-over age bracket, which works out to only about $313 per birth.[108]

Quebec's draft legislation also requires a positive psychosocial assessment of would-be parents prior to initiating IVF, but only in cases where donated gametes are used or where the physician has reasonable grounds to believe that the parents will endanger the child's security or development. The cost of the assessment would be borne by the would-be parents. Critics have noted that this regulation will target same-sex couples disproportionately, and have rightly observed that a comparable state intrusion into the lives of parents who conceive through intercourse is unimaginable.

Conclusions

The federal laws struck down by the SCC and existing provincial regulations all fail or failed to address adequately concerns about quality and safety, informed consent, and consumer protection that are inherent in the private, for-profit IVF sector. The context of privately financed for-profit delivery, rather than galvanizing greater regulatory force, ironically seems to have justified a light regulatory approach among the Canadian provinces. And even where there is specific IVF regulation, the primary effect of the regulation is not to regulate better quality and safety in the IVF sector, or to ameliorate the concerns associated with a for-profit health industry, but rather to limit the reproductive freedom of women and infertile couples. In attempting to accomplish all that the federal regulations would have accomplished, the province of Quebec restricted itself to banning harms and perceived moral wrongs; in doing so, it, neglected many real concerns arising from the context of for-profit delivery and the reasons why the provinces are best suited to regulate them. We conclude with several observations and recommendations for future regulation of IVF.

First, there is a need for regulations that address patient safety and quality of care so that the pressure to achieve a certain profit margin does not result in insufficient or otherwise inadequate (i.e., less qualified) staffing, or in practices that exacerbate the risks of IVF in the hope of obtaining certain results or attracting more customers. There should also be input regulations and guaranteed inspections that ensure a reasonable standard of care, with public transparency as to the results.

Furthermore, there should be regulations that set out exactly what is required for consent to IVF to be "informed." This must go further than the Quebec regulations, stating exactly what measures of success ought to be reported and at what level (physician, clinic, provincial average). Information given to patients must be tailored to their particular prognosis, age, and other relevant factors. Even where this is already informally practised, the nature of for-profit medicine is such that an explicit legal rule is demanded. Related to this, there is a need for regulations that focus on consumer protection; specifically, we need regulation regarding what information ought to be provided in advertising. In the case of IVF, there should be more consistency in the definition of "success rate" and how it is reported.

Regulation must also address the conflicts of interest encountered in private, for-profit health care. There need to be checks on the relationships between facilities, diagnostic centres, and family doctors; provisions that prevent doctors from recommending their own clinic, or at least require them to provide a number of options; and provisions that require facilities that offer their own diagnostics as well as treatment to fully explain all of the medical and non-medical options, emphasizing the purposes and risks of costly add-ons.

Enforcement is critical for all of these proposed reforms but is presently lacking in the status quo. Relying on customer complaints is insufficient, as patients will often not have the medical know-how to identify when malpractice has occurred or when the law has been breached or may fear jeopardizing the physician–patient relationship. Therefore, an independent enforcement body is required that conducts regular evaluations and that reports to the government and, critically, to patients and the general public. This body must have the authority to impose sanctions, including shutting down clinics that are not in compliance. Of course, it is not desirable to have cumbersome or expensive regulatory requirements that will increase the cost of IVF, placing it beyond the reach of even more individuals. However, a system of regular inspections is not, in our view, unreasonable in this regard.

Both levels of government that have attempted to regulate IVF have focused on moral and ethical harms unduly, without sufficiently attending to the risks faced by the thousands of individuals who undergo IVF treatments in private, for-profit facilities across Canada. The emphasis has been on restriction and on banning certain activities rather than on safely enabling access to care. Going forward, policy-makers in Canada must acknowledge not only the need to render illegal that which is considered morally problematic but also the need to have regulations that admit of the real-world context for the delivery of IVF services and that seriously consider the health and safety of those seeking IVF services, their need for consumer protection, and their rights to reproductive freedom. More broadly, the status quo in Canada has been to impose lighter regulations on privately financed care delivered in the for-profit sector. This is illogical and runs in the face of solid evidence from health services research. It is high time for lawmakers to reconsider this regulatory bias, in the IVF context and beyond.

NOTES

1 *Reference Re Assisted Human Reproduction Act*, 2010 SCC 61 at para 294, [2010] 3 SCR 457, 327 DLR (4d) 257; *Assisted Human Reproduction Act*, SC 2004, c 2.

2 *Regulation respecting the application of the Health Insurance Act*, RRQ 2011, c A-29, r. 5, s 34.4; "FAQ," *McGill Reproductive Centre*, http://www.mcgillivf.com/home.html . Ontario also provides some funding for IVF, but only if both fallopian tubes are blocked by natural causes, just 20 per cent of all IVF cycles performed in 2004 in Ontario: Medical Advisory Secretariat, Ministry of Health and Long-Term Care, "In Vitro Fertilization and Multiple Pregnancies: An Evidence-Based Analysis" (2006) 6:18 Ontario Health Technology Assessment Series 2006 at 21, http://www.hqontario.ca/english/providers/program/mas/tech/reviews/pdf/rev_ivf_101906.pdf.

3 Bill 20, *An Act to enact the Act to promote access to family medicine and specialized medicine services and to amend various legislative provisions relating to assisted procreation*, 1st Sess., 41st Leg., Quebec, 2014 (introduced by Hon Gaétan Barrette, Minister of Health and Social Services, 28 November 2014). See Kelly Grant, "Quebec to Cut *In Vitro* Fertilization Insurance Coverage," *Globe and Mail*, 28 November 2014, 2014 WLNR 33673554; Kelly

Grant, "Quebec Moves to Ban IVF for Women over 42," *Globe and Mail*, 5 December 2014, 2014 WLNR 34345749.

4 See, for example, Rene Almeling, *Sex Cells: The Medical Market for Eggs and Sperm* (Berkeley: University of California Press, 2011).

5 Colleen M. Flood, Bryan Thomas, and Leigh Harrison-Wilson, "Cosmetic Surgery Regulation and Regulation Enforcement in Ontario" (2010) 36 Queen's LJ 31 at 33.

6 Bill 89 on assisted human reproduction was introduced in the Quebec legislature in April 2005. Its stated aim was to promote quality of IVF services, specifically, to address the problem of multiple births: Bill 89, *An Act respecting clinical and research activities as regards assisted human reproduction and amending other legislative provisions*, 1st Sess., 37th Leg., Quebec, 2005 (introduced by Hon Philippe Couillard, Minister of Health and Social Services, 16 December 2004). It is quite possible that the imperative to regulate IVF in Quebec had its genesis as a political move to oppose federal attempts to legislate in this area. Indeed, the Hansard discussion of Bill 89 specifically refers to the province's objections to the regulatory aspects of the federal regime and mentions that the province filed a reference against the *AHRA* in December 2004. Following the introduction of Bill 89, in the fall of 2008, the provincial government made a commitment to pay for IVF. Consequently it could be argued, contrary to our thesis, that the province's decision to regulate IVF predated the initiative to fund IVF; however, the final bill vis-à-vis regulation was not passed until June 2009, and it was not set to come into effect until the *Regulation modifying the Regulation respecting the Application of the Health Insurance Act* (i.e., the funding aspect) was also passed and in effect. Thus, both the funding provisions and the new regulations came into effect in August 2010. Quebec, National Assembly, *Journal des débats* (Hansard), 37th Parl., 1st Sess., No. 136 (12 April 2005) (Philippe Couillard); "Assisted Procreation," *Santé et Services Sociaux Québec*, http://www.assnat.qc.ca/fr/travaux-parlementaires/journaux-debats/index-jd/recherche.html?cat=ex&Session=jd37l1se&Section=sujets&Requete=7597-9&Hier=Procr%C3%A9ation+assist%C3%A9e_Projet+de+loi+n%C2%B0+89_7597-9.

7 The reader should note that there may be many more clinics that offer IVF; however, these clinics do not perform the procedure themselves but rather are affiliated with one of the thirty or so clinics that do. Joanne Gunby, "Assisted Reproductive Technologies (ART) in Canada: 2010 Results from the Canadian ART Register," Canadian Fertility and Andrology Society, http://www.cfas.ca/index.php?option=com_content

&view=article&id=1206%3Acartr-annual-report-2009&catid=1012%3Acartr&Itemid=668; private correspondence between the authors and various clinics.

8 Gunby, *ibid*; Ministry of Health and Long Term Care Ontario, "Classification of Hospitals," http://www.health.gov.on.ca/en/common/system/services/hosp/group_q.aspx; "Fertility Specialist Resources" *IVF.ca*, http://www.ivf.ca/clinicprov.php. In Canada, "public hospital" refers to a hospital that operates on a not-for-profit basis, not a hospital that belongs necessarily to the public sector; see Raisa B. Deber, Commission on the Future of Health Care in Canada, "Delivering Health Care Services: Public, Not-for-Profit, or Private?" (2002), Discussion Paper No. 17, CIHR Team in Community Care and Health Human Resources, http://webcache.googleusercontent.com/search?q=cache:P5iPshr2zsEJ:teamgrant.ca/M-THAC%2520Greatest%2520Hits/Bonus%2520Tracks/Delivering%2520Health%2520Care%2520Services.pdf+&cd=1&hl=en&ct=clnk&gl=ca&client=firefox-b-ab.

9 Gunby, *ibid*.

10 Quebec Ministry of Health and Social Services, Press Release, "Dès le 5 Août 2010, les couples infertiles du Québec pourront bénéficier de la couverture des traitements de procréation assistée pour réaliser leur rêve d'voir un enfant," CNW Telbec, 13 July 2010.

11 Robin Hilborn, "Provincial Help for the Infertile in Canada: Free IVF in Quebec, Tax Help in Manitoba, Ontario Balks" *Fertility Helper*, 16 September 2010, http://www.familyhelper.net/iy/news/100917quebecivf.html.

12 Regional Fertility Program, http://regionalfertilityprogram.ca/faqs/ivficsi-faq/.

13 Hilborn, *supra* note 12.

14 Medical Advisory Secretariat, *supra* note 2 at 21.

15 *Ibid* at 21. This study (at 33) moreover indicated that the actual demand for IVF is not reflected in the number of cycles performed, as demand would increase if the treatment were more affordable. The 2006 report predicted that the number of cycles in Ontario would increase threefold if every indicator of infertility received public financing. It is likely, therefore, that bilateral tube blockage describes far fewer than 20 per cent of all infertile couples in Ontario.

16 *Regulation respecting the application of the Health Insurance Act*, RRQ 2011, c A-29, r. 5, s 34.4; "FAQ," McGill Reproductive Centre, http://www.mcgillivf.com.

17 "Fees," McGill Reproductive Centre, http://www.mcgillivf.com/home.html.

18 Grant, "Quebec to Cut *In Vitro* Fertilization Insurance Coverage," *supra* note 3.
19 Paula Corabian and David Hailey, "The Efficacy and Adverse Effects of *In Vitro* Fertilization and Embryo Transfer" (1999) 15:1 Int'l J of Technology Assessment in Health Care 66 at 78; Ivica Tadin *et al.*, "Fetal Reduction in Multifetal Pregnancy: Ethical Dilemmas" (2002) 43:2 Yonsei Medical Journal 252 at 252.
20 Simone E. Buitendijk, "Children after *In Vitro* Fertilization" (1999) 15:1 Int'l J of Technology Assessment in Health Care 52 at 53; Tadin *et al.*, *ibid*, at 252.
21 Emma Sowerby and John Parsons, "IVF: How Can We Reduce the Risks of Infection?" (2006) 8:3 The Obstetrician & Gynaecologist 159 at 160.
22 The precise mortality rate of ovarian hyperstimulation syndrome is unknown and difficult to quantify; however, a 2005 report suggests that the figure is probably approximately 1/450,000 in the UK. Adam Balen, "Ovarian Hyper Stimulation Syndrome: A Short Report for the HFEA," http://www.hfea.gov.uk/docs/OHSS_UPDATED_Report_from_Adam_Balen_2008.pdf.
23 P.J. Devereaux *et al.*, "A Systematic Review and Meta-Analysis of Studies Comparing Mortality Rates of Private For-Profit and Private Not-for-Profit Hospitals" (2002) 166:11 CMAJ 1399 at 1400, 1402.
24 *Ibid* at 1400.
25 *Ibid* at 1404.
26 *Ibid* at 1404.
27 *Ibid* at 1401.
28 *Ibid* at 1402, 1405.
29 P.J. Devereaux *et al.*, "Comparison of Mortality between Private For-Profit and Private Not-for-Profit Hemodialysis Centers: A Systematic Review and Meta-analysis" (2002) 288:19 JAMA 2449 at 2449.
30 *Ibid* at 2449, 2452.
31 *Ibid* at 2450.
32 *Ibid* at 2449, 2452.
33 *Ibid* at 2456.
34 *Ibid* at 2456.
35 Michael Hillmer *et al.*, "Nursing Home Profit Status and Quality of Care: Is There Any Evidence of an Association?" (2005) 62:2 Medical Care Research and Review 139 at 140.
36 *Ibid* at 156.
37 *Ibid* at 157–8.
38 *Ibid* at 158.

39 Mark B. McClellan and Douglas O. Staiger, "Comparing Hospital Quality at For-Profit and Not-for-Profit Hospitals," in *The Changing Hospital Industry: Comparing For-Profit and Not-for-Profit Institutions*, ed. David M Cutler (Chicago: University of Chicago Press, 2000), 93 at 95.
40 *Ibid* at 102.
41 *Ibid* at 102.
42 *Ibid* at 111.
43 *Ibid* at 109; Pauline Allen similarly noted in a study of the English NHS that the presence of for-profit providers encourages NHS providers to "raise their game" to mimic the more efficient practices of the for-profit clinics. See Pauline Allen *et al.*, "Provider Diversity in the English NHS: A Study of Recent Developments in Four Local Health Economies" (2011) 17 (Supp 1) J Health Serv Res Pol'y 23 at 28.
44 Jane Henderson and Stavros Petrou, "Assisted Reproduction – Counting the Cost: Economic Implications of Multiple Births" (2001) 4:3 Twin Research and Human Genetics 187. See also John Collins, "Cost Efficiency of Reducing Multiple Births" (2007) 15(Supp 3) Reprod BioMed Online 35.
45 Gunby, *supra* note 8.
46 Sujit Choudhry *et al.*, "Unregulated Private Markets for Health Care in Canada? Rules of Professional Misconduct, Physician Kickbacks and Physician Self-Referral" (2004) 170:7 CMAJ 1115 at 1115.
47 See, for example, Astra Fertility Group, http://www.astrafertility.com/diagnostic.html.
48 *Supra* note 1 at paras 7, 327; *Constitution Act, 1867* (UK), 30 & 31 Vict, c 3, reprinted in RSC 1985, App II, No. 5.
49 *Reference Re Assisted Human Reproduction Act*, *ibid* at paras 6, 327.
50 *Ibid* at paras 227, 327.
51 *Ibid* at paras 236, 238, 243, 327.
52 *Ibid* at paras 250, 327.
53 *Assisted Human Reproduction Act*, *supra* note 1, ss 5–7.
54 "First Test-Tube Babies Born in Canada Turn 25," Canadian Press, 24 March 2007, CTV News, : http://www.ctvnews.ca/first-test-tube-babies-born-in-canada-turn-25-1.234615.
55 *Regulated Health Professions Act, 1991*, SO 1991, c 18, s 10.
56 *Medicine Act General Regulation*, O Reg 114/94, s 27.
57 Flood *et al.*, *supra* note 5 at 48.
58 *Ibid* at 48.
59 *Independent Health Facilities Act*, RSO 1990, c I.3.
60 *Independent Health Facilities Act*, O Reg 650 (Facility Fees), s 1(23).

61 O Reg 114/94; "Out-of-Hospital Premises Inspection Program," http://www.cpso.on.ca/policies-publications/positions-initiatives/cosmetic-procedures-improving-patient-safety; IVF uses local anesthesia. See Georgia Reproductive Specialists, www.ivf.com/ivffaq.html.
62 "Out-of-Hospital Premise Standards," CPSO http://www.cpso.on.ca/uploadedfiles/policies/guidelines/office/ohp_standards.pdf.
63 Theresa Boyle, "Safety Inspections Find 13% of Private Clinics Don't Meet Provincial Standards," *Toronto Star*, 2 November 2014, WLNR 30679112.
64 *Health Care Consent Act*, SO 1996, c 2, Sched A.
65 *Ibid* at ss 11(1), (2), (3).
66 *Canadian Health Facilities Law Guide* (Toronto: CCH Canadian, 2003) at 1510.
67 *Medicine Act Professional Misconduct Regulation*, O Reg 856/93, s 1(1), para 9.
68 Colleen M. Flood and Bryan Thomas, "Canadian Medical Malpractice Law in 2011: Missing the Mark on Patient Safety" (2011) 86:3 Chicago-Kent L Rev 1053 at 1066, 1068.
69 See *ibid* at 1075–8.
70 *Code of ethics of physicians*, RRQ 2008, c M-9, r. 4.1, ss 28–9; *Act respecting health services and social services*, RSQ 2011, c S-4.2, ss 8, 9; article 11 CCQ.
71 *Medicine Act General Regulations*, O Reg 114/94.
72 *Regulated Health Professions Act*, SO 1991, c 18, Sched II, ss 85.11(1), 85.12.
73 *Supra* note 72 at s 17(1).
74 *An Act respecting clinical and research activities relating to assisted procreation*, RSQ 2010, c A-5.01.
75 *Regulation respecting clinical activities related to assisted procreation*, RRQ 2010, c A-5.01, r. 1.
76 *Supra* note 75 at s 20.
77 *Ibid* at ss 19, 32.
78 *Ibid* at ss 4–5.
79 *Ibid* at s 4.
80 *Supra* note 76 at s 2.
81 *Supra* note 75 at ss 6, 15, 36.
82 Jon M. Ford and David L. Kaserman, "Ownership Structure and the Quality of Medical Care: Evidence from the Dialysis Industry" (2000) 43 Journal of Economic Behavior & Organization 279 at 291–2.
83 J.M. Mitchell and T.R. Sass, "Physician Ownership of Ancillary Services: Indirect Demand Inducement or Quality Assurance?" (1995) 14:3 Journal of Health Economics 263 at 263.
84 Note: It was suggested to the authors at a presentation of this paper that a certain percentage of the owners had to work in the clinics. We found

nothing in the regulations to suggest that this is the case; however, even if it were the case, such an arrangement would only serve to cement the conflict of interest between doctors and their patients by requiring that the physicians have a personal interest in making the clinic as profitable as possible. Studies suggest that physician ownership of the specialty facilities in which they work leads to an increased use of diagnostic and ancillary services and an increase in procedures performed. This causes an increase in health care expenditures for the patients without any evidence of improvement to patient health. See J.M. Mitchell, "Do Financial Incentives Linked to Ownership of Specialty Hospitals Affect Physicians' Practice Patterns?" (2008) 46:7 Medical Care 732 at 736–7.

85 *Supra* note 76 at s 17.

86 *Ibid* at ss 20(1), (2).

87 Note: For example, according to the most recent information on their respective websites, the clinical pregnancy rate for women under thirty-five using fresh embryo transfers is 51 per cent at CReATe: http://www.createivf.com/ivf/index.htm; 60.1 per cent at ReproMed, http://www.repromed.ca/fertility_success.html; and 54.6 per cent at Astra Fertility, www.astrafertility.com/success_rates.html .

88 *Supra* note 75 at s 31.

89 *Ibid* at s 37.

90 P.J. Devereaux *et al., supra* note 31 at 2450, 2452.

91 *Assisted Human Reproduction Act, supra* note 1 at ss 6–7; *supra* note 75 at s 10; *supra* note 76 at s 17.

92 In March 2012 the federal government announced that the Assisted Human Reproduction Agency would be closed by March 2013 and all of its remaining functions taken over by Health Canada. This change has been implemented. See http://www.hc-sc.gc.ca/dhp-mps/brgtherap/legislation/reprod/index-eng.php . See for example Tom Blackwell, "Government Shutters Agency That Oversees Canada's Fertility and Assisted Reproduction Industry," *National Post*, 3 March 2012, http://news.nationalpost.com/news/government-shutters-agency-that-oversees-canadas-fertility-and-assisted-reproduction-industry. The relevant provision was amended to remove the reference to the Agency and licences issued by the Agency, leaving compensation to be addressed in regulations made by the Governor in Council: *Jobs, Growth and Long-term Prosperity Act*, SC 2012, c 19, s 719.

93 *Supra* note 1 at s 12, as amended by *Jobs, Growth and Long-term Prosperity Act*, SC 2012, c 19, s 719.

94 Art 25 CCQ.

95 Roger Collier, "Sperm Donor Pool Shrivels When Payments Cease" (2010) 182:3 CMAJ 233 at 233–4.

96 *Ibid* at 109–10; Toronto Institute For Reproductive Medicine, "Semen Donor Catalogue," http://www.repromed.ca/sperm_donor_catalogue.

97 See CTV News, "Surrogacy in Canada: What Are the Laws?" 11 August 2014, http://www.ctvnews.ca/canada/surrogacy-in-canada-what-are-the-laws-1.1954565.

98 MacKenna Roberts, "Canada Turns a Blind Eye to Egg 'Donor' Grey Market," *BioNews* 550, 22 March 2010, http://www.bionews.org.uk/page_56702.asp.

99 "Semen Donor Catalogue," *supra* note 98.

100 Sharon Kirkley, "Desperate Canadians Resort to Foreign Surrogates," *Ottawa Citizen*, 12 December 2010, http://webcache.googleusercontent.com/search?q=cache:FHxw_TZgEcIJ:embamex.sre.gob.mx/canada/index.php/home/208-domingo-12-diciembre-2010/1855-desperate-canadians-resort-to-foreign-surrogates-ottawa-citizen%3Fformat%3Dpdf+&cd=1&hl=en&ct=clnk&gl=us&client=firefox-b-ab.

101 John von Radowitz, "2 Embryos Better Than One for IVF Success," *Irish Examiner*, 13 January 2012, http://www.irishexaminer.com/ireland/kfidauaueykf/rss2.

102 *Supra* note 76 at s 10.

103 Grant, "Quebec Moves to Ban IVF for Women over 42," *supra* note 3.

104 Richard J. Paulson *et al.*, "Pregnancy in the Sixth Decade of Life: Obstetric Outcomes in Women of Advanced Reproductive Age" (2002) 288:18 JAMA 2320 at 2320–1, 2322.

105 *Ibid* at 2320–1, 2322.

106 Grant, "Quebec Moves to Ban IVF for Women over 42," *supra* note 3.

107 CIHI, *In Due Time: Why Maternal Age Matters* (Ottawa: CIHI, 2011) at 8.

108 *Ibid* at 11.

15 Great Expectations: Access to Assisted Reproductive Services and Reproductive Rights

SARAH HUDSON

We live in a country of great expectations, expectations that are fed by the advances of technology – health care is a prime example – and by the dissemination of knowledge and growing awareness, imperfect as they may be. Law benefits from technology and it is also the object of great expectations.[1]

Assisted human reproduction enables possibilities in family formation that did not previously exist. This rapidly advancing field has been described as "a victim of its own success." As J.F. Daar suggests, "increasing the technical ability to produce biological parenthood for those who could not previously have dared to include such joys in their life plans, only makes its unavailability more stinging."[2] This sentiment is particularly strong in jurisdictions, such as most Canadian provinces, where assisted human reproduction (AHR) services are not covered by public health insurance plans.

Canada began developing its legal response to AHR more than two decades ago. Even at that time, the issue of access to these services and public funding was already top of mind. It remains, however, far from resolved. When expectations of access to AHR are foisted upon the law, the invocation of a rights discourse invariably follows. While "few might dissent from a rhetorical assertion that men and women have a right to found a family," dispute resurfaces when debating what exactly that right entails, where it finds legal foundation, and who enjoys it.[3] This chapter examines the accessibility of AHR services in Canada and considers what past rights-based claims for funded AHR services reveal about the vitality and influence of a rhetoric of reproductive rights in this country. After all, the existence, nature, and scope of rights vis-à-vis access to AHR services are a means of managing and assessing the legitimacy of expectations of access to them.[4]

This chapter posits that rights claims are unlikely to secure funding for AHR services where none exists. A stand-alone right to access these technologies has not, and likely will not, be recognized at law. But when policy-makers and legislators do come to design a funding policy in this area, then a rights discourse – particularly related to equality – will be an important tool for ensuring equitable access to reproductive services for all potential users.

I. Infertility and AHR Services

In Canada, 1 to 2 per cent of all births are the result of AHR, principally through artificial insemination (AI) (non-intercourse insemination leading to fertilization within a woman's body) or *in vitro* fertilization (IVF) (fertilization outside of a woman's body; literally, fertilization "in glass").[5] These procedures may be undertaken using a couple's own gametes or those of a donor. While infertile heterosexual couples account for the majority of users of AHR services, there are estimates suggesting single women and same-sex couples account for 25 to 30 per cent of clientele at some urban fertility centres.[6] On the traditionally presupposed medical model, infertility is "a disease of the reproductive system,"[7] defined by the failure to achieve pregnancy after one year of regular unprotected heterosexual intercourse.[8] Linked to this definition is the oft-cited statistic about the prevalence of infertility – that one in every seven to eight couples currently struggles to conceive.[9]

The consequences of adopting a medical definition of infertility to determine access to AHR services will be highlighted below. For the moment, it suffices to introduce those who do not satisfy the medical definition and who may yet be candidates for reproductive assistance: single women, lesbian partners, individuals or couples with a genetic condition they do not wish to pass on to a child, or individuals about to undergo cancer treatment that risks rendering them infertile.[10] What these groups have in common with the physically infertile is an unfulfilled desire for a child and the need for external medical assistance to reproduce.[11] The experience of childlessness for single women and lesbian partners is frequently referred to as "social" infertility. For them, donor insemination (DI) is the first-choice treatment, but they may require IVF.

II. Public Funding of AHR Services in Canada

A. Canada Health Act

To fully appreciate the context in which decisions about public funding for AHR services are made, a brief overview of the Canadian Medicare system is essential. The *Canada Health Act* (*CHA*)[12] is the legal foundation of Canada's public health care system. Its primary objective is "to protect, promote and restore the physical and mental well-being of residents of Canada and to facilitate reasonable access to health services without financial or other barriers."[13] The primary constitutional responsibility for the provision of health care rests with the provinces.[14] Each operates a health insurance plan and qualifies for a cash contribution from the federal government if the plan satisfies five criteria: public administration, comprehensiveness, universality, portability, and accessibility.[15] The comprehensiveness criterion requires provinces to insure all medically necessary services provided by physicians and hospitals.[16]

The concept of "medically necessary" is deeply embedded in Medicare, although neither the *CHA* nor any of its counterpart provincial enactments offers an operational definition of this term.[17] It is a concept of "beguiling simplicity" – one that has defied clear analysis.[18] Although effectively the gatekeeper of public funding, it is a shifting platform from which individuals advocate for various policy goals; much of the discussion of medical necessity is undertaken "to decide whether treatment should be paid for out of the public purse."[19] Beyond seeking to understand how this concept operates in practice (some have described it as allowing "black box" decision-making,[20] generally driven by physician recommendations but liable to provincial variation[21]), the law has a role to play in "shaping and configuring the boundaries of Medicare" by ensuring that funding decisions comply with the requirements of constitutional and human rights law.[22]

B. The History of AHR Funding in Canada: Scientific Progress and Financial Regress

In 1989 the Government of Canada gave the Royal Commission on New Reproductive Technologies (RCNRT) a mandate to examine, *inter alia*, the rights of people using reproductive services, such as the right to access procedures and "rights" to parenthood, as well as the issue of funding infertility treatment.[23] In its final report, *Proceed With Care*, the RCNRT expressed the belief that Canada's health care system could accommodate AHR services: "If having children is important to most Canadians, as we have found it is, and if safe and effective means exist to help people who would otherwise not be able to have children to do so, then the ethic of care directs us to take this into account in societal decisions about how our collective resources are allocated, including those allocated to the health care system."[24]

Experts put forward to the RCNRT various concerns about equitable access to AHR services. They submitted that failure to adopt a "pro-active approach to ensuring accessibility" would result in "an unfair allocation of social and medical resources." They suggested that "family forms desired or utilized by others, such as single parent families, or homosexual families, will face discriminatory treatment."[25] The RCNRT's position was that "the criteria used to determine access to publicly funded medical services must be fair and applied equally to all."[26] In the particular context of DI, the RCNRT noted that

> there are no medical indications for the service, in that, other than in rare cases, it is performed on healthy women who are fertile. Whether heterosexual or homosexual, married or single, all women undergoing DI are in the same situation – they are unable to have a child, either because their partner is infertile or because they do not have a male partner. The Commission believes it is wrong to forbid some people access to medical services on the basis of social factors while others are permitted to use them; using criteria such as a woman's marital status or sexual orientation to determine access to DI, based on historical prejudices and stereotypes, amounts to discrimination as defined under human rights law and contravenes the Commission's guiding principle of equality ... Our recommendations are to ensure that services provided and funded by provinces' health budgets are not offered in a discriminatory way contravening the Canadian Charter ... Forming a family is of deep importance to the vast majority of Canadians, regardless of their sexual orientation, marital status, or financial situation.[27]

Finding that IVF's effectiveness was proven only in cases of bilateral fallopian tube blockage (BFTB),[28] the RCNRT recommended that IVF be insured in those cases only and specifically recommended that Ontario "defund" IVF for indications other than BFTB.[29] Ontario implemented the RCNRT's recommendations to reduce its coverage,[30] but no other province complied by introducing the minimal recommended coverage. *Proceed With Care* was published almost twenty years ago, yet access to publicly funded reproductive services in Canada today falls below the RCNRT's recommendations for funding based upon 1993 (and now out-of-date) evidence.[31] This state of affairs undermines the RCNRT's commitment to evidence-based medicine, and arguably, its ethic of care.

C. The Current Situation and Recent Developments

When it challenged the constitutionality of the federal legislation,[32] Quebec also introduced legislation regulating AHR, as well as complementary regulations listing AHR as an insured service.[33] This move set Quebec apart from most other Canadian provinces, which trail their counterparts in the industrialized world with regard to public funding of AHR.[34] In 2010, Quebec became the first province to provide comprehensive funding for AHR services; that funding covered three stimulated IVF cycles, egg retrieval from a donor, and AI.[35] In November 2015, however, Quebec's progressive funding commitment for AHR services came to an abrupt end with the assent of Bill 20, *An Act to enact the Act to promote access to family medicine and specialized medicine services and to amend various legislative provisions relating to assisted procreation*.[36] Public funding became limited to assisted insemination and fertility preservation services.

The Quebec experience may have a chilling effect on other provinces that are inclined to move forward with public funding of AHR services. That said, more than five years on from the *Reference re Assisted Human Reproduction Act* (the *Reference*),[37] there has been only modest action elsewhere in Canada to keep pace with Quebec's advances in this area, despite the Supreme Court of Canada's confirmation of a provincial mandate to do so. In 2010, Manitoba implemented a fertility tax credit.[38] In 2014, New Brunswick announced the Special Assistance Fund for Infertility Treatment, a one-time maximum grant of $5,000. The eligibility criteria for this fund include a medical diagnosis of "fertility problems."[39]

Up until 2014, the Ontario government had been conspicuously quiet, considering the recommendations made to it in a 2009 report titled *Raising Expectations* by a government-assembled Expert Panel on Infertility and Adoption (the Expert Panel).[40] The subtitle for the section on infertility and assisted reproduction, "Care to Proceed," is an inversion of the title of the RNCRT's report, signalling the strength of the call for progress beyond the limited funding for IVF in cases of BFTB[41] – a problem occurring in 1 per cent of the infertile population.[42] Noting that cost is the "single greatest barrier"[43] to accessing AHR services, the Expert Panel called for Ontario to remove this barrier by funding evidence-based AHR services, including

(i) up to three cycles of IVF for women aged forty-one years and twelve months or younger, including ancillary services when appropriate;
(ii) up to four cycles of AI/DI for women aged forty-one years and twelve months or younger (including the costs of sperm wash).

Rather than promptly acting on these recommendations, Ontario filed a response in a test case in which the complainants, a married couple experiencing infertility, were seeking coverage for prescribed cycles of IVF with intra-cytoplasmic sperm injection (ICSI) in line with the Expert Panel's recommendations. Ontario's response did not refer to *Raising Expectations*.[44] But in April 2014, the Ontario Ministry of Health and Long-Term Care announced plans to expand its funding for infertility services to improve affordability and access.[45] Under its new Fertility Program, Ontario commits to funding AI, one IVF cycle per patient per lifetime, and fertility preservation services.[46] Insured IVF cycles include single embryo transfers to reduce the risk of multiple births. This, the government stated, would "improve the safety of IVF … and may help reduce the health costs associated with multiple births."[47] Most notably, access under the new funding policy is expanded to include both medical and non-medical infertility: "While single people or people in same-sex partnerships may not be medically infertile, they may use fertility treatments in order to build their families."[48]

In launching its Fertility Program, Ontario downplayed the policy rationales heretofore considered the most persuasive when it comes to adding AHR services to public health insurance plans – namely, that infertility is a medical condition, and that covering it is cost-effective. Since these rationales still dominate much of the public discourse about public funding, a closer examination of their shortcomings – particularly their inequitable consideration of all potential users of AHR services – is merited.

1. ECONOMIC CONSIDERATIONS ECLIPSE RIGHTS RHETORIC

Economic factors are central to the debate about public financing of AHR services.[49] Canadian advocacy efforts emphasize the cost-efficiency of funding AHR services, with a particular focus on the health care costs of treating complications arising from multiple pregnancies.[50] Since public funding encourages single embryo transfers in IVF, the message has been: "We cannot afford not to fund."[51]

To be sure, dollars and cents are the political vernacular, but aside from the methodological and evidentiary limitations of cost-effectiveness studies,[52] there is the principled concern about the adequacy of singular responses to complex problems. For example, the UK's experience shows that while an economic rationale unlocks public funding for AHR services, that rationale is then overcome by a Pandora's box of considerations: Should a publicly funded health care system support such treatment? For whom? Should the treatment be limited to heterosexual couples?[53] Legal and ethical considerations proliferate. When a British academic pointed out that "it might be that lesbians and single women are more cost effective to treat than infertile heterosexual couples because they are less likely to have a physiological cause for their unwanted childlessness," but that these women were excluded from qualifying for such treatment under the UK's funding guideline, it quickly became apparent that economics alone is not up to the task.[54]

2. THE ILLNESS RATIONALE IS UNDERINCLUSIVE

Canadians are still campaigning for public funding or financial support for AHR services on the basis that infertility is a disease or medical condition. In March 2010 the Canadian Fertility and Andrology Society (CFAS), Canada's recognized authority on reproductive medicine, released a position statement in support of publicly funded IVF treatment across Canada:

> Infertility has been defined by the World Health Organization as a disease of the reproductive system defined by the failure to achieve a clinical pregnancy after 12 months or more of regular unprotected sexual intercourse. Since infertility has been defined as a disease, and its associated diagnostic and surgical management deemed "medically necessary" by provincial medical insurance plans,[55] full infertility treatment including IVF and ICSI must also be made available as a funded service, and easily accessible to all Canadians.[56]

New Brunswick's special assistance fund for infertility treatment is in line with this framework. The application form requires the applicant to declare that "I have been diagnosed by a physician with fertility problems" and that "I have attached documentation indicating that I have been diagnosed with infertility."[57]

AHR is a catalyst of significant social change. It has "emancipat[ed] procreation from the usual conditions of heterosexual commerce."[58] But a medical definition of infertility reasserts the connection between heterosexuality and reproduction and in the process eclipses the socially infertile, whose requests for access arise from the very existence of AHR.[59] Increasingly, the "unconventional families" enabled by AHR services are being accommodated by existing legal frameworks. In its opening statement of principles, the *Assisted Human Reproduction Act* (*AHRA*) recognizes the diverse users of reproductive services and declares that "persons who seek to undergo assisted reproductive procedures must not be discriminated against, including on the basis of their sexual orientation or marital status."[60] Buttressing this legislative design for equitable access are efforts to revamp parentage provisions in provincial family relations statutes to accommodate diverse families formed through AHR.[61] But the public funding of AHR services is a separate institutional concern from their statutory regulation, and the illness rationale risks creating an institutionalized discrepancy in equitable access to AHR services by privileging the medically infertile heterosexual couple when it comes to receiving *subsidized* reproductive assistance. The *Canadian Charter of Rights and Freedoms*[62] is a useful touchstone for evaluating the rationality of these discrepancies. The following section contends that while *Charter* rights are unlikely to secure public funding for AHR services where none exists, the equality guarantee both provides a critical check on underinclusive funding policies and serves as an important tool going forward, as equitable policies are designed.

D. Rights-Based Claims for Funding

There are three constitutional arguments that could support claims for access to publicly funded AHR services. Two – a right to health care and a right to reproductive autonomy – are not explicitly protected in the *Charter* but cast legal anchor in s. 7, which guarantees everyone "the right to life, liberty and security of the person and the right not to be deprived thereof except in accordance with the principles of fundamental justice." The third is the s. 15 equality guarantee:

"(1) Every individual is equal before and under the law and has the right to equal protection and equal benefit of the law without discrimination and, in particular, without discrimination based on race, national or ethnic origin, colour, religion, sex, age or mental or physical disability." Sexual orientation and marital status have been held to be analogous grounds to those enumerated in s. 15.[63]

1. RIGHT TO REPRODUCTIVE AUTONOMY

The decision to reproduce – and, it follows here, to seek reproductive assistance – is the kind of fundamental life decision that s. 7 protects, particularly when it comes to the liberty and security of the person.[64] To date, the concept of reproductive autonomy has been considered by the highest court in contexts such as criminalization of abortion[65] and forced sterilization,[66] in which the claim to reproductive autonomy has been conceived as a negative one – to be free from state interference. Generally speaking, the SCC has displayed a preference for negative liberties and has, in majority opinions, dismissed claims to positive rights under s. 7. This is especially well demonstrated in cases involving socio-economic rights, such as the right to health care. As Lorne Sossin explains, "on this view, state action is subject to constitutional constraint, but ... state inaction, by contrast, is a question of policy."[67] The question of whether reproductive autonomy gives rise to a "positive" right of access to subsidized AHR services remains unanswered in Canada, but it appears unlikely, on the current state of the law, that it will find favourable answer in s. 7.

2. RIGHT TO HEALTH CARE

The question of whether s. 7 encompasses a right to health care has been the subject of considerable academic and judicial debate.[68] Discussion surged in the wake of the SCC's divided 2005 ruling in *Chaoulli v Quebec (Attorney General)* [*Chaoulli*].[69] The case concerned the right to purchase private health insurance to avoid the risk of delays in the public system. Although it was decided on the basis of the Quebec *Charter of Human Rights and Freedoms*,[70] three of the four majority judges also found that Quebec's arbitrary prohibition on private insurance conspired with its failure to deliver public health care in a reasonable, timely manner to violate s. 7: "The *Charter* does not confer a freestanding constitutional right to health care. However, where the government puts in place a scheme to provide health care, that scheme must comply with the *Charter*."[71]

From this statement and prior case law, current constitutional conditions appear unfavourable for claimants who would seek to access a particular kind of treatment in the Medicare system on the basis of a s. 7 right to health care.[72] While Martha Jackman has described the SCC's approach to s. 7 as "inconclusive," and interpreted the Court as leaving open the possibility of adopting a "novel" interpretation of s. 7 that places positive obligations on governments to provide funding for socio-economic benefits, the Court has so far sidestepped the issue.[73] A s. 7 claim to achieve government funding for AHR services thus risks failing for similar reasons today as in 1999 in *Cameron v Nova Scotia* [*Cameron*]: "finding the public funding of particular medical services to be considered an element of the right to life, liberty or security of person would expand the parameters of judicial review, well beyond its present scope."[74] Roxanne Mykitiuk and Albert Wallrap go even further, hypothesizing that

> even if s. 7 of the Charter is found to guarantee the right to health care, it is unlikely that access to RTs [reproductive technologies] would be included under the framework of protected services. Rather, it is likely that a distinction will be drawn between basic health care services which are necessary to sustain life and basic well-being, and those services such as RTs, whose absence, while impoverishing one's quality of life, do not threaten life itself. Therefore, it is not likely that the courts will interpret the Charter in a manner that requires legislatures to provide access to RTs.[75]

3. RIGHT TO EQUALITY

Section 15 has been the most commonly used *Charter* section in claims to health services, albeit with a dismal record of success. *Eldridge v British Columbia (Attorney General)* [*Eldridge*][76] was an early win and remains the only decision of the SCC in a right-to-therapy challenge to impose a positive obligation on governments to expend public health funds.[77] From *Eldridge* comes the important proposition that the *Charter* may be infringed not only by legislation itself, but also by the actions of a delegated decision-maker in applying legislation.[78] Thus, coverage policies and decisions of medical necessity, which flow from the administration of provincial health insurance legislation, constitute "law" for the purposes of subs. 15(1).[79]

The claimants in *Eldridge* were deaf patients who contended the British Columbia government's failure to fund sign language interpreters as part of their medical treatment amounted to adverse effects discrimination on the basis of physical disability. Significantly, *Eldridge* did not concern the *scope* of insured services (in the sense of seeking to have a new treatment added to the roster); rather, it concerned equal access to *existing* insured services. Donna Greschner has labelled the government policy challenged in *Eldridge* as "rationing by characteristic": "a particular health care service is insured, but not everyone who can benefit from the service can access it." She explains further that "governments also engage in 'rationing by service' – a specific medical treatment for a particular illness or condition is not funded for anyone."[80] Challenges to this latter kind of policy under the *Charter* have not found ultimate success in the courts.[81] One significant failed AHR claim was *Cameron*. At the 2009 National Health Law Conference, Colleen Flood commented that the unsuccessful challenge in *Cameron* arguably has been a factor in Canada's outlier approach in the public funding of AHR services: the case "appeared to stymie political action and policy initiatives."[82]

a. Cameron v Nova Scotia. In the late 1990s, Cameron and Smith, a married couple, brought an action in Nova Scotia seeking reimbursement for certain medical and hospital services – namely, ICSI and frozen embryo transfers – and a declaration that those procedures were insured services under that province's *Health Services and Insurance Act*.[83] ICSI is a micromanipulation technique performed in combination with IVF and involves the selection of a single sperm for injection into the egg. It is clinically indicated in cases of male-factor infertility, from which Cameron suffered.[84]

The appellants' argument was twofold. They claimed first that the proper interpretation of the governing public health legislation required that IVF/ICSI be an insured service. The Court of Appeal rejected a narrow definition of "medical necessity" as "medical means for medical ends," which the government advanced to support its position that IVF/ICSI was not medically necessary as it did not impact a medical condition (the cause of infertility persists) but rather a non-medical one (childlessness). Justice Chipman did not venture to define "medical necessity," offering only the opinion that IVF/ICSI "*could* qualify as being medically necessary": "Surely the end of all medical treatment is to improve the quality of life. The immediate end may or may not be medical, but this seems to me to be a distinction without much, if any, difference."[85] Despite these general comments, Chipman JA did not find the government's decision that IVF/ICSI was not medically necessary to be in error. Rather, it involved an assessment of factors such as costs, success rates, and risks.[86]

The appellants alternatively argued that the government's refusal to provide insurance coverage for these services constituted a breach of their s. 7 and s. 15 *Charter* rights. The s. 7 claim was rejected at trial and was not pursued on appeal.[87] Regarding their s. 15 claim, Cameron and Smith compared themselves to fertile persons, for whom "every aspect of having children" was covered by Medicare.[88] Infertile persons did not have access to the full array of reproductive services and had to pay for significant procedures that for them held out the "only real hope of having a child."[89] Justice Chipman found that the health insurance legislation and policy, although neutral on their face, failed to take into account the position of the infertile, and differentiated between the appellants and others on the basis of an enumerated ground of discrimination – physical disability: "I do not think it can be seriously disputed that a person unable to have a child has a physical disability."[90] This comment, it should be noted, applied to both appellants, even though Smith, as far as the facts reveal, was not physically infertile, but experienced infertility through Cameron. Justice Bateman, dissenting on the s. 15 analysis, accepted that the policy to not fund IVF had an adverse effect on the appellants but did not accept that infertile persons were excluded from mainstream society in a way that made them disabled. She also was unable to find that infertility constituted an analogous ground under s. 15.[91]

Moving to the substantive discrimination inquiry, Chipman JA further found that the policy reinforced the disadvantage of the infertile. Focusing in particular on the contextual factor of "pre-existing disadvantage," Chipman JA observed the social stigma and grief associated with involuntary childlessness and concluded that the impact of the denial of these procedures perpetuated the view that the infertile are less worthy of recognition or value.[92] Fuelling the discrimination analysis was Chipman JA's determination that what was being denied the claimants was an opportunity to become parents. This was a key point of divergence between the majority and Bateman JA, the trial judge, and the defendants, all of whom divorced the benefit from its social context and maintained that what was being denied the claimants was simply funding to cover their specific treatment.[93] Despite finding a violation of subs. 15(1), Chipman JA found it to be justified under s. 1. Characterizing the objective of the policy as being to provide the best possible health coverage to

Nova Scotians in the context of limited financial resources, Chipman JA rested heavily on extreme budgetary pressures in the Department of Health.[94]

b. Funding Claims Post-Cameron. As one commentator has noted, by refusing leave to appeal in *Cameron* the SCC

> missed an opportunity to resolve some of this controversy about the nature of infertility, and in particular whether it amounts to a disability that would trigger scrutiny under section 15(1). In addition, by hearing and rendering judgment in *Cameron*, the Court could have developed its jurisprudence on questions regarding the funding of health services, and when denial of such funding might be discriminatory.[95]

Since *Cameron*, the Federal Court has considered a claim for AHR funding under the *Canada Human Rights Act*[96] in *Canada (Attorney General) v Buffett* [*Buffett*].[97] Buffett was a Warrant Officer with the Canadian Forces (CF) who suffered male-factor infertility: "The only realistic chance he had to father a child was by [IVF] with [ICSI]."[98] The CF health care plan[99] funded IVF for its female members with BFTB. By comparison to this group, Buffett claimed he was being denied an employment benefit and that such denial constituted adverse differential treatment based on his disability and sex.[100] The Canadian Human Rights Tribunal agreed and ordered the CF to fund up to three cycles of IVF/ICSI for the Buffetts and to take measures to "amend their policy for the funding of IVF treatments so that members with male-factor infertility receive substantially equal benefits as members with [BFTB], or all female members, as the case may be."[101]

On judicial review, Harrington J declined to recognize that the benefit of AHR has as its "essential purpose" the offer of a "real opportunity to have a child." Rather, its objective is to remove physiological "roadblocks" to conception.[102] Justice Harrington held that the CF, having decided to give female members the benefit of IVF, could not deny its male members ICSI. However, since "health services are provided to patients[,] to individuals," only the costs related to Buffett's sperm should be covered; the costs related to the egg and womb should not (just as for female members requiring IVF, the costs related to the sperm were not covered).[103] This reasoning provides an interesting contrast to Chipman JA's finding in *Cameron* that both appellants' subs. 15(1) rights were violated when funding was denied to them for reproductive services, even though the physiological problem lay with the male partner. Justice Harrington's decision might appear to dilute judicial support for the *Cameron* majority's characterization of the objectives of AHR as parenthood and a child. A key distinguishing feature, however, is that the object of the claim in *Buffett* was to equalize a benefit that was *already provided* by the CF. This alleviated the need for a deeply normative discussion of the benefit of AHR services. Justice Harrington simply extended the benefit program on its own terms (as he understood them). This was quite a different task than the one before the court in *Cameron*.

III. Rights in Reproduction: The Promise and Potential of Equality

The *Charter* does not explicitly guarantee a right to found a family, nor does s. 7 appear to be fertile ground for claims of a right to health care or a right to reproduce. Given the restricted protection of such socio-economic rights under the *Charter*, courts are unlikely to find that the state has an obligation to supply subsidized reproductive services on demand. Section 15 also has had very limited success in securing public funds for previously unfunded health-related services. It is realistic, therefore, to acknowledge that the initial commitment of public funds for AHR services in Canada depends on political will, not on the success of a *Charter* challenge.

This does not mean that would-be parents are without rights as Canadian legislatures begin to engage with the brave new world of AHR, by regulating it and providing public funding. In particular, all users of AHR services are entitled to expect fair and equal treatment from those who allocate what the state does supply.[104] Although there is considerable philosophical and jurisprudential uncertainty about a stand-alone right *to* reproduce,[105] there are indeed rights *in* reproduction. These are familiar rights – namely, equality rights – applied in a new context. That is, human rights guarantees of equality and non-discrimination provide a gateway to legal and justiciable "reproductive rights."

A. The Continued Relevance of Cameron

The rhetoric of equality rights has the potential to re-vision the objective of AHR services. More specifically, the reflections of Chipman JA in *Cameron* regarding the nature of the benefit and interests at stake remain instructive in a landscape in which diverse users of AHR services seek equitable access to them. Critically important to the recognition of socially infertile claimants' rights in reproduction is a decision-maker's, or policy-maker's, acceptance that the socially infertile are in an analogous position to the medically infertile. This, in turn, depends on the successful characterization of the objective of medical assistance for all infertility, even where there is a physiological root, as a social one – to alleviate involuntary childlessness.[106] In *Cameron*, Chipman JA acknowledged that "[t]he goal of IVF and ICSI treatment is not to treat disease or correct a condition or dysfunction, but to attain ... a 'non medical end' – the birth of a child. The infertile person's condition is not treated at all. The disease or dysfunction still remains. Nevertheless, if the procedure succeeds the infertile couple becomes parents."[107] Moreover, at various points in his reasons, Chipman JA described the appellants' condition as one of childlessness.[108] The RCNRT made similar comments with respect to DI.[109]

An examination of the subject matter of the benefit at stake is a foundational step in a s. 15 analysis; this in turn guides the selection of a relevant and appropriate comparator. Equality, after all, is an inherently comparative concept. As explained in *Withler v Canada (Attorney General)*, "comparison may bolster the contextual understanding of a claimant's place within a legislative scheme and society at large, and thus help to determine whether the impugned law perpetuates disadvantage or stereotyping."[110] Consider the similarities between a single woman or same-sex partner and a heterosexual female who is involuntarily childless on account of her male partner's physical infertility:

(i) the wish to avoid sexual relations considered personally, socially or morally unacceptable and the emotional complications they might entail (fidelity to one's partner appears as a common concern);
(ii) the wish to overcome the limitations imposed by one's personal and sexual preferences, in particular that of having chosen an infertile partner or form of relationship; and
(iii) the wish for *a child of one's own*, understood as a child emanating from the would-be parents' body and/or gametes.[111]

This comparison helps expose that AHR services *do* have social ends. The heteronomative bias in a medical definition of infertility has a prejudicial impact on the socially infertile, who, on account of their marital status or sexual orientation, are unable to demonstrate physical infertility.

Where a policy for public funding is devised on the illness rationale, the challenges for a socially infertile claimant to gain access will be particularly steep. The ready justification that fertility treatment is a "medical treatment for a medical condition" has the potential to stultify the discrimination claim. The rhetoric of equality rights and the framework of an equality analysis help recast the objective of AHR services, allowing for the design of more equitable funding and access policies.

It is worth noting that an appreciation that all infertility is a social condition has consequences not only for access to funding by diverse users, but also for levels of funding support for those who *do* satisfy a medical definition of fertility. For example, in *Buffett*, strict criteria focusing on physiological reproductive dysfunction gave only partial support to couples seeking access to IVF/ICSI (only the costs of the sperm were covered). *Buffett*-type reasoning also presumably would not support funding for third party reproductive services, such as donor–egg IVF, where medical procedures are performed on a person outside the infertile couple.

B. Developing Charter *Compliant Funding Policies*

Litigation has been a driver of social change in Canada – sometimes successfully, as in the case of same-sex marriage, and sometimes less so, as in the case of court challenges for Medicare funding for new therapies. But litigation is not the only way. Pearl Eliadis has observed that in Canada, the law has fallen short as a "policy driver," the result being "an impoverished policy process that fails to 'front-load' legal norms, including fundamental rights and freedoms, into policy development."[112] As some policy-makers and legislators now move to have AHR services included on the list of "insured services" – a development the *Charter* alone was unable to compel a decade ago – and if and when other provinces follow suit, Canada has an opportunity to proactively inscribe *Charter* values in its policy formation. Consider that non-discrimination is specifically included in the *AHRA*'s opening statement of principles, alongside a more general reference to "dignity and rights":

> (*b*) the benefits of assisted human reproductive technologies … for individuals, for families and for society in general can be most effectively

secured by taking appropriate measures for the protection and promotion of human health, safety, dignity and rights in the use of these technologies ...; and

(*e*) persons who seek to undergo assisted reproduction procedures must not be discriminated against, including on the basis of their sexual orientation or marital status.[113]

Of course, human rights are not all that are in play in policy development, and to formulate a policy that is coherent from all institutional perspectives is no easy task. Law, as a policy perspective, is unique in its concern for the many disciplines that contribute to a societal issue and in its purpose of resolving normative conflicts between them.[114] In Canada, formulating a funding policy for AHR services that respects both *Charter* values and the standard of "medical necessity" at the heart of public health insurance is a highly complex task. Nola Ries has articulated the theoretical quandary: "What comes first, the necessity or the dignity? ... Is human dignity demeaned because a claimant is denied access to a medically necessary health care service or is a service medically necessary because a person's dignity will be infringed if they do not have access to that service?"[115] It could be, as Barbara von Tigerstrom has noted, that *Charter* values require provinces to insure services even when they are not medically necessary by some definitions – such as with the treatment of social infertility – or it may be that through an interactive, interpretive process, the *Charter* impacts the very meaning of medical necessity.[116] It is regrettable that the Expert Panel's recommendations for Ontario did not even mention the concept of "medically necessary" in Ontario's *Health Insurance Act*, nor did they grapple with the interaction between medical necessity and equality rights. (Nor was this particular issue raised by the Advisory Process for Infertility Services in its report leading to Ontario's current funding program.)[117] Thus, while equality rights identify deficiencies in current approaches to the funding of AHR services, they do not provide a blueprint for how to respect *Charter* rights and at the same time satisfy other applicable legal frameworks. This is the work ahead.

IV. Conclusion

The guarantees of equality and non-discrimination are among the strongest in human rights law, and together they provide the surest foundation for a conception of "rights in reproduction." Although

s. 15 is a tool for the minority groups who do not satisfy the criteria for medical infertility to seek equal access to AHR services, to overcome the harms of exclusion that can result from mainstream thinking, and to widen the population of concern in policy formation, these are not "minority" rights for "minority" problems.[118] Indeed, a principal contribution of the right to equality in the context of access to AHR services is to emphasize the universal nature of the interests and rights at stake and to advance an understanding of *all* infertility, whatever its cause, as a social condition. As the group most affected by a lack of funding for AHR services, heterosexual couples experiencing physical infertility have been the most likely claimants and the principal population of concern. But Canadian provinces must continue to assess the stability of a funding policy's orbit around medical infertility in an atmosphere where dignity is the lodestar of rights protection.[119] The law must now do what it has not always so effectively done in Canada: assume the role of policy driver and front-load equality rights into the development of funding and access policies.[120] The possibilities presented by AHR are great; expectations of equitable access to AHR services are not only legitimate but also a matter of fundamental human rights.

NOTES

This chapter was adapted from a longer comparative piece prepared as an LLM dissertation at the University of Cambridge. The author gratefully acknowledges the Law Foundation of British Columbia for its award of a Graduate Fellowship.

1 The Honourable Charles D. Gonthier, "The Governance of Health Care: Fundamental Values, Law and Ethics, Courts, Parliament, and the *Charter*" in *Health Law at the Supreme Court of Canada*, ed. Jocelyn Downie & Elaine Gibson (Toronto: Irwin Law Inc, 2007), 7 at 7.
2 Judith F. Daar, "Accessing Reproductive Technologies: Invisible Barriers, Indelible Harms" (2008) 23 Berkeley J Gender L & Just 18 at 35.
3 Sheelagh Mcguinness and Amel Alghrani, "Gender and Parenthood: The Case for Realignment" (2008) 16 Med L Rev 261.
4 Athena Liu, *Artificial Reproduction and Reproductive Rights* (Aldershot: Dartmouth, 1991), 5.
5 Expert Panel on Infertility and Adoption, *Raising Expectations: Recommendations of the Expert Panel on Infertility and Adoption* (Ontario:

Ministry of Child and Youth Services, 2009), http://www.children.gov.on.ca/htdocs/english/documents/infertility/RaisingExpectationsEnglish.pdf 101–2.

6 Uniform Law Conference of Canada, Civil Law Section, *Assisted Human Reproduction*, Report of the ULCC-CCSO (Uniform Law Conference of Canada – Coordinating Committee of Senior Officials) Working Group, Ottawa, Ontario, 9–13 August 2009, http://www.ulcc.ca/en/uniform-acts-new-order/current-uniform-acts/637-child-status/1497-assisted-human-reproduction-working-group-report-2009; and see in this volume S. Marvel *et al.*, "Listening to LGBTQ People on Assisted Human Reproduction."

7 F. Zegers-Hochschild *et al.*, "The International Committee for Monitoring Assisted Reproductive Technology (ICMART) and the World Health Organization (WHO) Revised Glossary on ART Terminology, 2009" (2009) 24:11 Human Reproduction 2683–7 at 2686.

8 Canadian Fertility and Andrology Society, "Position Statement on Publicly-Funded IVF Treatment in Canada" (2010), http://www.cfas.ca.

9 Health Canada, "Assisted Human Reproduction" (2013), http://www.hc-sc.gc.ca/dhp-mps/brgtherap/legislation/reprod/index-eng.php.

10 As surrogacy introduces an additional host of legal and ethical issues, it is beyond the scope of this discussion.

11 Self-insemination is possible, but for the purposes of the access issues described herein ought not to be considered a prerequisite for clinical AHR services. AI in a regulated clinical setting offers health and safety protection (such as screening of sperm). (In fact, until declared unconstitutional in the *Reference, infra* note 32, s 10 of the AHRA, *infra* note 60, appeared to make it illegal to perform inseminations outside of a clinical setting.) Moreover, under parentage provisions in provincial family law legislation addressing assisted human reproduction, a clinically documented procedure involving donor gametes may also evidence parentage agreements, particularly with respect to "additional parents." See, for example, *Family Law Act*, SBC 2011, c 25, Part 3. See also *Uniform Child Status Act*, Uniform Law Conference of Canada, Civil Law Section, A Joint Project of the Uniform Law Conference of Canada and the Federal/Provincial/Territorial Coordinating Committee of Senior Officials on Family Justice, Halifax, Nova Scotia, 22–26 August 2010, http://www.ulcc.ca/en/uniform-acts-en-gb-1/86-child-status-act/1371-child-status-act-2010.

12 RSC 1985, c C-6.

13 *Ibid*, s 3.

14 *The Constitution Act, 1867* (UK), 30 & 31 Vict, c 3, ss 92(7), (13), (16); *Chaoulli v Quebec (Attorney General)*, 2005 SCC 35, [2005] 1 SCR 791 at para 18.

15 *Supra* note 12, s 7.

16 *Ibid*, s 9.

17 Colleen M. Flood, Caroyln Tuohy, and Mark Stabile, "What Is In and Out of Medicare? Who Decides?," in *Just Medicare: What's In, What's Out, How We Decide*, ed. Colleen M Flood (Toronto: University of Toronto Press, 2006), 15 at 17.

18 Glenn Griener, "Defining Medical Necessity: Challenges and Implications" (2002) 10 Health L Rev 6; Timothy Caulfield, "Wishful Thinking: Defining 'Medically Necessary' in Canada" (1996) 4 Health LJ 63; Nola M. Ries, "The Uncertain State of the Law Regarding Health Care and Section 15 of the *Charter*" (2003) 11 Health LJ 217.

19 Griener, *ibid*.

20 Colleen M. Flood, "Introduction," in *Just Medicare: What's In, What's Out, How We Decide*, ed. Colleen M. Flood (Toronto: University of Toronto Press, 2006), 3 at 4.

21 William Lahey, "Medicare and the Law: Contours of an Evolving Relationship," in *Canadian Health Law and Policy*, ed. Jocelyn Downie, Timothy Caulfield, and Colleen M Flood, 3rd ed. (Toronto: LexisNexis Canada, 2007), 1 at 37–9.

22 *Supra* note 20 at 11.

23 Order in Council No. PC 1989–2150; Royal Commission on New Reproductive Technologies, *Proceed with Care: Final Report of the Royal Commission on New Reproductive Technologies* (Ottawa: Minister of Government Services Canada, 1993), 3 [*Proceed with Care*].

24 *Ibid* at 70.

25 Margrit Eichler, "Human Rights and the New Reproductive Technologies – Individual or Collective Choices," in *Human Rights in the Twenty-first Century: A Global Challenge*, ed. Kathleen E. Mahoney and Paul Mahoney (Netherlands: Kluwer Academic, 1993), 875 at 876–7.

26 *Supra* note 23 at 455.

27 *Ibid* at 455–7.

28 *Ibid* at 518.

29 *Ibid* at 526, 564 (Recommendations 106–7, 128–9). At the time, Ontario was covering all IVF treatments for clinically qualified recipients.

30 Sharon Ikonomidis and Bernard Dickens, "Ontario's Decision to Defund *In Vitro* Fertilization Treatment Except for Women with Bilateral Fallopian Tube Damage" (1995) 21:3 Can Pub Pol'y 379 at 380.

31 Jeff Nisker, "Distributive Justice and Infertility Treatment in Canada" (2008) 30:5 Journal of Obstetrics and Gynaecology Canada 425 at 426.
32 *Reference re Assisted Human Reproduction Act*, 2010 SCC 41, [2010] 3 SCR 457 at paras 7–8.
33 *Act respecting clinical and research activities relating to assisted procreation*, RSQ c A-5.01; *infra* note 35.
34 Erin Nelson, "Regulating Reproduction" in *Canadian Health Law and Policy*, 3rd ed., ed. Jocelyn Downie, Timothy Caulfield, and Colleen M. Flood (Toronto: LexisNexis Canada, 2007), 367 at 396–7; Nisker, *supra* note 31.
35 Regulation respecting the application of the *Health Insurance Act*, RRQ, c A-29, r. 4, ss 34.3–34.6.
36 SQ 2015, c 25.
37 *Supra* note 32.
38 Manitoba Finance, *Personal Tax Credits*, https://www.gov.mb.ca/finance/personal/pcredits.html#fertility.
39 Service New Brunswick, *Infertility Treatment – Special Assistance Fund*, https://www.pxw1.snb.ca/snb7001/e/1000/infoTe.asp.
40 *Supra* note 5.
41 See RRO 1990, Reg 552, s 24(1), under the *Health Insurance Act*, RSO 1990, c H.6.
42 Edward G. Hughes and Mita Giacomini, "Funding *In Vitro* Fertilization for Persistent Subfertility: the Pain and the Politics" (2001) 76:3 Fertility & Sterility 431at 434.
43 *Supra* note 5 at 109.
44 *Attaran v Her Majesty the Queen in Right of Ontario as represented by the Minister of Health and Long-Term Care*, Human Rights Tribunal of Ontario File No. 2009–03240-I; *Ilha v Her Majesty the Queen in Right of Ontario as represented by the Minister of Health and Long-Term Care*, Human Rights Tribunal of Ontario File No. 2009–03239-I.
45 Ontario Ministry of Health and Long-Term Care, New Release, "Improving Access to Safe Fertility Treatments: Ontario Sharing Cost of IVF to Help People Who Cannot Conceive Children," 10 April 2014, http://news.ontario.ca/mohltc/en/2014/04/improving-access-to-safe-fertility-treatments.html?utm_source=ondemand&utm_medium=email&utm_campaign=o.
46 Ontario Ministry of Health and Long-Term Care, "Fertility Services," http://www.health.gov.on.ca/en/public/programs/ivf/.
47 *Supra* note 45.
48 *Supra* note 46.

49 Philipa Mladovsky and Corinna Sorenson, "Public Financing of IVF: A Review of Policy Rationales" (2010) 18:2 Health Care Analysis 113.
50 *Supra* note 5; Renda Bouzayen and Laura Eggerston, "*In Vitro* Fertilization: A Private Matter Becomes Public" (2009) 181:5 CMAJ 243; Edward Hughes, "Access to Effective Fertility Care in Canada" (2008) 30:5 Journal of Obstetrics and Gynaecology Canada 389–90.
51 *Supra* note 5.
52 *Supra* note 49.
53 Joan Mahoney, "Great Britain's National Health Service and Assisted Reproduction" (2009) 35:2 Wm Mitchell L Rev 403.
54 J.R. McMillan, "NICE, the Draft Fertility Guideline and Dodging the Big Question" (2003) 29 J Med Ethics 313. See also Laura Riley, "Equality of Access to NHS-Funded IVF Treatment in England and Wales," in *Human Fertilisation and Embryology: Reproducing Regulation*, ed. Kirsty Horsey and Hazel Biggs (London: Routledge-Cavendish, 2007), 83. For an update on the UK funding position to include same-sex couples, see National Institute for Health and Clinical Excellence, NICE Clinical Guideline 156, *Fertility: Assessment and Treatment for People with Fertility Problems* (London: 2013), https://www.nice.org.uk/guidance/cg156/chapter/1-recommendations.
55 Government health care plans cover costs of investigating and diagnosing infertility, as well as surgical interventions such as tubal surgery in a female. See Arthur Leader, "New Reproductive Technologies: Why Are We Limiting Choices for Infertile Couples?" (1999) 161:11 Canadian Medical Association Journal 1411.
56 *Supra* note 8.
57 Government of New Brunswick, Special Assistance Fund for Infertility Treatment, Application for Special Assistance (Funding) for Infertility Treatment, https://www.pxw1.snb.ca/snb7001/e/1000/9756E.pdf.
58 Simon Bateman, "When Reproductive Freedom Encounters Medical Responsibility: Changing Conceptions of Reproductive Choice" in *Current Practices and Controversies in Assisted Reproduction: Report of a WHO Meeting on "Medical, Ethical and Social Aspects of Assisted Reproduction"* held at World Health Organization Headquarters in Geneva, Switzerland, 17–21 September 2001, ed. Effy Vayena, Patrick J. Rowe, and P. David Griffin, http://hal.archives-ouvertes.fr/docs/00/27/67/15/PDF/WHO_Ch_30.pdf, 320 at 330.
59 *Ibid* at 322.
60 SC 2004, c 2, s 2(e).
61 *Supra* note 6.

62 *Canadian Charter of Rights and Freedoms*, Part I of the *Constitution Act, 1982*, being Schedule B to the *Canada Act 1982* (UK), 1982, c 11.

63 *Egan v Canada*, [1995] 2 SCR 513; *Miron v Trudel*, [1995] 2 SCR 418.

64 Katherine van Heugten and Judy Hunter, "Assisted Human Reproduction" in *A Brave New World: Where Biotechnology and Human Rights Intersect* (Ottawa: Government of Canada, 2005), http://publications.gc.ca/collections/Collection/Iu199-6-2005E_Biotech_CH2.pdf, 2–9; Glenn Rivard and Judy Hunter, *The Law of Assisted Human Reproduction* (Markham: LexisNexis, 2005), 105; Dana Hnatiuk, "Proceeding with Insufficient Care: A Comment on the Susceptibility of the Assisted Human Reproduction Act to Challenge under Section 7 of the Charter" (2007) 65:1 U Toronto Fac L Rev 39; *Doe v Canada (Attorney General)* (2006), 79 OR (3d) 586 (SC), aff'd 2007 ONCA 11, 84 OR (3d) 81, finding the s 7 liberty interest was engaged in the decision to conceive a child with the person of one's choice.

65 *R v Morgentaler*, [1988] 1 SCR 30.

66 *Re Eve*, [1986] 2 SCR 388.

67 Lorne Sossin, "Towards a Two-Tier Constitution? The Poverty of Health Rights," in *Access to Care, Access to Justice: The Legal Debate over Private Health Insurance in Canada*, ed. Colleen M Flood, Kent Roach, and Lorne Sossin (Toronto: University of Toronto Press, 2005), 161 at 170.

68 Martha Jackman, "The Constitution and the Regulation of New Reproductive Technologies," in Royal Commission on New Reproductive Technologies, *Overview of Legal Issues in New Reproductive Technologies* (Ottawa: Minister of Supply and Services Canada, 1993), Research Studies vol. 3, 18–41; Tamara Friesen, "The Right to Health Care" (2001) 9 Health LJ 205; Martha Jackman, "The Implications of Section 7 of the *Charter* for Health Care Spending in Canada," Discussion Paper No. 31, Commission on Future of Health Care in Canada (2002), http://www.collectionscanada.gc.ca/webarchives/20071206063524/http://www.hc-sc.gc.ca/english/care/romanow/hcc0381.html; Donna Greschner, "How Will the Charter of Rights and Freedoms and Evolving Jurisprudence Affect Health Care Costs?," Discussion Paper No. 20, Commission on Future of Health Care in Canada (2002), http://www.collectionscanada.gc.ca/webarchives/20071206063524/http://www.hc-sc.gc.ca/english/care/romanow/hcc0381.html; *Auton v British Columbia (Attorney General)*, 2002 BCCA 538, 6 BCLR (4th) 201 at paras 68–74, Saunders J.A., rev'd 2004 SCC 78, [2004] 3 SCR 657 [*Auton*].

69 Nola Ries, "Charter Challenges," in *Canadian Health Law and Policy*, 3rd ed., ed. Jocelyn Downie, Timothy Caulfield, and Colleen M. Flood (Toronto: LexisNexis Canada, 2007), 539 at 547.

70 RSQ c C-12.
71 *Chaoulli*, *supra* note 14 at para 104.
72 Van Heugten and Hunter, *supra* note 60 at 2-12–2-13; Nola Ries, "Section 7 of the Charter: A Constitutional Right to Health Care? Don't Hold Your Breath" (2003) 12:1 Health L Rev 29; *Brown v British Columbia* (1990), 42 BCLR (2d) 294 (SC) [*Brown*].
73 Martha Jackman and Bruce Porter, "Socio-Economic Rights under the Canadian Charter" (Fall 2007) Canadian Issues 26 at 28–9.
74 (1999), 172 NSR (2d) 227 (SC) at para 160, aff'd (1999), 177 DLR (4th) 611 (NSCA), leave to appeal to SCC refused (29 June 2000), motion for reconsideration of the application for leave to appeal dismissed (15 November 2001). *Cameron* will be discussed later in this chapter in the context of s 15 claims.
75 Roxanne Mykitiuk and Albert Wallrap, "Regulating Reproductive Technologies in Canada," in *Canadian Health Law and Policy*, 2nd ed., ed. Jocelyn Downie, Timothy Caulfield, and Colleen Flood (Markham: Butterworths, 2002), 367 at 395.
76 [1997] 3 SCR 624.
77 Ann Silversides, "Outcome of Health-Related Legal Challenges Is Sometimes Surprising" (2009) 181:11 CMAJ E-247; Flood, Stabile, and Tuohy, *supra* note 21 at 28. There is disagreement among commentators whether Eldridge is properly understood as recognizing a positive right or a negative one. See, for example, Cara Wilkie and Meryl Zisman Gary, "Positive and Negative Rights under the Charter: Closing the Divide to Advance Equality" (2011) 30 Windsor Rev Legal & Soc Issues 37 at 53, conceiving negative and positive rights as forming a spectrum: "While the claims in [*Eldridge* and another case] cannot be classified as strictly negative, they fall closer to the negative rights end of the spectrum, because a finding of discrimination does not mean that the government is under a constitutional obligation to provide the benefit sought. Instead, once the government has provided a benefit, it is under a constitutional obligation to do so in a non-discriminatory manner."
78 *Supra* note 76 at paras 20–1.
79 *Cameron* (NSCA), *supra* note 74 at para 124.
80 Greschner, *supra* note 68 at 7.
81 *Auton*, *supra* note 68 (s 15 claim for funding of applied behavioural therapy for autism); *Brown*, *supra* note 71 (s 15 claim by AIDS patients to have Azidothymidine included as an eligible drug under a Pharmacare Plan). See also Wilkie and Gary, *supra* note 77 at 52–4.
82 Silversides, *supra* note 77.

83 RSNS 1989, c 20.

84 *Cameron* (NSCA), *supra* note 74 at paras 5–6.

85 *Ibid* at para 85.

86 *Ibid* at paras 87–90.

87 *Ibid* at para 28; Ries, *supra* note 71 at 31, commented on the s 7 claim in *Cameron*: "it seems likely the facts and interests at play ... (a professional couple seeking fertility treatment to fulfill a desire to have a biologically related child) may not be sufficiently compelling to warrant imposing a constitutional obligation on government to fund the treatment."

88 *Cameron* (NSCA), *supra* note 74 at para 158.

89 *Ibid* at para 204.

90 *Ibid* at para 145.

91 *Ibid* at paras 258–69.

92 *Ibid* at paras 182–202.

93 *Ibid* at paras 84, 287.

94 *Ibid* at paras 218–36. For a critical comment on this approach, see Barbara von Tigerstrom, "Equality Rights and the Allocation of Scarce Resources in Health Care: A Comment on *Cameron v. Nova Scotia*" (1999) 11:1 Constitutional Forum 30 at 38–9.

95 Angela Campbell, "Pathways to and from the Supreme Court of Canada for Health Law Litigants," in *Health Law at the Supreme Court of Canada*, ed. Jocelyn Downie and Elaine Gibson (Toronto: Irwin Law, 2007), 365 at 375.

96 RSC 1985, c H-6, ss 7, 10(a).

97 2007 FC 1061, 78 Admin LR (4th) 54, varying 2006 CHRT 39.

98 *Ibid* at para 1.

99 *Ibid* at paras 11–12. CF members are explicitly excluded from the definition of "insured person" under the CHA. The federal government's responsibility for national defence includes military health (*The Constitution Act, 1867*, s 91(7)).

100 *Supra* note 97 at paras 1, 11–20.

101 2006 CHRT 39 at para 123.

102 *Supra* note 97 at paras 30, 55.

103 *Ibid* at paras 49, 53, 56, 62.

104 The Right Hon the Baroness Hale of Richmond, *From the Test Tube to the Coffin: Choice and Regulation in Private Life*, the Hamlyn Lectures (London: Sweet and Maxwell, 1996), 8–9.

105 See, for example, Laura Shanner, "The Right to Procreate: When Rights Claims Have Gone Wrong" (1995) 40 McGill LJ 823.

106 Maurice Rickard, "Is It Medically Legitimate to Provide Assisted Reproductive Treatments to Fertile Lesbians and Single Women?,"

Research Paper No. 23 (Australia: Department of the Parliamentary Library, 2001), http://www.aph.gov.au/binaries/library/pubs/rp/2000-01/01rp23.pdf.

107 *Cameron* (NSCA), *supra* note 74 at para 84.

108 *Ibid* at paras 143, 184, 203.

109 *Supra* note 23 at 455–7.

110 2011 SCC 12, [2011] 1 SCR 396 at para 65.

111 *Supra* note 58 at 322–3.

112 Pearl Eliadis, "Inserting Charter Values in Policy Processes," in *Diminishing Returns: Inequality and the Canadian Charter of Rights and Freedoms*, ed. Sheila McIntyre and Sanda Rodgers (Markham: LexisNexis Canada, 2006), 229 at 229–30.

113 *Supra* note 60.

114 *Supra* note 112 at 231.

115 Ries, *supra* note 18 at 233.

116 *Ibid*; von Tigerstrom, *supra* note 94 at 35.

117 Advisory Process for Infertility Services, Key Recommendations Report, 23 June 2015, http://www.health.gov.on.ca/en/public/programs/ivf/docs/ivf_report.pdf.

118 Stanley M. Corbett, *Canadian Human Rights Law and Commentary* (Markham: LexisNexis Canada, 2007), 12.

119 *R v Kapp*, 2008 SCC 41, [2008] 2 SCR 483 at para 21.

120 *Supra* note 112.

16 The Commodification of Gametes: Why Prohibiting Untrammelled Commercialization Matters

TRUDO LEMMENS

Introduction

In January 2012 the Royal Canadian Mounted Police raided the offices of Canadian Fertility Consultants (CFC).[1] The RCMP subsequently charged CFC's owner, Leia Picard, with twenty-seven offences, including violation of the prohibitions imposed by ss. 6 and 7 of Canada's *Assisted Human Reproduction Act* (*AHRA*) against the commercial buying and selling of gametes (ova and sperm) and providing surrogacy services.[2] Although the criminal charges were a Canadian first, media reports had documented the Canadian commercial market surrounding gametes and surrogacy services for many years. In a 2010 article in *The Walrus*, for example, Alison Motluk described the prevalence of commercial assisted human reproduction (AHR) transactions in Canada and the role of Canadians in the international fertility business.[3] Surveys conducted around the same period with support from the (since abolished) federal agency Assisted Human Reproduction Canada also confirmed that national and international AHR commercial transactions were occurring, including the sale, purchase, and cross-border transfer of gametes.[4] Reports of commercial practices in Canada continue to emerge.[5]

In this context, it is surprising that the 2012 raids were the Canadian government's first serious attempt to use the *AHRA* to address either national or transnational commercial AHR transactions.[6] Enforcement of the prohibitions against commercial AHR transactions may have previously been lax partly because of uncertainty about the constitutionality of some of the *AHRA*'s key components, including those provisions in s. 12 relating to the regulation of allowable reimbursements to gamete donors or surrogates.[7] Perhaps the constitutional challenge also provided an easy excuse for the federal government at the time to postpone thorny regulations detailing what forms of reimbursement would be acceptable and how these reimbursements should be organized. However, in the 2010 *Reference re Assisted Human Reproduction Act*,[8] the Supreme Court upheld the constitutionality of the reimbursement provisions, which enabled the government to develop more detailed provisions related to reimbursement. More than five years later, it is puzzling that enforcement remains lax and that the government has still enacted no regulations relating to reimbursements.

If some of the prosecutions move ahead, they might result in a new constitutional challenge, this time not to the provisions implementing a regulatory regime surrounding reproduction, but rather to the criminal prohibition on the commercial sale of gametes and surrogacy itself. For example, Ms Picard originally stated on a publicly accessible Facebook page her intent to challenge the constitutionality of the *AHRA*, although she ended up settling the criminal prosecution by paying a $60,000 penalty.[9]

This chapter explores some of the key arguments that would be made to challenge the constitutionality of a prohibition on the commercialization of gametes. It aims primarily at providing a defence of the ban on untrammelled commercialization, based on a moderate liberal approach towards the regulation of so-called contested commodities, one that recognizes the special nature of the goods involved in reproduction. The analysis builds on Margaret Jane Radin's work. Radin provides in my view convincing arguments as to why governments can reasonably restrict market transactions of "contested commodities," goods that arguably have a special meaning in society. I will explore here more specifically how these arguments play out in the context of gamete commercialization. My defence of the restrictions on market-based gamete exchanges runs counter to the arguments of several scholars who have criticized – including in this volume – the restrictions on commercial transactions in the context of AHR. Following a more theoretical discussion of the impact of commercialization, one that focuses particularly on the concerns associated with the concept of commodification, I will engage more fully with the arguments made by some of these scholars that a prohibition on commercial transactions in this context violates *Charter* rights. I put forward in this chapter that the potential impact of commercialization on the nature of the AHR goods should provide sufficient justification for market restrictions.

I will argue that the approach taken in the *AHRA* – a combination of a prohibition on sheer commercialization with a state-regulated compensation regime – is reasonable and even desirable public policy. Section 12, I will put forward, provides a basis for regulations that allow compensation in the context of an exchange system aimed at promoting access to reproductive services but that also protect core moral and public health–related interests.

While this chapter focuses on the commercialization of gametes, I will from time to time touch on the debate around commercial surrogacy. Even though several of the arguments made about the commercial sale of gametes are relevant in the surrogacy context, a ban on the commercial sale of gametes always seemed to me more difficult to justify than a ban on commercial surrogacy, because concerns over exploitation seem starker in the surrogacy context. Interestingly, however, at a 2011 Conference on the Supreme Court's reference, some Canadian commentators appeared very sceptical about the rationale behind prohibiting surrogacy, even outright rejecting concerns about exploitation.[10] More recent Canadian publications, including empirical studies on surrogacy, also challenge the idea that surrogacy contracts tend to be exploitative.[11] This suggests that the arguments I develop here, which focus much more on the nature of the "goods" involved in AHR and the concerns about commodification – and less on exploitation – are also more relevant for surrogacy than I originally conceived.

The *AHRA Reference:* The Supreme Court's Divergent Views on the Commercialization of AHR

Even though the Supreme Court's decision did not address the constitutionality of the criminal prohibition on the commercialization of specific reproductive practices, parts of the judgment still provide a hint of the contrasting views of the judges on the use of a prohibitive criminal law–based approach. The different opinions also give us a sense of the very divergent views about the concerns associated with commercialization. The key provision with respect to commodification of gametes is s. 7 of the *AHRA*. It stipulates that "[n]o person shall purchase, offer to purchase, or advertise for the purchase of sperm or ova from a donor or a person acting on behalf of a donor."[12] The provision uses the narrow language of "sale" and "purchase," but Jocelyn Downie and Françoise Baylis have reasonably argued that the section also applies to payment for third party egg production services, thus also targeting the business enterprises surrounding the marketing of gametes.[13] The penalties associated with violating s. 7 are severe, and include a fine of up to $500,000 and imprisonment of up to ten years, as well as forfeiture and disposition of the materials or information used in the offence.

In the *AHRA Reference*, Quebec did not challenge the constitutionality of s. 7, seemingly accepting that the core criminal law provisions are a legitimate exercise of federal jurisdiction. However, the province did challenge the provisions relating to the regulation of allowable reimbursements in s. 12, as well as various other provisions. As is discussed elsewhere in this volume,[14] a majority of the Supreme Court suspended the various licensing provisions, but Cromwell J switched sides when it came to the constitutionality of s. 12, thus upholding this provision.[15] Both McLachlin CJ and Cromwell J characterized s. 12 as related to the prohibition of various forms of commercialization of reproduction and as a legitimate exercise of the criminal law power. For McLachlin CJ, all of the *AHRA*'s provisions relate to the dominant purpose of the Act, namely, the aversion of "serious damage to the fabric of our society by prohibiting practices that tend to devalue human life and degrade participants."[16] With respect to s. 12, the Chief Justice emphasized that the provision draws the line between "inappropriate commodification" and acceptable reimbursement and is therefore related to the same concerns as those addressed by the non-contested ss. 6 and 7 of the *AHRA*, which prohibit payment for surrogacy and the purchase of gametes. Section 12 is seen by her, as well as by Cromwell J, as a "carve-out" that removes certain forms of payment from the strict prohibition.[17]

Chief Justice McLachlin explicitly mentioned "commodification" as the core rationale behind the prohibition of mere commercialization and the regulation of reimbursement. No definition of commodification is provided in the judgment, but it is clear that the term is situated within what some might describe as the fuzzier realm of morality. Chief Justice McLachlin quoted explicitly from the Baird Report: "To allow commercial exchanges of this type [buying and selling embryos, use of financial incentives, etc.] would undermine respect for human life and dignity and lead to the commodification of woman and children."[18] She also rebutted her colleagues who suggested that this was not about morality but about the regulation of medicine: "'Playing God' with genetic manipulation engages moral concerns that my colleagues' example of risky bypass surgery does not."[19]

But that does not mean that McLachlin CJ and her colleagues saw moral concerns as the sole rationale behind the *AHRA*'s general use of the criminal law, including with respect to the exchange of gametes. The Chief Justice stated more generally that "s. 12 is rooted in the same concerns as ss. 6 and 7,"[20] provisions that generally "criminalize conduct that Parliament has found to be fundamentally immoral, a public health evil, a threat to personal security, or some combinations of these factors."[21] In the discussion of the other sections of the *AHRA*, she frequently mentioned other factors that can be associated with concerns about payment for gametes and that overlapped with the commodification arguments that were more squarely within the realm of "moral concerns."

In discussing potential harms associated with AHR, McLachlin CJ mentioned the "dehumanization of motherhood," the "devaluation of persons with disabilities," discrimination based on ethnicity or genetic status, and "exploitation of the vulnerable,"[22] all concerns that can to some extent be connected to the commercialization issue, as discussed below.

Justices Lebel and Deschamps provided a diametrically opposed view of the possible impact of AHR. They did not recognize that s. 12 has a clear connection to the explicit prohibition on commercialization of surrogacy, gamete donation, and embryo creation. For them, s. 12 is, like all other impugned provisions, simply about the regulation of health. The easy comparison made with ordinary medical practice, various strong statements about the lack of moral concerns ("from the standpoint of morality," they state, "no evil has been identified."[23]), and the firm and broad rejection of the sufficient link to moral issues of all the impugned provisions seem to reflect a view that there are very few serious moral and societal concerns in the context of AHR that threaten to undermine important values.

Contested Commodities and Commercialization Concerns

Considering these very divergent views, it is essential to clarify first why commercialization of AHR material might be problematic and warrant intervention. Radin's *Contested Commodities: The Trouble with Trade in Sex, Children, Body Parts, and Other Things* contains one of the most sophisticated explorations of the concerns associated with the framing of all human interactions and exchanges in market terms.[24] In her book and related articles, she explores why and in what circumstances it can be morally problematic to use market rhetoric and market mechanisms to determine the appropriate distribution of socially and culturally valued goods. Although she recognizes that the market language embraced, for example, by law and economics scholars is largely rhetoric, she suggests that we cannot completely separate concerns about the rhetorical language of the market from concerns about when we concretely should allow money to be used as the main tool for regulating valued transactions. Concerns over rhetorical or metaphorical conceptualizations of goods as marketable items give us a sense of why we can reasonably opt for legislative or regulatory restrictions on market transactions in relation to these goods.

Radin discusses the complex relationship between the concepts of commodification, personhood, and human flourishing, and she shows, with a detailed discussion of the moral debates surrounding, among other things, the regulation of prostitution, baby-selling, and free speech, how "the way humans value things important to personhood"[25] cannot be captured fully in market terms. This suggests also why using the market as a concrete distribution mechanism can undermine the role these goods play in our self-realization and human flourishing.

In order to determine how goods ought to be distributed, Radin posits, we have to evaluate how they contribute to or play a role in creating the conditions for human flourishing. Under her "positive liberty," "identity-constructive," and pragmatic contextual approach, it is crucial to examine how specific goods carry specific meanings in specific social and cultural contexts, as well as how commodifying these goods may affect their meaning and undermine how they contribute to our personhood. The concept of market inalienability is thereby key: it reflects the idea that with respect to some types of goods, we may accept the legal and physical transfer of these goods, and even property-based control, but not untrammelled market trading. Market-inalienable goods are distinct from commodities in that not all three key characteristics of commodities apply: alienability, fungibility, and commensurability. Alienability refers to the right to sell, transfer, mortgage, or donate goods. Fungibility means that commodities can be exchanged without loss of value. Commensurability is the ability to determine the value of a good according to a common scale that applies to all commodities. Radin suggests that with respect to many goods that have a particular meaning in society, "we may decide that [they] ... are or should be market-inalienable only to a degree, or only in some aspects."[26] In relation to many of the "contested commodities," where there is debate over the appropriateness of selling and buying, society tends to allow some but not all market transactions.

Radin's view is directly connected to a specific view on liberty. She takes issue with the concept of personhood that is embedded in the "universal commodification" approach. For Radin, those who argue that all transactions can be measured in terms of their monetary value embrace a view of personhood in which identity and a particular view of freedom are intertwined; freedom, for universal commodifiers, is associated with an absolute separation from others and from the objects surrounding us, and with the idea that free choice is the key moral value. In this conceptualization of freedom, the autonomous person is able to engage in transactions in the marketplace without strings attached to persons or to goods that have a particular meaning. All choices made by this atomic individual, all relations, all personal attributes, can be weighed and measured according to objective market criteria. Everything is, in other words, commensurable and fungible. Freedom in this view of personhood is the freedom to engage in "unfettered trades of commodified objects."[27] In contrast, a more positive conception of freedom emphasizes the value of engaging in relationships with others and of exchanging objects in such a way that self-development is promoted. This freedom is connected to a view of personhood as fundamentally connected to others and to objects and exchanges in society that have a particular meaning to us, which cannot be captured in monetary terms. As human beings, we construct our lives communally, and we flourish through engaging in meaningful relations that necessarily involve the exchange of symbolically important (and often not monetarily assessable) goods. In fact, these more meaningful interactions shape our personhood much more than the exchange of commodified objects.

A detailed discussion of all the ramifications of Radin's theory exceeds the scope of this chapter. But a crucial element of her analysis, to be emphasized for our discussion here, is that for her, positive liberty is associated with a society that enables the structural context in which we develop our liberty, in which we can flourish. For law as a tool of social ordering, this means that legal institutions and legal rules should contribute to creating the conditions in which people can exercise meaningful choices that enable them to flourish. Autonomy is always an autonomy that unfolds itself and finds its shape in the context of a supportive societal structure.[28] The legal order can therefore never be entirely neutral; rather, it fundamentally contributes to the context in which some decisions are facilitated and others are discouraged – that is, those we think hamper the types of interactions that promote flourishing or that are essential to personhood and to what it means to be a human being.[29] Restrictions on specific market exchanges may be essential to promote and preserve a more meaningful positive liberty.

Radin is clearly not alone in her emphasis on how the market may affect important social goods. Michael Sandel, for example, argues in *What Money Can't Buy: The Moral Limits of Markets* in the same vein that "some of the good things in life are corrupted or degraded if turned into commodities"[30] – particularly those goods that are pivotal in our communal deliberations about the good society and the good life. Yet Radin tends to be more pragmatic, as well as more nuanced in her identification of the concrete ways in which market mechanisms ought to be restricted with respect to these items and often in specific contexts.[31]

A last important point Radin makes is that concerns about commodification and about the treatment of human attributes and other important goods as marketable items are generally connected to other concerns we have, in particular concerns about racial or gender subordination.[32] Concerns about the commodification of "motherhood," for example, are for her often directly connected to concerns about subordination of women.[33] She suggests that while we can theoretically imagine how mere commodification of motherhood may not necessarily undermine personhood, it will usually be connected to troublesome subordination. Disentangling these different concerns may often be impossible. The concerns about commodification, in other words, are rarely just about the "objectification" of important interactions into monetary relations.

Radin, Sandel, and others[34] emphasize the need for context-specific analysis of the value of goods, of their specific role in society, and of the potential corrupting impact of the commercial market on the nature of these goods. As mentioned earlier, Radin does not outright reject the use of markets as a distributive mechanism even with regard to so-called contested commodities, but she points to the need to evaluate what market distribution will really do, and to what extent and in what circumstances those goods should reasonably be excluded from market transactions and for what reasons.

Radin discusses various justifications we can invoke to restrict market transactions and how these apply in the context of specific transactions related to various contested commodities. I will discuss now the key arguments that can be connected to these justifications in the context of the sale of gametes.

Liberal Justifications for Market Restrictions: Market Efficiency and Noxious Markets

The first reason why market transactions can be restricted, Radin argues, is one that many moderate market liberals will agree with: market corrections.[35] Since for market liberals, contractual liberty is an essential component of the morality of the market, corrections may be needed when specific market-related situations undermine this liberty. A related argument is that market corrections can be acceptable because markets are often "noxious," as Debra Satz puts it.[36] Satz distinguishes various and somewhat overlapping reasons why this can be the case. A first reason is that markets sometimes have extremely harmful results, either for individuals or for society. With this concept of "harmful outcomes" to society, Satz moves more in the direction of recognizing that law sometimes restricts markets because of a commitment to important societal values, which I will discuss further in more detail. She gives as an example of "harms to society" how market distortions may undermine crucial egalitarian values. As an example of market restrictions justified through this secondary effect, one could think of limits imposed on commercialized health care. Allowing the wealthy to access the most luxurious form of care, when the most basic form of health care is not available to the poor, may rightly be seen as an affront to our societal commitment to equality. Another context that can render markets noxious, Satz argues, is when there are extreme vulnerabilities. This can happen either when there is very significant knowledge asymmetry or when one of the contracting parties is in an extremely vulnerable situation and cannot really be considered to act as an equal in the transaction. In such a situation, people's desperation to engage in commercial transactions undermines their autonomy. Emphasizing the unique concerns when people are pushed into negotiating about their own bodily integrity, Anne Phillips questions even whether there can ever really be meaningful equality in the context of the commercialization of human organs:

> Markets in human organs rely on a systemic inequality between recipients and vendors that has the effect of denying our moral equality. The fact that it is the body that is up for sale matters, not because our identities are intimately bound up with all the parts of our bodies, but because we all have bodies. If some of us nonetheless become positioned as sellers and others as buyers, the only conceivable explanation lies in our inequality.[37]

Arguments about the exploitation of poverty or financial need, and thus the vulnerability of the parties, have often been emphasized in AHR. One of the most common arguments is that a commercialization of reproduction will primarily push the unemployed, those living in poverty, students with increasingly high debts, and so on, to engage in these transactions out of a lack of alternatives.[38] Three different concepts are often used in this context: coercion, undue influence, and exploitation. I cannot discuss the difference between these connected terms here in detail, but they all reflect the idea of an absence or at least corruption of meaningful autonomous decision-making because of circumstances of vulnerability.[39]

The concern that offering excessive payment will particularly induce poor, vulnerable women to offer surrogacy services, or sell ova, "against their better judgment" or "because they feel they have no choice," is inevitably connected to the potential impact of these transactions. To speak of exploitation, there has to be some sense that a person's vulnerability has been used in a way that caused some level of physical, psychological, or dignitary harm. The idea is that the person's vulnerability has pushed the person to act in such a way that she would never have done if she had been in a less vulnerable position. If the outcome of the choice is fully satisfactory to those who consented to a transaction and there is no reason to argue that there is something fundamentally unfair about the context in which the transaction took place, it is clearly difficult to talk about exploitation.

What could arguably be the problem of offering significant payment in the context of gamete donation? Two issues can be distinguished here. One is the risk of serious physical harm associated with gamete donation. The other issue is that payment pushes people to engage in actions, the serious consequences and implications of which they don't fully grasp and may experience only much later.

To start with the latter, these concerns appear to relate to what Satz describes as the potential existence of highly asymmetric knowledge and agency on the part of some of the market participants. Satz herself gives the example of surrogacy contracts: "If agency is weak in surrogacy contracts, and the surrogate is now devastated by the thought of giving up a child she has borne, we will be less likely to think that we can justify enforcement of the contract simply on the basis that there was an agreement."[40] Is this as much of a concern in the context of gamete sale? We may indeed question whether eighteen-year-old students in need of some money fully grasp what it may mean for them to have a biological connection to future children; that these children may one day show up at their door; and that these children or they themselves may feel the need to establish a meaningful connection with them later in life. As Naomi Kahn puts it, "donors may feel somewhat unprepared for the short- and long-term moral, physical, and psychological effects of donation."[41] This can indeed also be the case in non-commercialized reproduction. It does not justify legal restrictions on, for example, sexual intercourse, which can also have life-changing implications that people may not always fully grasp in the moment. The difficulty of grasping the possible outcome (i.e., creating children who may have an identity interest in connecting later in life) is in other words not sufficient to make the transaction itself completely suspect and is not necessarily unique to the situation of paid gamete donation. In addition, as I will discuss further, those providing gametes may not be as vulnerable and as affected by the "outcome" of the contract as, say, a woman who has carried a child for nine months and is then forced to hand it over to others. Moreover, even in the context of surrogacy, the concept of exploitation is increasingly contested. Angela Campbell emphasizes that we may all too easily stereotype surrogates as vulnerable and disempowered, while evidence from various industrialized countries suggests the opposite.[42]

But surely it is reasonable to be concerned that excessive payment risks affecting people's judgments about the nature of gamete donation and the consequences of engaging in it. Turning gamete donation into an untrammelled and lucrative sales transaction conducted in the sterile environment of a laboratory may disconnect people from the profoundly human implications of their actions,[43] and perhaps more so than engaging in consensual sexual intercourse, which still involves a physical and most often to some degree psychological interaction with "the other." The government may legitimately try to counter this risk of complete detachment from the consequences of one's actions through regulatory intervention. That is, while significant payment does not obfuscate consent, we have to keep in mind that these are highly value-laden transactions that can have a significant impact on others, including resultant offspring. This concern adds a layer of justification to an overall regulatory and restrictive approach that tries to address the complex and multifaceted impact on others. These concerns could clearly be a rationale for governmental initiatives with respect to education and creating awareness. It also would, it seems, justify more extensive regulation that ensures particular informed consent procedures promoting awareness about what is at stake.[44]

With respect to the concern about exploitation, more commentators have referred to the physical risks involved in the harvesting of ova.[45] Ova retrieval does create significant risks to women's health. Downie and Baylis point out that the procedures involved not only are painful and uncomfortable but also create significant long-term risks, including damage to organs, infertility, hemorrhage, thromboembolism, and various forms of cancer.[46] Chief Justice McLachlin explicitly mentions the ova retrieval risks in her judgment, "including ovarian hyperstimulation syndrome, a potentially dangerous condition."[47] A qualitative study of the long-term psychological and physical impact of egg donation in the United States found that a majority of donors reported long-term side effects of donation, including impaired fertility, chronic pelvic pain, and ovarian cysts.[48]

Do these risks provide a sufficient basis to justify a ban on commercialization? It seems reasonable for the state to reduce the likelihood that poverty will drive women to donate eggs if there is a significant associated risk of health consequences. The possibility that poverty leads women to engage in frequent extraction of ova could be a particular concern in the context of a potential commercial harvesting of ova for research, if this market targets more marginalized women. It may be harder, though, to argue that women who provide eggs for AHR are among the most vulnerable in society and are particularly in need of additional protection. Indeed, for AHR purposes, women who donate ova tend to be students at top-rated universities in highly selective programs. They may need funding to cover high tuition and accumulated student loans, but they are also more likely to have other options to gain revenue. They may have some temporal vulnerability, which may require particular forms of societal support, not in the least perhaps for increasingly excessive tuition fees. But it is hard to argue that they represent a category of extremely vulnerable women who have no other choice but to sell their ova. In addition, these women tend to be highly educated, which makes it harder (but not necessarily impossible) to invoke fundamental knowledge asymmetry as the most important justification for market restrictions.

As mentioned, the idea that primarily vulnerable women will be driven to engage in AHR services has certainly been questioned by empirical evidence in the context of surrogacy.[49] In addition, several authors have suggested that the idea that restrictions are appropriate because of the risks involved stereotypically treats women as incapable of making their own rational reproductive choices.[50] Even in a commercialized market, restrictions could be placed on the number of procedures women can be involved with, to reduce the risk of harm. The risks involved in egg donation seem to be a valid reason to exercise regulatory control and impose restrictions, but are unlikely sufficient to justify a complete ban on the commercial sale of ova.

But even if the risk of harm is not the core reason to prohibit commercialization, I would suggest here again that these risks add to some more fundamental reasons why commercialization can reasonably be restricted. As Radin emphasizes, the concerns about commercialization are usually complex and rarely isolated.

Risk of Undermining the Altruistic Market

A second argument for restricting certain commercial transactions is that commercialization may undermine an altruistic market or even render it impossible. Richard Titmuss famously made this argument in the context of health care systems.[51] Building on his study of blood donations, he argued that commercial markets tend to undermine altruistic systems. Once people are confronted with the fact that others sell blood according to market criteria, they appear less inclined to see blood donation as an important civic duty they have to engage in to promote the public good.[52] Institutional commitment to promote altruistic donation will also be reduced if a commercial market is available. Titmuss's analysis has been very influential and is frequently invoked in discussions about the need to restrict commercial markets in specific health care circumstances, particularly in relation to blood donation, human organ donation, and other contexts related to the human body.[53]

There is value to the argument that a commercial sale may reduce the willingness of some to engage in altruistic donation, as well as the interest of many others, including institutional players, in investing sufficiently to promote altruistic donation. Radin is somewhat sceptical that this argument can be sufficient to prohibit commercial markets in most contested commodities. For her, it is often doubtful that people will stop donating altruistically because of the existence of a commercial market. It is certainly hard to predict whether and to what extent a commercialized sector will drive out altruism and destroy a non-commercialized sphere. In the context of AHR, it does not appear that this has completely happened. In the United States and Canada, practices of altruistic donation among people who know one another remain common, notwithstanding the widespread commercialization of the practice. Finally, as Angela Campbell, among others, has argued in the context of commercial surrogacy, altruistic and financial motivations are often intertwined and may interact with each other in complex ways.[54]

The Nature of Reproductive Goods

In my view, the strongest argument for banning commercialization is related to the nature of "reproductive goods" and the values associated with the transactions and the exchange of gametes. For Radin, legal restrictions on the market distribution of specific goods can be justified because commodification will fundamentally alter the goods. The idea that law can place restrictions on liberty for value-related reasons reflects a specific view of the complex interaction between law and society. "Law not only reflects culture but also shapes it," Radin argues. "It expresses conventional understandings of value and at the same time influences conventional understandings of value."[55] For Radin, untrammelled commercialization may affect things such as friendship, love, sexuality, and parenting, but also housing and work. She urges us to think about the extent to which commercialization may undermine the essential role some of these value-laden goods play in relation to our personhood. She invites us to be pragmatic, though, in assessing how important the restrictions on the market are, and to investigate concretely the specific ways in which we use and transfer these goods. This analysis, she emphasizes, has to be contextual. How do we apply her approach to the context of the prohibition of payment for AHR services and, for the purposes of this chapter, to gametes in particular?

A Contextual Analysis of Commercialization of Gametes: The Link with the Human Body

A contextual exploration should start with a more general observation about the nature of the debate. Clearly, discussions about the sale of gametes are connected to the debate surrounding the status of the human body. There is a long-standing legal tradition according to which the human body is unique and should not be treated as an ordinary market good. Without entering into this more general debate, it is sufficient here to point to the law's treatment of the body as something "special," at least of a different category than, say, cars, furniture, or luxury food. Although traditions should not be determinative of how we deal with a particular issue, they hint at a certain moral "attitude" we tend to have towards "goods" that play a particular role for personhood and human flourishing. It is clear that our existence and identity are fundamentally intertwined with our body.[56] We experience ourselves, our interactions with the outside world, and our relations, all through our body. As Anne Phillips states it, "we are all embodied beings, encountering the world through our bodies, and irretrievably shaped by the experiences, assumptions, and expectations attached to them."[57] Our embodied self, to some degree separated from but at the same time also fundamentally connected to others and to the outside world, is the basis also of our exercise of autonomy – hence the prohibition against selling ourselves into slavery. If we accept that the body has this unique role and status, we should also be cautious when dealing with separate components of the human body. Alastair Campbell, who also invokes Radin in his discussion of the status of the body in bioethics, frames it succinctly: "If we hold this richer view of the self we are bound to regard with concern attempts to treat all aspects of the individuals, including the person's bodily parts, as readily detachable from the whole, as no more than tradeable items."[58]

That doesn't mean, of course, that all body-related goods have the same meaning and value and that none of them should ever be alienated or sold on the market. It is widely accepted that some parts of our body, such as hair, nail clippings, and organs, can be transferred to others for a variety of reasons, and that particularly in the context of medicine, they can become part of a network of market transactions. Yet it seems reasonable to take as an approach that intimate connections to the human body force us to think more carefully about the specific meaning of the body and its parts and about the appropriateness of exchanging them on the market. From a values perspective, it seems fair to take a more "precautionary" approach to commercial transactions in relation to the body and its parts. As Radin argues – and Alastair Campbell agrees – whether and the extent to which those parts can be treated as commodities is "contested." We have to carefully consider at what stage in the process commercial transactions become appropriate and for what reason.

Gametes and Human Flourishing

So, what do gametes mean to us? What particular role do they play in human flourishing, and how could commercial sales affect their value in this regard? We can begin by observing that gametes have a peculiar connection to our body and to our being in the world. We now know that all of our body's tissues contain our genetic material, but these tissues do not all have the same direct connection as gametes to who we are, to where we come from, and to who may come after us. Gametes contain a wealth of genetic material that – at least in part – determines some of the core characteristics of a person, including appearance, health vulnerabilities, and personality traits. This argument does not have to be seen as an expression of genetic determinism. Without suggesting that genes truly determine who we are, we can fairly state that gametes carry important components of our past and the potential future of those that may come after us.[59] They contain genetic material from two other people – the biological parents – that directly contributes to the development of a new person – the offspring. This clearly creates a higher level of connectedness to others than ordinary body parts, with quite a unique meaning.

In fact, the special nature of reproductive goods and their connection to human flourishing is apparent from many of the debates surrounding AHR. For example, people who argue for allocating resources to AHR or who invoke equality rights to argue for access to reproductive services for, say, single women or gay couples, rightly emphasize the unique importance of this form of reproduction and its relationship to human flourishing. The fact that AHR creates a biological connection and that this connection carries a unique importance is implicit in these arguments. If this biological connection were not so important, one could very easily imagine advocates arguing that we should invest in better allocation of adoptive children and better adoption services to compensate for problems or inherent limitations that people may encounter with traditional reproduction. But very often these do not seem to be considered acceptable alternatives. Accordingly, biological links between sperm and ova donors and offspring are perceived as having some unique value. Gametes have a particular status because of their crucial relation-creating nature.

AHR does indeed create a complex web of personal relations: not just relations between parents and offspring, but also between donors and offspring; donors and recipients; surrogates and offspring; surrogates and prospective parents; and offspring and other potential biological relatives. While some of these relations are more intimate and more important for who we are and how we flourish than others, and while people often experience the importance of these relations in unique ways, they do have a uniform identity-connected significance.[60] These relations tend to have a special meaning and help shape who we are and what we value. It is in part through these relations that we realize ourselves in the world, that we situate ourselves with a particular past and a potential future.

Even if social, cultural, and historical contexts determine how important some of these relations are, and even if individuals differ with respect to the value they attach to the wide spectrum of relations, many people feel a desire to have a sense of whom they are connected to, even biologically. Without entering the debate here about the acceptability of anonymous gamete donation, it is fair to state that the growing criticism of anonymous sperm donation confirms that many people attach special value to biological connectedness.[61] As some have pointed out, including in this book, the right to know one's origins has even been recognized as one of the fundamental rights of children.[62]

The importance of these connections is confirmed in the types of meaningful relations that are increasingly being developed among those who are involved in AHR itself. People are constructing new ways to value the role of many of those who are connected to the children born from AHR, including the biological donors and surrogates. Parents are now routinely remaining in contact with surrogates and with those who provided gametes for AHR. More and more, they are trying to create and maintain different forms of meaningful relationships, often creating new rituals surrounding the novel ways in which people are connected through AHR, recognizing thereby how important this is for their children and for everyone involved.

Commercialization Practices and Their Impact

The question remains, of course, whether valuing these relations means that we should exclude the commercial sale of the gametes that are the foundational basis of these relations. Some examples of the practices that are already taking place offer us a good basis for exploring the problematic nature of untrammelled commercialization. One of the most extreme examples that received quite some attention in the media around the turn of the century,[63] spurring discussions in the medical, bioethics, and health policy literature,[64] was the "auctioning" of the sperm and ova of a number of donors by an American fashion photographer.[65] The website "Ronsangels.com" offered the sperm and ova of eight female and one male "donors" (in the website's words, sperm and ova with "beauty and brains") to the highest bidders. Bids had to start at $30,000, and the expectation was that they would rise to around $150,000. The potential donors were scantily dressed, showing off their good looks, and the website described their proper upbringing, their excellent university degrees, the absence of alcoholism and mental illness in their families, and so on. With respect to the sperm donor, people could bid for an exclusive sale of his allegedly high-quality sperm. The organizer, Ron Harris, explicitly defended the auction idea as a legitimate response to the desire of individuals to have genetically superior offspring.[66] "If you could increase the chance of reproducing beautiful children, and thus giving them an advantage in society, would you?,"[67] the website quipped in Nozickean terms. In an interview with the *New York Times*, Harris reported that he had received an offer of $45,000 early on. The auction may very well have been a publicity stunt, organized by a photographer who wanted to draw attention to some of his other products. But it became the subject of a heated debate in the United States and highlighted the legality of this type of practice. As Kenneth Baum reports, reactions among bioethicists and health policy commentators were overwhelmingly negative.[68]

Other, more clearly serious examples of commercialization practices that come close to the auction idea have become standard. Around the same time as this controversy, an American couple advertised in student newspapers at MIT as well as Yale, Harvard, and other Ivy League schools that they were willing to pay $50,000 for ova from a tall (5′5″ or higher), athletic, intelligent (SAT test result of 1400 or higher) college student with no significant family medical history.[69] "Auction"-like sales to higher bidders also occur in the context of standard sperm banks, where prospective parents can pay higher fees for an "exclusive" sperm or ova donation (as opposed to a standard donation by a donor whose gametes are also used by others).[70] Regardless of high payments for exclusivity and for auctions, careful selection of gametes, based on college degrees, good looks, and optimal health, appears to have become the norm. Advertisements soliciting sperm and ova continue to cover billboards in many Ivy League universities. The auction idea may have stirred controversy because it confronted us more starkly with the perverse logic of full commercialization. Yet we seem to be increasingly confronted with practices that are not so categorically different.[71]

Another revealing example of the potential impact of commercialization of gametes is the 2015 lawsuit launched by two Port Hope parents against an American sperm bank called Xytex Corp. In this lawsuit, the parents of a then seven-year-old child born through artificial insemination sought damages for pain, suffering, and financial losses because of fraud and misrepresentation related to the attributes of the donor whose sperm they had used to conceive a child. The parents allegedly had bought the sperm based on Xytex Corp.'s representation of the donor as a PhD student in neuroscience engineering, with a master's degree in artificial intelligence and an impeccable health history.[72] They later received by mistake an e-mail from the sperm bank from which they learned that the donor was in fact a school dropout who had previously been arrested for burglary and who had a history of schizophrenia, and that the picture representing him had been doctored to remove a large mole on his cheek. Rather than getting "ideal" sperm for the creation of their child, they had bought sperm with a lot of "genetic baggage" and without the associated good looks they had paid for. Many other parents had used the donor's sperm, and several of them indicated they would join the lawsuit. The lawyer for the parents suggested that they were primarily upset about the child's increased risk for schizophrenia, that the damages they were seeking were primarily to cover preventive screening for the illness, and that the lawsuit was also aimed at raising awareness about the lack of proper screening. Yet it seems naive to think that concerns about schizophrenia were the only important complaint the parents had. Several newspaper articles reported on this case, with legal commentators focusing exclusively on the need to have better regulation and screening of donors. Some even used the occasion to complain about the Canadian dependence on American sperm and ova importation, and suggested that these problems were really the result of the inappropriate restrictions on sperm and ova banks in Canada, thus making the case for a lifting of prohibitions. None of the articles expressed even the slightest concern about the child's future perception of this lawsuit. Personally, my first reaction was to think about the awkwardness of the future conversation between the parents and the child in which they had to explain their legal action. How do you explain to your child that you went to court because you really didn't get what you bargained for and that 50 per cent of her genetic building blocks were of lower than expected quality?[73]

What seems troubling in these cases is that an essential component of the process of procreation is treated as a commercial good just like any other marketable item, to be bought and sold according to market processes and prices. Human qualities of existing people are monetized with an expectation that these characteristics will be transferred to their offspring. Important characteristics of identity and personhood become commensurable, as if these characteristics can really be translated into a certain price without loss of value. Intelligence, good looks, size, family history, and even social or ethnic background become marketable items to be bought with payment commensurate to the desirability of the traits. As Mary Lyndon Shanley argues, allowing or even encouraging price variations for different kinds of genetic variations, as the commercialized market clearly does, undermines equal human dignity.[74] Lawsuits focusing on the flaws in the genetic material embedded in the gametes indirectly emphasize the perceived inequality embedded in human genetic material.

Concerns about a new form of eugenics add onto these concerns about objectification of essential components of personhood. In this system, the wealthy will be able to purchase the most "interesting" gametes, with the highest "genetic potential."[75] Even if we reject genetic determinism, and recognize that it is too simplistic to reduce future children to the characteristics associated with the gametes from which they originate, there is something disturbing, something dehumanizing about the practice. It also constitutes an affront to our sense of equality. In this system, we permit the wealthy to exercise more control over the types of offspring that are deemed to have a better "potential" in life, adding to already existing inequality based on wealth and social status. Several authors have rightly suggested that this this opens the door to a new form of free market eugenics.[76]

One could argue that even in natural reproduction, selection of "traits" happens through the tendency to select partners from similar social and cultural circles. Indeed, one reason why the wealthy send their children to elite private schools and colleges may very well be that these shape their relationships in the future. Social and cultural selection does indeed happen "naturally." "Sperm" or "ova" of graduates from esteemed faculties of medicine, engineering, or law can also be sought outside of the commercial market, of course, through traditional sexual relations. But is there really no categorical difference between the buying of sperm or ova through a seller's brochure with a list of enumerated optimal traits, and the "selection" of "sexual partners" with whom we reproduce through intimate human interactions with others, in a process of mutual exploration and discovery, with its rituals of seduction and engagement, and with its inherent uncertainty and need for some level of mutual respect and acceptance?[77]

Even if it is naive to think that buyers really control so much more the "product" when they buy gametes, the process of sale still creates some level of expectation that the product will meet the standards promised in the sales brochure. It also clearly sends the message that there is some increased level of control. The idea of selection of specific traits in offspring is clearly heightened, which confirms stereotypes of genetic determinism. A commercial market for traits that are so intimately connected to personhood seems to dehumanize what is at stake. The commercial nature of transactions surrounding surrogacy and gamete donation risks rendering these into depersonalized investments with a monetary value and a "quid pro quo": the higher the price, the more exclusive and qualitatively better the traits. Certainly, not everyone who pays for gametes will do it with this mindset, and a commercial transaction may not always devalue what is at stake. But it seems reasonable to argue that the fundamentally different nature of the "transaction" tends to make us think differently about the "product" we expect.

The commercial nature also affects other components of the transaction. As mentioned before, the debate over commercialization has a connection to the debate over the appropriateness of anonymous gamete donation. When biological donors see themselves as sellers of a product, it becomes much easier for them to dissociate from the "end product" that will follow. We are much less likely to have a sense of ethical connection to the reproductive process when we see ourselves as transferring a detachable good or as providing a mere market-based service in exchange for money. It makes it easier to think there is no other obligation as donor than to deliver the "product" according to the sales specifications; that there is no need to approach the "outcome" of this action as a new human being, and to appreciate how the process creates new, complex, but essentially human and often intimate relations, with all their promises and perils. It makes it much easier to reject the idea that those created have specific moral claims towards us. As Shanley argues, "payment suggests that the transfer is a complete and discrete event, that the action of the person providing gametes has no intrinsic relationship to that of the person receiving the gametes."[78]

Arguments against the Criminal Prohibition

Liberty as Sacrosanct Value and the Need to Provide Evidence of Harm

Several arguments have been invoked against the criminal ban on commercial sale of gametes. I will not discuss commercial surrogacy in any detail, but many of the arguments developed here can also be invoked in that context. The most basic argument is that a criminal prohibition restricts individual liberty and that the state can only restrict liberty when there is harm to others. For the most zealous libertarians, liberty restrictions are only acceptable for concrete measureable harms to others. For others, harm may include more complex harms to society, including to some of our core values, but there has to be evidence that state intervention is necessary. In my discussion of Radin's contextual approach, I already hinted at why I believe the first argument should be rebutted. If law contributes to creating a societal context in which we can flourish,[79] and if human reproduction, with all its complexities and its fundamental human connection-creating characteristics, is an important and value-laden component of our flourishing, which can be negatively affected by commercialization practices, it seems reasonable to argue that the state has a role to play. The more nuanced view – that restrictions are acceptable only if there is evidence that the measures reduce measurable harms – can be associated with, for example, Canadian Supreme Court jurisprudence, which I will briefly come back to at the end of this chapter. An important question arises in this context: What type of evidence is needed?

I would suggest here that caution has to be exercised with respect to the level of evidence required. Radin also hints at this when she argues: "To the extent that we are stubbornly committed to the idea that these things that are very important to human life, health, and self – and community development ought not to be completely monetized [–] regulation that does not (theoretically) meet an efficiency test can in principle be justified. Then the response of the political order in imposing constraints may be seen as a good-faith working out of the cultural values."[80]

I have provided arguments as to why untrammelled commercialization affects the important personhood-related values involved in reproduction. It evokes concerns about our commitment to an egalitarian society. And it risks reducing a fundamental identity- and human-relation–creating transaction into a commercial one. Those who insist on "empirical evidence" of harm often seem to rely on the fact that people can always consciously and individually measure the extent to which they are emotionally or psychologically affected by the practice and then adequately report on those effects. It also presumes that they can somehow translate how commercialization undermines their human flourishing. But the harm I have been describing here is intrinsically hard to measure. It is certainly hard to identify at the individual level. As Susanne Holland puts it, "the harm of commodification is socio-cultural,"[81] which is "to be found at the macro level."[82] It cannot be reduced to individual perception. It risks harming – often only in the long run – our way of being in the world. Once the harm is present, it is impossible to step out of who we are to measure how it has affected us. Those who invoke "empirical studies" to provide evidence that people who are involved in commercial transactions in the context of AHR do not "feel" commodified are therefore misconstruing what the concern over commodification really is about. The impact of commodification is complex, open-ended, more societal in nature, and long-term. That people do not "feel" commodified is not determinant in our inquiry into the harm of commodification.

Impact on Reproductive Rights and Interests of Others

A second set of arguments is that a ban on commercialization seriously affects the reproductive rights and interests of those who want access to AHR and those who are involved in it. We can identify two distinct arguments on this point. The first is that a ban affects access to sperm and ova. The second is that a ban leads to a booming black market in reproductive products and services, and therefore to greater exploitation of vulnerable women.

Impact on Access to Gametes

With respect to the first argument, it seems fair to state, as several authors have done,[83] that a ban on commercial sale can create a shortage of gametes. The commercial ban appears to have affected gamete availability in Canada, at least in the short term and in the current context.[84] Compensation appears to be a key motivating factor for young women and men participating in the transfer of gametes.[85] Canadian commentators have further argued that the prohibition in the *AHRA* makes us dependent on foreign importation of gametes.[86] It particularly impacts those who depend on AHR for procreation, including infertile and LGBTQ couples, as well as single mothers, for whom fewer gametes may be available and even then only at a much higher cost. This is not only a practical problem. It may have legal implications: *Charter*-related arguments are being made in this context, including in this volume, in relation to the impact of commercialization restrictions.[87] I will come back to this point later.

Interestingly, even commercial sperm and ova banks feel the need to emphasize that many donors "donate" because they see it as a contribution to an important "good" – that is, helping infertile couples, or those who cannot conceive traditionally, to have children of their own. This suggests, in a way, that sperm banks recognize the important values associated with gamete donation. It seems at least an indirect and prudent admission of the somewhat troubling nature of purely commercial gamete sale. The question then becomes: How important is it for the state to prevent this commercialization? Whether one accepts some impact on the availability of gametes as reasonable will obviously depend on the importance attached to avoiding commercial sale. The more we accept that commercialization undermines important components of personhood and human flourishing, the more we should find restrictions on sales reasonable, even if this may have a greater impact on some already disadvantaged groups.

With respect to the equality argument, I want to make two small observations. The first is that the idea of ensuring access to AHR appears different from ensuring access to other forms of medical care, or to most other important social goods. As argued earlier, AHR does involve, in the end, the creation of a new human being, who will be integrated into a complex web of social relations that are intimately connected to her own personhood. If commercialization risks affecting the nature of this activity, which has direct implications for the personhood and human flourishing of those who will be created, as well as implications for justice and equity in society at large, we should be cautious about the use of individual rights claims. Is it really appropriate to approach the coming into being of another human person who risks being affected by how we construct in law one of the crucial components of her creation, in line with how we deal with other important individual rights claims? I would argue that the relational nature of this human flourishing–related activity forces us to engage in a very careful balancing act.[88] It would justify, in my view, a more precautionary approach and more careful societal debate. Clearly, this is not just about the rights and liberty of parents. It is also about the interests and future rights of those who will be brought into existence, and about the impact of individual commercial transactions on reproductive practices more generally and thus also on society at large.[89] It seems somewhat odd to put forward equality arguments of prospective parents, while ignoring the more complex ways in which commercialized sperm and ova markets precisely build on an already existing structural inequality and risk reaffirming stereotypical views of biological determinism. As Marcy Darnowsky emphasizes, "championing rights in the abstract, without considering the political and social inequities with which we live, can undermine our commitments to social justice and solidarity, and to the democratic principle that we can and ought to participate in decisions about the basic conditions of our polity and collective life."[90] If we are committed to equality, we also ought to accept that our individual rights and interests may have to be restricted in order to facilitate the creation and maintenance of a social structure in which more fundamental and enduring equality and justice can flourish.

The importance of looking at the "third party" affected by AHR practices is also recognized by those who suggest that donor anonymity can be considered a violation of the rights of the child.[91] Granted, focusing on the interests of future children in the context of reproduction could also be done to argue for restrictions in the abortion context. But here again, we should be careful to make distinctions and to avoid all-too-easy generalizations. There is a categorical difference between the state interfering with the bodily integrity of a pregnant woman (as in the abortion context) and the state limiting the use of commercial market mechanisms for a transaction that is precisely aimed at a successful pregnancy and ultimately the creation of a new human being, with her own interests and rights.

The second point I want to make is that we may very well be in a transition phase with respect to AHR practices. These practices have clearly changed over time. In its early days, AHR was largely a secret, hidden practice, only accessible to married heterosexual couples. Children born through *in vitro* fertilization were not always informed that they were not fully biologically related to their legal parents. A sense of shame and embarrassment often prevented parents from informing their children. Anonymous and more detached "sale" of gametes fits within this context. Sperm and ova donors were not to be identified, and remained hidden. Yet, as mentioned, we clearly see a growing recognition of the importance of the variety of complex relations created through AHR and an increasing valuing and embracing of these relations. Is it premature to presume that we can stimulate much more altruistic donations, with perhaps some focus on mobilization within the communities of those who want to have access to reproduction?[92] Is it far-fetched to imagine the type of donor promotion that we see in the context of organ donation, where some countries have managed to promote much better results through inventive and active campaigns?

We may reach a very different, committed community of potential donors if we clearly express appreciation for the uniquely valuable contributions of donors to AHR. This also may require, as Stu Marvel and colleagues convincingly argue in this volume,[93] a more flexible regulatory scheme that doesn't necessarily impose the same rigid safety standards on known donor sperm donation as on sperm donated through a sperm bank. Critiques of commercial prohibition all too easily and superficially presume that "a law like Canada's requiring sperm donors to be altruists willing to assist infertile couples would deprive thousands of couples desperate to start a family."[94] The fluctuations in the number of donations in countries that introduced legislation banning anonymous donation are worth noting here. As Kahn discusses in some detail, countries that moved to mandatory identification of gamete providers have been faced with an initial significant decline in donations. Yet in several of these countries, the numbers have gradually increased again, showing, according to Kahn, that "predictions of drastic long-term effects appear overblown."[95]

The Need to Avoid a Black Market in AHR Services

The second argument is that a criminal prohibition stimulates a black market of AHR services in the country, including illegal and more hidden sale of gametes and paid surrogacy. The stricter approach in Canada also results in the use of international donors and surrogates, often affecting far more vulnerable women. There is some validity to these concerns. And as several recent cases confirm, the jurisprudence indicates a willingness of the courts to look at the indirect impact of strict governmental approaches on the rights and interests of individuals, particularly when members of vulnerable groups are involved.[96] The issue, I suggest, is again one of balancing. If we believe that untrammelled commercialization has a clearly pernicious impact, and that a strong prohibition is truly essential to help counter this impact, we may have to accept that there are some undesirable consequences to this approach. It then becomes important to look at how the negative consequences of this prohibitory approach can be mitigated and countered. One also has to keep in mind that AHR services are likely easier to control than, for example, prostitution. It takes some level of sophistication with respect to health care infrastructure to offer AHR services, at least when it involves storage of ova and sperm and *in vitro* fertilization.[97] Controlling these services to some extent should be feasible.

The Canadian government seems to have engaged in a laissez-faire approach to AHR and has rarely aggressively intervened to enforce the *AHRA*. It has even failed to implement regulations that would provide a clearer reimbursement scheme for gamete donors and surrogates. But all of this does not mean that stricter intervention that would offer greater protection against abuse is impossible.

The argument about the international implications also has some value. Yet the fact that Canadians may be more inclined to exploit people in other countries as a result of restrictions back home clearly does not always justify a more lenient approach in Canada. If the existence of a thriving international exploitative scheme were sufficient to abandon Canadian regulations, we should also get rid of child labour standards, workplace safety regulations, organ sale restrictions, and even some age-related sex restrictions. In all of these contexts, we have Canadians travelling abroad to circumvent Canadian law. Again: if we believe that the untrammelled commercial sale of gametes strongly undermines societal values, it seems appropriate to enact Canadian legislation, while being realistic about its impact and aware of the need to also intervene in a more global context, and while carefully considering how we can use domestic law to counter international exploitation.

With respect to the international impact, clearly, the government would not be able to physically restrain anyone interested in AHR from travelling abroad. But as Downie and Baylis demonstrate in an article on the topic, it can participate more actively in international actions to limit the negative impact of AHR, and it can try to reduce the practice through a variety of Canadian initiatives.[98] Most fundamentally, Downie and Baylis argue that the government can and should clarify, complete, and enforce the *AHRA*. They also argue that the government can stimulate the supply of Canadian non-commercial AHR transactions while simultaneously reducing the demand for these services, including through educational efforts as well as initiatives to reduce the incidence of infertility. Finally, they suggest that in some circumstances the government can apply Canadian law to extraterritorial activities, even though this is a hotly contested approach.[99]

The *Charter* Arguments and the Harm of Restrictions

Would the arguments I have provided survive a *Charter* challenge? Several *Charter*-related claims have been made against the commercialization prohibitions in the *AHRA*. They tend to focus on the prohibition against paid surrogacy, which raises somewhat different issues than paid gamete transfer, issues that are particularly relevant when discussing whether the prohibition constitutes a justifiable infringement on individual rights. I cannot discuss in detail here how all arguments would play out in both contexts, but I will comment briefly on the main arguments, which do deserve a fuller discussion, focusing specifically on gamete sales.

The general claims are that the commercialization prohibitions violate the s. 7 liberty and security rights of gamete donors or surrogates and that they violate the liberty and security rights and the s. 15 equality rights of prospective parents. A first observation, as Sarah Hudson also makes in this volume,[100] is that the Supreme Court explicitly rejected the right to free procreative choice as a positive right in *E (Mrs.) v Eve*.[101] This affects the likely success of liberty-based claims from both prospective parents and surrogates. A second important observation is that, in the context of the *AHRA* prohibitions, the state can hardly be seen as directly restricting the choice of future parent(s). The prohibition affects the liberty of a third party to offer a service in a specific form – that is, with *market-based payment* – that will facilitate a reproductive choice. Gamete providers can still transfer gametes, even in exchange for some level of compensation. The liberty restrictions of prospective parent(s) are only indirect.

Dave Snow emphasizes that the decision to be a surrogate falls within the right to reproductive autonomy and is among the fundamental and intimately personal decisions that the liberty right should protect.[102] Two objections can be made. One objection is that the decision to become a surrogate, and thus to function as a "conduit" for parenthood by others, is not exactly the same type of fundamental life choice as the choice to become a parent oneself, particularly if the main motive is financial compensation. More importantly, the law does not prevent the surrogate from carrying a child. It simply prohibits her from receiving market-based payment for doing so. In the context of gamete donation, the type of action involved (sperm or ova donation) appears to move even further away from the sorts of fundamental life choices the liberty interest traditionally protects. And again, the prohibition on commercialization does not prevent anyone from donating gametes. What Snow and others are arguing is that the liberty interest protects surrogates and gamete donors' ability to turn their reproductive capacities into a profit-making venture. Does this really deserve the same type of *Charter* protection as more fundamental life choices?

Superficially stronger *Charter* claims are based on the "security" interests of those involved. With respect to the security of the prospective parent(s), Snow argues that there is growing evidence that the inability to have children is associated with "risk of serious psychological and social consequences."[103] But at worst, the prohibition on commercial sale merely indirectly reduces the likelihood that third parties will engage in AHR activities that facilitate access to reproductive services for prospective parents. It seems a stretch to argue that this is sufficiently connected to the alleged harms associated with infertility to be seen as infringing on the prospective parents' security of the person. Typical "security interest" cases involve state intervention that directly intrudes on people's physical or mental integrity, or that prevents them from taking action to protect themselves against serious harm to their person (e.g., abortion). In fact, as I will discuss, the prohibition on commercialization actually aims, at least in part, at promoting the security interests of ova donors and surrogates.

What about the security interests of the surrogates or gamete providers? At least in the surrogacy context, the arguments here are perhaps somewhat stronger. Regulations can infringe on security interests when they expose people to significant harm, even indirectly, including through reducing people's options to protect themselves. The argument that Snow and others make is that the commercial prohibition pushes surrogates underground and thereby exposes them to a higher risk of exploitation and related harms. We can make comparisons here with the *Bedford* case, where the Supreme Court struck down laws prohibiting bawdyhouses, living on the avails of prostitution, and communicating for purposes of prostitution, because they prevented prostitutes from taking steps that would increase their security.

However, there are arguably some important differences between our situation and *Bedford*. In discussing the causality between the criminal prohibitions challenged in *Bedford* and the harm to the security interests of prostitutes, the Court suggested that many women involved in the sex trade "are not people who can be said to be truly 'choosing' a risky line of business." The Court emphasized their vulnerability and lack of choice to gain other income.[104] Yet, as Snow and others have argued elsewhere, empirical research suggests that (Canadian) surrogates are generally not a vulnerable class of people without other options. As I argued before, gamete donors, who tend to be successful college or university students, are even less likely to be as vulnerable because they probably have alternative sources of income. More importantly, the court in *Bedford* emphasized that security interests are triggered when "legislative provisions … aggravate the risk of disease, violence and death."[105] Even if the prohibition on payment would increase the risk of exploitation, I am aware of no evidence that commercialization prohibitions are exposing Canadians to the same level of very serious risk that women involved in the sex trade face because of the impugned laws in *Bedford*. Pregnancy is clearly a very serious risk factor in and of itself. Donation of ova also creates significant risks. But there is no reason to see the criminal prohibition against commercial payment as the cause of these serious risks. On the contrary, it is actually commercial payments that risk pushing people towards greater dangers such as multiple surrogacy contracts and frequent ova extraction. Particularly in the Canadian context, there is also no reason to think that the criminal prohibition on payment of surrogates or gamete donors prevents them from seeking publicly funded health care when they need it. The black market in surrogacy may contribute to some level of exploitation, but it does not create the same level of risk as back street abortions and dark alley sex. Finally, I also note that the Supreme Court has rejected the idea that an economic interest – for example, basic pay for work – is protected under the security interest. But economic interests seem to be the essence of the claim here. That is, surrogates want to be paid according to market criteria and not merely in line with governmentally restricted compensation. For these reasons, security of the person is unlikely to be triggered by the commercial prohibition.

A more likely avenue is a *Charter* claim based on discrimination. There are two components to a s. 15 discrimination challenge. First, a legislative provision has to distinguish people based on enumerated or analogous grounds; and second, the distinction has to "create[s] a disadvantage by perpetuating prejudice or stereotyping."[106] Hudson argues that infertility or the lack of capacity to reproduce naturally can be seen as a social condition, and not just a medical condition, and therefore supports a *Charter*-based claim of equal access to reproductive services for all of those for whom natural reproduction is not an option (i.e., the infertile and LBGTQ people).[107] One could argue that the category is perhaps too broad to be identifiable under one enumerated or analogous ground, but the broad concept of disability embraced by the Supreme Court makes this requirement relatively easy to meet. With respect to the second step, Snow argues that since the prohibitions "exclude a reproductive avenue for the infertile and LGBT individuals, it is easy to characterize them as demeaning on these grounds."[108] This is a clear overstatement, since only commercialized gamete sales and surrogacy services are prohibited. State-regulated donation and surrogacy with compensation are allowed. Yet the failure of government to actively implement a regulatory scheme and promote and protect this non-commercialized approach surely does not help here. It seems fair to argue, then, that the prohibition does affect to some extent the availability of gametes and surrogates, and thus creates a practical disadvantage. But is it a disadvantage associated with stereotyping and prejudices? I am not convinced it is, precisely in light of the very wide group of people affected. Is infertility really still surrounded by stereotyping and prejudices?

But let us presume, for the sake of argument, that the prohibitions are discriminatory, or that they infringe on liberty or security interests. We must still ask if the prohibition can be saved under the "reasonableness tests" embedded in ss. 7 and 1. Under s. 7, the question is whether the restriction of individual rights is in accordance with the principles of fundamental justice. The s. 1 analysis requires an evaluation of the compatibility of the restrictions with reasonable limits that can be imposed in a democratic society. I cannot discuss the nuances of these different tests in detail here, but I will try to provide some tentative responses to arguments made in the context of both of them, focusing primarily on s. 7.

In *Bedford*, the Supreme Court summarized the key questions commonly raised in the context of the concept of fundamental justice in the following way: "The overarching lesson that emerges from the case law is that laws run afoul of our basic values when the means by which the state seeks to attain its objective is fundamentally flawed, in the sense of being arbitrary, overbroad, or having effects that are grossly disproportionate to the legislative goal."[109]

The first criterion, arbitrariness, requires us to determine whether there is a real link between the prohibitions and a legitimate legislative goal. In his analysis of surrogacy, Snow focuses on the prevention of exploitation of vulnerability as the legislative goal.[110] He rejects the claim that women who engage in surrogacy are vulnerable, citing relevant studies showing that this is not the case. If, as he argues, the law actually increased vulnerability, one could invoke this as an example of arbitrariness. But for the reasons mentioned earlier, I find the argument of increased vulnerability and exploitation because of a prohibition on commercial sale of ova questionable. This argument is even less convincing with respect to payment for gametes. Being paid less, and according to a rigid legislative scheme, is not necessarily exploitative. More importantly, this argument focuses narrowly on the prohibition as a means to protect against exploitation and physical harm. In fact, the prohibition also targets the more general societal harms associated with commodification, which I discussed at length earlier. In essence, Snow is reflecting a narrow, "empiricist" view of commodification, as if commodification is a question of "feeling commodified." He ignores that the legislation also protects a societal commitment to equality and justice and that the different goals are fundamentally intersected in a complex way that makes it hard to discuss them in isolation, as I argued.

It is true that the increased emphasis in Supreme Court jurisprudence on the need for evidence makes this commitment to the vaguer values associated with commodification and to a broader concept of equality more contentious. As I pointed out earlier, these are harms to the fabric of our society, to our commitment to promote human flourishing. In some liberal circles these arguments are increasingly frowned upon and viewed as leading to the imposition of conservative values. A detailed discussion of this argument exceeds the scope of this chapter. Let me simply note that the state's promotion of non-commercialized reproduction fits perfectly with the widely accepted commitment in Canadian *Charter* jurisprudence to substantive (and not just formal) equality. State neutrality in this context constitutes indirect support for market-driven, for-profit reproductive services, which – as Lisa Ikemoto aptly demonstrates in her discussion of the blatantly commercial US AHR market[111] – demean our humanity and our societal commitment to equality. Untrammelled commercialization turns profoundly human characteristics into commercializable assets, reinforces stereotypes that smack of genetic determinism and social Darwinism, and turns a process that profoundly affects our being in the world and some of our most crucial human relations into a commercial contract.

Turning to gross disproportionality, Snow also stresses that the restrictions could infringe on this principle of fundamental justice for several reasons. One is that exploitation also happens outside the paid context (he mentions family pressures as an example).[112] The second is that the prohibition drives surrogacy underground, thus making surrogates more vulnerable, which relates to the point made earlier. Third, he suggests that a less restrictive regulatory regime may be possible. A general objection to Snow's argument here is that the Supreme Court has explicitly stated, in the context of the proportionality assessment, that Parliament has "broad latitude" to enact legislation as it deems fit.[113] Furthermore, as the Supreme Court emphasizes in *Bedford*, the rule "only applies in extreme cases where the seriousness of the deprivation is totally out of sync with the objective of the measure," and where the measure (i.e., prohibition of commercial pay) falls "outside the norms accepted in our free and democratic society."[114] Canada is clearly no outlier with respect to prohibiting or severely restricting commercialization of AHR. It can hardly be argued that the Canadian statute is completely "out of sync" with the acceptable norms of a free and democratic society.

The arguments made here in relation to the principles of fundamental justice give us a good sense of several of the arguments that one could make in a s. 1 analysis.[115] The only issue that I still want to address with respect to s. 1 is the question of whether the criminal prohibition would survive the "minimal impairment" test. In other words, if we accept that the prohibitions pursue a legitimate state goal or interest, and are rationally connected to this interest, is there nonetheless a less restrictive way to obtain the same result? This also gives us a sense of whether the criminal law restrictions on commercialization are really disproportionate.

If, as I argued, commercialization risks affecting crucial components of personhood and our societal commitment to equal dignity, then it seems appropriate to use the criminal law. Remember that the prohibition is not complete. The reimbursement system in s. 12 is crucial in this respect. The system allows for some level of fair compensation, while also using a criminal law provision to reconfirm the values associated with non-commodified human reproduction. This seems sufficient to meet the minimal impairment requirement.

Conclusion

In this chapter, I argued that the most crucial reasons for a prohibition on the commercial sale of gametes relate to the unique nature of reproductive goods. I argued that reproductive goods are fundamentally connected to our personhood and to our physical and moral being in the world. They are intimately connected to human flourishing, which occurs in part through a variety of complex relations with significant others. Untrammelled commercialization risks compromising the value-laden relational nature of gametes and reduces gametes to ordinary consumer goods with specific quality-related expectations.

It demeans the "outcome" of the AHR process, a process that is a fundamental and essential building block of the human person. The sale of gametes according to market criteria also affects underlying values of equality with regard to important societal activities and the intrinsic equal value of human beings, regardless of personal traits, whether they are related to health, personality, or ethnicity.

I also indicated that these concerns are intertwined with concerns about exploitation, undue influence, and potential harm to ova providers. These may, in and of themselves, not provide the strongest justification, but as Radin points out, it is often hard to disentangle all concerns. It seems reasonable, as McLachlin CJ also appears to suggest, for governments to enact regulation that aims at capturing a host of difficulties, some more serious than others.[116]

Prohibitions aimed at banning untrammelled commercialization of gametes ought not to excessively hinder practices that are predominantly based on altruism. A prohibition on commercial sales does not mean that gametes cannot be transferred to others and cannot be the subject of some "reimbursement" or some limited level of fair compensation in line with regulations. The most important component of a prohibitory approach is that it constitutes a strong symbolic recognition of the fact that human reproduction is not a proper fit for commercial sale. It reflects the values embedded in a state-supported and organized, largely altruistic donation system as a means to allow individuals to have equitable access to AHR, but in a context of non–market-based transactions. A regulatory approach to compensation emphasizes that it is only fair to recognize the contributions made by people who act as surrogates or who donate gametes, including the hardship they may suffer in the context of a socially valued service, while also recognizing the values that may be undermined by sheer commercial practices in this context. It is therefore very disconcerting that the Canadian government has failed to do anything with its power to regulate reimbursements in the many years since the *AHRA* was adopted, for it has thereby created legal uncertainty and difficulties in determining what constitutes proper reimbursement. The frequent controversies erupting in Canada around largely uncontrolled AHR practices, including the importation of gametes and surrogacy services, are perhaps not so much an unavoidable and inevitable result of what critics see as a wrong-headed prohibitory approach. They may simply be the result of the government's failure to introduce a more tightly regulated system that reflects a commitment to non-commercialization but that still allows some controlled level of fair compensation.

Where exactly to draw the line between acceptable compensation and unacceptable commercialization should be the subject of further discussion. As McLachlin CJ puts it: "The act of drawing [the] line [between commodification and acceptable reimbursement] raises fundamental moral questions. Though there are differing views on where the line should be drawn, it is difficult to argue that the criminal law power does not permit Parliament to prohibit that which falls on the wrong side of it."[117]

NOTES

Author's note: I would like to thank Natasha Chin and Michelle Jackson for excellent background research and Dov Kagan for very diligent editing, research, and work on the references. I am also grateful to Pascale Chapdelaine, Andrew Flavelle Martin, and colleagues at various institutions where I presented earlier versions of this paper, including the Faculties of Law of the Universities of Antwerpen, the KULeuven, Oxford, Tilburg, and Torcuato di Tella, for critical comments on earlier drafts.

1 Tom Blackwell, "Pregnant Surrogates 'Left in the Lurch' after RCMP Raid Fertility Consultant's Office," *National Post*, 1 March 2012, http://news.nationalpost.com/news/canada/pregnant-surrogates-left-in-the-lurch-after-rcmp-raid-fertility-consultants-office.
2 *Assisted Human Reproduction Act*, SC 2004, c 2, ss 6, 7 [*AHRA*].
3 Alison Motluk, "The Human Egg Trade: How Canada's Fertility Laws Are Failing Donors, Doctors and Parents," *The Walrus*, April 2010, http://thewalrus.ca/the-human-egg-trade.
4 See Eric Blyth, "Fertility Patients' Experiences of Cross-Border Reproductive Care" (2010) 94:1 Fertil Steril e11; Edward G. Hughes and Deirdre DeJean, "Cross-Border Fertility Services in North America: A Survey of Canadian and American Providers" (2010) 94:1 Fertil Steril e16; Jocelyn Downie and Françoise Baylis, "Transnational Trade in Human Eggs: Law, Policy, and (In)Action in Canada" (2013) 41:1 J Law Med Ethics 224 at 226.
5 See, for example, CBC News, "Canadians Pay Egg Donors on the Grey Market," 26 March 2014, http://www.cbc.ca/news/canada/montreal/canadians-pay-egg-donors-on-the-grey-market-1.2587853; CTV News,

"Canadian Women Flout Laws to Donate Eggs," 27 March 2012, http://www.ctvnews.ca/canadian-women-flout-laws-to-donate-eggs-1.787923.

6 Transnational transactions are also a concern as these often have substantial links to Canada. See Downie and Baylis, *supra* note 4 at 234.

7 Section 12 of the *AHRA* currently reads as follows:

12. (1) No person shall, except in accordance with the regulations,
  (a) reimburse a donor for an expenditure incurred in the course of donating sperm or an ovum;
  (b) reimburse any person for an expenditure incurred in the maintenance or transport of an *in vitro* embryo; or
  (c) reimburse a surrogate mother for an expenditure incurred by her in relation to her surrogacy.
(2) No person shall reimburse an expenditure referred to in subsection (1) unless a receipt is provided to that person for the expenditure.
(3) No person shall reimburse a surrogate mother for a loss of work-related income incurred during her pregnancy, unless
  (a) a qualified medical practitioner certifies, in writing, that continuing to work may pose a risk to her health or that of the embryo or foetus; and
  (b) the reimbursement is made in accordance with the regulations.

8 2010 SCC 61, [2010] 3 SCR 457 [*AHRA Reference*].

9 See Tom Blackwell, "'Business Has Boomed': Canadian Surrogacy Agent Facing 27 Charges Continues Her Controversial Work," *National Post*, 17 March 2013, http://news.nationalpost.com/news/canada/business-has-boomed-canadian-surrogacy-agent-facing-27-charges-continues-her-controversial-work; and Tom Blackwell, "Canadian Fertility Consultant Received $31K for Unwittingly Referring Parents to U.S. 'Baby-Selling' Ring," *National Post*, 15 December 2013, http://news.nationalpost.com/news/canada/canadian-fertility-consultant-received-about-30000-for-unwittingly-referring-parents-to-u-s-baby-selling-ring.

10 See, for example, the introduction in this volume by Trudo Lemmens and Andrew Flavelle Martin.

11 See, for example, Angela Campbell, who discusses various empirical studies related to surrogacy in the chapter "Engaging with Surrogates' Choices: Tracing and Proscribing Viable Mothers in Law," in *Sister Wives, Surrogates and Sex Workers: Outlaws by Choice?* (Vermont: Ashgate, 2013) at 97; see also Karen Busby and Delaney Vun, who discuss the results of empirical studies associated with surrogacy in Canada, in "Revisiting the

Handmaid's Tale: Feminist Theory Meets Empirical Research on Surrogate Mothers" (2010) 26 Can J Fam L 13 at 52–5.

12 *AHRA*, s 7. It is worth noting that unlike the prohibition on the commercialization of surrogacy, which includes a prohibition of both "sale" and "purchase," section 7 only targets the purchase of gametes. The alleged rationale for this difference is that the section specifically targets the commercial buyers of gametes. Legislators felt less need to penalize those who could be inclined to sell their eggs or sperm. The idea may also have been that prohibiting the purchase would create a sufficient incentive. One of the results has been that at least on one occasion, a young woman advertising her eggs for sale in a newspaper advertisement invoked the lack of prohibition to justify her actions, raising questions about the coherence of this approach. Perhaps it also reflects how the sale of reproductive services has been deemed more troubling than the sale of gametes.

13 *Supra* note 4 at 227–8.

14 See the chapters in Part 1 of this volume.

15 See Ian B. Lee's chapter in this volume, "Licensing and the *AHRA Reference*," which describes how Cromwell J came to this conclusion differently than McLachlin CJ. The Chief Justice, with Justices Binnie, Fish, and Charron concurring, would have upheld the constitutionality of the entire act.

16 *AHRA Reference*, *supra* note 8 at para 61.

17 Justice Cromwell: "sets out an extension of the regime established by s 6 and 7; s 12 is a form of exemption from the strictness of the regime which they impose and, to some extent, defines the scope of the prohibitions provided for in those sections." *Ibid* at para 290.

18 *Ibid* at para 111, citing Canada, *Proceed with Care: The Final Report of the Royal Commission on New Reproductive Technologies* (Ottawa: Canada Communications Group, 1993), 718 (the "Baird Report").

19 *AHRA Reference*, *supra* note 8 at para 74.

20 *Ibid* at para 112.

21 *Ibid* at para 88.

22 *Ibid* at para 100.

23 *Ibid* at para 250.

24 Margaret J. Radin, *Contested Commodities: The Trouble with Trade in Sex, Children, Body Parts, and Other Things* (Cambridge, MA: Harvard University Press, 1996).

25 *Ibid* at 9.

26 *Ibid* at 20.

27 *Ibid* at 56.
28 See the discussion in Jacob D. Rendtorff, "The Limitations and Accomplishments of Autonomy as Basic Principle in Bioethics and Biolaw," in *Autonomy and Human Rights in Health Care*, ed. David N. Weisstub and Guillermo Diaz Pintos (Dordrecht: Springer, 2008), 75 at 81.
29 See also, for example, Naomi Kahn, "The New Kinship" (2012) 100 Georgetown L J 367 at 407, who argues that "even in the absence of explicit regulation, the law still defines the space for flourishing" [reference omitted].
30 Michael Sandel, *What Money Can't Buy: The Moral Limits of Markets* (London: Allen Lane, 2012), 10.
31 This also sets Radin apart from Michael Walzer, who is more categorical in his classification of the nature of goods. See Michael Walzer, *Spheres of Justice: A Defence of Pluralism and Equality* (Oxford: Martin Robertson, 1983).
32 *Supra* note 24 at 154–63.
33 See also Debra Satz, *Why Some Things Should Not Be For Sale: The Moral Limits of the Market* (Oxford: Oxford University Press, 2010), 115–34; and Donna Dickinson, *Property in the Body: Feminist Perspectives* (Cambridge: Cambridge University Press, 2007), who discusses in more detail the gender implications of commodification of reproduction.
34 See, for example, Satz, *supra* note 33.
35 *Supra* note 24 at 49–53.
36 *Supra* note 33 at 91–112.
37 Anne Phillips, "It's My Body and I'll Do What I Like With It: Bodies as Objects and Property" (2011) 39:6 Political Theory 724 at 739.
38 See, for example, National Bioethics Advisory Committee, *Ethical Issues in Human Stem Cell Research*, vol. 1 (Rockville: National Bioethics Advisory Committee, 1999), 36. For some narrative examples of students selling ova to pay off debts, see Suzanne Holland, "Contested Commodities at Both Ends of Life: Buying and Selling Gametes, Embryos, and Body Tissues" (2001) 11:3 Kennedy Inst Ethics J 263 at 263–4.
39 The Canadian Supreme Court itself has used the terms jointly, without making a clear distinction. For example, consider the Supreme Court case of *Norberg v Wynrib*, [1992] 2 SCR 226 [*Norberg*]. In *Norberg*, an opinion supported by three of the six judges applied the contract law–based "doctrines of duress, undue influence, and unconscionability [that] have arisen to protect the vulnerable when they are in a relationship of unequal power" (para 28) to determine whether a drug-addicted patient could genuinely consent to sexual activity with a doctor who prescribed opioids in exchange. They ruled that the vulnerability and the dependency of

the patient in a power relation vitiated consent. More specifically, in the *AHRA Reference*, McLachlin CJ refers to the fact that s 9, which prohibits the donation of reproductive material by "youth," aims at protecting them from exploitation and undue pressure. See *AHRA Reference*, *supra* note 8 at para 92.

40 *Supra* note 33 at 96.

41 Kahn, *supra* note 29 at 376.

42 Angela Campbell, *supra* note 11 at 98–104, 124–5. See also Busby and Vun, *supra* note 11; Erin Nelson, *Law, Policy, and Reproductive Autonomy* (Oxford: Hart, 2013) at 331–2 and at 302 (discussing the argument about exploitation of gamete donors); and in this volume Stu Marvel *et al.*, "Listening to LGBTQ People on Assisted Human Reproduction."

43 In fact, Angela Campbell suggests that this is one of the advantages of payment for surrogacy services. For her, it facilitates the surrogate's "reasoned choice" and "emotional detachment" from the child. See Angela Campbell, *supra* note 11 at 134–5. This is obviously only an advantage if emotional ties and connectedness are seen as inappropriate burdens or as improperly hindering an efficient surrogacy system. The argument also seems to emphasize, in my view in a problematic way, a disjunction between "reasoned" and "emotional" choices. In sharp contrast, Mary Lyndon Shanley emphasizes how altruistic transfer is ethically preferable over payment precisely because "it leads society at large, not only provider and recipient, to reflect on and discuss what participation in human procreation means. Subsuming collaborative procreation into other kinds of buying and selling commodifies either human gametes or the use of the body, or both. Payment suggests that the transfer is a complete and discrete event, that the action of the person providing gametes has no intrinsic relationship to that of the person receiving the gametes." Shanley, "Collaboration and Commodification in Assisted Procreation: Reflections on an Open Market and Anonymous Donation in Human Sperm and Eggs" (2002) 36:2 Law & Soc'y Rev 257 at 279. Joan Raphael-Leff suggests that this emotional separation is a defence mechanism, in the context of a capitalist system of commercialized reproduction in which gametes become commodified. Raphael-Leff, "The Gift of Gametes: Unconscious Motivation, Commodification and Problematics of Genealogy" (2010) 94 Feminist Review 117 at 126–8.

44 Kahn also argues more generally that the relational impact of AHR transactions provides a strong rationale for state regulation. See Kahn, *supra* note 29, in particular at 407–17.

45 It seems appropriate to exclude sperm donation from this discussion. Sperm providers usually engage in an activity that has been described by one sperm bank as "America's most pleasant part time job" and can hardly be identified as dangerous to a man's health.
46 *Supra* note 4 at 224. See also Nelson, *supra* note 42, at 301–2.
47 See *AHRA Reference*, *supra* note 8 at para 97.
48 Nancy Kenney and Michelle McGown, "Looking Back: Egg Donors' Retrospective Evaluations of their Motivations, Expectations, and Experiences during Their First Donation Cycle" (2010) 93:2 Fertil Steril 455 at 465.
49 See Busby and Vun, *supra* note 11 at 52–5.
50 See, for example, Dave Snow, "Reproductive Autonomy and the Evolving Family of the Supreme Court of Canada: Implications for Assisted Reproductive Technologies" (2014) 41:1 Journal of Canadian Studies 153 at 159.
51 Richard M. Titmuss, *The Gift Relationship: From Human Blood to Social Policy* (London: Allen & Unwin, 1970).
52 Others have also made this argument. For Sandel, for example, "markets leave their mark. Sometimes, market values crowd out nonmarket values worth caring about." Sandel, *supra* note 30 at 9.
53 See, for example, the detailed discussion in Alastair Campbell, *The Body in Bioethics* (London: Routledge-Cavendish, 2009), 19–26; Satz, *supra* note 33 at 192–3; and Radin, *supra* note 24 at 96–9.
54 *Supra* note 11.
55 *Supra* note 24 at 220.
56 Consider the interesting discussion by Alastair Campbell, who calls for a reconceptualization of the body based on insights from phenomenology, feminism, and postmodernism. Campbell, *supra* note 53 at 4–10.
57 *Supra* note 37 at 729.
58 *Supra* note 52 at 19.
59 Mary Lyndon Shanley argues that there is a need as embodied beings for us to connect to our human history: "The right to learn the identity of one's genetic forebear stems from some people's desire to be able to connect themselves to human history concretely as embodied beings, not only abstractly as rational beings or as members of large social (national, ethnic, religious) groups." Shanley, *supra* note 43 at 268.
60 See also the discussion in Kahn, *supra* note 29, in particular at 413–17.
61 See in this volume Giroux and Milne, "The Right to Know One's Origins, the *AHRA Reference* and *Pratten v AGBC*"; Gruben, "A Number but No Name?"; and Guichon, "The Priority of the Health and Well-being of

Offspring." See in general Juliet R. Guichon, Ian Mitchell, and Michelle Giroux, eds., *The Right to Know One's Origin: Assisted Human Reproduction and the Best Interests of Children* (Brussels: Academic and Scientific Publishers, 2012). For an interesting discussion of the connection between the debate about gamete commercialization and donor anonymity, see Shanley, *supra* note 43.

62 See, for example, Veronica B. Pinero, "This Is Not Baby Talk: Canadian International Rights Obligations Regarding the Rights to Health, Identity and Family Relations," in Guichon, Mitchell and Giroux, *ibid*, 251; Michelle Giroux and Mariana De Lorenzi, "The Recognition of the Right to Identity of Children Born of Assisted Procreation: A Provincial Responsibility," in Guichon, Mitchell, and Giroux, *ibid*, 310; and Giroux and Milne, *supra* note 61.

63 See, for example, Carey Goldberg, "On Web, Models Auction Their Eggs to Bidders for Beautiful Children," *New York Time*, 23 October 1999, http://www.nytimes.com/1999/10/23/us/on-web-models-auction-their-eggs-to-bidders-for-beautiful-children.html.

64 See, for example, Peter Singer, "Foreword: Shopping at the Genetic Supermarket," in *The Ethics of Inheritable Genetic Modification: A Dividing Line?*, ed. John Rasko, Gabrielle O'Sullivan, and Rachel Ankeny (Cambridge: Cambridge University Press, 2006), xiii; and Kenneth Baum, "Golden Eggs: Towards the Rational Regulation of Oocyte Donation" (2001) BYU L Rev 107.

65 The website is no longer available, but a more detailed description of what it contained can be found in Singer, *supra* note 64 at xxii–xxiii; and in Baum, *supra* note 64 at 109. I accessed this website many years ago, after reading a critical review of it in the medical literature. Like Singer, I also experienced later that the link to the female "ova-models" had been interrupted and had become available only for paid subscribers, and seemed clearly interested in bringing browsers to a soft-porn website. It raises questions about the seriousness of the "auction" idea, but symbolizes in a way the gross commercialization that takes place in both these seemingly very different areas of social life.

66 See Goldberg, *supra* note 63.

67 *Ibid*.

68 Baum, *supra* note 64 at 111.

69 *Ibid* at 108.

70 This raises an obvious legal question about the enforcement of such an exclusivity contract!

71 Kahn gives various US examples, *supra* note 29, in particular at 374–9.

72 Canadian Press, "Canadian Couple Sues U.S. Sperm Bank for Alleged False Donor Details," *Globe and Mail*, 6 April 2015, http://www.theglobeandmail.com/news/national/canadian-couple-sues-us-sperm-bank-for-alleged-false-donor-details/article23810189.

73 I was interviewed twice by one of the journalists who reported on this case, and indicated that it really evokes moral concerns along the lines mentioned here. It was not reported in any of the articles on the case.

74 *Supra* note 43 at 272.

75 As Anna Curtis argues (even if she is generally in favour of significant compensation of donors and critical of the gendered emphasis on "altruism"): "the debates about compensating egg donors preclude discussions of the more serious moral and ethical issues involved. Egg donors are chosen based on their genetic desirability, the eugenic aspects of which are thinly veiled at best. The exorbitant costs of reproductive technology mean that only the wealthy can access these services [reference omitted]." In "Giving 'Til It Hurts: Egg Donation and the Cost of Altruism" (2010) 2 Feminist Formations 8 at 94.

76 See David S. King, "Preimplantation Genetic Diagnosis and the 'New' Eugenics" (1999) 25:2 J Med Ethics 176; see also Sandel, *supra* note 30.

77 See Raphael-Leff, *supra* note 43 at 117: "Institutionalized asexual reproduction alters unconscious conceptualizations of the act of procreation – converting the passionate intimacy of a primal scene into a clinical coupling of gametes in a mechanized area."

78 *Supra* note 43 at 279.

79 Debra Satz portrays Radin's view of the role of the state in enabling human flourishing as "a view that the purpose of the state is to make people happy." Satz, *supra* note 33 at 142. That seems a serious utilitarian reduction of the idea that the state has some role to play with respect to enabling people to create meaningful lives. It is not clear where Satz gets this portrayal of human flourishing as being reduced to "making people happy."

80 Radin, *supra* note 24 at 110, 113.

81 Holland, *supra* note 38 at 277. Holland also extensively relies on Radin's concept of human flourishing in her analysis of the impact of commodification of gametes, embryos, and body tissue.

82 *Ibid* at 276.

83 See, in this volume, Marvel *et al.*, *supra* note 42. See also Samantha Yee, Jason A. Hitkari, and Ellen M. Greenblatt, "A Follow-Up Study of Women Who Donated Oocytes to Known Recipient Couples for Altruistic Reasons" (2007) 22:7 Hum Reprod 2040 at 2041; Nelson, *supra* note 42 at

301; and Alan C. Milstein, "Op-Ed: Sperm Donor Industry Needs More Regulation," *National Law Journal*, 20 April 2015.

84 As I will argue further, this shortage may in part be the result of the failure of the government to enact appropriate regulations that enable reasonable compensation in the context of surrogacy and gamete donation. For an example of an unnuanced claim in that respect, see Milstein, *ibid*, who simply assumes that banning commercialization in the United States, as Canada has done, would create huge shortages.

85 Empirical studies confirm this. See, for example, Kenney and McGown, *supra* note 48. See also the discussion of the empirical literature on commercial surrogacy by Angela Campbell, *supra* note 11 at 98–102. Campbell emphasizes, however, that contrary to quite common held views, financial compensation for paid surrogacy is just one among several other factors that motivates women to act as surrogates. At the same time, the motivation to act as surrogate may be more complex and multifaceted than the decision to provide gametes.

86 See the discussion in Marvel *et al.*, *supra* note 42. See also Yee, Hitkari, and Greenblatt, *supra* note 83 at 2041; and Downie and Baylis, *supra* note 4 at 234.

87 See in particular in this volume the chapter by Sarah Hudson, "Great Expectations"; as well as the chapter by Marvel *et al.*, *supra* note 42. A detailed discussion of *Charter* rights can be found in Snow, *supra* note 50 at 173–8.

88 With this emphasis on the relational nature of assisted human reproduction, and the rejection of the atomistic liberty model, my approach makes clear overtures to relational theory. For a recent detailed discussion, see Jennifer Nedelsky, *Relational Theory: A Theory of Self, Autonomy, and Law* (Oxford: Oxford University Press, 2011). In this chapter, I do not develop in any detail how a relational theory approach can contribute to other legal disputes in the context of assisted human reproduction. But note that with my emphasis on the need to recognize and value the multiple, complex ways in which new relations are created in AHR, I distance myself from those who would argue that law needs to preserve traditional relationships in this context. With reference to the discussion about the enforcement of surrogacy contracts, Robert Leaky argues convincingly that there are "normative commitments within relational theory" "to diverse forms of relationships, to critical examination of background conditions," and to a more sophisticated view of autonomy. See Lecky, *Contextual Subjects: Family, State and Relational Theory* (Toronto: University of Toronto Press, 2008), 114. My rejection of untrammelled commercialization and my

support of a pragmatic inalienability approach, based on a contextual analysis, which I develop in this chapter, are in my view in line with relational theory.

89 I. Glenn Cohen rejects arguments related to the need for restrictions on AHR practices based on rights or best interests of future children, except perhaps in relation to the potential argument of a "life not worth living." For Cohen, since these children would not exist but for the AHR intervention, the process to create them cannot be seen to harm them. See "Regulating Reproduction: The Problem with Best Interests" (2001) 96:2 Minn L Rev 423 at 426. Yet he underappreciates thereby in my view the idea of wider societal ethical commitments to fostering the conditions in which human beings (current and future) can most appropriately flourish, which is, as I argue in this chapter, a proper basis also for state regulation. One can argue that it is in the interests of children as a category to be born in a societal system that is committed to protecting and promoting their interests (including their equality interests and their interests in connecting with biological relatives) and their capacity to flourish. Kahn puts forward (*supra* note 29 at 422) that Cohen also ignores how we have moral obligations to help maximize human capabilities of those who are there.

90 Marcy Darnovsky, "Human Rights in a Post-Human Future," in *Rights and Liberties in the Biotech Age: Why We Need a Genetic Bill of Rights*, ed. Sheldon Krimsky & Peter Shorett (Lanham: Rowman and Littlefield, 2005), 209 at 213.

91 See references, *supra* note 61.

92 For a discussion of the various alternative ways in which assisted human reproduction is already organized in LGBTQ communities, see the chapter in this volume by Marvel *et al.*, *supra* note 42.

93 *Ibid*.

94 Milstein, *supra* note 83. Milstein also completely fails to acknowledge in his short commentary on the Canadian case discussed earlier that Canadian law allows for some level of compensation.

95 Kahn, *supra* note 29 at 421.

96 See, for example, the approach of the Supreme Court in *Canada (Attorney General) v Bedford*, 2013 SCC 72, [2013] 3 SCR 1101 [*Bedford*].

97 One could object that restrictions on commercialization may push human reproduction underground and lead, at least when it comes to sperm donation, to more primitive selection of donors, transfer of sperm, and self-injections at home. This can obviously not easily be controlled. But is this not the same situation that we face in non-assisted human reproduction?

It is worth pointing out here that it is estimated that 20 to 30 per cent of lesbian couples already use home insemination from a known donor. See Snow, *supra* note 50 at 173; see also Motluk, *supra* note 3.

98 *Supra* note 4 at 230–5.

99 Specifically, Downie and Baylis observe that under the doctrine of "qualified territorial application," extra-territorial activities can be subject to Canadian law if two conditions are met: there is a "real and substantial link" between Canada and the behaviour in question, and if the enforcement of the law does not offend against "international comity." However, although Downie and Baylis also observe that at least some international AHR behaviour will meet this test, it is unclear where precisely to draw the line. *Ibid* at 230–1. For a critique on extra-territorial application of criminal law, see, for example, Robert J. Currie and Stephen Coughlan, "Extraterritorial Criminal Jurisdiction: Bigger Picture or Smaller Frame?" (2007) 11:2 Can Crim L Rev 141; and Alejandro Chehtman, "Chapter 18: Jurisdiction," in *The Oxford Handbook of Criminal Law*, ed. Markus Dubber and Tatjana Hörnle (New York: Oxford University Press, 2014), 399.

100 *Supra* note 87; see also Snow, *supra* note 50 at 162–3.

101 *E (Mrs.) v Eve* (1986), [1986] 2 SCR 388 at para 96.

102 Snow, *supra* note 50 at 174.

103 [Reference omitted.] Snow, *supra* note 50 at 176.

104 *Bedford*, *supra* note 96 at para 86.

105 *Ibid* at para 88.

106 *R v Kapp*, 2008 SCC 41 at para 17, [2008] 2 SCR 483.

107 *Supra* note 87.

108 *Supra* note 50 at 178.

109 *Bedford*, *supra* note 96 at para 105.

110 *Supra* note 50 at 175–6.

111 See, in this volume, Lisa Ikemoto, "Assisted Reproductive Technology Use among Neighbours."

112 Snow, *supra* note 50 at 175. Angela Campbell also makes this point. See *supra* note 11 at 103.

113 See, for example, *R v Malmo Levine; R v Caine*, 2003 SCC 74 at para 175, [2003] 3 SCR 571.

114 See *Bedford*, *supra* note 96 at para 120.

115 As is well known, under a section 1 analysis, the inquiry is whether (1) the rights restricting measures have a pressing and substantial objective; and (2) the means to obtain that objective are proportional. Proportionality assessment involves an evaluation of a rational

connection; a minimal impairment; and proportionality between the infringement and the objective.

116 See *AHRA Reference, supra* note 8 at para 36: "The complexity of modern problems often requires a nuanced scheme consisting of a mixture of absolute prohibitions, selective prohibitions based on regulations, and supporting administrative provisions. Such schemes permit flexibility, vital in a field of evolving technologies."

117 *Ibid* at para 111.

APPENDIX

Expert Reports

Appendix 1 Quebec: A Pioneer in the Regulation of AHR and Research in Canada [Expert Opinion for the Government of Quebec]

BARTHA MARIA KNOPPERS AND ÉLODIE PETIT

Foreword

In 1978, when I began my doctoral studies in assisted human reproduction (AHR) and published my first article on artificial insemination and its impact on filiation, people would sometimes ask me why I was interested in "science fiction." The birth of Louise Brown by AHR in 1978, the cloning of Dolly the sheep in 2001, and the South Korean egg donor controversy in 2005 have by now shown that my chosen field was far from being science fiction.

The Quebec government first began to legislate AHR procedures in the early 1980s (through the Civil Code of Québec). At that time, the *Ministére de la Santé et des Services sociaux* (MSSS) and the Bar of the Province of Quebec established focus groups, of which I was a part. The growing phenomenon of surrogacy contracts between American couples and Quebec women had made regulation an urgent priority.

In 1989, the Canadian government established the Royal Commission on New Reproductive Technologies (RCNRT), of which I was also a member. The Commission was divided from the start, making consensus difficult – if not impossible – to achieve. The Commission was also under pressure to accelerate the production of its report; as a result, this document was produced in an atmosphere of stress and compromise. Indeed, compromise was the only way a group of experts who held opposing viewpoints could work together effectively and harmoniously.

One of the points the RCNRT chose to make in its final report was that close cooperation with the provinces and other partners, such as health professionals, was essential. Among Commission members,

I was alone in advocating the establishment of an interprovincial agency, as opposed to a "national" body. I advocated the criminalization of certain morally reprehensible practices such as human reproductive cloning. The work of the Commission ended with the tabling of its final report on November 30, 1993.

The new Civil Code of Québec, which came into force in 1994, addressed a number of other issues the RCNRT had raised (such as filiation and the regulation of research). Around the same time, Health Canada declared a moratorium on certain AHR activities and potential abuses.

The "quality" of the work produced by federal government committees between 1993 and 2004 is a reflection of the complexity and problematic nature of this field, not to mention the pressure that was exerted by the government in its desire to control and limit abuses (e.g., the Raelians, the proposal for an international UN convention, etc.). Several draft bills were tabled before federal legislation was finally adopted in 2004.

Ten years after the RCNRT's final report, I found that I was alone in urging the Senate of Canada to abandon the "flawed" legislation now in force in Canada. In particular, I felt that the controlled activities listed in the federal legislation, not to mention the power of the Agency to infringe on the privacy of infertile couples and their potential offspring, as well as the ambiguity of certain definitions (e.g., genes), might result in undue intrusion on the part of the Government of Canada.

The Government of Quebec's interest in the civil law implications of assisted human reproduction goes back to 1981. Professional bodies (such as the *Ordre des médecins*) and research groups (such as the *Réseau de médecine génétique* of the *Fonds de la recherche en santé du Québec* (FRSQ)) have adopted research guidelines. Universities have established training programs in bioethics and genetic counselling. Quebec's Bill 89 completes the work of regulating the quality and safety of tests and services in Quebec. Together, the prohibitions contained in the federal legislation and the provisions of Bill 89 will afford the public an appropriate level of protection, while also respecting their liberties and personal values.

B.M. Knoppers, O.C.
Research Chair in Law and Medicine
Professor, Law Faculty, *Université de Montréal*

Introduction

It is difficult – perhaps even impossible – to draw a clear line between health and disease, that is[,] to distinguish between a normal state and an abnormal state. Words like "health" and "disease" are arbitrary, representing both an individual's subjective assessment of his or her condition and a collective judgment on the existence or non-existence of pathology. In short, these essentially sociological terms are far from static. The (decidedly utopian) definition of health established by the World Health Organization (WHO) – "a state of complete physical, mental and social well-being" – also reflects this binary assessment.

Is infertility a disease? The question may seem pointless to some, but the answer will in fact determine the importance that is given to remedying infertility and the means that are employed to achieve that goal. From an individual standpoint, infertility is invariably a source of psychological distress for the couples involved. Those who find themselves in this situation may experience infertility as a threat to their very "well-being." From a collective standpoint, the issue is far less clear. Some view infertility not as a disease but as a consequence of disease (e.g., endometriosis, STDs), while others argue that infertility can never truly be called a disease since, aside from thwarting a couple's desire to have children, infertility does not express itself. In our view, such ideas are at odds with [the] increasingly widespread concept of medicine that considers health, disease, and treatment from a holistic perspective in which biopsychosocial factors are taken into account. Assisted human reproduction (AHR) technologies therefore offer a palliative solution for this increasingly widespread disease. Research into ways of improving these technologies is ongoing and new forms of research on embryos are now possible through the creation of surplus embryos for in vitro fertilization. Indeed, research into embryonic stem cells and cloning has elicited considerable interest of late, due to its considerable therapeutic potential.

The *Act respecting assisted human reproduction and related research*, adopted by the federal government in 2004, is a response to concerns that this area needs to be regulated and is part of a growing legislative trend at the international level. This legislation is intended as a tool to regulate the new reproductive technologies for the "protection and promotion of human health, safety, dignity and rights." However, the wisdom of combining prohibitive measures with regulatory ones is questionable. While no one is challenging its constitutional authority in criminal matters, the activities that are regulated in this legislation interfere with the body of rules that already exists in Quebec. Our purpose here is to highlight two essential characteristics of the Quebec approach, which are its regulatory effectiveness and its coherent and innovative vision of assisted reproduction, both of which have placed Quebec in the forefront of this field.

I. Quebec: Opting for Regulatory Effectiveness

The decision to regulate a particular field must begin with the selection of an appropriate vehicle with which to effect the desired reforms. Several regulatory models are available to decision-makers. Also, every choice and every regulatory system constitutes a unique amalgam of cultural, historical and political elements. When Quebec began to look for the most suitable model to regulate assisted human reproduction (AHR), it opted for a strategy that reinforces regulatory effectiveness. Building on the idea that regulatory instruments can be different without being mutually exclusive, and that a combined approach may enhance effectiveness all around, Quebec chose to privilege a multi-institutional regulatory partnership that allies (A) government action, (B) empowered professional organizations, (C) committed research ethics committees, and (D) the *Fonds de la recherche en santé du Québec* (FRSQ).

A. Government Action

In the interest of regulatory coherence, the government pursues actions on two fronts: (1) the legislative and (2) the administrative/institutional.

(1) LEGISLATIVE ACTION: A BODY OF COHERENT RULES

Quebec took an interest in the impact of new reproductive technologies early on. Its initial interventions were in the area of family law and, more particularly, filiation. In 1980, the government took measures to bestow a stable legal status on children conceived by means of these technologies, by incorporating section 586, which prohibits disavowal or contestation of paternity in the case of children conceived by means of artificial insemination, into the Civil Code of Québec. Later, in its major reforms of 1991, Quebec generalized this filial protection, taking into account the new reality brought about by another important innovation in the field of assisted reproduction, namely in vitro fertilization. Finally, in 2002, Quebec legislators showed considerable initiative by adopting the *Act Instituting civil unions and establishing new rules of filiation*, which amended the Civil Code, guaranteeing the right of access to reproductive technologies of single persons and formalizing recognition of the filiation of children born to lesbian couples by means of AHR.

In addition to the innovative nature of these provisions, to which we shall return later, their integration into the Civil Code had symbolic resonance since, by associating these provisions with "[translation] a system of private law that is coherent and relatively complete," Quebec legislators wished to signal the fact that they viewed this new area of law as an important priority. Accordingly, the 1991 Civil Code amendments included several important additions designed to address the ethical concerns raised by these technologies. Thus, the nullity of surrogacy contracts, the confidentiality of nominative information relating to medically assisted procreation, and the principle of non-commercialization of [the] human body took their place within the regulatory universe of Quebec, in the form of common law rules.

In 1997, the National Assembly voted to amend the *Public Health Protection Act*. The amendments would have required centres that store gametes and embryos to obtain an operating licence from the Minister of Health (section 31) and would have authorized the Minister to establish standard[s] for equipment, operations and the inspection of these centres (section 69). Although these provisions never came into force – the *Act respecting medical laboratories, organ, tissue, gamete and embryo conservation, and the disposal of human bodies* (the new title of the *Public Health Protection Act* since April 2002) makes no reference to them – we can confidently state that there is a strong desire in Quebec to effectively regulate AHR-related clinical and research activities carried out in the private sector. This proactive attitude is currently reflected in Bill 89, *An Act respecting clinical and research activities as regards assisted human reproduction and amending other legislative provisions*. This legislation would not only require private clinics to obtain a permit from the Minister of Health in order to pursue assisted reproduction activities, but would extend this requirement to the entire public sector as well. It would also require these centres to obtain accreditation for their assisted reproduction activities, in this case extending to the private sector provisions first introduced in 2002 for all health and social services delivered in institutional settings. The body of provisions that have been adopted, culminating with Bill 89, will ensure that practices in this area are coherent, of high quality and safe throughout Quebec.

The aim of the Quebec government has been to go further in the direction of AHR regulation. In addition to wanting to ensure that only services of the highest quality are delivered, the government has sought to provide financial assistance for infertile couples who may want to use these services. The *Régie de l'assurance maladie du Québec* began to cover artificial insemination services in 1971. In 2001, the Quebec government introduced a system of refundable tax credits to cover the often prohibitive costs associated with artificial insemination and in vitro fertilization. The tax credit reimburses 30% of such costs, up to a maximum of $6,000 per year. Although the *Taxation Act* does not cover these costs in their entirety, the government's efforts in this direction are commendable; indeed, Quebec is the only province in Canada that offers reimbursement for a range of assisted reproduction procedures.

(2) ADMINISTRATIVE AND INSTITUTIONAL ACTIONS: PROOF OF AN ONGOING COMMITMENT

Quebec's dynamic legislative approach to assisted reproduction is supported by ongoing administrative and institutional action on the clinical and research fronts, an indication of Quebec's commitment to its Quebeckers.

As early as 1989, the *Ministére de la Santé et des Services sociaux* (MSSS) introduced its *Orientations pour améliorer la santé et le bien-être au Québec* [orientations for improving health and well-being in Quebec], which contained a number of initiatives that related directly to reproductive technologies. These initiatives were based on fundamental principles that must guide government action at all times, including:

- the principle of respect and protection for the dignity and interests of children conceived by means of reproductive technologies;
- the principle of non-commodification of the human body;
- the notion that all actions in this area, from infertility prevention to the use of reproductive technologies, must be coherent;
- the essential right to obtain information that is clear, accurate and comparable from centre to centre.

These principles – which were partly derived from the *Rapport du comité de travail sur les nouvelles technologies de reproduction humaine* [report of the working committee on human reproductive technologies], a committee established by MSSS, as well as several documents produced by the *Conseil du statut de la femme* – remain the cornerstone of Quebec's legislative and administrative action in this area and reflect a consistent commitment to comply with the highest ethical standards in matters related to reproduction.

In 1997, in a further effort to ensure that the AHR services delivered to the Quebec population would be safe and of the highest quality, MSSS began to exercise its power to restrict the delivery of certain services or drugs to certain facilities. Accordingly, it designated the public health facilities that would be authorized to provide donor artificial insemination (15 hospitals in all), and those that would be authorized to deliver in vitro fertilization and its variants, or collect, store, and distribute gametes and embryos (4 university hospitals).

The *Plan d'action ministériel en éthique de la recherche et en intégrité scientifique* (MSSS, 1998), which followed on the Deschamps report, introduced a number of important changes in the research field, particularly with respect to the use of human embryos. This action plan addresses two key objectives:

- to protect the safety and integrity of persons who participate in research activities;
- to clarify the different levels of responsibility and put in place means of fulfilling these responsibilities.

These two objectives underlie many provisions that are designed to secure the involvement of all research stakeholders and to instil in them a sense of responsibility with regards to the protection of the person, a *sine qua non* condition of ethically acceptable research. The introduction of a triple (scientific, ethical and financial) review system for all research involving persons or embryos that is carried out within the health and social services system again reflects Quebec's abiding desire to ensure that its population benefits from research of the highest quality.

In order to promote discussion of the legislative and administrative measures undertaken in the area of new health technologies, the Quebec government has established a number of multidisciplinary institutions whose role is to ensure that medical and scientific practices are governed by appropriate ethical standards. In 1988, for example, Quebec established the *Conseil d'évaluation des technologies de la santé* (CETS) in order to promote and support the evaluation of health technologies. The *Conseil*, which is composed of independent experts, was given a dual mandate:

- The first component of this mandate is aimed at all health system stakeholders, including members of the public (as recipients of care), health care providers and health service managers. It consists of "promoting and supporting the evaluation of health technologies, by disseminating results and encouraging their use in the decision making of all stakeholders involved in the use of these technologies."
- The second component relates to the advice given to the "Minister on issues with respect to the introduction, dissemination and use of health technologies, including expert advice on the effectiveness, safety, costs and health system impacts of these technologies, as well their economic, ethical and social implications[.]"

In 2000, the CETS was replaced by the *Agence d'évaluation des technologies et des modes d'intervention en santé* (AETMIS), an agency with a broader mandate that includes the assessment of service organization and delivery procedures. The new Agency was also given the responsibility of evaluating technical aids for disabled persons, a task formerly performed by the now-dissolved *Conseil consultatif sur les aides techniques*.

In 1996, at the request of the Minister of Health, the CETS produced a memorandum on the best means of using evaluative data in the field of reproductive technology. Reports dealing with the broader perinatal issue were also published and widely disseminated to stakeholders. With its freedom to choose the topics of its reports, as well as its ability to include social and ethical data in its work, this institution constitutes a privileged forum for discussion and a guarantor of safe and acceptable practices in the field of reproductive health for Quebeckers.

However, ethical deliberation must extend beyond the sphere of health technology assessment. Indeed, sectoral and specialized practices must be informed by "open, plural and ongoing discussion and reflection on ethical issues as they relate to scientific and technological advancement." It was this concern that led to the creation of the *Commission de l'éthique de la science et de la technologie* (CEST) in 2001. Operating under the stewardship of the *Conseil de la science et de la technologie* (CST), the Commission enjoys full moral independence. Its mission consists of:

- informing, sensitizing, gathering opinions, fostering reflection and organizing debates on the ethical issues raised by developments in science and technology; and

– proposing orientations to guide stakeholders in their decision making.

This dual mandate and autonomy confer on the CEST the latitude needed to analyse ethically sensitive issues in considerable depth. While the newly created Commission has yet to examine reproductive issues, its very existence ensures that Quebec's specific cultural context will be taken into account when ethical issues associated with medical technologies are analysed.

In April 2004, as a further sign of the importance placed on ethical discussion in Quebec, MSSS created an administrative unit entirely dedicated to the ethical issues facing the health and social services sector. The mission of this unit, which is part of the *Direction générale adjointe de l'évaluation*, is to develop and implement ethics-related policies, orientations and intervention strategies. Its mandate, which is intentionally defined in broad terms, is to implement and monitor Quebec's ethics regime for research activities in the field of health and social services, as well as to develop a regulatory regime that is specific to assisted reproduction. This unique institutional feature attests to Quebec's rigorous commitment to ethics.

B. Empowerment of Professional Organizations

As a complement to government measures, the multi-institutional regulatory partnership established by Quebec also places considerable emphasis on the empowerment of professional organizations. There are several reasons for this. First, by virtue of their extensive training and knowledge, professionals have a thorough understanding of the technical issues that arise in connection with new reproductive technologies. Second, as the *Collège des médecins du Québec* has pointed out, guidelines, codes of clinical practice and ethical obligations cannot stand still; they must evolve along with practices and ways of thinking. Finally, when such mechanisms are permitted to evolve according to criteria that are meaningful to the scientific and medical community, they are more likely to be accepted and appropriately applied by the members of that community.

The empowerment of professional organizations is effected in two ways: through specific guidelines and through more general texts of an administrative or ethical nature that govern medical and research practices in Quebec. In the first category, two documents are worthy of mention; (a) the *Politique concernant l'infertilité et la fécondation in vitro* (1993) of the Association of Obstetricians and Gynecologists of Quebec, which defines infertility as a disease, and considers the procedures carried out to correct it as medical procedures (this position reflects the view expressed by most professional organizations in the debate around the nature of infertility); and (b) the 1994 guidelines on artificial insemination issued by the *Collège des médecins du Québec,* which review the primary legal and ethical parameters established to guide medical practitioners in Quebec. This document also had a didactic purpose: the *Collège* felt that if doctors provided a better explanation of artificial insemination, couples would be better prepared to deal with an unfavourable outcome. Few resources of this nature have been provided by Quebec medical authorities and the *Collège des médecins du Québec* itself reminds us, in this regard, that: "[translation] at the scientific level, guidelines on assisted reproduction are usually developed by Canada-wide organizations and are generally consistent with those recognized internationally by the medical community."

Alongside this international standardization of scientific practice, Quebec has also developed its own ethics documents. These texts of a general nature constitute a coherent set of ethical and administrative rules designed to protect the public. The *Collège des médecins* has at its disposal a range of documents that enable it to fulfil its mission at every stage of medical intervention and to oversee AHR practices in Quebec. The *Collège* is also empowered to grant licensure to practice, based on personal qualifications. Bill 89 consolidates this legitimacy, since it stipulates that assisted reproduction centres must be directed by a member of the *Ordre des médecins* who holds a certificate of specialization in obstetrics–gynecology conferred by the *Collège des médecins*. To ensure the quality of medical practice, the *Collège* actively exercises its power of inspection over "[translation] every aspect of medical ethics, member discipline, and the honour and dignity of the profession." The *Collège* can impose disciplinary sanctions as it sees fit, the most serious sanction being the withdrawal of a member's licence to practice.

This circularity in the area of accountability is designed to ensure that practices adhere to the very highest standards. In light of the proven effectiveness of these mechanisms, Bill 89 broadens the *Collège*'s mandate to include an advisory and investigative role with respect to: quality assessment; safety and ethics in assisted reproduction centres; the professional competency of physicians who work in these centres; and the quality standards with which such facilities must comply.

Beyond such mechanisms, the Code of Ethics of Physicians constitutes a crucial and ever-evolving instrument in the "[translation] service of the ethical creativity and moral responsibility of professionals." In addition to the binding nature of its rules, the Code constitutes an essential guarantee that awareness of the moral issues associated with the practice of medicine will continue to grow within the profession. The reforms introduced in 2002 also took place [in] the context of the growing bioethics movement; as such, they included a series of measures that require physicians to comply with ethical mechanisms in the performance of their clinical or research duties. For example, sections 28 and 31 strengthen requirements related to subject consent in the context of treatment and research. The new Code also requires physicians who wish to carry out research involving human beings to first obtain approval for their projects from a research ethics committee that observes current standards in terms of its composition and its operating procedures. Physicians are further required to spell out their ethical obligations to collaborators. The revision of the Code of Ethics of Physicians has had a domino effect on other health professions, such as nursing, prompting them to undertake similar initiatives in the area of ethical accountability.

A consensus has emerged around administrative and ethical rules of this kind [that has made] AHR practices safer and more ethical and encourage[d] physicians to reflect on their moral obligations as practitioners. Still, Quebec has not delegated to these organizations the power to make decisions on issues that require democratic debate, such as the determination of ethically acceptable health risks or, on a broader level, the choice of approaches to the area of infertility. Scientific experts are not experts in societ[al] values, and ethical questioning is not, in any fundamental sense, central to scientific activity, a field [in which] the standards adopted are more likely to reflect practical concerns having to do with the management of new technologies within a given profession rather than broader socio-ethical considerations.

C. Role of Research Ethics Committees

Research ethics committees (RECs) play a central role in the multi-institutional regulatory partnership. Indeed, these committees represent a cornerstone of the *Plan d'action ministériel en éthique de la recherche et en intégrité scientifique*; as such, their mission consists of actively promoting research ethics rules and principles. The mandate of these committees comprises three major components:

- an evaluative component: the committees are called on to ethically and scientifically evaluate research projects involving human subjects that are carried out in the health and social services system;
- an oversight component: the committee[s] provide ongoing monitoring for approved research projects, through passive measures (e.g., reviewing project modifications and annual reports submitted by researchers), as well as active measures (e.g., distributing questionnaires to research subjects, conducting on-site visits of research centres); and
- a regulatory and informative component; research ethics committees develop guidelines, consent form templates, and information guides for researchers. They also carry out information and awareness activities on ethical issues for the benefit of the scientific community.

The purview of research ethics committees is broad, encompassing the entire range of research activities involving human subjects (be they competent, incompetent or minors), human cadavers and remains, organic human tissues and fluids, gametes, embryos and fetuses, as well as all related personal information. All research projects in the field of assisted reproduction, whether they involve infertile couples, embryos or embryonic cells, are evaluated ethically and scientifically and monitored by ethics committees.

The central role assigned to RECs in the field of assisted reproduction is linked to the crucial function they perform in the area of bioethics. These committees orient their deliberations towards consensus-building, which is considered to be the only valid decision-making process in the field of ethics. A consensus, which can sometimes take the form of a minor compromise, reflects the shared values of committee members. A diversity of disciplines and views is a characteristic requirement of research ethics committees. When a variety of background sand opinions are represented, there is a greater likelihood that decisions related to research on embryos or embryonic stem cells will meet with acceptance. Research ethics committees promote continuity in ethical reflection, which in turn leads to greater flexibility in the analysis and resolution of existing or prospective ethical issues. Moreover, the relative independence of RECs – an inherent feature of their identity – gives them greater credibility as a regulatory mechanism in the eyes of the various stakeholders in the field of reproductive technology.

While research ethics committees pursue a holistic vocation, the law may determine that certain highly sensitive types of research – such as those involving minors or legally incompetent adults – must be evaluated by a research ethics committee that has been designated or established by the Minister of Health and Social Services. For legislators, assisted procreation clearly falls into the category of research that is sensitive and in need of special treatment. Accordingly, Bill 89 stipulates that "a research project on assisted human reproduction must be approved and supervised by a recognized research ethics committee or a research ethics committee established by the Minister." The impact of these provisions is threefold: in addition to the symbolic character of this approach, limiting these responsibilities to recognized RECs should ensure a minimum and pluralistic representation of members, as well as the involvement of persons with broad knowledge of research methods and fields in the area of assisted reproduction. Moreover, the likely transposition of the requirement that designated RECs submit annual reports to the Minister, and the Minister's power to revoke the designation of committees that fail to comply with established operating conditions, provide added assurance that the highest scientific and ethical research standards will be applied in the area of assisted reproduction. An important aspect in this regard is the dual accountability mechanism that Bill 89 introduces with respect to AHR, namely the requirement that centres for AHR submit annual reports of their activities, as a complement to the annual reports required of research ethics committees. This allows for the comparative analysis of research projects as disclosed by centres and examined by committees.

Added to the authority of research ethics committees in the area of AHR is an expansion of their field of intervention; they will evaluate not only AHR research projects carried out within the health system, but also those conducted in private clinics, a category not previously covered under the MSSS action plan.

Finally, it should be noted that the ethics unit of MSSS employs a full-time resource person whose duties revolve specifically around the work of RECs. The mandate of this resource person is to support ethics committees in their mission, to act as an expert advisor for inquiries and difficulties encountered in the area of research ethics, as well as to assess designation requests and monitor designated RECs. The very existence and complementarity of these functions fosters recognition of the essential nature of the work performed by RECs. Given the crucial function performed by research ethics committees in Quebec, expanding that role to include all AHR research carried out in the public and private sectors seem an entirely appropriate development.

D. Role of the Fonds de la recherche en santé du Québec

The *Fonds de la recherche en santé du Québec* (FRSQ) is a quasi-public organization that provides funding for health research. Established by the *Ministére de la Santé* in 1964 under the name *Conseil de recherches médicales*, its mandate was originally limited to advising the Minister on matters related to health research. Oversight changes at the *Ministére* provided an opportunity to redefine and broaden the mandate of the FRSQ, which now encompasses health research planning and coordination. The FRSQ plays an important role in the multi-institutional AHR partnership in Quebec, owing to its strategic position as an intermediary between government and the scientific community. Public funding for health research in Quebec is accompanied by legal and administrative rules, as well as monitoring procedures (audits)[,] with which researchers and institutions are required to comply. This is an important point: the mission of the FRSQ is inseparable from the promotion of research ethics. "Acknowledgement that 'ethics' and 'scientific integrity' are inextricably linked is a sign of the maturity of research communities and their stakeholders. Indeed, these investigators view the promotion of these two basic values and their application (best practices) as an additional guarantee of the quality of their work and of their reputation."

Moreover, the role of the FRSQ as a promoter of research ethics was endorsed by MSSS in its 1998 action plan, which enlarged the organization's responsibilities, entrusting it with the mandate to set research standards (in the form of a quality assurance system) and monitoring procedures. To this end, the FRSQ published *Research Ethics and Scientific Integrity Guidelines* (2001, revised 2003) that apply to researchers and ethics committees operating in public health institutions in Quebec. The fundamental principle that underlies these guidelines is that FRSQ funding for projects involving human subjects is conditional upon approval and follow-up by an REC affiliated with the health care institution in which the project is to be carried out. In addition to complying with standards, institutions must [...] implement a regulatory framework for research activities, as prescribed in the ministerial action plan. The *Cadre réglementaire des bonnes practiques de la recherche dans les établissements universitaires de santé du Québec* [regulatory framework for good research practices in university health institutions in Quebec], developed by the FRSQ, addresses the goal of providing guidance and support to university health institutions in this implementation. Indeed, this type of regulatory framework for institutional health research is the only mechanism of its kind in Canada.

The field of intervention of the FRSQ is fairly broad, encompassing not only research conducted in FRSQ research centres affiliated with university hospitals and non-university hospitals, but also research carried out by FRSQ research groups on university campuses in Quebec. The ethical and administrative standards adopted by the FRSQ complement the articulated, multi-partner mechanisms established to promote research quality in Quebec. Moreover, the FRSQ plays an active role in monitoring AHR research and helped to draft *Human Pluripotent Stem Cell Research: Recommendations for CIHR-Funded Research*, a document issued by the federal government.

The FRSQ's involvement in the drafting of the above-mentioned document and the adherence of its advisory committee on research ethics and scientific integrity to the ethical standards articulated in its pages prompted the FRSQ board of directors to recognize and adopt the document as well. The FRSQ encouraged its research ethics committees to adopt these recommendations in the assessment of research projects dealing with pluripotent human stem cells, while adding its own comments regarding implementation mechanisms. Accordingly, the FRSQ does not fund projects involving:

- research to create human embryos solely for the purpose of derivation and use of embryonic stem cell lines;
- research involving somatic cell nuclear transfer into human oocytes for the purposes of developing human embryonic stem cell lines (so-called "therapeutic" cloning);
- research involving the directed donation of stem cell lines or cell lines of a pluripotent nature to particular individuals (except in the case of autologous donations); or
- research involving the creation of hybrid species.

Public agencies that fund research have a fundamental role to play. The mandate of these bodies requires that they remain informed about new scientific developments and respond quickly to techno-scientific innovations and the ethical problems such innovations can occasion. Their importance from a regulatory standpoint relates not only to their enforcement of established administrative and ethical rules, but also to their role as catalysts (e.g.[,] when funding guidelines fill a legislative gap, as in the case of embryonic stem cell research). The FRSQ's ability to explicitly or implicitly communicate to government the needs of the Quebec scientific community in the area of standards amply justifies the role it has been assigned in the area of AHR.

The primacy of the multi-institutional regulatory partnership is equal to Quebec's ambition, which is to ensure that its population benefits from research and services of the highest quality in the area of assisted reproduction. Bill 89 strengthens this strategy, by linking these mechanisms to the Quebec reality, resulting in a more effective system that will add to Quebec's standing as a pioneer in this field.

II. Quebec: A Coherent and Innovative Vision

Quebec's vision in the area of assisted human reproduction (AHR) goes beyond the mere organization of services and research activities: it seeks to establish a system that is both coherent and innovative. The system needs to be coherent because the sensitive nature of AHR makes it imperative that all Quebec stakeholders adhere to ethical and legal standards that are consistent with the highest international standards (see A). It needs to be innovative so that Quebec can maintain its leading role in the field of reproductive technologies, both in Canada and internationally (see B).

A. Integration of Quebec Rules with International Standards

Integrating Quebec rules with international standards in AHR achieves two objectives[:] the symbolic objective confirming the expression of a transnational consensus, and the practice objective of providing a reference guide for the various stakeholders in this field. While there are many noteworthy aspects to this interregulatory dialogue, we will examine three[:] (1) consent in AHR services and research; (2) non-commercialization of the human body; and (3) the monitoring of research on embryos and embryonic stem cell lines.

(1) CONSENT IN AHR SERVICES AND RESEARCH

One of the essential ethical principles that must guide action in the health field is undoubtedly respect for the autonomy of the individual. Whether in the context of treatment or research, consent must be based on the liberty of human beings who "[translation] assume their own destiny, by demonstrating intelligence and a sense of responsibility." For the health professional, this vision of the person, which is at once legalistic and Kantian, primarily take[s] the form of an obligation to secure the voluntary consent of patients, which is to say their free and informed consent, before undertaking any therapeutic or experimental procedure. This (initially legal) requirement is in fact a reaction against the paternalistic attitude of the medical profession[,] for which any act "[translation] is, and must be, based on the patient's trust and the physician's conscience." As a result of such attitudes, the concept of consent did not even figure in the medical codes of ethics throughout the 19th century and the early part of the 20th century.

The moral requirement to secure consent differs depending on whether it relates to treatment or research. In the first instance, it relates to individual medical necessity, while in the second[,] it relates to a dynamic of solidarity, even though benefit may be derived by individual research subjects. The desire to establish a distinct approach and to emphasize the protection of research subjects is understandable given the many abuses that have taken place in the past, including the experiments carried [out] by the Nazis during WWII and those reported by H.K. Beecher in 1966.

In Quebec, the need to obtain a person's free and informed consent is expressed through the principle of the inviolability of the person, as enshrined in the Civil Code. Absence of coercion and the requirement to divulge sufficient information to permit responsible decision making are constants in all international standards documents. While the principle is clear, its implementation is all the more important in the field of reproductive technology, where the long-term risks for women and children are still imperfectly understood. Given the unique nature of gamete and embryo donation, health professionals are entirely justified in stressing the importance of donor consent. In fact, Quebec is one of the few jurisdictions that limits the possibility of even giving one's consent as a donor to instances where the risks incurred are not out of proportion to the benefits that are reasonably expected. The health of potential egg donors must prevail over their altruistic aims, given the high risks they must incur. Moreover, by stipulating that a minor or an incompetent adult cannot alienate a part of their body unless that part can be regenerated and the procedure poses no grave risk to their health, Quebec is *de facto* prohibiting egg donations by minors and thereby reducing the [chances] that pressure will be brought to bear on minors by family members, given the scarcity of such donations.

The principle of respect for autonomy is nowhere more important than in the research field. The conditions under which individuals exercise free and informed consent in research settings are in fact a distillation of the recommendations made in international documents on this subject. Vulnerable populations, such as minors and legally incompetent adults, are protected by severe restrictions concerning the experiments to which they may consent. In AHR, practitioners generally deal with competent adults; however, great vigilance needs to be exercised, given the vulnerability of couples and the potential blurring of physician/researcher roles. Indeed, such concern is entirely appropriate in light of the recent scandal in South Korea, where ova taken from staff members of investigator Hwang Woo-Suk were used in cloning experiments. The multi-partner mechanisms adopted by Quebec promote a precautionary approach and combine the principle of respect for autonomy with the principle of beneficence. Legislators establish the relevant parameters in this area, including: the legal requirement that potential research subjects must give their consent in writing; the right of subjects to withdraw their consent at any time; and the provisions regarding the proportionality of research risks to benefits. Furthermore, the requirement that AHR projects be submitted to designated research ethics committees, the influence exerted by the FRSQ through its ethical standards, and the regulatory framework applied to institutions within the health system, provide optimal protection for research subjects and fully meet the standards articulated in international documents. These mechanisms, which are unique to Quebec, are designed to protect the right of people to make their own decisions with respect to AHR treatment and research and to determine what is best for them within ethically appropriate parameters.

(2) NON-COMMERCIALIZATION OF HUMAN BODY

The use of gametes and embryos in AHR services and research has created a growing demand for these human materials. While the demand for them has grown exponentially since the therapeutic potential of embryonic stem cells became clear, scarcity remains an issue, given the difficulty inherent in obtaining ova and embryos. This imbalance between supply and demand has given rise to a market that Quebec intends to eradicate. Section 25 of the Civil Code of Québec seeks to counteract the commercial lure of this market by stipulating that alienation by a person of a part or product of his body shall be gratuitous [freely given], and by further requiring that experiments must not give rise to any financial rewards, other than the payment of compensation for the loss or inconvenience suffered.

In giving concrete expression to the principle that the human body is not a commodity, Quebec has adopted standards that are consistent with international texts: the symbolic meaning ascribed to the human body excludes it from the realm of commerce. This appeal to the altruism of Quebeckers is intended to address two concomitant objectives (while also adhering to the underlying principle of justice) [–] solidarity with the sick and the protection of vulnerable persons against all forms of exploitation [–] thereby ensuring that the burdens associated with medical progress are fairly distributed.

Still, this Quebec conception comes up against the view that prevails in the United States, namely that the individual has the exclusive right to dominion over his or her own body and that obstacles to this right should be as few as possible. This supremacy of liberal philosophy translates into the idea that only the individual is capable of assessing the risks and benefits that an action (a donation in this instance) poses for him or her. From this point of view, financial incentives constitute an effective means of regulating supply and demand. However, to recognize the wisdom of the Quebec approach, one need only consider the plight of poor women[,] who might be tempted to sell their eggs as a means of subsistence, or that of couples who might take part in experimental protocols for AHR in order to fund their own fertility treatments. The risks in this area are so great that the European Parliament has adopted a resolution that deals specifically with commerce in human eggs. In it, the EU urges its member states to adopt measures to prevent the exploitation of women in the application of life science and stresses that any woman forced to sell any part of her body, including reproductive cells, become[s] prey to organized crime networks that traffic in people and organs. Quebec's rule prohibiting commercial gain for donors and research subjects constitutes a presumption of ethical behaviour.

(3) MONITORING OF EMBRYO AND EMBRYONIC STEM CELL RESEARCH

Embryo research has attracted an unprecedented amount of attention in the scientific community since the remarkable therapeutic potential of embryonic stem cells was first discovered. The avid response to these developments has prompted international bodies to (re)position themselves with regard to the acceptability of this form of research and to consider the imposition of restrictions and conditions on its pursuit. A number of key points emerge from this analysis, highlighting the consonance of Quebec rules with the highest international ethical standards. Among these, we should mention the clear preference for research that uses supernumerary embryos created for reproductive purposes and no longer needed for such purposes. The ethical justification for this preference is that these embryos are destined to be destroyed, since the in vitro fertilization process often results in the creation of more embryos than are needed. Moreover, the creation of embryos specifically for research purposes evokes the idea of instrumental use, which explains the considerable resistance that this approach has encountered. Quebec shares such misgivings and has taken measures to restrict the production of embryos for research purposes. Its first intervention in this area was carried out through its funding body, the *Fonds de recherce en santé du Québec* (FRSQ), when the latter announced that it would not fund projects in which embryos are created specifically for research, nor projects involving any form of cloning. Bill 89 reiterates this ethical orientation and would only allow "research projects on embryos and embryonic stem cells resulting from assisted human reproduction activities and not used for that purpose."

While permissible in principle, this type of research must comply with a number of conditions in Quebec, conditions that largely echo those found in international guidelines. As stated earlier, free and informed consent, given without coercion, is crucial in terms of respecting the moral and religious convictions of donors. While section 22 of the Civil Code of Québec stipulates that a body part removed from a person as part of the care he or she received may be used for research purposes if the person so consents, the FRSQ specifies how these provisions are to be applied in the specific context of embryo and embryonic stem cell research. First, it proposes that consent for reproductive activities and consent for research activities be secured at different times to avoid confusion or undue pressure; second, it proposes that embryos created from the gametes of third donors not be retained, since securing consent in these cases would imperil donor anonymity.

Research on embryos and embryonic stem cells is generally considered acceptable only when alternative methods of comparable efficacy are not available. In other words, this type of research should serve a palliative purpose and not be viewed as a casual option. Indeed, the unique status of the embryo justifies special protective measures. Quebec is in favour of such measures and, as such, requires investigators to justify the use of embryonic cells over postnatal or adult stem cells.

All research projects in which embryos are used to extract stem cells must undergo ethical and scientific evaluation. However, this requirement does not meet with unanimous approval in regards to research on previously extracted stem cells. Whereas Canada has determined that evaluation is not necessary in these cases, Quebec has chosen to take a more restrictive approach by requiring that all research projects involving embryos and embryonic stem cells be reviewed by an REC. In adopting such a comprehensive approach, Quebec has given itself the ability to regulate new fields of scientific research, while also providing assurance to its population that the research being carried out in the field of AHR is of the highest quality, is respectful of people's convictions, and meets the highest international ethical standards.

B. Quebec: A Leader in the Field of AHR

The integration of Quebec rules with international standards in the area of AHR (a few examples of which have been provided in these pages) is crucial in that it sends a proactive message about Quebec's desire to participate in efforts to promote coherence in a sensitive field where the geopolitical boundaries do not necessarily constitute an effective defence against rapid technological development. These essential efforts to achieve coherence include a number of Quebec initiatives that are worthy of note both in Canada (1) and internationally (2); these initiatives also reflect Quebec's standing as a leader in the field of assisted reproduction.

(1) IN CANADA

Quebec can take pride in the pioneering role it has played in three distinct areas of AHR in Canada, namely[,] (a) research governance[,] (b) surrogacy[,] and (c) filiation of children born out of AHR.

a) Research Governance. The role that international documents set out for research ethics committees in the regulation of research is a crucial one. As proponents of research subject protection and of ethical conduct in research, these committees are entrusted with the very important responsibility of approving research protocols. Some commentators have criticized the power conferred upon these committees or even questioned whether these bodies actually play a useful role. Such questions arise when committees take questionable positions owing to incompetence or lack of accountability. The idea of legally regulating research mechanisms in order to ensure that the highest ethical standards are met is currently being studied in Canada. Two proposals have emerged: the Public Assurance System for Research Involving Humans in Council-Funded Institutions[,] developed by the Social Sciences and Humanities Research Council of Canada (SSHRC)[,] and the Accreditation System for Human Research Protection Programs[,] established by the National Council on Ethics in Human Research (NCEHR). While the two differ in terms of their selected means of implementation, the audiences they target (the SSHRC targets the RECs, while the NCEHR targets all stakeholders in the research field), and the reference standards that apply (the Police Statements of three councils in the case of the SSHRC and all formal documents produced in Canada in the case of the NCEHR), [...] share the idea that sound governance is based on efficacy, transparency and accountability. Quebec can therefore boast that it is a true leader in the area of research governance.

Indeed, the REC designation procedure and the requirement that institutions and organizations within the Quebec health system adopt a regulatory framework for their research activities together constitute a solid and effective basis for ensuring compliance with the highest ethical standards. Ministerial recognition confers upon research ethics committees the exclusive authority to evaluate sensitive research projects, such as those involving minors or legally incompetent adults and, in the near future, research projects in the field of medically assisted reproduction. As we have seen, ministerial recognition necessitates compliance with a number of requirements, including a committee membership that is multidisciplinary, independent and qualified, as well as annual reporting to MSSS. Similarly, the adoption of a regulatory framework requires institutions and organizations within the health system to establish and comply with a range of standards in areas such as[] the compulsory reporting of research activities; the handling of scientific misconduct and ethical breaches; and the management of data banks and research records. Other measures in the area of AHR research include the research licence-granting process, as well as the accountability and accreditation procedures provided for in Bill 89. All of these measures will undeniably contribute to the creation of a transparent, effective and accountable process in the research field. Moreover, the NCERH has explicitly acknowledged Quebec's position as a leader in this area, having indicated that the Quebec system may be used as a basis or regulatory reference for the development of a Canadian accreditation system.

b) Surrogacy. Views concerning surrogacy are divided, with the Anglo-Saxon tradition and its strong emphasis on the principle of autonomy frequently clashing with the Latin tradition and its greater emphasis on the protection of the person. Quebec is the first jurisdiction in Canada to have adopted a legal position with respect to surrogacy. Opting for a forward-looking approach in anticipation of potential abuses, Quebec incorporated into its 1991 reforms provisions that specifically declare contracts entered into by surrogate mothers to be null and void. This determination is of considerable symbolic importance for, in seeking to protect the general interest, it also explicitly signals that surrogacy contracts constitute an infringement on the principles of respect for human dignity. While advocates of individual autonomy may view such contracts as a private matter and may choose to ignore issues of social inequality, Quebec has determined that it cannot ignore such issues.

Surrogacy represents the instrumentalization of the child and the woman. The child is instrumentalized by virtue of the fact that it is being created for the specific purpose of being turned over to others. The woman is instrumentalized because the surrogacy contract leads to exploitation of her body, on the basis of her reproductive capacity. The female body is used as a matrix, a technical tool for the fulfilment of the wishes of others, while the emotional bond between mother and child is discounted. The social and financial inequality frequently observed between commissioning couples and surrogate mothers increases the likelihood of exploitation. Addressing this problem by limiting such contracts to those that involve no remuneration seems an ineffective solution at best. Where does one draw the fine line between remuneration and financial compensation? Even financial compensation can constitute an incentive to this type of transaction for women whose economic situation is precarious. Declaring all such contracts null and void seems a far more judicious approach. Indeed, making such contracts impossible to carry out effectively discourages potential parties: the commissioning couple may fear that the surrogate mother will renege, while the surrogate mother has no real assurance that the promised sum will be paid or that she will not be left with a child she may not want (as in the case of a child born with trisomy or when the commissioning couple separates). Discouraging such contracts by declaring them legally null and void and adding the threat of legal sanctions under the *Youth Protection Act* constitutes a strong disincentive. At present, the only arrangement that is possible under Quebec law is the adoption of a child born to a surrogate mother. By imposing legal sanctions against those who profit from adoption, Quebec is effectively attacking potential problems at their source.

c) Filiation of Children Conceived by Means of AHR. Formally recognizing the filiation of children born by means of assisted reproduction is a crucial breakthrough that Quebec can take pride in having pioneered in Canada. In 1980, Quebec became the first jurisdiction to introduce legal provisions prohibiting the disavowal or contestation of paternity in the case of children conceived by means of artificial insemination, with or without a donor, when both spouses have consented to the procedure. This enshrinement in law of paternal filiation goes beyond mere legal functionality and touches on a symbolic dimension that is essential to the construction of an individual's social and psychological identity. Such recognition also clarifies the position of [the] sperm donor, exempting [him] from the establishment of any bond of filiation between [him] and the children born of [his] donated sperm, provided that the spouses have jointly consented to the procedure.

This was a legal innovation in Canada, one that was followed by other equally forward-looking measures, such as the Civil Code amendments of 1991, which determined that donation of genetic material does not create a bond of filiation between the donor and the child born of the parental project. Making this legal point became necessary in light of emerging in vitro fertilization techniques that were little known when the 1980 Code amendments were introduced. In vitro techniques, which involve removing eggs or embryos from a woman's body for fertilization with donor sperm, raised new questions regarding filiation since, until then, the biological mother and the legal mother had been one and the same. Whereas the 1980 provisions addressed the issue of paternal filiation, the amendments introduced by Quebec in 1991 broke new ground by addressing the issue of maternal filiation in the case of children conceived by means of donated eggs or embryos: Quebec established that no bond of filiation exists between any donor (be it of sperm, eggs or embryos) and the children conceived by means of such donations. This legal enshrinement of the primacy of the parental project – that is of emotional and social reality over biological reality in reproductive technology – is another Quebec breakthrough.

(2) THE INTERNATIONAL DIMENSION

Filiation is an area of assisted reproduction in which Quebec has taken a number of very bold steps. The *Act instituting civil unions and establish new rules of filiation* (2002) introduced [...] a revolutionary concept of filiation into the Civil Code by recognizing the dual filiation of children born to lesbian couples by means of AHR.

Although no legal provisions had previously barred lesbian couples from accessing AHR services, the reality faced by these couples was quite different; at least three clinics had refused to provide services to lesbians before the enactment of this legislation in 2002. Providing unchallenged access to these technologies for lesbian couples is an important step, but Quebec did not stop there in its quest to become an international leader. It went on to prescribe that the child's birth certificate must bear not only the name of the woman who gave birth to the child, but also that of her same-sex partner in the parental project. Both are designated as the mothers, with all of the rights and obligations that apply in the case of filiation by blood. Rights which the law specifically attributes to the father are assumed by the same-sex partner of the woman who bears the child. This dual filiation is granted the same legal presumption regardless of whether the couple is married or in a civil union. Such legal recognition goes further than any other international provisions in this area. Quebec has again shown that it can act as a bold international catalyst in the regulation of reproductive technologies.

Conclusion

Quebec has adopted a comprehensive approach to AHR, one not tainted by exceptionalism relative to other areas of health, and the Quebec government has shown that it is interested in and committed to monitoring the development of reproductive technologies and related fields of research. Clearly, Quebec has taken up the challenge of addressing the ethical issues associated with these technologies and has fully assumed its decision-making powers in this area. The points reviewed in this document attest to this unwavering commitment.

- *Quebec has been overseeing AHR and related research since 1980.* A review of key events illustrates the continuity of the Quebec government's actions in this area:
  - 1980: *Civil Code of Québec*, S.Q. 1980, c. 39, s. 586 on the disavowal or contestation of paternity in cases of artificial insemination.
  - 1991: *Civil Code of Québec*, S.Q. 1991, c. 64, s. 538 to 542 on the filiation of children conceived by means of AHR; surrogacy contracts; the donation of gametes; and the principle of non-commercialization of the human body.
  - 1997: Designation of public health institutions authorized to offer donor artificial insemination services (15 hospitals), as well as those authorized to provide in vitro fertilization and gamete/embryo storage services (4 university hospitals).
  - 1997: *An Act to Amend the Public Health Protection Act*, S.Q. 1997, c. 77, s. 2 and 8, on the need to obtain a licence from the Minister of Health to operate a gamete/embryo storage centre and authorizing the Minister to establish standards pertaining to equipment, operations and inspection of such centres.
  - 1998: Ministerial action plan for research ethics and scientific integrity (MSSS). This action plan introduced a triple review system (scientific, ethical, financial) for all research on persons or embryos carried out within the health and social services system.
  - 2002: *An Act instituting civil unions and establishing new rules of filiation*, S.Q. 2002, c. 6, s. 30[,] on access to reproductive technologies for single persons and the filiation of children born to lesbian couples by means of AHR.
  - 2004: Bill 89 – *An Act respecting clinical and research activities as regards assisted human reproduction and amending other legislative provisions.*
- *Quebec has opted for effective standards by privileging a multi-stakeholder partnership.* Multiple stakeholders in the AHR and research fields share responsibility and pursue a discussion process designed to ensure that effective ethical and legal parameters

are established. Such cooperation with professional organizations, research ethics committees and the *Fonds de la recherche du Québec* promotes infertility prevention, as well as the development of research and clinical practices in AHR, within a framework that is ethically acceptable to the Quebec population.

- *Quebec's ethical standards are consistent with the highest international standards.* Mobilizing the entire range of Quebec stakeholders towards compliance with ethical standards that meet the highest international standards (subject consent in treatment and research, affirmation of the principle of non-commercialization of the human body, restrictions pertaining to research on embryos and embryonic stem cells) sends a proactive message about Quebec's desire to promote coherence in the area of AHR.
- *The incorporation of standards into the Civil Code reflects the priority given to AHR and scientific research.* A civil code articulates key concepts, transcendent principles, guidelines and the ideals that inform a legal tradition. The choice of this medium to accommodate most of the provisions relating to AHR and research clearly demonstrates the symbolic importance Quebec has striven to confer on the regulation of these sensitive practices since 1980.
- *Quebec is in the forefront of regulatory efforts around AHR and research.* Quebec's status as a leader in Canada (regulation of research, surrogacy and filiation of children conceived by means of AHR) and internationally (recognition of the dual filiation of children born to lesbian couples by means of AHR) demonstrates that its decision making in matters related to research and reproductive technologies is informed by truly innovative ideas.

Appendix 2 The Regulation of Assisted Human Reproductive Technologies and Related Research: A Public Health, Safety and Morality Argument [Expert Opinion for the Federal Government]

FRANÇOISE BAYLIS

On December 15, 2004, the Québec government filed a reference with the Québec Court of Appeal in which it challenged the constitutionality of the *Assisted Human Reproduction Act* (*AHR Act*),[1] specifically sections 8–19, 40–53, 60, 61, and 68. In support of this challenge, the Québec government obtained an expert report from Professor Bartha Maria Knoppers and Ms Petit. In response, the federal government solicited an expert report from me in which I argued that federal legislation was needed to protect and promote public health, safety, and morality for current and future generations of Canadians through the pursuit of ethical and therapeutic science and technologies.

Arguments presented to the Québec Court of Appeal in support of the constitutional validity of the *AHR Act* did not succeed. The Court held that all of the challenged provisions were unconstitutional.[2] In the wake of this advisory opinion, the Government of Canada appealed to the Supreme Court of Canada (SCC). The SCC handed down its ruling on December 22, 2010.[3] In a 4–4–1 decision, it determined that many (but not all) of the challenged provisions were *ultra vires* the federal government. Below is my expert report, which is cited in the SCC decision.

Statement of Expertise

I am a philosopher with ethics expertise on assisted human reproductive technologies, genetic technologies, and embryo research. This expertise dates back to the mid[-]1980s and includes both academic research and national policy work. Some of the work is briefly detailed below in chronological order.

From 1987 to 1988, I was Academic Secretary for the Medical Research Council of Canada Working Group on Guidelines for Somatic Cell Gene Therapy (the Working Group was chaired by Dr. Patricia Baird,] who later chaired the Royal Commission on New Reproductive Technologies).[4] In 1989, I completed my Philosophy PhD dissertation on "The Ethics of Ex Utero Research on 'IVF' Human Embryos[.]" In the dissertation, the main chapter of which is published in *Bioethics*,[5] I introduced a novel ethical distinction between viable and non-viable human embryos.

In 1990 and 1991, I was a consultant to the University of Western Ontario research team on early Pre-Implantation Cell Screening – the first Canadian site to do research on pre-implantation genetic diagnosis. In 1991, I was a consultant to the Royal Commission on New Reproductive Technologies. My work on informed choice is included in Volume 1 of the Commission's Research Studies.[6]

From the mid[-]1990s onward I developed an independent peer-reviewed research program with funding primarily from: Associated Medical Services Inc., the Social Science and Humanities Research Council of Canada, the Canadian Institutes of Health Research, and the Stem Cell Network, a member of the Network of Centres of Excellence program. This research has focused on women's reproductive health, the ethics of research involving women, embryo research, gene transfer research, stem cell research, human cloning, and obligations to future generations.

In tandem with this research, I continued to be involved in national policy work. For example, from 1994 to 1997 I was a member of the Ethics Committee of the Society of Obstetricians and Gynaecologists of Canada and from 1997 to 1998 I was a Consultant with the Society of Obstetricians and Gynaecologist[s] of Canada and the Canadian Fertility and Andrology Society on their *Joint Policy Statement: Ethical Issues in Assisted Reproduction*.[7] From 1998 to 2000 I was a member of the National Council on Ethics in Human Research.

On the strength of this record, in January 1999, I was invited to testify before the US National Bioethics Advisory Commission on the ethics of embryonic stem cell research.[8]

In the same year, I was appointed by the Governor in Council to the Canadian Biotechnology Advisory Committee.[9] I then served on the Science and Industry Advisory Committee of Genome Canada from

2000 till 2003. In the Fall of 2000, I was named to the Canadian Institutes of Health Research (CIHR) *Ad hoc* Working Group on Stem Cell Research and I co-authored the guidelines published in 2002.[10] From 2001 to 2004 I was a member of the CIHR Governing Council appointed by the Governor in Council (prior to this I completed a year of service in 2001 on the CIHR Genetics Institute Advisory Board).

From 2002 to 2004, as the federal legislation on assisted human reproductive technologies and related research was being developed, I was consulted by Health Canada on various aspects of Bill C-6 (formerly Bill C-13; formerly Bill C-56). I also testified, by invitation, in support of the draft legislation before the Standing Committee on Health and the Senate Committee on Social Affairs, Science and Technology.[11] Since the *Assisted Human Reproduction Act* received Royal Assent March 29, 2004, I have continued to be consulted by the government of Canada on various aspects of the legislation.

In 2004, I was awarded a Canada Research Chair in Bioethics and Philosophy to explore fundamental philosophical questions concerning our obligations to future generations in the development and use of biotechnologies.[12]

It is on the basis of this extensive and wide[-]ranging academic research and national policy experience that I offer the following opinion. I have read the décret #73-2006 of February 14, 2006 "Renvoi à la Cour d'appel du Québec relatif à la Loi sur la procréation assistée" (L.C. 2004, ch. 2) and the expert report (both the original French text and the English translation) filed by Professor Knoppers and Ms Petit. The purpose of my ethics expert report is to answer this report.

Françoise Baylis, PhD
Professor and Canada Research Chair in
Bioethics and Philosophy,
Dalhousie University

Introduction

The Province of Québec has challenged the constitutionality of the *Assisted Human Reproduction Act* (hereafter, the *AHR Act*),[13] specifically Sections 8–19, 40–53, 60, 61, and 68. From an ethical perspective this challenge is deeply problematic as the federal legislation is clearly needed to protect and promote public health, safety, and morality for current and future generations of Canadians through the pursuit of ethical and therapeutic science and technologies. This need is articulated by the Commissioners of the Royal Commission on New Reproductive Technologies (including Professor Knoppers)[14] and echoed in subsequent Health Canada documents, parliamentary committee reports, an open letter from Canadian health care ethics and health law experts, and the legislation itself.

In the 1993 Final Report of the Royal Commission on New Reproductive Technologies, *Proceed With Care*, the following statement appears:

> Given what we have learned through extensive consultation, data collection, and analysis over the life of our mandate, we share the widely held public view that new reproductive technologies raise issues of a magnitude and importance that not only warrant but *require a national response*. We reject the argument that new reproductive technologies as a general matter should continue to be subdivided into component parts and left to the provincial legislatures, or delegated to self-governing professional bodies, for regulation on a province-by-province or even an institution-by-institution basis. Considering the overarching nature, profound importance, and fundamental inter-relatedness of the issues involved, we consider that federal regulation of new reproductive technologies – under the national concern branch of the peace, order, and good government power, as well as under *the criminal law*, trade and commerce, spending, and other relevant federal constitutional powers – is clearly warranted.[15] [emphasis added]

The Commissioners re-emphasize the point in concluding their report and recommending criminal legislation including federal regulatory oversight:

> We have judged that certain activities conflict so sharply with the values espoused by Canadians and by this Commission, and are so potentially harmful to the interests of individuals and of society, that they must be prohibited by the federal government under threat of criminal sanction. These actions include human zygote/embryo research related to ectogenesis, cloning, animal/human hybrids, the transfer of zygotes to another species, or the maturation and fertilization of eggs from human fetuses; the sale of human eggs, sperm, zygotes, fetuses, and fetal tissue; and advertising for or acting as an intermediary to bring about a preconception arrangement, receiving payment or any financial or commercial benefit for acting as an intermediary, and making payment for a preconception arrangement.[16] [emphasis added]

In 1996, with the introduction of Bill C-47, the *Human Reproductive and Genetic Technologies Act*, Health Canada published *New Reproductive and Genetic Technologies: Setting Boundaries, Enhancing Health* outlining the government's intention to introduce a regulatory framework. The following statement, explaining the purpose of the legislation, appears in this document:

> The major objectives of the new legislation are the following: first, *to protect the health and safety of Canadians in the use of human reproductive materials for assisted reproduction, other medical procedures and medical research*; second, to ensure the appropriate treatment of human reproductive materials outside the body; and third, *to protect the dignity and security of all persons, especially women and children*. These goals are best accomplished through legislation where certain practices are criminalized.[17] [emphasis added]

In May 2001, the Minister of Health presented the Standing Committee on Health with a draft legislative proposal -- Bill C-56, *An Act Respecting Assisted Human Reproduction* – for review and discussion. At this time, Health Canada published "Frequently Asked Questions" and directly addressed the purpose of federal legislation in the area of assisted human reproduction:

> Why is the federal government legislating in this area – isn't it an area where the provinces have control? The draft legislation is *founded upon the federal responsibility for criminal law, as is other federal health protection legislation such as the Food and Drug Act and the Tobacco Act*. In Canada, the courts have affirmed that the criminal law power will support the creation of prohibitions which serve a public purpose, including public peace, order, security, health and morality. The draft legislation on assisted human reproduction contains prohibitions pertaining to a number of unacceptable activities including cloning and commercial surrogacy. *The proposal that is now before the Standing Committee on Health is the result of consultations with the provinces and territories, as well as with numerous stakeholder groups and concerned members of the public. A consensus exists that the Government of Canada should provide leadership by putting in place a legislative framework that would ensure consistency of measures governing assisted human reproduction.*
>
> Which activities would be regulated? One of the main purposes of the regulations would be to *protect the health and safety of Canadians – particularly of women and of the children* who are born through assisted human reproductive procedures.[18] [emphasis added]

Later the same year, in December 2001, the House of Commons Standing Committee on Health issued the following recommendations:

> The Minister of Health introduce legislation on assisted human reproduction and related research as a priority.
>
> The Preamble be replaced by a Statutory Declaration enacted in the body of the legislation.
>
> The Statutory Declaration set forth the following guiding principles:
>
> … (f) human reproductive technologies provide benefits to individuals, families, and society in general; (g) those benefits can be most effectively secured by taking appropriate measures for *the protection and promotion of human health, safety, dignity, and rights in the use of such technologies.*[19] [emphasis added]

And, correspondingly, Bill C-13 (as reported to the House on December 12, 2002), later Bill C-6, and finally the *AHR Act* (as assented to March 29, 2004) declare:

> 2(b) the benefits of assisted human reproductive technologies and related research for individuals, for families and for society in general can be most effectively secured by *taking appropriate measures for the protection and promotion of human health, safety, dignity and rights in the use of these technologies and related research.* [emphasis added]

Significantly, the general purpose of Bill C-13 found favour with health care ethics and health law academics and consultants in Canada who, in an open letter dated October 26, 2003, applauded the Government for introducing the assisted human reproduction legislation and insisted that "the safety and well-being of Canadian women and children depends upon them passing the legislation now."[20] Never before, or since, have members of the Canadian bioethics community taken a public stance on a matter of bioethical import.[21]

In sum, extensive studies and reports (including a Royal Commission) have concluded that the legislation now being challenged by the Province of Québec is needed to protect and promote public health, safety and morality. This conclusion not only remains valid today, but is even more urgent and persuasive given the changing technology landscape, and the current political and economic climate.

To explain, assisted human reproduction is different from other medical technologies and areas of research insofar as reproduction plays a central role in the lives of women, families, and society. As a result, it is anticipated that assisted human reproduction will have a direct impact on: women's reproductive health and well-being, particular groups of women, children, family structure, people with disabilities and society in general in terms of our understanding of how we relate to each other. Second, the ever expanding range of available technologies requires us to confront profound moral questions about the extent to which human life can be created, manipulated, redesigned and commodified. Third, the risks associated with assisted human reproductive technologies and related research are serious, new, and complex, not only for those who access the technologies or participate in the research, but for all Canadians given the potential use of these technologies to alter fundamental species characteristics and thereby call into question our understanding of personhood and humanness. Fourth, the potential commercial opportunities in this area of practice and research allow unusual threats of conflict of interest on the part of clinicians and researchers. These concerns, taken together, underscore the need for federal legislation.

Outline

The ethical argument in defence of the federal government's decision to legislate in this area is in three parts.

Part One explains how federal oversight of assisted human reproductive technologies and related research is necessary for both principled and practical reasons to protect and promote public health and safety for all Canadians, especially women and children (irrespective of their place of residence).[22] Further, Part One explains the need to protect and promote public morality especially in relation to the commercialization and commodification of human reproduction, human reproductive materials and human embryos. The alternative to federal legislation – a fragmented, variable, province-by-province-by-territory approach – is morally unsound. As explained below, diversity among the provinces and territories in regard to the regulation of assisted human reproductive technologies and related research is contrary to the health and safety interests of Canadians, and to Canadian social values – i.e., "the ideals that we as a society espouse and consider fundamental to our ability to thrive both individually and collectively."[23]

Part Two explains why the provincial "multi-institutional regulatory partnership" constructed by Professor Knoppers and Ms Petit is not a sound alternative to the current federal legislation. Part Two also draws attention to the fact that Professor Knoppers herself elsewhere concedes that the federal government has jurisdiction in this area. Indeed, in places she has even advocated for the exercise of this jurisdiction (both through controlled and prohibited activities).[24] It follows that her expert report can only be taken to be presenting an alternative approach to federal legislation. The existence of an alternative approach, however, does not in any way undermine the claim of federal jurisdiction.

Part Three highlights the moral foundation for the current federal legislation. The *AHR Act* is the fruit of an unprecedented, comprehensive, public consultation initiated in the late 1980s and culminating in the 1993 Final Report of the Royal Commission on New Reproductive Technologies, *Proceed with Care*.[25] Canadian social values, as recorded in the Commission's Final Report (and reaffirmed in subsequent parliamentary committee reports, government policy papers, as well as expert testimony before the Standing Committee on Health), underpin the current federal legislation.

1. The Need for Federal Oversight of Assisted Human Reproductive Technologies and Related Research to Protect and Promote Public Health, Safety and Morality

The *AHR Act* is needed to protect and promote the public health and safety of current and future generations of Canadians through the pursuit of ethical and therapeutic science and technologies. Indeed, the development and use (or non use) of assisted human reproductive technologies and the pursuit (or non pursuit) of related research raise significant public health and safety concerns that need to be addressed in a comprehensive and consistent manner. To briefly illustrate this point, consider the risk of zoonosis – the transfer of an infectious disease from nonhuman animals to humans – when creating interspecific hybrids, transgenics or chimeras.[26] This is a significant public health and safety concern that knows no geopolitical boundaries. No less significant a public health risk is sex selection for non-medical reasons, as this could alter the usual ratio of boys to girls. Indeed, in India and China where sex determination followed by female foeticide, infanticide and homicide is practiced, there is a significant imbalance in the boy–girl ratio[27] as well as an increase in gender discrimination.

Second, the *AHR Act* is also needed to safeguard Canadian social values. Assisted human reproductive technologies and related research raise profound moral questions about the extent to which human life can be created, manipulated, redesigned and commodified, and the answers to these questions have profound implications for the values of respect for human life and human dignity. For example, while the possibility of human cloning to produce children raises important health concerns, it is the ethical issues and the anticipated social and legal consequences that are most troubling and that render policymaking about human cloning a federal priority. The same can be said of commercial surrogacy (i.e., contractual pregnancy) where, for a fee, a woman agrees to become pregnant and bear a child for another. She does so not only at increased health risk to herself, but in a context of increased risk of coercion and exploitation for all women. In addition, there are worries about the commodification of human reproductive labour as well as the commodification of human reproductive materials and embryos.

The *AHR Act* addresses these public health, safety and morality concerns by enacting clear prohibitions and by introducing a federal regulatory framework for the responsible and ethical use of those assisted human reproductive technologies and services that are permitted.

1.1 The Appointment of a Royal Commission on New Reproductive Technologies

In the late 1980s, the Canadian government established a Royal Commission on New Reproductive Technologies (Commission) with a broad and expansive mandate. In its own words, the Commission understood its mandate as follows:

> The appointment of a royal commission was an opportunity to collect much-needed information, to foster the public awareness and debate that are necessary to create an informed social consensus, and, above all, to provide a principled framework for Canadian public policy on the use or restriction of these technologies. The Commission was thus placed squarely in the gap between technological development and policy development, with the task of helping to close it.[28]
>
> ....
>
> A royal commission's role is to clarify facts and issues, to analyze them from an ethical and social perspective, and to make principled

recommendations chosen from among clearly described alternatives. The over-riding goal of the Royal Commission on New Reproductive Technologies was to do this for the consideration of the Government, Parliament, and the people of Canada.[29]

After several years of research, consultation and deliberation, the Commission concluded that the individual and collective interests of Canadians were best served by developing comprehensive policies and regulations at the federal level.

> … the research, development, and use of new reproductive technologies involve national concerns that cut across social, ethical, legal, medical, economic, and other considerations and institutions. This characteristic of new reproductive technologies generates the needs for a *distinct* regulatory and organizational response – one capable of responding to and dealing with the issues in a comprehensive way.[30] [emphasis added]

The following are among the many reasons given by the Commission for the broad national framework it proposed:

Canada's response to reproductive technologies must reflect constitutional values with respect to promoting equality and accommodating diversity, in the overall context of establishing congruence and consistency with Canadians' values and priorities and Canada's changing social fabric.

Finally, no existing legislation or regulatory regime is broad enough and no public or private organization is equipped or has demonstrated the capacity to deal with these questions in the comprehensive, timely fashion we believe is necessary.[31]

1.2 The Need for Federal Oversight, and the Problems with Independent Provincial or Territorial Oversight

Over the course of its mandate, the Commission was repeatedly reminded "of the *dangerous* and inequitable situation created by the existing patchwork of laws, standards, programs, and services across Canada"[32] [emphasis added]. The *AHR Act* corrects this problem by ensuring a pan-Canadian approach to the regulation of assisted human reproduction and related research. The *AHR Act* introduces minimum federal safety and ethical standards for controlled activities. These regulations apply in all provinces and territories, except for those provinces that: "agree in writing that there are law of the province in force that are equivalent to those sections and the corresponding provisions of the regulations."[33]

The most significant problem with independent provincial or territorial oversight is reproductive and scientific tourism. Indeed, the need for comprehensive, coherent, harmonized standards of practice across the country to discourage any form of reproductive tourism was identified by the provinces and territories in consultation with Health Canada as a reason for federal leadership.[34] In the realm of therapy, the *AHR Act* seeks to prevent an interprovincial and territorial human resource drain (which could result in shortages not only for assisted reproduction but also for basic reproductive care) by eliminating the incentive for clinicians to move to another province or territory simply to practice in a place with no rules or "less onerous" rules. In the realm of research, the *AHR Act* seeks to avoid similar mobility issues for researchers and research sponsors and achieves this for human embryo research (whether the research involves the use of human reproductive materials for the purpose of creating an embryo (including a transgenic embryo), or research on existing embryos), by having this be a controlled activity for which a license is required. This is an important achievement given emerging evidence in the United States of the ways in which a regulatory patchwork of research policies can affect the mobility of stem cell researchers interested in embryo research. Indeed, a recent study shows that researchers are being actively solicited to relocate to countries and states with permissive embryonic stem cell research policies.[35] In addition to the issue of mobility, there is the issue of standards. With research involving humans it has already been noted that "if provinces and territories continue to vary in their oversight of research, we will likely see a 'race to the bottom' as research sponsors will disproportionately situate research in jurisdictions perceived to be the most 'research friendly' or, put differently, with the lowest standards."[36] The same risk applies to human embryo research.

Consider now the public health, safety and morality protection and promotion aspects of some of the sections of the *AHR Act* contested by the Québec government.

Section 8 of the *AHR Act* requires written consent from gamete donors to use reproductive material (from a live donor or from a donor's body after death) to create an embryo, as well as written consent to use in vitro embryos. This requirement is clearly in the interest of those who use assisted human reproductive technologies. Without this federal legislation, the disposition of reproductive materials and in vitro embryos might not be under the legal control of the gamete providers, but under the legal control of IVF clinic directors. Persons unable to produce their own gametes might seek out clinic directors prepared to give them donor gametes with no attention being paid to the wishes of the donors. Also, without the current federal legislation (with its coherent set of national norms) moribund patients or corpses might be transported from one province or territory that would prohibit the posthumous use of reproductive material to create an embryo, to another province or territory that would allow this practice. In neither scenario would the public health, safety, and morality interests of Canadians be protected or promoted.

Section 9 prohibits obtaining gametes from minors (i.e., persons under 18 years of age) "except for the purpose of preserving the sperm or ovum or for the purpose of creating a human being that the person reasonably believes will be raised by the donor."[37] Without the federal legislation that is currently being challenged, there might be no age limit and young girls at the age of menarche might be approached to donate gametes for others' reproductive or research use. This could hardly be consistent with their health and safety interests, especially when one considers both the short- and long-term health risks of ovulation induction and oocyte retrieval. One reasonably well-documented short-term risk of ovulation induction is ovarian hyperstimulation syndrome (OHSS). Mild forms of OHSS include: "transient lower abdominal discomfort, mild nausea, vomiting, diarrhea, and abdominal distention (observed in up to a third of superovulation cycles)."[38] These symptoms may persist or worsen resulting in serious illness marked by one or more of the following: "rapid weight gain, tense ascites, hemodynamic instability (orthostatic hypotension, tachycardia), respiratory difficulty, progressive oliguria and laboratory abnormalities. Life-threatening complications of OHSS include renal failure, adult respiratory distress syndrome (ARDS), hemorrhage from ovarian rupture, and thromboembolism."[39] The long-term risks to women of OHSS are less well documented, but there are two studies that suggest a link between ovarian stimulation and ovarian cancer.[40] In addition to these physical risks, there are the twin risks of coercion and exploitation. Taken together, these risks speak loudly to the need for clear, legislated limits on the permissible as found in the *AHR Act*.

Section 10 provides the framework for the regulations concerning the alteration, manipulation, treatment, use, obtention, storage, transfer, destruction, import or export of human reproductive materials and in vitro embryos in order to address the health and safety risks associated with these procedures. Consider the option of cryostorage of excess embryos (i.e., embryos in excess of the maximum for transfer in a single cycle). Women who undergo the painful and risky procedure of ovarian stimulation as part of infertility treatment in the hope of building a family have a strong interest in cryopreserving embryos that are not transferred in the original stimulated cycle.[41] Failure to cryopreserve embryos for future reproductive use means: (i) an increase in the number of uncomfortable, painful or risky procedures that women undergo in pursuit of their reproductive project (physical harms); (ii) an increase in the psychological stress associated with the use of assisted human reproductive technologies (psychological harm); (iii) a decrease in the chance of pregnancy (psychological and social harm); (iv) an increase in the social disruption associated with the use of assisted human reproductive technologies (social harm); and (v) an increase in the financial burden of infertility treatment (economic harm).[42] It is important that the regulations pursuant to the *AHR Act* protect and promote the health and safety of women whilst safeguarding them from the twin risks of coercion and exploitation by researchers who would prefer that women donate their fresh embryos to research instead of cryopreserving them for later reproductive use.[43]

Section 11 provides the framework for regulations concerning the combination of "any part or any proportion of the human genome specified in the regulations with any part of the genome of a species specified in the regulations."[44] Without the *AHR Act* transgenic research might go unregulated and this could result in serious public health consequences (consider, for example, the possibility of zoonosis).[45] Research that involves crossing species boundaries is not only potentially dangerous, it is also ethically controversial. Many perceive this research as a threat to human dignity because it raises fundamental questions about who we are and will become as a species. Allowing unregulated transgenic research would be clearly inconsistent with the public health, safety, and morality interests of Canadians.

Section 12 is about setting limits on reimbursement for expenditures incurred in relation to gamete donation or embryo transfer as well as surrogacy (i.e., contract pregnancy). The purpose of limiting reimbursement (in addition to prohibiting outright payment for reproductive materials and services), is to further minimize the commodification of women's reproductive materials and reproductive labour as well as minimize the risks of coercion and exploitation. Without this legislation, reimbursement or payment practices in some provinces or territories might make gamete and embryo selling as well as contract pregnancy very attractive options for some women who will be at increased risk of commodification. In turn, this commodification can lead to objectification and exploitation because where there is a market for gametes, embryos or contract pregnancy women in certain economic conditions may "agree to use their bodies in ways that demean their humanity."[46] The Commission writes most eloquently on this point with specific reference to contract pregnancy:

> Allowing or ignoring the practice of preconception agreements in one province while it is prohibited elsewhere would have a harmful impact, not only on gestational mothers and other women in the province in question, but on Canadian women generally. Such permissiveness in one jurisdiction – quite apart from the "reproductive tourism" it would encourage – would convey tacit acceptance, or even affirmative state sanction, of a practice that is likely to undermine the value, dignity, reproductive capacity, and bodily integrity of Canadian women. Again, because of the great mobility of Canadians, failure to impose adequate controls on the safety of assisted conception technologies in one province or region would inevitably have social, health, and economic consequences as those affected moved elsewhere.[47]

Section 13 establishes the need for uniform high quality standards for the clinics and research facilities where assisted human reproductive technologies are provided and related research is conducted. Canadian families, women and children are entitled to access high quality treatment and research premises across the country. Indeed, their health and safety depends on it.

Section 14 mandates the collection of health reporting information from persons providing human reproductive material and in vitro embryos. This mandatory reporting of health information on a national scale is crucial to the public health and safety of Canadians as this means data will be available on the basis of which to assess safety, efficacy and effectiveness.

Section 15 addresses privacy issues. More specifically, it aims to protect the personal identity of persons providing health reporting information. The promise of anonymity means that gamete donors are not at risk of having parental responsibilities for genetic offspring with whom they have no social, familial ties. It also means, however, that children born of donor gametes can only have access to non-identifying health information about the donor. The balance of harms and benefits in relation to this issue remains contested; for now the legislation serves to ensure a consistent approach across the country which arguably is preferable to the current situation in Canada with adoption.

Sections 16 to 19 deal with a range of issues concerning access to health reporting information, the destruction of such information, the destruction of human reproductive material, the maintenance of a health information registry, the use of information in the registry, the disclosure of such information, and so on. These issues are absolutely critical to the public health, safety, and morality interests of Canadians. It is only through careful, comprehensive, standardized, national reporting and data analysis that we can come to understand the long-term safety, efficacy and effectiveness of various interventions and identify risks to public health and safety, or possible human rights abuses. Mandating health reporting information from all clinics across the country ensures the largest, most reliable database (which is needed to develop sound, evidence-based standards of care). It also permits identification of clinics that have unusually high incidence of poor health outcomes which may indicate that they are engaging in excessively risky interventions. Also, with a national registry there can be important economies of scale. Considerable public resources are required to develop and maintain a health information registry, a monitoring system, a cadre of expert inspectors, etc. Resources saved in this context, might be available to respond to other public health needs.

In sum, a fragmented, variable, province-by-province-by-territory approach to the regulation of assisted human reproductive technologies and related research raises important health and safety concerns for Canadians (especially women and children) and potentially undermines the dignity and rights of Canadians. In contrast, the AHR Act serves to protect and promote public health, safety, and morality for current and future generations of Canadians. It does so by introducing comprehensive, coherent, harmonized standards of practice across the country for both therapy and research involving assisted human reproductive technologies.

2. A Multi-Institutional Regulatory Partnership as an Alternative to Federal Legislation

The expert report prepared by Professor Knoppers and Ms Petit describes a "multi-institutional regulatory partnership" in Québec for the regulation of assisted human reproductive technologies and related research. This regulatory partnership involves the provincial government, provincial professional organizations, local research ethics boards (REBs), and the provincial research funding organization, Fonds de la recherche en santé du Québec. Professor Knoppers and Ms Petit suggest that together these provincial "institutions" provide sufficient regulatory oversight.

Below I carefully review the regulatory partnership approach. First, I critically examine the limitations of provincial legislative action, as well as administrative and institutional actions. I then summarize the problems with relying on provincial professional organizations' ethics codes and guidelines. Next, I rehearse some of the problems with the role of research ethics boards (REBs), and then I identify the problem of conflict of interest with the Fonds de la recherche en santé du Québec. Finally, I comment on the apparent inconsistency in Professor Knoppers' views on the regulation of assisted human reproductive technologies and related research.

2.2.1 Provincial Legislative Action and Administrative and Institutional Actions

Professor Knoppers and Ms Petit briefly summarize current provincial legislative action in Québec in the area of family law (addressing the legal status of children born of assisted human reproduction), public health protection law (with the *Act respecting medical laboratories, organ, tissue, gamete and embryo conservation, and the disposal of human bodies*), and tax law (introducing a system of refundable tax credits to help defray the costs of certain reproductive technologies). They also refer to general laws of the province, and they mention Bill 89, *An Act respecting clinical and research activities as regards assisted human reproduction and amending other legislative provisions*.

The problem with this summary of provincial legislative action is that it looks at Québec in isolation from the other Canadian provinces and territories. This is problematic because the ultimate issue is not what is acceptable for one province (in this case Québec), but rather what is acceptable for all ten provinces, for all three territories, and for Canada as a country. More precisely, the issue in this case is whether to allow a fragmented, variable, province-by-province-by-territory approach to the regulation of assisted human reproductive technologies and related research, or whether to embrace a comprehensive and coherent federal legislative approach as found in the *AHR Act* that will protect and promote public health, safety and morality for Canadians whilst preserving the provinces' ability to legislate in this area. The *AHR Act* allows the Governor in Council to "declare that any or all of sections 10 to 16, 46 to 53 and 61 and any corresponding provisions of the regulations do not apply in a province ... [where] the Minister and the government of that province agree in writing that there are law[s] of the province in force that are equivalent to those sections and the corresponding provisions of the regulations."[48]

The same criticism applies to provincial administrative and institutional actions in Québec. It follows that diversity and full flexibility in the regulation of assisted human reproductive technologies and related research is contrary to the collective interests of current and future generations of Canadians. This does not mean that provincial or territorial legislation should be precluded, but simply that it should be part of a coherent, consistent, national framework. To quote the Commission on this point:

> This [i.e., the need for national leadership] does not obviate the need for decisive action by provinces and professional bodies as well, but action at the national level must provide the leadership and impetus for a new approach to managing reproductive technologies.[49]

In brief, provincial government action, should harmonize with federal legislation so as to further protect and promote public health, safety and morality, in a manner consistent with the *AHR Act*. Provincial action (in Québec or any other province) is insufficient in the absence of national legislation that (i) is consistent with Canadian social values, (ii) is protective of the public health, safety, and morality of Canadians, and (iii) ensures equal access and non-discrimination. Only with national legislation providing minimum ethical and safety standards is it possible to guard against (i) reproductive and scientific tourism, (ii) potentially harmful assisted human reproductive technologies and related research, and (iii) the attendant risks to women and children that a fragmented, variable, province-by-province-by-territory approach would allow for.

2.2.2 *Provincial Professional Organizations*

A common problem for self-regulating professions, especially when setting the rules for safety, quality assessment, and ethics is conflict of interest. In very general terms, professional health organizations have a primary interest in promoting the health of patients. They also have a secondary interest in protecting their members' professional monopoly. When the primary and secondary interests conflict, decisions regarding the dominant interest (improved health care) may be unduly influenced by professional self-interest in maintaining professional power and privilege. Deference to professional interests is evident in the expert report prepared by Professor Knoppers and Ms Petit where they suggest that regulatory mechanisms (such as guidelines and codes) are accepted and adhered to by the members of the scientific and medical community as they are consonant with their interests, "ces dispositifs évoluent selon des critères propres à la communauté médicale et scientifique, lesquels sont gages d'une acceptabilité et d'une mise en oeuvre appropriée par ces membres."[50] But why privilege criteria of interest to the scientific and medical community over and above criteria of interest to infertile patients, especially as these criteria may diverge significantly from those of researchers and clinicians?

Another point worth noting is that in the past when there was an absence of legislation, the codes of ethics and ethical practice guidelines of relevant professional organizations were not particularly effective in promoting public health, safety and morality. Consider, for example, the long-term failure of relevant professional health organizations to develop sound ethical practice guidelines and policies regarding the maximum number of embryos for transfer per cycle. Indeed, to this day [2006], despite considerable evidence of the harmful consequences associated with multiple pregnancy and multiple birth for both women and children,[51] there is nothing mandating Canadian clinicians to limit the number of embryos transferred per cycle.[52] Indeed, in a 2005 publication summarizing 2001 Canadian data, the IVF Directors Group of the Canadian Fertility and Andrology Society eschews responsibility for directing Canadian centers to reduce the number of embryos transferred per cycle:

> One issue of great concern to all providers and consumers of ART is that of multiple pregnancy. Although it is not the role of CARTR [Canadian Assisted Reproductive Technologies Register] to encourage its member

centers to reduce their multiple pregnancy rates through limiting the number of embryos transferred, it is our responsibility to provide data to inform centers about the situation in Canada. Whereas many policy makers, in Europe especially, are pushing for single-embryo transfers to virtually eliminate multiple pregnancy, in Canada, more than half of the fresh ETs [embryo transfers] in 2001 involved three or more embryos.[53] [emphasis added]

To date [2006], there are no professional guidelines in Canada dealing with this important public health issue.

Further long-standing evidence of the failure of professional organizations to promote public health, safety and morality include (i) the failure to develop and to enforce uniform standards for reporting fertilization, clinical pregnancy, live birth and multiple birth rates, (ii) the failure to insist upon the practice of evidence-based medicine, (iii) the failure to clearly distinguish research interventions from therapeutic interventions, and (iv) the failure to develop uniform consent procedures for both therapy and research (with, for example, standardized descriptions of the potential harms and benefits). Now, in recent years, some of the failures noted above have been addressed. For example, for the first time, in 2005, the IVF Directors Group of the Canadian Fertility and Andrology Society published aggregate data for 2001 for 19 of the 22 clinics providing assisted reproductive technologies at that time (the three Québec clinics elected not to provide any data). Hereafter, these data are to be published on an annual basis.

As professional standards and practices have been developed, however, there has been an evident interest in shielding members of the profession "from outside knowledge of their deviance [from standards, as this] also shields the profession from embarrassment, with its potential for precipitating a decline in public trust."[54] For example, in Canada the data on fertilization, clinical pregnancy, live birth and multiple birth rates are provided as aggregate data (i.e., data that is combined from several measurements), not per clinic data.[55] In other jurisdictions (including the United States and the United Kingdom), these data are provided separately per clinic which allows patients to make comparisons between clinics. In this way, there is information about the performance of individual clinics as well as general information about all clinics taken together. While the IVF Directors Group of the Canadian Fertility and Andrology Society offers several reasons for this difference in practice, the fact remains that there is clear professional self-interest (especially in a context of voluntary reporting) in not making clinic specific data publicly available in Canada.

The *AHR Act* overcomes problems of professional conflict of interest. The regulations pursuant to the legislation are developed by government, not interest groups (though relevant stakeholders have been, and no doubt will continue to be, consulted). As well, Assisted Human Reproduction Canada (AHRC) – a federal regulatory body mandated "(a) to protect and promote the health and safety, and the human dignity and human rights, of Canadians, and (b) to foster the application of ethical principles, in relation to assisted human reproduction and other matters to which this [AHR] Act applies"[56] [–] is governed by an independent board of experts. Excluded from membership on the board are persons who "hold a licence or are an applicant for a licence or a director, officer, shareholder or partner of a licensee or applicant for a licence."[57] In these ways the *AHR Act* addresses some of the failures noted above. For example, AHRC would have both individual and aggregate data about a range of therapeutic and research practices undertaken in Canadian clinics and could use this data to effectively protect and promote the health and safety of Canadians.

2.2.3 Role of Research Ethics Boards

There are 105 health care institutions in Québec with REBs (9 of which are mixed research and clinical ethics committees).[58] The problems these local REBs face are many and include (i) the lack of expert ethics review owing, in part, to the absence of a *required* education and certification program for REB members to ensure that they are adequately trained for the job,[59] (ii) the potential for compromised ethics review depending upon the volume of protocols submitted for review (too few protocols and REB members may not develop the requisite expertise; too many protocols and REB members may "cut corners"), (iii) the failure to effectively promote the collectivization of learning and thereby reduce ad hoc decision-making owing, in part, to the isolation of REBs and the absence of an accreditation program for REBs, (iv) the lack of appropriate administrative support and operating funds for REBs to do the job well, (v) continued, inappropriate reliance on volunteer REB members, and (vi) the inability of REBs (that rely on volunteers and are typically under-staffed and under-funded) to properly monitor the research they approve (which raises significant problems of accountability).[60] Indeed, in a 2001–2002 study of the day-to-day challenges faced by Québec REBs, only published in 2004, 100% of REBs surveyed reported major problems resulting from inadequate financial resources (and explained how this had a direct impact on the ability of REBs to maintain an adequate level of expertise); 96% reported major problems resulting from inadequate human resources (in part because of continued reliance on volunteers); 84% reported problems to do with the isolation of independent REBs; 82% reported problems owing to the lack of time for proper ethics review; and the list goes on.[61]

Importantly, the *AHR Act* addresses some of these problems, at least with respect to embryo research. Such research is a controlled activity for which a license must be issued by AHRC. AHRC is to be adequately resourced both in terms of finances and personnel. Moreover, AHRC has the authority to set terms and conditions on any license it issues and is also empowered to amend, suspend or revoke a licence, as appropriate. Further, AHRC "may take all reasonable measures that [it] … considers necessary to prevent, reduce or mitigate any threat to human health or safety that results, or may reasonably be expected to result from a controlled activity."[62] This cannot but count as an improvement on the *status quo* where review by local REBs is potentially lacking in adequate resources, expertise and authority. AHRC can also designate inspectors and analysts for the purpose of enforcing the *AHR Act* and monitoring research facilities, thereby effectively addressing the issue of accountability[,] which remains a significant challenge for local REBs that struggle to meet the mandated requirement that "les comités d'éthique de la recherche verront a préparer et mettre en place un mécanisme de suivi éthique pour les projets de recherche en cours."[63]

2.2.4. *Role of the Provincial Research Funding Organization*

The Fonds de la recherche en santé du Québec (FRSQ) has fairly comprehensive ethics guidelines that apply to researchers and research institutions that receive FRSQ funding.[64] However, as with other research ethics guidelines in Canada, there are problems with enforcement as well as conflict of interest.

As regards enforcement, there are questions about compliance with the ethics guidelines and about the failure to impose serious sanctions on researchers and research institutions that violate the ethics guidelines. These concerns extend beyond the provincial FRSQ ethics guidelines, and include the national ethics guidelines – the Tri-Council Policy Statement (TCPS)[65] – which apply to all Québec researchers and research institutions that receive federal funding from the Canadian Institutes of Health Research, the Natural Sciences and Engineering Research Council of Canada, or the Social Sciences and Humanities Research Council of Canada. Evidence of noncompliance with the TCPS notwithstanding,[66] as at 2005, there were no documented cases of Québec research institutions having been disciplined through freezing or withdrawal of research funding for noncompliance with the TCPS.[67]

A further problem with enforcement is that the FRSQ guidelines only apply to researchers and research institutions that receive FRSQ funding. Meanwhile, a significant proportion of research and innovative practice involving reproductive technologies and human embryos is conducted in private clinics that may not rely on public (provincial or federal) funding, in which case the provincial and federal ethics guidelines simply have no force. Article 21 of the *Code civil du Québec*[68] requires REB approval of publicly- and privately-funded research, but only for research that involves minors and incompetent persons. Nothing in this law or any other Québec law requires REB approval for privately-funded research involving competent persons.

Second, there is the problem of structural conflict of interest. The FRSQ is an agency of the government of Québec, created under the *Act Respecting the Ministère du Développement économique et régional et de la Recherche.*[69] It is an organization with competing interests and obligations, such that the protection of public health, safety and morality is not clearly its sole or even primary obligation. The FRSQ's mission is not only to promote and provide financial support for scientifically and ethically sound research, it is also to contribute to Québec's economic growth:

> Le FRSQ n'est pas un conseil de recherche mais bien un Fonds dont la mission est de contribuer au développement de la recherche scientifique et technologique dans le domaine de la santé des personnes et des populations et de participer au développement économique du Québec.[70]

These are laudable goals, but what happens when ethics and economics conflict as with research involving assisted human reproductive technologies and related research?

Importantly, with the *AHR Act*, embryo research is not plagued with problems of enforcement or conflict of interest. The *AHR Act* introduces clear prohibitions on certain types of research and creates enforceable rules for all research that is a controlled activity. The criminal prohibitions and research regulations apply equally to publicly- and privately-funded research and any person who contravenes the *AHR Act* is potentially subject to a significant fine or term of imprisonment.[71] As well, there is AHRC with the power to issue, amend, suspend, or revoke research licenses, and to monitor research sites for compliance with the *AHR Act*.[72]

2.2.5 *Conclusion*

In response to the above analysis, Professor Knoppers and Ms Petit might object that it is inappropriate to assess the merits of each regulatory mechanism in isolation given that they have proposed a "regulatory partnership" in which the weaknesses of one regulatory mechanism might be compensated for by the strengths of another. However, as the Commission argued [including Professor Knoppers, as one of the Commissioners]:

> ... *it is unrealistic to expect self-regulating professional bodies, or the provinces, individually or together, to provide the necessary level of regulation and control on issues that transcend not only provincial but national and intergenerational boundaries and that have implications for all Canadians*, regardless of where they live. It is the view of Canadians, and Commissioners' view as well, that given rapidly expanding knowledge and rapid dissemination of technologies, immediate intervention and concerted leadership are required at the national level.[73] [emphasis added]

In their expert report, Professor Knoppers and Ms Petit do not contest the need for "concerted leadership at the national level," nor do they challenge the federal government's authority in criminal matters. Indeed, in the Foreword, Professor Knoppers is supportive of (at least some of) the criminal prohibitions in the *AHR Act*. She writes (in reference to her work with the Commission), « J'adhérais par ailleurs à la proposition visant à criminaliser certaines activités moralement répréhensibles notamment, le clonage reproductif humain. »[74] Also, the closing sentence in the Foreword states: « Les activités prohibées par la législation fédérale et les dispositions du project de loi n° 89 offriront ensemble une protection adéquate des citoyens et citoyenne tout en respectant leur liberté et valeurs individuelles. »[75] Bill 89 is surely irrelevant, however, to any analysis of whether the legal patchwork in Québec meets the federal standard of equivalence and adequately promotes and protects public health, safety and morality for Canadians living in Québec. The Bill has not been passed and so could still be significantly modified or even abandoned. As such, it can play no role in a debate about the sufficiency of the proposed multi-institutional regulatory partnership.

In any case, the point I wish to make here is that Professor Knoppers and Ms Petit appear to be of the view that criminal prohibitions are a matter of federal jurisdiction, while the controlled activities are in provincial jurisdiction, and are best handled by a conglomeration of provincial government action, professional organization ethics codes and guidelines, REBs, and the Fonds de la recherche en santé du Québec.

Interestingly, this perspective contrasts markedly with Professor Knoppers' earlier writings for the public[,] which support a federal approach to controlled activities. In an August 2001 Comment for *The Globe and Mail* Professor Knoppers writes:

> The law has many positive attributes. Unfortunately, these are outweighed by one major problem, the continued reliance on criminal prohibitions … The federal government could create a regulatory body empowered to both issue licences for a defined set of activities (similar to what is currently proposed) and produce, modify and monitor a "moratorium list" … *a regulatory scheme with some criminal sanctions aimed at responding to legitimate public health concerns of all citizens would still be within federal jurisdiction. It would parallel other areas of federal oversight, such as Ottawa's work to protect the environment and control the marketing of tobacco and pharmaceuticals.*[76] [emphasis added]

Slightly less than a year later, in May 2002, also in *The Globe and Mail,* Professor Knoppers writes:

> As one of the last Western countries to legislate in the area, Canada can learn from the mistakes of others and *produce a regulatory system* that could be a model for the world.[77] [emphasis added]

A week later, still in *The Globe and Mail,* Professor Knoppers writes:

> *We urge the [Canadian] government not to criminalize nuclear transfer, but to tightly regulate it* … It is *possible to regulate controversial technologies* such as

nuclear transfer without using criminal bans. The U.K. Human Fertilization and Embryology Authority is a working model of a regulatory body, one with a long and honourable history.[78] [emphasis added]

Together, these excerpts advocate support for federal criminal initiatives, with regulatory authority, and also concede that a federal law with some criminal sanctions is within federal jurisdiction.[79] These writings are therefore inconsistent with the perspective that federal regulations for assisted human reproduction and related research are not warranted because the development of such regulations is a provincial responsibility.

In my opinion, a federal approach to assisted human reproduction and related research that includes some criminal sanctions, and to which regulatory powers attach, is necessary to protect and promote public health, safety and morality for Canadians. And, until recently, it would appear that Professor Knoppers was also of this opinion.

In sum, the proposed alternative to the AHR Act – a multi-institutional regulatory partnership – is not a sound alternative. Only comprehensive, coherent, harmonized standards of practice across the country for both therapy and research involving assisted human reproductive technologies effectively serves to protect and promote public health, safety, and morality for current and future generations of Canadians.

3. The Moral Underpinnings of the Current Federal Legislation

The *AHR Act* includes six explicit and one implicit guiding principles: the principles of autonomy, equality, respect for human life and dignity, protection of the vulnerable, non-commercialization of reproduction, balancing individual and collective interests, and accountability. These principles mirror those of the Commission and as such (as at 1993) they (i) cohere with Canadian views and values, (ii) are consistent with ethical principles in other international inquiries, and (iii) are grounded in sound ethical reasoning.[80] These points all lend the current legislation unique moral credibility. It is also worth noting that in the years between the Commission's Final Report and the enactment of the *AHR Act* there is no evidence of a shift in core social values. For example, in 2001, the House of Commons Standing Committee on Health, identified the following overarching considerations for federal legislation: [r]espect for human individuality, dignity and integrity; precautionary approach to protect and promote health; non-commodification and non-commercialization; informed choice; and accountability and transparency.[81]

3.1 The Commission's Ethical Framework and Guiding Principles

In 1993, following nearly four years of research, consultation and deliberation on a wide range of scientific, medical, ethical, legal, social, and economic aspects of assisted human reproductive technologies and related research, the Commission published its Final Report *Proceed with Care*. This report explains in considerable detail the ethical framework and guiding principles that informed the Commission's deliberations and policy recommendations.

The Commission adopted a modified ethic of care – a theoretical perspective with currency "in secular mainstream ethics, in feminist theory, and in religious thinking" that sees people as "connected to one another in families, communities, and social bonds of all sorts."[82] An ethic of care, in contrast to other ethical frameworks, prioritizes mutual care and connectedness; it aims to recognize interdependent interests, to build relationships and to prevent (or at the very least reduce) conflict. Not all conflict is avoidable, however. When there is conflict, the Commission recommends the use of guiding principles within the overall perspective of an ethic of care where the priority remains "on helping human relationships to flourish by seeking to foster the dignity of the individual and the welfare of the community."[83]

The guiding principles that, in the Commission's view, give "concrete expression to the ideal of care"[84] are individual autonomy, equality, respect for human life and dignity, protection of the vulnerable, non-commercialization of reproduction, appropriate use of resources, accountability, and balancing individual and collective interests.[85] These principles, which are to serve "as a sort of bottom line of social justice when all else fails,"[86] were identified through public hearings (oral testimony and written submissions), a review of reports from other countries, and a review of the bioethics literature. Most importantly, the Commission found that

> the eight principles we identified ... reflect widespread consensus in Canadian society on the ethical basis that should guide decision making.
>
> Indeed, these principles were endorsed by a very broad range of groups – professionals and laypeople, women and men, religious and secular

groups, members of racial and ethnic minorities, people with disabilities, doctors, and patients. That these principles were endorsed by groups with diverse experiences and interests confirms our belief that they capture important ethical considerations.[87]

Indeed, an important feature of these mid-level principles is that they can be supported by multiple ethical theories.

In addition to identifying Canadian views and values regarding the use of assisted human reproductive technologies and related research, the Commission also carefully researched and reviewed myriad ethical issues surrounding the use (or non use) of human reproductive technologies in a Canadian legal, political, economic and cultural context with particular attention to Canadian systems and institutions. In this way, the Commission sought to provide the public, those working in the field of assisted human reproductive technologies (clinicians and researchers), and federal policy makers with a clear account of the moral reasoning and ethical analysis informing its deliberations and underlying its policy recommendations – the goal being to provide a morally sound basis for establishing uniquely Canadian "humane and caring" policies on assisted human reproductive technologies and related research.

Of note in this regard is the fact that the Commission identified balancing individual and collective interests as the area in which their most difficult social policy decisions arose. The Commission recognized the interests of infertile persons, and persons at risk of having a child afflicted with a genetic disease, in using reproductive technologies. The Commission also recognized the interests of researchers in having access to human reproductive materials and embryos to research and develop therapeutic interventions for persons afflicted with certain diseases or disorders. But no less important than these individual interests are our collective (societal) interests in the just allocation of finite health resources and the safety of the population and future generations. According to the Commission, sometimes, for the good of Canadian society (or specific groups within Canadian society), individual interests must be curtailed as when these interests are "harmful or prohibitively costly for the rest of society."[88]

Following wide consultation with Canadians, careful research into the ethical, legal, social, scientific and medical issues, the Commission "found consistent and widespread demand for national leadership and action in relation to assisted human reproductive technologies."[89] The Commission concluded that

> Canada must move forward into the new reality with a clear, coordinated approach that permits us to resolve and manage the critical issues involved. To allow Canada's response to be delayed or fragmented by the existing web of jurisdictional and administrative arrangements would, in the view of Commissioners [again, including Professor Knoppers as one of the Commissioners], be a mistake of enormous proportions. Failure to intervene constructively and decisively would amount to an abdication of social responsibility and a failure of political will.[90]

In the years that followed, in consultation with the provinces and territories, as well as various interested stakeholder organizations, the federal government undertook to develop legislation on reproductive and genetic technologies.[91] During the consultation process, there was general acknowledgment of the need for federal leadership in this morally charged arena, and a desire on the part of most stakeholders for this leadership to be manifested through legislation.[92] Among the reasons for federal leadership were (i) the need for leadership "rooted in Canadian societal values such as respect for human rights," (ii) "the need for consistency and coherence across the country to discourage any form of 'reproductive tourism,'" and (iii) the lack of resources to self-regulate.[93]

3.2 Principles in the AHR Act

The fruit of the Commission's work – to develop a perspective that policy makers could apply in developing public policy for assisted human reproductive (and other emerging) technologies and related research – is the *AHR Act*[,] which received Royal Assent March 29, 2004. The *AHR Act* entrenches the care perspective and seven of the eight guiding principles found in the Commission's Final Report. As such, the *AHR Act* is congruous with the views and values of Canadians as carefully researched and documented by the Commission.

In the Principles section of the *AHR Act*, there is explicit reference to the following six principles: protection for the vulnerable; respect for human life and dignity; individual autonomy; equality; non-commercialization of reproduction; and balancing individual and collective interests. The principle of accountability though not explicitly identified in the Principles section is clearly important as evidenced by the requirement to create AHRC to:

> **22...** (a) to protect and promote the health and safety, and the human dignity and human rights, of Canadians, and,
> (b) to foster the application of ethical principles,
> in relation to assisted human reproduction and other matters to which this Act applies.

In pursuit of these objectives, AHRC is empowered to issue licences to persons providing assisted reproduction services and conducting research involving in vitro human embryos, to inspect clinics and research laboratories, to collect, analyse and manage health reporting information, and to monitor and review ethical and scientific issues as they emerge and evolve.[94]

The only principle in the Commission's Final Report that is not an integral part of the *AHR Act* is the principle of appropriate use of resources – a principle relevant to resource decision-making concerning the provision of new assisted reproductive services and technologies in relation to a broad range of clearly defined reproductive and other health needs and priorities. The absence of this principle is not surprising as this is clearly an area of provincial jurisdiction.

The principle of *protection for the vulnerable* finds its clearest expression in the first and third principles of the *AHR Act*:

> **2** (a) the health and well-being of children born through the application of assisted human reproductive technologies must be given priority in all decision respecting their use;
> **2** (c) while all persons are affected by these technologies, women more than men are directly and significantly affected by their application and the health and well-being of women must be protected in the application of these technologies;

The second principle articulated in the *AHR Act* provides further endorsement for the principle of *protection for the vulnerable* and also entrenches the principle of *respect for human life and dignity*:

> **2** (b) the benefits of assisted human reproductive technologies and related research for individuals, for families and for society in general can be most effectively secured by taking appropriate measures for the protection and promotion of human health, safety, dignity and rights in the use of these technologies and in related research;

The principle of *individual autonomy* is understood in terms of a commitment to promote informed consent. The fourth principle in the *AHR Act* stipulates that

> **2** (d) the principle of free and informed consent must be promoted and applied as a fundamental condition of the use of human reproductive technologies;

Next comes the principle of *equality*:

> **2** (e) persons who seek to undergo assisted reproduction procedures must not be discriminated against, including on the basis of their sexual orientation or marital status;

The principle of *non-commercialization of reproduction*:

> **2** (f) trade in the reproductive capabilities of women and men and the exploitation of children, women and men for commercial ends raise health and ethical concerns that justify their prohibition;

Finally, there is the principle of *balancing individual and collective interests*:

> **2** (g) human individuality and diversity, and the integrity of the human genome, must be preserved and protected.

In sum, the AHR Act is based on the findings of the Commission, findings that (i) continue to cohere with Canadian social values, (ii) were consistent with ethical principles found in other international inquiries at the time of writing, and (iii) remain well grounded in sound ethical reasoning. More generally, the AHR Act not only effectively protects and promotes public health and safety for Canadians (especially women and children), it also protects and promotes morality for current and future generations of Canadians.

Conclusion

Notwithstanding claims to the contrary, the issue in this case is not whether the province of Québec has a demonstrated interest in, or commitment to monitoring the development of, assisted human reproductive technologies and related research, nor is it whether the various provincial regulatory mechanisms described by Professor Knoppers and Ms Petit taken together (with or without some version of Bill 89) could make for a coherent regulatory framework in Québec. Rather, the issue in this case is whether the *AHR Act* is needed to protect and promote public health, safety, and morality for Canadians. My answer to this question is a resounding "yes."

In closing, I agree with the prescient remarks made by the Commission more than a dozen years ago when it noted that how our country regulates assisted human reproductive technologies and related research "will say much about Canada as a society – what we value, what our priorities are, what kind of society we want to live in." "How we choose to use, or not to use, these technological capacities will shape society for our children and for their children."[95] Indeed, no less than who we are as a people is evidenced by our response to the ever increasingly complex array of available (and possible) scientific and medical developments related to assisted human reproductive technologies.

The AHR Act is based on clear, explicit and ethically sound principles and coheres with Canadian social values. It effectively protects and promotes public health, safety and morality for all Canadians.

NOTES

1 *Assisted Human Reproduction Act*, S.C. 2004, c 2.
2 *Renvoi relative à la Loi sur la procreation assistée (Canada)*, [2008] J.Q.J. No. 5489, 2008 QCCA 1157, 298 D.L.R. (4th) 712 (Q.C.C.A.)
3 Reference re *Assisted Human Reproduction Act*, 2010 SCC 61.
4 Canada, Medical Research Council of Canada, Guidelines for Research on Somatic Cell Gene Therapy in Humans (Ottawa: Minister of Supply and Services Canada, 1990).
5 Françoise Baylis, "The Ethics of Ex Utero Research on Spare 'Non Viable' IVF Human Embryos" (1990) 4:4 Bioethics 311.
6 Françoise Baylis, "Assisted Reproductive Technologies: Informed Choice" in New Reproductive Technologies: Ethical Aspects Vol. 1 of the research

studies of the Royal Commission on New Reproductive Technologies (Ottawa: Minister of Government Services Canada, 1993) 47.

7 Society of Obstetricians and Gynaecologist of Canada and Canadian Fertility and Andrology Society, "Joint Policy Statement: Ethical Issues in Assisted Reproduction," http://www.cfas.ca/english/library/jps%20Ethical%20Issues.pdf [subscription required] [SOGC & CFAS Joint Statement].

8 Françoise Baylis, "Research Involving Human Embryonic Material: Ethical Considerations" (Paper presented to the National Bioethics Advisory Commission, Washington, D.C., January 19, 1999) [unpublished]; and F. Baylis, "Embryological Viability" (2005) 5:6 American Journal of Bioethics 17.

9 Françoise Baylis, "In Brief. The Canadian Biotechnology Advisory Committee" (2000) 30:3 Hastings Center Report 52.

10 Canada, Canadian Institutes of Health Research, Ad Hoc Working Group on Stem Cell Research. Human Pluripotent Stem Cell Research: Recommendations for CIHR-Funded Research, http://www.cihr.ca/about_cihr/ethics/stem_cell/stem_cell_recommendations_e.shtml [no longer available online].

11 Françoise Baylis, "Bill C-6 An Act respecting assisted human reproduction and related research" (Paper presented to the Government of Canada, Senate Committee on Social Affairs, Science and Technology, Ottawa, February 26, 2004) [unpublished]; Françoise Baylis, "Bill C-13 An Act respecting assisted human reproduction" (Paper presented to the Government of Canada, Standing Committee on Health, Ottawa, November 19, 2002) [unpublished]; and Françoise Baylis, "Assisted Human Reproduction" (Paper presented to the Government of Canada, Standing Committee on Health, Ottawa, May 31, 2001) [unpublished]. See, Françoise Baylis, "Brickbats and Bouquets for the Draft Legislation on Assisted Human Reproduction" (2001) 10:1 Health Law Review 3.

12 Canada Research Chairs, http://www.chairs.gc.ca/web/home_e.asp [now http://www.chairs-chaires.gc.ca/home-accueil-eng.aspx].

13 Assisted Human Reproduction Act, S.C. 2004, c 2 [AHR Act].

14 In her expert opinion "Le Québec: pionnier dans l'encadrement de la PMA et de la recherche au Canada," at ii et iii, Professor Bartha Maria Knoppers disavows the Commission's finding that the regulation of assisted reproductive technologies should not happen on a province-by-province basis. She further states that during the Commission's deliberations « J'étais la seule à promouvoir l'institution d'une agence interprovinciale plutôt que 'nationale' » [Knoppers & Petit, "Le Québec:

pionnier"]. This view is not recorded in the Commission's Final Report; nor is there a dissenting opinion from Professor Knoppers explaining her perspective (an option that was available to her and indeed was exercised by Commissioner Suzanne Scorsone in relation to different concerns).

15 Canada, Royal Commission on New Reproductive Technologies, *Proceed with Care: Final Report of the Royal Commission on New Reproductive Technologies*, vol. 1 (Ottawa: Minister of Government Services Canada, 1993) at 18; see similar passages at 17, 22, and 124 [Commission, *Proceed With Care*, vol. 1]. (Commission royale sur les nouvelle techniques de reproduction, Un virage à prendre en douceur (Rapport final), vol. 1, à la p. 20. Voir également pp. 19, 24-25 et 141-42 [Virage en douceur, vol. 1]).

16 Canada, *Proceed With Care: Final Report of the Royal Commission on New Reproductive Technologies*, vol. 2 (Ottawa: Minister of Government Services Canada, 1993) at 1022 [Commission, *Proceed With Care*, vol. 2]. (Commission royale sur les nouvelle techniques de reproduction, Un virage à prendre en douceur (Rapport final), vol. 2, à la p. 1159 [Virage en douceur, vol. 2]).

17 Canada, Health Canada, *New Reproductive and Genetic Technologies: Setting Boundaries, Enhancing Health* (Ottawa: Minister of Government Services Canada, 1996) at 25, http://www.hc-sc.gc.ca/dhp-mps/alt_formats/cmcd-dcmc/pdf/tech_reprod_e.pdf [no longer available online].

18 Canada, Health Canada, "Frequently Asked Questions" May 2001, http://www.hc-sc.gc.ca/ahc-asc/media/nr-cp/2001/2001_44bk2_e.html [no longer available online].

19 Canada, House of Commons, Standing Committee on Health, *Assisted Human Reproduction: Building Families* (December 2001), http://www.parl.gc.ca/InfocomDoc/37/1/HEAL/Studies/Reports/healrp01/08-rap-e.htm#SECTION%201 [now http://www.parl.gc.ca/content/hoc/Committee/371/HEAL/Reports/RP1032041/healrp02/healrp02-e.pdf] [Standing Committee on Health, Building Families].

20 Open Letter from 65 Canadian Health Care Ethics and Health Law Experts on Bill C-13. October 26, 2003 Press Release; distributed to members of Parliament [on file with the author].

21 This open letter was drafted by Professor Jocelyn Downie and myself the evening of October 25th while attending the Joint Meeting of the American Society for Bioethics and Humanities and the Canadian Bioethics Society in Montréal. We wrote this letter in response to a heightened concern about the future of Bill C-13. A draft of the letter was given to Mr. Timothy Caulfield to review, and minor amendments were negotiated. On the last day of the Joint Meeting, during the final coffee break and as people

were leaving the meeting, Professor Downie and I invited Canadian colleagues still in attendance (many had already left the meeting) to sign the open letter. The response was very positive and we garnered a total of 65 signatures. Professor Knoppers was invited to sign the open letter but declined to do so. On October 28, 2003 the House of Commons passed Bill C-13; all members of the House had received a copy of the open letter.

22 Though all persons who avail themselves of assisted reproductive technologies are affected by their use, it is widely recognized that women and children are more directly and significantly affected by their use. This fact is explicitly recognized in the *AHR Act, see supra* note 1, s 2(c).

23 Angela Campbell, "A Place for Criminal Law in the Regulation of New Reproductive Technologies" (2002) 10 *Health Law Journal* 77 at 82.

24 Bartha Knoppers and Timothy Caulfield, "Don't Make Science a Crime: Criminal Law Is Too Blunt a Tool to Cope with Genetic Research," *Globe and Mail*, 20 August 2001, A13 [Knoppers and Caulfield, "Don't Make Science a Crime"]; Timothy Caulfield, Abdallah Daar, Bartha Knoppers, and Peter Singer, "MPs Have the Wrong Focus," *Globe and Mail*, 2 May 2002, A21 [Caulfield, Daar, Knoppers, and Singer, "MPs Have the Wrong Focus"]; Abdallah Daar, Timothy Caulfield, Bartha Knoppers, and Peter Singer, "Ban Cloning, Not Its Life-Saving Cousin," *Globe and Mail*, 9 May 2002, A21 [Daar, Caulfield, Knoppers, and Singer, "Ban Cloning"] *infra* notes 58, 59, 60.

25 Canada, Royal Commission on New Reproductive Technologies, *Proceed with Care: Final Report of the Royal Commission on New Reproductive Technologies*, vol. 1 (Ottawa: Minister of Government Services Canada, 1993) at 18; see similar passages at 17, 22, and 124.

26 Françoise Baylis and Jason Scott Robert, "Primer on Ethics and Crossing Species Boundaries," *ActionBioscience*, May 2006, http://www.actionbioscience.org/biotech/baylis_robert.html [now http://www.actionbioscience.org/biotechnology/baylis_robert.html].

27 The usual ratio of boys to girls is 102–106 boys to 100 girls. In China in 2000 the ratio was 117 boys to 100 girls (with the ratio as high as 135 boys to 100 girls in some regions). Parliamentary Office of Science and Technology, "Sex Selection," *Postnote*,July 2003, no. 198, 4pp, http://www.parliament.uk/post/pn198.pdf [now http://researchbriefings.files.parliament.uk/documents/POST-PN-198/POST-PN-198.pdf].

28 See *supra* note 25 at 4.

29 See *ibid* at 9.

30 See *ibid* at 16.

31 See *ibid* at 12.

32 See *ibid* at 124.
33 See *supra* note 1, s 68.
34 Canada, Health Canada, *Feedback Report: Discussion and Written Comments on Proposed Federal RGTs Legislation*, Ottawa, June 2000, at 2.
35 Aaron Levine, "Research Policy and the Mobility of US Stem Cell Scientists" (2006) 24 *Nature Biotechnology* 865.
36 Jocelyn Downie, "The Canadian Agency for the Oversight of Research Involving Humans: A Reform Proposal" (2006) 13 *Accountability in Research* 75 at 81.
37 See *supra* note 1, s 9.
38 Practice Committee of the American Society for Reproductive Medicine, "Ovarian Hyperstimulation Syndrome" (2003) 80:5 *Fertility and Sterility* 1309.
39 *Ibid.*
40 A.S. Whittemore, R. Harris, and J. Itnyre *et al.*, "Characteristics Relating to Ovarian Cancer Risk: Collaborative Analysis of 12 US Case-control Studies. II Invasive Epithelial Ovarian Cancers in White Women" (1996) 136:10 *American Journal of Epidemiology* 1184; M.A. Rossing, J.R. Darling, N.S. Weiss *et al.*, "Ovarian Tumors in a Cohort of Infertile Women" (1994) 331:12 *New England Journal of Medicine* 771.
41 Ian S. Tummon, Mark Wentworth, and Alan Thornhill, "Frozen-Thawed Embryo Transfer and Live Birth: Long-term Follow-Up after One Oocyte Retrieval" (2006) 86:1 *Fertility and Sterility* 239.
42 Carolyn McLeod and Françoise Baylis, "Donating Fresh Versus Frozen Embryos to Stem Cell Research: In Whose Interests?" (2007) 21 *Bioethics* 465.
43 See *ibid.* See also Françoise Baylis and Caroline McInnes, "Women at Risk: Embryonic and Fetal Stem Cell Research in Canada" (2007) 1 *McGill Journal of Law and Health* 53.
44 See *supra* note 1, s 11.
45 See *supra* note 26.
46 Ann Alpers and Bernard Lo, "Commodification and Commercialization in Human Embryos Research" (1994) 6 *Stanford Law and Policy Review* 39.
47 See *supra* note 25 at 21.
48 See *supra* note 1, s 68.
49 See *supra* note 25 at 12–13.
50 Bartha Maria Knoppers and Elodie Petit, Expert Report "Le Québec: pionnier dans l'encadrement de la PMA et de la recherche au Canada" at 13.
51 E.Y. Adashi, P.N. Barri, R. Berkowitz, P. Braude, *et al.*, "Infertility Therapy-Associated Multiple Pregnancies (Births): An Ongoing Epidemic"

(2003) 7 *Reprod BioMed Online* 515; M. Garel, C. Salobir, and B. Blondel, "Psychological Consequences of Having Triplets: A 4-Year Follow-Up Study" (1997) 67 *Fertility and Sterility* 1162; M.A. Ellison and J.E. Hall, "Social Stigma and Compounded Losses: Quality-of-Life Issues for Multiple-Birth Families" (2003) 80 *Fertility and Sterility* 405; and T.L. Callhan, J.A. Hall, S.L. Ettner, *et al.*, "The Economic Impact of Multiple Gestation Pregnancies and the Contribution of Assisted-Reproduction Technologies to Their Incidence" (1994) 331 *New England Journal of Medicine* 244.

52 In practice, the maximum number of embryos transferred varies from clinic to clinic and, more specifically, from patient to patient (based on age, reason for treatment, number of previous cycles, etc.). In policy, a maximum of three embryos is mentioned. See Society of Obstetricians and Gynaecologists of Canada and Canadian Fertility and Andrology Society, *Joint Policy Statement: Ethical Issues in Assisted Reproduction* (p. 19), http://www.cfas.ca/images/stories/pdf/joint_policy_statement_ethical_issues.pdf.

53 Joanne Gunby and Salim Daya on behalf of the IVF Directors Group of the Canadian Fertility and Andrology Society, "Assisted Reproductive Technologies (ART) in Canada: 2001 Results from the Canadian ART Register" (2005) 84:3 *Fertility and Sterility* 590.

54 Mark S. Frankel, "Professional Codes: Why, How, and with What Impact?" (1989) 8 *Journal of Business Ethics* 109 at 113.

55 Some clinics will make some of this information available on an elective basis.

56 See *supra* note 1, s 22.

57 See *supra* note 1, s 26(8).

58 Présentation du répertoire des comités d'éthique du Québec, http://ethique.msss.gouv.qc.ca/site/repertoire.phtml [now http://ethique.msss.gouv.qc.ca/lethique-de-la-recherche/repertoire-des-etablissements-du-rsss-des-cer-et-des-cec.html].

59 In May 2005, the Quebec government introduced an elective online tutorial on research ethics review, http://ethique.msss.gouv.qc.ca/didacticiel. Some REBs have made this a mandatory requirement for their members (personal communication Carolyn Ells, Assistant Professor, Biomedical Ethics Unit, McGill University, and co-author of the online tutorial). As at 24 April 2006, four hundred people had registered for the tutorial (these registrants may or may not be REB members, and they may or may not have completed the online tutorial).

60 Comité d'experts sur l'évaluation des mécanismes de contrôle en matière de recherche clinique. Rapport sur l'évaluation des mécanismes de

contrôle en matière de recherche clinique, présente au Ministre de la Santé et des Services sociaux du Québec 1995, http://www.frsq.gouv.qc.ca/fr/ethique/pdfs_ethique/Deschamps.pdf [now http://ethique.msss.gouv.qc.ca/fileadmin/documents/rapports/Rapport_DESCHAMPS_1995.pdf]; Marie-Hélène Parizeau, "Rapport d'enquête concernant les activités des comités d'éthique clinique et des comités d'éthique de la recherche au Québec," Québec, Direction générale de la planification et de l'évaluation, ministère de la Santé et des Services sociaux, 1999, http://www.frsq.gouv.qc.ca/en/ethique/pdfs_ethique/rapport_enquete.pdf [now https://www.bibliotheque.assnat.qc.ca/DepotNumerique_v2/AffichageFichier.aspx?idf=104432]; Eryck Malouin, "Rapport d'étude 2001–2002 Les comités d'éthique de la recherche du réseau québécois de la santé et des services sociaux," Direction générale adjointe de l'évaluation, de la recherche et des affaires extérieures, Ministère de la Santé et des Services sociaux, 2004, http://publications.msss.gouv.qc.ca/acrobat/f/documentation/2004/04-714-01.pdf [now http://publications.msss.gouv.qc.ca/msss/fichiers/2004/04-714-01.pdf]; see *supra* note 18.

61 See *supra* note 60 [Malouin]. Note: In October 2005 the Ministre de la Santé et des Services sociaux du Québec announced that it would be updating this report, and that it expected the update to be completed in Spring 2006.

62 See *supra* note 1, s 44.

63 Ministre de la Santé et des Services sociaux du Québec. Plan d'action ministériel en éthique de la recherche et en intégrité scientifique, 1998, p. 14.

64 Fonds de la recherce en santé du Québec, Éthique, intégrité scientifique et bonnes pratiques de la recherche, http://www.frsq.gouv.qc.ca/fr/ethique/ethique.shtml [now http://www.frqs.gouv.qc.ca/ethique].

65 Canada, Canadian Institutes of Health Research, Natural Sciences and Engineering Research Council of Canada, Social Sciences and Humanities Research Council of Canada, *Tri-Council Policy Statement: Ethical Conduct for Research Involving Humans*, 1998 with 2000, 2002, and 2005 amendments, http://www.pre.ethics.gc.ca/archives/tcps-eptc/docs/TCPS%20October%202005_E.pdf. The second edition of the TCPS was published in December 2010.

66 Trudo Lemmens, *Report of the Three Granting Agencies from the Ethics Review Committee Regarding the Assessment of Institutional Policies with the Tri-Council Policy Statement: Ethical Conduct for Research Involving Humans* (2002) (unpublished, on file with the author).

67 Michael McDonald, "Canadian Governance for Ethical Research Involving Humans" (2005) 13:2&3 *Health Law Review* 5 at 8.

68 Code civil du Québec, L.Q., 1991, art. 21.
69 L.R.Q., c M-30.01.
70 Fonds de la recherce en santé du Québec, Mission intégrale, http://www.frsq.gouv.qc.ca/fr/a_propos/popup/mission_integrale.html.
71 See *supra* note 1, ss 60 and 61.
72 See *supra* note 1, ss 40–53.
73 See *supra* note 25 at 12–13. In her expert report, see *supra* note 50 at ii and iii. Knoppers disavows the commission's finding that the regulation of assisted reproductive technologies should not happen on a province-by-province basis. She further states that during the Commission's deliberations « j'étais la seule à promouvoir l'institution d'une agence interprovinciale plutôt que 'nationale.' » This view is not recorded in the commission's Final Report; nor is there a dissenting opinion from Professor Knoppers explaining her perspective (an option that was available to her and indeed was exercised by commissioner Suzanne Scorsone in relation to different concerns).
74 See *supra* note 50 at i.
75 See *ibid* at iii and iv.
76 See *supra* note 24 (Knoppers and Caulfield, "Don't Make Science a Crime").
77 See *supra* note 24 (Caulfield, Daar, Knoppers, and Singer, "MPs Have the Wrong Focus").
78 See *supra* note 24 (Daar, Caulfield, Knoppers, and Singer, "Ban Cloning").
79 To my knowledge these claims (which have also been made in oral presentations) have not been repudiated.
80 Will Kymlicka, "Approaches to the Ethical Issues Raised by the Royal Commission's Mandate," in *New Reproductive Technologies: Ethical Aspects*, vol. 1 of the research studies of the Royal Commission on New Reproductive Technologies (Ottawa: Minister of Government Services Canada, 1993) 1, at 18–27; and see *supra* note 7 at 53 and 58–9.
81 Canada, House of Commons, Standing Committee on Health, *Assisted Human Reproduction: Building Families* (December 2001), http://www.parl.gc.ca/InfocomDoc/37/1/HEAL/Studies/Reports/healrp01/08-rap-e.htm#SECTION%201 [now http://www.parl.gc.ca/content/hoc/Committee/371/HEAL/Reports/RP1032041/healrp02/healrp02-e.pdf].
82 See *supra* note 25 at 51, 50, respectively.
83 See *ibid* at 52.
84 See *ibid* at 52.
85 See *ibid* at 53.
86 See *ibid* at 50.
87 See *ibid* at 58.

88 See *ibid* at 63.
89 See *ibid* at 11.
90 See *ibid* at 10.
91 See *supra* note 16.
92 Provinces and territories, although supportive of federal legislation, were concerned about the possible impact of such legislation on their health care system and existing laws. Quebec officials were not supportive of federal regulations governing reproductive and genetic technologies. They did recognize, however, that this was not an area of practice with geopolitical borders, hence their interest in having standards and regulations that were coherent with those developed in other provinces and territories. See *supra* note 34 at 3.
93 See *ibid* at 2.
94 See *supra* note 1, s 24.
95 See *supra* note 25 at 1, 2, respectively.

Appendix 3 Response to the Second Opinion of Françoise Baylis Entitled "The Regulation of Assisted Human Reproductive Technologies and Related Research: A Public Health, Safety and Morality Argument"

BARTHA MARIA KNOPPERS

- The expert report submitted by F. Baylis does not, indeed cannot – despite her assertions to the contrary – constitute a response to our own expert report. Our presentation was meant to shed light on an intervention articulated and pioneered in Quebec as part of the *legal* regulation of assisted human reproduction (AHR) and related research, while Ms. Baylis' report clearly falls within the ethical realm.
- A significant point of confusion underlies Ms. Baylis' report. The construction of her ethical intervention as to the merits of federal oversight appears to presume that we refuse to recognize that the federal government has any legitimate role to play. As we stated in our introduction, neither our report, nor the referral to the Court of Appeal, challenges the legitimacy of limited criminal prohibitions for non-controversial activities. Therefore, to present the federal law as an indivisible whole, an "all or nothing" proposition, including its criminal prohibitions, its contested provisions, and sections 13–19 (p. 10–18) without making any distinctions, is an attempt to discredit Quebec's multi-institutional partnership by suggesting that the latter is meant to be an alternative to the federal legislation in its entirety. This is completely groundless.
- Ms. Baylis speaks of the need for sections 8–12 of the federal Act, indicating that there would be a risk of "inter-provincial tourism" if these sections were omitted. Let us cite, for example, the reference

to the transportation of patients or dead bodies from one province to another in order to harvest gametes (p. 14), the donation of eggs by young women upon their first menstruation (p. 14), the failure to cryopreserve embryos by Canadian researchers eager to work with fresh embryos (p. 15), and so on. Such generalizations are without scientific foundation and reflect a catastrophizing and alarmist attitude that is intended to frighten readers and obscure alternative approaches. While we recognize that such risks are always possible and must be taken into consideration, it is instructive to consider the Canadian situation during the period between the 1980s (when in vitro fertilization (IVF) first began) and March 2004, when the federal legislation was adopted. If, during that period, we were in a state of normative chaos that seriously jeopardized the health and morality of Canadians – a situation comparable to that which Ms. Baylis fears would obtain if provincial jurisdiction were to be recognized in this field – why were there so few controversies or binding federal interventions during this period?

- One can only assume that there existed, in Quebec and elsewhere, provincial legal standards (in such areas as consent and confidentiality), not to mention professional standards, that held potential hazards in check throughout those years. One can also assume that the Canadian values of dignity, health and safety that underlie the federal legislation are not foreign to Canadian researchers and physicians (who are also members of the Canadian population), as their professionally responsible conduct makes clear.
- In her second opinion, Ms. Baylis states that the primary challenge of regulation in the field of AHR and related research is not to determine what is acceptable to Quebec but rather what is "acceptable" to all 10 provinces (p. 19). This assertion is based on the false premise that any federal legislation will necessarily be acceptable to every province. We believe, on the contrary, that the regional and provincial specificities that are the very foundation of any federal system must be taken into account. The soundness of a piece of legislation is not synonymous with homogeneity. Canada's multiculturalist tradition stands as a convincing illustration of this. Moreover, shared philosophies and common values can be lived and implemented differently in different provinces. Are we to assume that provincial laws are unacceptable or that diversity in the regulation of AHR is contrary to the collective interests of current and future generations?

The numerous references made to the work and conclusions of the Royal Commission on New Reproductive Technologies also warrant comment. Here, it is necessary to recontextualize a statement of the Commission which is cited in the second opinion in an effort to justify the need for federal legislation, namely that "no existing legislation or regulatory regime is broad enough and no public or private organization is equipped or has demonstrated the capacity to deal with these questions, in the comprehensive, timely fashion we believe is necessary" (p. 12). This conclusion dates back to 1993 and reflects the provisions that applied at that time. Clearly it does not reflect the significant normative developments that have taken place in Quebec since then, such as the implementation of the new Civil Code, the Ministère's action plan on research ethics and scientific integrity (1998), the creation of the *Commission de l'éthique de la science et de la technologie*, the Ministère's decision to authorize public health facilities to provide donor artificial insemination services, IVF services, gamete and embryo distribution, etc. Applying the Commission's conclusions to the current situation is therefore problematic. One cannot legitimately assume that the Commission would arrive at the same conclusions were it to examine the situation that exists today in 2006.

- In Ms. Baylis' report, Quebec's multi-institutional partnership is criticized on the basis of its component parts: *professional associations* are depicted as unaccountable and as promoting values that favour the interests of their community over those of infertile patients (p. 21). This comment disregards the legal reality, namely that the technical provisions of the laws that govern AHR (and other areas of medicine) are generally based on the requirements of good clinical practices developed by (or in partnership with) professional organizations. The federal Act is no exception: its regulations, such as those pertaining to practice requirements and materials (section 65(1)) are necessarily influenced by the highest technical standards.

  According to Ms. Baylis, Quebec's 105 research ethics committees (RECs) are not in the best position to evaluate protocols because they lack training and financial resources (p. 23–25). We wish to point out, on this score, that Quebec's Bill 89 would restrict the performance of such evaluations to committees that are recognized by the Ministère, thereby ensuring that these committees are competent to perform this function. If the competence of RECs is so problematic, why did Health Canada, in an information entitled *Proposed Act Respecting Assisted Human Reproduction – AHR-related Research* (May 2002), stipulate that all projects to be submitted to the Agency for consideration should first be reviewed by an REC? What is more, lack of funding is a problem that cannot justify federal encroachment in this area of jurisdiction. Nothing would prevent the federal authorities from increasing funding for RECs through a grant program that respects provincial jurisdiction in this area, or through an equalization system.

As for the *Fonds de la recherche en santé du Québec* (FRSQ) (p. 25), its strengths and limitations in this area are no different from those of the Canadian Institutes of Health Research (CIHR), and yet the usefulness of the latter is never called into question, neither in the second opinion, nor in the federal legislation, which stipulates that consent requirements for embryonic stem cell research must be those articulated in the 2002 CIHR guidelines (section 40(3.1)). We note, however, that no reference is made to the numerous provisions contained in the Quebec Civil Code, a coherent legal instrument of considerable symbolic force whose provisions with respect to AHR and related research are a matter of public record.

- Ms. Baylis herself recognizes the limitations of analyzing individual mechanisms of Quebec's multi-institutional model (p. 27) when she states that "[i]t is inappropriate to assess the merits of each regulatory mechanism in isolation given that they have proposed a 'regulatory partnership' in which the weaknesses of one regulatory mechanism might be compensated for by the strengths of another." What is more, linking the conclusions articulated by the federal Commission in 1993 to this essential admission strikes us, once again, as beside the point.
- The final portion of Ms. Baylis' defence of the soundness of the present federal Act deals with the moral values that underlie this legislation (p. 30 et seq.) Ms. Baylis cites the protection of vulnerable persons, the principles of respect for human life and dignity, autonomy, equality, the non-commercialization of the human body, and the balancing of individual and collective interests. This explanation strikes us as essential, since it ultimately illustrates the bias which would have us believe that respect for these various principles can only be assured through federal intervention. Are we to assume that Quebec's standards are not guided by these same ideals, despite their symbolic inclusion in the Civil Code and the

Quebec Charter of Human Rights and Freedoms of 1975? Are we to conclude that the provinces are unfit to implement these principles, which extend well beyond the realm of reproduction?

- Ms. Baylis goes on to challenge the integrity of my expert report by quoting from articles published in the *Globe and Mail*, from which she has deduced that I recognize the federal government's jurisdiction over both prohibited and regulated activities (p. 28). First of all, I wish to reiterate that our report does not contest the federal government's right to enact criminal prohibitions. Then, Ms. Baylis makes the mistake of over-interpreting these newspaper articles which examine the potential consequences of the federal government's criminalization of therapeutic cloning rather than the jurisdiction or role of the provinces. The titles of the cited articles are in fact quite clear as to the subject matter to follow: *Don't Make Science a Crime: Criminal Law Is Too Blunt a Tool to Cope with Genetic Research; Ban Cloning, Not Its Life-Saving Cousin.* The title of a more recent article from the newspaper *Le Devoir* (February 28, 2003) is similarly eloquent: *Le Projet de loi C-13 sur la procréation assistée: une interdiction pénale injustifiée, au détriment de la science.*

  It is within this very narrow framework that the co-authors of these articles and I have proposed a regulatory scheme that would include criminal penalties for therapeutic cloning, as a means of avoiding the drawbacks of criminalizing therapeutic cloning outright, particularly in view of the fact that the need for such criminalization is not universally recognized.
- It is important to recall that this proposal was shaped by a realistic understanding of the very narrow margin of manoeuvre that was available in terms of amending this Act. We specified, in fact, that "this approach … would require only minor modifications to the current proposal" (*Don't Make Science a Crime: Criminal Law Is Too Blunt a Tool to Cope with Genetic Research*). In the article published in *Le Devoir*, we "[translation] recognize that amendments to this bill are highly unlikely at this time, particularly with regard to therapeutic cloning." Therefore, to conclude that these articles contradict my contention that the provinces have the capacity and the jurisdiction to regulate authorized practices in the area of AHR and related research is entirely unwarranted.
- In fact, we clearly stated that "of course, the real, unspoken justification for criminal prohibitions is the perennial Canadian problem of federal/provincial jurisdiction. The *Constitution Act of 1867* gives

the provinces the power to enact laws in the area of health and the federal government the power to enact criminal laws. Ottawa may feel that 'criminal-like' prohibitions are necessary in order to secure jurisdiction" (*Don't Make Science a Crime: Criminal Law Is Too Blunt a Tool to Cope with Genetic Research*).

- On February 18, 2004, when I testified before the Standing Senate Committee on Social Affairs, Science and Technology, which was examining Bill C-6, I indicated that I firmly believed there was no legal void in the provinces of Canada with respect to AHR (e.g., health information legislation, various provincial laws governing medical practices and research) and reiterated my confidence in the system of multi-institutional regulation. As I am in favour of the enactment of criminal prohibitions when a social consensus exists (e.g., for reproductive cloning), I have called for the creation of an *interprovincial* body to safeguard the health of women and children. Moreover, to answer the question raised by the Committee Chair as to the appropriateness of adopting this federal legislation as it exists today, I was the only witness who spoke in favour of abandoning the bill.

October 23, 2006

Contributors

Françoise Baylis, Professor, Departments of Bioethics and Philosophy, Dalhousie University

Bernard M. Dickens, Professor Emeritus of Health Law and Policy, University of Toronto

Susan G. Drummond, Associate Professor, Osgoode Hall Law School, Toronto

Rachel Epstein, Banting Postdoctoral Fellow, Brock University; Founding Coordinator, LGBTQ Parenting Network, Sherbourne Health Centre; "Creating Our Families" Research Team, Toronto

Colleen M. Flood, Professor and Canada Research Chair in Health Law and Policy, Common Law Section, Faculty of Law, University of Ottawa

Michelle Giroux, Lawyer and Full Professor, Civil Law Section, Faculty of Law, University of Ottawa; Member of the Interdisciplinary Research Laboratory on the Rights of the Child (IRLRC)

datejie green, PhD candidate, Faculty of Information and Media Studies, Western University; "Creating Our Families" Research Team, Toronto

Vanessa Gruben, Associate Professor, Common Law Section, Faculty of Law, University of Ottawa

Juliet R. Guichon, Assistant Professor, Department of Community Health Sciences, Cumming School of of Medicine, University of Calgary

Sarah Hudson, Lawyer, Vancouver, British Columbia

Lisa C. Ikemoto, Professor of Law, University of California-Davis School of Law

Bartha Maria Knoppers, Director, Centre of Genomics and Policy, Department of Human Genetics, Faculty of Medicine, McGill University

Hoi L. Kong, Associate Professor of Law, McGill University

Ian B. Lee, Associate Professor, Faculty of Law, University of Toronto

Trudo Lemmens, Professor and Scholl Chair in Health Law and Policy, Faculty of Law and Dalla Lana School of Public Health, University of Toronto

Andrew Flavelle Martin, SJD Candidate, Faculty of Law, University of Toronto

Stu Marvel, Postdoctoral Fellow, School of Law, Emory University, Atlanta; "Creating Our Families" Research Team, Toronto

Cheryl Milne, Executive Director, David Asper Centre for Constitutional Rights at the Faculty of Law, University of Toronto; formerly Counsel, Justice for Children and Youth legal clinic, Toronto

Élodie Petit, Ethics consultant; Co-Chair, Clinical Ethics Committee, Montreal Heart Institute

Glenn Rivard, Barrister and Solicitor, Ontario

Carol Rogerson, Professor, Faculty of Law, University of Toronto

Lori E. Ross, Associate Professor, Social and Behavioural Health Sciences Division, Dalla Lana School of Public Health, University of Toronto; "Creating Our Families" Research Team, Toronto

Jeanne Snelling, Research Fellow in Bioethics and Health Law, Bioethics Centre and Adjunct Lecturer, Faculty of Law, University of Otago

Jennifer M. Speirs, Research Associate, Centre for Research on Families and Relationships, University of Edinburgh

Leah S. Steele, St Michael's Hospital, Toronto; Department of Family and Community Medicine, University of Toronto; "Creating Our Families" Research Team, Toronto

Lesley A. Tarasoff, PhD candidate, Dalla Lana School of Public Health, University of Toronto; Social & Epidemiological Research Department, Centre for Addiction and Mental Health; "Creating Our Families" Research Team, Toronto

Bryan Thomas, Research Associate, Common Law Section, Faculty of Law, University of Ottawa

Index